CORPORATION
• FOR •
ENTERPRISE
DEVELOPMENT

D0101044

THE 1995 DEVELOPMENT REPORT CARD FOR THE STATES

ECONOMIC
BENCHMARKS
FOR STATE
AND
CORPORATE
DECISION–
MAKERS

Ninth

Edition

ISSN: 1045-4691
ISBN: 1-883187-05-2

CORPORATION
• FOR •
ENTERPRISE
DEVELOPMENT

National Office
777 North Capitol Street, NE
Suite 410
Washington, DC 20002
Phone: (202) 408-9788
Fax: (202) 408-9793

Table of Contents

(continued)

The Corporation for Enterprise Development
Copyright 1995 by CFED. All rights reserved.

Introduction

The 1995 Development Report Card for the States

The Development Report Card for the States is an annual assessment of the strengths and weaknesses of each state's economy and its potential for future growth using state-by-state comparisons based upon over 50 socioeconomic data measures. The Report Card's methodology is a comparative one in which each state's performance is evaluated relative to the performance of all the others. This type of assessment, called *comparative benchmarking*, is very powerful in its ability to take into account broad macroeconomic cycles and to highlight relative strengths and weaknesses. For example, is a state's moderate employment growth over the last couple of years actually a positive sign if all other states are growing at twice the rate? Doesn't that imply that this state is lagging behind?

The Report Card compares and grades all states in each of three indexes measuring different aspects of its economic health. This analysis is supplemented by a general rating of each state's tax and fiscal system's ability to support long-term economic development, as well as supplementary (but ungraded) measures of quality of life. The three graded indexes are structured to measure:

Economic Performance: *What are the economic benefits and opportunities provided by the state's economy to its citizens?*

Business Vitality: *How vital and dynamic is the state's business sector?*

Development Capacity: *What is the state's capacity for future growth and recovery from economic adversity?*

Each of these graded indexes is comprised of three or more subindexes, also graded (with the exception of the Environmental, Social & Health Conditions subindex), providing a more detailed understanding of the facets of a state's economy.

The Environmental, Social & Health Conditions subindex is not graded or included in any calculations. It is presented along side the Economic Performance Index to round out the picture of a state's economic benefits by providing an understanding of the state's quality of life. Unfortunately, these data measures are not as well-developed and robust as the other Economic Performance data, and therefore they are not included in calculations for the Economic Performance Index's ranks or grades.

Because the Tax & Fiscal System Index compares financial systems, not economic outcomes, and because relevant data is often not as precise and as frequently updated, we do not grade the Tax & Fiscal System Index as we do the three main economic indexes. Rather, the states are ranked and given a plus for an exemplary system, a minus for a poor one, and a check for those in the middle.

The Report Card's framework is based upon two key assumptions. The first is that the goal of any state development policy is increased economic well-being for its citizens. The second is that businesses flourish in healthy economies and not in poor, stagnant ones. Thus, the goals of state development officials and the business community are complementary. Policymakers want a strong economy to fulfill their public mandate. Businesses want to be in a healthy economy as a means of encouraging their own economic success.

The success of a state's economy depends upon the vitality of its businesses and the strength of its physical infrastructure and human, financial, and technological resources. Yet, there is not a direct, simple causal relationship between development capacity, business vitality, and economic performance. There are too many external forces beyond the control of state or federal government affecting national and regional economies and the activities of individual businesses. Nevertheless, there is a strong correlation between them, especially between economic performance and development capacity. States with the requisite resources can better develop competitive, dynamic, and vital businesses – the underpinning of future economic prosperity. The Report Card's three indexes reflect this relationship.

It is important to note that the recognition of a strong relationship between development capacity and economic performance, one of the primary considerations behind the Report Card's structure, is not merely a hopeful supposition. Rather, scholarly research on the economic impact of investments in public services and infrastructure has demonstrated a powerful link between the two. For example, an important study by researcher Alicia Munnell (*The New England Economic Review*, September/October 1990), found that states investing more in public infrastructure tend to have greater output, more private investment, and more employment growth. (See also Timothy Bartik, *Who Benefits from State and Local Development Policies*, 1991.)

It is important to realize that a state's position in each of the three indexes changes at different paces. Economic Performance can exhibit noticeable annual changes, and Business Vitality can swing dramatically in a single year. Yet Development Capacity, the fundamentals, takes much longer to grow and flourish. Ironically, it is this slowest moving index which is most susceptible to direct policy intervention. Business Vitality can be affected but much less directly than resource development, and Economic Performance is almost impossible to directly impact via specific policies. Yet it is the investments in development capacity, made for the long haul, which can lead to

stronger, more sustainable performance and recovery.

The Tax & Fiscal System Index measures how well-equipped a state's financial system is to provide solid support for future economic development. Contrary to popular belief, a good business climate depends less on the size of the tax bite than it does on the mix of taxes and quality of government services provided. In other words, simply lowering or raising tax rates will not necessarily change economic health and business vitality. Rather, a tax and fiscal system that is balanced, equitable, and stable can sustain necessary long-term investments and help minimize uncertainties. As the National Conference of State Legislatures and the National Governors' Association write:

> "...generally acknowledged principles of good state tax policy...hold that a state tax system should provide appropriate and timely revenues, distribute burdens equitably, promote economic efficiency and growth, be easily administered and ensure accountability." (*Financing State Government in the 1990's*, 1993, page vii)

Therefore, the Report Card's Tax & Fiscal System Index uses over 15 measures to assess the stability, balance, fairness, and equity of a state's tax and fiscal system.

Results, Not Just Efforts

Unlike many other studies, such as the old Grant Thornton Manufacturing Index, the Report Card is built on outcome-based measures. It shows how healthy a state's economy actually is, not how hard everyone has worked at improving it. Thus, the Report Card measures an increase in employment, *not* the number of business recruitment offices in a state; it measures the increase in new businesses and *not* new tax incentives being offered; and it measures the education of the work force, *not* the availability and quality of training. Knowing what and how well states are practicing economic development is important, but it is not the bottom line. Instead, the Report Card concentrates on the differences these efforts make to both citizens and business.

As a result, the Report Card does not distinguish between states that are conscientiously investing in the future and those that are coasting off their past. Many states that currently rank at the bottom of the Development Capacity Index are actually among the most active pioneers in education reform, public-private partnerships, and industrial modernization. Their efforts are making them exciting places to live, work, and grow a business, but the results of their initiatives may not show up in the aggregate statistics for perhaps even another decade.

The Report Card Framework

The Report Card framework was first developed several years ago based upon an extensive literature review and on the review of a technical advisory board comprised of economic development experts and business, labor, government, and community development officials. Each year we have revised and honed the measures used and the presentation of the book based upon reader response and CFED's own hands-on experience in policy development across the nation.

The core of the Report Card is in the grades and ranks for every state in all three indexes and each individual measure. These are presented on individual state Report Cards at the book's center and summarized in the National Findings. As before, the book presents national and regional findings – the overall patterns and lessons discernible each year for the entire nation and each geographic region – plus detailed source notes and measure descriptions for each index, and an in-

depth discussion of the appropriate state tax and fiscal systems for economic development.

Although grades and ranks are given for each subindex and index, no single overall grade is given because it overly condenses the complex facets of each state's economy. We give grades because they give a quick and immediate sense of a state's overall comparative position in each area, which can easily be used as a guide to further exploration – both within and outside of the Report Card data – into the complex economic forces at work in each state. They should not be used as an excuse to avoid further investigation.

Who Should Use the Report Card?

The Report Card has been designed as a tool to help people and organizations interested in assessing and evaluating a state's economic progress and development. The Report Card is recommended reading for:

- economic development officials;
- policy analysts;
- strategic planners;
- elected and appointed officials;
- state and local chambers of commerce:
- utility executives;
- community and labor leaders;
- corporate site planners; and
- researchers.

In short, the Report Card is for everyone who wants to know how a state is doing in providing a healthy economic environment for its citizenry and businesses, or for anyone who wants some initial guidance on what needs to be done for improvement.

How Should the Report Card be Used?

The Report Card does not offer prescriptions, nor does it provide detailed descriptions of individual states and their economic histories. Rather, the Report Card presents a comparative assessment of each state's overall economic performance, the vitality and dynamism in its business community, and the relative strength of its resources necessary for its future economic health, all relative to other states. The Report Card's ranking methodology allows comparison of a state to its neighbors and competitors.

Another way to assess a state's efforts over the years is to compare all of the states in its region using the five-year data in the Regional Findings. This data can also be used to compare a state's economic performance to that of other states with similar development capacity resources and business vitality, illustrating whether a state has fallen behind or overachieved.

Whom do you want to emulate? Find states with similar resource levels in previous years but better economic performance. Why are they doing better? Find the overall leaders in the nation and your geographic region and ask why they are doing so well.

Thinking of expanding your company? How do the states you are considering rate in the resources which are most important to you? How do the states compare in overall economic conditions? How do they compare in relation to their neighbors?

There are a host of other questions to be asked: What have been a particular state's strong points recently? Where is it weakest? Where has it improved or declined dramatically? What do recent changes in Development Capacity and Business Vitality present for the future?

Some warnings: The Report Card is not a crystal ball. It does not predict the future; it only indicates in which direction a state has been traveling and how well it is prepared to meet upcoming challenges. Additionally, the current economic performance indicators do not reflect economic conditions this week, nor last month, but rather over the past year or two. Data collection and time limitations prohibit "real time" evaluation akin to stock prices. Finally, the indicators use data from different years, so care should be taken when comparing individual measures.

The Report Card is best used as a tool to explore important economic questions about where a state's economy is and where it is going.

National Findings

The 1995 Development Report Card

| STATE | INDEXES | | | STATE | INDEXES | | |
	Economic Performance	Business Vitality	Development Capacity		Economic Performance	Business Vitality	Development Capacity
Alabama	C	B	D	Montana	B	B	B
Alaska	B	F	D	Nebraska	A	C	C
Arizona	C	C	B	Nevada	B	A	D
Arkansas	C	F	F	New Hampshire	C	C	C
California	D	C	B	New Jersey	C	C	A
Colorado	A	A	A	New Mexico	D	C	D
Connecticut	B	D	A	New York	D	C	C
Delaware	A	C	A	North Carolina	C	D	C
Florida	D	D	C	North Dakota	C	F	C
Georgia	C	A	C	Ohio	C	C	B
Hawaii	A	F	B	Oklahoma	F	B	F
Idaho	A	A	B	Oregon	B	B	A
Illinois	D	B	A	Pennsylvania	C	A	B
Indiana	A	B	D	Rhode Island	C	D	C
Iowa	A	C	C	South Carolina	D	B	D
Kansas	C	C	D	South Dakota	B	C	D
Kentucky	F	D	D	Tennessee	B	A	C
Louisiana	F	C	F	Texas	D	A	C
Maine	D	D	D	Utah	A	C	A
Maryland	A	D	B	Vermont	C	F	C
Massachusetts	C	B	A	Virginia	A	C	B
Michigan	C	B	C	Washington	D	B	A
Minnesota	B	A	A	West Virginia	F	D	F
Mississippi	D	A	F	Wisconsin	A	D	B
Missouri	D	C	C	Wyoming	B	A	C

For information on how grades are calculated, see the Methodology section.
For a detailed explanation of indexes, refer to the individual index sections.

The National Story

The Mountain West: Cooking at High Altitudes

East of the California coast, west of the plains, the economy of the Mountain West has risen like a gigantic soufflé. Of all six regions in the U.S., the Mountain West easily claims the blue ribbon in best overall economic performance for 1994. It is tops in job creation, and average pay rose in six of the region's eight states. More than that, the Mountain West nudged past the Industrial Midwest, last year's "Comeback Kid," in Business Vitality. The region has the best physical infrastructure, second best human resources, and second best technological base – some of the most important ingredients for future growth. When their broad-based and equitable tax and fiscal systems are added to the mix, the Mountain West virtually sweeps the top awards on this year's Report Card.

The emergence of the Mountain West as the country's top region for economic development represents quite a reversal of fortune. As late as 1991, the Mountain West was wallowing in the bottom half of the nation in economic performance. Since then, Colorado, Idaho, and Montana have all risen at least two letter grades in Economic Performance; Utah and Wyoming up one. In fact the only state in the region which fails to do well in Economic Performance is New Mexico, suffering extreme poverty. Even so, New Mexico is number two in the nation in average annual pay growth, which may eventually take some of the sting out of its painfully low wage structure.

Evidence suggests that, even if California had not been battered by economic and environmental catastrophes, the Mountain West, with its strong entrepreneurship, excellent resources, and growing hi-tech centers (such as the "Software Valley" between Provo and Salt Lake City) would still have been positioning itself as one of the country's most attractive places to establish and conduct business. Entrepreneurial energy in the region has improved steadily since 1990 to explosive levels of new company formation and the jobs that go with them. Since the *1992 Development Report Card*, every Mountain West state but two has frequently ranked in the top ten in entrepreneurship in the last four years – and the two that did not, Arizona and Nevada, finally do so this year.

At the same time, the resources these new businesses need to be competitive are also exceptional, and getting better. Human resources in the northern half of the region continue to be excellent, where most people have at least a high school degree. For the last several years, Colorado, New Mexico, and Utah have led the nation with excellent high technology resources, while Idaho and Montana have steadily improved since 1993. Add strong recent improvements in physical infrastructure – low energy costs, low sewage treatment needs, low rates of deficiencies on the region's highways and bridges – and you have a very powerful mixture to fuel future economic growth.

These trends have not gone unnoticed. Last November, a *Money* magazine article on the "Top 20 Spots for Entrepreneurs" found that the key factors to economic success were a diverse economy, an educated workforce, access to capital, construction activity, good transportation networks, and good quality of life – and that most of the best places for entrepreneurs were "west of the Continental Divide." (*Money*, November 1994, pp. 126-134).

Some may call this independent confirmation of the infamous "splash back" – the exodus of harried California businesses to the friendlier business climates of neighboring states. No one (including the *Development Report Card*) can definitively answer that claim, but it is important to remember that while California lost 240,000 jobs between late 1989 and late 1994 – during the same period the Mountain West *added 990,000.*

One question remains for the Mountain West. With employment on the West Coast, particularly California, having hit bottom and now on the way back up, will the entrepreneurs of the Mountain West pull up stakes and move to the coast? Will the soufflé fall? Most likely not. The Mountain West has been building a solid infrastructure for business for years and is bursting with entrepreneurial energy. The Mountain West is clearly cooking up its own successes.

Following a Winning Formula: The South Improves Its Development Capacity

Year after year, the *Development Report Card* has shown a strong relationship between investments in development capacity (physical infrastructure, as well as human, technology, and financial resources) and future economic performance. Yet, it is extremely difficult for a state to alter the landscape of these development resources. Improvements take place only after decades of sustained investment, often with precious little to show for the effort in the short run. It's even harder for late-comers to the race when the leading states are running as fast as they can. The South's leaders are painfully aware of this truth. Many have worked hard – in some states for more than two decades – to shake the region's legacy of poverty, illiteracy, and lack of technological sophistication. Modern southern leaders have been outspoken champions of education reform and job training. Regional banking was born in the capital-starved South and southern leaders have played major roles in promoting the information superhighway and technology utilization in firms and classrooms.

Although the South continues to receive a disproportionate share of Ds and Fs in Development Capacity, *The 1995 Development Report Card* offers them some cause for optimism. For the first time, a cluster of southern states improve their grades in Development Capacity. Florida, Kentucky, North Carolina, Tennessee, and

Virginia each advance one letter grade. Only three other states in the nation are able to do the same (Delaware, Idaho, Wyoming). Now, five out of twelve southern states rate a C or better. Moreover, although nine U.S. states step down a grade in Development Capacity this year, *no southern state was among them.* Since Development Capacity rankings change infrequently and almost never by more than one grade at a time, this regional shift is a remarkable accomplishment.

Although many of the Southern states show gains in the sixteen measures used to compose the Development Capacity grade, Tennessee and North Carolina stand out as making improvements this year in Financial Resources, Technology Resources, and Infrastructure & Amenities – three of the four "subindexes" in the Development Capacity Index. The shift can be traced to improvements in bank deposits, commercial loans, venture capital investments, highways, and the number of scientists and engineers in the southern workforce.

Improvements in Human Resources – the fourth subindex – were less sweeping in the South, yet Arkansas, Florida, and Tennessee each jumped two or three notches in their high school graduation rankings. Since K-12 education is highly correlated to economic prosperity, these improvements are a very encouraging trend for the South. The other good news is that Arkansas and West Virginia, which suffered from some of the country's highest rates of illiteracy in past generations, now rank *above the national average* in high school graduation.

Perhaps the best news of all, however, is that the South's improvements in Development Capacity have been part of a small but discernible climb in the states' Human Resources, Financial Resources, and Infrastructure & Amenity Resources rankings the last three to four years. Grades that were unchanged on the *Development Report Card* in previous years have masked these important improvements in rankings. This should be especially encouraging for southern leaders. The Mountain West and Industrial Midwest – this year's leader and last year's runner-up in economic performance, respectively – had also made sustained improvements in Development Capacity in the years preceding their strong Economic Performance showing. Arkansas, Georgia, and Tennessee – already tops in job growth and lowest in unemployment – may eventually lead the region into the winner's circle in Economic Performance.

Following a Losing Formula: Distorted Tax Structures and Eroding Infrastructure

When it comes to taxes, the issue is not simply low or no taxes. State and local leaders, along with businesses, often approach taxes from a very narrow perspective, focusing only on the negatives on the cost side of the tax equation. This perspective can be short-sighted given that quality public services, such as education and infrastructure, though costly, are critical for business success. And although the Report Card does not assess whether or not a state is taking in enough money, it does measure the soundness of a state's tax and fiscal system: whether its revenue sources are balanced and stable, how equitable it is, and how well it promotes local government fiscal capacity.

What happens when a state's tax and fiscal structure limits its ability to make these investments? The Northeast and the Pacific provide two interesting cases in point.

The Northeast: Although not the nation's worst region on this year's Tax & Fiscal System Index, the Northeast is decidedly mediocre. Maine is the only state in the region to earn an above average rating (+), while 70 percent of the states earn an average rating (✓). While the Northeast can claim the nation's best Tax Fairness, with half of the region's states ranking above average and no states below average, the region ranks last on Fiscal Equalization, with no states above average

and 70 percent of the states below average. With a large number of revenue-starved urban areas, yet few mechanisms to compensate for local tax differentials, the Northeast has been losing ground faster than any other region on Development Capacity. Between 1988 and 1995, the region experienced the greatest decrease in average Development Capacity rankings. Yet, looking closer at the measures, it becomes apparent that this drop in ranking was caused almost exclusively by a drop in physical infrastructure, in particular the quality of the region's bridges, highways, and the affordability of its urban housing.

The Pacific: As was the case last year, the Pacific has the nation's poorest ratings on this year's Tax & Fiscal System Index. Of the region's five states, only one receives an above average (+) rating, while two states (40 percent of the region) receive a below average (–) rating. In particular, Washington, with an over-reliance on sales taxes, and Oregon, with an over-reliance on property and income taxes, have very unbalanced revenue raising structures. As one might predict, the Pacific, though still leading the nation in the Development Capacity Index, has been losing ground to other regions. Over the period 1988 to 1995, the Pacific experienced the second highest decrease in average Development Capacity rankings. Again, looking closer at the measures, it appears that this drop in ranking can be largely accounted for by a decrease in the quality of the region's infrastructure.

Of course, a weak infrastructure does not automatically relegate a state or region to economic decline. While the Northeast has indeed been on the decline in Economic Performance since the early 1990s, the Pacific is again one of this year's top performers. Thus, the lesson here is that a bad tax and fiscal structure may not doom a state in the upswing of a business cycle, but it can limit its ability to adapt to changing economic fortunes.

The 1995 Honor Roll

Five states make the Honor Roll (straight As and Bs in the three Report Card indexes) this year – Colorado, Idaho, Minnesota, Montana, and Oregon. For Colorado and Minnesota, this represents a repeat performance from last year. Reflecting the last two years' regional trends, three of these top five states (60 percent) are in the Mountain West, with one each in the Pacific and Industrial Midwest. Meanwhile, seven more states earn an honorable mention with two honor grades and a C: Delaware, Massachusetts, Pennsylvania, Tennessee, Utah, Virginia, and Wyoming.

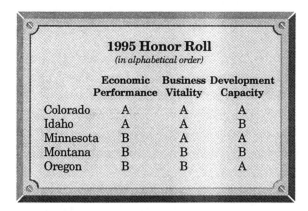

1995 Honor Roll
(in alphabetical order)

	Economic Performance	Business Vitality	Development Capacity
Colorado	A	A	A
Idaho	A	A	B
Minnesota	B	A	A
Montana	B	B	B
Oregon	B	B	A

- **Colorado:** The valedictorian of this year's class is Colorado. For the third straight year, Colorado has the best grades in the nation, and for the second consecutive year, it earns all As. Even Colorado's superlative grades do not provide an adequate gauge of the overall strength of its economy. Colorado's Economic Performance ranks first in the country, while its Development Capacity is second and Business Vitality is third. Still one of the top four states in Human Resources, Technology Resources, and Infrastructure & Amenities, Colorado is unlikely to leave the Honor Roll any time soon. The Rocky Mountain state's only current weakness is in Financial Resources – due to low loan activity – and now is the time to fix it.

- **Idaho:** Idaho is on the upswing – of the five Honor Roll states, it improved the most since last year. It leaps from a C to an A in Economic Performance, as its pay growth outpaces most other states, its poverty rate declines, and income disparities are shrinking. But most noticeably, Idaho improves its rank by over 30 places in Rural\Urban Disparity – meaning the state has tempered job and income disparities between its urban and rural areas. Idaho ranks in the top five in Employment, Competitiveness of Existing Business, and Entrepreneurial Energy. However, there are some signs of weakness in this vibrant economy, especially its great lack of economic diversity, which leaves it vulnerable to cyclical downturns.

- **Minnesota:** An annual Report Card stand-out, Minnesota earns its fourth Honor Roll appearance in the last five years. In 1988, Minnesota ranked first in Development Capacity; it has not relinquished that top ranking since. The current strength of the Gopher state's Development Capacity (in particular its Human Resources, Financial Resources, and Infrastructure & Amenities) bodes well for its future economic performance. Minnesota improves its Business Vitality grade from a B to an A by boosting its Entrepreneurial Energy two letter grades (from D to B). A lower rank in Economic Performance is due largely to declining equity, especially a worsening income distribution between rich and poor.

- **Montana:** The biggest surprise on this year's Honor Roll, Montana makes its first appearance on the listing of top achievers. Five years ago, Montana had below average grades in all three indexes and seemed light-years away from honors consideration. However, Montana improved its Development Capacity ranking every year since 1992, raising its overall grade from a D to a B. Meanwhile, Montana now ranks 17th in

Economic Performance, earning a solid B. Now that there are opportunities at home, people are coming back, reversing years of detrimental outmigration.

- **Oregon:** The only Honor Roll state from the Pacific region, Oregon joins the top performers with a jump from a D to a B in Business Vitality. Oregon achieved this by improving its ranking in all three Business Vitality subindexes, and in particular, by climbing 14 places in Entrepreneurial Energy (only Colorado ranks higher). With all this entrepreneurial energy, jobs are plentiful in Oregon. Indeed, it seems as if the Oregon economy has left all the hubbub about timber and spotted owls behind. Of all the Pacific states, only Oregon receives an A in the Employment subindex this year. This is a grade up from last year, and the culmination of steady improvements since 1992. Moreover, the A in Employment is paired with a solid B in the Earnings subindex. Oregon may be benefiting from the California "splash-back" phenomena, but success can also be attributed to encouraging key industries, especially high value-added ones like software and bio-technology. Moreover, Oregon's rates of new business formation were high even before 1993, when California fell from first to twenty-second in state rankings for Entrepreneurial Energy.

Worthy of mention is yet another Mountain West state, Wyoming, which posts the greatest improvement in the country during the past year:

- **Wyoming:** By improving its grades in all three indexes, Wyoming is just a grade away from Honor Roll consideration with one A, one B, and one C. Wyoming's leap from thirty-five to five in Business Vitality is among the largest improvements in this year's Report Card. This was accomplished with a jump from a D to a B in Entrepreneurial Energy and from a B to an A in the Competitiveness of Existing Business subindex.

Gold Stars for Tax & Fiscal Systems

This year's top performers on the Tax & Fiscal System Index – which evaluates state tax systems based on their stability, fairness, and their policies for sharing revenues (to equalize local fiscal capacity) – are California, Idaho, and Minnesota. These three states were also the top ranking states on last year's index. At the head of the class on Tax & Fiscal System for the fourth year in a row is Minnesota, which draws strength from the third highest ranking on Fiscal Stability & Balanced Revenue and the second highest ranking on Tax Fairness. Just behind Minnesota, in second place, is Idaho, which earns above average (+) ratings on all three Tax & Fiscal System subindexes. California lands firmly in third place, with a balanced tax structure and the nation's most equitable tax policies. It is interesting to note that the two top-ranking states on this year's Tax & Fiscal System Index (Minnesota and Idaho) also make the Honor Roll. In fact, three of the five Honor Roll states earn above average (+) ratings on their tax and fiscal systems. Oregon, with poor rankings on Fiscal Stability & Balanced Revenue and Fiscal Equalization, is the only Honor Roll state with a below average tax and fiscal system. It must be noted that the Tax & Fiscal System Index *does not* measure whether the revenues raised by a state's tax system are *adequate* to meet a state's spending needs. Thus, while California's tax and fiscal system is fair and well balanced, the state continues to struggle with structural deficits.

The Class Of 1991 – Where Are They Now?

The 1991 Honor Roll was dominated by the Northeast with half of its states on the list and two of the remaining five Honor Roll states, Virginia and Pennsylvania, bordering the Northeast region. Since then, regional dominance has changed dramatically, as the significant improvements in the Mountain West have been accompanied by a steep decline in the formerly dominant Northeast.

All of the Northeast's 1991 honor states experienced significant declines in their ranks for every index. The Northeast's fall from glory has been most pronounced in the Business Vitality Index. While the five 1991 Northeastern leaders still managed to remain moderately strong in Economic Performance and Development Capacity, none of these five states receives an honor grade in Business Vitality this year.

The remaining five 1991 Honor Roll states have fared somewhat better. Minnesota is the lone 1991 Honor Roll state to make the 1995 Honor Roll. Meanwhile, Nevada, Pennsylvania, Virginia, and Utah each earn two honor grades this year.

At the opposite end in 1991, five states received failing grades in each index: Arkansas, Louisiana, Montana, Oklahoma, and West Virginia. Regrettably, only Montana (a 1995 Honor Roll performer) has improved significantly. The other four states remain at the bottom of the class, each receiving two Fs in 1995.

A snapshot of the states with the best overall Development Capacity in 1991 illustrates the importance of human, technology, and financial resources and infrastructure for future economic success. Of the ten states earning As in Development Capacity in 1991, 60 percent earn an A or B in Economic Performance in 1995 and only California, receives a poor grade as it battles back from natural disasters (last year's F in Economic Performance is now a D).

Although Economic Performance rankings have dropped in the Pacific and Northeast regions, the regions' Development Capacity rankings are still tops. If strong resources are so important to economic growth, why then has performance in these regions declined? Perhaps the answer lies in Development Capacity *trends*. Development Capacity is the least fluid of the three main indexes; policy innovations directed at improving human, technology, financial resources, and infrastructure take years to produce concrete results. Yet, by improving its development capacity more rapidly than other regions, a region can boost its economic competitiveness. Conversely, those regions that fail to keep pace with development capacity improvements will slip economically. During the last eight years, the Development Capacity-Economic Performance link has been evident.

THE 1991 HONOR ROLL STATES – WHERE ARE THEY NOW?

1991 Honor Roll States	1991 Grades			1995 Grades		
	Economic Performance	Business Vitality	Development Capacity	Economic Performance	Business Vitality	Development Capacity
Connecticut	A	A	A	B	D	A
Delaware	A	B	A	A	C	A
Maryland	A	A	A	A	D	B
Minnesota	B	A	A	B	A	A
Nevada	A	B	B	B	A	D
New Hampshire	A	A	B	C	C	C
New Jersey	A	A	A	C	C	A
Pennsylvania	B	B	A	C	A	B
Utah	B	A	A	A	C	A
Virginia	B	B	B	A	C	B

Current 1995 Economic Performance Grades of 1991 Top Development Capacity States

State	1991 Development Capacity Grade	1995 Economic Performance Grade
MINNESOTA	A	B
Washington	A	C
UTAH	A	A
Massachusetts	A	C
CONNECTICUT	A	B
COLORADO	A	A
California	A	D
DELAWARE	A	A
MARYLAND	A	A
Pennsylvania	A	C

Capitalization indicates states with 1995 honor grades in Economic Performance.

The Mountain West, the region with the best Development Capacity Index growth trend, now ranks at the top of the Economic Performance Index. Meanwhile, the Pacific and Northeast, with the worst Development Capacity growth trends, are the only regions whose Economic Performance rankings have dropped since 1991.

Average Development Capacity Rankings By Region

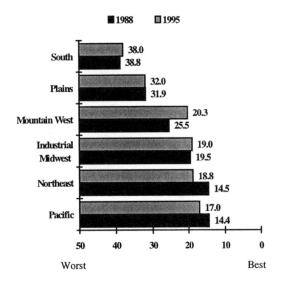

■ 1988   ▨ 1995

South	38.0 / 38.8
Plains	32.0 / 31.9
Mountain West	20.3 / 25.5
Industrial Midwest	19.0 / 19.5
Northeast	18.8 / 14.5
Pacific	17.0 / 14.4

50   40   30   20   10   0
Worst   Best

Final Observations

Some defense-dependent states have healthy, growing economies despite cutbacks. Thirteen state economies could be classified as defense-dependent – states that in 1991 had over five percent of their labor force in defense employment *and* above average ratios of defense contracts to total personal income. These states vary markedly in their performance in the Employment subindex, which measures changes in short- and long-term job growth as well as unemployment rates and the duration of unemployment. Four defense-dependent states – Connecticut, California, Maine, Massachusetts – suffer from very low rankings in almost every Employment subindex measure, resulting in Ds and Fs overall. Yet, four other defense-dependent states – Arizona, Colorado, Virginia, Utah – excel in most of these measures, earning As and Bs in Employment. The remaining five states, Alaska, Maryland, Mississippi, Missouri, and New Mexico, earn Cs.

Defense spending in the Mountain West, like the Northeast, has been focused on high-tech strategic command, intelligence, or weapons research and development. It is possible that these defense dollars served as an investment in building technological capacity, which the Mountain West was better able to convert into commercial purposes. Unfortunately for Connecticut and Maine, the only defense-dependent states to earn an F in the Employment subindex, recent rankings in Entrepreneurial Energy are discouragingly mediocre.

At the same time, regional economies built around troop training and movement may not have to resign themselves to permanent economic damage. Contrary to what state economists had anticipated, the region surrounding the Charleston base experienced a bloom in new business growth in 1994. Aiding new business formation may help mitigate the loss of military jobs.

Technical training for the "high performance workplace" may be the critical factor in reducing growing income disparity. For more than a decade, the top 20 percent of all U.S. households, ranked by income, have been garnering an ever greater share of total income while, at the same time, the bottom 20 percent of households have taken home proportionately less. This phenomena has been observed around the world, in industrialized and developing countries alike, but the United States and United Kingdom stand out from all other developed countries as having by far the worst record. This trend is reflected in the *Development Report Card* measures, with 32 states showing an increasingly skewed income distribution.

The cause of growing income disparity is a hotly debated issue, but recent work by the Federal Reserve Banks of New York and Boston suggests that "technology" accounts for more than half the deterioration in this equity measure. In other words, modern industry and business, dependent on the technical competence of its workers and managers to manipulate computers, ideas, and information, offer a wage premium to high skilled workers and "no way in" for unskilled workers.

Thus, it is interesting to note which states are registering improvements in income distribution, and to speculate why. Of the 18 states where income levels of the top and bottom households are converging, seven were western states that have a strikingly homogeneous population – very little ethnic diversity or unemployment – and substantial growth in average annual pay (SD, MT, CO, WY, IA, NE, ND). For these states, the upswing in the economy has distributed benefits in the 1950s-style pattern where even the lowest earning households share in the expansion. This occurred even as the states imported skilled workers from California and elsewhere.

The real kudos in equity, however, should go to Michigan and Indiana plus four southern states – Alabama, Arkansas, Louisiana, and Tennessee. Each state, under far less favorable circumstances, is showing improvement in income disparity and is also experiencing job and/or pay growth. It is not clear why these states are doing well. In some cases the economic recovery may have put unemployed technicians back on the job, and in other cases the unskilled worker may have found new job opportunities. If, as expected, the majority of new jobs being created in the 1990s are skilled positions, then the South's legendary customized job training programs may account for part of the success.

In any event, for the 32 states where the rich and the poor are growing farther apart, planners should not count on a rising tide lifting all boats. Those workers – and state economies – unable to navigate the rough waters of the high performance workplace will drift, if not sink.

Low costs don't equal more jobs and vice versa. Despite the importance of labor *productivity* – the amount of output per worker – the myth persists that the best path to a strong economy is simply a low-cost labor climate. Just looking at the Northeast, one would be inclined to believe this. On this year's Report Card, all five Fs on the Employment subindex go to states in the Northeast, and of those five, four earn As or Bs on Earnings & Job Quality. Yet, the relationship between jobs and wages is not so simple. Of the states *outside* the Northeast that earn an A on this year's Earnings & Job Quality subindex, none receive below a C on the Employment subindex. Moreover, of the four states with the lowest grades for Earnings & Job Quality (OK, WV, LA, AR), only Arkansas earns above a D on Employment. This should not be surprising. Labor, after all, accounts for less than a quarter of production costs in manufacturing. Much more important is a state's mix of industries – how the economy is diversified – and the competitiveness of its firms and industries and the skills of its workforce.

1995 Economic Performance Index

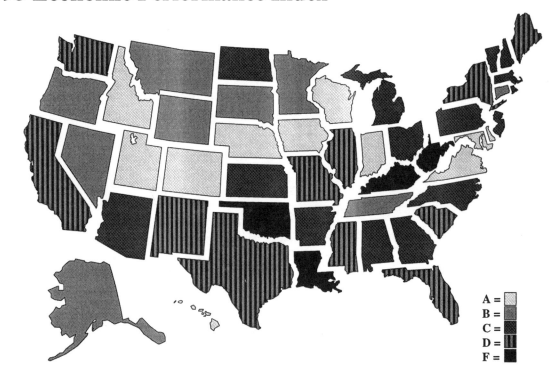

A =
B =
C =
D =
F =

Economic Performance: *How many economic benefits and opportunities for growth is the state economy providing its populace?* The bottom line on how an economy is doing, and an indicator of whether a state offers a good place for businesses to grow, is a state's current performance – that is, how well it does its job of providing citizens opportunities for employment, earnings, and widely shared growth.

Percent of States

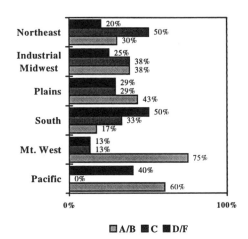

■ A/B ■ C ■ D/F

- This year's leader in Economic Performance is the Mountain West, as 75 percent of its states earn an A or B – double the number of honor grades from last year. Not far behind is last year's leader, the Pacific, where 60 percent of the states score an A or B. Grades have slipped in the Pacific region, though in an interesting twist – the Pacific (with two out of five states earning a D or an F) now also vies with the South for the highest percentage of poor grades.

- In the middle of the pack, the Plains (43 percent of the states have As and Bs) repeats last year's solid performance, while the Northeast continues its descent into mediocrity (50 percent of the states earn Cs versus only 30 percent last year).

- Once again, the South has the nation's poorest overall Economic Performance. Only Virginia and Tennessee earn above a C. At the same time, half of the states earn a D or F – an increase in poor grades from last year.

1995 Economic Performance Report Card

Overall Index			Employment Subindex		Earnings & Job Quality Subindex		Equity Subindex	
Grade	Rank		Rank	Grade	Rank	Grade	Rank	Grade
A	1	Colorado	4	A	9	A	3	A
	2	Wisconsin	8	A	3	A	20	B
	3	Hawaii	26	C	1	A	8	A
	4	Indiana	10	A	11	B	19	B
	5	Virginia	17	B	9	A	15	B
	6	Utah	1	A	32	C	9	A
	7	Delaware	19	B	4	A	22	C
	8	Idaho	3	A	27	C	17	B
	8	Iowa	20	B	20	B	7	A
	10	Maryland	31	C	11	B	6	A
	10	Nebraska	13	B	34	C	1	A
B	12	Wyoming	21	C	29	C	2	A
	13	Nevada	14	B	6	A	33	C
	13	South Dakota	6	A	36	D	11	B
	15	Minnesota	5	A	18	B	32	C
	15	Oregon	6	A	16	B	33	C
	17	Montana	15	B	37	D	5	A
	18	Alaska	33	C	21	C	4	A
	19	Tennessee	2	A	23	C	35	C
	20	Connecticut	46	F	4	A	13	B
C	21	North Dakota	11	B	43	D	10	A
	22	Massachusetts	43	D	11	B	13	B
	23	Michigan	29	C	2	A	37	D
	24	Kansas	35	C	23	C	17	B
	24	New Hampshire	28	C	23	C	24	C
	26	Arizona	8	A	41	D	27	C
	27	Georgia	18	B	30	C	29	C
	27	Ohio	37	D	15	B	25	C
	29	North Carolina	16	B	21	C	42	D
	30	Alabama	23	C	35	C	23	C
	31	Arkansas	12	B	50	F	21	C
	32	Pennsylvania	44	D	14	B	26	C
	33	New Jersey	47	F	8	A	30	C
	34	Vermont	35	C	40	D	16	B
	35	Rhode Island	50	F	7	A	35	C
D	36	Washington	34	C	30	C	30	C
	37	Illinois	39	D	17	B	41	D
	38	Florida	29	C	42	D	27	C
	39	Texas	24	C	37	D	39	D
	40	Missouri	26	C	27	C	49	F
	41	Maine	48	F	45	D	11	B
	42	New Mexico	22	C	39	D	46	F
	43	South Carolina	37	D	32	C	43	D
	44	California	42	D	23	C	50	F
	45	Mississippi	25	C	44	D	47	F
	45	New York	49	F	19	B	48	F
F	47	Kentucky	32	C	45	D	44	D
	48	Oklahoma	41	D	47	F	38	D
	49	Louisiana	40	D	49	F	40	D
	50	West Virginia	44	D	47	F	44	D

1995 Business Vitality Index

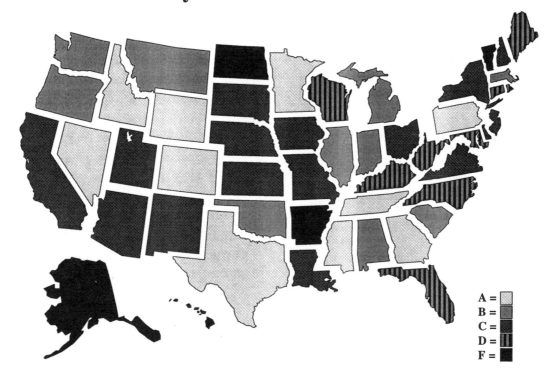

A =
B =
C =
D =
F =

Business Vitality: *How vital is the state's business sector?* The vitality of any state economy is determined by the strength and dynamism of the businesses located there – that is, how competitive they are, how diversified, and how many new ones are being created each year.

- For the second year in a row, the Mountain West and Industrial Midwest lead the nation in Business Vitality. In both regions, 63 percent of the states earn an honor grade of A or B. Impressively, the Mountain West actually improves on last year's outstanding grades – now no state in the region earns below a C.

- The Pacific and the South also have relatively strong Business Vitality grades. In both regions, roughly 40 percent of the states receive an A or B. Yet, the underlying trends differ. The South, with an increase in Ds and Fs from last year, is moving towards either very good or very bad grades. The Pacific's performance, meanwhile, is improving as two Cs became Bs or As.

- After modest scores last year, the Northeast receives the lowest scores on Business Vitality this year. With Massachusetts the only state with a grade above C, the region also has the nation's highest percentage of Ds and Fs – 50 percent.

Percent of States

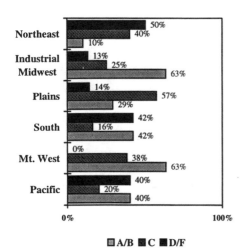

Northeast 50% / 40% / 10%

Industrial Midwest 13% / 25% / 63%

Plains 14% / 57% / 29%

South 42% / 16% / 42%

Mt. West 0% / 38% / 63%

Pacific 40% / 20% / 40%

0%   100%

■ A/B ■ C ■ D/F

1995 Business Vitality Report Card

Overall Index			Competitiveness of Existing Business Subindex		Entrepreneurial Energy Subindex		Structural Diversity Subindex	
Grade	Rank		Rank	Grade	Rank	Grade	Rank	Grade
A	1	Texas	11	B	14	B	4	A
	2	Tennessee	14	B	18	B	8	A
	3	Colorado	41	D	1	A	1	A
	4	Mississippi	31	C	14	B	6	A
	5	Georgia	29	C	9	A	14	B
	5	Wyoming	3	A	18	B	31	C
	7	Minnesota	18	B	17	B	18	B
	8	Idaho	4	A	4	A	46	F
	9	Nevada	1	A	5	A	50	F
	10	Pennsylvania	8	A	49	F	2	A
B	11	South Carolina	10	A	29	C	21	C
	12	Alabama	22	C	31	C	8	A
	12	Indiana	6	A	44	D	11	B
	14	Michigan	2	A	27	C	35	C
	14	Montana	20	B	3	A	41	D
	16	Washington	18	B	5	A	45	D
	17	Illinois	11	B	48	F	10	A
	17	Oregon	36	D	2	A	31	C
	19	Oklahoma	36	D	23	C	12	B
	20	Massachusetts	8	A	36	D	29	C
C	21	Missouri	45	D	22	C	7	A
	22	New Jersey	16	B	30	C	30	C
	23	California	32	C	27	C	19	B
	23	Delaware	24	C	13	B	41	D
	23	Kansas	43	D	18	B	17	B
	23	Ohio	5	A	49	F	24	C
	23	Utah	50	F	7	A	21	C
	28	New Mexico	34	C	12	B	35	C
	29	Louisiana	13	B	34	C	35	C
	29	New York	7	A	40	D	35	C
	31	Nebraska	47	F	8	A	28	C
	31	South Dakota	26	C	11	B	46	F
	33	Arizona	35	C	10	A	40	D
	33	Iowa	45	D	25	C	15	B
	33	New Hampshire	30	C	24	C	31	C
	33	Virginia	44	D	38	D	3	A
D	37	Kentucky	38	D	45	D	4	A
	37	Maine	21	C	41	D	25	C
	37	North Carolina	38	D	37	D	12	B
	37	Wisconsin	23	C	39	D	25	C
	41	Florida	48	F	21	C	19	B
	42	Connecticut	14	B	31	C	44	D
	42	Maryland	28	C	45	D	16	B
	44	West Virginia	17	B	34	C	43	D
	45	Rhode Island	27	C	31	C	39	D
F	46	Vermont	32	C	43	D	25	C
	47	Arkansas	25	C	45	D	31	C
	48	Alaska	40	D	16	B	48	F
	49	North Dakota	42	D	42	D	23	C
	50	Hawaii	49	F	26	C	49	F

1995 Development Capacity Index

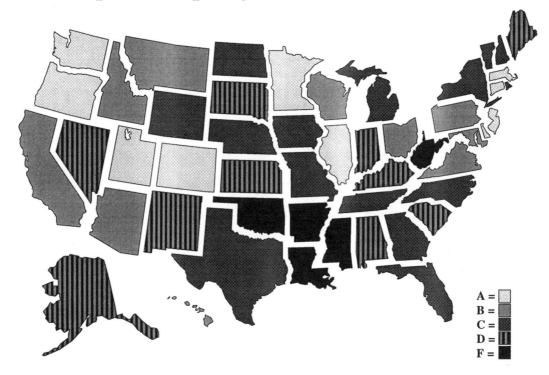

A =
B =
C =
D =
F =

Development Capacity: *What is the state's capacity for continued growth and recovery from economic adversity?* The future of both today's and tomorrow's businesses is tied directly to the quality and availability of the "building blocks" of economies – a skilled workforce, technology resources, financial resources, and physical infrastructure and amenity resources.

Percent of States

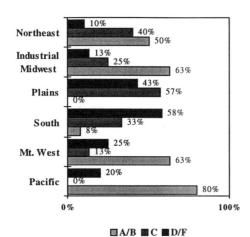

- For the fourth year in a row, the Pacific leads the nation in Development Capacity, with 80 percent of the region's states receiving an A or B. Last year no state in the region received a D or F; Alaska now receives a D.

- Not far behind the Pacific are the Industrial Midwest and the Mountain West – in each region 63 percent of the states earn an A or B. While the Industrial Midwest's strong grades are a virtual repeat from last year, the Mountain West's grades are an improvement, representing yet another area in which the region is gaining ascendancy.

- Though still the region with the most Ds and Fs (58 percent), the South can claim a moral victory this year with more than double the amount of C or above grades compared with last year. Perhaps the biggest disappointment this year comes from the Plains, which continues to have mostly average grades, but can now claim no state with an A or B.

1995 Development Capacity Report Card

Overall Index			Human Resources Subindex		Technology Resources Subindex		Financial Resources Subindex		Infrastructure & Amenity Resources Subindex	
Grade	Rank		Rank	Grade	Rank	Grade	Rank	Grade	Rank	Grade
A	1	Minnesota	8	A	21	C	2	A	4	A
	2	Colorado	4	A	2	A	32	C	2	A
	3	Washington	5	A	17	B	12	B	9	A
	4	Massachusetts	1	A	1	A	1	A	45	D
	5	Utah	3	A	5	A	41	D	1	A
	6	New Jersey	5	A	12	B	11	B	37	D
	7	Illinois	27	C	24	C	10	A	7	A
	7	Oregon	21	C	22	C	6	A	19	B
	9	Connecticut	2	A	7	A	21	C	40	D
	10	Delaware	28	C	10	A	19	B	17	B
B	11	Ohio	34	C	18	B	9	A	17	B
	12	Wisconsin	20	B	27	C	12	B	20	B
	13	Virginia	24	C	11	B	18	B	27	C
	14	Montana	10	A	31	C	38	D	3	A
	15	Hawaii	9	A	29	C	20	B	25	C
	16	Pennsylvania	29	C	16	B	3	A	36	D
	17	Arizona	23	C	12	B	39	D	11	B
	18	Idaho	18	B	22	C	21	C	25	C
	18	Maryland	16	B	4	A	34	C	32	C
	20	California	25	C	9	A	23	C	30	C
C	21	Texas	40	D	19	B	25	C	7	A
	22	Georgia	39	D	33	C	7	A	13	B
	22	New York	30	C	8	A	8	A	46	F
	22	Rhode Island	31	C	6	A	5	A	50	F
	25	Iowa	21	C	30	C	36	D	6	A
	25	Vermont	5	A	15	B	31	C	42	D
	27	North Dakota	18	B	24	C	37	D	15	B
	28	Nebraska	14	B	35	C	27	C	20	B
	29	Missouri	35	C	36	D	14	B	16	B
	30	New Hampshire	10	A	14	B	35	C	49	F
	31	Tennessee	46	F	37	D	16	B	14	B
	31	Wyoming	15	B	32	C	46	F	20	B
	33	Michigan	37	D	20	B	15	B	42	D
	34	North Carolina	43	D	26	C	3	A	46	F
	35	Florida	38	D	39	D	30	C	12	B
D	36	Kansas	12	B	40	D	39	D	29	C
	36	New Mexico	32	C	3	A	50	F	35	C
	38	Alabama	46	F	28	C	17	B	32	C
	39	Nevada	32	C	42	D	49	F	4	A
	40	Alaska	13	B	34	C	43	D	38	D
	41	South Dakota	25	C	46	F	26	C	32	C
	42	Maine	17	B	43	D	29	C	41	D
	43	Indiana	42	D	40	D	28	C	24	C
	44	South Carolina	48	F	45	D	33	C	9	A
	45	Kentucky	45	D	49	F	24	C	23	C
F	46	Oklahoma	36	D	38	D	42	D	30	C
	47	Arkansas	41	D	50	F	47	F	28	C
	48	West Virginia	44	D	48	F	45	D	39	D
	49	Louisiana	50	F	44	D	44	D	42	D
	50	Mississippi	48	F	47	F	48	F	48	F

Regional Findings

The following is a regional listing of states and state abbreviations found in the *1995 Development Report Card for the States*.

The Northeast

Connecticut	CT
Delaware	DE
Maine	ME
Maryland	MD
Massachusetts	MA
New Hampshire	NH
New Jersey	NJ
New York	NY
Rhode Island	RI
Vermont	VT

The Industrial Midwest

Illinois	IL
Indiana	IN
Michigan	MI
Minnesota	MN
Missouri	MO
Ohio	OH
Pennsylvania	PA
Wisconsin	WI

The Plains

Iowa	IA
Kansas	KS
Nebraska	NE
North Dakota	ND
Oklahoma	OK
South Dakota	SD
Texas	TX

The South

Alabama	AL
Arkansas	AR
Florida	FL
Georgia	GA
Kentucky	KY
Louisiana	LA
Mississippi	MS
North Carolina	NC
South Carolina	SC
Tennessee	TN
Virginia	VA
West Virginia	WV

The Mountain West

Arizona	AZ
Colorado	CO
Idaho	ID
Montana	MT
Nevada	NV
New Mexico	NM
Utah	UT
Wyoming	WY

The Pacific

Alaska	AK
California	CA
Hawaii	HI
Oregon	OR
Washington	WA

The Northeast

While other regions rebounded strongly from the recession in the early 1990s, the Northeast is still caught in an economic tailspin. In the past year, the already struggling Northeast seemingly hit rock bottom with 40 percent of its states dropping by two or more grades in one or more indexes (ME, NJ, NY, VT). This grade deterioration was largely due to a dramatic decline in Business Vitality, as the rate of new company formations is falling off precipitously. Moreover, existing new businesses are not contributing as significantly to job growth as elsewhere in the nation. Many parts of the region are still trying to coast off of their historically strong resources (its human resources are still the country's best). But recent disinvestment may soon come back to haunt them: infrastructure has declined sharply since 1990 and the financial sector is still shaken. But the worst may soon be over – business closings are among the nation's lowest, and many economists (including Dun & Bradstreet) are predicting continued recovery in 1995.

A =
B =
C =
D =
F =

Economic Performance:

- As recently as 1992, 70 percent of Northeastern states received an A or a B in Economic Performance; this year, 70 percent receive grades of C or less, marking an all-time low. In 1988, Northeastern states captured the top nine spots nationally in Economic Performance; this year, Connecticut, Delaware, and Maryland are the only states in the region to earn honor grades.

- While other regions (such as the Mountain West) have rebounded strongly from the early 1990s recession, the Northeast has not. The Northeast's ranking in the Employment subindex has dropped every year since 1989 and is currently the worst in the country – all five Fs in Employment are found in this region (CT, ME, NJ, NY, RI).

- Despite declining ranks in Earnings & Job Quality during the past year (70 percent of the states dropped in ranking), the Northeast still has some of the nation's best paying jobs: six of the top eleven states in Earnings & Job Quality are in the Northeast (CT, DE, MA, MD, NJ, RI).

Business Vitality:

- While last year four Northeastern states earned an A or B in Business Vitality, this year only Massachusetts (20th nationally) earns a grade higher than a C. A significant decline in entrepreneurship is primarily responsible for the steep drop in Business Vitality grades.

- Last year, with 60 percent of the states earning an A or B, the Northeast was one of the nation's most entrepreneurial regions. Now, Delaware's B is the only grade higher than C in Entrepreneurial Energy.

- Northeastern economic problems are compounded by a striking lack of balance in the regional economy. Maryland is the only state in the region to rank higher than 25 in Structural Diversity, with Connecticut and Delaware ranking among the ten worst.

Development Capacity:

- The Northeast remains one of the nation's strongest regions in Development Capacity with four states earning an A (CT, DE, MA, NJ) due to excellent human, technology, and financial resources. Six of the nine states with the highest college attainment rates are in the Northeast (CT, MA, MD, NH, NJ, VT).

- Despite inroads made by the Mountain West, the Northeast is still home to most of the nation's top high-technology jobs. Only Maine earns a non-honor mark in the Technology Resources subindex.

- The Northeast's rapidly deteriorating infrastructure may help explain why the region's economic performance has declined while its development capacity has remained strong. The Northeast's grades in Infrastructure & Amenity Resources have declined every year since 1990 so that the region now ranks last in this subindex with eight states receiving Ds and Fs (CT, ME, MA, NH, NJ, NY, RI, VT).

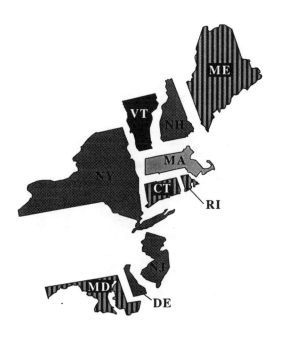

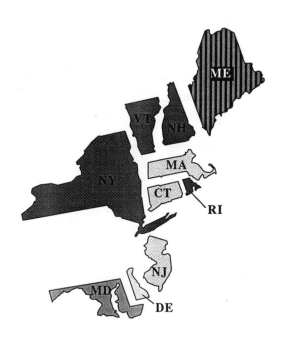

The Industrial Midwest

The "Rust Belt" certainly isn't rusting any longer. Proving that last year's comeback was no fluke, the Industrial Midwest has sustained its gains in all three indexes. A resurgent auto industry has led the charge, greatly boosting manufacturing employment and creating a plethora of mid- to high-wage positions. While job quality has consistently improved since 1992, income disparity between rich and poor has also grown. In order to sustain its growth and fill these high-skill positions, the region must reverse its decline in the Human Resources subindex by boosting the educational attainment of its residents. Although the region has been extraordinarily successful in chipping the rust off aging businesses (posting the lowest business failure rates in the country), it has not created many new firms. To keep pace with the surging Mountain West, the Industrial Midwest must resuscitate its stagnant entrepreneurial sector in much the same way it revitalized its manufacturing sector.

Economic Performance:

- The Industrial Midwest sustains last year's leap from the rear to the middle of the pack. Three states earn honor grades (IN, MN, WI), including two of the nation's top four (IN, WI), while two states earn Ds (MO, IL). None receive an F.

- High job quality remains a regional asset as every single Industrial Midwest state except Missouri (which receives a C) earns an honor grade in Earnings & Job Quality. Overall pay levels are good (only Wisconsin is below average), and health coverage is excellent (every state but Illinois is in the top 20).

- Equity is the region's weakest Economic Performance subindex. Three states receive failing grades (IL, MI, MO), with large gaps between the rich and poor and rural and urban areas.

A =
B =
C =
D =
F =

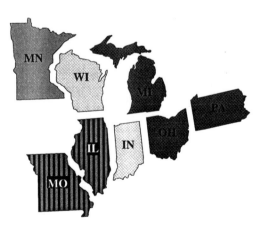

Business Vitality:

- The Industrial Midwest is one of the nation's best performers in Business Vitality despite a stagnant entrepreneurial sector. Only Wisconsin ranks below average in Business Vitality and five of eight states earn honor grades (IL, IN, MI, MN, PA).

- Competitiveness of Existing Business and Structural Diversity are both strong. Six states earn an A or a B in the former subindex (IL, IN, MI, MN, OH, PA) and five states do so in the latter (IL, IN, MN, MO, PA).

- Even though Entrepreneurial Energy has improved substantially from 1993 (when every state received a poor grade), the region still struggles in this subindex, with Minnesota the only state earning an honor grade and five states receiving poor grades (IL, IN, OH, PA, WI). Fewer new companies are formed in this region than anywhere else (all states rank in the bottom 15).

Development Capacity:

- The Industrial Midwest states earn only one failing grade (IN) and five honor grades (IL, MN, OH, PA, WI) in Development Capacity. Minnesota ranks first in the nation in this index for an unprecedented eighth consecutive year.

- The region's Financial Resources are the best in the country. Every state except Indiana earns an honor grade, including four As (IL, MN, OH, PA). Led by low urban housing costs and above-average urban mass transit availability, five states receive honor grades in Infrastructure & Amenity Resources (IL, MN, MO, OH, WI).

- With no states ranking in the top 20 in college attainment, Human Resources are the region's big weakness. Only Minnesota and Wisconsin receive honor grades while Indiana and Michigan receive Ds. Technology Resources are also cause for concern as every state except Indiana drops in ranking since last year.

The Plains

The Plains' economies are generally dominated by the cycles of boom and bust in agriculture, energy, and real estate. This may help explain their almost diametric split between north and south. At the same time that the northern Plains are thriving in economic performance with the lowest unemployment in the country, the southern Plains are sputtering, with large disparities between rich and poor, sub-par employment and declining performance. Texas seems to be breaking a little with tradition by hitching its wagon to Mexico and other export markets. Although the state is hurting now, the strategy may have begun to pay off – the state has experienced a rapid rise (though not as much as hoped for) over the past four years in business vitality and job growth. Future economic success will rest on the region's ability to match recent improvements in infrastructure with corresponding progressions in human, technology, and financial resources.

Economic Performance:

- Every state is above average in Economic Performance except for Oklahoma and Texas, which lag far behind the rest with a D and an F, respectively. The northern Plains (IA, ND, NE, SD) now all earn honor grades in Equity, mostly due to decreases in the gap between rich and poor. The northern Plains also saw strong improvements in employment conditions with very low unemployment rates. Again, only Oklahoma and Texas have below average employment situations.

- An abundance of low-paying jobs places the Plains' Earnings & Job Quality among the worst in the country with four states receiving failing grades (ND, OK, SD, TX). Four of the eight states with the nation's lowest annual wages are from this region (IA, NE, ND, SD).

A =
B =
C =
D =
F =

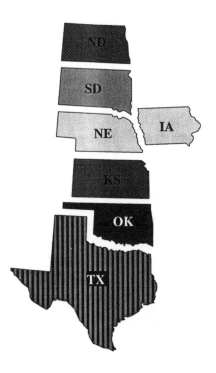

Business Vitality:

- Regional performance in Business Vitality is mixed, containing the good, the bad, and the ugly. Texas earns the nation's best Business Vitality grade, but North Dakota ranks second to last. Four of the other five states earn Cs (IA, KS, NE, SD).

- The Plains states are struggling in Competitiveness of Existing Business with four states dropping grades (KS, NE, ND, SD) in the past year. Five states receive failing grades (IA, KS, NE, ND, OK) and only Texas earns an honor grade.

- Entrepreneurial Energy is high in the Plains. Last year five states ranked in the bottom half nationally in this subindex, now only North Dakota does. Structural Diversity is also strong – four states earn honor grades (IA, KS, OK, TX).

Development Capacity:

- The region continues to show weakness in Development Capacity – last year only two states received honor grades and this year none do. Three states (43 percent) receive poor grades (Kansas and South Dakota earn Ds and Oklahoma an F).

- Technology and Financial Resources are the region's Achilles' heel. Only Texas, which receives a B in Technology Resources, earns an honor grade in either subindex. Four states earn Ds in Financial Resources (IA, KS, ND, OK). Four states in this region rank among the bottom ten in SBIC Financings (IA, ND, OK, SD) and three states completely lack a venture capital industry (KS, ND, SD).

- Infrastructure & Amenity Resources in the Plains is strong. No states rank at the bottom, and four states earn honor grades (IA, NE, ND, TX). Five states rank among the ten best in sewage treatment needs (IA, NE, ND, OK, SD), and energy is cheap (only Kansas has higher than average energy costs).

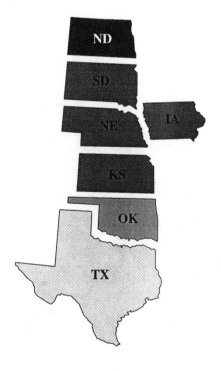

The South

The good news for the South is that it improved its Development Capacity grades during the past year and that it is again strong in the Tax & Fiscal System Index – the "enablers" of future growth. The bad news is that the South still has a long way to go – Economic Performance and Development Capacity rankings remain the worst in the country, as they have for the last decade. In particular, job quality in the South is alarmingly low, as measured by average pay, annual pay growth, and health insurance coverage. Interestingly, even omitting pay levels from the grade calculation – to neutralize any possible bias due to large cost of living differences – does little to change the South's poor Earnings & Job Quality rankings. The region still has poor health coverage and little movement in pay levels. On the brighter side, the region's performance in the Employment subindex remains respectably in the middle ranges with Arkansas, Georgia, and Tennessee leading the way. Alabama, Florida, and Mississippi are also creating jobs rapidly but are held back by poor unemployment rates.

A =
B =
C =
D =
F =

Economic Performance:

- Traditionally weak in Economic Performance, the South kept its two strong headliners (TN, VA) but saw Florida join last year's five failing states (KY, LA, MS, SC, WV). The problem remains poor Earnings & Job Quality and Equity; only Virginia can get above a C in those two subindexes. Not only are wages low, but they are increasing slower than elsewhere. Poverty remains a problem – nine of the eleven worst ranking states are southern (the other two are California and Oklahoma). There are positive signs, though, in Alabama, Arkansas, Louisiana, and Tennessee; these states can all point to a decrease in the gap between rich and poor.

- The good news is that the region's Employment outlook is brighter, with five states earning an A or B (AR, GA, NC, TN, VA). Arkansas, Georgia, and Tennessee, in particular, have seen very strong recent employment growth with unemployment rates that are 5 percent and below – structural full employment according to some.

Business Vitality:

- Business Vitality rankings in the South are a cause for both optimism and concern – five states (42 percent) earn honor grades (AL, GA, MS, SC, TN) while five states receive Ds or Fs (AR, FL, KY, NC, WV). The balance may tilt towards optimism, though, as three of the nation's five best Business Vitality rankings are in the South (TN, GA, MS), with Arkansas the only state ranking in the nation's five worst.

- Southern economies are generally well-balanced – eight states (67 percent) earn an A or a B in Structural Diversity (AL, FL, GA, KY, MS, NC, TN, VA); only West Virginia receives a failing grade. Income generated by the region's traded sector is spread over a variety of industries in the South with five top-ten performers in sectoral diversity (AL, KY, MS, TN, VA).

Development Capacity:

- While the South remains the nation's worst region for development resources, it has improved significantly during the past year – no southern state fell in ranking, and five states raised their grades (FL, KY, NC, TN, VA). However, ten of twelve states rank below 30 in the national rankings, including six of the nation's bottom seven (AR, KY, LA, MS, SC, WV). Only Virginia earns an honor grade.

- Human Resources are the South's biggest problem – only Virginia can earn a passing grade of C. Technology Resources are only marginally better with Virginia as the sole Honor Roll performer (again) and eight states earning failing grades (AR, FL, KY, LA, MS, SC, TN, WV).

- Great disparity exists in the financial resources available to Southern states. Alabama, Georgia, North Carolina, Tennessee, and Virginia earn honor grades in the subindex while Arkansas, Louisiana, Mississippi, and West Virginia have among the seven worst financial resources in the nation.

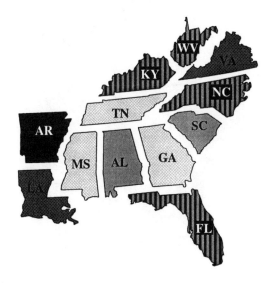

The Mountain West

Entrepreneurial energy in the Mountain West is brimming at its highest level in decades. Opportunities now abound and historical outmigration trends have reversed, as people are staying (and coming back) home. This year, the Mountain West jumped to the top of both the Economic Performance and Business Vitality indexes. The regional economy is firing on all cylinders – both long-term and short-term employment vastly exceed the levels in all other regions; new companies are continuing to spring up everywhere creating an abundance of well-paying jobs; unemployment is low; and there is less disparity between rich and poor than ever before. The region's only blemishes are a poorly diversified industrial base and one of the nation's worst financial bases (low deposits accompanied by even lower loan activity). However, with strong human and technology resources and an extraordinary infrastructure, the Mountain West appears poised to remain among the nation's economic leaders.

Economic Performance:

- The Mountain West is this year's star. Every state except Utah improved its Economic Performance ranking during the past year, so that now six of the eight states (75 percent) earn honor grades (CO, ID, MT, NV, UT, WY).

- Strong employment growth characterizes the region as every state ranked above average in the Employment subindex, with half of them in the top ten. Interestingly, despite having some of the highest employment growth rates, many Mountain West states had coomparativley high unemployment rates (including Arizona, Idaho, New Mexico, and Nevada).

- Although the region is improving in Earnings & Job Quality and Equity, it still lags behind much of the nation. Even though six states saw increases in Earnings & Job Quality, Colorado and Nevada (both earning As) are the only two states to currently rank in the top half nationally.

A =
B =
C =
D =
F =

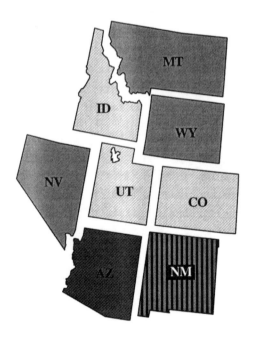

The Corporation for Enterprise Development

Business Vitality:

- Four states now earn As (CO, ID, NV, WY), up from two last year, and no state earns less than a C. The key is the Mountain West's outstanding Entrepreneurial Energy – all eight states are in the top twenty. In fact, 60 percent of the country's top ten entrepreneurial states were in the Mountain West (AZ, CO, ID, MT, NV, UT). With a focus on small companies, the region has one of the overall highest rates of new business job growth.

- The Competitiveness of Existing Business in the region, meanwhile, is more mixed. Over half of the states (AZ, CO, NM, MT, UT) receive very little income from industries that compete out of state (the traded sector), yet on the other hand, Idaho, Nevada, and Wyoming do very well in the traded sector strength measure.

- Structural Diversity is the Mountain West's weak subindex. Four states receive failing grades (AZ, ID, MT, NV). The region is among the worst in the country, dropping in rank since last year.

Development Capacity:

- Development Capacity is the Mountain West's weakest index, but even so, it is still strong due to the quality of its workforce and infrastructure. Five states earn an A or B (AZ, CO, ID, MT, UT), though two of its more southern states have Ds (NV, NM). Two-thirds of the region's states receive an A or B in Infrastructure & Amenity Resources (AZ, CO, MT, NV, UT), including the top four in the country (UT, CO, MT, NV), as the region boasts some of the best bridges and highways and lowest energy costs. Strong high school attainment and moderate college attainment also characterize most of the region.

- Financial Resources in the Mountain West are weak. No state earns an honor grade in this subindex and three-fourths actually receive failing grades (AZ, MT, NV, NM, UT, WY). Commercial bank deposits are low, commercial and industrial loan activity sluggish, and little venture capital is coming to the area (although the later may be changing).

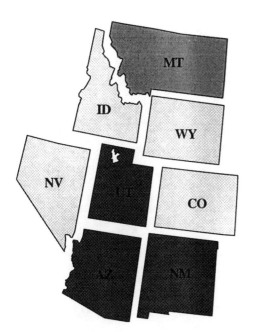

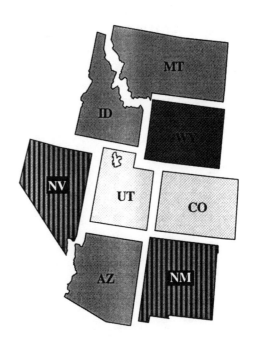

The Pacific

As distant economically as they are geographically, the Pacific states behave less like a regional unit than an eclectic collection of state economies. Alaska and Hawaii are highly dependent upon their unique natural resource endowments and serve largely domestic markets, while California is well diversified – almost a nation unto itself – and exports heavily. The economies of Oregon and Washington, meanwhile, are deeply affected by certain industrial sectors but are more industrialized and export-intensive than Alaska and Hawaii. Hawaii and Oregon performed well this year, but for entirely different reasons. Hawaii, despite struggling employment, improved its already strong Earnings & Job Quality and Equity, while Oregon moved into the nation's elite in Employment rankings, despite a drop in Equity. What the Pacific states do have in common, however, is a strong development capacity with unsurpassed human resources.

Economic Performance:

- There is no strong unified trend or pattern in the Pacific states' Economic Performance – the states are all very much products of their own individual circumstances. Alaska, Hawaii, and Oregon earn honor grades, but the first two states have unique and isolated economies from which it is difficult to draw regional conclusions. Washington earns a D, with Employment dragging it down, while Oregon, similar in many ways, receives a B. California's poor grade reflects its series of catastrophes.

- The region's Earnings & Job Quality ranks are generally good as Hawaii and Oregon earn an A and B and the other three states rank in the top 30. Equity, on the other hand, is mixed – California ranks last nationally, while Hawaii and Alaska earn As.

- Interestingly, Alaska and Hawaii had the nation's second and third most significant decreases in the gap between rich and poor, while Oregon, the other strong performing state, actually saw a marked increase in income disparity – more so than in California.

A =
B =
C =
D =
F =

Business Vitality:

- The Pacific's Business Vitality is almost a reverse mirror image of its Economic Performance, as top performing Alaska and Hawaii must contend with Fs in Business Vitality. Meanwhile, Washington has a D in Performance, but a B in Business Vitality. The only exception is Oregon, matching its B in Economic Performance with a B in Business Vitality.

- Entrepreneurial Energy in the region is very strong – whether in response to limited opportunities or economic growth. None of the five Pacific states receive a grade lower than a C, and three (AK, OR, WA) get an A or B, mostly due to job growth from new and young businesses.

- In contrast to entrepreneurship, existing businesses appear weak. Alaska, Hawaii, and Oregon receive failing grades in Competitiveness of Existing Business, and only Washington, with a B, earns a grade above a C. Poor grades are due to very high business closing rates (all five states are worse than average), but this may just reflect the high turnover associated with restructuring and/or growing economies.

Development Capacity:

- The one index in which the Pacific is relatively uniform is Development Capacity, with all the region's states except Alaska receiving an honor grade. Human resources are the region's main attraction. All five states rank in the top half for Human Resources, including Hawaii and Washington, who receive As. Technology Resources is next with none of the states scoring poorly and California and Washington among the top 20. The Pacific states are still strong in the necessary resources for high-technology industries.

- Alaska's D is the only non-honor grade. In fact, Alaska's Ds in Financial Resources and Infrastructure & Amenity Resources are the only failing grades among Pacific states in any of the four Development Capacity subindexes.

Regional & State Trends: 1991–1995
Economic Performance Index

	1991 Rank	Grade	1992 Rank	Grade	1993 Rank	Grade	1994 Rank	Grade	1995 Rank	Grade
Northeast										
Connecticut	10	A	8	A	11	B	15	B	20	B
Delaware	6	A	3	A	1	A	11	B	7	A
Maine	7	A	22	C	24	C	42	D	41	D
Maryland	3	A	2	A	5	A	32	C	10	A
Massachusetts	21	C	28	C	34	C	35	C	22	C
New Hampshire	2	A	12	B	21	C	10	A	24	C
New Jersey	5	A	16	B	24	C	24	C	33	C
New York	37	D	34	C	44	D	36	D	45	D
Rhode Island	16	B	20	B	32	C	39	D	35	C
Vermont	17	B	13	B	13	B	16	B	34	C
Industrial Midwest										
Illinois	35	C	26	C	36	D	40	D	37	D
Indiana	22	C	20	B	30	C	5	A	4	A
Michigan	27	C	31	C	40	D	32	C	23	C
Minnesota	18	B	11	B	23	C	6	A	15	B
Missouri	40	D	24	C	18	B	49	F	40	D
Ohio	35	C	25	C	26	C	25	C	27	C
Pennsylvania	13	B	15	B	22	C	17	B	32	C
Wisconsin	9	A	7	A	3	A	3	A	2	A
Plains										
Iowa	23	C	18	B	9	A	4	A	8	A
Kansas	15	B	13	B	17	B	28	C	24	C
Nebraska	12	B	5	A	6	A	8	A	10	A
North Dakota	30	C	37	D	45	D	36	D	21	C
Oklahoma	40	D	46	F	46	F	44	D	48	F
South Dakota	29	C	39	D	20	B	19	B	13	B
Texas	43	D	39	D	29	C	27	C	39	D
South										
Alabama	44	D	41	D	38	D	28	C	30	C
Arkansas	45	D	47	F	19	B	21	C	31	C
Florida	23	C	32	C	30	C	25	C	38	D
Georgia	28	C	30	C	43	D	32	C	27	C
Kentucky	47	F	42	D	50	F	46	F	47	F
Louisiana	50	F	49	F	49	F	50	F	49	F
Mississippi	46	F	50	F	48	F	44	D	45	D
North Carolina	19	B	17	B	14	B	22	C	29	C
South Carolina	23	C	34	C	40	D	41	D	43	D
Tennessee	34	C	38	D	34	C	19	B	19	B
Virginia	19	B	23	C	4	A	11	B	5	A
West Virginia	49	F	44	D	47	F	47	F	50	F
Mountain West										
Arizona	30	C	34	C	42	D	28	C	26	C
Colorado	39	D	33	C	15	B	6	A	1	A
Idaho	33	C	19	B	12	B	31	C	8	A
Montana	48	F	43	D	32	C	38	D	17	B
Nevada	1	A	1	A	15	B	17	B	13	B
New Mexico	40	D	48	F	37	D	43	D	42	D
Utah	13	B	9	A	10	A	2	A	6	A
Wyoming	30	C	27	C	26	C	22	C	12	B
Pacific										
Alaska	37	D	45	D	38	D	9	A	18	B
California	26	C	28	C	28	C	47	F	44	D
Hawaii	3	A	6	A	8	A	1	A	3	A
Oregon	11	B	9	A	6	A	14	B	15	B
Washington	8	A	4	A	2	A	13	B	36	D

Regional & State Trends: 1991–1995
Business Vitality Index

	1991		1992		1993		1994		1995	
	Rank	Grade	Rank	Grade	Rank	Grade	Rank	Grade	Rank	Grade
Northeast										
Connecticut	7	A	15	B	31	C	43	D	42	D
Delaware	19	B	9	A	43	D	11	B	23	C
Maine	17	B	17	B	6	A	17	B	37	D
Maryland	9	A	20	B	28	C	28	C	42	D
Massachusetts	12	B	39	D	20	B	30	C	20	B
New Hampshire	1	A	41	D	46	F	39	D	33	C
New Jersey	5	A	12	B	30	C	3	A	22	C
New York	6	A	24	C	19	B	9	A	29	C
Rhode Island	23	C	35	C	48	F	49	F	45	D
Vermont	21	C	16	B	16	B	23	C	46	F
Industrial Midwest										
Illinois	26	C	17	B	11	B	6	A	17	B
Indiana	30	C	6	A	26	C	2	A	12	B
Michigan	42	D	38	D	28	C	32	C	14	B
Minnesota	4	A	5	A	34	C	17	B	7	A
Missouri	35	C	30	C	40	D	20	B	21	C
Ohio	45	D	30	C	34	C	29	C	23	C
Pennsylvania	15	B	21	C	15	B	20	B	10	A
Wisconsin	40	D	24	C	40	D	37	D	37	D
Plains										
Iowa	41	D	3	A	43	D	38	D	33	C
Kansas	36	D	12	B	34	C	16	B	23	C
Nebraska	32	C	26	C	45	D	44	D	31	C
North Dakota	49	F	26	C	22	C	19	B	49	F
Oklahoma	47	F	45	D	40	D	47	F	19	B
South Dakota	26	C	10	A	20	B	39	D	31	C
Texas	24	C	1	A	1	A	1	A	1	A
South										
Alabama	13	B	23	C	2	A	6	A	12	B
Arkansas	42	D	34	C	5	A	39	D	47	F
Florida	15	B	33	C	37	D	32	C	41	D
Georgia	26	C	46	F	10	A	11	B	5	A
Kentucky	32	C	26	C	13	B	24	C	37	D
Louisiana	50	F	47	F	37	D	34	C	29	C
Mississippi	32	C	37	D	16	B	8	A	4	A
North Carolina	2	A	35	C	13	B	26	C	37	D
South Carolina	38	D	49	F	47	F	45	D	11	B
Tennessee	31	C	29	C	8	A	5	A	2	A
Virginia	11	B	19	B	26	C	20	B	33	C
West Virginia	46	F	42	D	16	B	46	F	44	D
Mountain West										
Arizona	26	C	50	F	49	F	50	F	33	C
Colorado	8	A	3	A	4	A	3	A	3	A
Idaho	36	D	7	A	7	A	10	A	8	A
Montana	39	D	30	C	8	A	14	B	14	B
Nevada	13	B	21	C	31	C	30	C	9	A
New Mexico	17	B	2	A	3	A	11	B	28	C
Utah	10	A	11	B	22	C	15	B	23	C
Wyoming	48	F	43	D	11	B	35	C	5	A
Pacific										
Alaska	20	B	14	B	39	D	26	C	48	F
California	3	A	8	A	25	C	35	C	23	C
Hawaii	44	D	48	F	50	F	48	F	50	F
Oregon	21	C	44	D	22	C	39	D	17	B
Washington	24	C	40	D	33	C	24	C	16	B

Regional & State Trends: 1991–1995
Development Capacity Index

	1991		1992		1993		1994		1995	
	Rank	Grade	Rank	Grade	Rank	Grade	Rank	Grade	Rank	Grade
Northeast										
Connecticut	5	A	12	B	8	A	9	A	9	A
Delaware	7	A	15	B	7	A	11	B	10	A
Maine	43	D	45	D	45	D	44	D	42	D
Maryland	9	A	9	A	6	A	11	B	18	B
Massachusetts	4	A	4	A	5	A	4	A	4	A
New Hampshire	14	B	25	C	30	C	33	C	30	C
New Jersey	10	A	18	B	11	B	8	A	6	A
New York	24	C	7	A	18	B	24	C	22	C
Rhode Island	16	B	23	C	23	C	20	B	22	C
Vermont	20	B	13	B	25	C	26	C	25	C
Industrial Midwest										
Illinois	19	B	11	B	17	B	6	A	7	A
Indiana	36	D	33	C	43	D	43	D	43	D
Michigan	25	C	22	C	31	C	30	C	33	C
Minnesota	1	A	1	A	1	A	1	A	1	A
Missouri	33	C	26	C	34	C	34	C	29	C
Ohio	12	B	17	B	15	B	17	B	11	B
Pennsylvania	10	A	21	C	13	B	15	B	16	B
Wisconsin	31	C	10	A	9	A	7	A	12	B
Plains										
Iowa	35	C	26	C	29	C	18	B	25	C
Kansas	25	C	29	C	32	C	29	C	36	D
Nebraska	25	C	33	C	22	C	16	B	28	C
North Dakota	42	D	46	F	42	D	30	C	27	C
Oklahoma	44	D	44	D	39	D	42	D	46	F
South Dakota	32	C	37	D	44	D	40	D	41	D
Texas	22	C	19	B	20	B	27	C	21	C
South										
Alabama	45	D	43	D	39	D	41	D	38	D
Arkansas	48	F	49	F	47	F	47	F	47	F
Florida	39	D	40	D	36	D	36	D	35	C
Georgia	34	C	31	C	21	C	23	C	22	C
Kentucky	46	F	42	D	46	F	46	F	45	D
Louisiana	47	F	47	F	49	F	49	F	49	F
Mississippi	50	F	50	F	50	F	50	F	50	F
North Carolina	29	C	24	C	37	D	37	D	34	C
South Carolina	41	D	41	D	41	D	45	D	44	D
Tennessee	40	D	26	C	37	D	39	D	31	C
Virginia	16	B	6	A	19	B	22	C	13	B
West Virginia	49	F	47	F	48	F	48	F	48	F
Mountain West										
Arizona	20	B	20	B	13	B	18	B	17	B
Colorado	5	A	5	A	4	A	2	A	2	A
Idaho	28	C	38	D	26	C	27	C	18	B
Montana	38	D	36	D	26	C	14	B	14	B
Nevada	16	B	32	C	26	C	32	C	39	D
New Mexico	36	D	39	D	35	C	35	C	36	D
Utah	3	A	3	A	2	A	4	A	5	A
Wyoming	22	C	35	C	23	C	37	D	31	C
Pacific										
Alaska	30	C	29	C	33	C	25	C	40	D
California	7	A	8	A	9	A	20	B	20	B
Hawaii	14	B	16	B	12	B	13	B	15	B
Oregon	13	B	14	B	16	B	10	A	7	A
Washington	2	A	2	A	3	A	3	A	3	A

1995 State Report Cards

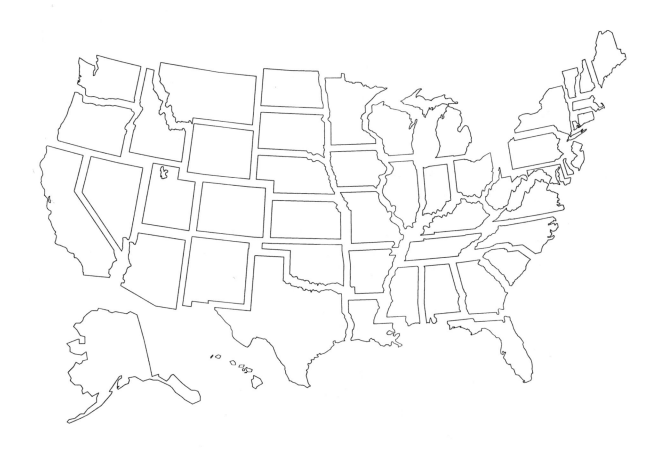

ALABAMA 1995 REPORT CARD

ECONOMIC PERFORMANCE	C

Employment C
Earnings & Job Quality C
Equity C

BUSINESS VITALITY	B

Business Competitiveness C
Entrepreneurial Energy....................................C
Structural Diversity ....A

DEVELOPMENT CAPACITY	D

Human Resources..F
Technology Resources C
Financial Resources..B
Infrastructure & Amenity Resources.................C

Tax & Fiscal System	√

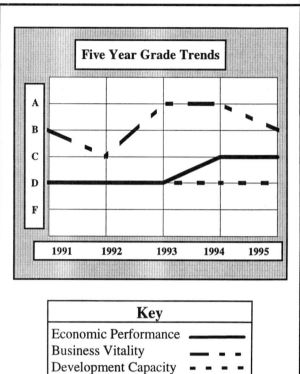

Five Year Grade Trends

1991 1992 1993 1994 1995

Key	
Economic Performance	——————
Business Vitality	— ▪ ▪ ▪
Development Capacity	▪ ▪ ▪ ▪

- **Economic Performance:** For the second year in a row, Alabama earns average grades in all facets of Economic Performance. Alabama's improving unemployment rate and short-term employment growth now rank in the top 20. Moreover, for the second year in a row, the gap between the rich and the poor is shrinking faster in Alabama than in all but eight states. Due largely to poor social indicators, the quality of life in Alabama is below average.

- **Business Vitality:** Due to a decrease in the competitiveness of its existing businesses, Alabama's grade drops to a B. Although manufacturing capital investments remain high, the diminished competitiveness of the state's businesses is reflected largely in the nation's sixth worst number of business closings. Entrepreneurial Energy remains only modest in Alabama, but the state's industries are well diversified.

- **Development Capacity:** For the sixth year in a row, Alabama receives a below average grade for its development resources. The state's primary weakness, Human Resources, receives a failing grade with a very low high school graduation rate and the nation's fourth lowest college attainment. Nevertheless, the state's Financial Resources remain above average and, with rapidly improving highway quality, the state's infrastructure resources have improved to an average mark.

- **Tax & Fiscal System:** Alabama receives an average mark for its Tax & Fiscal System. While the state has one of the least equitable tax structures, it has above average stability and policies to equalize fiscal capacity among local governments.

For information on how grades and ranks are calculated, see the Methodology section.
For a detailed explanation of indexes, refer to the individual index section.

WHERE ALABAMA RANKS – MEASURE BY MEASURE

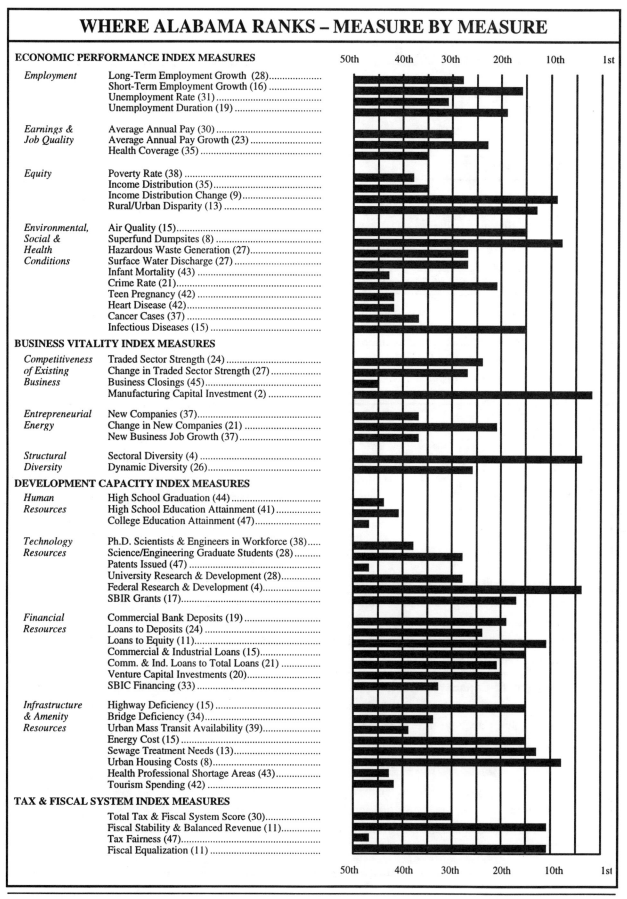

ECONOMIC PERFORMANCE INDEX MEASURES

50th   40th   30th   20th   10th   1st

Employment
Long-Term Employment Growth (28)....................
Short-Term Employment Growth (16) ....
Unemployment Rate (31) ....
Unemployment Duration (19) ....

Earnings &
Job Quality
Average Annual Pay (30) ....
Average Annual Pay Growth (23) ....
Health Coverage (35) ....

Equity
Poverty Rate (38) ....
Income Distribution (35) ....
Income Distribution Change (9) ....
Rural/Urban Disparity (13) ....

Environmental,
Social &
Health
Conditions
Air Quality (15) ....
Superfund Dumpsites (8) ....
Hazardous Waste Generation (27) ....
Surface Water Discharge (27) ....
Infant Mortality (43) ....
Crime Rate (21) ....
Teen Pregnancy (42) ....
Heart Disease (42) ....
Cancer Cases (37) ....
Infectious Diseases (15) ....

BUSINESS VITALITY INDEX MEASURES

Competitiveness
of Existing
Business
Traded Sector Strength (24) ....
Change in Traded Sector Strength (27) ....
Business Closings (45) ....
Manufacturing Capital Investment (2) ....

Entrepreneurial
Energy
New Companies (37)..
Change in New Companies (21) ....
New Business Job Growth (37) ....

Structural
Diversity
Sectoral Diversity (4) ....
Dynamic Diversity (26)...

DEVELOPMENT CAPACITY INDEX MEASURES

Human
Resources
High School Graduation (44) ....
High School Education Attainment (41) ....
College Education Attainment (47)........................

Technology
Resources
Ph.D. Scientists & Engineers in Workforce (38).....
Science/Engineering Graduate Students (28) ....
Patents Issued (47) ....
University Research & Development (28)................
Federal Research & Development (4)......................
SBIR Grants (17)..

Financial
Resources
Commercial Bank Deposits (19) ....
Loans to Deposits (24) ....
Loans to Equity (11)..
Commercial & Industrial Loans (15).......................
Comm. & Ind. Loans to Total Loans (21) ....
Venture Capital Investments (20)..........................
SBIC Financing (33) ....

Infrastructure
& Amenity
Resources
Highway Deficiency (15) ....
Bridge Deficiency (34)...
Urban Mass Transit Availability (39).....................
Energy Cost (15) ....
Sewage Treatment Needs (13)..............................
Urban Housing Costs (8).......................................
Health Professional Shortage Areas (43)................
Tourism Spending (42) ....

TAX & FISCAL SYSTEM INDEX MEASURES

Total Tax & Fiscal System Score (30).....................
Fiscal Stability & Balanced Revenue (11)...............
Tax Fairness (47)..
Fiscal Equalization (11) ....

50th   40th   30th   20th   10th   1st

ALASKA 1995 REPORT CARD

ECONOMIC PERFORMANCE	B

Employment C
Earnings & Job Quality C
Equity ....A

BUSINESS VITALITY	F

Business Competitiveness ....D
Entrepreneurial Energy...B
Structural Diversity ....F

DEVELOPMENT CAPACITY	D

Human Resources...B
Technology Resources C
Financial Resources...D
Infrastructure & Amenity Resources ....D

Tax & Fiscal System	√

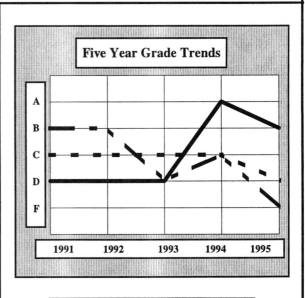

Five Year Grade Trends

1991   1992   1993   1994   1995

Key	
Economic Performance	——————
Business Vitality	— — —
Development Capacity	- - - -

- **Economic Performance:** Due to slowing short-term job growth and continued high unemployment, Alaska's grade drops to a B this year. Earnings & Job Quality remain mixed, with strong average annual pay, but low pay growth. The state's strength lies in its extremely low poverty rate and good income distribution. Alaska's quality of life is mixed, with the nation's lowest cancer rate, but high crime and lots of superfund dumpsites.

- **Business Vitality:** Alaska's Business Vitality plummets to the third worst in the nation. Although entrepreneurial energy and new company formation remain strong, the competitiveness of the state's businesses is weak, with low manufacturing capital investment and decreasing income from the industries that compete out of state (the traded sector). In addition, the state's poorly diversified economy remains a glaring weakness.

- **Development Capacity:** With the quality of its Infrastructure & Amenity Resources weakening, including worsening highways and increasing housing costs, Alaska now receives a D in Development Capacity – the Pacific's worst grade. Financial Resources are also poor, with the nation's worst ratio of loans to equity. The state's strongest development resource is its people – it continues to lead the nation in high school education attainment.

- **Tax & Fiscal System:** Alaska receives an average grade in the Tax & Fiscal System. Without a personal income tax, the state's tax and fiscal structure lacks stability; yet, with strong policies to equalize revenues among local governments, Alaska ranks third on fiscal equalization.

For information on how grades and ranks are calculated, see the Methodology section.
For a detailed explanation of indexes, refer to the individual index section.

WHERE ALASKA RANKS – MEASURE BY MEASURE

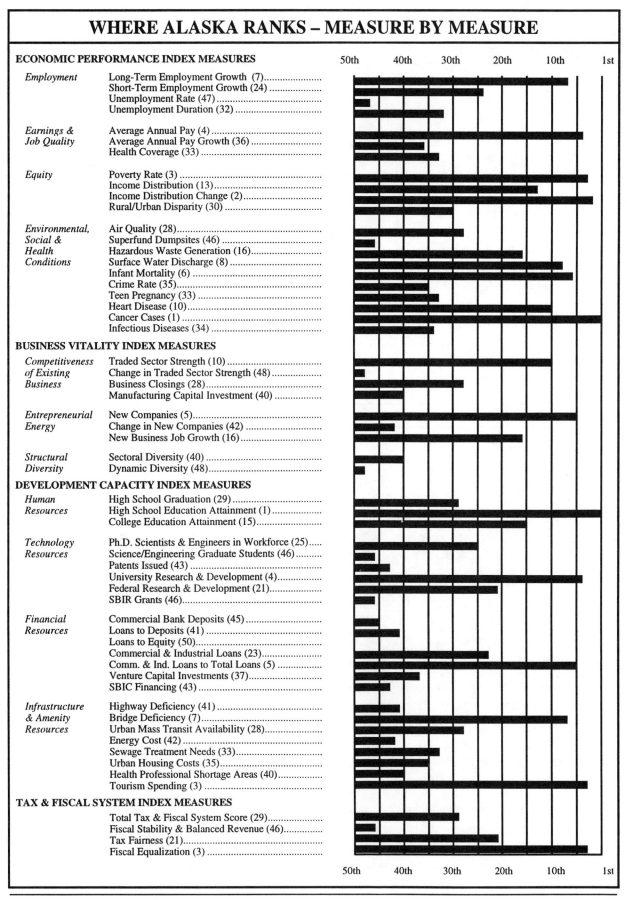

ECONOMIC PERFORMANCE INDEX MEASURES

		50th 40th 30th 20th 10th 1st

Employment
Long-Term Employment Growth (7)
Short-Term Employment Growth (24)
Unemployment Rate (47)
Unemployment Duration (32)

Earnings & Job Quality
Average Annual Pay (4)
Average Annual Pay Growth (36)
Health Coverage (33)

Equity
Poverty Rate (3)
Income Distribution (13)
Income Distribution Change (2)
Rural/Urban Disparity (30)

Environmental, Social & Health Conditions
Air Quality (28)
Superfund Dumpsites (46)
Hazardous Waste Generation (16)
Surface Water Discharge (8)
Infant Mortality (6)
Crime Rate (35)
Teen Pregnancy (33)
Heart Disease (10)
Cancer Cases (1)
Infectious Diseases (34)

BUSINESS VITALITY INDEX MEASURES

Competitiveness of Existing Business
Traded Sector Strength (10)
Change in Traded Sector Strength (48)
Business Closings (28)
Manufacturing Capital Investment (40)

Entrepreneurial Energy
New Companies (5)
Change in New Companies (42)
New Business Job Growth (16)

Structural Diversity
Sectoral Diversity (40)
Dynamic Diversity (48)

DEVELOPMENT CAPACITY INDEX MEASURES

Human Resources
High School Graduation (29)
High School Education Attainment (1)
College Education Attainment (15)

Technology Resources
Ph.D. Scientists & Engineers in Workforce (25)
Science/Engineering Graduate Students (46)
Patents Issued (43)
University Research & Development (4)
Federal Research & Development (21)
SBIR Grants (46)

Financial Resources
Commercial Bank Deposits (45)
Loans to Deposits (41)
Loans to Equity (50)
Commercial & Industrial Loans (23)
Comm. & Ind. Loans to Total Loans (5)
Venture Capital Investments (37)
SBIC Financing (43)

Infrastructure & Amenity Resources
Highway Deficiency (41)
Bridge Deficiency (7)
Urban Mass Transit Availability (28)
Energy Cost (42)
Sewage Treatment Needs (33)
Urban Housing Costs (35)
Health Professional Shortage Areas (40)
Tourism Spending (3)

TAX & FISCAL SYSTEM INDEX MEASURES

Total Tax & Fiscal System Score (29)
Fiscal Stability & Balanced Revenue (46)
Tax Fairness (21)
Fiscal Equalization (3)

		50th 40th 30th 20th 10th 1st

ARIZONA 1995 REPORT CARD

ECONOMIC PERFORMANCE	C
Employment	A
Earnings & Job Quality	D
Equity	C

BUSINESS VITALITY	C
Business Competitiveness	C
Entrepreneurial Energy	A
Structural Diversity	D

DEVELOPMENT CAPACITY	B
Human Resources	C
Technology Resources	B
Financial Resources	D
Infrastructure & Amenity Resources	B

Tax & Fiscal System	+

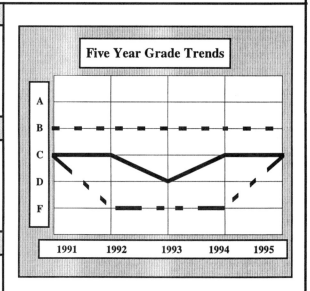

Five Year Grade Trends

Key	
Economic Performance	————
Business Vitality	▬ ▬ ▬
Development Capacity	▪ ▪ ▪ ▪

- **Economic Performance:** Arizona's economy is thriving, but unfortunately, the impacts are still not being fully shared. Arizona ranks second in the nation in short-term employment growth. But, as in previous years, the state has poor Earnings & Job Quality ranks. Arizona is also still struggling to overcome a unfavorable poverty rate and a large gap between the rich and poor. Not surprisingly, the state fairs poorly in Social Conditions (although Environmental and Health Conditions are good).

- **Business Vitality:** Arizona's Business Vitality jumps from worst in the nation last year to near average, an improvement due mostly to very strong new company formation (the source of all those new jobs). But, with little money coming in from businesses that compete out of state (45th in traded sector strength), and with the top industries growing and contracting at the same time, Arizona is still vulnerable and not as vital as it may need to be.

- **Development Capacity:** Led by excellent Technology Resources (12th best in the nation) and Infrastructure & Amenity Resources (11th best), Arizona has strong development resources: a lot of R&D funding, patents, and science and engineering graduate students, and a sturdy physical infrastructure (including the lowest level of bridge deficiencies in the nation). Improved loan activity and high school graduation would make Human and Financial Resources competitive as well.

- **Tax & Fiscal System:** Arizona's Tax & Fiscal System ranks among the top five in the country – its system is well balanced and is among the more equitable systems in the country.

For information on how grades and ranks are calculated, see the Methodology section.
For a detailed explanation of indexes, refer to the individual index section.

WHERE ARIZONA RANKS – MEASURE BY MEASURE

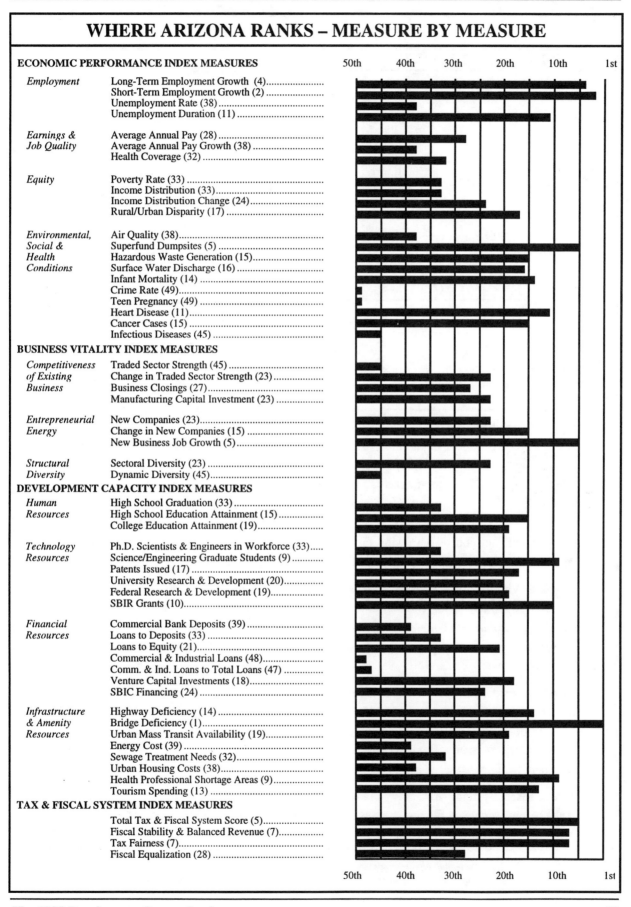

ECONOMIC PERFORMANCE INDEX MEASURES

		50th 40th 30th 20th 10th 1st
Employment	Long-Term Employment Growth (4)	
	Short-Term Employment Growth (2)	
	Unemployment Rate (38)	
	Unemployment Duration (11)	
Earnings & Job Quality	Average Annual Pay (28)	
	Average Annual Pay Growth (38)	
	Health Coverage (32)	
Equity	Poverty Rate (33)	
	Income Distribution (33)	
	Income Distribution Change (24)	
	Rural/Urban Disparity (17)	
Environmental, Social & Health Conditions	Air Quality (38)	
	Superfund Dumpsites (5)	
	Hazardous Waste Generation (15)	
	Surface Water Discharge (16)	
	Infant Mortality (14)	
	Crime Rate (49)	
	Teen Pregnancy (49)	
	Heart Disease (11)	
	Cancer Cases (15)	
	Infectious Diseases (45)	

BUSINESS VITALITY INDEX MEASURES

Competitiveness of Existing Business	Traded Sector Strength (45)	
	Change in Traded Sector Strength (23)	
	Business Closings (27)	
	Manufacturing Capital Investment (23)	
Entrepreneurial Energy	New Companies (23)	
	Change in New Companies (15)	
	New Business Job Growth (5)	
Structural Diversity	Sectoral Diversity (23)	
	Dynamic Diversity (45)	

DEVELOPMENT CAPACITY INDEX MEASURES

Human Resources	High School Graduation (33)	
	High School Education Attainment (15)	
	College Education Attainment (19)	
Technology Resources	Ph.D. Scientists & Engineers in Workforce (33)	
	Science/Engineering Graduate Students (9)	
	Patents Issued (17)	
	University Research & Development (20)	
	Federal Research & Development (19)	
	SBIR Grants (10)	
Financial Resources	Commercial Bank Deposits (39)	
	Loans to Deposits (33)	
	Loans to Equity (21)	
	Commercial & Industrial Loans (48)	
	Comm. & Ind. Loans to Total Loans (47)	
	Venture Capital Investments (18)	
	SBIC Financing (24)	
Infrastructure & Amenity Resources	Highway Deficiency (14)	
	Bridge Deficiency (1)	
	Urban Mass Transit Availability (19)	
	Energy Cost (39)	
	Sewage Treatment Needs (32)	
	Urban Housing Costs (38)	
	Health Professional Shortage Areas (9)	
	Tourism Spending (13)	

TAX & FISCAL SYSTEM INDEX MEASURES

	Total Tax & Fiscal System Score (5)	
	Fiscal Stability & Balanced Revenue (7)	
	Tax Fairness (7)	
	Fiscal Equalization (28)	

50th 40th 30th 20th 10th 1st

The 1995 Development Report Card

ARKANSAS 1995 REPORT CARD

ECONOMIC PERFORMANCE	C
Employment	B
Earnings & Job Quality	F
Equity	C

BUSINESS VITALITY	F
Business Competitiveness	C
Entrepreneurial Energy	D
Structural Diversity	C

DEVELOPMENT CAPACITY	F
Human Resources	D
Technology Resources	F
Financial Resources	F
Infrastructure & Amenity Resources	C

Tax & Fiscal System	√

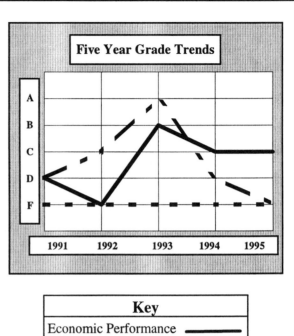

Five Year Grade Trends

1991 1992 1993 1994 1995

Key
Economic Performance ———
Business Vitality — — —
Development Capacity - - - -

- **Economic Performance:** Led by short-term employment growth (10th in the nation) and an unemployment rate among the top 20, Arkansas' strong job market is the second best in the region. However, ranking among the worst five in pay, pay growth, and employer provided health coverage, the state's Earnings & Job Quality rank is the nation's worst. While the gap between rich and poor is narrowing faster than in all but seven other states, Arkansas still ranks very poorly on poverty. The quality of life in Arkansas is poor as well.

- **Business Vitality:** In the last two years, Arkansas has dropped from an A to an F in Business Vitality. Arkansas' Entrepreneurial Energy is the South's weakest – marked by the nation's second smallest growth in new company formations. On the bright side, with strong manufacturing capital investments and a relatively low rate of business closings, the competitiveness of Arkansas' businesses is average.

- **Development Capacity:** Arkansas receives a failing grade for its development resources for the sixth straight year. Despite a top 20 high school graduation rate, low overall education attainment leads to poor Human Resources. Moreover, Technology and Financial Resources earn a failing grade. Only the state's Infrastructure & Amenity Resources, with strong highways and sewage treatment facilities, earns an average mark.

- **Tax & Fiscal System:** Arkansas' Tax & Fiscal System is average. While the state's tax structure ranks below average on fairness, it rates above average on stability and is among the best at sharing revenues with local governments.

For information on how grades and ranks are calculated, see the Methodology section.
For a detailed explanation of indexes, refer to the individual index section.

WHERE ARKANSAS RANKS – MEASURE BY MEASURE

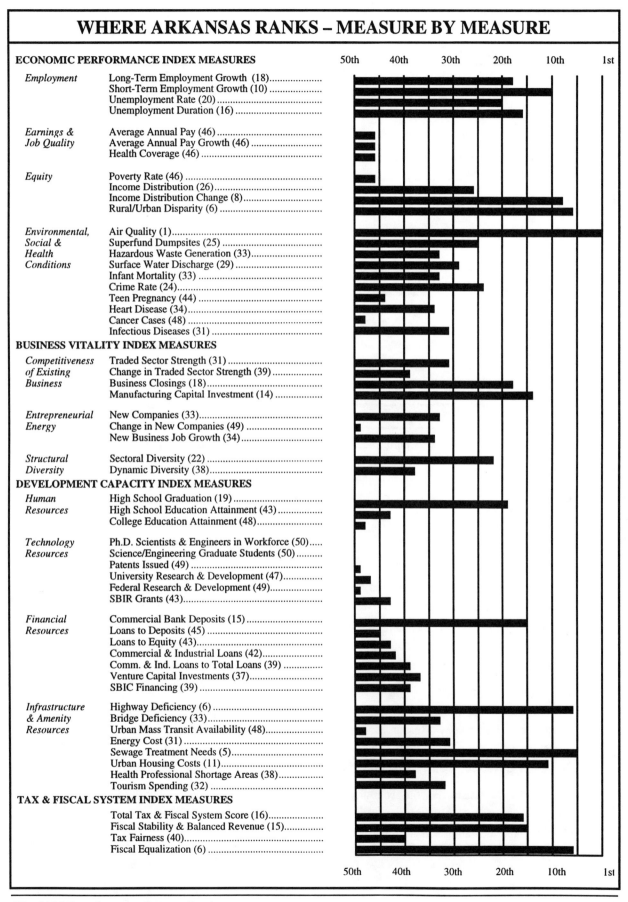

ECONOMIC PERFORMANCE INDEX MEASURES

Employment	Long-Term Employment Growth (18)	
	Short-Term Employment Growth (10)	
	Unemployment Rate (20)	
	Unemployment Duration (16)	
Earnings &	Average Annual Pay (46)	
Job Quality	Average Annual Pay Growth (46)	
	Health Coverage (46)	
Equity	Poverty Rate (46)	
	Income Distribution (26)	
	Income Distribution Change (8)	
	Rural/Urban Disparity (6)	
Environmental,	Air Quality (1)	
Social &	Superfund Dumpsites (25)	
Health	Hazardous Waste Generation (33)	
Conditions	Surface Water Discharge (29)	
	Infant Mortality (33)	
	Crime Rate (24)	
	Teen Pregnancy (44)	
	Heart Disease (34)	
	Cancer Cases (48)	
	Infectious Diseases (31)	

BUSINESS VITALITY INDEX MEASURES

Competitiveness	Traded Sector Strength (31)	
of Existing	Change in Traded Sector Strength (39)	
Business	Business Closings (18)	
	Manufacturing Capital Investment (14)	
Entrepreneurial	New Companies (33)	
Energy	Change in New Companies (49)	
	New Business Job Growth (34)	
Structural	Sectoral Diversity (22)	
Diversity	Dynamic Diversity (38)	

DEVELOPMENT CAPACITY INDEX MEASURES

Human	High School Graduation (19)	
Resources	High School Education Attainment (43)	
	College Education Attainment (48)	
Technology	Ph.D. Scientists & Engineers in Workforce (50)	
Resources	Science/Engineering Graduate Students (50)	
	Patents Issued (49)	
	University Research & Development (47)	
	Federal Research & Development (49)	
	SBIR Grants (43)	
Financial	Commercial Bank Deposits (15)	
Resources	Loans to Deposits (45)	
	Loans to Equity (43)	
	Commercial & Industrial Loans (42)	
	Comm. & Ind. Loans to Total Loans (39)	
	Venture Capital Investments (37)	
	SBIC Financing (39)	
Infrastructure	Highway Deficiency (6)	
& Amenity	Bridge Deficiency (33)	
Resources	Urban Mass Transit Availability (48)	
	Energy Cost (31)	
	Sewage Treatment Needs (5)	
	Urban Housing Costs (11)	
	Health Professional Shortage Areas (38)	
	Tourism Spending (32)	

TAX & FISCAL SYSTEM INDEX MEASURES

	Total Tax & Fiscal System Score (16)	
	Fiscal Stability & Balanced Revenue (15)	
	Tax Fairness (40)	
	Fiscal Equalization (6)	

CALIFORNIA 1995 REPORT CARD

ECONOMIC PERFORMANCE	D

Employment ....D
Earnings & Job Quality C
Equity ....F

BUSINESS VITALITY	C

Business Competitiveness C
Entrepreneurial Energy..C
Structural Diversity ....B

DEVELOPMENT CAPACITY	B

Human Resources...C
Technology Resources ....A
Financial Resources...C
Infrastructure & Amenity Resources.....................C

Tax & Fiscal System	+

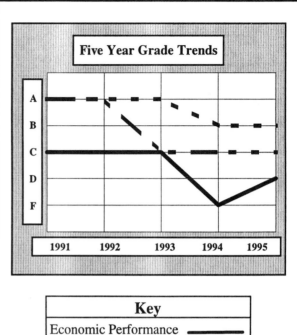

Five Year Grade Trends

1991   1992   1993   1994   1995

Key

Economic Performance ——————
Business Vitality — - -
Development Capacity - - - -

- **Economic Performance:** California is showing signs of a rebound. While unemployment remains the second worst in the nation, short-term job growth has improved, and for those with jobs, pay is very good. Yet, the state seems to be dividing into the haves and have-nots – poverty is high and income distribution is poor and getting worse. The quality of life in California is mixed – the state compares well on most health indicators, but the crime rate is high and air quality is the nation's worst.

- **Business Vitality:** Though the state's overall grade is unchanged from last year, California shows improvement on several measures of Business Vitality. The competitiveness of the state's businesses has improved due to a decrease in business closings and the persistent strength among industries that trade outside the state. Moreover, with continued efforts to diversify away from defense industries, Structural Diversity has improved.

- **Development Capacity:** California's strength rests with its above average development resources. With federal R&D money still pouring into the state and a top ten ranking on patents issued, California's Technology Resources are excellent. Due to improved highways, the state's Infrastructure & Amenity Resources grade has improved from last year. However, the state's Human Resources are mixed – college attainment is high, but high school graduation is low.

- **Tax & Fiscal System:** For the second straight year, California has the nation's third highest ranking tax and fiscal climate. In addition to having a fairly balanced and stable revenue raising structure, California has the nation's most equitable tax system.

For information on how grades and ranks are calculated, see the Methodology section.
For a detailed explanation of indexes, refer to the individual index section.

WHERE CALIFORNIA RANKS – MEASURE BY MEASURE

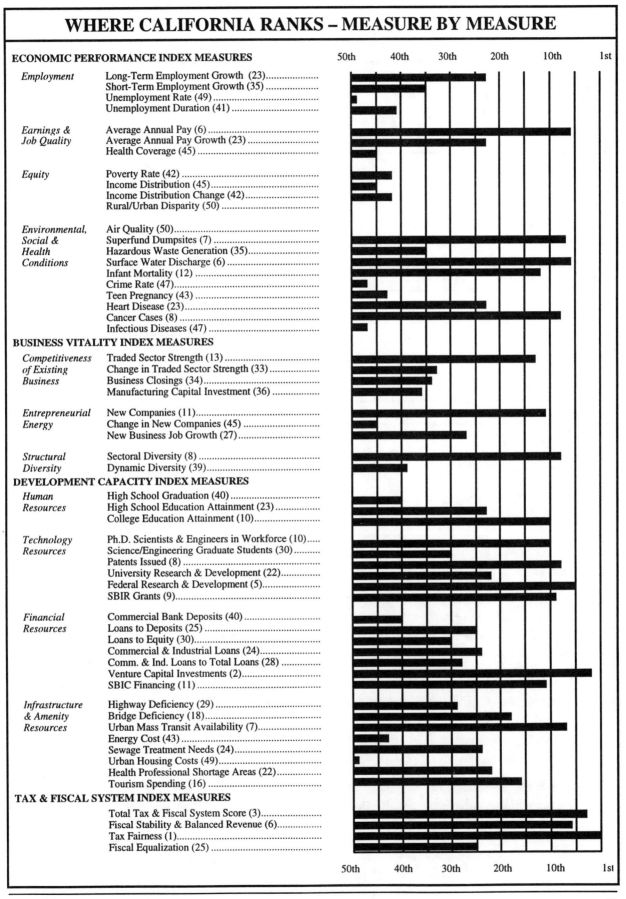

ECONOMIC PERFORMANCE INDEX MEASURES

Employment	Long-Term Employment Growth (23)
	Short-Term Employment Growth (35)
	Unemployment Rate (49)
	Unemployment Duration (41)
Earnings & Job Quality	Average Annual Pay (6)
	Average Annual Pay Growth (23)
	Health Coverage (45)
Equity	Poverty Rate (42)
	Income Distribution (45)
	Income Distribution Change (42)
	Rural/Urban Disparity (50)
Environmental, Social & Health Conditions	Air Quality (50)
	Superfund Dumpsites (7)
	Hazardous Waste Generation (35)
	Surface Water Discharge (6)
	Infant Mortality (12)
	Crime Rate (47)
	Teen Pregnancy (43)
	Heart Disease (23)
	Cancer Cases (8)
	Infectious Diseases (47)

BUSINESS VITALITY INDEX MEASURES

Competitiveness of Existing Business	Traded Sector Strength (13)
	Change in Traded Sector Strength (33)
	Business Closings (34)
	Manufacturing Capital Investment (36)
Entrepreneurial Energy	New Companies (11)
	Change in New Companies (45)
	New Business Job Growth (27)
Structural Diversity	Sectoral Diversity (8)
	Dynamic Diversity (39)

DEVELOPMENT CAPACITY INDEX MEASURES

Human Resources	High School Graduation (40)
	High School Education Attainment (23)
	College Education Attainment (10)
Technology Resources	Ph.D. Scientists & Engineers in Workforce (10)
	Science/Engineering Graduate Students (30)
	Patents Issued (8)
	University Research & Development (22)
	Federal Research & Development (5)
	SBIR Grants (9)
Financial Resources	Commercial Bank Deposits (40)
	Loans to Deposits (25)
	Loans to Equity (30)
	Commercial & Industrial Loans (24)
	Comm. & Ind. Loans to Total Loans (28)
	Venture Capital Investments (2)
	SBIC Financing (11)
Infrastructure & Amenity Resources	Highway Deficiency (29)
	Bridge Deficiency (18)
	Urban Mass Transit Availability (7)
	Energy Cost (43)
	Sewage Treatment Needs (24)
	Urban Housing Costs (49)
	Health Professional Shortage Areas (22)
	Tourism Spending (16)

TAX & FISCAL SYSTEM INDEX MEASURES

	Total Tax & Fiscal System Score (3)
	Fiscal Stability & Balanced Revenue (6)
	Tax Fairness (1)
	Fiscal Equalization (25)

COLORADO 1995 REPORT CARD

ECONOMIC PERFORMANCE — A

Employment ....A
Earnings & Job Quality ....A
Equity ....A

BUSINESS VITALITY — A

Business Competitiveness ....D
Entrepreneurial Energy......................................A
Structural Diversity ....A

DEVELOPMENT CAPACITY — A

Human Resources..A
Technology Resources ....A
Financial Resources...C
Infrastructure & Amenity Resources.....................A

Tax & Fiscal System — +

Five Year Grade Trends

(Graph: vertical axis A, B, C, D, F; horizontal axis 1991, 1992, 1993, 1994, 1995)

Key
Economic Performance ——————
Business Vitality — -- --
Development Capacity - - - -

- **Economic Performance:** Colorado ranks number one in Economic Performance this year, with top ten performances in Employment, Earnings & Job Quality, and Equity. While both short-term and long-term employment growth are excellent (6th and 8th best), average annual pay growth is improving (7th), and the gap between the rich and poor is shrinking (4th). Colorado compares well in Environmental, Social & Health Conditions, led by low rates of cancer and heart disease.

- **Business Vitality:** Spurred partly by explosive new company formation, Colorado has one of the most vital business sectors in the nation. The state's only weaknesses are a relatively high level of business closings and a sluggish increase in income from sectors competing out of state (although the former may simply reflect the high turnover of a bustling economy).

- **Development Capacity:** With the nation's second best technology resources, second best Infrastructure & Amenity Resources, and fourth best Human Resources, Colorado only trails Minnesota in the quality of its development resources. The state's one resource deficiency is relatively low commercial and industrial loan activity (45th), though high venture capital and SBIC financing may supply enough capital.

- **Tax & Fiscal System:** Colorado has balanced and stable revenue raising systems, accompanied by the ninth most equitable tax system. Unfortunately, the state does a poor job of equalizing its local governments' fiscal capacities.

For information on how grades and ranks are calculated, see the Methodology section.
For a detailed explanation of indexes, refer to the individual index section.

WHERE COLORADO RANKS – MEASURE BY MEASURE

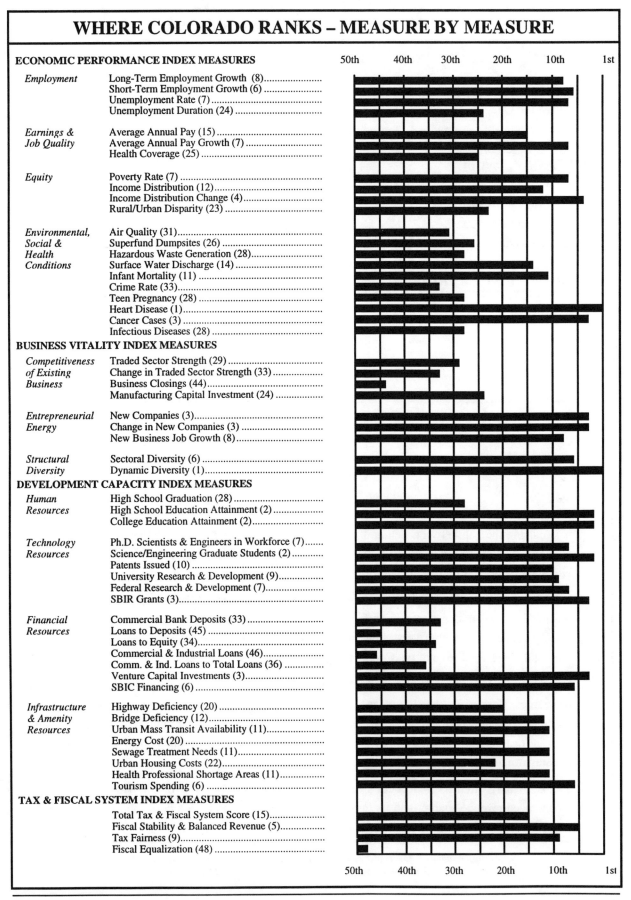

ECONOMIC PERFORMANCE INDEX MEASURES

Employment
Long-Term Employment Growth (8)
Short-Term Employment Growth (6)
Unemployment Rate (7)
Unemployment Duration (24)

Earnings & Job Quality
Average Annual Pay (15)
Average Annual Pay Growth (7)
Health Coverage (25)

Equity
Poverty Rate (7)
Income Distribution (12)
Income Distribution Change (4)
Rural/Urban Disparity (23)

Environmental, Social & Health Conditions
Air Quality (31)
Superfund Dumpsites (26)
Hazardous Waste Generation (28)
Surface Water Discharge (14)
Infant Mortality (11)
Crime Rate (33)
Teen Pregnancy (28)
Heart Disease (1)
Cancer Cases (3)
Infectious Diseases (28)

BUSINESS VITALITY INDEX MEASURES

Competitiveness of Existing Business
Traded Sector Strength (29)
Change in Traded Sector Strength (33)
Business Closings (44)
Manufacturing Capital Investment (24)

Entrepreneurial Energy
New Companies (3)
Change in New Companies (3)
New Business Job Growth (8)

Structural Diversity
Sectoral Diversity (6)
Dynamic Diversity (1)

DEVELOPMENT CAPACITY INDEX MEASURES

Human Resources
High School Graduation (28)
High School Education Attainment (2)
College Education Attainment (2)

Technology Resources
Ph.D. Scientists & Engineers in Workforce (7)
Science/Engineering Graduate Students (2)
Patents Issued (10)
University Research & Development (9)
Federal Research & Development (7)
SBIR Grants (3)

Financial Resources
Commercial Bank Deposits (33)
Loans to Deposits (45)
Loans to Equity (34)
Commercial & Industrial Loans (46)
Comm. & Ind. Loans to Total Loans (36)
Venture Capital Investments (3)
SBIC Financing (6)

Infrastructure & Amenity Resources
Highway Deficiency (20)
Bridge Deficiency (12)
Urban Mass Transit Availability (11)
Energy Cost (20)
Sewage Treatment Needs (11)
Urban Housing Costs (22)
Health Professional Shortage Areas (11)
Tourism Spending (6)

TAX & FISCAL SYSTEM INDEX MEASURES

Total Tax & Fiscal System Score (15)
Fiscal Stability & Balanced Revenue (5)
Tax Fairness (9)
Fiscal Equalization (48)

50th 40th 30th 20th 10th 1st

CONNECTICUT 1995 REPORT CARD

ECONOMIC PERFORMANCE	B
Employment	F
Earnings & Job Quality	A
Equity	B

BUSINESS VITALITY	D
Business Competitiveness	B
Entrepreneurial Energy	C
Structural Diversity	D

DEVELOPMENT CAPACITY	A
Human Resources	A
Technology Resources	A
Financial Resources	C
Infrastructure & Amenity Resources	D

Tax & Fiscal System	√

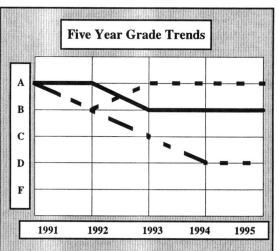

Five Year Grade Trends

1991　1992　1993　1994　1995

Key
Economic Performance ——————
Business Vitality ― ― ―
Development Capacity ▪ ▪ ▪ ▪

- **Economic Performance:** Defense restructuring is taking its toll on Connecticut. Short and long-term employment growth are third and second worst in the nation, respectively, and the state has the highest ratio of long-term unemployment in the country. Meanwhile, the state is behind most states' average annual pay growth and in the rate it is closing the gap between rich and poor. The good news is that Connecticut's average annual pay and health coverage are still the best in the nation, and poverty rate ranks second best. However, poor environmental conditions are a burden on the quality of life.

- **Business Vitality:** Connecticut continues its free-fall in Business Vitality despite strong existing businesses – the traded sector is performing well and few business are closing. Entrepreneurial Energy is mediocre with a very slow increase in new companies, and Structural Diversity is still among the worst in the country. Connecticut's economy needs to become more vibrant.

- **Development Capacity:** With the country's second best Human Resources and strong Technology Resources, Connecticut has the means to bounce back. It has the second highest level of college graduates, strong R&D activity, and increased venture capital to channel into new ventures. Only poor infrastructure, especially high energy costs, heavy sewage treatment needs and expensive housing, might hamper improvement.

- **Tax & Fiscal System:** Connecticut's Tax & Fiscal System compares favorable with other states' in its balanced revenue sources and its fairness. However, the state does a poor job of equalizing the fiscal capacity of local governments.

For information on how grades and ranks are calculated, see the Methodology section.
For a detailed explanation of indexes, refer to the individual index section.

WHERE CONNECTICUT RANKS – MEASURE BY MEASURE

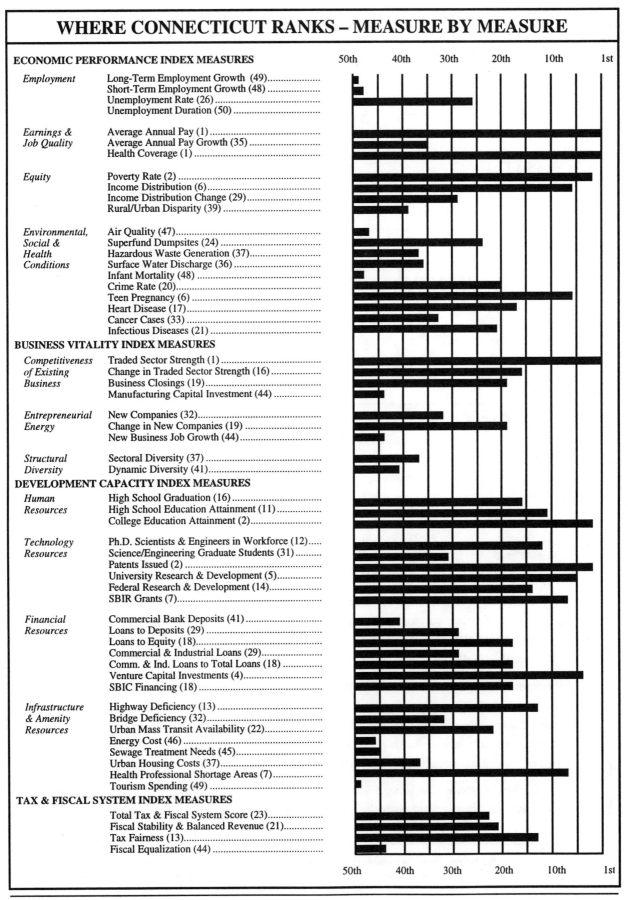

ECONOMIC PERFORMANCE INDEX MEASURES

Employment
Long-Term Employment Growth (49)
Short-Term Employment Growth (48)
Unemployment Rate (26)
Unemployment Duration (50)

Earnings & Job Quality
Average Annual Pay (1)
Average Annual Pay Growth (35)
Health Coverage (1)

Equity
Poverty Rate (2)
Income Distribution (6)
Income Distribution Change (29)
Rural/Urban Disparity (39)

Environmental, Social & Health Conditions
Air Quality (47)
Superfund Dumpsites (24)
Hazardous Waste Generation (37)
Surface Water Discharge (36)
Infant Mortality (48)
Crime Rate (20)
Teen Pregnancy (6)
Heart Disease (17)
Cancer Cases (33)
Infectious Diseases (21)

BUSINESS VITALITY INDEX MEASURES

Competitiveness of Existing Business
Traded Sector Strength (1)
Change in Traded Sector Strength (16)
Business Closings (19)
Manufacturing Capital Investment (44)

Entrepreneurial Energy
New Companies (32)
Change in New Companies (19)
New Business Job Growth (44)

Structural Diversity
Sectoral Diversity (37)
Dynamic Diversity (41)

DEVELOPMENT CAPACITY INDEX MEASURES

Human Resources
High School Graduation (16)
High School Education Attainment (11)
College Education Attainment (2)

Technology Resources
Ph.D. Scientists & Engineers in Workforce (12)
Science/Engineering Graduate Students (31)
Patents Issued (2)
University Research & Development (5)
Federal Research & Development (14)
SBIR Grants (7)

Financial Resources
Commercial Bank Deposits (41)
Loans to Deposits (29)
Loans to Equity (18)
Commercial & Industrial Loans (29)
Comm. & Ind. Loans to Total Loans (18)
Venture Capital Investments (4)
SBIC Financing (18)

Infrastructure & Amenity Resources
Highway Deficiency (13)
Bridge Deficiency (32)
Urban Mass Transit Availability (22)
Energy Cost (46)
Sewage Treatment Needs (45)
Urban Housing Costs (37)
Health Professional Shortage Areas (7)
Tourism Spending (49)

TAX & FISCAL SYSTEM INDEX MEASURES

Total Tax & Fiscal System Score (23)
Fiscal Stability & Balanced Revenue (21)
Tax Fairness (13)
Fiscal Equalization (44)

DELAWARE 1995 REPORT CARD

ECONOMIC PERFORMANCE	A
Employment ....B	
Earnings & Job Quality ....A	
Equity C	

BUSINESS VITALITY	C
Business Competitiveness C	
Entrepreneurial Energy..................................B	
Structural Diversity ....D	

DEVELOPMENT CAPACITY	A
Human Resources...C	
Technology Resources ....A	
Financial Resources.....................................B	
Infrastructure & Amenity Resources.................B	

Tax & Fiscal System	–

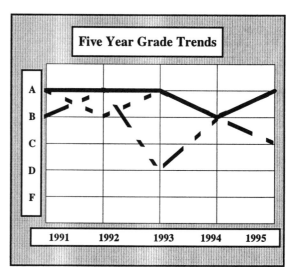

Five Year Grade Trends

1991 1992 1993 1994 1995

Key

Economic Performance ————
Business Vitality ▬ ▪ ▪ ▪
Development Capacity ▪ ▪ ▪ ▪

- **Economic Performance:** After a temporary decline last year, Delaware is back. Its employment conditions have turned around (long-term employment ranks 15th and unemployment ranks 13th). Earnings & Job Quality also improves to the country's fifth best: Delaware has the tenth highest average annual pay and the fifth most extensive health coverage. The one dampener is the state's extremely poor Environmental Conditions (the nation's worst surface water discharge and worst ratio of superfund dumpsites) and Health Conditions (44th in both cancer rates and infectious diseases).

- **Business Vitality:** Delaware drops a grade from last year, but still boasts strong entrepreneurship and vigorous existing businesses (in particular, the money it gets from traded sectors, or those competing out of state). The only concern is that Delaware has the third least diversified economy in the country.

- **Development Capacity:** Average Human Resources (poor high school graduation offset by many college graduates); excellent Technology Resources (including number one in patents); good Financial Resources (first in deposits, loans to deposits, and total commercial and industrial loans); and solid Infrastructure & Amenity Resources make Delaware one of the best all-around states in terms of resources for the future.

- **Tax & Fiscal System:** Delaware's Tax & Fiscal System rates poorly because its revenue sources are relatively unbalanced and unstable, but does compare well in fairness measures.

For information on how grades and ranks are calculated, see the Methodology section.
For a detailed explanation of indexes, refer to the individual index section.

WHERE DELAWARE RANKS – MEASURE BY MEASURE

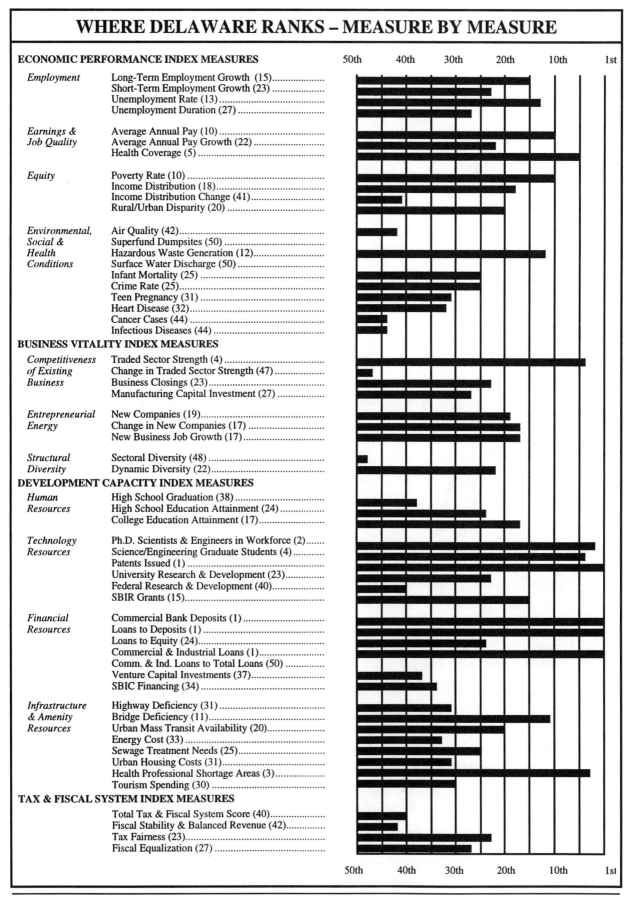

FLORIDA 1995 REPORT CARD

ECONOMIC PERFORMANCE	D

Employment C
Earnings & Job Quality ....D
Equity C

BUSINESS VITALITY	D

Business Competitiveness ....F
Entrepreneurial Energy..C
Structural Diversity ....B

DEVELOPMENT CAPACITY	C

Human Resources...D
Technology Resources ....D
Financial Resources...C
Infrastructure & Amenity Resources.......................B

Tax & Fiscal System	–

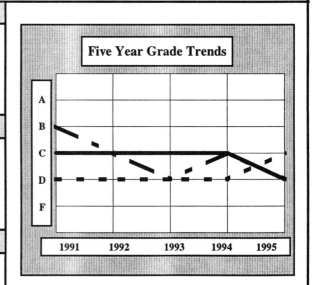

Five Year Grade Trends

Key
Economic Performance ————
Business Vitality ▬ ▪ ▪ ▬
Development Capacity ▪ ▪ ▪ ▪ ▪

- **Economic Performance:** With decreasing strength in its job market, Florida now ranks below average in Economic Performance. The state still boasts strong long-term job growth, but short-term job growth has slowed and unemployment is up. Moreover, pay is below average in Florida and growing slowly. Despite strong environmental quality, overall quality of life rates poorly, particularly in measures such as crime and cancer.

- **Business Vitality:** Despite improving diversification among the state's businesses, Florida now rates below average on Business Vitality. With the nation's worst rank for income in industries that trade outside the state (traded sector) and a high rate of business closings, the competitiveness of the state's businesses is third worst. Moreover, while new company formation is among the top ten, overall Entrepreneurial Energy is only average.

- **Development Capacity:** Florida is one of a handful of southern states that has moved up to an average level on Development Capacity. The change came about through marginal improvements in the state's rank on some key indicators such as the high school graduation rate, university R&D spending, commercial bank deposits, and highway deficiency. Overall, while the state's Infrastructure & Amenity Resources are strong, Human and Technology Resources remain poor.

- **Tax & Fiscal System:** Florida's Tax & Fiscal System rates below average and is among the worst in the region. The state has one of the nation's least equitable tax systems, and with no personal income tax, it also ranks below average on stability.

For information on how grades and ranks are calculated, see the Methodology section.
For a detailed explanation of indexes, refer to the individual index section.

WHERE FLORIDA RANKS – MEASURE BY MEASURE

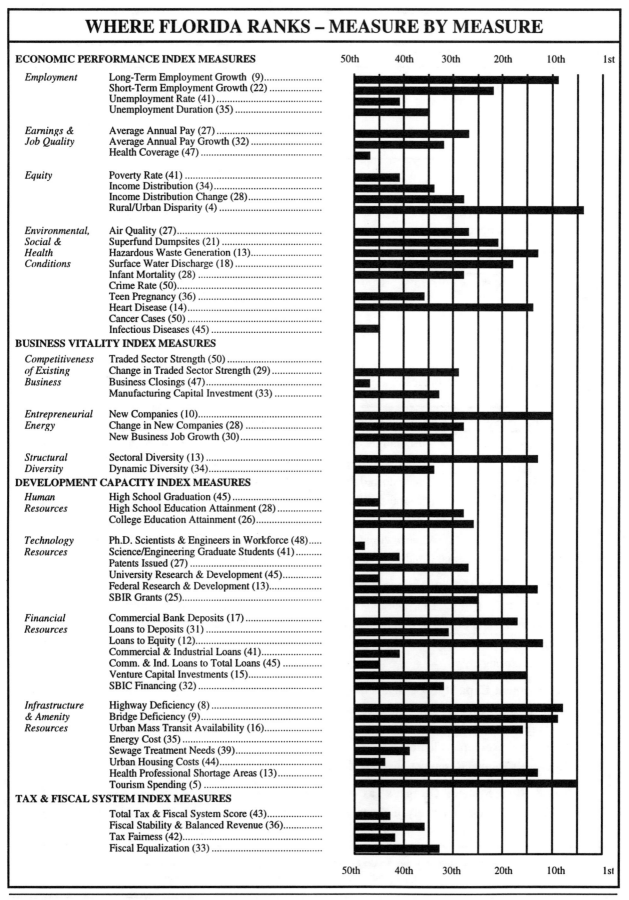

ECONOMIC PERFORMANCE INDEX MEASURES

| | | 50th | 40th | 30th | 20th | 10th | 1st |

Employment
- Long-Term Employment Growth (9)
- Short-Term Employment Growth (22)
- Unemployment Rate (41)
- Unemployment Duration (35)

Earnings & Job Quality
- Average Annual Pay (27)
- Average Annual Pay Growth (32)
- Health Coverage (47)

Equity
- Poverty Rate (41)
- Income Distribution (34)
- Income Distribution Change (28)
- Rural/Urban Disparity (4)

Environmental, Social & Health Conditions
- Air Quality (27)
- Superfund Dumpsites (21)
- Hazardous Waste Generation (13)
- Surface Water Discharge (18)
- Infant Mortality (28)
- Crime Rate (50)
- Teen Pregnancy (36)
- Heart Disease (14)
- Cancer Cases (50)
- Infectious Diseases (45)

BUSINESS VITALITY INDEX MEASURES

Competitiveness of Existing Business
- Traded Sector Strength (50)
- Change in Traded Sector Strength (29)
- Business Closings (47)
- Manufacturing Capital Investment (33)

Entrepreneurial Energy
- New Companies (10)
- Change in New Companies (28)
- New Business Job Growth (30)

Structural Diversity
- Sectoral Diversity (13)
- Dynamic Diversity (34)

DEVELOPMENT CAPACITY INDEX MEASURES

Human Resources
- High School Graduation (45)
- High School Education Attainment (28)
- College Education Attainment (26)

Technology Resources
- Ph.D. Scientists & Engineers in Workforce (48)
- Science/Engineering Graduate Students (41)
- Patents Issued (27)
- University Research & Development (45)
- Federal Research & Development (13)
- SBIR Grants (25)

Financial Resources
- Commercial Bank Deposits (17)
- Loans to Deposits (31)
- Loans to Equity (12)
- Commercial & Industrial Loans (41)
- Comm. & Ind. Loans to Total Loans (45)
- Venture Capital Investments (15)
- SBIC Financing (32)

Infrastructure & Amenity Resources
- Highway Deficiency (8)
- Bridge Deficiency (9)
- Urban Mass Transit Availability (16)
- Energy Cost (35)
- Sewage Treatment Needs (39)
- Urban Housing Costs (44)
- Health Professional Shortage Areas (13)
- Tourism Spending (5)

TAX & FISCAL SYSTEM INDEX MEASURES
- Total Tax & Fiscal System Score (43)
- Fiscal Stability & Balanced Revenue (36)
- Tax Fairness (42)
- Fiscal Equalization (33)

| | | 50th | 40th | 30th | 20th | 10th | 1st |

GEORGIA 1995 REPORT CARD

ECONOMIC PERFORMANCE	C

Employment ....B
Earnings & Job Quality C
Equity C

BUSINESS VITALITY	A

Business Competitiveness C
Entrepreneurial Energy..A
Structural Diversity ....B

DEVELOPMENT CAPACITY	C

Human Resources...D
Technology Resources C
Financial Resources..A
Infrastructure & Amenity Resources.....................B

Tax & Fiscal System	√

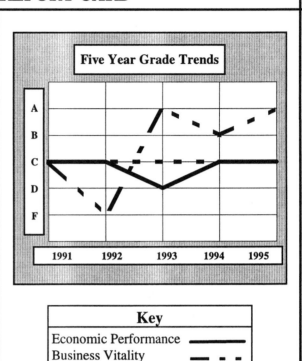

Five Year Grade Trends

Key

Economic Performance	———
Business Vitality	— - -
Development Capacity	- - - -

- **Economic Performance:** With an above average job market and improving measures of Equity, Georgia earns a C. While job growth has slowed marginally, the state's Employment picture is still above average and among the top five in the region. Earnings & Job Quality are average, but the state boasts a sharply reduced poverty rate and a narrowing gap between rich and poor. The quality of life is average but uneven – Environmental Conditions are good, but Social Conditions are poor.

- **Business Vitality:** With a strong burst of entrepreneurial activity, Georgia has the nation's fifth best Business Vitality. The state ranks among the top ten in new company formations, and ranks second in the rate of increase in new companies. At the same time, the state's industries are well diversified. The competitiveness of the state's business is average, but Georgia does rank last in business closings.

- **Development Capacity:** Georgia's development resources are the second strongest in the South. With strong lending activity, Financial Resources continue to be excellent. The state's Infrastructure & Amenity Resources, with the best highway quality, rank above average. Technology Resources, led by a boost in federal R&D spending, moves up to an average grade. The state's Human Resources are poor, though, with the fifth lowest high school graduation.

- **Tax & Fiscal System:** Georgia's Tax & Fiscal System receives an average rank. While the state's tax structure ranks relatively high on stability and its policies for sharing revenue with local governments, it is one of the nation's least equitable.

For information on how grades and ranks are calculated, see the Methodology section.
For a detailed explanation of indexes, refer to the individual index section.

WHERE GEORGIA RANKS – MEASURE BY MEASURE

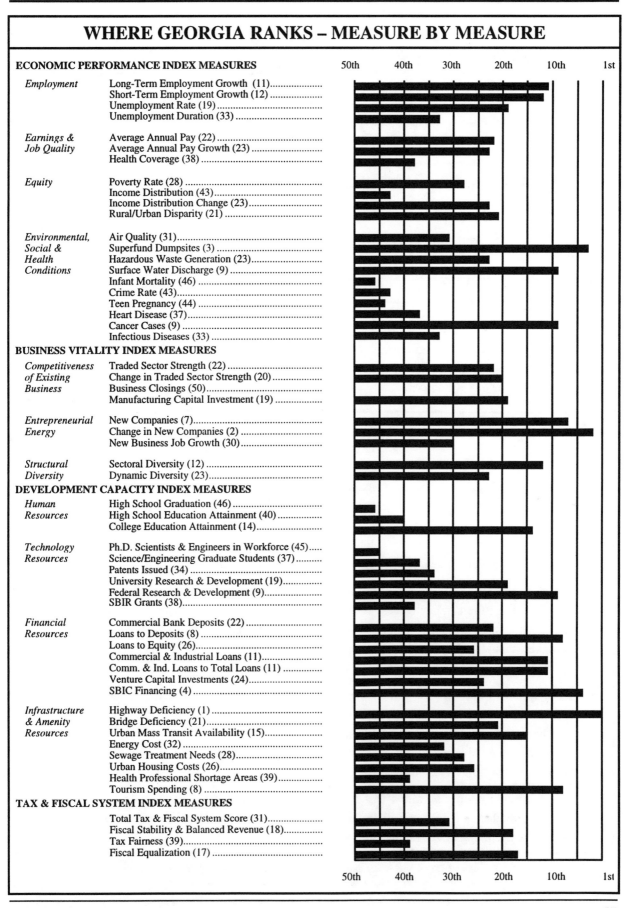

ECONOMIC PERFORMANCE INDEX MEASURES

		50th 40th 30th 20th 10th 1st
Employment	Long-Term Employment Growth (11)	
	Short-Term Employment Growth (12)	
	Unemployment Rate (19)	
	Unemployment Duration (33)	
Earnings & Job Quality	Average Annual Pay (22)	
	Average Annual Pay Growth (23)	
	Health Coverage (38)	
Equity	Poverty Rate (28)	
	Income Distribution (43)	
	Income Distribution Change (23)	
	Rural/Urban Disparity (21)	
Environmental, Social & Health Conditions	Air Quality (31)	
	Superfund Dumpsites (3)	
	Hazardous Waste Generation (23)	
	Surface Water Discharge (9)	
	Infant Mortality (46)	
	Crime Rate (43)	
	Teen Pregnancy (44)	
	Heart Disease (37)	
	Cancer Cases (9)	
	Infectious Diseases (33)	

BUSINESS VITALITY INDEX MEASURES

Competitiveness of Existing Business	Traded Sector Strength (22)	
	Change in Traded Sector Strength (20)	
	Business Closings (50)	
	Manufacturing Capital Investment (19)	
Entrepreneurial Energy	New Companies (7)	
	Change in New Companies (2)	
	New Business Job Growth (30)	
Structural Diversity	Sectoral Diversity (12)	
	Dynamic Diversity (23)	

DEVELOPMENT CAPACITY INDEX MEASURES

Human Resources	High School Graduation (46)	
	High School Education Attainment (40)	
	College Education Attainment (14)	
Technology Resources	Ph.D. Scientists & Engineers in Workforce (45)	
	Science/Engineering Graduate Students (37)	
	Patents Issued (34)	
	University Research & Development (19)	
	Federal Research & Development (9)	
	SBIR Grants (38)	
Financial Resources	Commercial Bank Deposits (22)	
	Loans to Deposits (8)	
	Loans to Equity (26)	
	Commercial & Industrial Loans (11)	
	Comm. & Ind. Loans to Total Loans (11)	
	Venture Capital Investments (24)	
	SBIC Financing (4)	
Infrastructure & Amenity Resources	Highway Deficiency (1)	
	Bridge Deficiency (21)	
	Urban Mass Transit Availability (15)	
	Energy Cost (32)	
	Sewage Treatment Needs (28)	
	Urban Housing Costs (26)	
	Health Professional Shortage Areas (39)	
	Tourism Spending (8)	

TAX & FISCAL SYSTEM INDEX MEASURES

	Total Tax & Fiscal System Score (31)	
	Fiscal Stability & Balanced Revenue (18)	
	Tax Fairness (39)	
	Fiscal Equalization (17)	

50th 40th 30th 20th 10th 1st

The 1995 Development Report Card

HAWAII 1995 REPORT CARD

ECONOMIC PERFORMANCE	A
Employment	C
Earnings & Job Quality	A
Equity	A

BUSINESS VITALITY	F
Business Competitiveness	F
Entrepreneurial Energy	C
Structural Diversity	F

DEVELOPMENT CAPACITY	B
Human Resources	A
Technology Resources	C
Financial Resources	B
Infrastructure & Amenity Resources	C

Tax & Fiscal System	√

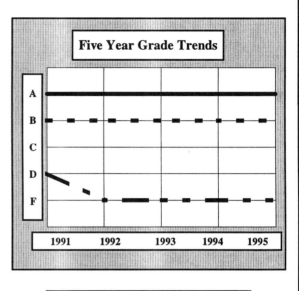

Five Year Grade Trends

1991   1992   1993   1994   1995

Key

Economic Performance	————
Business Vitality	— - -
Development Capacity	- - - -

- **Economic Performance:** Hawaii still has one of the nation's strongest economies, but problems are beginning to appear in its job market. With a big deterioration in unemployment (5th to 33rd) and the fourth weakest short-term job growth, Hawaii rates average on Employment. On the bright side, Earnings & Job Quality are the nation's best and poverty the nation's lowest. Only a high crime rate mars what is otherwise an excellent quality of life.

- **Business Vitality:** Hawaii's Business Vitality is the nation's worst. The state receives failing grades both for the competitiveness of existing businesses (low manufacturing capital investment and weakness in industries that trade outside the state) and for the diversity of its economy. However, though only average on Entrepreneurial Energy, Hawaii led the nation in new business job growth (measured between 1989 and 1993).

- **Development Capacity:** Hawaii's Development Capacity receives a B for the sixth straight year. Its Human Resources are excellent, led by the nation's sixth best high school attainment. Its Financial Resources, marked by strong lending activity, are good. In contrast, Hawaii's Infrastructure & Amenity Resources rate only so-so, with several widely divergent scores (first in health care availability, last in urban housing costs).

- **Tax & Fiscal System:** Hawaii's Tax & Fiscal System receives an average grade. While the state ranks among the top ten for its policies to equalize revenues among local governments, it receives a below average rating on tax fairness.

For information on how grades and ranks are calculated, see the Methodology section.
For a detailed explanation of indexes, refer to the individual index section.

WHERE HAWAII RANKS – MEASURE BY MEASURE

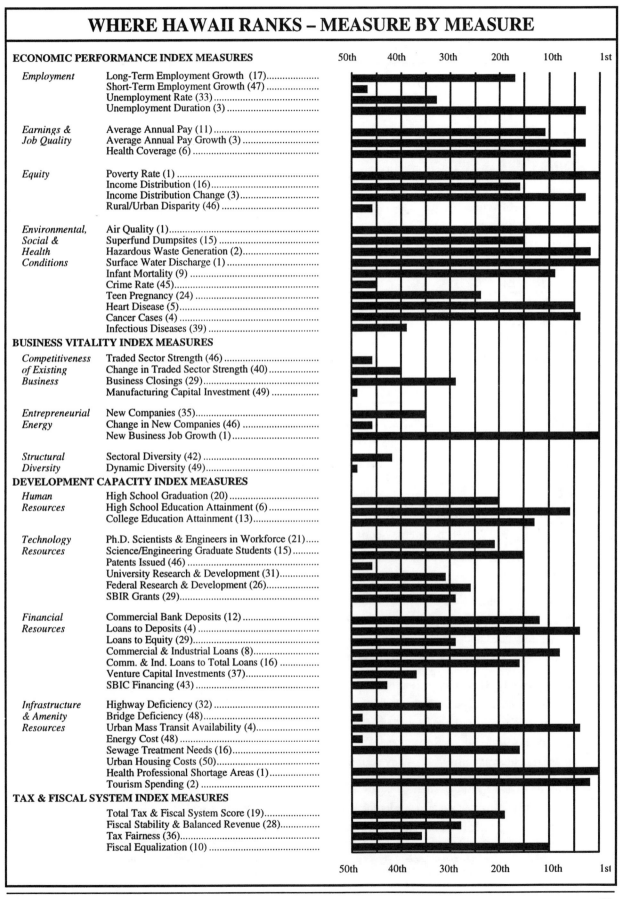

ECONOMIC PERFORMANCE INDEX MEASURES

Employment
- Long-Term Employment Growth (17)
- Short-Term Employment Growth (47)
- Unemployment Rate (33)
- Unemployment Duration (3)

Earnings & Job Quality
- Average Annual Pay (11)
- Average Annual Pay Growth (3)
- Health Coverage (6)

Equity
- Poverty Rate (1)
- Income Distribution (16)
- Income Distribution Change (3)
- Rural/Urban Disparity (46)

Environmental, Social & Health Conditions
- Air Quality (1)
- Superfund Dumpsites (15)
- Hazardous Waste Generation (2)
- Surface Water Discharge (1)
- Infant Mortality (9)
- Crime Rate (45)
- Teen Pregnancy (24)
- Heart Disease (5)
- Cancer Cases (4)
- Infectious Diseases (39)

BUSINESS VITALITY INDEX MEASURES

Competitiveness of Existing Business
- Traded Sector Strength (46)
- Change in Traded Sector Strength (40)
- Business Closings (29)
- Manufacturing Capital Investment (49)

Entrepreneurial Energy
- New Companies (35)
- Change in New Companies (46)
- New Business Job Growth (1)

Structural Diversity
- Sectoral Diversity (42)
- Dynamic Diversity (49)

DEVELOPMENT CAPACITY INDEX MEASURES

Human Resources
- High School Graduation (20)
- High School Education Attainment (6)
- College Education Attainment (13)

Technology Resources
- Ph.D. Scientists & Engineers in Workforce (21)
- Science/Engineering Graduate Students (15)
- Patents Issued (46)
- University Research & Development (31)
- Federal Research & Development (26)
- SBIR Grants (29)

Financial Resources
- Commercial Bank Deposits (12)
- Loans to Deposits (4)
- Loans to Equity (29)
- Commercial & Industrial Loans (8)
- Comm. & Ind. Loans to Total Loans (16)
- Venture Capital Investments (37)
- SBIC Financing (43)

Infrastructure & Amenity Resources
- Highway Deficiency (32)
- Bridge Deficiency (48)
- Urban Mass Transit Availability (4)
- Energy Cost (48)
- Sewage Treatment Needs (16)
- Urban Housing Costs (50)
- Health Professional Shortage Areas (1)
- Tourism Spending (2)

TAX & FISCAL SYSTEM INDEX MEASURES
- Total Tax & Fiscal System Score (19)
- Fiscal Stability & Balanced Revenue (28)
- Tax Fairness (36)
- Fiscal Equalization (10)

(Horizontal axis labels: 50th, 40th, 30th, 20th, 10th, 1st)

IDAHO 1995 REPORT CARD

ECONOMIC PERFORMANCE	A

Employment ....A
Earnings & Job Quality C
Equity ....B

BUSINESS VITALITY	A

Business Competitiveness ....A
Entrepreneurial Energy..................................A
Structural Diversity ....F

DEVELOPMENT CAPACITY	B

Human Resources...B
Technology Resources C
Financial Resources.......................................C
Infrastructure & Amenity Resources..............C

Tax & Fiscal System	+

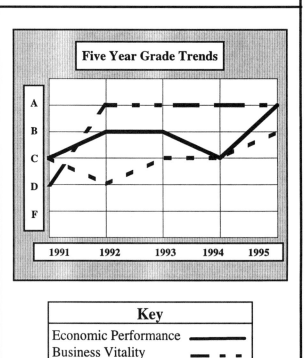

Five Year Grade Trends

1991   1992   1993   1994   1995

Key

Economic Performance ————
Business Vitality — - -
Development Capacity - - - -

- **Economic Performance:** A leader in the Mountain West's surge to the top, Idaho jumps two grades to an A with strong, yet broad-based, economic growth. Many new companies and relocations led to the country's highest short-term employment growth, while also improving the state's rank in average annual pay growth from twenty-seventh to seventh. Benefits seem broadly shared as the gap between the rich and poor is small. Meanwhile, the quality of life is excellent, with the best overall Health Conditions, and good Social and Environmental Conditions.

- **Business Vitality:** Idaho's vigor is highlighted in its fourth Business Vitality A in a row. Existing businesses are still competitive, and entrepreneurship is strong due to the second highest rate of new companies and strong new business job growth. Only poor diversity may leave the economy vulnerable, as the state's top industries are highly concentrated and on similar business cycles.

- **Development Capacity:** Finally, Idaho has an above average grade in development resources. While Financial, Technology, and Infrastructure & Amenity Resources have all remained steady Cs, in-migration and the twelfth best high school graduation rate combine to give the state an excellent set of Human Resources. There may be some future problems, with poor highways, little mass transit availability, and many people without ready access to primary health care.

- **Tax & Fiscal System:** Idaho's balanced and stable revenue system also happens to be one of the most fair and best at equalizing its local governments' different fiscal capacities – resulting in the second best Tax & Fiscal System score in the nation.

For information on how grades and ranks are calculated, see the Methodology section.
For a detailed explanation of indexes, refer to the individual index section.

WHERE IDAHO RANKS – MEASURE BY MEASURE

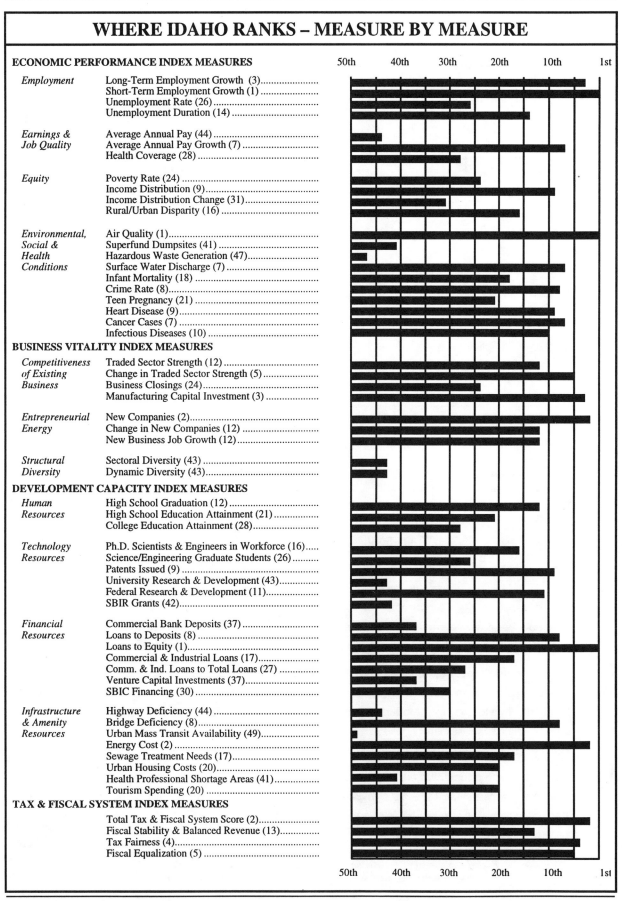

ECONOMIC PERFORMANCE INDEX MEASURES

		50th	40th	30th	20th	10th	1st

Employment
Long-Term Employment Growth (3).......................
Short-Term Employment Growth (1) ....
Unemployment Rate (26) ....
Unemployment Duration (14) ....

Earnings & Job Quality
Average Annual Pay (44) ....
Average Annual Pay Growth (7) ....
Health Coverage (28) ....

Equity
Poverty Rate (24) ....
Income Distribution (9).......................................
Income Distribution Change (31)..........................
Rural/Urban Disparity (16) ....

Environmental, Social & Health Conditions
Air Quality (1)..
Superfund Dumpsites (41)....................................
Hazardous Waste Generation (47).........................
Surface Water Discharge (7) ....
Infant Mortality (18) ....
Crime Rate (8)..
Teen Pregnancy (21) ....
Heart Disease (9)..
Cancer Cases (7) ....
Infectious Diseases (10) ....

BUSINESS VITALITY INDEX MEASURES

Competitiveness of Existing Business
Traded Sector Strength (12) ....
Change in Traded Sector Strength (5) ....
Business Closings (24)...
Manufacturing Capital Investment (3) ....

Entrepreneurial Energy
New Companies (2)..
Change in New Companies (12) ....
New Business Job Growth (12).............................

Structural Diversity
Sectoral Diversity (43) ....
Dynamic Diversity (43)..

DEVELOPMENT CAPACITY INDEX MEASURES

Human Resources
High School Graduation (12).................................
High School Education Attainment (21) ....
College Education Attainment (28).........................

Technology Resources
Ph.D. Scientists & Engineers in Workforce (16).....
Science/Engineering Graduate Students (26) ....
Patents Issued (9) ....
University Research & Development (43)...............
Federal Research & Development (11)....................
SBIR Grants (42)...

Financial Resources
Commercial Bank Deposits (37) ....
Loans to Deposits (8) ....
Loans to Equity (1)..
Commercial & Industrial Loans (17)......................
Comm. & Ind. Loans to Total Loans (27) ....
Venture Capital Investments (37).........................
SBIC Financing (30)..

Infrastructure & Amenity Resources
Highway Deficiency (44) ....
Bridge Deficiency (8)..
Urban Mass Transit Availability (49).....................
Energy Cost (2) ....
Sewage Treatment Needs (17)..............................
Urban Housing Costs (20)....................................
Health Professional Shortage Areas (41)...............
Tourism Spending (20) ....

TAX & FISCAL SYSTEM INDEX MEASURES

Total Tax & Fiscal System Score (2).......................
Fiscal Stability & Balanced Revenue (13)..............
Tax Fairness (4)..
Fiscal Equalization (5) ....

		50th	40th	30th	20th	10th	1st

ILLINOIS 1995 REPORT CARD

ECONOMIC PERFORMANCE	D
Employment	D
Earnings & Job Quality	B
Equity	D

BUSINESS VITALITY	B
Business Competitiveness	B
Entrepreneurial Energy	F
Structural Diversity	A

DEVELOPMENT CAPACITY	A
Human Resources	C
Technology Resources	C
Financial Resources	A
Infrastructure & Amenity Resources	A

Tax & Fiscal System	–

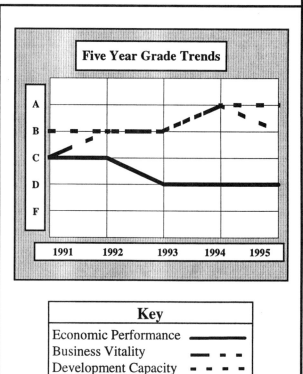

Five Year Grade Trends

1991 1992 1993 1994 1995

Key	
Economic Performance	———
Business Vitality	— - -
Development Capacity	- - - -

- **Economic Performance:** For the third straight year, Illinois earns a poor grade in Economic Performance. The state's job market is poor, with low employment growth and high unemployment. In addition, while average annual pay remains top notch, pay growth now ranks 32nd in the nation. One bright spot for the state is a decrease in the poverty rate. The quality of life in Illinois is below average, comparing particularly poorly on social indicators such as infant mortality and crime.

- **Business Vitality:** Despite continued strength in the competitiveness of its businesses and the diversity of its economy, Illinois' grade drops to a B this year. In particular, with slow new business job growth and a steep drop in the rate of new company formations, Illinois now ranks third worst on Entrepreneurial Energy.

- **Development Capacity:** Illinois' Development Capacity is the seventh best in the nation. Led by strong mass transit availability and quality bridges, Illinois' Infrastructure & Amenity Resources are excellent. In addition, with top ten rankings for both bank deposits and commercial/industrial loans, Illinois' Financial Resources also earn the highest grade. The state's Human Resources and Technology Resources are both average.

- **Tax & Fiscal System:** Illinois' system rates below average and is the second worst in the Industrial Midwest. In particular, the state's revenue raising structure is poorly balanced and the state ranks among the worst ten states in terms of equalizing local fiscal capacity.

For information on how grades and ranks are calculated, see the Methodology section.
For a detailed explanation of indexes, refer to the individual index section.

WHERE ILLINOIS RANKS – MEASURE BY MEASURE

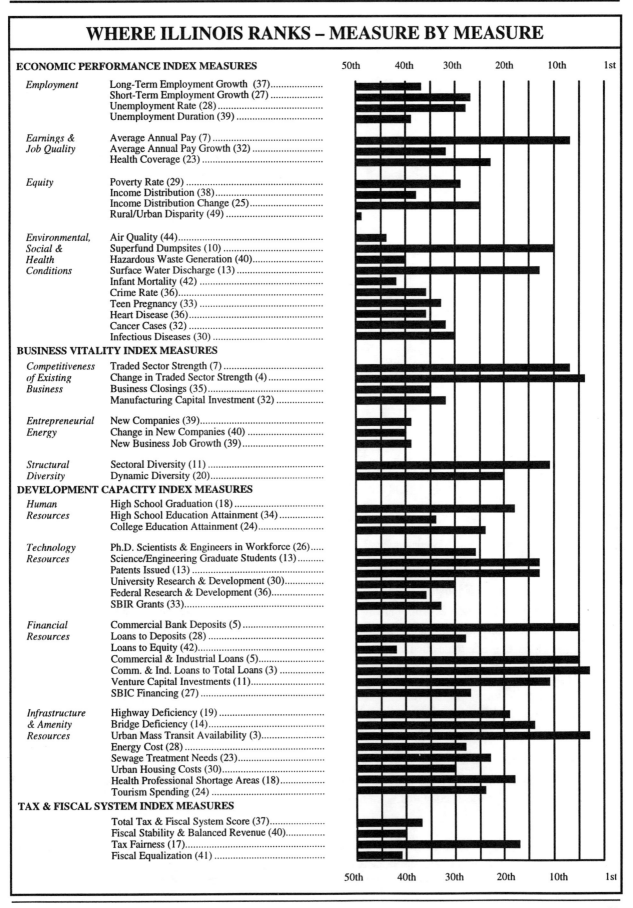

ECONOMIC PERFORMANCE INDEX MEASURES

| | | 50th | 40th | 30th | 20th | 10th | 1st |

Employment
- Long-Term Employment Growth (37)
- Short-Term Employment Growth (27)
- Unemployment Rate (28)
- Unemployment Duration (39)

Earnings & Job Quality
- Average Annual Pay (7)
- Average Annual Pay Growth (32)
- Health Coverage (23)

Equity
- Poverty Rate (29)
- Income Distribution (38)
- Income Distribution Change (25)
- Rural/Urban Disparity (49)

Environmental, Social & Health Conditions
- Air Quality (44)
- Superfund Dumpsites (10)
- Hazardous Waste Generation (40)
- Surface Water Discharge (13)
- Infant Mortality (42)
- Crime Rate (36)
- Teen Pregnancy (33)
- Heart Disease (36)
- Cancer Cases (32)
- Infectious Diseases (30)

BUSINESS VITALITY INDEX MEASURES

Competitiveness of Existing Business
- Traded Sector Strength (7)
- Change in Traded Sector Strength (4)
- Business Closings (35)
- Manufacturing Capital Investment (32)

Entrepreneurial Energy
- New Companies (39)
- Change in New Companies (40)
- New Business Job Growth (39)

Structural Diversity
- Sectoral Diversity (11)
- Dynamic Diversity (20)

DEVELOPMENT CAPACITY INDEX MEASURES

Human Resources
- High School Graduation (18)
- High School Education Attainment (34)
- College Education Attainment (24)

Technology Resources
- Ph.D. Scientists & Engineers in Workforce (26)
- Science/Engineering Graduate Students (13)
- Patents Issued (13)
- University Research & Development (30)
- Federal Research & Development (36)
- SBIR Grants (33)

Financial Resources
- Commercial Bank Deposits (5)
- Loans to Deposits (28)
- Loans to Equity (42)
- Commercial & Industrial Loans (5)
- Comm. & Ind. Loans to Total Loans (3)
- Venture Capital Investments (11)
- SBIC Financing (27)

Infrastructure & Amenity Resources
- Highway Deficiency (19)
- Bridge Deficiency (14)
- Urban Mass Transit Availability (3)
- Energy Cost (28)
- Sewage Treatment Needs (23)
- Urban Housing Costs (30)
- Health Professional Shortage Areas (18)
- Tourism Spending (24)

TAX & FISCAL SYSTEM INDEX MEASURES

- Total Tax & Fiscal System Score (37)
- Fiscal Stability & Balanced Revenue (40)
- Tax Fairness (17)
- Fiscal Equalization (41)

| | 50th | 40th | 30th | 20th | 10th | 1st |

INDIANA 1995 REPORT CARD

ECONOMIC PERFORMANCE	A

Employment ....A
Earnings & Job Quality ....B
Equity ....B

BUSINESS VITALITY	B

Business Competitiveness ....A
Entrepreneurial Energy...D
Structural Diversity ....B

DEVELOPMENT CAPACITY	D

Human Resources..D
Technology Resources ....D
Financial Resources..C
Infrastructure & Amenity Resources.....................C

Tax & Fiscal System	–

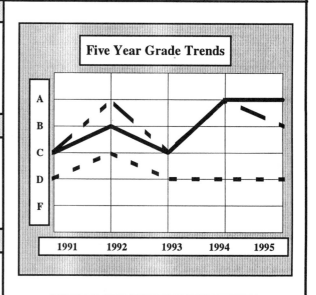

Five Year Grade Trends

A
B
C
D
F

1991   1992   1993   1994   1995

Key

Economic Performance ————
Business Vitality — – —
Development Capacity ▪ ▪ ▪ ▪

- **Economic Performance:** Indiana earns an A for the second year in a row. Led by strong short-term job growth and low unemployment, the state has the nation's tenth best job market. In addition, Earnings & Job Quality are strong, marked by the ninth best health coverage. On measures of quality of life, however, Indiana is below average, particularly with poor Environmental Conditions such as surface water discharge.

- **Business Vitality:** Due to sagging Entrepreneurial Energy – particularly a drop in new business job growth and slowdown in new company formation – Indiana's grade drops to a B this year. Despite this drop, Indiana's economy is well diversified and receives an excellent mark for the competitiveness of its existing business with a top ten rank in the strength of its traded sector (those industries that trade outside the state).

- **Development Capacity:** Indiana's weakness continues to be Development Capacity, which receives a poor grade for the third straight year. While the state's Infrastructure & Amenity and Financial Resources are both average, its Technology Resources are poor. Moreover, with the nation's third worst college attainment, Indiana's Human Resources rank among the bottom ten in the nation.

- **Tax & Fiscal System:** Indiana's Tax & Fiscal System rates below average and is the lowest ranking in the region. While the state's revenue raising structure rates above average in terms of balance, it is one of the nation's least equitable.

For information on how grades and ranks are calculated, see the Methodology section.
For a detailed explanation of indexes, refer to the individual index section.

WHERE INDIANA RANKS – MEASURE BY MEASURE

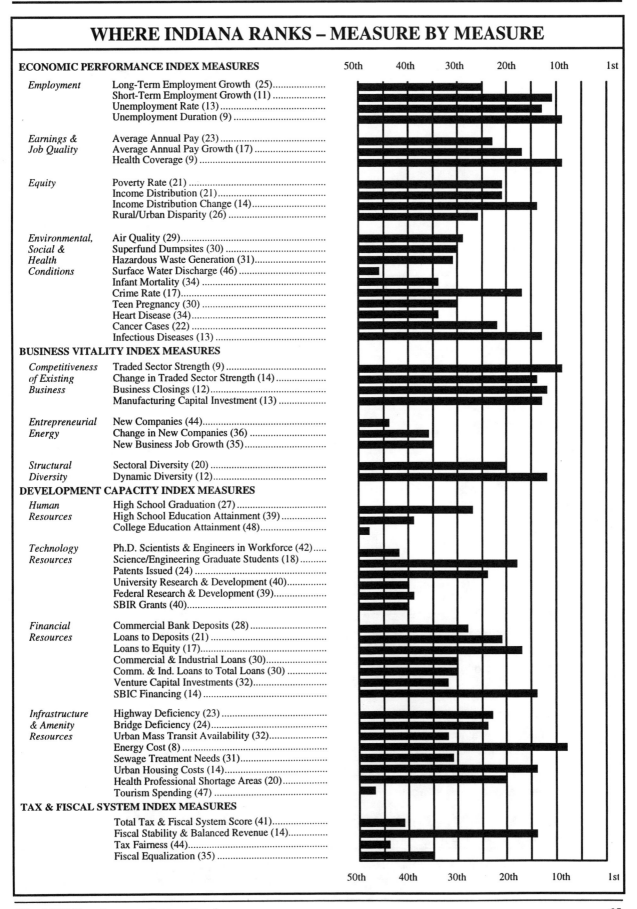

ECONOMIC PERFORMANCE INDEX MEASURES

| | | 50th | 40th | 30th | 20th | 10th | 1st |

Employment
Long-Term Employment Growth (25)....................
Short-Term Employment Growth (11)....................
Unemployment Rate (13) ....
Unemployment Duration (9) ....

Earnings & Job Quality
Average Annual Pay (23) ....
Average Annual Pay Growth (17) ....
Health Coverage (9) ....

Equity
Poverty Rate (21) ....
Income Distribution (21)................................
Income Distribution Change (14)........................
Rural/Urban Disparity (26) ....

Environmental, Social & Health Conditions
Air Quality (29)................................
Superfund Dumpsites (30) ....
Hazardous Waste Generation (31)........................
Surface Water Discharge (46) ....
Infant Mortality (34) ....
Crime Rate (17)................................
Teen Pregnancy (30) ....
Heart Disease (34) ....
Cancer Cases (22) ....
Infectious Diseases (13) ....

BUSINESS VITALITY INDEX MEASURES

Competitiveness of Existing Business
Traded Sector Strength (9) ....
Change in Traded Sector Strength (14) ....
Business Closings (12)................................
Manufacturing Capital Investment (13) ....

Entrepreneurial Energy
New Companies (44)................................
Change in New Companies (36) ....
New Business Job Growth (35)........................

Structural Diversity
Sectoral Diversity (20) ....
Dynamic Diversity (12)................................

DEVELOPMENT CAPACITY INDEX MEASURES

Human Resources
High School Graduation (27) ....
High School Education Attainment (39) ....
College Education Attainment (48)........................

Technology Resources
Ph.D. Scientists & Engineers in Workforce (42).....
Science/Engineering Graduate Students (18) ....
Patents Issued (24) ....
University Research & Development (40)................
Federal Research & Development (39)................
SBIR Grants (40)................................

Financial Resources
Commercial Bank Deposits (28) ....
Loans to Deposits (21) ....
Loans to Equity (17)................................
Commercial & Industrial Loans (30)....................
Comm. & Ind. Loans to Total Loans (30) ....
Venture Capital Investments (32)....................
SBIC Financing (14) ....

Infrastructure & Amenity Resources
Highway Deficiency (23) ....
Bridge Deficiency (24)................................
Urban Mass Transit Availability (32)....................
Energy Cost (8) ....
Sewage Treatment Needs (31)........................
Urban Housing Costs (14)................................
Health Professional Shortage Areas (20)................
Tourism Spending (47) ....

TAX & FISCAL SYSTEM INDEX MEASURES

Total Tax & Fiscal System Score (41)....................
Fiscal Stability & Balanced Revenue (14)..............
Tax Fairness (44)................................
Fiscal Equalization (35) ....

| | | 50th | 40th | 30th | 20th | 10th | 1st |

IOWA 1995 REPORT CARD

ECONOMIC PERFORMANCE	A

Employment ....B
Earnings & Job Quality ....B
Equity ....A

BUSINESS VITALITY	C

Business Competitiveness ....D
Entrepreneurial Energy..........................C
Structural Diversity ....B

DEVELOPMENT CAPACITY	C

Human Resources.....................................C
Technology Resources C
Financial Resources.................................D
Infrastructure & Amenity Resources.....................A

Tax & Fiscal System	√

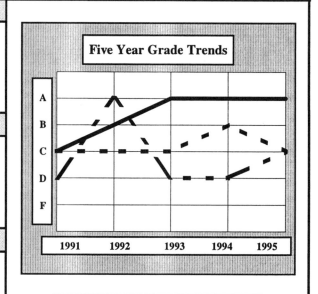

Five Year Grade Trends

Key
Economic Performance ————
Business Vitality ▬ ▬ ▬ ▪
Development Capacity ▪ ▪ ▪ ▪

- **Economic Performance:** With plentiful jobs and good Equity ratings, Iowa has the best Economic Performance in the Plains. The state appears to have reached full employment (3.7% – third lowest in the nation), although job quality has not yet caught up – annual pay still ranks only 43rd. The state ranks third in income distribution – it has one of the smallest gaps between the rich and poor – and boasts a low poverty rate. Excellent Social Conditions and good Health and Environmental Conditions contribute to a superior quality of life.

- **Business Vitality:** Slight improvements in entrepreneurship and Structural Diversity move Iowa up to a C in Business Vitality. New business job growth is good (7th) and the state's economy is becoming less concentrated. The existing businesses are still not very competitive as little money comes from out of state (the traded sector) and upgrading of manufacturing equipment is below average.

- **Development Capacity:** Iowa lost out on a B by just one rank this year. It still boasts solid Human Resources (with the 2nd highest high school graduation rate) and excellent Infrastructure & Amenity Resources (2nd best on deficient highways and the nation's lowest sewage treatment needs). Technology and Financial Resources are only average, with few scientists and engineers in the work force and below average loan activity, despite the nation's seventh highest deposits.

- **Tax & Fiscal System:** Iowa does a good job of equalizing the different fiscal capacities of local governments and has a fairly stable and balanced revenue system.

For information on how grades and ranks are calculated, see the Methodology section.
For a detailed explanation of indexes, refer to the individual index section.

WHERE IOWA RANKS – MEASURE BY MEASURE

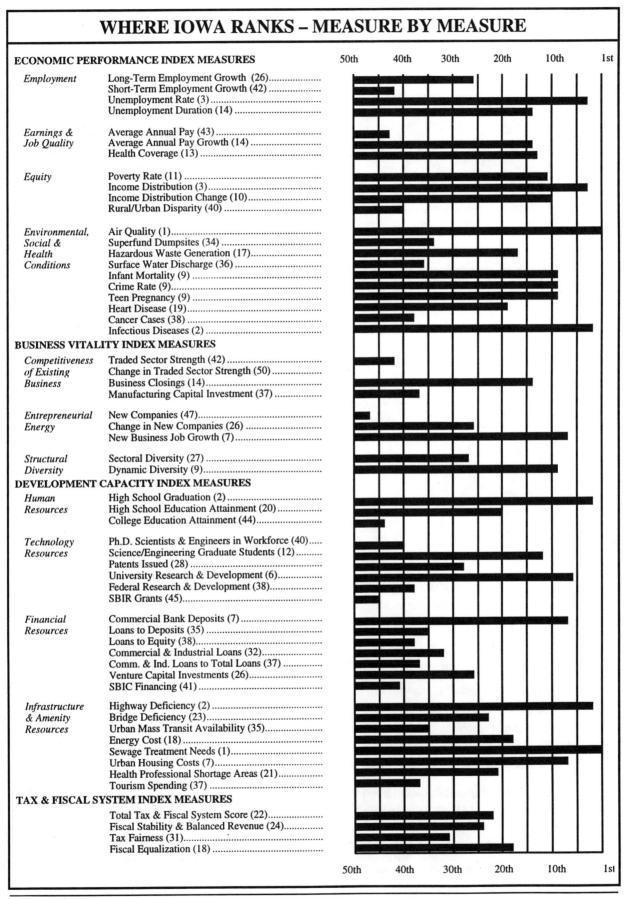

ECONOMIC PERFORMANCE INDEX MEASURES

Employment
- Long-Term Employment Growth (26)
- Short-Term Employment Growth (42)
- Unemployment Rate (3)
- Unemployment Duration (14)

Earnings & Job Quality
- Average Annual Pay (43)
- Average Annual Pay Growth (14)
- Health Coverage (13)

Equity
- Poverty Rate (11)
- Income Distribution (3)
- Income Distribution Change (10)
- Rural/Urban Disparity (40)

Environmental, Social & Health Conditions
- Air Quality (1)
- Superfund Dumpsites (34)
- Hazardous Waste Generation (17)
- Surface Water Discharge (36)
- Infant Mortality (9)
- Crime Rate (9)
- Teen Pregnancy (9)
- Heart Disease (19)
- Cancer Cases (38)
- Infectious Diseases (2)

BUSINESS VITALITY INDEX MEASURES

Competitiveness of Existing Business
- Traded Sector Strength (42)
- Change in Traded Sector Strength (50)
- Business Closings (14)
- Manufacturing Capital Investment (37)

Entrepreneurial Energy
- New Companies (47)
- Change in New Companies (26)
- New Business Job Growth (7)

Structural Diversity
- Sectoral Diversity (27)
- Dynamic Diversity (9)

DEVELOPMENT CAPACITY INDEX MEASURES

Human Resources
- High School Graduation (2)
- High School Education Attainment (20)
- College Education Attainment (44)

Technology Resources
- Ph.D. Scientists & Engineers in Workforce (40)
- Science/Engineering Graduate Students (12)
- Patents Issued (28)
- University Research & Development (6)
- Federal Research & Development (38)
- SBIR Grants (45)

Financial Resources
- Commercial Bank Deposits (7)
- Loans to Deposits (35)
- Loans to Equity (38)
- Commercial & Industrial Loans (32)
- Comm. & Ind. Loans to Total Loans (37)
- Venture Capital Investments (26)
- SBIC Financing (41)

Infrastructure & Amenity Resources
- Highway Deficiency (2)
- Bridge Deficiency (23)
- Urban Mass Transit Availability (35)
- Energy Cost (18)
- Sewage Treatment Needs (1)
- Urban Housing Costs (7)
- Health Professional Shortage Areas (21)
- Tourism Spending (37)

TAX & FISCAL SYSTEM INDEX MEASURES
- Total Tax & Fiscal System Score (22)
- Fiscal Stability & Balanced Revenue (24)
- Tax Fairness (31)
- Fiscal Equalization (18)

50th   40th   30th   20th   10th   1st

KANSAS 1995 REPORT CARD

ECONOMIC PERFORMANCE	C

Employment C
Earnings & Job Quality C
Equity ....B

BUSINESS VITALITY	C

Business Competitiveness ....D
Entrepreneurial Energy...B
Structural Diversity ....B

DEVELOPMENT CAPACITY	D

Human Resources..B
Technology Resources ....D
Financial Resources..D
Infrastructure & Amenity Resources......................C

Tax & Fiscal System	+

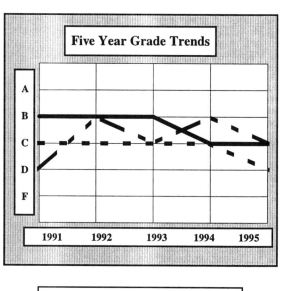

Five Year Grade Trends

| | 1991 | 1992 | 1993 | 1994 | 1995 |

Key	
Economic Performance	⎯⎯⎯
Business Vitality	▬ ▪ ▪
Development Capacity	▪ ▪ ▪ ▪

- **Economic Performance:** Kansas repeats last year's average performance, though it improved its Equity rating. The gap between the rich and the poor began to significantly shrink, as did the economic disparity between its urban and rural areas (from 39th to 18th). Only employment growth remains low, as do average earnings. Kansas' quality of life is very good (as are most Plains states'), especially its Health Conditions.

- **Business Vitality:** Kansas' Business Vitality is only average this year, as existing businesses lost some of their competitive edge. Businesses competing out-of-state (the traded sector) are falling behind in the amount of income they bring into the state, while business closings were just below average. Fortunately, entrepreneurship is high, led by an increase in new businesses, and the economy's key sectors are on different business cycles, making it less vulnerable to outside shocks.

- **Development Capacity:** Resources remain mostly average in Kansas, with the state's Infrastructure & Amenity Resources ranking near the middle. Poor Technology Resources (below average in every measure but science/engineering graduate students) and weak Financial Resources (due to very low loan activity) are offset by strong Human Resources. In fact, Kansas has the ninth highest high school attainment in the country, while college attainment ranks twentieth.

- **Tax & Fiscal System:** Kansas has one of the 15 best revenue systems – it has balanced and stable revenue sources and is fairly equitable as well.

For information on how grades and ranks are calculated, see the Methodology section.
For a detailed explanation of indexes, refer to the individual index section.

WHERE KANSAS RANKS – MEASURE BY MEASURE

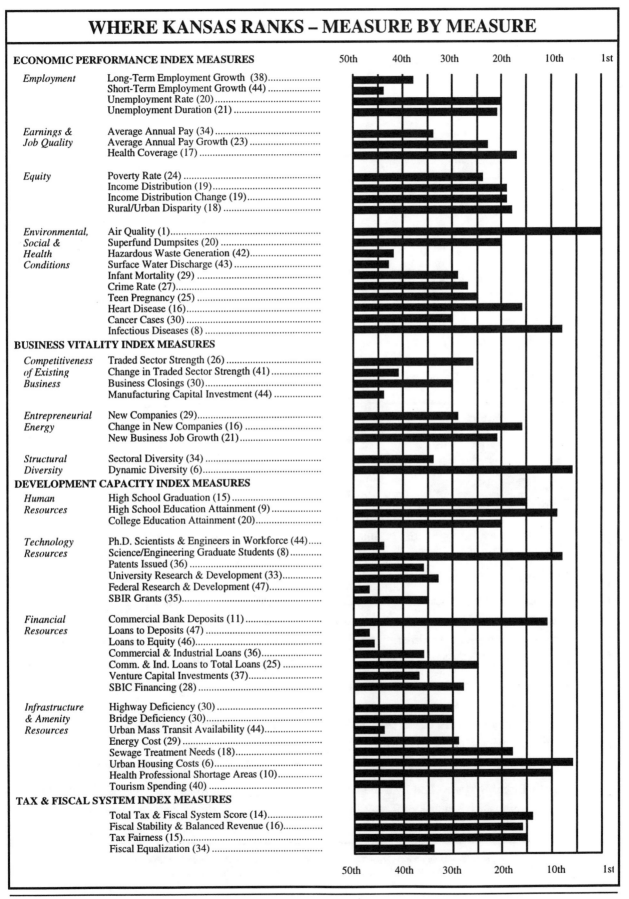

ECONOMIC PERFORMANCE INDEX MEASURES

Employment
Long-Term Employment Growth (38)
Short-Term Employment Growth (44)
Unemployment Rate (20)
Unemployment Duration (21)

Earnings & Job Quality
Average Annual Pay (34)
Average Annual Pay Growth (23)
Health Coverage (17)

Equity
Poverty Rate (24)
Income Distribution (19)
Income Distribution Change (19)
Rural/Urban Disparity (18)

Environmental, Social & Health Conditions
Air Quality (1)
Superfund Dumpsites (20)
Hazardous Waste Generation (42)
Surface Water Discharge (43)
Infant Mortality (29)
Crime Rate (27)
Teen Pregnancy (25)
Heart Disease (16)
Cancer Cases (30)
Infectious Diseases (8)

BUSINESS VITALITY INDEX MEASURES

Competitiveness of Existing Business
Traded Sector Strength (26)
Change in Traded Sector Strength (41)
Business Closings (30)
Manufacturing Capital Investment (44)

Entrepreneurial Energy
New Companies (29)
Change in New Companies (16)
New Business Job Growth (21)

Structural Diversity
Sectoral Diversity (34)
Dynamic Diversity (6)

DEVELOPMENT CAPACITY INDEX MEASURES

Human Resources
High School Graduation (15)
High School Education Attainment (9)
College Education Attainment (20)

Technology Resources
Ph.D. Scientists & Engineers in Workforce (44)
Science/Engineering Graduate Students (8)
Patents Issued (36)
University Research & Development (33)
Federal Research & Development (47)
SBIR Grants (35)

Financial Resources
Commercial Bank Deposits (11)
Loans to Deposits (47)
Loans to Equity (46)
Commercial & Industrial Loans (36)
Comm. & Ind. Loans to Total Loans (25)
Venture Capital Investments (37)
SBIC Financing (28)

Infrastructure & Amenity Resources
Highway Deficiency (30)
Bridge Deficiency (30)
Urban Mass Transit Availability (44)
Energy Cost (29)
Sewage Treatment Needs (18)
Urban Housing Costs (6)
Health Professional Shortage Areas (10)
Tourism Spending (40)

TAX & FISCAL SYSTEM INDEX MEASURES

Total Tax & Fiscal System Score (14)
Fiscal Stability & Balanced Revenue (16)
Tax Fairness (15)
Fiscal Equalization (34)

50th   40th   30th   20th   10th   1st

KENTUCKY 1995 REPORT CARD

ECONOMIC PERFORMANCE	F

Employment C
Earnings & Job Quality ....D
Equity ....D

BUSINESS VITALITY	D

Business Competitiveness ....D
Entrepreneurial Energy.............................D
Structural Diversity ....A

DEVELOPMENT CAPACITY	D

Human Resources......................................D
Technology Resources ....F
Financial Resources..................................C
Infrastructure & Amenity Resources.........C

Tax & Fiscal System	+

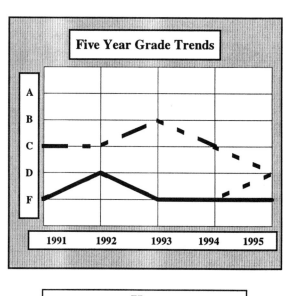

Five Year Grade Trends

1991   1992   1993   1994   1995

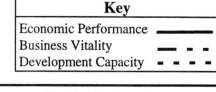

Key	
Economic Performance	————
Business Vitality	— - -
Development Capacity	- - - -

- **Economic Performance:** For the third straight year, Kentucky receives a failing grade. While the state's job market remains average, Earnings & Job Quality, marked by low pay and slowing pay growth, now receives a poor rating. In addition, given the state's high poverty and second worst rank on income distribution, its strong score for minimizing disparities among urban and rural areas is little consolation. While the state ranks well on social indicators such as crime, overall quality of life in Kentucky is below average.

- **Business Vitality:** Despite having the nation's fourth most diversified economy, Kentucky's overall Business Vitality grade dropped to a D. With particularly low rates of new company formation, Entrepreneurial Energy in Kentucky is poor. In addition, the poor competitiveness of the state's existing businesses is reflected in a relatively high rate of business closings.

- **Development Capacity:** Kentucky is one of a handful of southern states which showed improvement on Development Capacity. Though the change was not dramatic, the state showed marginal improvements on several key indicators, such as college attainment, SBIR grants, and lending activity (particularly SBIC financing). Despite these improvements, Kentucky is still hampered by poor Human Resources and the nation's second worst Technology Resources.

- **Tax & Fiscal System:** Led by a top ten ranking for its policies to equalize the fiscal capacity of local governments, Kentucky's Tax & Fiscal System receives an above average rating.

For information on how grades and ranks are calculated, see the Methodology section.
For a detailed explanation of indexes, refer to the individual index section.

WHERE KENTUCKY RANKS – MEASURE BY MEASURE

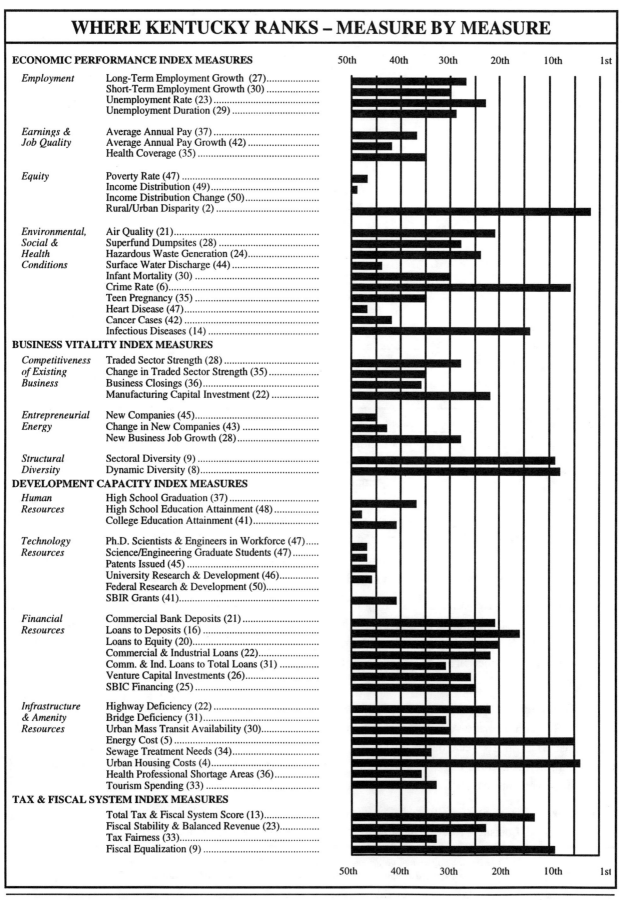

ECONOMIC PERFORMANCE INDEX MEASURES

| | | 50th | 40th | 30th | 20th | 10th | 1st |

Employment
- Long-Term Employment Growth (27)
- Short-Term Employment Growth (30)
- Unemployment Rate (23)
- Unemployment Duration (29)

Earnings & Job Quality
- Average Annual Pay (37)
- Average Annual Pay Growth (42)
- Health Coverage (35)

Equity
- Poverty Rate (47)
- Income Distribution (49)
- Income Distribution Change (50)
- Rural/Urban Disparity (2)

Environmental, Social & Health Conditions
- Air Quality (21)
- Superfund Dumpsites (28)
- Hazardous Waste Generation (24)
- Surface Water Discharge (44)
- Infant Mortality (30)
- Crime Rate (6)
- Teen Pregnancy (35)
- Heart Disease (47)
- Cancer Cases (42)
- Infectious Diseases (14)

BUSINESS VITALITY INDEX MEASURES

Competitiveness of Existing Business
- Traded Sector Strength (28)
- Change in Traded Sector Strength (35)
- Business Closings (36)
- Manufacturing Capital Investment (22)

Entrepreneurial Energy
- New Companies (45)
- Change in New Companies (43)
- New Business Job Growth (28)

Structural Diversity
- Sectoral Diversity (9)
- Dynamic Diversity (8)

DEVELOPMENT CAPACITY INDEX MEASURES

Human Resources
- High School Graduation (37)
- High School Education Attainment (48)
- College Education Attainment (41)

Technology Resources
- Ph.D. Scientists & Engineers in Workforce (47)
- Science/Engineering Graduate Students (47)
- Patents Issued (45)
- University Research & Development (46)
- Federal Research & Development (50)
- SBIR Grants (41)

Financial Resources
- Commercial Bank Deposits (21)
- Loans to Deposits (16)
- Loans to Equity (20)
- Commercial & Industrial Loans (22)
- Comm. & Ind. Loans to Total Loans (31)
- Venture Capital Investments (26)
- SBIC Financing (25)

Infrastructure & Amenity Resources
- Highway Deficiency (22)
- Bridge Deficiency (31)
- Urban Mass Transit Availability (30)
- Energy Cost (5)
- Sewage Treatment Needs (34)
- Urban Housing Costs (4)
- Health Professional Shortage Areas (36)
- Tourism Spending (33)

TAX & FISCAL SYSTEM INDEX MEASURES

- Total Tax & Fiscal System Score (13)
- Fiscal Stability & Balanced Revenue (23)
- Tax Fairness (33)
- Fiscal Equalization (9)

| | | 50th | 40th | 30th | 20th | 10th | 1st |

LOUISIANA 1995 REPORT CARD

ECONOMIC PERFORMANCE	F

Employment ....D
Earnings & Job Quality ....F
Equity ....D

BUSINESS VITALITY	C

Business Competitiveness ....B
Entrepreneurial Energy...................................C
Structural Diversity C

DEVELOPMENT CAPACITY	F

Human Resources..F
Technology Resources ....D
Financial Resources..D
Infrastructure & Amenity Resources...............D

Tax & Fiscal System	–

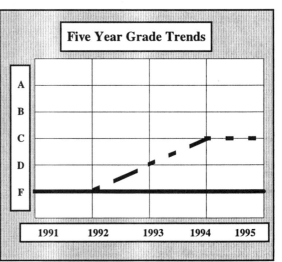

Five Year Grade Trends

1991 1992 1993 1994 1995

Key
Economic Performance ———
Business Vitality – – –
Development Capacity ▪ ▪ ▪ ▪

- **Economic Performance:** Louisiana's overall Economic Performance is the nation's second weakest. With the worst rate of employer-provided health coverage and below average pay, Earnings & Job Quality receive a failing mark. Moreover, the state's job market, despite improving short-term job growth, rates poor overall. On measures of Equity, the state rates poorly, though a narrowing gap between rich and poor is a positive trend. With the worst social indicators in the U.S., the quality of life is also among the worst.

- **Business Vitality:** Louisiana's strength lies in its Business Vitality. Though rating only average overall, the state benefits, in particular, from businesses that rank above average on competitiveness (e.g., low business closings and the fourth highest level of manufacturing capital investments). However, on measures of Entrepreneurial Energy and Structural Diversity, Louisiana is only average.

- **Development Capacity:** Louisiana's development resources continue to rank second worst in the U.S. With the nation's lowest high school graduation rate, the state's Human Resources rank dead last. The state's Technology and Infrastructure & Amenity Resources are not much better – both earn below average marks. One positive sign is the state's Financial Resources which, with small improvements in bank deposits and venture capital investments, now receive a passing grade.

- **Tax & Fiscal System:** With below average marks for both the stability and fairness of its tax structure, Louisiana receives a below average rating in the Tax & Fiscal System.

For information on how grades and ranks are calculated, see the Methodology section.
For a detailed explanation of indexes, refer to the individual index section.

WHERE LOUISIANA RANKS – MEASURE BY MEASURE

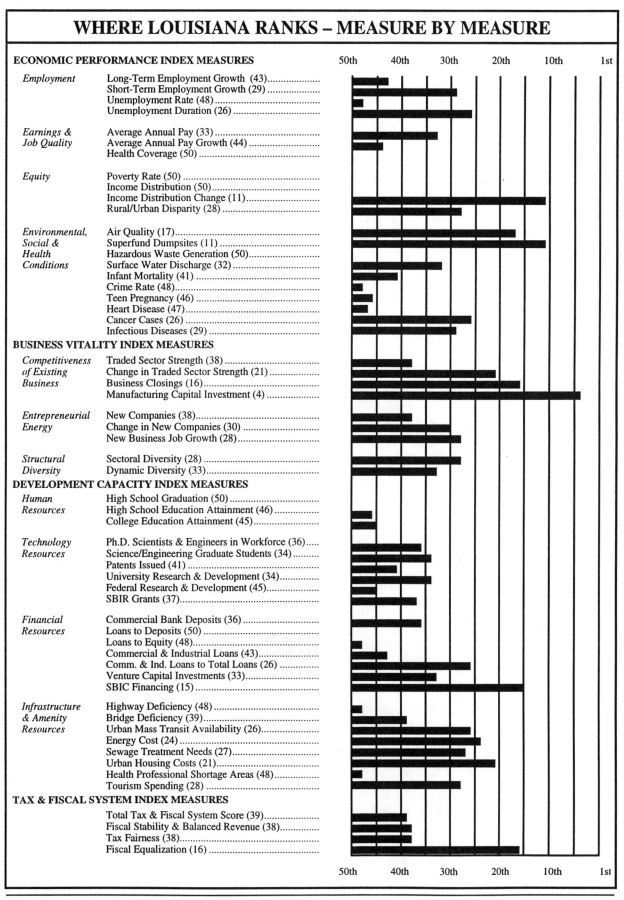

ECONOMIC PERFORMANCE INDEX MEASURES

Employment
Long-Term Employment Growth (43)
Short-Term Employment Growth (29)
Unemployment Rate (48)
Unemployment Duration (26)

Earnings & Job Quality
Average Annual Pay (33)
Average Annual Pay Growth (44)
Health Coverage (50)

Equity
Poverty Rate (50)
Income Distribution (50)
Income Distribution Change (11)
Rural/Urban Disparity (28)

Environmental, Social & Health Conditions
Air Quality (17)
Superfund Dumpsites (11)
Hazardous Waste Generation (50)
Surface Water Discharge (32)
Infant Mortality (41)
Crime Rate (48)
Teen Pregnancy (46)
Heart Disease (47)
Cancer Cases (26)
Infectious Diseases (29)

BUSINESS VITALITY INDEX MEASURES

Competitiveness of Existing Business
Traded Sector Strength (38)
Change in Traded Sector Strength (21)
Business Closings (16)
Manufacturing Capital Investment (4)

Entrepreneurial Energy
New Companies (38)
Change in New Companies (30)
New Business Job Growth (28)

Structural Diversity
Sectoral Diversity (28)
Dynamic Diversity (33)

DEVELOPMENT CAPACITY INDEX MEASURES

Human Resources
High School Graduation (50)
High School Education Attainment (46)
College Education Attainment (45)

Technology Resources
Ph.D. Scientists & Engineers in Workforce (36)
Science/Engineering Graduate Students (34)
Patents Issued (41)
University Research & Development (34)
Federal Research & Development (45)
SBIR Grants (37)

Financial Resources
Commercial Bank Deposits (36)
Loans to Deposits (50)
Loans to Equity (48)
Commercial & Industrial Loans (43)
Comm. & Ind. Loans to Total Loans (26)
Venture Capital Investments (33)
SBIC Financing (15)

Infrastructure & Amenity Resources
Highway Deficiency (48)
Bridge Deficiency (39)
Urban Mass Transit Availability (26)
Energy Cost (24)
Sewage Treatment Needs (27)
Urban Housing Costs (21)
Health Professional Shortage Areas (48)
Tourism Spending (28)

TAX & FISCAL SYSTEM INDEX MEASURES

Total Tax & Fiscal System Score (39)
Fiscal Stability & Balanced Revenue (38)
Tax Fairness (38)
Fiscal Equalization (16)

MAINE 1995 REPORT CARD

ECONOMIC PERFORMANCE	D

Employment ....F
Earnings & Job Quality ....D
Equity ....B

BUSINESS VITALITY	D

Business Competitiveness C
Entrepreneurial Energy....................................D
Structural Diversity C

DEVELOPMENT CAPACITY	D

Human Resources..B
Technology Resources ....D
Financial Resources..C
Infrastructure & Amenity Resources.................D

Tax & Fiscal System	+

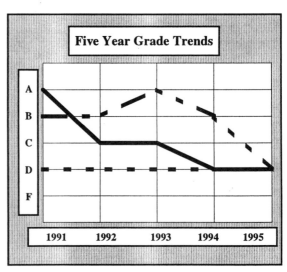

Five Year Grade Trends

| | 1991 | 1992 | 1993 | 1994 | 1995 |

Key

Economic Performance	———
Business Vitality	— - -
Development Capacity	- - - -

- **Economic Performance:** Maine's economy continues its downward slide. The nation's worst short-term employment growth and a very poor unemployment rate keep Maine's employment outlook dismal. At the same time, Earnings & Job Quality measures have suffered so that the state now also ranks among the country's worst (average annual pay growth dropped from 37th to 47th). The only good news is that the gap between rich and poor is decreasing. The quality of life is good, with good Social and Health Conditions.

- **Business Vitality:** Maine's economy is becoming less dynamic, which does not help prospects for a recovery. Although the number of business closings are third in the nation, new company formations are slowing down (ranked 41st) and new business job growth is poor (49th). As a result, Maine has one of the worst entrepreneurial economies in the nation. Meanwhile, the economy also became less diverse, making it less flexible and adaptable.

- **Development Capacity:** The good news is that Maine's development resources – the tools for its long-term recovery – are slowly inching upwards. Human Resources have improved and now rank among the nation's best. Technology Resources have improved, as has Infrastructure & Amenity Resources (from an F to a D), even though it has declined elsewhere in the region.

- **Tax & Fiscal System:** Maine has one of the country's most equitable tax systems. Yet, the balance of its revenue-raising structure is below average as are the state policies for equalizing local governments fiscal capacity.

For information on how grades and ranks are calculated, see the Methodology section.
For a detailed explanation of indexes, refer to the individual index section.

WHERE MAINE RANKS – MEASURE BY MEASURE

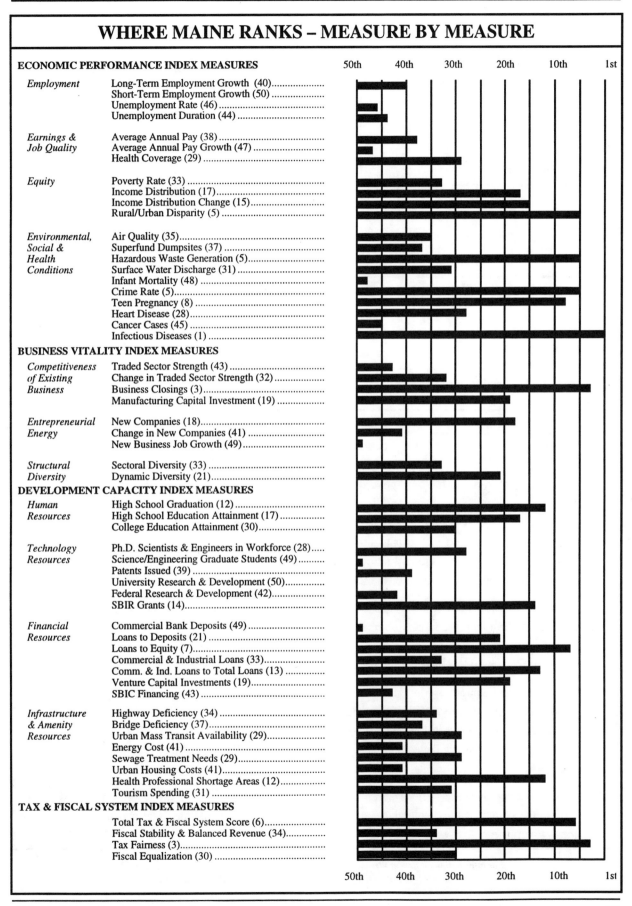

		50th	40th	30th	20th	10th	1st

ECONOMIC PERFORMANCE INDEX MEASURES

Employment
- Long-Term Employment Growth (40)
- Short-Term Employment Growth (50)
- Unemployment Rate (46)
- Unemployment Duration (44)

Earnings & Job Quality
- Average Annual Pay (38)
- Average Annual Pay Growth (47)
- Health Coverage (29)

Equity
- Poverty Rate (33)
- Income Distribution (17)
- Income Distribution Change (15)
- Rural/Urban Disparity (5)

Environmental, Social & Health Conditions
- Air Quality (35)
- Superfund Dumpsites (37)
- Hazardous Waste Generation (5)
- Surface Water Discharge (31)
- Infant Mortality (48)
- Crime Rate (5)
- Teen Pregnancy (8)
- Heart Disease (28)
- Cancer Cases (45)
- Infectious Diseases (1)

BUSINESS VITALITY INDEX MEASURES

Competitiveness of Existing Business
- Traded Sector Strength (43)
- Change in Traded Sector Strength (32)
- Business Closings (3)
- Manufacturing Capital Investment (19)

Entrepreneurial Energy
- New Companies (18)
- Change in New Companies (41)
- New Business Job Growth (49)

Structural Diversity
- Sectoral Diversity (33)
- Dynamic Diversity (21)

DEVELOPMENT CAPACITY INDEX MEASURES

Human Resources
- High School Graduation (12)
- High School Education Attainment (17)
- College Education Attainment (30)

Technology Resources
- Ph.D. Scientists & Engineers in Workforce (28)
- Science/Engineering Graduate Students (49)
- Patents Issued (39)
- University Research & Development (50)
- Federal Research & Development (42)
- SBIR Grants (14)

Financial Resources
- Commercial Bank Deposits (49)
- Loans to Deposits (21)
- Loans to Equity (7)
- Commercial & Industrial Loans (33)
- Comm. & Ind. Loans to Total Loans (13)
- Venture Capital Investments (19)
- SBIC Financing (43)

Infrastructure & Amenity Resources
- Highway Deficiency (34)
- Bridge Deficiency (37)
- Urban Mass Transit Availability (29)
- Energy Cost (41)
- Sewage Treatment Needs (29)
- Urban Housing Costs (41)
- Health Professional Shortage Areas (12)
- Tourism Spending (31)

TAX & FISCAL SYSTEM INDEX MEASURES
- Total Tax & Fiscal System Score (6)
- Fiscal Stability & Balanced Revenue (34)
- Tax Fairness (3)
- Fiscal Equalization (30)

		50th	40th	30th	20th	10th	1st

MARYLAND 1995 REPORT CARD

ECONOMIC PERFORMANCE	A

Employment C
Earnings & Job Quality ....B
Equity ....A

BUSINESS VITALITY	D

Business Competitiveness C
Entrepreneurial Energy...D
Structural Diversity ....B

DEVELOPMENT CAPACITY	B

Human Resources..B
Technology Resources ....A
Financial Resources..C
Infrastructure & Amenity Resources....................C

Tax & Fiscal System	√

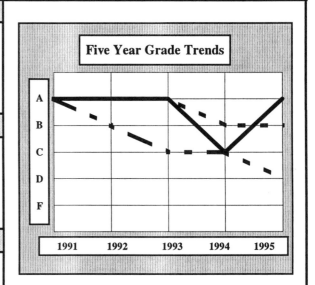

Five Year Grade Trends

Key
Economic Performance ———
Business Vitality ▬ ▬ ▬
Development Capacity ▬ ▬ ▬ ▬

- **Economic Performance:** Maryland's Economic Performance improved as Equity measures stabilized with the fourth best poverty rank and a smaller than average gap between rich and poor. While employment opportunities are moderate, jobs are good for those who have them. The state has the ninth highest average annual pay and the seventeenth highest rate of health coverage. Employment growth in 1993-1994 was near average and many looking for work were unemployed long-term. The state has good Environmental Conditions, and is just below average in Social and Health Conditions.

- **Business Vitality:** Entrepreneurship declined impacting the state's Business Vitality. Maryland had the smallest increase in new companies and below average new business job growth. Existing companies held their own as business closings decreased and the money from companies competing out of state increased. The economy remains one of the country's most diversified.

- **Development Capacity:** Maryland has very strong resources, led by the fourth best Technology Resources in the country, (with high ranks in university R&D funding, federal R&D funding, and scientists and engineers in the work force). The state has excellent Human Resources to match, (with the sixth highest college attainment rate in the nation). Financial Resources are a little below average (except venture capital) and the state's physical infrastructure is mediocre.

- **Tax & Fiscal System:** The Maryland Tax & Fiscal System is moderately well-balanced and among the country's most equitable, but it does a poor job of equalizing fiscal capacity among its local governments.

For information on how grades and ranks are calculated, see the Methodology section.
For a detailed explanation of indexes, refer to the individual index section.

WHERE MARYLAND RANKS – MEASURE BY MEASURE

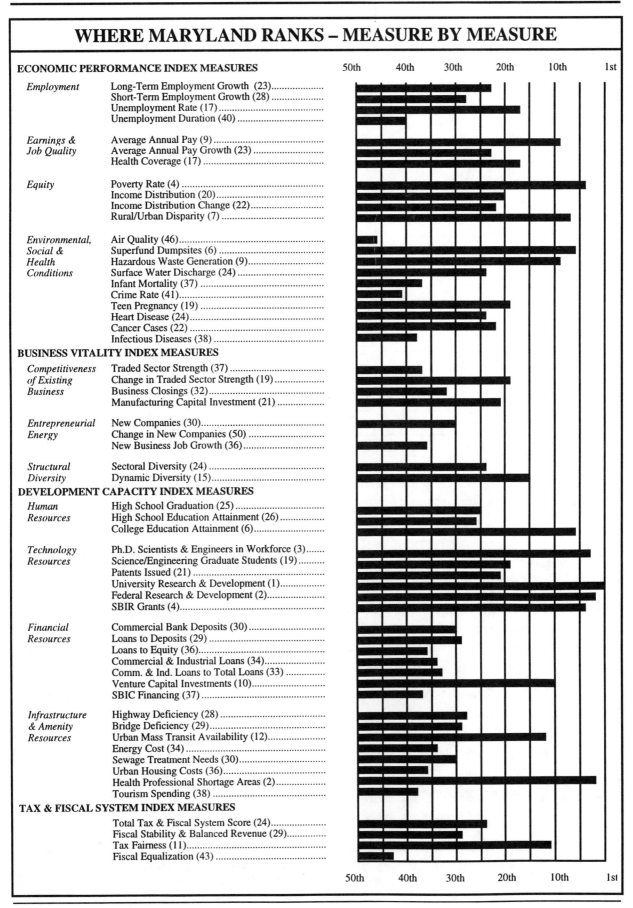

ECONOMIC PERFORMANCE INDEX MEASURES

50th 40th 30th 20th 10th 1st

Employment
Long-Term Employment Growth (23)
Short-Term Employment Growth (28)
Unemployment Rate (17)
Unemployment Duration (40)

Earnings & Job Quality
Average Annual Pay (9)
Average Annual Pay Growth (23)
Health Coverage (17)

Equity
Poverty Rate (4)
Income Distribution (20)
Income Distribution Change (22)
Rural/Urban Disparity (7)

Environmental, Social & Health Conditions
Air Quality (46)
Superfund Dumpsites (6)
Hazardous Waste Generation (9)
Surface Water Discharge (24)
Infant Mortality (37)
Crime Rate (41)
Teen Pregnancy (19)
Heart Disease (24)
Cancer Cases (22)
Infectious Diseases (38)

BUSINESS VITALITY INDEX MEASURES

Competitiveness of Existing Business
Traded Sector Strength (37)
Change in Traded Sector Strength (19)
Business Closings (32)
Manufacturing Capital Investment (21)

Entrepreneurial Energy
New Companies (30)
Change in New Companies (50)
New Business Job Growth (36)

Structural Diversity
Sectoral Diversity (24)
Dynamic Diversity (15)

DEVELOPMENT CAPACITY INDEX MEASURES

Human Resources
High School Graduation (25)
High School Education Attainment (26)
College Education Attainment (6)

Technology Resources
Ph.D. Scientists & Engineers in Workforce (3)
Science/Engineering Graduate Students (19)
Patents Issued (21)
University Research & Development (1)
Federal Research & Development (2)
SBIR Grants (4)

Financial Resources
Commercial Bank Deposits (30)
Loans to Deposits (29)
Loans to Equity (36)
Commercial & Industrial Loans (34)
Comm. & Ind. Loans to Total Loans (33)
Venture Capital Investments (10)
SBIC Financing (37)

Infrastructure & Amenity Resources
Highway Deficiency (28)
Bridge Deficiency (29)
Urban Mass Transit Availability (12)
Energy Cost (34)
Sewage Treatment Needs (30)
Urban Housing Costs (36)
Health Professional Shortage Areas (2)
Tourism Spending (38)

TAX & FISCAL SYSTEM INDEX MEASURES

Total Tax & Fiscal System Score (24)
Fiscal Stability & Balanced Revenue (29)
Tax Fairness (11)
Fiscal Equalization (43)

50th 40th 30th 20th 10th 1st

The 1995 Development Report Card

MASSACHUSETTS 1995 REPORT CARD

ECONOMIC PERFORMANCE	C

Employment ....D
Earnings & Job Quality ....B
Equity ....B

BUSINESS VITALITY	B

Business Competitiveness ....A
Entrepreneurial Energy...................................D
Structural Diversity C

DEVELOPMENT CAPACITY	A

Human Resources...A
Technology Resources ....A
Financial Resources.......................................A
Infrastructure & Amenity Resources.................D

Tax & Fiscal System	√

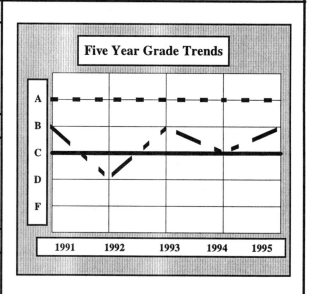

Five Year Grade Trends

1991 1992 1993 1994 1995

Key

Economic Performance ——————
Business Vitality ▬ ▬ ▬
Development Capacity ▪ ▪ ▪ ▪

- **Economic Performance:** Although harder to get, jobs in Massachusetts pay well. Employment growth is slow and unemployment duration is below average. However, the state has the fifth best paying jobs and good health coverage for those who do work, coupled with one of the lowest poverty rates in the nation. Social Conditions compare favorably (3rd in infant mortality and 5th in teen pregnancy), Health Conditions are fair but Environmental Conditions, especially air quality, are poor.

- **Business Vitality:** The vitality of the business sector improves as existing businesses become more competitive, the rate of business closings declines, and the businesses that compete out of state (the traded sector) increases significantly. Additionally, the overall economy remains diverse. But new enterprises are not developing – Massachusetts has the ninth lowest rate of new companies.

- **Development Capacity:** Massachusetts has the best overall rank in Human Resources, the best Technology and Financial Resources, but the fifth *worst* Infrastructure & Amenity Resources. The state ranks in the top 20 for all but one of 16 measures, and first in college attainment, science and engineering graduate students, and venture capital. But it ranks in the bottom six for half of the infrastructure measures (49th in bridge deficiency and sewage treatment needs).

- **Tax & Fiscal System:** Massachusetts has a moderately balanced revenue-raising system which is also fairly equitable, but is one of the worst states at equalizing the different fiscal capabilities of its local governments.

For information on how grades and ranks are calculated, see the Methodology section.
For a detailed explanation of indexes, refer to the individual index section.

WHERE MASSACHUSETTS RANKS – MEASURE BY MEASURE

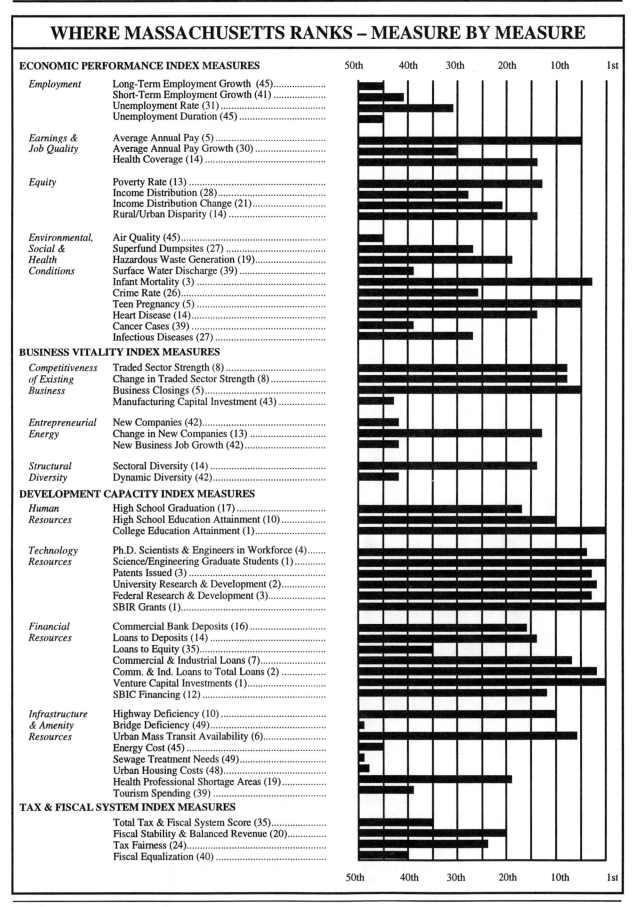

ECONOMIC PERFORMANCE INDEX MEASURES

| | | 50th | 40th | 30th | 20th | 10th | 1st |

Employment
Long-Term Employment Growth (45)
Short-Term Employment Growth (41)
Unemployment Rate (31)
Unemployment Duration (45)

Earnings & Job Quality
Average Annual Pay (5)
Average Annual Pay Growth (30)
Health Coverage (14)

Equity
Poverty Rate (13)
Income Distribution (28)
Income Distribution Change (21)
Rural/Urban Disparity (14)

Environmental, Social & Health Conditions
Air Quality (45)
Superfund Dumpsites (27)
Hazardous Waste Generation (19)
Surface Water Discharge (39)
Infant Mortality (3)
Crime Rate (26)
Teen Pregnancy (5)
Heart Disease (14)
Cancer Cases (39)
Infectious Diseases (27)

BUSINESS VITALITY INDEX MEASURES

Competitiveness of Existing Business
Traded Sector Strength (8)
Change in Traded Sector Strength (8)
Business Closings (5)
Manufacturing Capital Investment (43)

Entrepreneurial Energy
New Companies (42)
Change in New Companies (13)
New Business Job Growth (42)

Structural Diversity
Sectoral Diversity (14)
Dynamic Diversity (42)

DEVELOPMENT CAPACITY INDEX MEASURES

Human Resources
High School Graduation (17)
High School Education Attainment (10)
College Education Attainment (1)

Technology Resources
Ph.D. Scientists & Engineers in Workforce (4)
Science/Engineering Graduate Students (1)
Patents Issued (3)
University Research & Development (2)
Federal Research & Development (3)
SBIR Grants (1)

Financial Resources
Commercial Bank Deposits (16)
Loans to Deposits (14)
Loans to Equity (35)
Commercial & Industrial Loans (7)
Comm. & Ind. Loans to Total Loans (2)
Venture Capital Investments (1)
SBIC Financing (12)

Infrastructure & Amenity Resources
Highway Deficiency (10)
Bridge Deficiency (49)
Urban Mass Transit Availability (6)
Energy Cost (45)
Sewage Treatment Needs (49)
Urban Housing Costs (48)
Health Professional Shortage Areas (19)
Tourism Spending (39)

TAX & FISCAL SYSTEM INDEX MEASURES

Total Tax & Fiscal System Score (35)
Fiscal Stability & Balanced Revenue (20)
Tax Fairness (24)
Fiscal Equalization (40)

| | | 50th | 40th | 30th | 20th | 10th | 1st |

MICHIGAN 1995 REPORT CARD

ECONOMIC PERFORMANCE	C

Employment C
Earnings & Job Quality ....A
Equity ....D

BUSINESS VITALITY	B

Business Competitiveness ....A
Entrepreneurial Energy................................C
Structural Diversity C

DEVELOPMENT CAPACITY	C

Human Resources...D
Technology Resources ....B
Financial Resources.....................................B
Infrastructure & Amenity Resources.....................D

Tax & Fiscal System	–

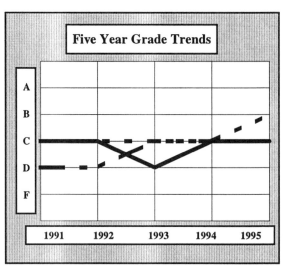

Five Year Grade Trends

| | 1991 | 1992 | 1993 | 1994 | 1995 |

Key	
Economic Performance	————
Business Vitality	▬ ▪ ▪
Development Capacity	▪ ▪ ▪ ▪

- **Economic Performance:** Michigan's economy continues to receive an average grade. Its strength lies in Earnings & Job Quality which, with strong pay and pay growth, now ranks second best in the nation. However, the state's job market remains mediocre and, on measures of Equity, the state ranks poor. With the nation's third worst scores for Environmental Conditions, the overall quality of life also rates poor.

- **Business Vitality:** With increasing Entrepreneurial Energy, ranking 11th in the rate of change in new company formations, Michigan's grade improves to a B this year. In addition, the state continues to benefit from the nation's second most competitive businesses (it has the lowest number of business closings and the third best income in sectors that trade outside the state).

- **Development Capacity:** Michigan's average grade reflects mixed development resources. With a top ten ranking for patents issued, the state's Technology Resources are above average. In addition, the state's Financial Resources, led by strong commercial lending activity, are also above average. However, with a below average high school graduation rate and poor highways, the state's Human and Infrastructure & Amenity Resources are poor.

- **Tax & Fiscal System:** Michigan's Tax & Fiscal System rates below average. While the state ranks in the middle based on the stability and fairness of its tax system, it does a poor job of promoting equal fiscal capacity among local governments.

For information on how grades and ranks are calculated, see the Methodology section.
For a detailed explanation of indexes, refer to the individual index section.

WHERE MICHIGAN RANKS – MEASURE BY MEASURE

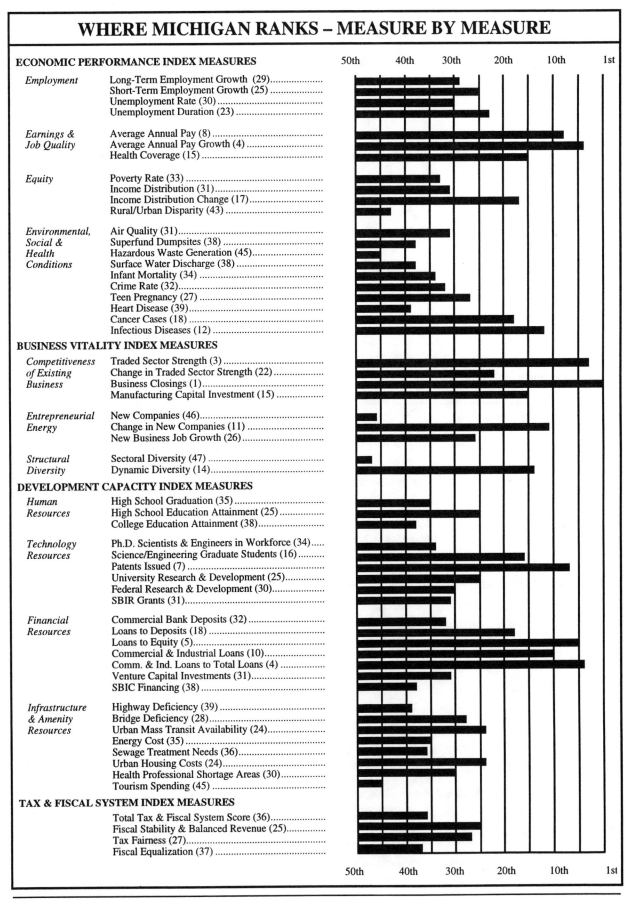

ECONOMIC PERFORMANCE INDEX MEASURES

Employment
- Long-Term Employment Growth (29)
- Short-Term Employment Growth (25)
- Unemployment Rate (30)
- Unemployment Duration (23)

Earnings & Job Quality
- Average Annual Pay (8)
- Average Annual Pay Growth (4)
- Health Coverage (15)

Equity
- Poverty Rate (33)
- Income Distribution (31)
- Income Distribution Change (17)
- Rural/Urban Disparity (43)

Environmental, Social & Health Conditions
- Air Quality (31)
- Superfund Dumpsites (38)
- Hazardous Waste Generation (45)
- Surface Water Discharge (38)
- Infant Mortality (34)
- Crime Rate (32)
- Teen Pregnancy (27)
- Heart Disease (39)
- Cancer Cases (18)
- Infectious Diseases (12)

BUSINESS VITALITY INDEX MEASURES

Competitiveness of Existing Business
- Traded Sector Strength (3)
- Change in Traded Sector Strength (22)
- Business Closings (1)
- Manufacturing Capital Investment (15)

Entrepreneurial Energy
- New Companies (46)
- Change in New Companies (11)
- New Business Job Growth (26)

Structural Diversity
- Sectoral Diversity (47)
- Dynamic Diversity (14)

DEVELOPMENT CAPACITY INDEX MEASURES

Human Resources
- High School Graduation (35)
- High School Education Attainment (25)
- College Education Attainment (38)

Technology Resources
- Ph.D. Scientists & Engineers in Workforce (34)
- Science/Engineering Graduate Students (16)
- Patents Issued (7)
- University Research & Development (25)
- Federal Research & Development (30)
- SBIR Grants (31)

Financial Resources
- Commercial Bank Deposits (32)
- Loans to Deposits (18)
- Loans to Equity (5)
- Commercial & Industrial Loans (10)
- Comm. & Ind. Loans to Total Loans (4)
- Venture Capital Investments (31)
- SBIC Financing (38)

Infrastructure & Amenity Resources
- Highway Deficiency (39)
- Bridge Deficiency (28)
- Urban Mass Transit Availability (24)
- Energy Cost (35)
- Sewage Treatment Needs (36)
- Urban Housing Costs (24)
- Health Professional Shortage Areas (30)
- Tourism Spending (45)

TAX & FISCAL SYSTEM INDEX MEASURES
- Total Tax & Fiscal System Score (36)
- Fiscal Stability & Balanced Revenue (25)
- Tax Fairness (27)
- Fiscal Equalization (37)

MINNESOTA 1995 REPORT CARD

ECONOMIC PERFORMANCE	B

Employment ....A
Earnings & Job Quality ....B
Equity C

BUSINESS VITALITY	A

Business Competitiveness ....B
Entrepreneurial Energy.........................B
Structural Diversity ....B

DEVELOPMENT CAPACITY	A

Human Resources....................................A
Technology Resources C
Financial Resources...............................A
Infrastructure & Amenity Resources.....................A

Tax & Fiscal System	+

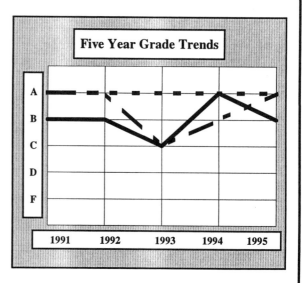

Five Year Grade Trends

Key

Economic Performance ──────
Business Vitality ── ── ──
Development Capacity ▬ ▬ ▬ ▬

- **Economic Performance:** Down from an A last year, Minnesota's economy continues to benefit from good jobs and good wages. In fact, with low unemployment and rapid short-term job growth, Minnesota's job market is the nation's fifth best. Moreover, though pay growth has slowed, Earnings & Job Quality remain above average. The state's only weakness is below average and falling income distribution. Nevertheless, the quality of life is the region's best, with the nation's best ranking on Health Conditions.

- **Business Vitality:** With a big jump in Entrepreneurial Energy, led by a top ten ranking for the increase in new company formations, Minnesota now ranks seventh nationally on Business Vitality. Though the industries that trade outside the state show a decrease in strength, the competitiveness of Minnesota's businesses is still above average. On measures of Structural Diversity, the state also receives an above average grade.

- **Development Capacity:** Once again, Minnesota's development resources are the best in the nation. With the nation's best high school graduation rate, the state's Human Resources are excellent. In addition, Minnesota's Financial Resources (strong venture capital activity) and Infrastructure & Amenity Resources (top ten in bridge quality and health care availability) also receive the highest grade.

- **Tax & Fiscal System:** Minnesota has the nation's highest ranking Tax & Fiscal System. Minnesotans can be proud of the nation's second most equitable tax system and the third most stable revenue raising structure.

For information on how grades and ranks are calculated, see the Methodology section.
For a detailed explanation of indexes, refer to the individual index section.

WHERE MINNESOTA RANKS – MEASURE BY MEASURE

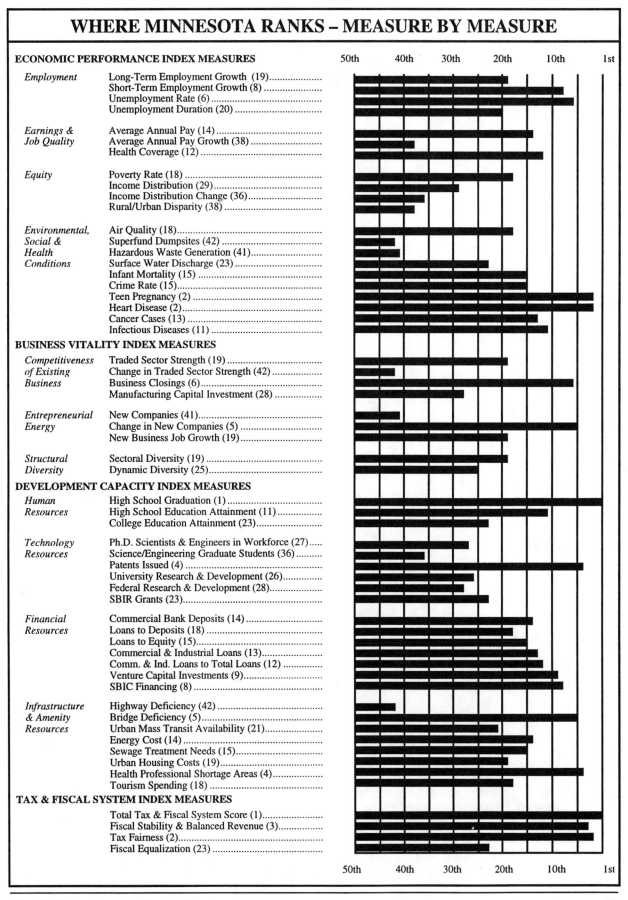

		50th	40th	30th	20th	10th	1st

ECONOMIC PERFORMANCE INDEX MEASURES

Employment
- Long-Term Employment Growth (19)
- Short-Term Employment Growth (8)
- Unemployment Rate (6)
- Unemployment Duration (20)

Earnings & Job Quality
- Average Annual Pay (14)
- Average Annual Pay Growth (38)
- Health Coverage (12)

Equity
- Poverty Rate (18)
- Income Distribution (29)
- Income Distribution Change (36)
- Rural/Urban Disparity (38)

Environmental, Social & Health Conditions
- Air Quality (18)
- Superfund Dumpsites (42)
- Hazardous Waste Generation (41)
- Surface Water Discharge (23)
- Infant Mortality (15)
- Crime Rate (15)
- Teen Pregnancy (2)
- Heart Disease (2)
- Cancer Cases (13)
- Infectious Diseases (11)

BUSINESS VITALITY INDEX MEASURES

Competitiveness of Existing Business
- Traded Sector Strength (19)
- Change in Traded Sector Strength (42)
- Business Closings (6)
- Manufacturing Capital Investment (28)

Entrepreneurial Energy
- New Companies (41)
- Change in New Companies (5)
- New Business Job Growth (19)

Structural Diversity
- Sectoral Diversity (19)
- Dynamic Diversity (25)

DEVELOPMENT CAPACITY INDEX MEASURES

Human Resources
- High School Graduation (1)
- High School Education Attainment (11)
- College Education Attainment (23)

Technology Resources
- Ph.D. Scientists & Engineers in Workforce (27)
- Science/Engineering Graduate Students (36)
- Patents Issued (4)
- University Research & Development (26)
- Federal Research & Development (28)
- SBIR Grants (23)

Financial Resources
- Commercial Bank Deposits (14)
- Loans to Deposits (18)
- Loans to Equity (15)
- Commercial & Industrial Loans (13)
- Comm. & Ind. Loans to Total Loans (12)
- Venture Capital Investments (9)
- SBIC Financing (8)

Infrastructure & Amenity Resources
- Highway Deficiency (42)
- Bridge Deficiency (5)
- Urban Mass Transit Availability (21)
- Energy Cost (14)
- Sewage Treatment Needs (15)
- Urban Housing Costs (19)
- Health Professional Shortage Areas (4)
- Tourism Spending (18)

TAX & FISCAL SYSTEM INDEX MEASURES

- Total Tax & Fiscal System Score (1)
- Fiscal Stability & Balanced Revenue (3)
- Tax Fairness (2)
- Fiscal Equalization (23)

		50th	40th	30th	20th	10th	1st

MISSISSIPPI 1995 REPORT CARD

ECONOMIC PERFORMANCE	D

Employment C
Earnings & Job Quality ....D
Equity ....F

BUSINESS VITALITY	A

Business Competitiveness C
Entrepreneurial Energy...........................B
Structural Diversity ....A

DEVELOPMENT CAPACITY	F

Human Resources....................................F
Technology Resources ....F
Financial Resources................................F
Infrastructure & Amenity Resources ....F

Tax & Fiscal System	+

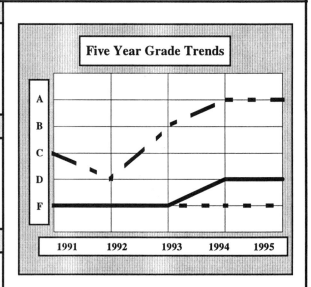

Five Year Grade Trends

1991 1992 1993 1994 1995

Key	
Economic Performance	———
Business Vitality	– – -
Development Capacity	- - - -

- **Economic Performance:** Mississippi's Economic Performance is below average. While the state's jobs rate average, slowing short-term job growth and high unemployment mean a drop from last year's B mark. Earnings & Job Quality are below average (though with strong pay growth, show signs of improvement). The state does poorly on measures of Equity, with the nation's second highest poverty and third worst income distribution. Despite the best Environmental Conditions in the South, the overall quality of life is also below average.

- **Business Vitality:** Mississippi's strength continues to lie in its Business Vitality, which ranks fourth in the nation. The state's businesses are well diversified, and with improving ranks for new company formations, Entrepreneurial Energy now rates above average.

- **Development Capacity:** Once again, Mississippi's development resources are the weakest in the nation. In fact, the state receives a failing mark on every Subindex of Development Capacity – Human Resources, Technology Resources, Financial Resources and Infrastructure & Amenity Resources. Some hopeful signs include improving ranks on college education attainment, bank deposits, and commercial lending.

- **Tax & Fiscal System:** Mississippi's Tax & Fiscal System ranks above average. Though the state's tax structure ranks below average in terms of fairness, it is the fourth best in the nation in its policies to equalize fiscal capacity among local governments.

For information on how grades and ranks are calculated, see the Methodology section.
For a detailed explanation of indexes, refer to the individual index section.

WHERE MISSISSIPPI RANKS – MEASURE BY MEASURE

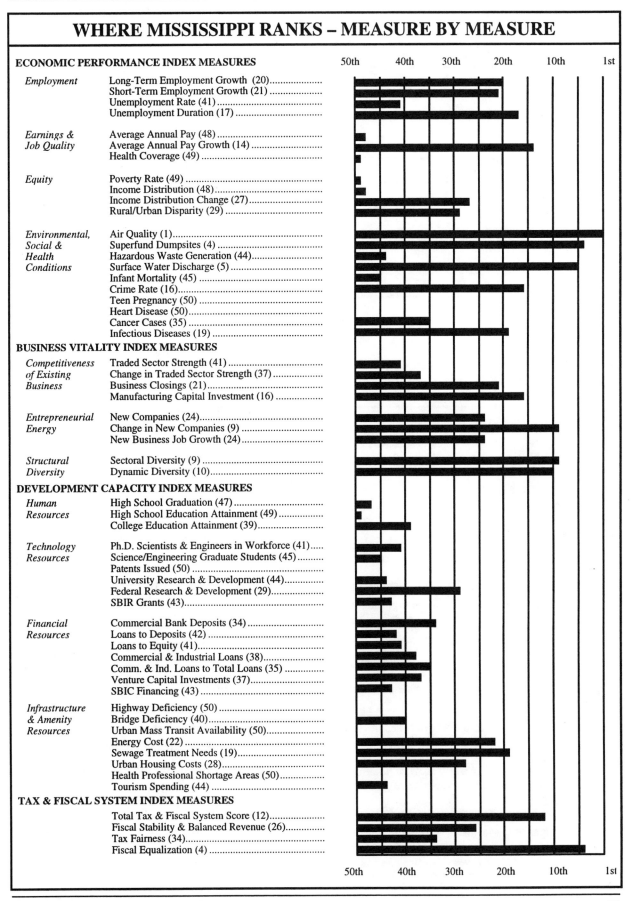

		50th	40th	30th	20th	10th	1st

ECONOMIC PERFORMANCE INDEX MEASURES

Employment
- Long-Term Employment Growth (20)
- Short-Term Employment Growth (21)
- Unemployment Rate (41)
- Unemployment Duration (17)

Earnings & Job Quality
- Average Annual Pay (48)
- Average Annual Pay Growth (14)
- Health Coverage (49)

Equity
- Poverty Rate (49)
- Income Distribution (48)
- Income Distribution Change (27)
- Rural/Urban Disparity (29)

Environmental, Social & Health Conditions
- Air Quality (1)
- Superfund Dumpsites (4)
- Hazardous Waste Generation (44)
- Surface Water Discharge (5)
- Infant Mortality (45)
- Crime Rate (16)
- Teen Pregnancy (50)
- Heart Disease (50)
- Cancer Cases (35)
- Infectious Diseases (19)

BUSINESS VITALITY INDEX MEASURES

Competitiveness of Existing Business
- Traded Sector Strength (41)
- Change in Traded Sector Strength (37)
- Business Closings (21)
- Manufacturing Capital Investment (16)

Entrepreneurial Energy
- New Companies (24)
- Change in New Companies (9)
- New Business Job Growth (24)

Structural Diversity
- Sectoral Diversity (9)
- Dynamic Diversity (10)

DEVELOPMENT CAPACITY INDEX MEASURES

Human Resources
- High School Graduation (47)
- High School Education Attainment (49)
- College Education Attainment (39)

Technology Resources
- Ph.D. Scientists & Engineers in Workforce (41)
- Science/Engineering Graduate Students (45)
- Patents Issued (50)
- University Research & Development (44)
- Federal Research & Development (29)
- SBIR Grants (43)

Financial Resources
- Commercial Bank Deposits (34)
- Loans to Deposits (42)
- Loans to Equity (41)
- Commercial & Industrial Loans (38)
- Comm. & Ind. Loans to Total Loans (35)
- Venture Capital Investments (37)
- SBIC Financing (43)

Infrastructure & Amenity Resources
- Highway Deficiency (50)
- Bridge Deficiency (40)
- Urban Mass Transit Availability (50)
- Energy Cost (22)
- Sewage Treatment Needs (19)
- Urban Housing Costs (28)
- Health Professional Shortage Areas (50)
- Tourism Spending (44)

TAX & FISCAL SYSTEM INDEX MEASURES
- Total Tax & Fiscal System Score (12)
- Fiscal Stability & Balanced Revenue (26)
- Tax Fairness (34)
- Fiscal Equalization (4)

		50th	40th	30th	20th	10th	1st

MISSOURI 1995 REPORT CARD

ECONOMIC PERFORMANCE	D
Employment	C
Earnings & Job Quality	C
Equity	F

BUSINESS VITALITY	C
Business Competitiveness	D
Entrepreneurial Energy	C
Structural Diversity	A

DEVELOPMENT CAPACITY	C
Human Resources	C
Technology Resources	D
Financial Resources	B
Infrastructure & Amenity Resources	B

Tax & Fiscal System	√

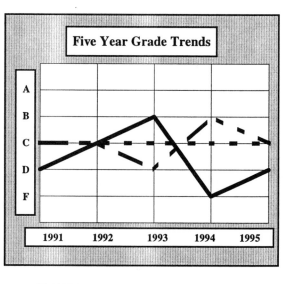

Five Year Grade Trends

1991   1992   1993   1994   1995

Key
Economic Performance ———
Business Vitality — — —
Development Capacity - - - -

- **Economic Performance:** Although improved from last year's failing grade, Missouri's economy is still poor. Wages are average and growing slowly, and the job market, despite improving short-term employment (20th in the nation) and lower unemployment, receives only average grades. Moreover, with a high poverty rate and income distribution that is poor and getting worse, Missouri earns the nation's second worst score on measures of Equity. The quality of life in Missouri is poor as well.

- **Business Vitality:** Missouri's average grade reflects uneven performance in Business Vitality. On one hand, with worse than average business closings and weakness in those industries that trade outside the state, the Competitiveness of Existing Business is poor. On the other hand, the state's businesses are very well diversified, and with a rank of 11th on new business job growth, Entrepreneurial Energy earns a high C grade.

- **Development Capacity:** Missouri earns a C in Development Capacity, but the make-up is changing. With improving highway quality and the nation's lowest urban housing costs, Missouri's Infrastructure & Amenity Resources improved to a B. Similarly, Financial Resources earn an above average grade this year, with increased venture capital activity and SBIC financing. However, due to a below average high school graduation rate, Human Resources are only average, and Technology Resources now rate as poor.

- **Tax & Fiscal System:** Missouri's Tax & Fiscal System is average across the board, with average rankings for tax fairness, stability and policies to equalize fiscal capacity among local governments.

For information on how grades and ranks are calculated, see the Methodology section.
For a detailed explanation of indexes, refer to the individual index section.

WHERE MISSOURI RANKS – MEASURE BY MEASURE

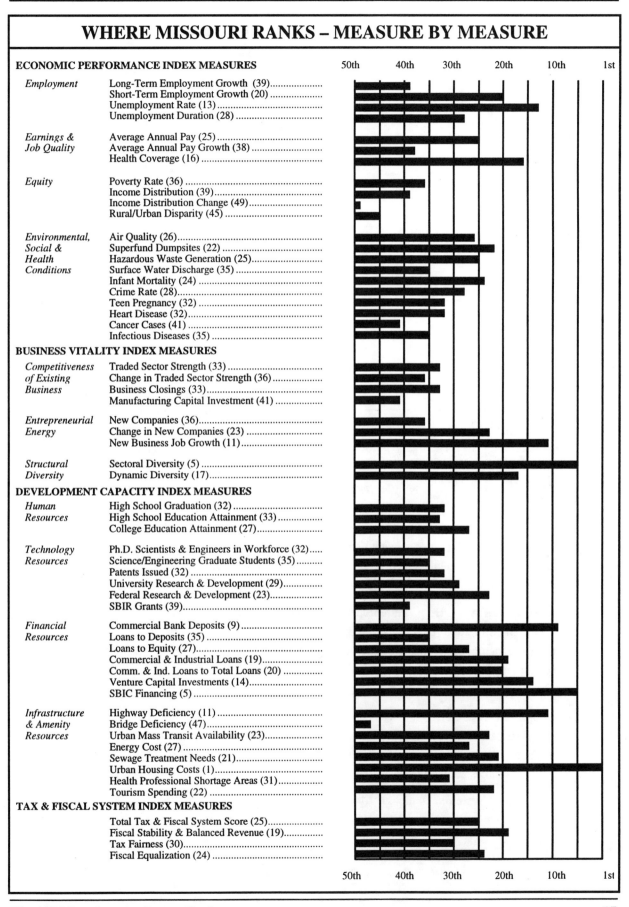

ECONOMIC PERFORMANCE INDEX MEASURES

Employment
Long-Term Employment Growth (39)
Short-Term Employment Growth (20)
Unemployment Rate (13)
Unemployment Duration (28)

Earnings & Job Quality
Average Annual Pay (25)
Average Annual Pay Growth (38)
Health Coverage (16)

Equity
Poverty Rate (36)
Income Distribution (39)
Income Distribution Change (49)
Rural/Urban Disparity (45)

Environmental, Social & Health Conditions
Air Quality (26)
Superfund Dumpsites (22)
Hazardous Waste Generation (25)
Surface Water Discharge (35)
Infant Mortality (24)
Crime Rate (28)
Teen Pregnancy (32)
Heart Disease (32)
Cancer Cases (41)
Infectious Diseases (35)

BUSINESS VITALITY INDEX MEASURES

Competitiveness of Existing Business
Traded Sector Strength (33)
Change in Traded Sector Strength (36)
Business Closings (33)
Manufacturing Capital Investment (41)

Entrepreneurial Energy
New Companies (36)
Change in New Companies (23)
New Business Job Growth (11)

Structural Diversity
Sectoral Diversity (5)
Dynamic Diversity (17)

DEVELOPMENT CAPACITY INDEX MEASURES

Human Resources
High School Graduation (32)
High School Education Attainment (33)
College Education Attainment (27)

Technology Resources
Ph.D. Scientists & Engineers in Workforce (32)
Science/Engineering Graduate Students (35)
Patents Issued (32)
University Research & Development (29)
Federal Research & Development (23)
SBIR Grants (39)

Financial Resources
Commercial Bank Deposits (9)
Loans to Deposits (35)
Loans to Equity (27)
Commercial & Industrial Loans (19)
Comm. & Ind. Loans to Total Loans (20)
Venture Capital Investments (14)
SBIC Financing (5)

Infrastructure & Amenity Resources
Highway Deficiency (11)
Bridge Deficiency (47)
Urban Mass Transit Availability (23)
Energy Cost (27)
Sewage Treatment Needs (21)
Urban Housing Costs (1)
Health Professional Shortage Areas (31)
Tourism Spending (22)

TAX & FISCAL SYSTEM INDEX MEASURES

Total Tax & Fiscal System Score (25)
Fiscal Stability & Balanced Revenue (19)
Tax Fairness (30)
Fiscal Equalization (24)

50th   40th   30th   20th   10th   1st

MONTANA 1995 REPORT CARD

ECONOMIC PERFORMANCE — B

Employment ....B
Earnings & Job Quality ....D
Equity ....A

BUSINESS VITALITY — B

Business Competitiveness ....B
Entrepreneurial Energy....................................A
Structural Diversity ....D

DEVELOPMENT CAPACITY — B

Human Resources...A
Technology Resources C
Financial Resources...D
Infrastructure & Amenity Resources.....................A

Tax & Fiscal System — √

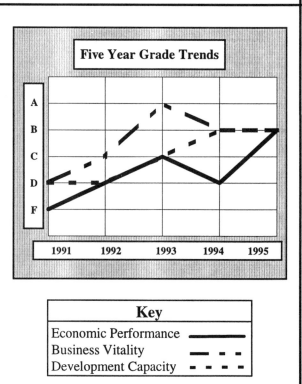

Five Year Grade Trends

| | 1991 | 1992 | 1993 | 1994 | 1995 |

Key

Economic Performance ——————
Business Vitality — - -
Development Capacity - - - -

- **Economic Performance:** Montana's economy mirrors its improving development resources. The state's explosive growth led to great improvements, including the fourth fastest growth in average annual pay (though, overall, pay is still only 47th) and the 13th best short-term employment growth. Equity is good, with the gap between rich and poor seventh smallest and still decreasing rapidly. Montana also has some of the best Environmental, Social & Health Conditions, including the lowest rate of surface water discharge and low hazardous waste generation.

- **Business Vitality:** High entrepreneurship and improved business competitiveness offset deteriorating Structural Diversity to keep Montana's Business Vitality above average. Large increases in income from businesses competing out of state (the traded sector), the sixth highest rate of new companies, and tenth highest rate of new business job growth make for a vibrant economy, although increasing concentration in key industries may make it vulnerable.

- **Development Capacity:** Excellent Human Resources (led by the 5th best high school graduation rate) are surpassed by the country's third best rank in Infrastructure & Amenity Resources (4th lowest energy costs, and sewage treatment needs, and 10th for bridge deficiency). Technology and financial resources are mediocre, as loan activity is weak and the state has little R&D funding.

- **Tax & Fiscal System:** Although Montana has one of the least well balanced revenue raising structures, it has one of the most equitable tax systems as well as a good record of equalizing the differing fiscal capacities of local governments.

For information on how grades and ranks are calculated, see the Methodology section.
For a detailed explanation of indexes, refer to the individual index section.

WHERE MONTANA RANKS – MEASURE BY MEASURE

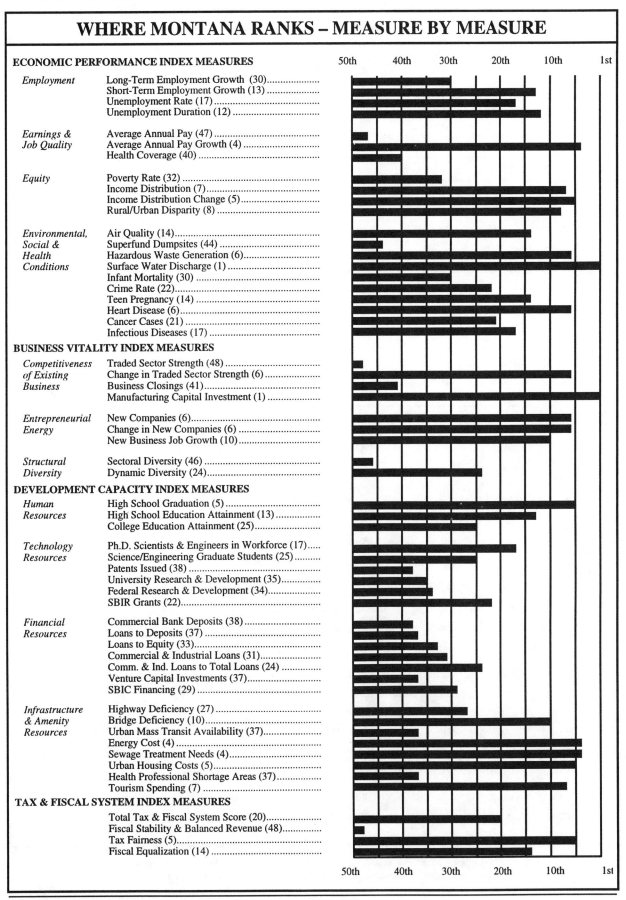

ECONOMIC PERFORMANCE INDEX MEASURES

| | | 50th | 40th | 30th | 20th | 10th | 1st |

Employment
Long-Term Employment Growth (30)
Short-Term Employment Growth (13)
Unemployment Rate (17)
Unemployment Duration (12)

Earnings & Job Quality
Average Annual Pay (47)
Average Annual Pay Growth (4)
Health Coverage (40)

Equity
Poverty Rate (32)
Income Distribution (7)
Income Distribution Change (5)
Rural/Urban Disparity (8)

Environmental, Social & Health Conditions
Air Quality (14)
Superfund Dumpsites (44)
Hazardous Waste Generation (6)
Surface Water Discharge (1)
Infant Mortality (30)
Crime Rate (22)
Teen Pregnancy (14)
Heart Disease (6)
Cancer Cases (21)
Infectious Diseases (17)

BUSINESS VITALITY INDEX MEASURES

Competitiveness of Existing Business
Traded Sector Strength (48)
Change in Traded Sector Strength (6)
Business Closings (41)
Manufacturing Capital Investment (1)

Entrepreneurial Energy
New Companies (6)
Change in New Companies (6)
New Business Job Growth (10)

Structural Diversity
Sectoral Diversity (46)
Dynamic Diversity (24)

DEVELOPMENT CAPACITY INDEX MEASURES

Human Resources
High School Graduation (5)
High School Education Attainment (13)
College Education Attainment (25)

Technology Resources
Ph.D. Scientists & Engineers in Workforce (17)
Science/Engineering Graduate Students (25)
Patents Issued (38)
University Research & Development (35)
Federal Research & Development (34)
SBIR Grants (22)

Financial Resources
Commercial Bank Deposits (38)
Loans to Deposits (37)
Loans to Equity (33)
Commercial & Industrial Loans (31)
Comm. & Ind. Loans to Total Loans (24)
Venture Capital Investments (37)
SBIC Financing (29)

Infrastructure & Amenity Resources
Highway Deficiency (27)
Bridge Deficiency (10)
Urban Mass Transit Availability (37)
Energy Cost (4)
Sewage Treatment Needs (4)
Urban Housing Costs (5)
Health Professional Shortage Areas (37)
Tourism Spending (7)

TAX & FISCAL SYSTEM INDEX MEASURES

Total Tax & Fiscal System Score (20)
Fiscal Stability & Balanced Revenue (48)
Tax Fairness (5)
Fiscal Equalization (14)

| | | 50th | 40th | 30th | 20th | 10th | 1st |

NEBRASKA 1995 REPORT CARD

ECONOMIC PERFORMANCE	A

Employment ....B
Earnings & Job Quality C
Equity ....A

BUSINESS VITALITY	C

Business Competitiveness ....F
Entrepreneurial Energy...A
Structural Diversity C

DEVELOPMENT CAPACITY	C

Human Resources...B
Technology Resources C
Financial Resources...C
Infrastructure & Amenity Resources.....................B

Tax & Fiscal System	√

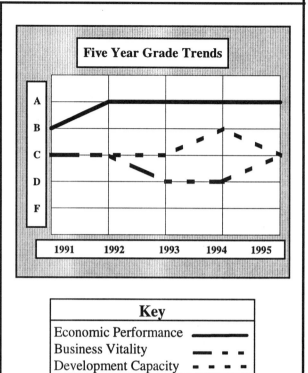

Five Year Grade Trends

Key
Economic Performance ————
Business Vitality ▬ ▬ ▬
Development Capacity ▪ ▪ ▪ ▪

- **Economic Performance:** Although Nebraska's economy is not growing very fast, it may be because it doesn't have to. After four years of A grades, Nebraska boasts the nation's lowest unemployment rate (2.9 percent), the lowest unemployment duration, and the second smallest gap between rich and poor. Even annual pay growth is improving (17th). An excellent quality of life rounds out the picture, as the state compares especially favorably on Social Conditions.

- **Business Vitality:** Nebraska moves up to a C this year due to very strong entrepreneurship (which was able to overcome a drop in the Competitiveness of Existing Business). The state had the nation's highest increase in new company formation (which was already solid), and above average new business job growth. Over-concentration in a few key industries may ruin the pretty picture in the future.

- **Development Capacity:** Nebraska slips a grade in Development Capacity, indicating that resources necessary for future growth, are declining. Human Resources fell some although high school graduation is still fourth in the country. The state's Infrastructure & Amenity Resources deteriorated with a significant increase in the number of deficient highways (from 10th to 35th). Rankings for bridge deficiency and mass urban transit availability stay below average.

- **Tax & Fiscal System:** While Nebraska's Tax & Fiscal System does a poor job of equalizing fiscal capacity among local governments, it receives above average marks for both stability and fairness.

For information on how grades and ranks are calculated, see the Methodology section.
For a detailed explanation of indexes, refer to the individual index section.

WHERE NEBRASKA RANKS – MEASURE BY MEASURE

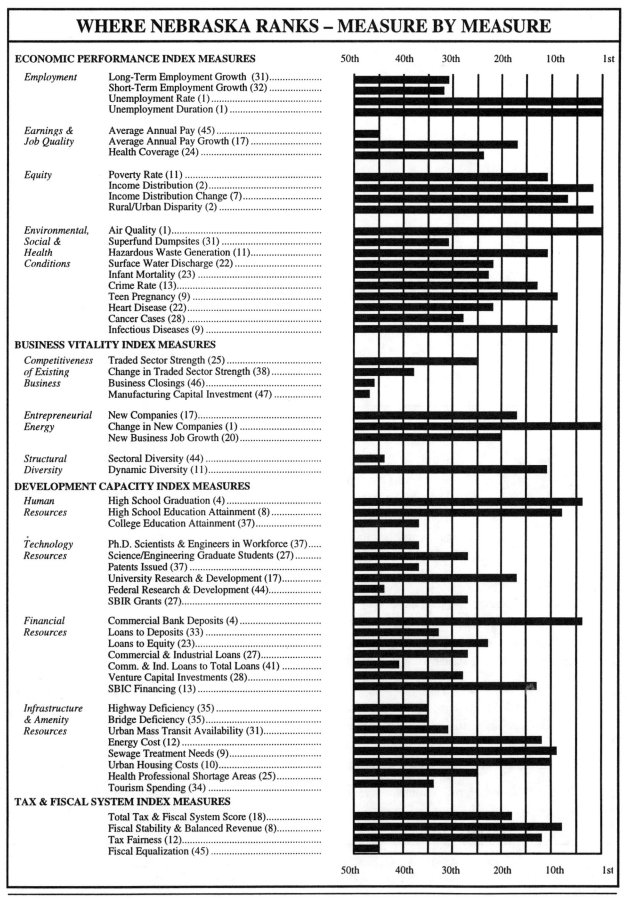

ECONOMIC PERFORMANCE INDEX MEASURES

	50th 40th 30th 20th 10th 1st

Employment
- Long-Term Employment Growth (31)
- Short-Term Employment Growth (32)
- Unemployment Rate (1)
- Unemployment Duration (1)

Earnings & Job Quality
- Average Annual Pay (45)
- Average Annual Pay Growth (17)
- Health Coverage (24)

Equity
- Poverty Rate (11)
- Income Distribution (2)
- Income Distribution Change (7)
- Rural/Urban Disparity (2)

Environmental, Social & Health Conditions
- Air Quality (1)
- Superfund Dumpsites (31)
- Hazardous Waste Generation (11)
- Surface Water Discharge (22)
- Infant Mortality (23)
- Crime Rate (13)
- Teen Pregnancy (9)
- Heart Disease (22)
- Cancer Cases (28)
- Infectious Diseases (9)

BUSINESS VITALITY INDEX MEASURES

Competitiveness of Existing Business
- Traded Sector Strength (25)
- Change in Traded Sector Strength (38)
- Business Closings (46)
- Manufacturing Capital Investment (47)

Entrepreneurial Energy
- New Companies (17)
- Change in New Companies (1)
- New Business Job Growth (20)

Structural Diversity
- Sectoral Diversity (44)
- Dynamic Diversity (11)

DEVELOPMENT CAPACITY INDEX MEASURES

Human Resources
- High School Graduation (4)
- High School Education Attainment (8)
- College Education Attainment (37)

Technology Resources
- Ph.D. Scientists & Engineers in Workforce (37)
- Science/Engineering Graduate Students (27)
- Patents Issued (37)
- University Research & Development (17)
- Federal Research & Development (44)
- SBIR Grants (27)

Financial Resources
- Commercial Bank Deposits (4)
- Loans to Deposits (33)
- Loans to Equity (23)
- Commercial & Industrial Loans (27)
- Comm. & Ind. Loans to Total Loans (41)
- Venture Capital Investments (28)
- SBIC Financing (13)

Infrastructure & Amenity Resources
- Highway Deficiency (35)
- Bridge Deficiency (35)
- Urban Mass Transit Availability (31)
- Energy Cost (12)
- Sewage Treatment Needs (9)
- Urban Housing Costs (10)
- Health Professional Shortage Areas (25)
- Tourism Spending (34)

TAX & FISCAL SYSTEM INDEX MEASURES

- Total Tax & Fiscal System Score (18)
- Fiscal Stability & Balanced Revenue (8)
- Tax Fairness (12)
- Fiscal Equalization (45)

	50th 40th 30th 20th 10th 1st

NEVADA 1995 REPORT CARD

ECONOMIC PERFORMANCE	B

Employment ....B
Earnings & Job Quality ....A
Equity C

BUSINESS VITALITY	A

Business Competitiveness ....A
Entrepreneurial Energy....................................A
Structural Diversity ....F

DEVELOPMENT CAPACITY	D

Human Resources..C
Technology Resources ....D
Financial Resources...F
Infrastructure & Amenity Resources ....A

Tax & Fiscal System	–

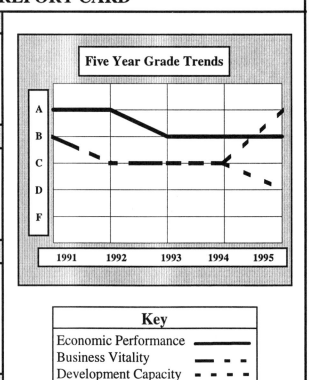

Five Year Grade Trends

1991 1992 1993 1994 1995

Key

Economic Performance ———
Business Vitality — — —
Development Capacity ▪ ▪ ▪ ▪

- **Economic Performance:** Nevada's economy is strong in Employment and Earnings & Job Quality. It had the nation's best long-term (and 4th best short-term) employment growth. But not everything is rosy – many people have difficulty finding work (the unemployment rate ranks 34th, with many unemployed long-term) and the gap between the rich and poor is still increasing significantly. While Environmental Conditions are among the best (few superfund dumpsites and little hazardous waste), Social and Health Conditions are not favorable (42nd in crime rate and 44th in heart disease).

- **Business Vitality:** Nevada has a very vital business sector – just an over-concentrated one. The state has the worst Structural Diversity for a second year, leaving it vulnerable to shocks and cyclical downswings. Nevada's businesses are among the nation's most competitive and entrepreneurship is stellar with large increases in new companies and new business job growth.

- **Development Capacity:** Nevada's development resources are mixed. It has the fourth best ranking in Infrastructure & Amenity Resources due to good bridges, highways, and low sewage treatment needs. But Financial Resources are very poor with some of the nation's worst loan activity (49th in commercial and industrial loans, 47th in loans to equity), and Technology Resources are weak from a lack of scientists/engineers in the workforce and low college attainment.

- **Tax & Fiscal System:** Without a personal or corporate income tax, Nevada's revenue generating system is very unbalanced. Combined with a relatively regressive system, Nevada is one of the worst performers in this index.

For information on how grades and ranks are calculated, see the Methodology section.
For a detailed explanation of indexes, refer to the individual index section.

WHERE NEVADA RANKS – MEASURE BY MEASURE

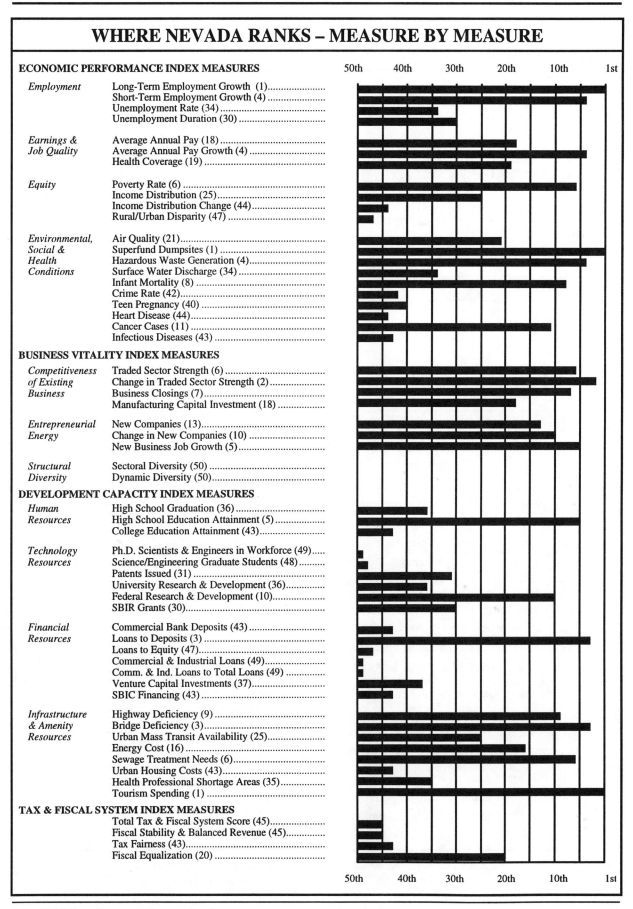

ECONOMIC PERFORMANCE INDEX MEASURES

| | | 50th | 40th | 30th | 20th | 10th | 1st |

Employment
- Long-Term Employment Growth (1)
- Short-Term Employment Growth (4)
- Unemployment Rate (34)
- Unemployment Duration (30)

Earnings & Job Quality
- Average Annual Pay (18)
- Average Annual Pay Growth (4)
- Health Coverage (19)

Equity
- Poverty Rate (6)
- Income Distribution (25)
- Income Distribution Change (44)
- Rural/Urban Disparity (47)

Environmental, Social & Health Conditions
- Air Quality (21)
- Superfund Dumpsites (1)
- Hazardous Waste Generation (4)
- Surface Water Discharge (34)
- Infant Mortality (8)
- Crime Rate (42)
- Teen Pregnancy (40)
- Heart Disease (44)
- Cancer Cases (11)
- Infectious Diseases (43)

BUSINESS VITALITY INDEX MEASURES

Competitiveness of Existing Business
- Traded Sector Strength (6)
- Change in Traded Sector Strength (2)
- Business Closings (7)
- Manufacturing Capital Investment (18)

Entrepreneurial Energy
- New Companies (13)
- Change in New Companies (10)
- New Business Job Growth (5)

Structural Diversity
- Sectoral Diversity (50)
- Dynamic Diversity (50)

DEVELOPMENT CAPACITY INDEX MEASURES

Human Resources
- High School Graduation (36)
- High School Education Attainment (5)
- College Education Attainment (43)

Technology Resources
- Ph.D. Scientists & Engineers in Workforce (49)
- Science/Engineering Graduate Students (48)
- Patents Issued (31)
- University Research & Development (36)
- Federal Research & Development (10)
- SBIR Grants (30)

Financial Resources
- Commercial Bank Deposits (43)
- Loans to Deposits (3)
- Loans to Equity (47)
- Commercial & Industrial Loans (49)
- Comm. & Ind. Loans to Total Loans (49)
- Venture Capital Investments (37)
- SBIC Financing (43)

Infrastructure & Amenity Resources
- Highway Deficiency (9)
- Bridge Deficiency (3)
- Urban Mass Transit Availability (25)
- Energy Cost (16)
- Sewage Treatment Needs (6)
- Urban Housing Costs (43)
- Health Professional Shortage Areas (35)
- Tourism Spending (1)

TAX & FISCAL SYSTEM INDEX MEASURES
- Total Tax & Fiscal System Score (45)
- Fiscal Stability & Balanced Revenue (45)
- Tax Fairness (43)
- Fiscal Equalization (20)

| | | 50th | 40th | 30th | 20th | 10th | 1st |

NEW HAMPSHIRE 1995 REPORT CARD

ECONOMIC PERFORMANCE	C

Employment C
Earnings & Job Quality C
Equity C

BUSINESS VITALITY	C

Business Competitiveness C
Entrepreneurial Energy......................................C
Structural Diversity C

DEVELOPMENT CAPACITY	C

Human Resources..A
Technology Resources ....B
Financial Resources..C
Infrastructure & Amenity Resources.................F

Tax & Fiscal System	–

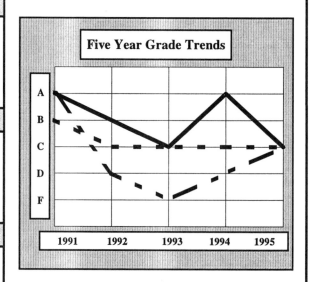

Five Year Grade Trends

1991 1992 1993 1994 1995

Key	
Economic Performance	———
Business Vitality	– ·· –
Development Capacity	▪ ▪ ▪ ▪

- **Economic Performance:** In past years, the quality of New Hampshire's existing jobs had compensated for declining opportunities. But no more – its poor grade in performance now reflects the lowest increase in pay and one of the biggest increases in the gap between rich and poor. Very strong employment figures (9th in unemployment, 18th in short-term employment growth) indicate that jobs are finally arriving – though whether they can repair the damage in Equity remains to be seen. The state still has an excellent quality of life.

- **Business Vitality:** The state's Business Vitality edged up a notch, as the economy diversified and existing businesses were more competitive (the income from businesses competing out of state improved significantly and business closings decreased). Entrepreneurship slipped a little but remains solid, with a high rate of new companies (although creating relatively few jobs).

- **Development Capacity:** Like much of New England, New Hampshire has excellent Human and Technology Resources but a decaying infrastructure. In fact, New Hampshire ranks in the bottom six in four separate Infrastructure & Amenity Resources measures: highway deficiency, sewage treatment needs, energy costs, and urban mass transit availability.

- **Tax & Fiscal System:** New Hampshire's Tax & Fiscal System rates very poorly. With no sales tax and a excessive reliance on property taxes, it has the most unbalanced and unstable revenue-generating structure. It is also the nation's worst at equalizing local government's different fiscal capabilities.

For information on how grades and ranks are calculated, see the Methodology section.
For a detailed explanation of indexes, refer to the individual index section.

WHERE NEW HAMPSHIRE RANKS – MEASURE BY MEASURE

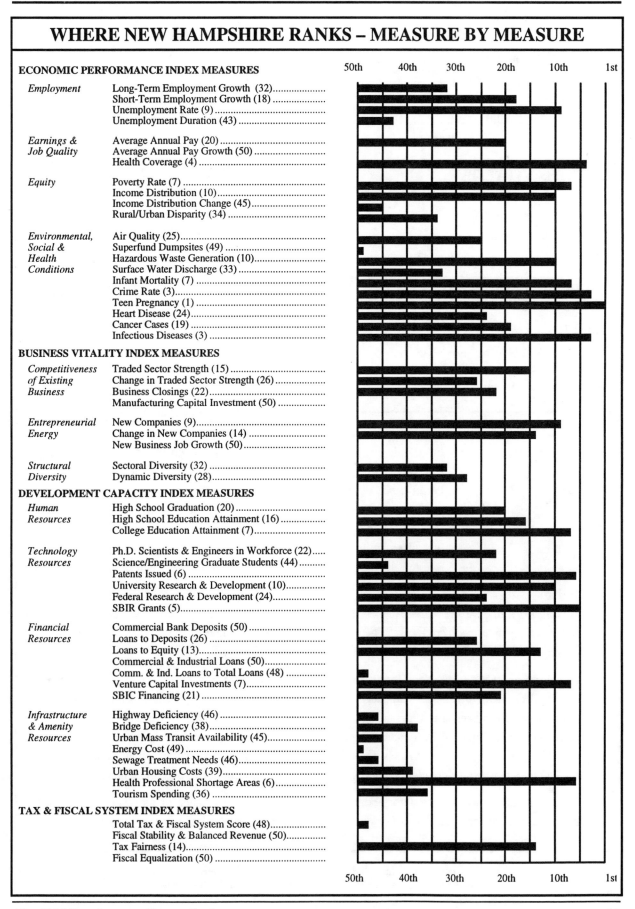

ECONOMIC PERFORMANCE INDEX MEASURES

Employment
Long-Term Employment Growth (32)
Short-Term Employment Growth (18)
Unemployment Rate (9)
Unemployment Duration (43)

Earnings & Job Quality
Average Annual Pay (20)
Average Annual Pay Growth (50)
Health Coverage (4)

Equity
Poverty Rate (7)
Income Distribution (10)
Income Distribution Change (45)
Rural/Urban Disparity (34)

Environmental, Social & Health Conditions
Air Quality (25)
Superfund Dumpsites (49)
Hazardous Waste Generation (10)
Surface Water Discharge (33)
Infant Mortality (7)
Crime Rate (3)
Teen Pregnancy (1)
Heart Disease (24)
Cancer Cases (19)
Infectious Diseases (3)

BUSINESS VITALITY INDEX MEASURES

Competitiveness of Existing Business
Traded Sector Strength (15)
Change in Traded Sector Strength (26)
Business Closings (22)
Manufacturing Capital Investment (50)

Entrepreneurial Energy
New Companies (9)
Change in New Companies (14)
New Business Job Growth (50)

Structural Diversity
Sectoral Diversity (32)
Dynamic Diversity (28)

DEVELOPMENT CAPACITY INDEX MEASURES

Human Resources
High School Graduation (20)
High School Education Attainment (16)
College Education Attainment (7)

Technology Resources
Ph.D. Scientists & Engineers in Workforce (22)
Science/Engineering Graduate Students (44)
Patents Issued (6)
University Research & Development (10)
Federal Research & Development (24)
SBIR Grants (5)

Financial Resources
Commercial Bank Deposits (50)
Loans to Deposits (26)
Loans to Equity (13)
Commercial & Industrial Loans (50)
Comm. & Ind. Loans to Total Loans (48)
Venture Capital Investments (7)
SBIC Financing (21)

Infrastructure & Amenity Resources
Highway Deficiency (46)
Bridge Deficiency (38)
Urban Mass Transit Availability (45)
Energy Cost (49)
Sewage Treatment Needs (46)
Urban Housing Costs (39)
Health Professional Shortage Areas (6)
Tourism Spending (36)

TAX & FISCAL SYSTEM INDEX MEASURES

Total Tax & Fiscal System Score (48)
Fiscal Stability & Balanced Revenue (50)
Tax Fairness (14)
Fiscal Equalization (50)

50th 40th 30th 20th 10th 1st

NEW JERSEY 1995 REPORT CARD

ECONOMIC PERFORMANCE	C

Employment ....F
Earnings & Job Quality ....A
Equity C

BUSINESS VITALITY	C

Business Competitiveness ....B
Entrepreneurial Energy....................................C
Structural Diversity C

DEVELOPMENT CAPACITY	A

Human Resources...A
Technology Resources ....B
Financial Resources...B
Infrastructure & Amenity Resources....................D

Tax & Fiscal System	√

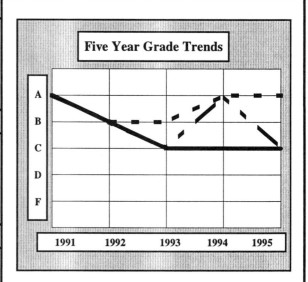

Five Year Grade Trends

1991 1992 1993 1994 1995

Key	
Economic Performance	———————
Business Vitality	– – –
Development Capacity	- - - -

- **Economic Performance:** Last year's improvements in Business Vitality and Development Capacity have yet to pull up New Jersey's Economic Performance grade. Employment conditions rank low (43rd in unemployment, 38th in short-term employment growth) and earnings show signs of losing ground as pay growth fell from third to 23rd. The quality of life suffers from the nation's worst Environmental Conditions (in the bottom five for all five measures) and Health Conditions remain poor (due to high cancer and infectious disease rates).

- **Business Vitality:** Last year's excellent Business Vitality grade was short-lived as entrepreneurship falls back down to mediocre levels. The competitiveness of existing businesses weakened as business closings fall to 43rd. The state's economic diversity remains average.

- **Development Capacity:** New Jersey retains some of the country's best development resources. Human Resources are ranked fifth due mostly to the fourth best college attainment. In addition, Technology Resources are very strong (top five in patents and scientists and engineers in the workforce), and Financial Resources are good with high deposits and strong venture capital activity. But, like the rest of the region, New Jersey's physical infrastructure is deteriorating, ranking among the worst eight in bridge deficiency, energy costs, sewage treatment needs, and urban housing costs.

- **Tax & Fiscal System:** New Jersey compares fairly well for the balance of its revenue-generating structure, and for the equity of its tax system and its policies for equalizing local governments' fiscal capabilities.

For information on how grades and ranks are calculated, see the Methodology section.
For a detailed explanation of indexes, refer to the individual index section.

WHERE NEW JERSEY RANKS – MEASURE BY MEASURE

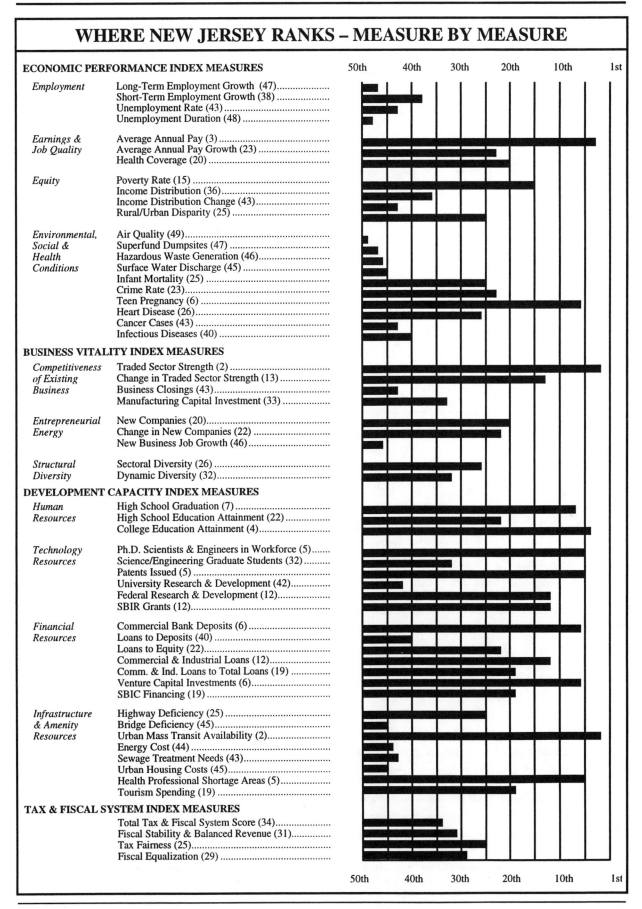

ECONOMIC PERFORMANCE INDEX MEASURES

		50th	40th	30th	20th	10th	1st

Employment
- Long-Term Employment Growth (47)
- Short-Term Employment Growth (38)
- Unemployment Rate (43)
- Unemployment Duration (48)

Earnings & Job Quality
- Average Annual Pay (3)
- Average Annual Pay Growth (23)
- Health Coverage (20)

Equity
- Poverty Rate (15)
- Income Distribution (36)
- Income Distribution Change (43)
- Rural/Urban Disparity (25)

Environmental, Social & Health Conditions
- Air Quality (49)
- Superfund Dumpsites (47)
- Hazardous Waste Generation (46)
- Surface Water Discharge (45)
- Infant Mortality (25)
- Crime Rate (23)
- Teen Pregnancy (6)
- Heart Disease (26)
- Cancer Cases (43)
- Infectious Diseases (40)

BUSINESS VITALITY INDEX MEASURES

Competitiveness of Existing Business
- Traded Sector Strength (2)
- Change in Traded Sector Strength (13)
- Business Closings (43)
- Manufacturing Capital Investment (33)

Entrepreneurial Energy
- New Companies (20)
- Change in New Companies (22)
- New Business Job Growth (46)

Structural Diversity
- Sectoral Diversity (26)
- Dynamic Diversity (32)

DEVELOPMENT CAPACITY INDEX MEASURES

Human Resources
- High School Graduation (7)
- High School Education Attainment (22)
- College Education Attainment (4)

Technology Resources
- Ph.D. Scientists & Engineers in Workforce (5)
- Science/Engineering Graduate Students (32)
- Patents Issued (5)
- University Research & Development (42)
- Federal Research & Development (12)
- SBIR Grants (12)

Financial Resources
- Commercial Bank Deposits (6)
- Loans to Deposits (40)
- Loans to Equity (22)
- Commercial & Industrial Loans (12)
- Comm. & Ind. Loans to Total Loans (19)
- Venture Capital Investments (6)
- SBIC Financing (19)

Infrastructure & Amenity Resources
- Highway Deficiency (25)
- Bridge Deficiency (45)
- Urban Mass Transit Availability (2)
- Energy Cost (44)
- Sewage Treatment Needs (43)
- Urban Housing Costs (45)
- Health Professional Shortage Areas (5)
- Tourism Spending (19)

TAX & FISCAL SYSTEM INDEX MEASURES
- Total Tax & Fiscal System Score (34)
- Fiscal Stability & Balanced Revenue (31)
- Tax Fairness (25)
- Fiscal Equalization (29)

		50th	40th	30th	20th	10th	1st

NEW MEXICO 1995 REPORT CARD

ECONOMIC PERFORMANCE   D

Employment C
Earnings & Job Quality ....D
Equity ....F

BUSINESS VITALITY   C

Business Competitiveness C
Entrepreneurial Energy...B
Structural Diversity C

DEVELOPMENT CAPACITY   D

Human Resources...C
Technology Resources ....A
Financial Resources...F
Infrastructure & Amenity Resources.....................C

Tax & Fiscal System   +

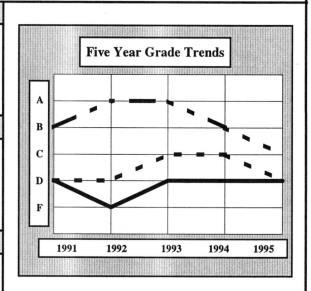

Five Year Grade Trends

Key	
Economic Performance	————
Business Vitality	— - -
Development Capacity	- - - -

- **Economic Performance:** Poor equity and mediocre earnings drag down New Mexico's performance. Increased poverty, an expanding gap between rich and poor, one of the ten lowest average annual pay rates, and very poor health coverage lead to the state's poor grade. There are signs of improvement, as Earnings & Job Quality are growing quickly (second in the nation) and employment growth is among the nation's strongest. New Mexico's Environmental and Health Conditions are excellent, but compare very poorly in Social Conditions (48th in teen pregnancy, 44th in crime rate, and 40th in infant mortality).

- **Business Vitality:** The state's Business Vitality declines some this year because so many of its key sectors have moved towards similar business cycles, making the economy more vulnerable to outside forces. But strong entrepreneurship (the eight largest increase in new company formations) and fairly competitive businesses keep New Mexico's Business Vitality near average.

- **Development Capacity:** New Mexico's development resources are a study in contrasts. It has the worst Financial Resources in the nation (ranking in the bottom ten in over half the financial measures), countered by the third best Technology Resources (due to the strength of Los Alamos). Human and Infrastructure & Amenity Resources are moderate with the second best rating in bridge deficiency but 49th in highway deficiency, and 42nd in high school graduation.

- **Tax & Fiscal System:** New Mexico has one of the better tax and fiscal systems, ranking first in equalizing local government's different fiscal capabilities, and in the top twenty in the balance of its revenue raising structure.

For information on how grades and ranks are calculated, see the Methodology section.
For a detailed explanation of indexes, refer to the individual index section.

WHERE NEW MEXICO RANKS – MEASURE BY MEASURE

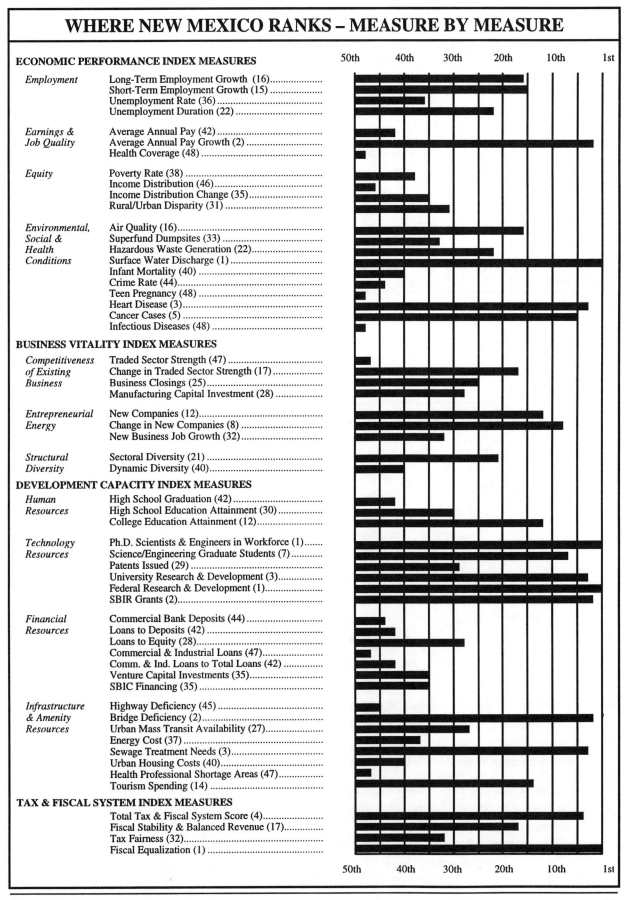

ECONOMIC PERFORMANCE INDEX MEASURES

| | | 50th | 40th | 30th | 20th | 10th | 1st |

Employment
- Long-Term Employment Growth (16)
- Short-Term Employment Growth (15)
- Unemployment Rate (36)
- Unemployment Duration (22)

Earnings & Job Quality
- Average Annual Pay (42)
- Average Annual Pay Growth (2)
- Health Coverage (48)

Equity
- Poverty Rate (38)
- Income Distribution (46)
- Income Distribution Change (35)
- Rural/Urban Disparity (31)

Environmental, Social & Health Conditions
- Air Quality (16)
- Superfund Dumpsites (33)
- Hazardous Waste Generation (22)
- Surface Water Discharge (1)
- Infant Mortality (40)
- Crime Rate (44)
- Teen Pregnancy (48)
- Heart Disease (3)
- Cancer Cases (5)
- Infectious Diseases (48)

BUSINESS VITALITY INDEX MEASURES

Competitiveness of Existing Business
- Traded Sector Strength (47)
- Change in Traded Sector Strength (17)
- Business Closings (25)
- Manufacturing Capital Investment (28)

Entrepreneurial Energy
- New Companies (12)
- Change in New Companies (8)
- New Business Job Growth (32)

Structural Diversity
- Sectoral Diversity (21)
- Dynamic Diversity (40)

DEVELOPMENT CAPACITY INDEX MEASURES

Human Resources
- High School Graduation (42)
- High School Education Attainment (30)
- College Education Attainment (12)

Technology Resources
- Ph.D. Scientists & Engineers in Workforce (1)
- Science/Engineering Graduate Students (7)
- Patents Issued (29)
- University Research & Development (3)
- Federal Research & Development (1)
- SBIR Grants (2)

Financial Resources
- Commercial Bank Deposits (44)
- Loans to Deposits (42)
- Loans to Equity (28)
- Commercial & Industrial Loans (47)
- Comm. & Ind. Loans to Total Loans (42)
- Venture Capital Investments (35)
- SBIC Financing (35)

Infrastructure & Amenity Resources
- Highway Deficiency (45)
- Bridge Deficiency (2)
- Urban Mass Transit Availability (27)
- Energy Cost (37)
- Sewage Treatment Needs (3)
- Urban Housing Costs (40)
- Health Professional Shortage Areas (47)
- Tourism Spending (14)

TAX & FISCAL SYSTEM INDEX MEASURES
- Total Tax & Fiscal System Score (4)
- Fiscal Stability & Balanced Revenue (17)
- Tax Fairness (32)
- Fiscal Equalization (1)

| | | 50th | 40th | 30th | 20th | 10th | 1st |

NEW YORK 1995 REPORT CARD

ECONOMIC PERFORMANCE   D

Employment ....F
Earnings & Job Quality ....B
Equity ....F

BUSINESS VITALITY   C

Business Competitiveness ....A
Entrepreneurial Energy................................D
Structural Diversity C

DEVELOPMENT CAPACITY   C

Human Resources..C
Technology Resources ....A
Financial Resources.....................................A
Infrastructure & Amenity Resources.....................F

Tax & Fiscal System   √

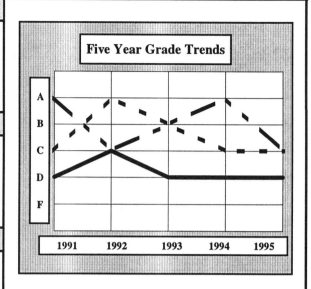

Five Year Grade Trends

1991   1992   1993   1994   1995

Key	
Economic Performance	————
Business Vitality	– ·· –
Development Capacity	– – –

- **Economic Performance:** New York's Economic Performance remains poor. Employment conditions are well below average. Earnings are affected as growth in annual average pay falls to 36th – though overall pay levels are still the nation's second highest. Equity conditions decrease as the poverty rate and income distribution deteriorate. The state's Environmental, Social & Health Conditions point to a poor quality of life.

- **Business Vitality:** A drop in entrepreneurship pulled New York's Business Vitality back down to a moderate level. The increase in new companies slowed considerably (falling from 16th to 37th) as did new business job growth (from 26th to 46th). New York ranks fifth in the number of businesses competing out of state. At the same time, the economy remains moderately diversified.

- **Development Capacity:** New York's development resources are mixed. Human Resources are good with high college attainment, but weak in high school graduation. Technology Resources are strong with many scientists and engineers in the work force and graduate school. Financial Resources are also strong with a high deposit rate and increased commercial and industrial loan activity. But infrastructure is poor, as New York has the worst bridges, high energy costs, and poor sewage treatment needs.

- **Tax & Fiscal System:** New York's Tax & Fiscal System compares moderately well, both in the balance of its revenue-raising structure and how it equalizes the differing fiscal capabilities of local governments.

*For information on how grades and ranks are calculated, see the **Methodology** section.*
For a detailed explanation of indexes, refer to the individual index section.

WHERE NEW YORK RANKS – MEASURE BY MEASURE

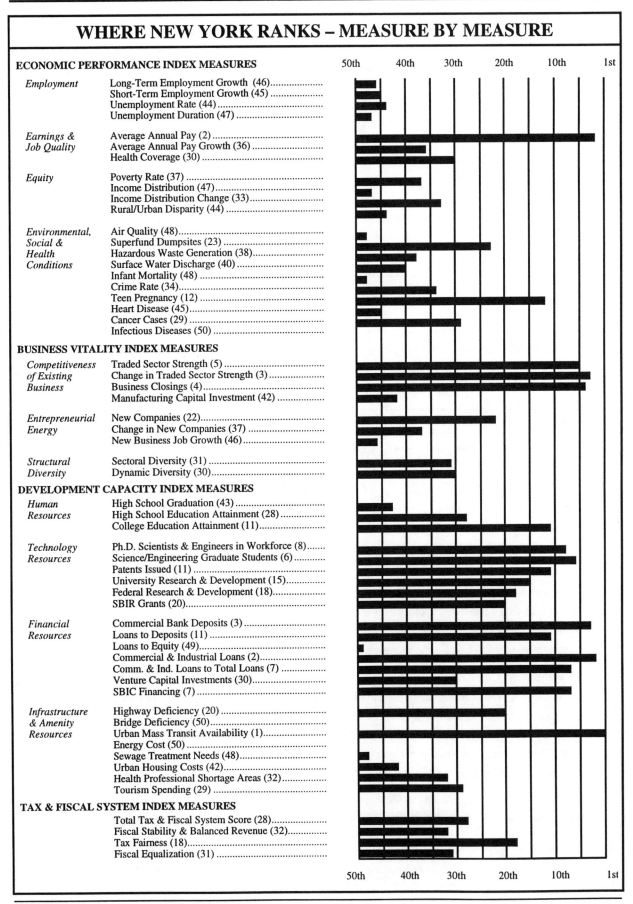

ECONOMIC PERFORMANCE INDEX MEASURES

Employment
- Long-Term Employment Growth (46)
- Short-Term Employment Growth (45)
- Unemployment Rate (44)
- Unemployment Duration (47)

Earnings & Job Quality
- Average Annual Pay (2)
- Average Annual Pay Growth (36)
- Health Coverage (30)

Equity
- Poverty Rate (37)
- Income Distribution (47)
- Income Distribution Change (33)
- Rural/Urban Disparity (44)

Environmental, Social & Health Conditions
- Air Quality (48)
- Superfund Dumpsites (23)
- Hazardous Waste Generation (38)
- Surface Water Discharge (40)
- Infant Mortality (48)
- Crime Rate (34)
- Teen Pregnancy (12)
- Heart Disease (45)
- Cancer Cases (29)
- Infectious Diseases (50)

BUSINESS VITALITY INDEX MEASURES

Competitiveness of Existing Business
- Traded Sector Strength (5)
- Change in Traded Sector Strength (3)
- Business Closings (4)
- Manufacturing Capital Investment (42)

Entrepreneurial Energy
- New Companies (22)
- Change in New Companies (37)
- New Business Job Growth (46)

Structural Diversity
- Sectoral Diversity (31)
- Dynamic Diversity (30)

DEVELOPMENT CAPACITY INDEX MEASURES

Human Resources
- High School Graduation (43)
- High School Education Attainment (28)
- College Education Attainment (11)

Technology Resources
- Ph.D. Scientists & Engineers in Workforce (8)
- Science/Engineering Graduate Students (6)
- Patents Issued (11)
- University Research & Development (15)
- Federal Research & Development (18)
- SBIR Grants (20)

Financial Resources
- Commercial Bank Deposits (3)
- Loans to Deposits (11)
- Loans to Equity (49)
- Commercial & Industrial Loans (2)
- Comm. & Ind. Loans to Total Loans (7)
- Venture Capital Investments (30)
- SBIC Financing (7)

Infrastructure & Amenity Resources
- Highway Deficiency (20)
- Bridge Deficiency (50)
- Urban Mass Transit Availability (1)
- Energy Cost (50)
- Sewage Treatment Needs (48)
- Urban Housing Costs (42)
- Health Professional Shortage Areas (32)
- Tourism Spending (29)

TAX & FISCAL SYSTEM INDEX MEASURES
- Total Tax & Fiscal System Score (28)
- Fiscal Stability & Balanced Revenue (32)
- Tax Fairness (18)
- Fiscal Equalization (31)

50th 40th 30th 20th 10th 1st

NORTH CAROLINA 1995 REPORT CARD

ECONOMIC PERFORMANCE   C

Employment ....B
Earnings & Job Quality C
Equity ....D

BUSINESS VITALITY   D

Business Competitiveness ....D
Entrepreneurial Energy...............................D
Structural Diversity ....B

DEVELOPMENT CAPACITY   C

Human Resources...D
Technology Resources C
Financial Resources.....................................A
Infrastructure & Amenity Resources......................F

Tax & Fiscal System   +

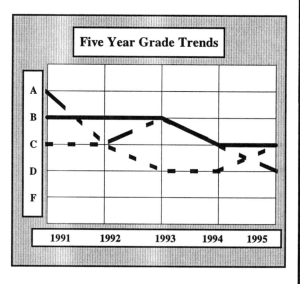

Five Year Grade Trends

Grade scale: A B C D F — Years: 1991 1992 1993 1994 1995

Key
Economic Performance ——————
Business Vitality — — —
Development Capacity - - - -

- **Economic Performance:** North Carolina's Economic Performance is average. While the state's job market – marked by strong long-term job growth and very low unemployment – is above average, its Earnings & Job Quality are only average. Moreover, due to above average poverty and a growing gap between rich and poor, the state now rates below average on measures of Equity. With the nation's best Environmental Conditions, but some of the worst Social Conditions, such as infant mortality, the quality of life is average.

- **Business Vitality:** Due to a slowing in Enterpreneurial Energy, particularly new business job growth, North Carolina's Business Vitality now earns a below average grade. While the state's businesses are well diversified, low manufacturing capital investments and the nation's third worst rate of business closings are signs of poor competitiveness.

- **Development Capacity:** North Carolina is one of a handful of southern states that shows improved strength in Development Capacity. This improvement is a result of modest changes in rankings on several key indicators, such as college attainment, scientists and engineers in the work force, university R&D spending, and venture capital investments. Overall, the state's Financial Resources are top-notch, but Human Resources continue to be poor and the state's Infrastructure & Amenity Resources now earns a failing mark.

- **Tax & Fiscal System:** With the second most balanced tax structure in the U.S. and an above average rating for policies to equalize local fiscal capacity, North Carolina's Tax & Fiscal System is above average.

For information on how grades and ranks are calculated, see the Methodology section.
For a detailed explanation of indexes, refer to the individual index section.

WHERE NORTH CAROLINA RANKS – MEASURE BY MEASURE

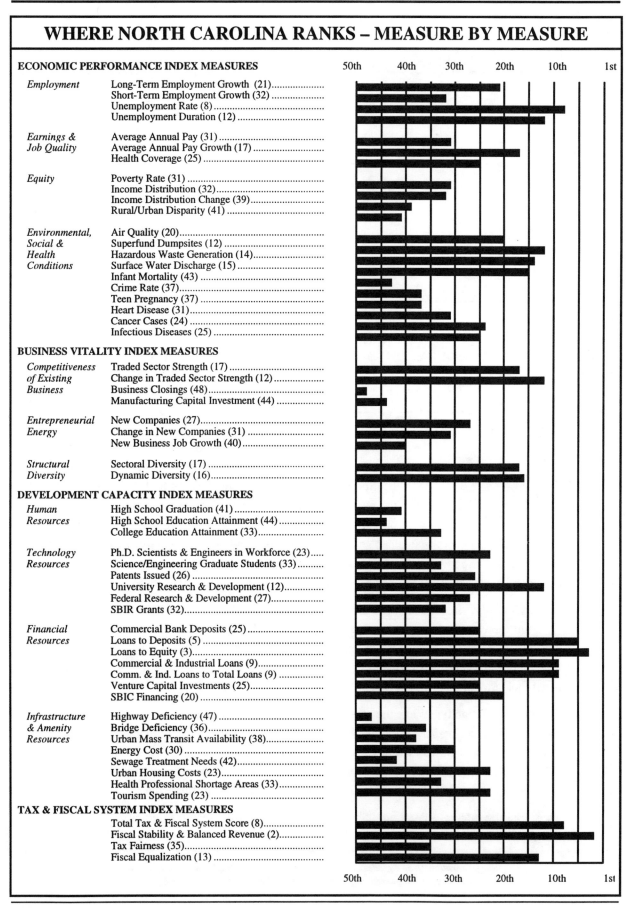

ECONOMIC PERFORMANCE INDEX MEASURES

| | | 50th | 40th | 30th | 20th | 10th | 1st |

Employment
- Long-Term Employment Growth (21)
- Short-Term Employment Growth (32)
- Unemployment Rate (8)
- Unemployment Duration (12)

Earnings & Job Quality
- Average Annual Pay (31)
- Average Annual Pay Growth (17)
- Health Coverage (25)

Equity
- Poverty Rate (31)
- Income Distribution (32)
- Income Distribution Change (39)
- Rural/Urban Disparity (41)

Environmental, Social & Health Conditions
- Air Quality (20)
- Superfund Dumpsites (12)
- Hazardous Waste Generation (14)
- Surface Water Discharge (15)
- Infant Mortality (43)
- Crime Rate (37)
- Teen Pregnancy (37)
- Heart Disease (31)
- Cancer Cases (24)
- Infectious Diseases (25)

BUSINESS VITALITY INDEX MEASURES

Competitiveness of Existing Business
- Traded Sector Strength (17)
- Change in Traded Sector Strength (12)
- Business Closings (48)
- Manufacturing Capital Investment (44)

Entrepreneurial Energy
- New Companies (27)
- Change in New Companies (31)
- New Business Job Growth (40)

Structural Diversity
- Sectoral Diversity (17)
- Dynamic Diversity (16)

DEVELOPMENT CAPACITY INDEX MEASURES

Human Resources
- High School Graduation (41)
- High School Education Attainment (44)
- College Education Attainment (33)

Technology Resources
- Ph.D. Scientists & Engineers in Workforce (23)
- Science/Engineering Graduate Students (33)
- Patents Issued (26)
- University Research & Development (12)
- Federal Research & Development (27)
- SBIR Grants (32)

Financial Resources
- Commercial Bank Deposits (25)
- Loans to Deposits (5)
- Loans to Equity (3)
- Commercial & Industrial Loans (9)
- Comm. & Ind. Loans to Total Loans (9)
- Venture Capital Investments (25)
- SBIC Financing (20)

Infrastructure & Amenity Resources
- Highway Deficiency (47)
- Bridge Deficiency (36)
- Urban Mass Transit Availability (38)
- Energy Cost (30)
- Sewage Treatment Needs (42)
- Urban Housing Costs (23)
- Health Professional Shortage Areas (33)
- Tourism Spending (23)

TAX & FISCAL SYSTEM INDEX MEASURES
- Total Tax & Fiscal System Score (8)
- Fiscal Stability & Balanced Revenue (2)
- Tax Fairness (35)
- Fiscal Equalization (13)

| | | 50th | 40th | 30th | 20th | 10th | 1st |

NORTH DAKOTA 1995 REPORT CARD

ECONOMIC PERFORMANCE	C

Employment ....B
Earnings & Job Quality ....D
Equity ....A

BUSINESS VITALITY	F

Business Competitiveness ....D
Entrepreneurial Energy...D
Structural Diversity C

DEVELOPMENT CAPACITY	C

Human Resources...B
Technology Resources C
Financial Resources...D
Infrastructure & Amenity Resources....................B

Tax & Fiscal System	+

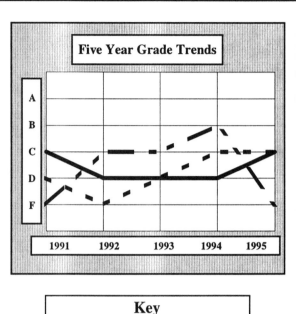

Five Year Grade Trends

1991   1992   1993   1994   1995

Key

Economic Performance ──────
Business Vitality   ── ─ ─
Development Capacity   ─ ─ ─ ─

- **Economic Performance:** Spurred by the impact of increased economic activity, North Dakota is now only one rank away from a B. Short-term employment growth is ninth in the country, pushing the unemployment rate down to fifth in the nation. The increased opportunities led to improvements in average annual pay growth (17th best) and some of the smallest gaps between the rich and poor. The only drawbacks are poor health coverage and pay levels which, despite increases, are still second lowest. North Dakotans have a good quality of life, comparing well in Environmental, Social & Health Conditions.

- **Business Vitality:** In contrast, the state takes a nose-dive in Business Vitality, due almost entirely to a large increase in business closings (from 4th to 31st) and the evaporation of last year's temporary increase in income from businesses that compete out-of-state (the traded sector). Meanwhile, entrepreneurship remains below average (bottom ten for both new companies and new business job growth), and diversity remains moderate.

- **Development Capacity:** While the other indexes fluctuated, North Dakota resources changed very little. The state maintains very good human resources (including the third highest high school graduation rate) and Infrastructure & Amenity Resources (good highways and the second lowest level of sewage treatment needs). Technology Resources are still average, and Financial Resources are still poor due to low loan activity and little untraditional forms of financing.

- **Tax & Fiscal System:** A very equitable tax system and a good record of equalizing the differing fiscal capabilities of local governments give the state's Tax & Fiscal System an excellent rating.

For information on how grades and ranks are calculated, see the Methodology section.
For a detailed explanation of indexes, refer to the individual index section.

WHERE NORTH DAKOTA RANKS – MEASURE BY MEASURE

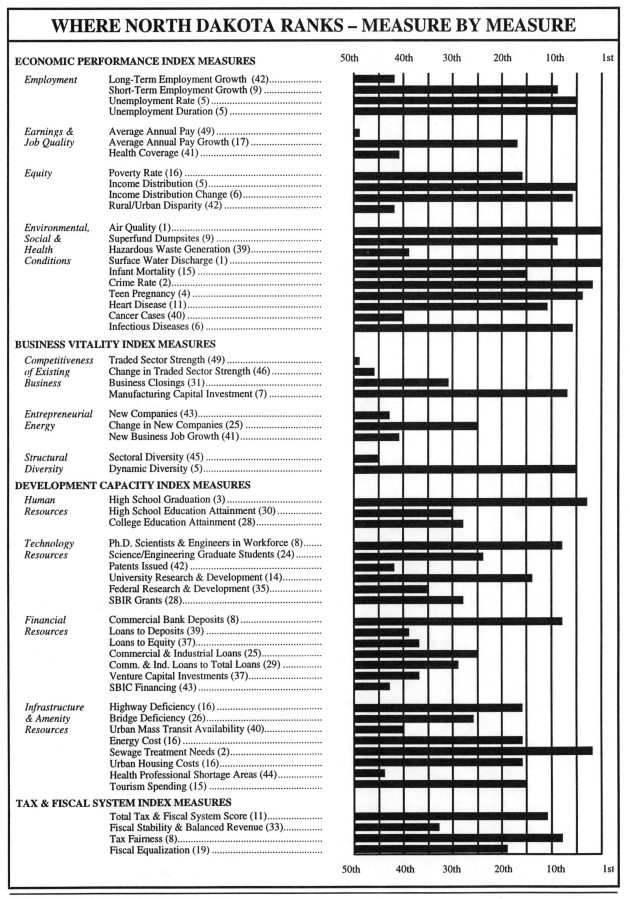

ECONOMIC PERFORMANCE INDEX MEASURES

Employment
Long-Term Employment Growth (42)
Short-Term Employment Growth (9)
Unemployment Rate (5)
Unemployment Duration (5)

Earnings & Job Quality
Average Annual Pay (49)
Average Annual Pay Growth (17)
Health Coverage (41)

Equity
Poverty Rate (16)
Income Distribution (5)
Income Distribution Change (6)
Rural/Urban Disparity (42)

Environmental, Social & Health Conditions
Air Quality (1)
Superfund Dumpsites (9)
Hazardous Waste Generation (39)
Surface Water Discharge (1)
Infant Mortality (15)
Crime Rate (2)
Teen Pregnancy (4)
Heart Disease (11)
Cancer Cases (40)
Infectious Diseases (6)

BUSINESS VITALITY INDEX MEASURES

Competitiveness of Existing Business
Traded Sector Strength (49)
Change in Traded Sector Strength (46)
Business Closings (31)
Manufacturing Capital Investment (7)

Entrepreneurial Energy
New Companies (43)
Change in New Companies (25)
New Business Job Growth (41)

Structural Diversity
Sectoral Diversity (45)
Dynamic Diversity (5)

DEVELOPMENT CAPACITY INDEX MEASURES

Human Resources
High School Graduation (3)
High School Education Attainment (30)
College Education Attainment (28)

Technology Resources
Ph.D. Scientists & Engineers in Workforce (8)
Science/Engineering Graduate Students (24)
Patents Issued (42)
University Research & Development (14)
Federal Research & Development (35)
SBIR Grants (28)

Financial Resources
Commercial Bank Deposits (8)
Loans to Deposits (39)
Loans to Equity (37)
Commercial & Industrial Loans (25)
Comm. & Ind. Loans to Total Loans (29)
Venture Capital Investments (37)
SBIC Financing (43)

Infrastructure & Amenity Resources
Highway Deficiency (16)
Bridge Deficiency (26)
Urban Mass Transit Availability (40)
Energy Cost (16)
Sewage Treatment Needs (2)
Urban Housing Costs (16)
Health Professional Shortage Areas (44)
Tourism Spending (15)

TAX & FISCAL SYSTEM INDEX MEASURES

Total Tax & Fiscal System Score (11)
Fiscal Stability & Balanced Revenue (33)
Tax Fairness (8)
Fiscal Equalization (19)

OHIO 1995 REPORT CARD

ECONOMIC PERFORMANCE	C

Employment ....D
Earnings & Job Quality ....B
Equity C

BUSINESS VITALITY	C

Business Competitiveness ....A
Entrepreneurial Energy...F
Structural Diversity C

DEVELOPMENT CAPACITY	B

Human Resources..C
Technology Resources ....B
Financial Resources..A
Infrastructure & Amenity Resources....................B

Tax & Fiscal System	√

Five Year Grade Trends

	1991	1992	1993	1994	1995

Key

Economic Performance ——————
Business Vitality ▬ ▬ ▬ ▬
Development Capacity ▪ ▪ ▪ ▪

- **Economic Performance:** For the fifth straight year, Ohio's economy earns an average grade. Earnings & Job Quality are above average, but with slow employment growth, the state's employment market continues to be poor. On measures of Equity, Ohio is only average, with income distribution that is below average and getting worse. Moreover, Ohio has a poor quality of life, particularly on indicators of teen pregnancy and heart disease.

- **Business Vitality:** Ohio's average grade reflects uneven performance in Business Vitality. On one hand, with increasing strength among those industries that trade outside the state, and the second lowest number of business closings, Ohio's businesses are among the most competitive. On the other hand, the state ranks second lowest in the nation on Entrepreneurial Energy and, for the second year in a row, is last in new company formation.

- **Development Capacity:** Ohio's Development Capacity resources are above average and show increasing strength. With improving rankings for bank deposits and venture capital activity, Ohio's Financial Resources are now among the top ten. Moreover, the state's Infrastructure & Amenity Resources, marked by improving highway quality, now rank above average. With a below average high school graduation rate, however, Human Resources continue to be only average.

- **Tax & Fiscal System:** Ohio's Tax & Fiscal System receives an average rating. While the state's tax fairness and policies for equalizing local fiscal capacity are average, it has the fourth most stable tax structure.

For information on how grades and ranks are calculated, see the Methodology section.
For a detailed explanation of indexes, refer to the individual index section.

WHERE OHIO RANKS – MEASURE BY MEASURE

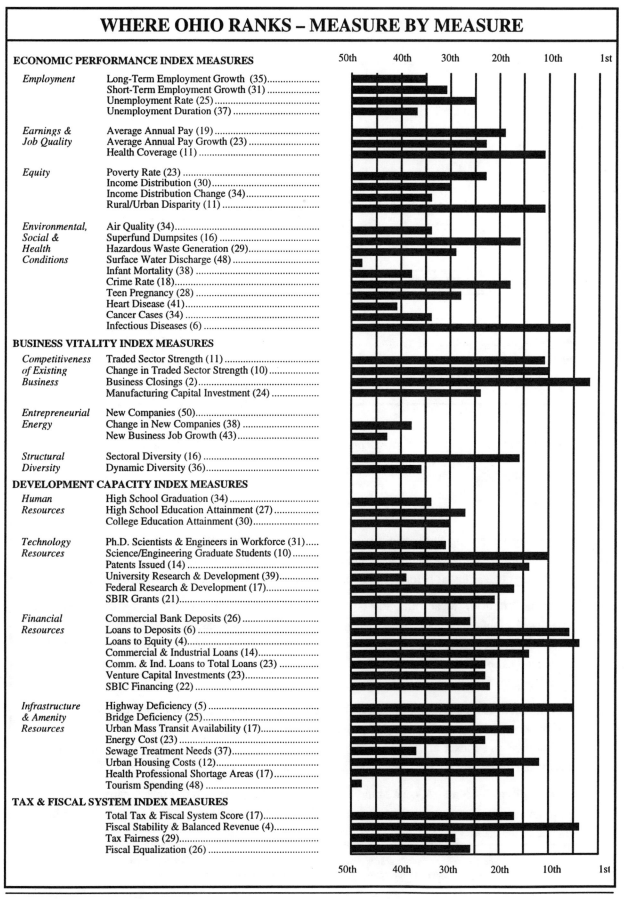

ECONOMIC PERFORMANCE INDEX MEASURES

Employment
Long-Term Employment Growth (35)
Short-Term Employment Growth (31)
Unemployment Rate (25)
Unemployment Duration (37)

Earnings & Job Quality
Average Annual Pay (19)
Average Annual Pay Growth (23)
Health Coverage (11)

Equity
Poverty Rate (23)
Income Distribution (30)
Income Distribution Change (34)
Rural/Urban Disparity (11)

Environmental, Social & Health Conditions
Air Quality (34)
Superfund Dumpsites (16)
Hazardous Waste Generation (29)
Surface Water Discharge (48)
Infant Mortality (38)
Crime Rate (18)
Teen Pregnancy (28)
Heart Disease (41)
Cancer Cases (34)
Infectious Diseases (6)

BUSINESS VITALITY INDEX MEASURES

Competitiveness of Existing Business
Traded Sector Strength (11)
Change in Traded Sector Strength (10)
Business Closings (2)
Manufacturing Capital Investment (24)

Entrepreneurial Energy
New Companies (50)
Change in New Companies (38)
New Business Job Growth (43)

Structural Diversity
Sectoral Diversity (16)
Dynamic Diversity (36)

DEVELOPMENT CAPACITY INDEX MEASURES

Human Resources
High School Graduation (34)
High School Education Attainment (27)
College Education Attainment (30)

Technology Resources
Ph.D. Scientists & Engineers in Workforce (31)
Science/Engineering Graduate Students (10)
Patents Issued (14)
University Research & Development (39)
Federal Research & Development (17)
SBIR Grants (21)

Financial Resources
Commercial Bank Deposits (26)
Loans to Deposits (6)
Loans to Equity (4)
Commercial & Industrial Loans (14)
Comm. & Ind. Loans to Total Loans (23)
Venture Capital Investments (23)
SBIC Financing (22)

Infrastructure & Amenity Resources
Highway Deficiency (5)
Bridge Deficiency (25)
Urban Mass Transit Availability (17)
Energy Cost (23)
Sewage Treatment Needs (37)
Urban Housing Costs (12)
Health Professional Shortage Areas (17)
Tourism Spending (48)

TAX & FISCAL SYSTEM INDEX MEASURES

Total Tax & Fiscal System Score (17)
Fiscal Stability & Balanced Revenue (4)
Tax Fairness (29)
Fiscal Equalization (26)

50th 40th 30th 20th 10th 1st

OKLAHOMA 1995 REPORT CARD

ECONOMIC PERFORMANCE	F
Employment ....D	
Earnings & Job Quality ....F	
Equity ....D	

BUSINESS VITALITY	B
Business Competitiveness ....D	
Entrepreneurial Energy...C	
Structural Diversity ....B	

DEVELOPMENT CAPACITY	F
Human Resources..D	
Technology Resources ....D	
Financial Resources..D	
Infrastructure & Amenity Resources.....................C	

Tax & Fiscal System	√

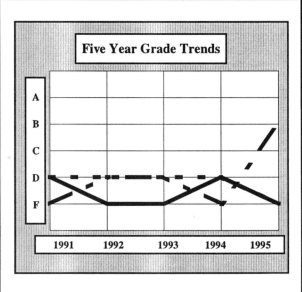

Five Year Grade Trends

1991 1992 1993 1994 1995

Key

Economic Performance ⎯⎯⎯
Business Vitality ▬ ▬ ▬
Development Capacity ▪ ▪ ▪ ▪

- **Economic Performance:** Oklahoma's economy is still sputtering. Employment conditions remain poor (third lowest long-term employment growth and below average unemployment) and the quality of the jobs that do exist, as a group, are not strong (health coverage and the growth of average annual pay are among the nation's worst ten). This has caused Equity to slip this year, as the economic disparities between rural and urban areas increased and the gap between the rich and poor is not closing quite as fast as before. Good Environmental Conditions elevate the quality of life.

- **Business Vitality:** Meanwhile, the business community is bouncing back. Existing businesses experience a jump in competitiveness. Those that compete out-of-state (the traded sector) bring much more money into the state and entrepreneurship soars with a large increase in the rate of new companies established and more jobs from new businesses. Dynamic diversity moved up to a solid B, completing the picture.

- **Development Capacity:** Unfortunately for future prospects, development resources have gone from bad to worse. Human Resources slip some (mostly due to a drop in college attainment), while Technology and Financial Resources remain poor. Infrastructure & Amenity Resources remain steady, led by low sewage treatment needs and inexpensive energy and urban housing costs.

- **Tax & Fiscal System:** A good ability to equalize between the differing fiscal capacities of local governments is unfortunately offset by a relatively inequitable tax system. This places the state in the middle of the pack.

For information on how grades and ranks are calculated, see the Methodology section.
For a detailed explanation of indexes, refer to the individual index section.

WHERE OKLAHOMA RANKS – MEASURE BY MEASURE

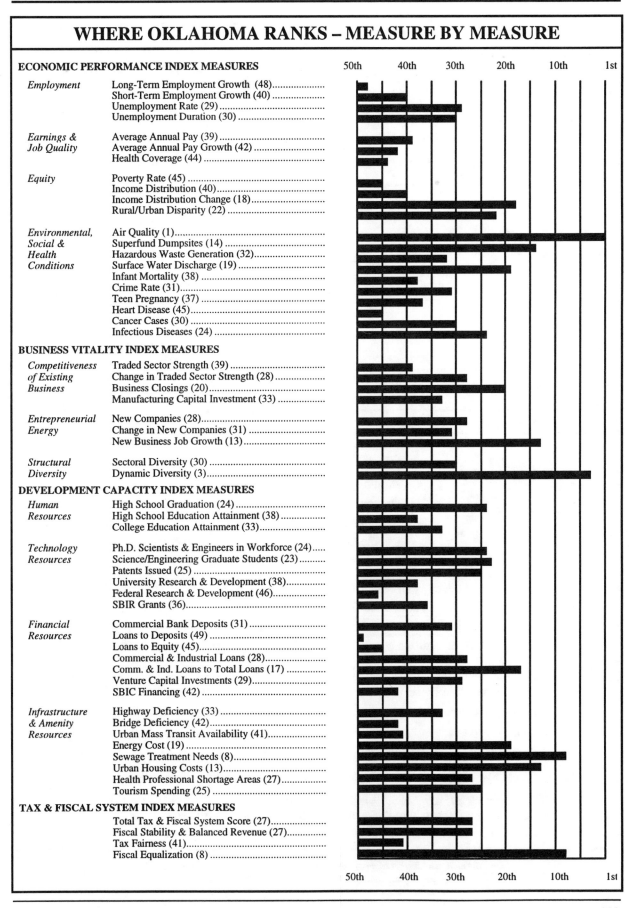

ECONOMIC PERFORMANCE INDEX MEASURES

		50th	40th	30th	20th	10th	1st

Employment
- Long-Term Employment Growth (48)
- Short-Term Employment Growth (40)
- Unemployment Rate (29)
- Unemployment Duration (30)

Earnings & Job Quality
- Average Annual Pay (39)
- Average Annual Pay Growth (42)
- Health Coverage (44)

Equity
- Poverty Rate (45)
- Income Distribution (40)
- Income Distribution Change (18)
- Rural/Urban Disparity (22)

Environmental, Social & Health Conditions
- Air Quality (1)
- Superfund Dumpsites (14)
- Hazardous Waste Generation (32)
- Surface Water Discharge (19)
- Infant Mortality (38)
- Crime Rate (31)
- Teen Pregnancy (37)
- Heart Disease (45)
- Cancer Cases (30)
- Infectious Diseases (24)

BUSINESS VITALITY INDEX MEASURES

Competitiveness of Existing Business
- Traded Sector Strength (39)
- Change in Traded Sector Strength (28)
- Business Closings (20)
- Manufacturing Capital Investment (33)

Entrepreneurial Energy
- New Companies (28)
- Change in New Companies (31)
- New Business Job Growth (13)

Structural Diversity
- Sectoral Diversity (30)
- Dynamic Diversity (3)

DEVELOPMENT CAPACITY INDEX MEASURES

Human Resources
- High School Graduation (24)
- High School Education Attainment (38)
- College Education Attainment (33)

Technology Resources
- Ph.D. Scientists & Engineers in Workforce (24)
- Science/Engineering Graduate Students (23)
- Patents Issued (25)
- University Research & Development (38)
- Federal Research & Development (46)
- SBIR Grants (36)

Financial Resources
- Commercial Bank Deposits (31)
- Loans to Deposits (49)
- Loans to Equity (45)
- Commercial & Industrial Loans (28)
- Comm. & Ind. Loans to Total Loans (17)
- Venture Capital Investments (29)
- SBIC Financing (42)

Infrastructure & Amenity Resources
- Highway Deficiency (33)
- Bridge Deficiency (42)
- Urban Mass Transit Availability (41)
- Energy Cost (19)
- Sewage Treatment Needs (8)
- Urban Housing Costs (13)
- Health Professional Shortage Areas (27)
- Tourism Spending (25)

TAX & FISCAL SYSTEM INDEX MEASURES
- Total Tax & Fiscal System Score (27)
- Fiscal Stability & Balanced Revenue (27)
- Tax Fairness (41)
- Fiscal Equalization (8)

	50th	40th	30th	20th	10th	1st

OREGON 1995 REPORT CARD

ECONOMIC PERFORMANCE	B

Employment .... A
Earnings & Job Quality .... B
Equity C

BUSINESS VITALITY	B

Business Competitiveness .... D
Entrepreneurial Energy................................ A
Structural Diversity C

DEVELOPMENT CAPACITY	A

Human Resources.. C
Technology Resources C
Financial Resources...................................... A
Infrastructure & Amenity Resources .... B

Tax & Fiscal System	–

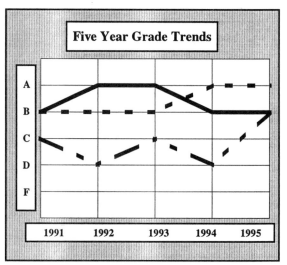

Five Year Grade Trends

1991   1992   1993   1994   1995

Key

Economic Performance	————
Business Vitality	– - -
Development Capacity	- - - -

- **Economic Performance:** Although its grade is unchanged from last year, Oregon's economy shows improving strength. With shrinking unemployment and continued strong job growth, Oregon's job market is excellent – the Pacific's best. Earnings & Job Quality remain above average. The state's only blemish is its income distribution, which is only average and getting worse. Despite a high crime rate, Oregon does well in most Environmental, Social, & Health Conditions.

- **Business Vitality:** Oregon is an Honor Roll state this year, largely on the strength of its dramatic jump in Business Vitality. Though the Competitiveness of Existing Business is still poor, Oregon now ranks second in the nation for its Entrepreneurial Energy (top ten in new companies and new business job growth). In addition, the state's top industries show improving diversity.

- **Development Capacity:** For the second year in a row, Oregon's Development Capacity receives an excellent grade. Led by strong lending activity and the nation's second highest rate of SBIC financing, the state's Financial Resources are top notch. In addition, with low energy costs and strong public transit availability, infrastructure resources are above average. Human Resources and Technology Resources rank near the middle.

- **Tax & Fiscal System:** Oregon receives a below average rating for its Tax & Fiscal System. With no sales tax and an over-reliance on property taxes, the revenue raising structure lacks balance. Moreover, while the tax structure ranks above average on fairness, the state is second worst in the nation at equalizing revenues among local governments.

For information on how grades and ranks are calculated, see the Methodology section.
For a detailed explanation of indexes, refer to the individual index section.

WHERE OREGON RANKS – MEASURE BY MEASURE

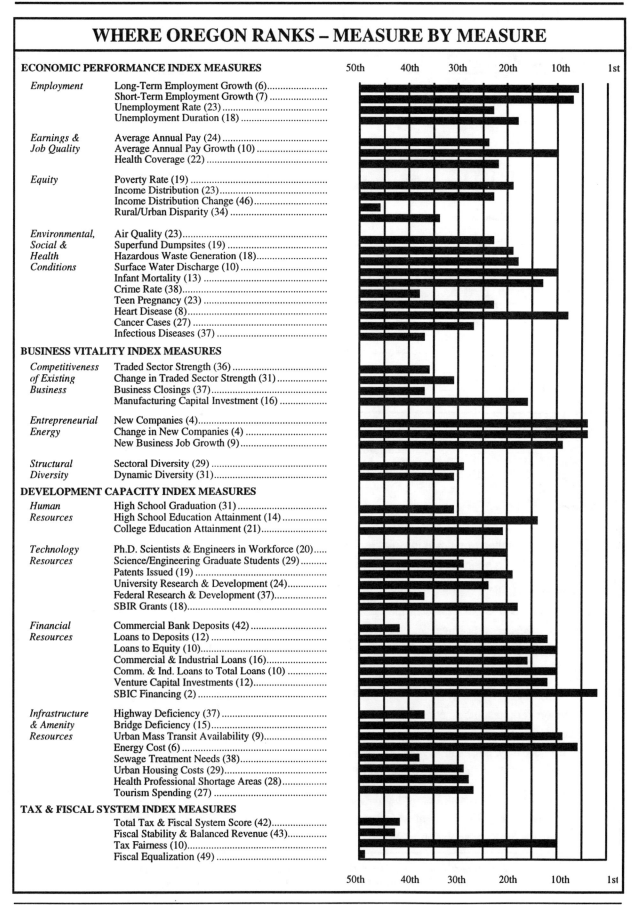

ECONOMIC PERFORMANCE INDEX MEASURES

Employment
- Long-Term Employment Growth (6)
- Short-Term Employment Growth (7)
- Unemployment Rate (23)
- Unemployment Duration (18)

Earnings & Job Quality
- Average Annual Pay (24)
- Average Annual Pay Growth (10)
- Health Coverage (22)

Equity
- Poverty Rate (19)
- Income Distribution (23)
- Income Distribution Change (46)
- Rural/Urban Disparity (34)

Environmental, Social & Health Conditions
- Air Quality (23)
- Superfund Dumpsites (19)
- Hazardous Waste Generation (18)
- Surface Water Discharge (10)
- Infant Mortality (13)
- Crime Rate (38)
- Teen Pregnancy (23)
- Heart Disease (8)
- Cancer Cases (27)
- Infectious Diseases (37)

BUSINESS VITALITY INDEX MEASURES

Competitiveness of Existing Business
- Traded Sector Strength (36)
- Change in Traded Sector Strength (31)
- Business Closings (37)
- Manufacturing Capital Investment (16)

Entrepreneurial Energy
- New Companies (4)
- Change in New Companies (4)
- New Business Job Growth (9)

Structural Diversity
- Sectoral Diversity (29)
- Dynamic Diversity (31)

DEVELOPMENT CAPACITY INDEX MEASURES

Human Resources
- High School Graduation (31)
- High School Education Attainment (14)
- College Education Attainment (21)

Technology Resources
- Ph.D. Scientists & Engineers in Workforce (20)
- Science/Engineering Graduate Students (29)
- Patents Issued (19)
- University Research & Development (24)
- Federal Research & Development (37)
- SBIR Grants (18)

Financial Resources
- Commercial Bank Deposits (42)
- Loans to Deposits (12)
- Loans to Equity (10)
- Commercial & Industrial Loans (16)
- Comm. & Ind. Loans to Total Loans (10)
- Venture Capital Investments (12)
- SBIC Financing (2)

Infrastructure & Amenity Resources
- Highway Deficiency (37)
- Bridge Deficiency (15)
- Urban Mass Transit Availability (9)
- Energy Cost (6)
- Sewage Treatment Needs (38)
- Urban Housing Costs (29)
- Health Professional Shortage Areas (28)
- Tourism Spending (27)

TAX & FISCAL SYSTEM INDEX MEASURES
- Total Tax & Fiscal System Score (42)
- Fiscal Stability & Balanced Revenue (43)
- Tax Fairness (10)
- Fiscal Equalization (49)

Scale: 50th 40th 30th 20th 10th 1st

PENNSYLVANIA 1995 REPORT CARD

ECONOMIC PERFORMANCE — C

Employment ....D
Earnings & Job Quality ....B
Equity C

BUSINESS VITALITY — A

Business Competitiveness ....A
Entrepreneurial Energy..................................F
Structural Diversity ....A

DEVELOPMENT CAPACITY — B

Human Resources..C
Technology Resources ....B
Financial Resources.......................................A
Infrastructure & Amenity Resources.............D

Tax & Fiscal System — √

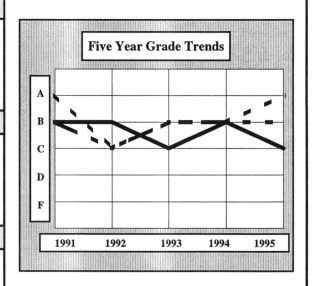

Five Year Grade Trends

1991 1992 1993 1994 1995

Key	
Economic Performance	———
Business Vitality	— — —
Development Capacity	- - - -

- **Economic Performance:** After an above average grade last year, Pennsylvania's grade returns to a C this year. With slow employment growth (46th on short-term growth), Pennsylvania now has the region's worst job market. Moreover, while Earnings & Job Quality remain a strength, the state is now below average on pay growth. Despite strong rankings on social indicators, such as crime rate and teen pregnancy, the quality of life is poor in Pennsylvania, with poor rankings on health and environmental measures.

- **Business Vitality:** Up a grade from last year, Pennsylvania continues to benefit from one of the most competitive businesses in the nation (strength in those industries that trade outside the state and low business closings) and the second most diversified economy. However, Entrepreneurial Energy is the second worst in the nation, with slow new business job growth and the second lowest number of new companies.

- **Development Capacity:** Led by the nation's third best Financial Resources, Pennsylvania's development resources continue to be strong. The state's Technology Resources are above average, and though ranking only average on Human Resources, the state's high school graduation rate ranks eleventh. Pennsylvania's biggest weakness is its Infrastructure & Amenity Resources which, due to high energy costs and poor bridge quality, rate as poor.

- **Tax & Fiscal System:** Pennsylvania has an average ranking Tax & Fiscal System. While the state's revenue raising structure is among the top ten in terms of balance, its policies for equalizing local fiscal capacity are below average.

For information on how grades and ranks are calculated, see the Methodology section.
For a detailed explanation of indexes, refer to the individual index section.

WHERE PENNSYLVANIA RANKS – MEASURE BY MEASURE

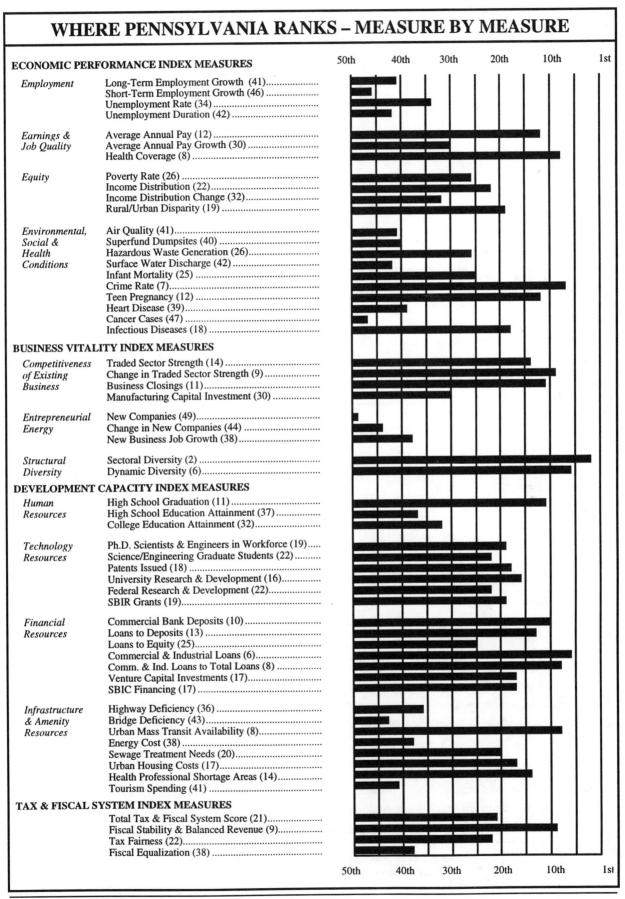

RHODE ISLAND 1995 REPORT CARD

ECONOMIC PERFORMANCE   C

Employment ....F
Earnings & Job Quality ....A
Equity C

BUSINESS VITALITY   D

Business Competitiveness C
Entrepreneurial Energy...C
Structural Diversity ....D

DEVELOPMENT CAPACITY   C

Human Resources..C
Technology Resources ....A
Financial Resources..A
Infrastructure & Amenity Resources.....................F

Tax & Fiscal System   √

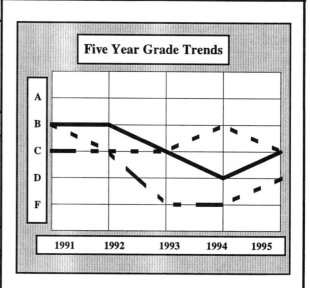

Five Year Grade Trends

| | 1991 | 1992 | 1993 | 1994 | 1995 |

Key

Economic Performance ⎯⎯⎯
Business Vitality ⎯ ⎯ ⎯
Development Capacity ▪ ▪ ▪ ▪

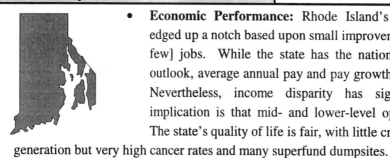

- **Economic Performance:** Rhode Island's Economic Performance has edged up a notch based upon small improvements in the quality of its [very few] jobs. While the state has the nation's worst overall employment outlook, average annual pay and pay growth have both actually improved. Nevertheless, income disparity has significantly increased. The implication is that mid- and lower-level opportunities are disappearing. The state's quality of life is fair, with little crime and little hazardous waste generation but very high cancer rates and many superfund dumpsites.

- **Business Vitality:** Rhode Island's improved Business Vitality is an encouraging sign. Entrepreneurship has increased with lots of new companies and more jobs associated with them. Existing businesses appear to be holding steady as closings are low and industries that compete out of state (the traded sector) are bringing increasing worker income into Rhode Island.

- **Development Capacity:** Rhode Island has a unique mix of strong and weak resources. Despite its high-end industries, it ranks below average in Human Resources. But its Technology Resources are the country's eighth best and its Financial Resources are fifth best. The state's Achilles' heel, though, is the nation's worst physical infrastructure (ranking in the bottom seven in highway deficiency, bridge deficiency, energy costs and sewage treatment needs).

- **Tax & Fiscal System:** Rhode Island's Tax & Fiscal System is fair, especially with a revenue-generating structure that is more balanced and stable than most, but the state has a somewhat weak record of equalizing different fiscal capacities of local governments.

For information on how grades and ranks are calculated, see the Methodology section.
For a detailed explanation of indexes, refer to the individual index section.

WHERE RHODE ISLAND RANKS – MEASURE BY MEASURE

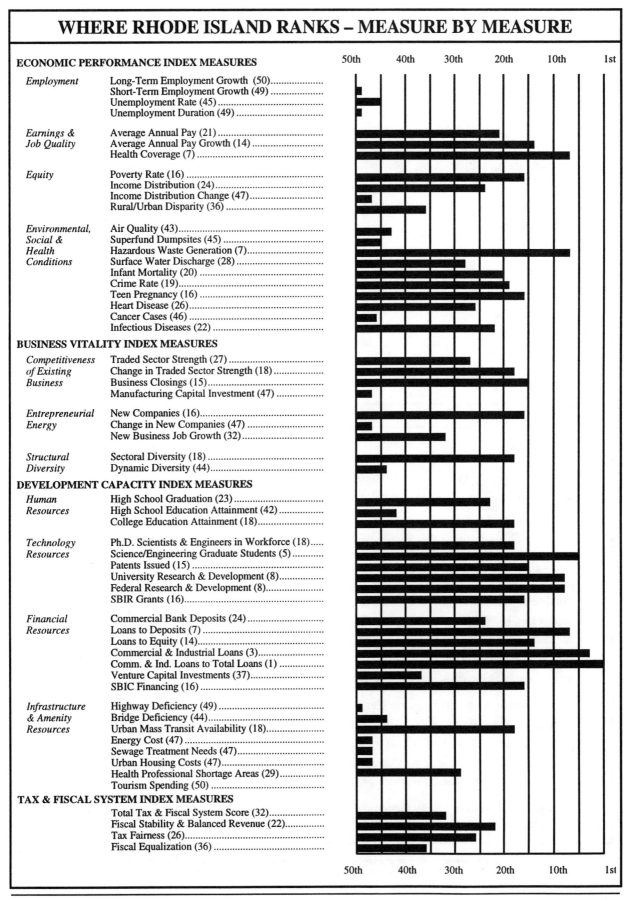

ECONOMIC PERFORMANCE INDEX MEASURES

		50th	40th	30th	20th	10th	1st

Employment
Long-Term Employment Growth (50)....................
Short-Term Employment Growth (49) ....
Unemployment Rate (45)....................................
Unemployment Duration (49) ....

Earnings & Job Quality
Average Annual Pay (21).....................................
Average Annual Pay Growth (14) ....
Health Coverage (7)...

Equity
Poverty Rate (16)..
Income Distribution (24)......................................
Income Distribution Change (47)...........................
Rural/Urban Disparity (36) ....

Environmental, Social & Health Conditions
Air Quality (43)..
Superfund Dumpsites (45) ....
Hazardous Waste Generation (7)...........................
Surface Water Discharge (28) ....
Infant Mortality (20) ....
Crime Rate (19)...
Teen Pregnancy (16) ....
Heart Disease (26)..
Cancer Cases (46)..
Infectious Diseases (22) ....

BUSINESS VITALITY INDEX MEASURES

Competitiveness of Existing Business
Traded Sector Strength (27) ....
Change in Traded Sector Strength (18) ....
Business Closings (15)..
Manufacturing Capital Investment (47) ....

Entrepreneurial Energy
New Companies (16)...
Change in New Companies (47) ....
New Business Job Growth (32).............................

Structural Diversity
Sectoral Diversity (18) ....
Dynamic Diversity (44)..

DEVELOPMENT CAPACITY INDEX MEASURES

Human Resources
High School Graduation (23) ....
High School Education Attainment (42) ....
College Education Attainment (18).........................

Technology Resources
Ph.D. Scientists & Engineers in Workforce (18).....
Science/Engineering Graduate Students (5) ....
Patents Issued (15) ....
University Research & Development (8).................
Federal Research & Development (8).....................
SBIR Grants (16)...

Financial Resources
Commercial Bank Deposits (24) ....
Loans to Deposits (7) ....
Loans to Equity (14)...
Commercial & Industrial Loans (3).......................
Comm. & Ind. Loans to Total Loans (1) ....
Venture Capital Investments (37)...........................
SBIC Financing (16) ....

Infrastructure & Amenity Resources
Highway Deficiency (49)......................................
Bridge Deficiency (44)...
Urban Mass Transit Availability (18).....................
Energy Cost (47) ....
Sewage Treatment Needs (47)..............................
Urban Housing Costs (47)....................................
Health Professional Shortage Areas (29).................
Tourism Spending (50) ....

TAX & FISCAL SYSTEM INDEX MEASURES

Total Tax & Fiscal System Score (32)....................
Fiscal Stability & Balanced Revenue (22)...............
Tax Fairness (26)...
Fiscal Equalization (36) ....

		50th	40th	30th	20th	10th	1st

SOUTH CAROLINA 1995 REPORT CARD

ECONOMIC PERFORMANCE	D

Employment ....D
Earnings & Job Quality C
Equity ....D

BUSINESS VITALITY	B

Business Competitiveness ....A
Entrepreneurial Energy......................................C
Structural Diversity C

DEVELOPMENT CAPACITY	D

Human Resources...F
Technology Resources ....D
Financial Resources...C
Infrastructure & Amenity Resources ....A

Tax & Fiscal System	+

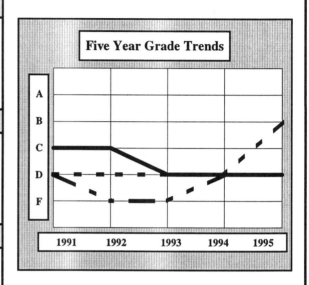

Five Year Grade Trends

1991 1992 1993 1994 1995

Key	
Economic Performance	———
Business Vitality	— - -
Development Capacity	- - - -

- **Economic Performance:** For the third straight year, South Carolina receives a below average grade. One promising trend, marked by the nation's tenth fastest pay growth and an increase in employer-provided health coverage, is an improvement in Earnings & Job Quality. However, with a slowing in long-term job growth and income distribution that is uneven and getting worse, both the state's job market and its performance on measures of Equity are poor. In addition, overall quality of life in South Carolina is below average.

- **Business Vitality:** Fueled by a turnaround on Entrepreneurial Energy, South Carolina's grade jumps two letters this year. Ranking 50th last year, South Carolina's Entrepreneurial Energy earns an average mark on the strength of robust new business job growth and shows an improving trend in new company formations. In addition, with a low rate of business closings, the state's businesses are now among the most competitive in the U.S.

- **Development Capacity:** South Carolina's development resources continue to receive a below average grade. Weakest of all are the state's Human Resources, which are held back by the nation's second worst high school graduation rate. Technology Resources are also below average. On the bright side, the state's Financial Resources are now average, and with high quality highways and bridges, its infrastructure is now among the best in the nation.

- **Tax & Fiscal System:** With the nation's most well balanced tax structure, South Carolina's Tax & Fiscal System earns an above average rating and is the South's best.

For information on how grades and ranks are calculated, see the Methodology section.
For a detailed explanation of indexes, refer to the individual index section.

WHERE SOUTH CAROLINA RANKS – MEASURE BY MEASURE

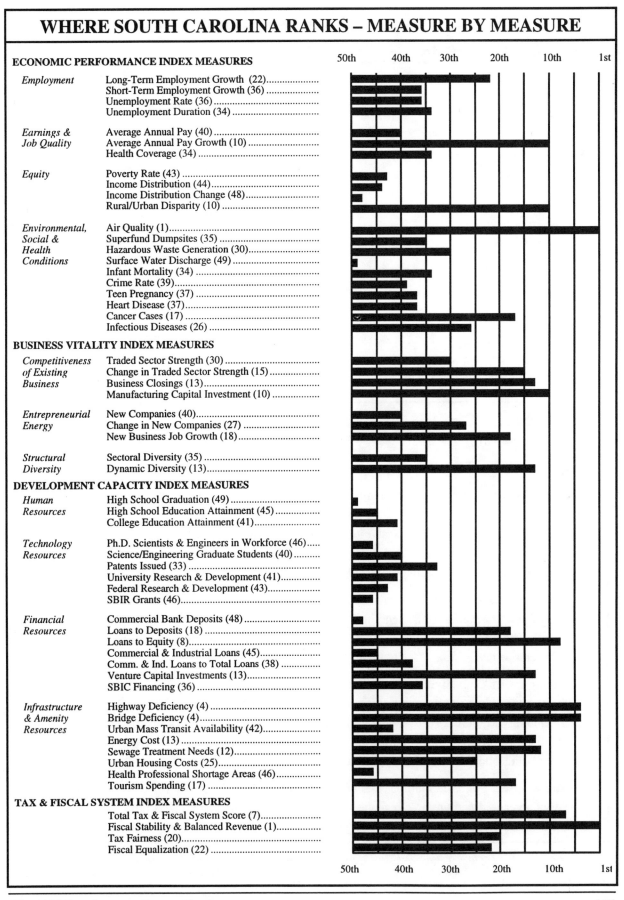

ECONOMIC PERFORMANCE INDEX MEASURES

Employment
Long-Term Employment Growth (22)
Short-Term Employment Growth (36)
Unemployment Rate (36)
Unemployment Duration (34)

Earnings & Job Quality
Average Annual Pay (40)
Average Annual Pay Growth (10)
Health Coverage (34)

Equity
Poverty Rate (43)
Income Distribution (44)
Income Distribution Change (48)
Rural/Urban Disparity (10)

Environmental, Social & Health Conditions
Air Quality (1)
Superfund Dumpsites (35)
Hazardous Waste Generation (30)
Surface Water Discharge (49)
Infant Mortality (34)
Crime Rate (39)
Teen Pregnancy (37)
Heart Disease (37)
Cancer Cases (17)
Infectious Diseases (26)

BUSINESS VITALITY INDEX MEASURES

Competitiveness of Existing Business
Traded Sector Strength (30)
Change in Traded Sector Strength (15)
Business Closings (13)
Manufacturing Capital Investment (10)

Entrepreneurial Energy
New Companies (40)
Change in New Companies (27)
New Business Job Growth (18)

Structural Diversity
Sectoral Diversity (35)
Dynamic Diversity (13)

DEVELOPMENT CAPACITY INDEX MEASURES

Human Resources
High School Graduation (49)
High School Education Attainment (45)
College Education Attainment (41)

Technology Resources
Ph.D. Scientists & Engineers in Workforce (46)
Science/Engineering Graduate Students (40)
Patents Issued (33)
University Research & Development (41)
Federal Research & Development (43)
SBIR Grants (46)

Financial Resources
Commercial Bank Deposits (48)
Loans to Deposits (18)
Loans to Equity (8)
Commercial & Industrial Loans (45)
Comm. & Ind. Loans to Total Loans (38)
Venture Capital Investments (13)
SBIC Financing (36)

Infrastructure & Amenity Resources
Highway Deficiency (4)
Bridge Deficiency (4)
Urban Mass Transit Availability (42)
Energy Cost (13)
Sewage Treatment Needs (12)
Urban Housing Costs (25)
Health Professional Shortage Areas (46)
Tourism Spending (17)

TAX & FISCAL SYSTEM INDEX MEASURES
Total Tax & Fiscal System Score (7)
Fiscal Stability & Balanced Revenue (1)
Tax Fairness (20)
Fiscal Equalization (22)

SOUTH DAKOTA 1995 REPORT CARD

ECONOMIC PERFORMANCE	B
Employment	A
Earnings & Job Quality	D
Equity	B

BUSINESS VITALITY	C
Business Competitiveness	C
Entrepreneurial Energy	B
Structural Diversity	F

DEVELOPMENT CAPACITY	D
Human Resources	C
Technology Resources	F
Financial Resources	C
Infrastructure & Amenity Resources	C

Tax & Fiscal System	–

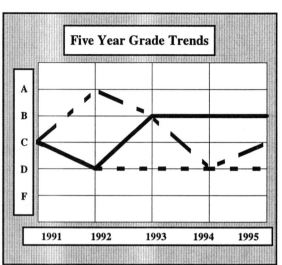

Five Year Grade Trends

1991 1992 1993 1994 1995

Key	
Economic Performance	————
Business Vitality	— - -
Development Capacity	- - - -

- **Economic Performance:** South Dakota maintains its strong performance with improved Employment, although Earnings & Job Quality are poor. The state's short-term employment growth improves dramatically and unemployment is second lowest. The state also has the number one increase in average annual pay – which it needs to maintain to shake its last place ranking in overall average annual pay. Equity slips, as the gap between rich and poor stops closing so fast. One of the poorer performing Plains states in quality of life, South Dakota still compares very well in Environmental Conditions.

- **Business Vitality:** South Dakota's Business Vitality improves due to a significant increase in the rate of new companies formed and in the number of jobs from small businesses (from 22nd to 2nd best). The damper is that the economy becomes slightly less diverse and existing businesses lose some competitiveness.

- **Development Capacity:** South Dakota's development resources remain below average for the fourth year. Financial Resources drop due to a slight decrease in commercial and industrial loans. Technology Resources are still among the worst in the nation (ranking 48th in R&D and patents), while Human Resources and Infrastructure & Amenity Resources rate only average (although high school graduation is the nation's 6th best).

- **Tax & Fiscal System:** South Dakota has one of the worst ranks in the Tax & Fiscal System, with very unbalanced and unstable revenue sources, an unequitable system, and little effort to equalize the differing fiscal capacities of its local governments.

For information on how grades and ranks are calculated, see the Methodology section.
For a detailed explanation of indexes, refer to the individual index section.

WHERE SOUTH DAKOTA RANKS – MEASURE BY MEASURE

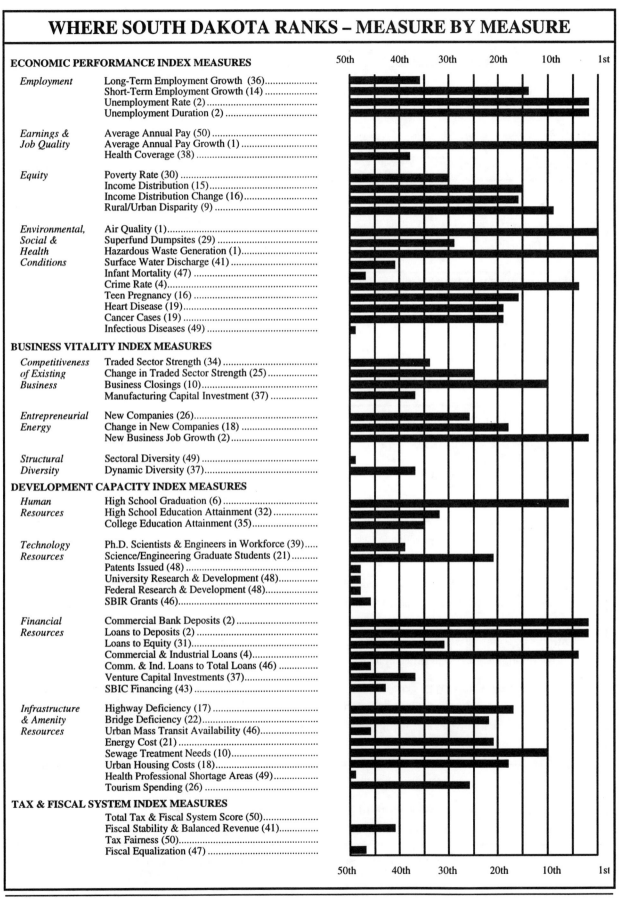

ECONOMIC PERFORMANCE INDEX MEASURES

| | 50th | 40th | 30th | 20th | 10th | 1st |

Employment
Long-Term Employment Growth (36)....................
Short-Term Employment Growth (14)..................
Unemployment Rate (2)....................................
Unemployment Duration (2)..............................

Earnings & Job Quality
Average Annual Pay (50)..................................
Average Annual Pay Growth (1)..........................
Health Coverage (38)......................................

Equity
Poverty Rate (30)..
Income Distribution (15)..................................
Income Distribution Change (16)..........................
Rural/Urban Disparity (9)................................

Environmental, Social & Health Conditions
Air Quality (1)..
Superfund Dumpsites (29)................................
Hazardous Waste Generation (1)..........................
Surface Water Discharge (41)............................
Infant Mortality (47)......................................
Crime Rate (4)..
Teen Pregnancy (16)......................................
Heart Disease (19)..
Cancer Cases (19)..
Infectious Diseases (49)..................................

BUSINESS VITALITY INDEX MEASURES

Competitiveness of Existing Business
Traded Sector Strength (34)..............................
Change in Traded Sector Strength (25)..................
Business Closings (10)....................................
Manufacturing Capital Investment (37)..................

Entrepreneurial Energy
New Companies (26)......................................
Change in New Companies (18)..........................
New Business Job Growth (2)............................

Structural Diversity
Sectoral Diversity (49)....................................
Dynamic Diversity (37)....................................

DEVELOPMENT CAPACITY INDEX MEASURES

Human Resources
High School Graduation (6)..............................
High School Education Attainment (32)..................
College Education Attainment (35)........................

Technology Resources
Ph.D. Scientists & Engineers in Workforce (39).....
Science/Engineering Graduate Students (21)..........
Patents Issued (48)..
University Research & Development (48)..............
Federal Research & Development (48)..................
SBIR Grants (46)..

Financial Resources
Commercial Bank Deposits (2)..........................
Loans to Deposits (2)....................................
Loans to Equity (31)......................................
Commercial & Industrial Loans (4)......................
Comm. & Ind. Loans to Total Loans (46)..........
Venture Capital Investments (37)........................
SBIC Financing (43)......................................

Infrastructure & Amenity Resources
Highway Deficiency (17)..................................
Bridge Deficiency (22)....................................
Urban Mass Transit Availability (46)..................
Energy Cost (21)..
Sewage Treatment Needs (10)............................
Urban Housing Costs (18)................................
Health Professional Shortage Areas (49)..............
Tourism Spending (26)....................................

TAX & FISCAL SYSTEM INDEX MEASURES

Total Tax & Fiscal System Score (50)....................
Fiscal Stability & Balanced Revenue (41)..............
Tax Fairness (50)..
Fiscal Equalization (47)....................................

| | 50th | 40th | 30th | 20th | 10th | 1st |

TENNESSEE 1995 REPORT CARD

ECONOMIC PERFORMANCE	B

Employment .... A
Earnings & Job Quality C
Equity C

BUSINESS VITALITY	A

Business Competitiveness .... B
Entrepreneurial Energy.................................... B
Structural Diversity .... A

DEVELOPMENT CAPACITY	C

Human Resources.. F
Technology Resources .... D
Financial Resources.. B
Infrastructure & Amenity Resources..................... B

Tax & Fiscal System	–

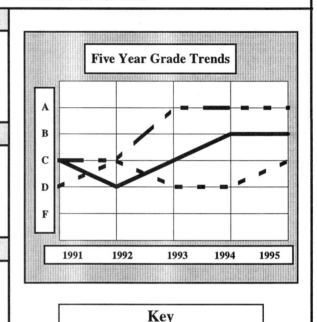

Five Year Grade Trends

1991   1992   1993   1994   1995

Key	
Economic Performance	——————
Business Vitality	— - -
Development Capacity	- - - -

- **Economic Performance:** For the second year, Tennessee's economy earns a B. With strong short-term job growth and an above average unemployment rate, its job market is the nation's second best. Moreover, pay growth is among the nation's top ten and, with a narrowing gap between the rich and poor, Tennessee no longer ranks below average on measures of Equity. Unfortunately, due to weak ranking health indicators, Tennessee's quality of life is among the nation's poorest.

- **Business Vitality:** Tennessee's Business Vitality is the second best in the nation. While business closings have increased somewhat, the competitiveness of the state's businesses is still above average. Moreover, the state's businesses are among the most well diversified in the U.S. and, with strong new business job growth and an improving trend in new company formations, the state is now among the top 20 in Enterpreneurial Energy.

- **Development Capacity:** Tennessee is one of a handful of southern states that shows improved strength on Development Capacity. This strength is particularly evident in the state's Financial Resources (first in SBIC financing) and its Infrastructure & Amenity Resources (improved highway quality and access to health care), both of which are now near average. Several glaring weaknesses persist, however – the state's Technology Resources are now below average and Human Resources continue to receive a failing grade.

- **Tax & Fiscal System:** With the third least equitable tax system, Tennessee has one of the nation's five worst ranking Tax & Fiscal System.

For information on how grades and ranks are calculated, see the Methodology section.
For a detailed explanation of indexes, refer to the individual index section.

WHERE TENNESSEE RANKS – MEASURE BY MEASURE

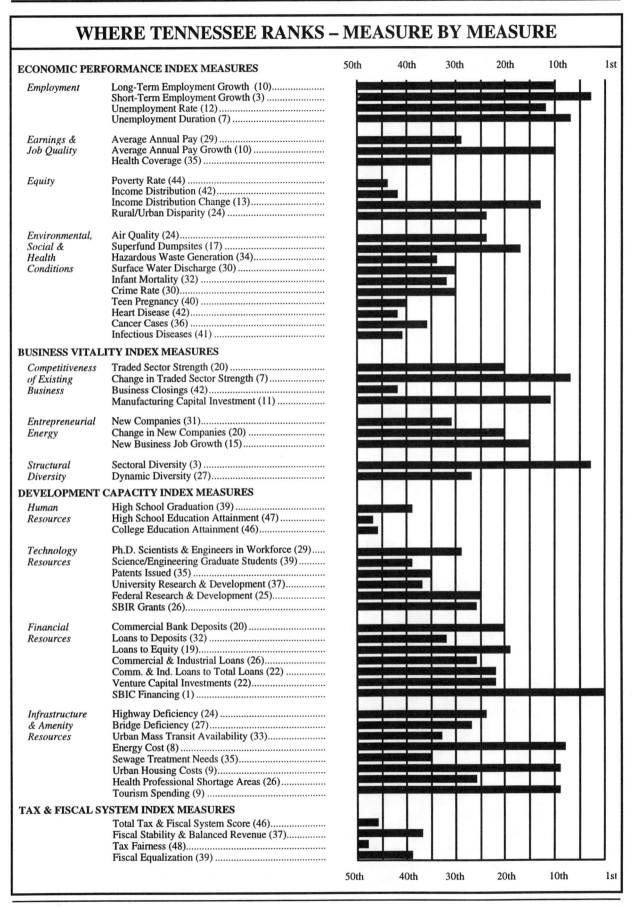

ECONOMIC PERFORMANCE INDEX MEASURES

Employment
- Long-Term Employment Growth (10)
- Short-Term Employment Growth (3)
- Unemployment Rate (12)
- Unemployment Duration (7)

Earnings & Job Quality
- Average Annual Pay (29)
- Average Annual Pay Growth (10)
- Health Coverage (35)

Equity
- Poverty Rate (44)
- Income Distribution (42)
- Income Distribution Change (13)
- Rural/Urban Disparity (24)

Environmental, Social & Health Conditions
- Air Quality (24)
- Superfund Dumpsites (17)
- Hazardous Waste Generation (34)
- Surface Water Discharge (30)
- Infant Mortality (32)
- Crime Rate (30)
- Teen Pregnancy (40)
- Heart Disease (42)
- Cancer Cases (36)
- Infectious Diseases (41)

BUSINESS VITALITY INDEX MEASURES

Competitiveness of Existing Business
- Traded Sector Strength (20)
- Change in Traded Sector Strength (7)
- Business Closings (42)
- Manufacturing Capital Investment (11)

Entrepreneurial Energy
- New Companies (31)
- Change in New Companies (20)
- New Business Job Growth (15)

Structural Diversity
- Sectoral Diversity (3)
- Dynamic Diversity (27)

DEVELOPMENT CAPACITY INDEX MEASURES

Human Resources
- High School Graduation (39)
- High School Education Attainment (47)
- College Education Attainment (46)

Technology Resources
- Ph.D. Scientists & Engineers in Workforce (29)
- Science/Engineering Graduate Students (39)
- Patents Issued (35)
- University Research & Development (37)
- Federal Research & Development (25)
- SBIR Grants (26)

Financial Resources
- Commercial Bank Deposits (20)
- Loans to Deposits (32)
- Loans to Equity (19)
- Commercial & Industrial Loans (26)
- Comm. & Ind. Loans to Total Loans (22)
- Venture Capital Investments (22)
- SBIC Financing (1)

Infrastructure & Amenity Resources
- Highway Deficiency (24)
- Bridge Deficiency (27)
- Urban Mass Transit Availability (33)
- Energy Cost (8)
- Sewage Treatment Needs (35)
- Urban Housing Costs (9)
- Health Professional Shortage Areas (26)
- Tourism Spending (9)

TAX & FISCAL SYSTEM INDEX MEASURES
- Total Tax & Fiscal System Score (46)
- Fiscal Stability & Balanced Revenue (37)
- Tax Fairness (48)
- Fiscal Equalization (39)

TEXAS 1995 REPORT CARD

ECONOMIC PERFORMANCE	D

Employment C
Earnings & Job Quality ....D
Equity ....D

BUSINESS VITALITY	A

Business Competitiveness ....B
Entrepreneurial Energy....................................B
Structural Diversity ....A

DEVELOPMENT CAPACITY	C

Human Resources..D
Technology Resources ....B
Financial Resources..C
Infrastructure & Amenity Resources.................A

Tax & Fiscal System	–

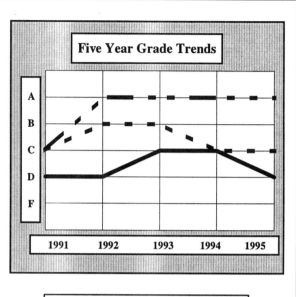

Five Year Grade Trends

1991   1992   1993   1994   1995

Key
Economic Performance —————
Business Vitality ▬ ▬ ▬
Development Capacity ▬ ▬ ▬

- **Economic Performance:** The performance of the Texas economy stumbles this past year. Despite strong employment growth, unemployment remains a problem and previous strong increases in average annual pay slips to below average. There are big gaps in Equity in Texas – the state has one of the ten largest gaps between rich and poor and a poverty rate worse than most of its peers. All the other Plains states compare well in quality of life measures, but Texas compares poorly in measures of Social and Environmental Conditions.

- **Business Vitality:** For the second year in a row, Texas ranks number one in Business Vitality. No longer a slave to oil, Texas has the fourth most diverse economy. Entrepreneurship is high, with the third highest rate of jobs from new companies. Existing businesses are also strong, pulling in money from out of state (the traded sector) with increased of investment in manufacturing equipment.

- **Development Capacity:** Texas misses a B by one rank this year, boding well for future economic growth. Although Human Resources are still weak (especially with the nation's third worst high school graduation), physical infrastructure is excellent (highway and bridge deficiency ranking 7th and 13th respectively), and Technology Resources are above average. The Financial Resource subindex shows that the state has a high degree of alternative financing activity.

- **Tax & Fiscal System:** Texas ranks among the bottom states due to a relatively unbalanced, unstable, and inequitable tax system.

For information on how grades and ranks are calculated, see the Methodology section.
For a detailed explanation of indexes, refer to the individual index section.

WHERE TEXAS RANKS – MEASURE BY MEASURE

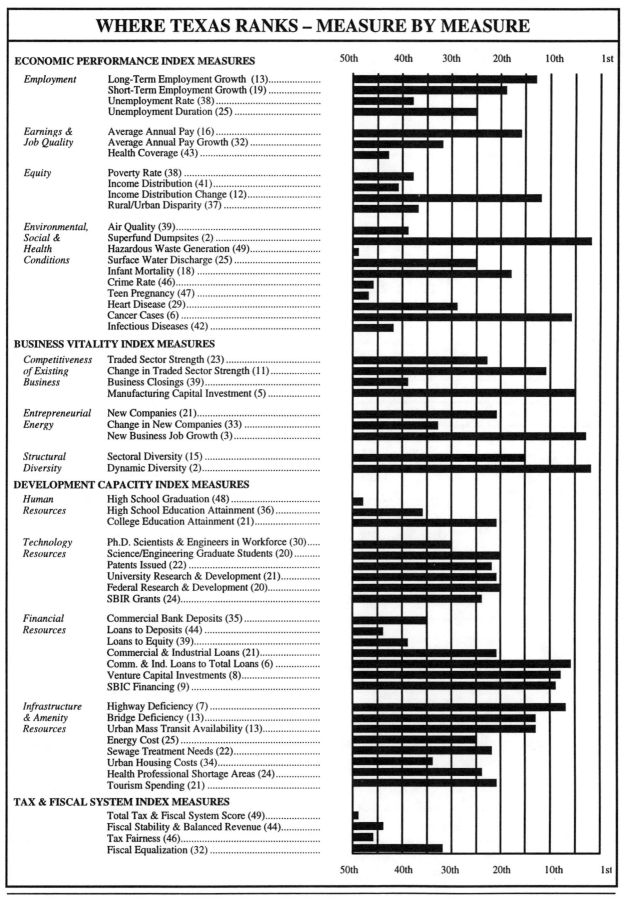

ECONOMIC PERFORMANCE INDEX MEASURES

Employment
Long-Term Employment Growth (13)
Short-Term Employment Growth (19)
Unemployment Rate (38)
Unemployment Duration (25)

Earnings &
Job Quality
Average Annual Pay (16)
Average Annual Pay Growth (32)
Health Coverage (43)

Equity
Poverty Rate (38)
Income Distribution (41)
Income Distribution Change (12)
Rural/Urban Disparity (37)

Environmental,
Social &
Health
Conditions
Air Quality (39)
Superfund Dumpsites (2)
Hazardous Waste Generation (49)
Surface Water Discharge (25)
Infant Mortality (18)
Crime Rate (46)
Teen Pregnancy (47)
Heart Disease (29)
Cancer Cases (6)
Infectious Diseases (42)

BUSINESS VITALITY INDEX MEASURES

Competitiveness
of Existing
Business
Traded Sector Strength (23)
Change in Traded Sector Strength (11)
Business Closings (39)
Manufacturing Capital Investment (5)

Entrepreneurial
Energy
New Companies (21)
Change in New Companies (33)
New Business Job Growth (3)

Structural
Diversity
Sectoral Diversity (15)
Dynamic Diversity (2)

DEVELOPMENT CAPACITY INDEX MEASURES

Human
Resources
High School Graduation (48)
High School Education Attainment (36)
College Education Attainment (21)

Technology
Resources
Ph.D. Scientists & Engineers in Workforce (30)
Science/Engineering Graduate Students (20)
Patents Issued (22)
University Research & Development (21)
Federal Research & Development (20)
SBIR Grants (24)

Financial
Resources
Commercial Bank Deposits (35)
Loans to Deposits (44)
Loans to Equity (39)
Commercial & Industrial Loans (21)
Comm. & Ind. Loans to Total Loans (6)
Venture Capital Investments (8)
SBIC Financing (9)

Infrastructure
& Amenity
Resources
Highway Deficiency (7)
Bridge Deficiency (13)
Urban Mass Transit Availability (13)
Energy Cost (25)
Sewage Treatment Needs (22)
Urban Housing Costs (34)
Health Professional Shortage Areas (24)
Tourism Spending (21)

TAX & FISCAL SYSTEM INDEX MEASURES

Total Tax & Fiscal System Score (49)
Fiscal Stability & Balanced Revenue (44)
Tax Fairness (46)
Fiscal Equalization (32)

50th   40th   30th   20th   10th   1st

UTAH 1995 REPORT CARD

ECONOMIC PERFORMANCE   A

Employment ....A
Earnings & Job Quality C
Equity ....A

BUSINESS VITALITY   C

Business Competitiveness ....F
Entrepreneurial Energy............................A
Structural Diversity C

DEVELOPMENT CAPACITY   A

Human Resources......................................A
Technology Resources ....A
Financial Resources..................................D
Infrastructure & Amenity Resources.....................A

Tax & Fiscal System   +

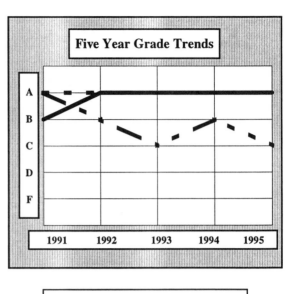

Five Year Grade Trends

1991   1992   1993   1994   1995

Key

Economic Performance	——
Business Vitality	– ··
Development Capacity	▪ ▪ ▪ ▪

- **Economic Performance:** After four years of excellent overall performance, Utah's economy is beginning to decline. Though maintaining explosive employment growth (ranking 2nd in long-term and 5th in short-term growth, with the 3rd lowest unemployment rate), Utah's average annual pay growth has slowed. Although Social and Health Conditions are good, high hazardous waste generation, poor air quality, and many superfund dumpsites are diminishing the state's quality of life.

- **Business Vitality:** Utah's existing business are weaker than in the past. Large decreases in the income from business competing out of state and the second worst number of business closings are cause for concern. But the economy is still fairly diverse and creating many new companies (though less than previously).

- **Development Capacity:** Utah has maintained its excellent development resources, giving the state tools to deal with economic pitfalls. The state has excellent Human Resources (4th highest high school attainment rate), excellent Technology Resources, and the best overall Infrastructure & Amenity Resources (3rd in highway deficiency and 7th in sewage treatment needs). Financial Resources are poor, with low deposits and venture capital. However, strong loan activity implies banks are making the best of what they have.

- **Tax & Fiscal System:** Utah has one of the best ranking Tax & Fiscal Systems, with a balanced source of revenues, a good record of equalizing its local governments fiscal capabilities and relatively equitable taxes.

For information on how grades and ranks are calculated, see the Methodology section.
For a detailed explanation of indexes, refer to the individual index section.

WHERE UTAH RANKS – MEASURE BY MEASURE

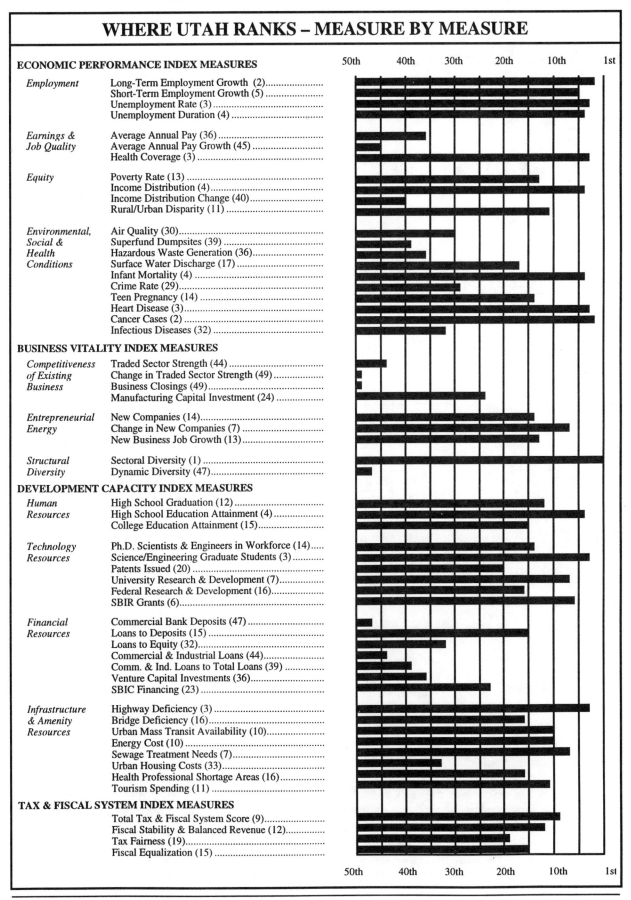

ECONOMIC PERFORMANCE INDEX MEASURES

Employment
Long-Term Employment Growth (2)
Short-Term Employment Growth (5)
Unemployment Rate (3)
Unemployment Duration (4)

Earnings & Job Quality
Average Annual Pay (36)
Average Annual Pay Growth (45)
Health Coverage (3)

Equity
Poverty Rate (13)
Income Distribution (4)
Income Distribution Change (40)
Rural/Urban Disparity (11)

Environmental, Social & Health Conditions
Air Quality (30)
Superfund Dumpsites (39)
Hazardous Waste Generation (36)
Surface Water Discharge (17)
Infant Mortality (4)
Crime Rate (29)
Teen Pregnancy (14)
Heart Disease (3)
Cancer Cases (2)
Infectious Diseases (32)

BUSINESS VITALITY INDEX MEASURES

Competitiveness of Existing Business
Traded Sector Strength (44)
Change in Traded Sector Strength (49)
Business Closings (49)
Manufacturing Capital Investment (24)

Entrepreneurial Energy
New Companies (14)
Change in New Companies (7)
New Business Job Growth (13)

Structural Diversity
Sectoral Diversity (1)
Dynamic Diversity (47)

DEVELOPMENT CAPACITY INDEX MEASURES

Human Resources
High School Graduation (12)
High School Education Attainment (4)
College Education Attainment (15)

Technology Resources
Ph.D. Scientists & Engineers in Workforce (14)
Science/Engineering Graduate Students (3)
Patents Issued (20)
University Research & Development (7)
Federal Research & Development (16)
SBIR Grants (6)

Financial Resources
Commercial Bank Deposits (47)
Loans to Deposits (15)
Loans to Equity (32)
Commercial & Industrial Loans (44)
Comm. & Ind. Loans to Total Loans (39)
Venture Capital Investments (36)
SBIC Financing (23)

Infrastructure & Amenity Resources
Highway Deficiency (3)
Bridge Deficiency (16)
Urban Mass Transit Availability (10)
Energy Cost (10)
Sewage Treatment Needs (7)
Urban Housing Costs (33)
Health Professional Shortage Areas (16)
Tourism Spending (11)

TAX & FISCAL SYSTEM INDEX MEASURES
Total Tax & Fiscal System Score (9)
Fiscal Stability & Balanced Revenue (12)
Tax Fairness (19)
Fiscal Equalization (15)

Scale (top and bottom): 50th 40th 30th 20th 10th 1st

VERMONT 1995 REPORT CARD

ECONOMIC PERFORMANCE	C
Employment C	
Earnings & Job Quality ....D	
Equity ....B	

BUSINESS VITALITY	F
Business Competitiveness C	
Entrepreneurial Energy.........................D	
Structural Diversity C	

DEVELOPMENT CAPACITY	C
Human Resources...................................A	
Technology Resources ....B	
Financial Resources...............................C	
Infrastructure & Amenity Resources.....D	

Tax & Fiscal System	√

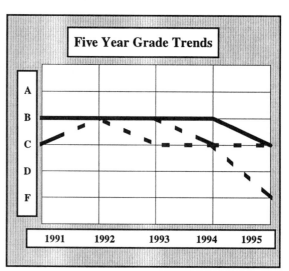

Five Year Grade Trends

| | 1991 | 1992 | 1993 | 1994 | 1995 |

Key

Economic Performance	————
Business Vitality	– - -
Development Capacity	- - -

- **Economic Performance:** Vermont's Economic Performance has fallen as employment growth slows and the quality of its jobs falls significantly in comparison to its neighbors. The good news is that previous years' job growth has now led to a better than average unemployment rate (4.7 percent). However, the state still ranks poorly in annual pay and pay growth. To the state's credit, Vermont has excellent Social and Health Conditions and a good Environmental Conditions, marred only by one of the nation's worst number of superfund dumpsites.

- **Business Vitality:** Vermont's Business Vitality plummets. Entrepreneurship falls from an A to a D as Vermont has one of the nation's smallest increases in new companies (48th) and one of the lowest amounts of new business job growth (48th). Existing businesses seem to be holding their own, with few closings in an economy which is moderately well diversified.

- **Development Capacity:** The quality of Vermont's development resources are classic for the Northeast – some of the nation's best Human Resources but poor Infrastructure & Amenity Resources. Vermont has the ninth best high school graduation rate and seventh best college attainment. The state ranks in the bottom ten in most Infrastructure & Amenity Resources. Meanwhile, Technology Resources are above average and Financial Resources moderate.

- **Tax & Fiscal System:** Vermont's Tax & Fiscal System compares moderately well – it is one of the nation's most equitable, but one of the worst for equalizing local governments' different fiscal capacity.

For information on how grades and ranks are calculated, see the Methodology section.
For a detailed explanation of indexes, refer to the individual index section.

WHERE VERMONT RANKS – MEASURE BY MEASURE

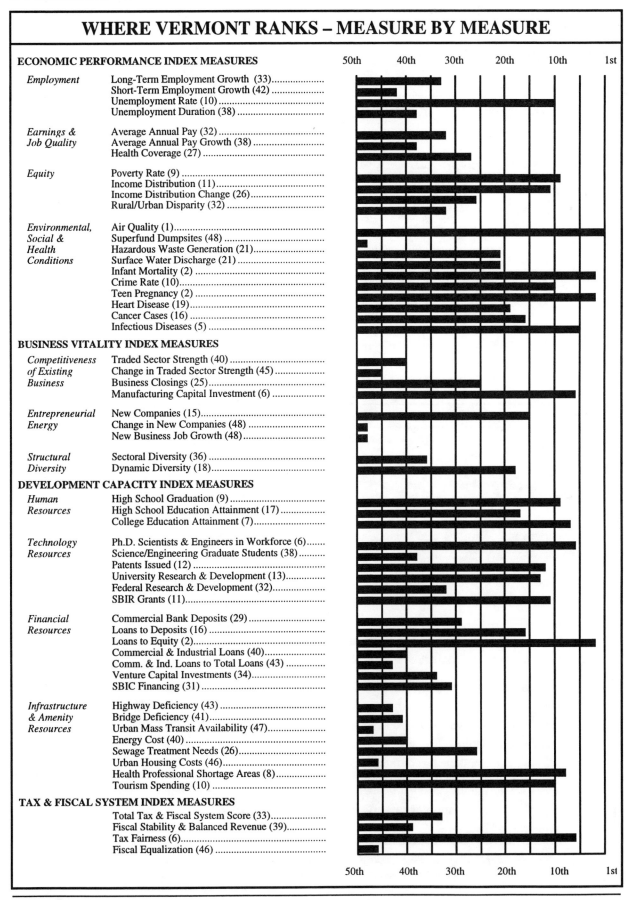

ECONOMIC PERFORMANCE INDEX MEASURES

		50th	40th	30th	20th	10th	1st

Employment
- Long-Term Employment Growth (33)
- Short-Term Employment Growth (42)
- Unemployment Rate (10)
- Unemployment Duration (38)

Earnings & Job Quality
- Average Annual Pay (32)
- Average Annual Pay Growth (38)
- Health Coverage (27)

Equity
- Poverty Rate (9)
- Income Distribution (11)
- Income Distribution Change (26)
- Rural/Urban Disparity (32)

Environmental, Social & Health Conditions
- Air Quality (1)
- Superfund Dumpsites (48)
- Hazardous Waste Generation (21)
- Surface Water Discharge (21)
- Infant Mortality (2)
- Crime Rate (10)
- Teen Pregnancy (2)
- Heart Disease (19)
- Cancer Cases (16)
- Infectious Diseases (5)

BUSINESS VITALITY INDEX MEASURES

Competitiveness of Existing Business
- Traded Sector Strength (40)
- Change in Traded Sector Strength (45)
- Business Closings (25)
- Manufacturing Capital Investment (6)

Entrepreneurial Energy
- New Companies (15)
- Change in New Companies (48)
- New Business Job Growth (48)

Structural Diversity
- Sectoral Diversity (36)
- Dynamic Diversity (18)

DEVELOPMENT CAPACITY INDEX MEASURES

Human Resources
- High School Graduation (9)
- High School Education Attainment (17)
- College Education Attainment (7)

Technology Resources
- Ph.D. Scientists & Engineers in Workforce (6)
- Science/Engineering Graduate Students (38)
- Patents Issued (12)
- University Research & Development (13)
- Federal Research & Development (32)
- SBIR Grants (11)

Financial Resources
- Commercial Bank Deposits (29)
- Loans to Deposits (16)
- Loans to Equity (2)
- Commercial & Industrial Loans (40)
- Comm. & Ind. Loans to Total Loans (43)
- Venture Capital Investments (34)
- SBIC Financing (31)

Infrastructure & Amenity Resources
- Highway Deficiency (43)
- Bridge Deficiency (41)
- Urban Mass Transit Availability (47)
- Energy Cost (40)
- Sewage Treatment Needs (26)
- Urban Housing Costs (46)
- Health Professional Shortage Areas (8)
- Tourism Spending (10)

TAX & FISCAL SYSTEM INDEX MEASURES
- Total Tax & Fiscal System Score (33)
- Fiscal Stability & Balanced Revenue (39)
- Tax Fairness (6)
- Fiscal Equalization (46)

		50th	40th	30th	20th	10th	1st

VIRGINIA 1995 REPORT CARD

ECONOMIC PERFORMANCE   A

Employment ....B
Earnings & Job Quality ....A
Equity ....B

BUSINESS VITALITY   C

Business Competitiveness ....D
Entrepreneurial Energy...D
Structural Diversity ....A

DEVELOPMENT CAPACITY   B

Human Resources...C
Technology Resources ....B
Financial Resources...B
Infrastructure & Amenity Resources.....................C

Tax & Fiscal System   –

Five Year Grade Trends

	1991	1992	1993	1994	1995
A					
B					
C					
D					
F					

Key

Economic Performance ————
Business Vitality ▬ ▬ ▬
Development Capacity ▪ ▪ ▪ ▪

- **Economic Performance:** Virginia bounces back as many of its long-term unemployed found work and wages improved. Though recent employment growth has been poor, the unemployment rate is low and few people are unemployed for a long time, implying that the economy may be at "full employment." Virginia also has one of the nation's most equitable economies (low poverty and income disparity) and a moderate quality of life.

- **Business Vitality:** The Virginia economy appears to have become more steady. A very diverse structure and an improvement in the rate of business closings could not fully offset significant deterioration in the increase of new companies and one of the worst level of jobs from new businesses. Weakening entrepreneurship counteracts improving competitiveness of the state's existing businesses, causing the state's Business Vitality grade to drop.

- **Development Capacity:** The quality of Virginia's development resources improves. Financial Resources improve due to an overall increase in loan activity and SBIC financing, while Technology Resources are above average with very high levels of Federal R&D and SBIR grants. The disparity in Human Resources may illustrate the vast differences between the northern suburbs near Washington and the rest of the state.

- **Tax & Fiscal System:** Virginia's Tax & Fiscal System ranks in the bottom 15 because it does little to equalize the different fiscal capabilities of its local governments and has a relatively unbalanced revenue-raising structure.

For information on how grades and ranks are calculated, see the Methodology section.
For a detailed explanation of indexes, refer to the individual index section.

WHERE VIRGINIA RANKS – MEASURE BY MEASURE

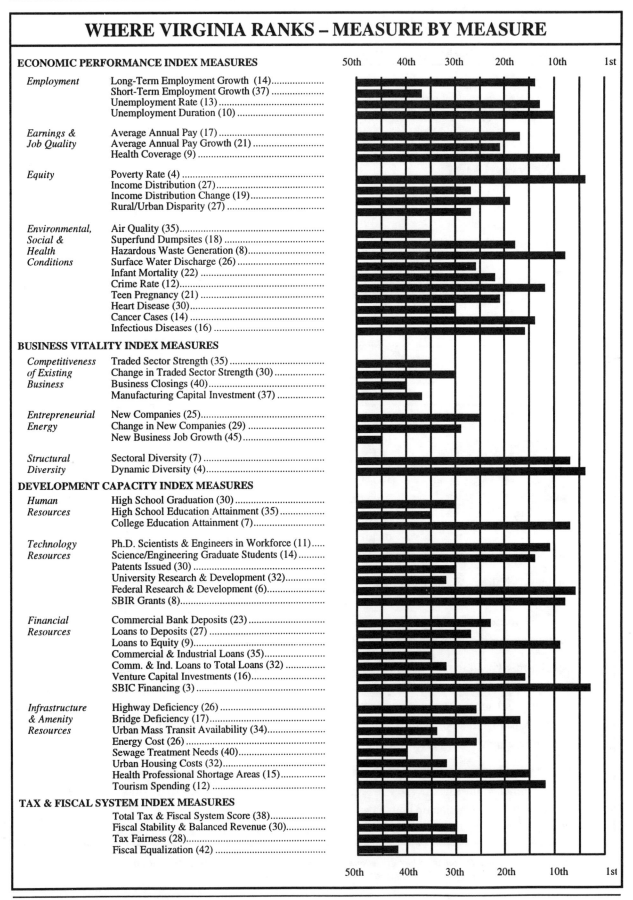

ECONOMIC PERFORMANCE INDEX MEASURES

		50th	40th	30th	20th	10th	1st

Employment
- Long-Term Employment Growth (14)
- Short-Term Employment Growth (37)
- Unemployment Rate (13)
- Unemployment Duration (10)

Earnings & Job Quality
- Average Annual Pay (17)
- Average Annual Pay Growth (21)
- Health Coverage (9)

Equity
- Poverty Rate (4)
- Income Distribution (27)
- Income Distribution Change (19)
- Rural/Urban Disparity (27)

Environmental, Social & Health Conditions
- Air Quality (35)
- Superfund Dumpsites (18)
- Hazardous Waste Generation (8)
- Surface Water Discharge (26)
- Infant Mortality (22)
- Crime Rate (12)
- Teen Pregnancy (21)
- Heart Disease (30)
- Cancer Cases (14)
- Infectious Diseases (16)

BUSINESS VITALITY INDEX MEASURES

Competitiveness of Existing Business
- Traded Sector Strength (35)
- Change in Traded Sector Strength (30)
- Business Closings (40)
- Manufacturing Capital Investment (37)

Entrepreneurial Energy
- New Companies (25)
- Change in New Companies (29)
- New Business Job Growth (45)

Structural Diversity
- Sectoral Diversity (7)
- Dynamic Diversity (4)

DEVELOPMENT CAPACITY INDEX MEASURES

Human Resources
- High School Graduation (30)
- High School Education Attainment (35)
- College Education Attainment (7)

Technology Resources
- Ph.D. Scientists & Engineers in Workforce (11)
- Science/Engineering Graduate Students (14)
- Patents Issued (30)
- University Research & Development (32)
- Federal Research & Development (6)
- SBIR Grants (8)

Financial Resources
- Commercial Bank Deposits (23)
- Loans to Deposits (27)
- Loans to Equity (9)
- Commercial & Industrial Loans (35)
- Comm. & Ind. Loans to Total Loans (32)
- Venture Capital Investments (16)
- SBIC Financing (3)

Infrastructure & Amenity Resources
- Highway Deficiency (26)
- Bridge Deficiency (17)
- Urban Mass Transit Availability (34)
- Energy Cost (26)
- Sewage Treatment Needs (40)
- Urban Housing Costs (32)
- Health Professional Shortage Areas (15)
- Tourism Spending (12)

TAX & FISCAL SYSTEM INDEX MEASURES
- Total Tax & Fiscal System Score (38)
- Fiscal Stability & Balanced Revenue (30)
- Tax Fairness (28)
- Fiscal Equalization (42)

		50th	40th	30th	20th	10th	1st

The 1995 Development Report Card

WASHINGTON 1995 REPORT CARD

ECONOMIC PERFORMANCE   D

Employment C
Earnings & Job Quality C
Equity C

BUSINESS VITALITY   B

Business Competitiveness ....B
Entrepreneurial Energy..A
Structural Diversity ....D

DEVELOPMENT CAPACITY   A

Human Resources..A
Technology Resources ....B
Financial Resources..B
Infrastructure & Amenity Resources.....................A

Tax & Fiscal System   –

Five Year Grade Trends

| | 1991 | 1992 | 1993 | 1994 | 1995 |

Key

Economic Performance	———
Business Vitality	— - -
Development Capacity	- - - -

- **Economic Performance:** Washington's grade drops to a D this year – the state's worst grade in the past five years. Earnings & Job Quality is marked by the nation's second smallest pay growth. At the same time, the job market remains flat with slow short-term job growth and a high unemployment rate. The quality of life, marked by strong health indicators, is above average, but suffers from several poor environmental rankings.

- **Business Vitality:** Washington improves a letter grade from last year and now leads the region in Business Vitality. Entrepreneurial Energy remains excellent, with the nation's highest rate of new company formations. Moreover, the state's economy shows improving diversification while its existing businesses, with a decrease in business closings, display increased competitiveness.

- **Development Capacity:** Washington's development resources are the third best in the country. Led by top ten rankings in both high school and college attainment, the state receives the highest grade for its Human Resources. In addition, with good highways and the nation's lowest energy costs, Washington's Infrastructure & Amenity Resources are also excellent. The state's Technology and Financial Resources are both above average.

- **Tax & Fiscal System:** Washington's Tax & Fiscal System is the fourth worst in the country. With an over-reliance on sales taxes – a regressive form of taxation – the state's tax structure is the second worst in the nation on both balance and fairness.

For information on how grades and ranks are calculated, see the Methodology section.
For a detailed explanation of indexes, refer to the individual index section.

WHERE WASHINGTON RANKS – MEASURE BY MEASURE

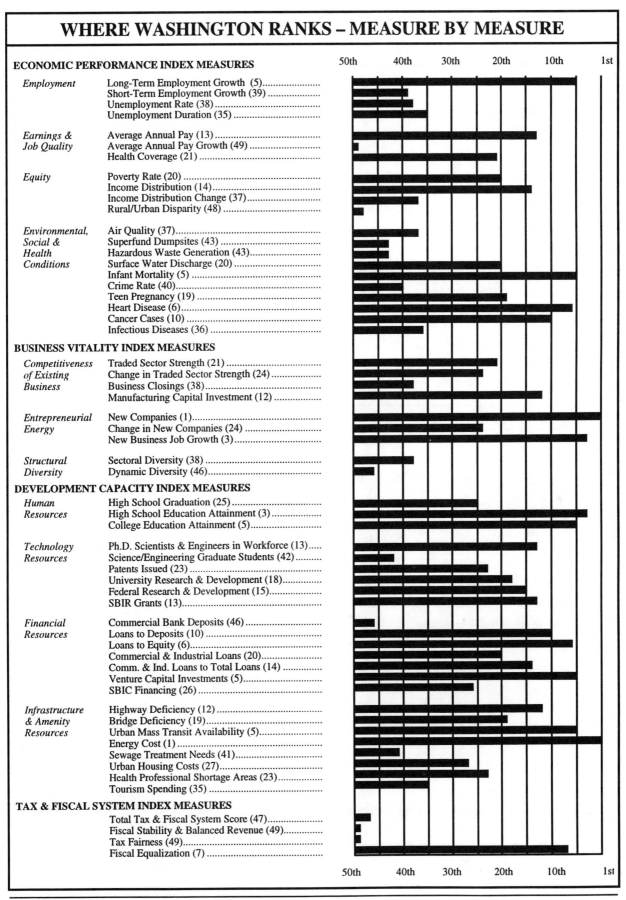

| | | 50th | 40th | 30th | 20th | 10th | 1st |

ECONOMIC PERFORMANCE INDEX MEASURES

Employment
Long-Term Employment Growth (5)
Short-Term Employment Growth (39)
Unemployment Rate (38)
Unemployment Duration (35)

Earnings & Job Quality
Average Annual Pay (13)
Average Annual Pay Growth (49)
Health Coverage (21)

Equity
Poverty Rate (20)
Income Distribution (14)
Income Distribution Change (37)
Rural/Urban Disparity (48)

Environmental, Social & Health Conditions
Air Quality (37)
Superfund Dumpsites (43)
Hazardous Waste Generation (43)
Surface Water Discharge (20)
Infant Mortality (5)
Crime Rate (40)
Teen Pregnancy (19)
Heart Disease (6)
Cancer Cases (10)
Infectious Diseases (36)

BUSINESS VITALITY INDEX MEASURES

Competitiveness of Existing Business
Traded Sector Strength (21)
Change in Traded Sector Strength (24)
Business Closings (38)
Manufacturing Capital Investment (12)

Entrepreneurial Energy
New Companies (1)
Change in New Companies (24)
New Business Job Growth (3)

Structural Diversity
Sectoral Diversity (38)
Dynamic Diversity (46)

DEVELOPMENT CAPACITY INDEX MEASURES

Human Resources
High School Graduation (25)
High School Education Attainment (3)
College Education Attainment (5)

Technology Resources
Ph.D. Scientists & Engineers in Workforce (13)
Science/Engineering Graduate Students (42)
Patents Issued (23)
University Research & Development (18)
Federal Research & Development (15)
SBIR Grants (13)

Financial Resources
Commercial Bank Deposits (46)
Loans to Deposits (10)
Loans to Equity (6)
Commercial & Industrial Loans (20)
Comm. & Ind. Loans to Total Loans (14)
Venture Capital Investments (5)
SBIC Financing (26)

Infrastructure & Amenity Resources
Highway Deficiency (12)
Bridge Deficiency (19)
Urban Mass Transit Availability (5)
Energy Cost (1)
Sewage Treatment Needs (41)
Urban Housing Costs (27)
Health Professional Shortage Areas (23)
Tourism Spending (35)

TAX & FISCAL SYSTEM INDEX MEASURES

Total Tax & Fiscal System Score (47)
Fiscal Stability & Balanced Revenue (49)
Tax Fairness (49)
Fiscal Equalization (7)

| | | 50th | 40th | 30th | 20th | 10th | 1st |

WEST VIRGINIA 1995 REPORT CARD

ECONOMIC PERFORMANCE	F

Employment ....D
Earnings & Job Quality ....F
Equity ....D

BUSINESS VITALITY	D

Business Competitiveness ....B
Entrepreneurial Energy............................C
Structural Diversity ....D

DEVELOPMENT CAPACITY	F

Human Resources...................................D
Technology Resources ....F
Financial Resources...............................D
Infrastructure & Amenity Resources.......D

Tax & Fiscal System	√

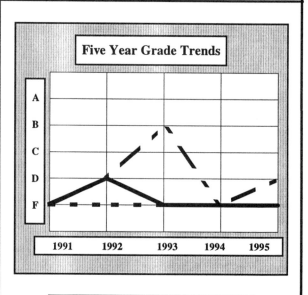

Five Year Grade Trends

1991   1992   1993   1994   1995

Key	
Economic Performance	——————
Business Vitality	— ·· — ··
Development Capacity	– – – –

- **Economic Performance:** West Virginia's efforts at improving resources and vitality have not yet been fully realized. Neighboring states have surged past the state in employment growth and increases in earnings. The good news is that the state has the excellent Social Conditions with the nation's lowest crime rate although poor Health and Environmental Conditions do impair quality of life.

- **Business Vitality:** The West Virginia economy has become more vital as increases in entrepreneurship reverberate. New company formation rates have improved and the state's level of jobs from new businesses jumped (from 40th to 23rd). At the same time, the rate of business closings was one of the lowest in the nation.

- **Development Capacity:** West Virginia's development resources remain poor. But changes are noticeable in the state's infrastructure. Its Human Resources are still poor (50th in college attainment) despite an above average high school graduation rate – young graduates may be leaving because of too few opportunities at home. Meanwhile, West Virginia's commercial banks appear to be too timid – the state has some of the nation's lowest loan activity *despite* one of the highest deposit rates (18th).

- **Tax & Fiscal System:** West Virginia's Tax & Fiscal System is one of the best at equalizing the different fiscal capabilities of its local governments, and does moderately well on the balance of its revenue-raising structure.

For information on how grades and ranks are calculated, see the Methodology section.
For a detailed explanation of indexes, refer to the individual index section.

WHERE WEST VIRGINIA RANKS – MEASURE BY MEASURE

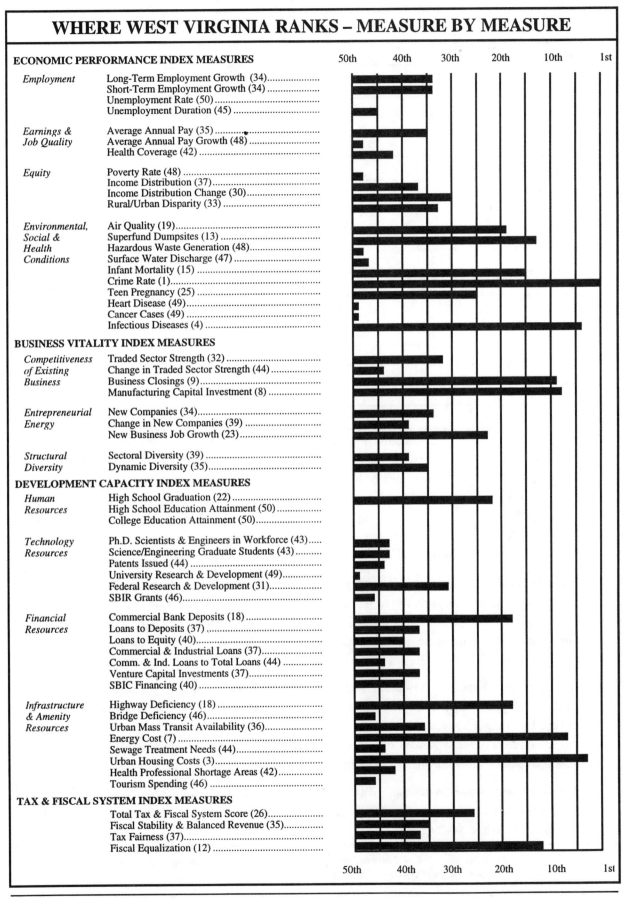

ECONOMIC PERFORMANCE INDEX MEASURES

Employment
Long-Term Employment Growth (34)
Short-Term Employment Growth (34)
Unemployment Rate (50)
Unemployment Duration (45)

Earnings & Job Quality
Average Annual Pay (35)
Average Annual Pay Growth (48)
Health Coverage (42)

Equity
Poverty Rate (48)
Income Distribution (37)
Income Distribution Change (30)
Rural/Urban Disparity (33)

Environmental, Social & Health Conditions
Air Quality (19)
Superfund Dumpsites (13)
Hazardous Waste Generation (48)
Surface Water Discharge (47)
Infant Mortality (15)
Crime Rate (1)
Teen Pregnancy (25)
Heart Disease (49)
Cancer Cases (49)
Infectious Diseases (4)

BUSINESS VITALITY INDEX MEASURES

Competitiveness of Existing Business
Traded Sector Strength (32)
Change in Traded Sector Strength (44)
Business Closings (9)
Manufacturing Capital Investment (8)

Entrepreneurial Energy
New Companies (34)
Change in New Companies (39)
New Business Job Growth (23)

Structural Diversity
Sectoral Diversity (39)
Dynamic Diversity (35)

DEVELOPMENT CAPACITY INDEX MEASURES

Human Resources
High School Graduation (22)
High School Education Attainment (50)
College Education Attainment (50)

Technology Resources
Ph.D. Scientists & Engineers in Workforce (43)
Science/Engineering Graduate Students (43)
Patents Issued (44)
University Research & Development (49)
Federal Research & Development (31)
SBIR Grants (46)

Financial Resources
Commercial Bank Deposits (18)
Loans to Deposits (37)
Loans to Equity (40)
Commercial & Industrial Loans (37)
Comm. & Ind. Loans to Total Loans (44)
Venture Capital Investments (37)
SBIC Financing (40)

Infrastructure & Amenity Resources
Highway Deficiency (18)
Bridge Deficiency (46)
Urban Mass Transit Availability (36)
Energy Cost (7)
Sewage Treatment Needs (44)
Urban Housing Costs (3)
Health Professional Shortage Areas (42)
Tourism Spending (46)

TAX & FISCAL SYSTEM INDEX MEASURES

Total Tax & Fiscal System Score (26)
Fiscal Stability & Balanced Revenue (35)
Tax Fairness (37)
Fiscal Equalization (12)

Scale: 50th 40th 30th 20th 10th 1st

WISCONSIN 1995 REPORT CARD

ECONOMIC PERFORMANCE	A
Employment	A
Earnings & Job Quality	A
Equity	B

BUSINESS VITALITY	D
Business Competitiveness	C
Entrepreneurial Energy	D
Structural Diversity	C

DEVELOPMENT CAPACITY	B
Human Resources	B
Technology Resources	C
Financial Resources	B
Infrastructure & Amenity Resources	B

Tax & Fiscal System	+

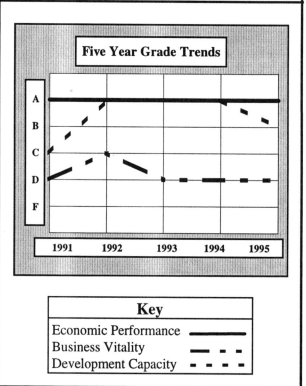

Five Year Grade Trends

1991   1992   1993   1994   1995

Key	
Economic Performance	———
Business Vitality	— - -
Development Capacity	- - - -

- **Economic Performance:** Wisconsin's performance was the second best in the nation. The state is one of two with excellent grades on Earnings & Job Quality (due to high pay growth and health coverage) and Employment (low unemployment and strong long-term job growth). Wisconsin also earns above average grades on Equity, but with an increasing poverty rate and a widening gap between rich and poor, their rank is declining. The quality of life is good – second best in the Industrial Midwest.

- **Business Vitality:** With grades unchanged from last year's below average results, Wisconsin continues to have the region's worst Business Vitality. The state's primary weakness is Enterpreneurial Energy, which is marked by the nation's third worst ranking on new company formation. While the state ranks in the top ten for fewest business closings, the overall Competitiveness of Existing Business is only average.

- **Development Capacity:** Wisconsin's development resources are strong, yet marginal changes result in a B grade after three straight years of As. Financial Resources are particularly strong, marked by strong lending activity and a top ten ranking on SBIC financing. Human Resources and Infrastructure & Amenity Resources also rank above average, but with a sharp drop in rankings on both college education attainment and highway deficiencies, both have weakened since last year.

- **Tax & Fiscal System:** Wisconsin's Tax & Fiscal System ranks among the nation's top ten. The state ranks above average on the stability of its revenue raising structure and is among the top twenty for the fairness of its taxes.

For information on how grades and ranks are calculated, see the Methodology section.
For a detailed explanation of indexes, refer to the individual index section.

WHERE WISCONSIN RANKS – MEASURE BY MEASURE

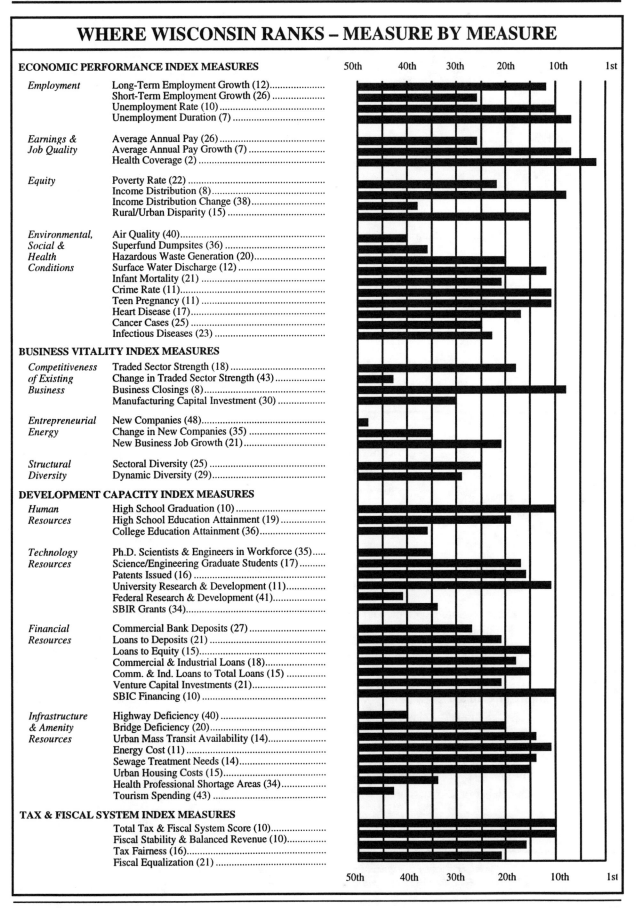

ECONOMIC PERFORMANCE INDEX MEASURES

Employment
Long-Term Employment Growth (12)
Short-Term Employment Growth (26)
Unemployment Rate (10)
Unemployment Duration (7)

Earnings & Job Quality
Average Annual Pay (26)
Average Annual Pay Growth (7)
Health Coverage (2)

Equity
Poverty Rate (22)
Income Distribution (8)
Income Distribution Change (38)
Rural/Urban Disparity (15)

Environmental, Social & Health Conditions
Air Quality (40)
Superfund Dumpsites (36)
Hazardous Waste Generation (20)
Surface Water Discharge (12)
Infant Mortality (21)
Crime Rate (11)
Teen Pregnancy (11)
Heart Disease (17)
Cancer Cases (25)
Infectious Diseases (23)

BUSINESS VITALITY INDEX MEASURES

Competitiveness of Existing Business
Traded Sector Strength (18)
Change in Traded Sector Strength (43)
Business Closings (8)
Manufacturing Capital Investment (30)

Entrepreneurial Energy
New Companies (48)
Change in New Companies (35)
New Business Job Growth (21)

Structural Diversity
Sectoral Diversity (25)
Dynamic Diversity (29)

DEVELOPMENT CAPACITY INDEX MEASURES

Human Resources
High School Graduation (10)
High School Education Attainment (19)
College Education Attainment (36)

Technology Resources
Ph.D. Scientists & Engineers in Workforce (35)
Science/Engineering Graduate Students (17)
Patents Issued (16)
University Research & Development (11)
Federal Research & Development (41)
SBIR Grants (34)

Financial Resources
Commercial Bank Deposits (27)
Loans to Deposits (21)
Loans to Equity (15)
Commercial & Industrial Loans (18)
Comm. & Ind. Loans to Total Loans (15)
Venture Capital Investments (21)
SBIC Financing (10)

Infrastructure & Amenity Resources
Highway Deficiency (40)
Bridge Deficiency (20)
Urban Mass Transit Availability (14)
Energy Cost (11)
Sewage Treatment Needs (14)
Urban Housing Costs (15)
Health Professional Shortage Areas (34)
Tourism Spending (43)

TAX & FISCAL SYSTEM INDEX MEASURES

Total Tax & Fiscal System Score (10)
Fiscal Stability & Balanced Revenue (10)
Tax Fairness (16)
Fiscal Equalization (21)

Chart scale: 50th, 40th, 30th, 20th, 10th, 1st

WYOMING 1995 REPORT CARD

ECONOMIC PERFORMANCE	B

Employment C
Earnings & Job Quality C
Equity ....A

BUSINESS VITALITY	A

Business Competitiveness ....A
Entrepreneurial Energy...B
Structural Diversity C

DEVELOPMENT CAPACITY	C

Human Resources...B
Technology Resources C
Financial Resources...F
Infrastructure & Amenity Resources ....B

Tax & Fiscal System	-

Five Year Grade Trends

Key	
Economic Performance	————
Business Vitality	— - -
Development Capacity	▪ ▪ ▪ ▪

- **Economic Performance:** The past couple of years have seen Wyoming's economy improving – not only in employment (17th in short-term employment growth, 44th in long-term) but also in wages (as the annual pay growth goes from 50th to 10th). The end result is the nation's smallest gap between rich and poor, (the state ranks 1st in income distribution *and* change in income distribution). The best overall Environmental, Social & Health Conditions illustrate that an excellent quality of life accompanies Wyoming's flowering economic opportunities.

- **Business Vitality:** Strong entrepreneurship, led by huge increases in new business job growth (1989-1993) and the eighth highest rate of new companies push Wyoming's Business Vitality to a top grade. Meanwhile, Structural Diversity remains near average and the income from businesses competing out of state (the traded sector) grew faster than any other state.

- **Development Capacity:** Wyoming's development resources improved – Financial Resources are weak as loan activity is very low despite high deposit levels (48th in loans to deposits and 39th in total commercial and industrial loans, yet 13th in deposits per capita). Human Resources are excellent (especially high school graduation and attainment), and Infrastructure & Amenity Resources are good (led by low energy costs and few deficient bridges). Technology Resources are moderate, mostly due to the high number of scientists in the work force and graduate school.

- **Tax & Fiscal System:** Wyoming's big weakness may be its unbalanced revenue generating system and relatively inequitable tax system, limiting its ability to adapt to changes and crises.

For information on how grades and ranks are calculated, see the Methodology section.
For a detailed explanation of indexes, refer to the individual index section.

WHERE WYOMING RANKS – MEASURE BY MEASURE

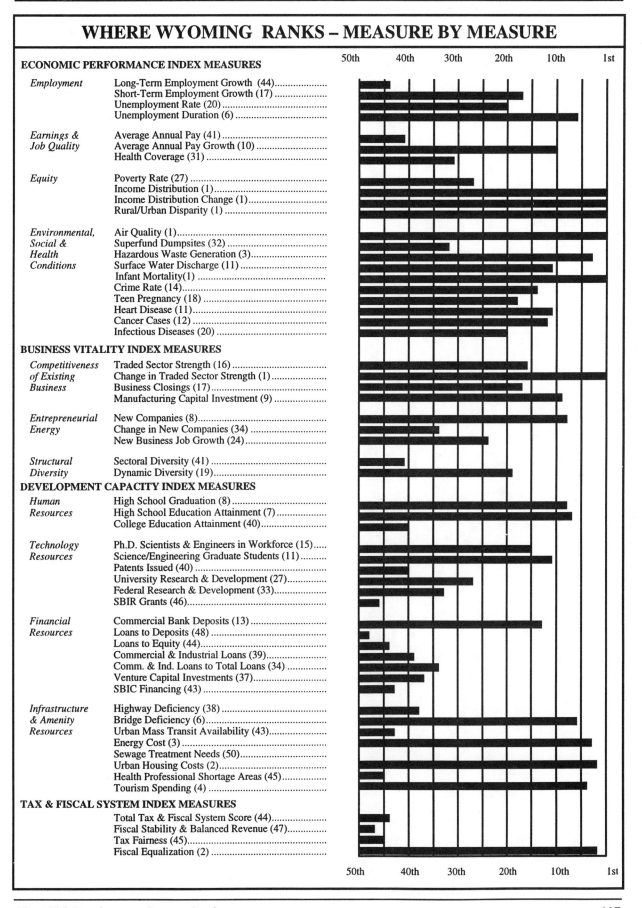

ECONOMIC PERFORMANCE INDEX MEASURES

		50th	40th	30th	20th	10th	1st

Employment
- Long-Term Employment Growth (44)
- Short-Term Employment Growth (17)
- Unemployment Rate (20)
- Unemployment Duration (6)

Earnings & Job Quality
- Average Annual Pay (41)
- Average Annual Pay Growth (10)
- Health Coverage (31)

Equity
- Poverty Rate (27)
- Income Distribution (1)
- Income Distribution Change (1)
- Rural/Urban Disparity (1)

Environmental, Social & Health Conditions
- Air Quality (1)
- Superfund Dumpsites (32)
- Hazardous Waste Generation (3)
- Surface Water Discharge (11)
- Infant Mortality (1)
- Crime Rate (14)
- Teen Pregnancy (18)
- Heart Disease (11)
- Cancer Cases (12)
- Infectious Diseases (20)

BUSINESS VITALITY INDEX MEASURES

Competitiveness of Existing Business
- Traded Sector Strength (16)
- Change in Traded Sector Strength (1)
- Business Closings (17)
- Manufacturing Capital Investment (9)

Entrepreneurial Energy
- New Companies (8)
- Change in New Companies (34)
- New Business Job Growth (24)

Structural Diversity
- Sectoral Diversity (41)
- Dynamic Diversity (19)

DEVELOPMENT CAPACITY INDEX MEASURES

Human Resources
- High School Graduation (8)
- High School Education Attainment (7)
- College Education Attainment (40)

Technology Resources
- Ph.D. Scientists & Engineers in Workforce (15)
- Science/Engineering Graduate Students (11)
- Patents Issued (40)
- University Research & Development (27)
- Federal Research & Development (33)
- SBIR Grants (46)

Financial Resources
- Commercial Bank Deposits (13)
- Loans to Deposits (48)
- Loans to Equity (44)
- Commercial & Industrial Loans (39)
- Comm. & Ind. Loans to Total Loans (34)
- Venture Capital Investments (37)
- SBIC Financing (43)

Infrastructure & Amenity Resources
- Highway Deficiency (38)
- Bridge Deficiency (6)
- Urban Mass Transit Availability (43)
- Energy Cost (3)
- Sewage Treatment Needs (50)
- Urban Housing Costs (2)
- Health Professional Shortage Areas (45)
- Tourism Spending (4)

TAX & FISCAL SYSTEM INDEX MEASURES
- Total Tax & Fiscal System Score (44)
- Fiscal Stability & Balanced Revenue (47)
- Tax Fairness (45)
- Fiscal Equalization (2)

		50th	40th	30th	20th	10th	1st

Methodology

The Report Card Framework

The Development Report Card's three index framework was based on the findings from an extensive literature review about the dynamics of development and economic growth in today's economy. The framework and indicators were reviewed by a technical advisory board composed of economic experts and representatives from business, labor, government, and community development organizations. CFED also drew upon its own hands-on-expertise in technical assistance and strategic policy design.

The Report Card weighs each measure equally in the calculation of each individual subindex. No assumption is made about one measure being more important to a subindex than the others. Similarly, each subindex is weighted equally in the compilation of each of the three major indexes. However, it is important to note that because each subindex is composed of a different number of measures (anywhere from two to eight), individual measures do not effect major indexes equivalently. For instance, Business Vitality is composed of three subindexes, one of which (Entrepreneurial Energy) is composed of three measures while another (Competitiveness of Existing Business) is composed of four measures. Thus each measure in Entrepreneurial Energy counts 1/9 towards the major Business Vitality Index (1/3 x 1/3), while each measure in Competitiveness of Existing Business counts 1/12 towards Business Vitality (1/4 x 1/3).

Readers should be aware that recent fiscal pressures on federal departments have made it more difficult than usual to update several data measures, and that this may become a greater problem in the future.

Cautions and Caveats

No Grade Point Average: Although a single summary grade would help capture the public imagination, it also unduly telescopes the very complex process of development and masks important changes, as well as each state's strengths and weaknesses. Thus, we provide grades only for individual indexes and subindexes.

The Quality of Data: The measures available to diagnose the health of state economies vary in quality and precision. Since we are driven by what needs to be known, not just by what is readily known, we sometimes have to resort to proxy measures – indirect ways of getting answers to important questions – because no one has asked or collected data on the measures before. It is also our policy to be as consistent as possible in the measures from year to year. However, in a few cases, because databases are discontinued, interrupted, or updated only biannually, we have elected to switch sources or repeat data from last year in order to maintain the highest data quality. The changes in this year's Report Card are explained in the Appendix at the end of the book.

The Timeliness of Data: Data provide a snapshot of the recent past, so some changes may have occurred, particularly for job-related measures like unemployment rate and employment growth, by the time data is available. The timeliness of each measure may also vary due to how it was collected. Economists call these "lags" in the data. Since the Report Card is based on, and thus limited by, available and collected measures, changes in economies which are dramatic by anecdote may appear slight in the Report Card.

Making the Grades

Here's how the Report Card grades are calculated:

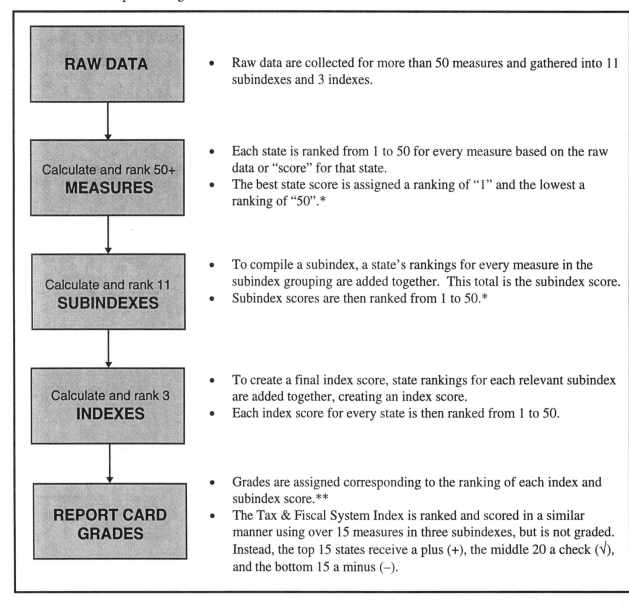

RAW DATA

- Raw data are collected for more than 50 measures and gathered into 11 subindexes and 3 indexes.

Calculate and rank 50+
MEASURES

- Each state is ranked from 1 to 50 for every measure based on the raw data or "score" for that state.
- The best state score is assigned a ranking of "1" and the lowest a ranking of "50".*

Calculate and rank 11
SUBINDEXES

- To compile a subindex, a state's rankings for every measure in the subindex grouping are added together. This total is the subindex score.
- Subindex scores are then ranked from 1 to 50.*

Calculate and rank 3
INDEXES

- To create a final index score, state rankings for each relevant subindex are added together, creating an index score.
- Each index score for every state is then ranked from 1 to 50.

REPORT CARD GRADES

- Grades are assigned corresponding to the ranking of each index and subindex score.**
- The Tax & Fiscal System Index is ranked and scored in a similar manner using over 15 measures in three subindexes, but is not graded. Instead, the top 15 states receive a plus (+), the middle 20 a check (√), and the bottom 15 a minus (–).

* *When a tie occurs, both states receive the same rank, and the next highest scoring state is ranked as if a tie had not occurred. For example, if two states both have the best score, they both receive a rank of 1 and the next best state is ranked 3.*

**	Rank	Grade
	1-10	A
	11-20	B
	21-35	C
	36-45	D
	46-50	F

Economic Performance Index

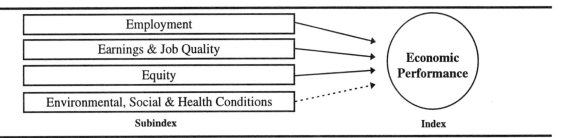

Employment	
Earnings & Job Quality	→
Equity	
Environmental, Social & Health Conditions	

Subindex   **Economic Performance**   **Index**

The Economic Performance Index is based on eleven individual measures gathered into three subindexes. For informational purposes, ten measures on environmental, social, and health conditions are also included.

> *The Economic Performance Index is a thorough review of a state's "profits and losses."*

Employment Subindex

The Employment subindex determines the extent to which the economy is providing work for those who seek it by measuring:

- *Long-Term Employment Growth*
- *Short-Term Employment Growth*
- *Unemployment Rate*
- *Unemployment Duration*

Earnings & Job Quality Subindex

This subindex determines how well people are compensated for the work they do based on the following three measures:

- *Average Annual Pay*
- *Average Annual Pay Growth*
- *Health Coverage*

Equity Subindex

Equity, or the extent to which the opportunity to attain a high standard of living is widely shared, is based on four measures:

- *Poverty Rate*
- *Income Distribution*
- *Income Distribution Change*
- *Rural/Urban Disparity*

Environmental, Social & Health Conditions Subindex

This subindex provides insights into the quality of life where people live. Because environmental, social, and health conditions are still too imprecise to characterize the overall quality of life, these measures are *not* included when grading the states. The three main areas explored are:

Environmental Quality:
- *Air Quality*
- *Superfund Dumpsites*
- *Hazardous Waste Generation*
- *Surface Water Discharge*

Social Conditions:
- *Infant Mortality*
- *Crime Rate*
- *Teen Pregnancy*

Health Conditions:
- *Heart Disease*
- *Cancer Cases*
- *Infectious Diseases*

Data tables, measures, and sources for each subindex can be found on the pages that follow.

Employment Data

State	Long-Term Employment		Short-Term Employment		Unemployment Rate		Unemployment Duration	
	%	Rank	%	Rank	%	Rank	%	Rank
Alabama	12.56	28	3.58	16	6.0	31	14.4	19
Alaska	22.71	7	2.55	24	7.8	47	19.0	32
Arizona	27.27	4	8.44	2	6.4	38	12.1	11
Arkansas	16.65	18	4.77	10	5.3	20	13.4	16
California	13.66	23	1.84	35	8.6	49	23.3	41
Colorado	21.78	8	6.16	6	4.2	7	16.7	24
Connecticut	-2.57	49	-1.98	48	5.6	26	32.4	50
Delaware	17.74	15	2.82	23	4.9	13	17.5	27
Florida	21.10	9	2.99	22	6.6	41	20.3	35
Georgia	20.02	11	3.90	12	5.2	19	19.9	33
Hawaii	17.09	17	-1.08	47	6.1	33	9.3	3
Idaho	29.17	3	8.56	1	5.6	26	12.9	14
Illinois	8.04	37	2.35	27	5.7	28	22.2	39
Indiana	12.94	25	4.20	11	4.9	13	11.0	9
Iowa	12.71	26	0.33	42	3.7	3	12.9	14
Kansas	7.87	38	0.16	44	5.3	20	15.8	21
Kentucky	12.58	27	2.19	30	5.4	23	18.1	29
Louisiana	3.12	43	2.24	29	8.0	48	17.1	26
Maine	6.78	40	-2.24	50	7.4	46	27.2	44
Maryland	13.66	23	2.32	28	5.1	17	22.3	40
Massachusetts	1.60	45	0.84	41	6.0	31	27.8	45
Michigan	11.69	29	2.52	25	5.9	30	16.6	23
Minnesota	16.63	19	4.86	8	4.0	6	15.7	20
Mississippi	14.90	20	3.08	21	6.6	41	14.2	17
Missouri	7.42	39	3.14	20	4.9	13	17.7	28
Montana	10.96	30	3.75	13	5.1	17	12.3	12
Nebraska	10.23	31	1.92	32	2.9	1	6.8	1
Nevada	46.20	1	6.56	4	6.2	34	18.3	30
New Hampshire	9.91	32	3.45	18	4.6	9	25.3	43
New Jersey	0.19	47	1.56	38	6.8	43	28.4	48
New Mexico	17.21	16	3.59	15	6.3	36	16.3	22
New York	1.35	46	0.11	45	6.9	44	28.2	47
North Carolina	14.73	21	1.92	32	4.4	8	12.3	12
North Dakota	3.51	42	4.85	9	3.9	5	9.6	5
Ohio	8.82	35	2.07	31	5.5	25	21.5	37
Oklahoma	-1.49	48	1.26	40	5.8	29	18.3	30
Oregon	24.82	6	5.00	7	5.4	23	14.3	18
Pennsylvania	4.13	41	-0.07	46	6.2	34	24.0	42
Rhode Island	-3.69	50	-2.08	49	7.1	45	31.1	49
South Carolina	14.66	22	1.78	36	6.3	36	20.0	34
South Dakota	8.71	36	3.72	14	3.3	2	7.3	2
Tennessee	20.47	10	7.73	3	4.8	12	10.6	7
Texas	18.60	13	3.31	19	6.4	38	16.8	25
Utah	32.30	2	6.35	5	3.7	3	9.5	4
Vermont	9.71	33	0.33	42	4.7	10	21.9	38
Virginia	18.28	14	1.62	37	4.9	13	11.3	10
Washington	25.57	5	1.52	39	6.4	38	20.3	35
West Virginia	9.47	34	1.85	34	8.9	50	27.8	45
Wisconsin	19.20	12	2.50	26	4.7	10	10.6	7
Wyoming	3.06	44	3.51	17	5.3	20	10.0	6

Employment Data Sources

The most basic measure of the economic health of a state is whether people can find work. Four measures of employment are used in this subindex:

- *Long-Term Employment Growth*
- *Short-Term Employment Growth*
- *Unemployment Rate*
- *Unemployment Duration*

Long-Term Employment Growth

Long-term employment growth shows how much an economy is expanding, a key indicator of economic health. This is *not* a measure of job creation, but rather of state residents gainfully employed. Measuring employment growth allows us to look at both employees and proprietors and to use more recent comparable state data than is available for job growth. Employment changes also better reflect the impact of growth on local citizens. Neither employment nor job growth tells us anything about the quality of jobs people are getting, or who is hired – and who isn't. To measure employment growth across similar cyclical conditions, we measure the change from the nation's emergence from the early 1980s recession to its emergence from the most recent one.

Measure: Percentage change in annual average employment, by place of residence, from the year 1986 to the year 1994.
Source: U.S. Department of Labor, Bureau of Labor Statistics, Local Area Unemployment Statistics. Washington, DC: February 1995.

Short-Term Employment Growth

To reflect the impact of recent events on the trend uncovered by long-term employment growth, we measure short-term changes in employment over the last year.

Measure: Percentage of change in average annual employment, by place of residence, 1993-1994.
Source: Same as Long-Term Employment Growth.

Unemployment Rate

The most commonly used measure of the mismatch between the number of jobs and job-seekers is the unemployment rate – the number of people looking for work or waiting to be called back to a job from which they have been laid off. Careful consideration should be given because this measure doesn't tell us anything about those who have never been a part of the labor force or those that have stopped looking entirely.

Measure: Annual average unemployment rate, 1994.
Source: U.S. Department of Labor, Bureau of Labor Statistics, Local Area Unemployment Statistics. Washington, DC: February 1995.

Unemployment Duration

Unemployment lasting for longer periods of time may indicate that the economy is failing to produce jobs, that the jobs being created and the skills of the workforce don't match, or that the hiring of some kinds of workers is being restricted in some way. Once again, because only those still looking for work are counted as unemployed, we do not have a way to identify those who have stopped looking.

Measure: Percentage of unemployed members of the labor force who were unemployed more than 27 weeks, annual average, 1993.
Source: U.S. Department of Labor, Bureau of Labor Statistics, *Geographic Profile of Employment and Unemployment 1993*. Washington, DC: GPO, September 1994 (Bulletin 2446).

Earnings & Job Quality Data

State	Average Annual Pay		Average Annual Pay Growth		Health Coverage	
	$	Rank	%	Rank	%	Rank
Alabama	22,786	30	2.0	23	58.7	35
Alaska	32,336	4	1.6	36	59.3	33
Arizona	23,501	28	1.5	38	59.8	32
Arkansas	20,337	46	1.1	46	53.2	46
California	29,468	6	2.0	23	53.3	45
Colorado	25,682	15	2.6	7	62.5	25
Connecticut	33,169	1	1.7	35	73.1	1
Delaware	27,143	10	2.1	22	69.6	5
Florida	23,571	27	1.8	32	52.8	47
Georgia	24,867	22	2.0	23	58.6	38
Hawaii	26,325	11	3.1	3	68.8	6
Idaho	21,188	44	2.6	7	61.7	28
Illinois	28,420	7	1.8	32	63.1	23
Indiana	24,109	23	2.3	17	67.0	9
Iowa	21,441	43	2.4	14	66.6	13
Kansas	22,430	34	2.0	23	65.3	17
Kentucky	22,170	37	1.4	42	58.7	35
Louisiana	22,632	33	1.3	44	46.3	50
Maine	22,026	38	1.0	47	61.0	29
Maryland	27,684	9	2.0	23	65.3	17
Massachusetts	30,229	5	1.9	30	66.4	14
Michigan	28,260	8	2.9	4	66.1	15
Minnesota	25,711	14	1.5	38	66.7	12
Mississippi	19,694	48	2.4	14	52.1	49
Missouri	23,898	25	1.5	38	65.6	16
Montana	19,932	47	2.9	4	57.6	40
Nebraska	20,815	45	2.3	17	62.9	24
Nevada	25,461	18	2.9	4	65.1	19
New Hampshire	24,962	20	0.4	50	70.8	4
New Jersey	32,716	3	2.0	23	64.6	20
New Mexico	21,731	42	3.2	2	52.5	48
New York	32,919	2	1.6	36	60.4	30
North Carolina	22,770	31	2.3	17	62.5	25
North Dakota	19,382	49	2.3	17	56.9	41
Ohio	25,339	19	2.0	23	66.9	11
Oklahoma	22,003	39	1.4	42	54.1	44
Oregon	24,093	24	2.5	10	63.9	22
Pennsylvania	26,274	12	1.9	30	67.8	8
Rhode Island	24,889	21	2.4	14	68.2	7
South Carolina	21,928	40	2.5	10	58.8	34
South Dakota	18,613	50	3.3	1	58.6	38
Tennessee	23,368	29	2.5	10	58.7	35
Texas	25,545	16	1.8	32	55.1	43
Utah	22,250	36	1.2	45	71.2	3
Vermont	22,704	32	1.5	38	61.8	27
Virginia	25,496	17	2.2	21	67.0	9
Washington	25,760	13	0.8	49	64.0	21
West Virginia	22,373	35	0.9	48	55.2	42
Wisconsin	23,610	26	2.6	7	71.6	2
Wyoming	21,745	41	2.5	10	60.2	31

Earnings & Job Quality Data Sources

The Earnings and Job Quality subindex explores the issue of whether America's economic restructuring is replacing well-paid, low-skill jobs with low-paying, moderate skill jobs. It goes beyond how many jobs are being created to gauge how good the jobs are in terms of wages and benefits by measuring the following:

- *Average Annual Pay*
- *Average Annual Pay Growth*
- *Health Coverage*

Average Annual Pay

Average annual pay is the total annual pay of all employees covered by unemployment insurance, divided by the average number of employees. In addition to wages, payroll data includes bonuses, tips and gratuities, paid vacation, and employer contributions to deferred compensation plans.

With few exceptions, all full-time and part-time employees in covered firms are reported, including production and sales workers, corporation officials, executives, supervisory personnel, and clerical workers. Excluded, due to limits on data, are agricultural workers on small farms, most railroad employees, most non-profit organization employees, self-employed workers, and all members of the Armed Forces.

Measure: Average annual pay (in dollars) for all workers covered by unemployment insurance, by location of establishment, 1993, preliminary data.

Source: U.S. Department of Labor, Bureau of Labor Statistics. "Average Annual Pay by State and Industry, 1993." *USDL 94-454 News Release*. Washington, DC: September 23, 1994.

Average Annual Pay Growth

This measure examines how fast average annual pay in a state is growing from year to year. Like employment growth, this measure aims to portray how much improvement, if any, is occurring in each state's economy.

Measure: Percentage of change in average annual pay for all workers covered by unemployment insurance, by location of establishment, 1992-1993.

Source: Same as Average Annual Pay.

Health Coverage

One important clue to job quality is the extent to which state economies are meeting the benefit needs of their citizens, which varies significantly from state to state. Of these benefits, employer-sponsored health coverage is perhaps the most important.

Measure: Percentage of non-elderly population covered by employer-based health plans, 1993.

Source: Employee Benefit Research Institute. *Sources of Health Insurance and Characteristics of the Uninsured.* Washington, DC: Employee Benefit Research Institute, February 1995.

Equity Data

State	Poverty Rate		Income Distribution		Income Distribution Change		Rural/Urban Disparity	
	%	Rank	Ratio	Rank	%	Rank	Score	Rank
Alabama	17.4	38	9.53	35	-8.00	9	13	13
Alaska	9.1	3	7.64	13	-18.60	2	30	30
Arizona	15.4	33	9.51	33	2.80	24	17	17
Arkansas	20.0	46	8.81	26	-8.40	8	6	6
California	18.2	42	11.28	45	14.20	42	50	50
Colorado	9.9	7	7.63	12	-10.80	4	23	23
Connecticut	8.5	2	7.18	6	7.40	29	39	39
Delaware	10.2	10	7.95	18	13.40	41	20	20
Florida	17.8	41	9.52	34	5.80	28	4	4
Georgia	13.5	28	10.97	43	2.20	23	21	21
Hawaii	8.0	1	7.87	16	-11.10	3	46	46
Idaho	13.1	24	7.51	9	8.00	31	16	16
Illinois	13.6	29	9.91	38	3.20	25	49	49
Indiana	12.2	21	8.41	21	-2.60	14	26	26
Iowa	10.3	11	6.54	3	-6.40	10	40	40
Kansas	13.1	24	8.08	19	0.80	19	18	18
Kentucky	20.4	47	12.82	49	27.80	50	2	2
Louisiana	26.4	50	14.07	50	-5.90	11	28	28
Maine	15.4	33	7.88	17	-2.50	15	5	5
Maryland	9.7	4	8.22	20	1.50	22	7	7
Massachusetts	10.7	13	8.90	28	1.20	21	14	14
Michigan	15.4	33	9.33	31	-0.80	17	43	43
Minnesota	11.6	18	8.91	29	11.90	36	38	38
Mississippi	24.7	49	11.97	48	4.50	27	29	29
Missouri	16.1	36	9.94	39	20.90	49	45	45
Montana	14.9	32	7.41	7	-10.00	5	8	8
Nebraska	10.3	11	6.48	2	-8.60	7	2	2
Nevada	9.8	6	8.59	25	15.20	44	47	47
New Hampshire	9.9	7	7.59	10	16.60	45	34	34
New Jersey	10.9	15	9.56	36	14.60	43	25	25
New Mexico	17.4	38	11.47	46	11.80	35	31	31
New York	16.4	37	11.53	47	9.40	33	44	44
North Carolina	14.4	31	9.44	32	12.90	39	41	41
North Dakota	11.2	16	7.15	5	-8.80	6	42	42
Ohio	13.0	23	9.20	30	10.10	34	11	11
Oklahoma	19.9	45	10.07	40	-0.30	18	22	22
Oregon	11.8	19	8.53	23	17.20	46	34	34
Pennsylvania	13.2	26	8.45	22	8.30	32	19	19
Rhode Island	11.2	16	8.56	24	17.90	47	36	36
South Carolina	18.7	43	11.16	44	19.00	48	10	10
South Dakota	14.2	30	7.75	15	-2.30	16	9	9
Tennessee	19.6	44	10.18	42	-3.70	13	24	24
Texas	17.4	38	10.12	41	-5.20	12	37	37
Utah	10.7	13	6.65	4	13.10	40	11	11
Vermont	10.0	9	7.60	11	4.40	26	32	32
Virginia	9.7	4	8.83	27	0.80	19	27	27
Washington	12.1	20	7.71	14	12.10	37	48	48
West Virginia	22.2	48	9.89	37	7.80	30	33	33
Wisconsin	12.6	22	7.45	8	12.80	38	15	15
Wyoming	13.3	27	6.03	1	-19.50	1	1	1

Equity Data Sources

Any evaluation of a state's economy must consider the distribution of opportunities to gain employment and income. To measure how widely economic opportunity is shared, four measures are used:

- *Poverty Rate*
- *Income Distribution*
- *Income Distribution Change*
- *Rural/Urban Disparity*

Poverty Rate

The number of individuals in a state who live below the federally-established poverty line presents a concrete measure of performance in general, and of equity in particular. An economy with a high percentage of people below this line – whether they work or not – is not fulfilling its basic purpose of providing people with opportunities for a better life.

Measure: Percentage of population living in households with incomes below the poverty line, 1993.

Source: U.S. Department of Commerce, Bureau of the Census. Data from March 1994 Current Population Survey. Washington, DC: 1994.

Income Distribution

This figure measures the variation between the wealthiest 20 percent and the poorest 20 percent of the population. The greater the variation, the less equitable the distribution of income.

Measure: Ratio of mean income of families (family income) in the top quintile to mean income of families in the bottom quintile, 1991-1993.

Source: Jon Haveman. Purdue University: Calculations based on merged U.S. Current Population Survey data tapes from 1992, 1993, and 1994.

Income Distribution Change

To capture a sense of whether economic development is increasing or decreasing the opportunity for people to obtain the elements of a better life, we examine the change in a state's income distribution from the late 1980s to the beginning of this decade.

Measure: Percentage of change in the ratio of mean income of families in the top quintile (family income) to mean income of families in the bottom quintile, from the 1988-1990 ratio to 1991-1993 ratio.

Source: Same as Income Distribution. Calculations based on merged U.S. Current Population Survey data tapes from March 1989, 1990, 1991, 1992, 1993, and 1994.

Rural/Urban Disparity

Economic development also needs to be widely shared across a state. This measure presents a composite score of the disparities in economic performance indicators between urban and rural areas in a state.

Measure: Composite index score of six economic performance measures that compare absolute value differences between nonmetropolitan and metropolitan counties within a state. Measures include long-term employment growth (1987-1993), short-term employment growth (1992-1993), unemployment rate (1993), average earnings (1992), long-term earnings growth (1987-1992), and short-term earnings growth (1991-1992).

Source: CFED: "Rural/Urban Disparity Index." *The 1995 Development Report Card for the States.* Washington, DC: 1995.

Note: See the Appendix: *Rural/Urban Disparity Index* for details and an explanation of New Jersey's score.

Environmental, Social & Health Conditions Data (part 1)

State	Air Quality		Superfund Dumpsites		Hazardous Waste Generation		Surface Water Discharge	
	Score	Rank	#	Rank	Metric Tons	Rank	%	Rank
Alabama	0.18	15	3.08	8	136.91	27	6.88	27
Alaska	0.79	28	13.11	46	42.35	16	1.89	8
Arizona	1.57	38	2.45	5	42.21	15	5.00	16
Arkansas	0.00	1	4.90	25	315.35	33	8.00	29
California	5.35	50	3.05	7	425.46	35	1.21	6
Colorado	1.15	31	4.92	26	141.65	28	4.67	14
Connecticut	4.30	47	4.57	24	632.68	37	9.57	36
Delaware	2.73	42	26.76	50	29.76	12	21.88	50
Florida	0.72	27	4.16	21	38.33	13	5.24	18
Georgia	1.15	31	1.84	3	114.43	23	2.76	9
Hawaii	0.00	1	3.39	15	1.79	2	0.00	1
Idaho	0.00	1	8.85	41	4,186.78	47	1.45	7
Illinois	3.17	44	3.15	10	1,123.94	40	4.48	13
Indiana	0.81	29	5.74	30	291.24	31	14.36	46
Iowa	0.00	1	6.71	34	45.14	17	9.57	36
Kansas	0.00	1	3.92	20	1,288.60	42	12.28	43
Kentucky	0.65	21	5.22	28	131.33	24	13.11	44
Louisiana	0.45	17	3.24	11	7,405.03	50	8.70	32
Maine	1.24	35	8.06	37	9.44	5	8.16	31
Maryland	3.37	46	2.59	6	15.62	9	6.19	24
Massachusetts	3.32	45	4.97	27	45.86	19	10.69	39
Michigan	1.15	31	8.11	38	3,401.21	45	10.38	38
Minnesota	0.51	18	8.97	42	1,277.67	41	6.17	23
Mississippi	0.00	1	1.87	4	3,106.03	44	1.18	5
Missouri	0.69	26	4.17	22	133.12	25	9.56	35
Montana	0.05	14	10.47	44	13.83	6	0.00	1
Nebraska	0.00	1	6.17	31	22.56	11	5.97	22
Nevada	0.65	21	0.68	1	7.75	4	9.09	34
New Hampshire	0.68	25	14.91	49	15.65	10	8.82	33
New Jersey	5.03	49	13.54	47	3,800.35	46	14.00	45
New Mexico	0.30	16	6.67	33	100.74	22	0.00	1
New York	4.44	48	4.51	23	998.78	38	12.02	40
North Carolina	0.54	20	3.25	12	41.84	14	4.89	15
North Dakota	0.00	1	3.13	9	1,079.14	39	0.00	1
Ohio	1.23	34	3.42	16	165.42	29	16.78	48
Oklahoma	0.00	1	3.37	14	293.93	32	5.26	19
Oregon	0.66	23	3.88	19	45.28	18	2.86	10
Pennsylvania	2.07	41	8.46	40	136.49	26	12.19	42
Rhode Island	3.01	43	12.00	45	14.60	7	6.90	28
South Carolina	0.00	1	7.10	35	169.79	30	18.95	49
South Dakota	0.00	1	5.56	29	1.39	1	12.12	41
Tennessee	0.67	24	3.47	17	342.70	34	8.05	30
Texas	1.59	39	1.63	2	5,999.15	49	6.39	25
Utah	1.11	30	8.38	39	508.84	36	5.13	17
Vermont	0.00	1	13.79	48	62.73	21	5.88	21
Virginia	1.24	35	3.82	18	15.30	8	6.45	26
Washington	1.33	37	10.30	43	2,934.75	43	5.38	20
West Virginia	0.52	19	3.30	13	4,230.87	48	15.69	47
Wisconsin	1.78	40	7.87	36	52.13	20	4.38	12
Wyoming	0.00	1	6.25	32	4.73	3	3.45	11

The Corporation for Enterprise Development

Environmental, Social & Health Conditions Data Sources

This "informational" subindex includes a wide array of environmental, social, and health factors that contribute to a state's quality of life. Ten measures in three areas are used:

Environmental Quality:
- *Air Quality*
- *Superfund Dumpsites*
- *Hazardous Waste Generation*
- *Surface Water Discharge*

Social Conditions:
- *Infant Mortality*
- *Crime Rate*
- *Teen Pregnancy*

Health:
- *Heart Disease*
- *Cancer Cases*
- *Infectious Diseases*

Environmental Quality

Only factors for which consistent state-by-state data can be collected are examined. Many other elements are needed to accurately portray the quality of the environment.

Air Quality

Measure: Score according to the degree to which state residents live in areas that exceeded national ambient air quality standards for ozone and/or carbon monoxide, 1993-1994.

Source: Environmental Protection Agency, Office of Air Quality Planning and Standards. *Ozone and Carbon Monoxide Areas Designated Nonattainment.* Washington, DC: August 15, 1994. Calculations by CFED.

Superfund Dumpsites

Measure: Number of final and proposed superfund dumpsites per one million population, 1994.

Source: Environmental Protection Agency, Office of Emergency and Remedial Response. *Supplementary Materials, National Priorities List, Final Rule.* Publication 9320.7-05I. Washington, DC: December 1994.

Hazardous Waste Generation

Measure: Hazardous waste (in metric tons) generated per 1,000 population, 1991.

Source: Environmental Protection Agency, Office of Solid Waste. *National Biennial RICAS Hazardous Waste Report* (based on 1991 data). Washington, DC: 1994.

Surface Water Discharge

Measure: Percentage of major municipal, nonmunicipal, and federal discharges in significant noncompliance with the established water quality standards specified on permit, 4th Quarter, Fiscal Year 1994 (ending June 1994).

Source: Environmental Protection Agency, Compliance Evaluation Section. Washington, DC: 1994.

Environmental, Social & Health Conditions Data (part 2)

State	Infant Mortality		Crime Rate		Teen Pregnancy	
	Rate	Rank	Rate	Rank	Rate	Rank
Alabama	10.0	43	4,678.8	21	73	42
Alaska	6.0	6	5,567.9	35	64	33
Arizona	7.2	14	7,431.7	49	82	49
Arkansas	8.8	33	4,810.7	24	75	44
California	6.7	12	6,456.9	47	74	43
Colorado	6.6	11	5,526.8	33	58	28
Connecticut	–	–	4,650.4	20	39	6
Delaware	8.2	25	4,872.1	25	60	31
Florida	8.3	28	8,351.0	50	66	36
Georgia	10.7	46	6,193.0	43	75	44
Hawaii	6.3	9	6,277.0	45	54	24
Idaho	7.4	18	3,845.1	8	52	21
Illinois	9.8	42	5,617.9	36	64	33
Indiana	9.0	34	4,465.1	17	59	30
Iowa	6.3	9	3,846.4	9	41	9
Kansas	8.4	29	4,975.3	27	56	25
Kentucky	8.5	30	3,259.7	6	65	35
Louisiana	9.7	41	6,846.6	48	76	46
Maine	–	–	3,153.9	5	40	8
Maryland	9.2	37	6,106.5	41	51	19
Massachusetts	5.2	3	4,893.9	26	38	5
Michigan	9.0	34	5,452.5	32	57	27
Minnesota	7.3	15	4,386.2	15	36	2
Mississippi	10.3	45	4,418.3	16	84	50
Missouri	8.1	24	5,095.4	28	63	32
Montana	8.5	30	4,790.0	22	46	14
Nebraska	8.0	23	4,117.1	13	41	9
Nevada	6.2	8	6,180.1	42	71	40
New Hampshire	6.1	7	2,905.0	3	31	1
New Jersey	8.2	25	4,800.8	23	39	6
New Mexico	9.5	40	6,266.1	44	80	48
New York	–	–	5,551.3	34	45	12
North Carolina	10.0	43	5,652.3	37	70	37
North Dakota	7.3	15	2,820.3	2	37	4
Ohio	9.4	38	4,485.3	18	58	28
Oklahoma	9.4	38	5,294.3	31	70	37
Oregon	6.8	13	5,765.6	38	53	23
Pennsylvania	8.2	25	3,271.4	7	45	12
Rhode Island	7.5	20	4,499.0	19	48	16
South Carolina	9.0	34	5,903.4	39	70	37
South Dakota	11.4	47	2,958.2	4	48	16
Tennessee	8.7	32	5,239.5	30	71	40
Texas	7.4	18	6,439.1	46	79	47
Utah	5.5	4	5,237.4	29	46	14
Vermont	4.8	2	3,972.4	10	36	2
Virginia	7.8	22	4,115.5	12	52	21
Washington	5.7	5	5,952.3	40	51	19
West Virginia	7.3	15	2,532.6	1	56	25
Wisconsin	7.6	21	4,054.1	11	42	11
Wyoming	4.7	1	4,163.0	14	50	18

Social Conditions

These indicators gauge aspects of a state's quality of life by examining factors related to the social conditions of adults and children.

Infant Mortality

Infant mortality correlates highly with the health and nutrition of the mother, which in turn, provides us with some insight about living conditions for families and the accessibility of prenatal care services.

Measure: Rate of infant (under one year) deaths per 1,000 live births, 12 months ending June 1994, provisional figures.

Source: National Center for Health Statistics. *Monthly Vital Statistics Report.* Vol. 43, No. 6. Hyattsville, MD: November 16, 1994.

Crime Rate

The higher the crime rate – whether it affects people personally or not – the less safe people are likely to feel. This crime rate, drawing on FBI data, addresses the most serious crimes: murder, rape, robbery, assault, burglary, larceny, and motor vehicle theft.

Measure: FBI index, rate of serious crimes per 100,000 population, 1993.

Source: Department of Justice, Federal Bureau of Investigation, *Crime in the United States, 1993.* Washington, DC: GPO, 1994.

Teen Pregnancy

Teenage pregnancies have soared in recent years, pointing to problems in family structure and in the inability of young mothers to gain the skills needed to be competitive workers in today's economy.

Measure: Birth rate per 1,000 females, aged 15-19, 1992.

Source: Child Trends, Inc., *Facts at a Glance.* Washington, DC: February 1995.

Environmental, Social & Health Conditions Data (part 3)

State	Heart Disease Rate	Heart Disease Rank	Cancer Cases Rate	Cancer Cases Rank	Infectious Diseases Rate	Infectious Diseases Rank
Alabama	170	42	502	37	24.9	15
Alaska	136	10	217	1	46.1	34
Arizona	138	11	445	15	61.6	45
Arkansas	161	34	578	48	41.4	31
California	148	23	397	8	71.7	47
Colorado	120	1	337	3	39.3	28
Connecticut	141	17	494	33	31.1	21
Delaware	160	32	543	44	57.3	44
Florida	139	14	599	50	61.6	45
Georgia	165	37	405	9	44.1	33
Hawaii	128	5	350	4	51.8	39
Idaho	133	9	382	7	22.8	10
Illinois	164	36	487	32	40.0	30
Indiana	161	34	473	22	24.1	13
Iowa	144	19	505	38	11.9	2
Kansas	140	16	486	30	19.5	8
Kentucky	177	47	528	42	24.7	14
Louisiana	177	47	477	26	39.6	29
Maine	153	28	557	45	11.2	1
Maryland	150	24	473	22	50.1	38
Massachusetts	139	14	516	39	37.4	27
Michigan	166	39	459	18	23.9	12
Minnesota	123	2	427	13	23.0	11
Mississippi	193	50	499	35	30.0	19
Missouri	160	32	525	41	47.1	35
Montana	131	6	465	21	28.6	17
Nebraska	145	22	479	28	22.6	9
Nevada	172	44	425	11	56.9	43
New Hampshire	150	24	462	19	13.5	3
New Jersey	151	26	533	43	53.1	40
New Mexico	126	3	359	5	72.5	48
New York	173	45	484	29	87.3	50
North Carolina	159	31	475	24	33.5	25
North Dakota	138	11	520	40	16.9	6
Ohio	167	41	496	34	16.9	6
Oklahoma	173	45	486	30	32.8	24
Oregon	132	8	478	27	49.4	37
Pennsylvania	166	39	573	47	28.9	18
Rhode Island	151	26	570	46	31.3	22
South Carolina	165	37	453	17	35.0	26
South Dakota	144	19	462	19	78.0	49
Tennessee	170	42	500	36	54.3	41
Texas	154	29	366	6	56.3	42
Utah	126	3	258	2	43.8	32
Vermont	144	19	451	16	15.2	5
Virginia	155	30	431	14	27.0	16
Washington	131	6	419	10	47.8	36
West Virginia	192	49	582	49	13.9	4
Wisconsin	141	17	476	25	31.6	23
Wyoming	138	11	426	12	30.8	20

Health Conditions

"How healthy are the people in each state?" To begin to answer this question, we look at the burden disease and illness place on the overall health of a population.

Heart Disease

Measure: Death rate from coronary heart disease, three-year running average, age- and race-adjusted, per 100,000 population, 1989-1991.

Source: National Center for Health Statistics, Hyattsville, MD, as cited in Northwestern National Life Insurance Company. *The NWNL State Health Rankings: 1994 Edition.* Minneapolis: Northwestern National Life Insurance Company, 1994.

Cancer Cases

Measure: Projected rate of cancer cases, all types, neither age- nor race-adjusted, per 100,000 population, 1994.

Source: American Cancer Society. "Cancer Facts and Figures - 1994." Atlanta GA: American Cancer Society, 1994. As cited in Northwestern National Life Insurance Company above.

Infectious Diseases

Measure: Occurrence of AIDS, tuberculosis, and hepatitis, three-year average rate, neither age- nor race-adjusted, per 100,000 population, 1990-1992.

Source: Centers for Disease Control. *Morbidity and Mortality Weekly.* Volumes 39-41. Atlanta, GA. As cited in Northwestern National Life Insurance Company above.

Business Vitality Index

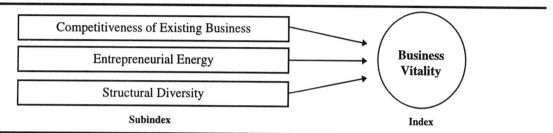

Subindex	Index
Competitiveness of Existing Business	
Entrepreneurial Energy	Business Vitality
Structural Diversity	

The Business Vitality Index is determined by using nine measures gathered into three subindexes.

The Business Vitality Index evaluates the "product line" – the businesses that constitute a state's economy.

Competitiveness of Existing Business Subindex

This subindex measures the strength of the state's traded sector (industries that compete with those out-of-state), whether it is investing in itself, and if businesses are being maintained. The four measures used are:

- *Traded Sector Strength*
- *Change in Traded Sector Strength*
- *Business Closings*
- *Manufacturing Capital Investment*

Entrepreneurial Energy Subindex

The Entrepreneurial Energy subindex evaluates the extent to which a state's economy is generating new firms, and whether they are contributing to employment growth. The three indicators are:

- *New Companies*
- *Change in New Companies*
- *New Business Job Growth*

Structural Diversity Subindex

Structural Diversity examines the economic base of the state economy to determine if it is sufficiently varied so the state can grow even if the market for products produced by one of its industries changes. Two measures are used:

- *Sectoral Diversity*
- *Dynamic Diversity*

Data tables, measures, and sources for each subindex can be found on the pages that follow.

Competitiveness of Existing Business Data

State	Traded Sector Strength $	Rank	Change in Traded Sector Strength $	Rank	Business Closings %	Rank	Capital Investment %	Rank
Alabama	9,481	24	738	27	16.92	45	12.0	2
Alaska	11,206	10	57	48	13.37	28	5.1	40
Arizona	7,464	45	857	23	13.23	27	6.9	23
Arkansas	8,904	31	586	39	12.42	18	7.9	14
California	10,457	13	677	33	14.57	34	5.3	36
Colorado	8,957	29	677	33	16.02	44	6.8	24
Connecticut	14,238	1	964	16	12.44	19	4.7	44
Delaware	12,523	4	236	47	12.92	23	6.5	27
Florida	6,174	50	708	29	17.02	47	5.5	33
Georgia	9,690	22	928	20	20.77	50	7.2	19
Hawaii	7,243	46	520	40	13.48	29	4.1	49
Idaho	10,588	12	1,544	5	13.06	24	11.2	3
Illinois	11,949	7	1,689	4	14.60	35	5.8	32
Indiana	11,568	9	1,043	14	11.85	12	8.1	13
Iowa	7,941	42	-947	50	11.96	14	5.2	37
Kansas	9,241	26	463	41	13.50	30	4.7	44
Kentucky	9,098	28	676	35	14.74	36	7.0	22
Louisiana	8,462	38	901	21	12.31	16	10.9	4
Maine	7,940	43	681	32	9.06	3	7.2	19
Maryland	8,546	37	933	19	13.78	32	7.1	21
Massachusetts	11,890	8	1,347	8	10.07	5	4.8	43
Michigan	12,573	3	865	22	7.00	1	7.6	15
Minnesota	10,039	19	424	42	10.26	6	6.4	28
Mississippi	8,146	41	661	37	12.53	21	7.5	16
Missouri	8,822	33	670	36	14.37	33	5.0	41
Montana	6,863	48	1,403	6	15.26	41	14.9	1
Nebraska	9,417	25	650	38	16.95	46	4.4	47
Nevada	12,215	6	2,073	2	10.52	7	7.3	18
New Hampshire	10,295	15	744	26	12.63	22	3.9	50
New Jersey	13,576	2	1,092	13	15.39	43	5.5	33
New Mexico	7,045	47	957	17	13.16	25	6.4	28
New York	12,223	5	2,010	3	9.88	4	4.9	42
North Carolina	10,231	17	1,114	12	17.46	48	4.7	44
North Dakota	6,511	49	271	46	13.73	31	10.2	7
Ohio	11,068	11	1,207	10	8.14	2	6.8	24
Oklahoma	8,380	39	732	28	12.48	20	5.5	33
Oregon	8,556	36	696	31	14.79	37	7.5	16
Pennsylvania	10,392	14	1,227	9	11.66	11	6.1	30
Rhode Island	9,236	27	946	18	12.25	15	4.4	47
South Carolina	8,913	30	980	15	11.94	13	8.9	10
South Dakota	8,567	34	752	25	11.52	10	5.2	37
Tennessee	10,038	20	1,364	7	15.36	42	8.7	11
Texas	9,535	23	1,116	11	15.07	39	10.8	5
Utah	7,513	44	-27	49	17.50	49	6.8	24
Vermont	8,220	40	298	45	13.16	25	10.5	6
Virginia	8,558	35	702	30	15.21	40	5.2	37
Washington	9,944	21	780	24	15.02	38	8.4	12
West Virginia	8,847	32	391	44	11.43	9	9.6	8
Wisconsin	10,224	18	400	43	11.32	8	6.1	30
Wyoming	10,288	16	2,474	1	12.37	17	9.1	9

Competitiveness of Existing Business Data Sources

Only if businesses are competitive out-of-state and investing in themselves will they be an engine for further economic growth and development. The four measures are:

- *Traded Sector Strength*
- *Change in Traded Sector Strength*
- *Business Closings*
- *Manufacturing Capital Investment*

Traded Sector Strength

The traded sector of each state is comprised of industries which compete in multistate, national and international markets. When these industries sell their goods and services, they bring wealth into the state and fuel the rest of the economy. Traded sector income per worker measures the economic strength of each state's traded sector.

Measure: Traded sector personal income (in dollars) per worker, 1993.

Source: U.S. Department of Commerce, Bureau of Economic Analysis. "State Personal Income Summary Tables 1968-1993." Washington, DC: August 1994; U.S. Department of Labor, Bureau of Labor Statistics. *Employment & Wages: Annual Averages, 1993.* Bulletin 2449. Washington, DC: October 1994, and *Geographic Profile of Employment & Unemployment, 1993.* Bulletin 2446. Washington, DC: September 1994. Calculations by Mt. Auburn Associates.

Note: See the Appendix: *Traded Sector and Structural Diversity* for more information.

Change in Traded Sector Strength

Traded sector strength does not suggest, however, whether a state's traded sector industries are faring better or worse than recent years. To get at the changing condition of a state's traded sector

industries, we examine the change in traded sector income per worker from 1990 to 1993.

Measure: Change (in dollars) in traded sector strength per worker, 1990-1993.

Source: Same as Traded Sector Strength.

Business Closings

Perhaps the most basic indicator of the competitiveness of the businesses in a state is simply whether businesses survive. The level of business closings in a state as reported by state employment security offices is measured.

Measure: Percentage rate of business closings from October 1993-September 1994.

Source: U.S. Department of Labor, Employment and Training Administration, Unemployment Insurance Service, ETA581, "Contributing Operations Reports." Washington, DC: 1994.

Note: "Closings" are businesses that either reported being out of business or reported no employment for two years.

Manufacturing Capital Investment

Quality and innovation create competitiveness and, therefore, business vitality. What drives innovation are the investments businesses make in people, products, and physical plants. Of these, the only investments that can currently be measured on a state-by-state basis are those in manufacturing machinery and equipment.

Measure: Investment in new and used machinery and equipment as a percentage of manufacturing value added, 1991.

Source: U.S. Department of Commerce, Bureau of the Census. *1991 Annual Survey of Manufacturers: Geographic Area Statistics.* Washington, DC: GPO, February 1993.

Entrepreneurial Energy Data

State	New Companies #	Rank	Change in New Companies %	Rank	New Business Job Growth %	Rank
Alabama	5.75	37	7.01	21	4.1	37
Alaska	10.45	5	-2.50	42	7.6	16
Arizona	6.75	23	10.72	15	10.1	5
Arkansas	6.15	33	-10.42	49	4.8	34
California	9.53	11	-4.10	45	5.9	27
Colorado	10.90	3	36.94	3	9.4	8
Connecticut	6.21	32	8.09	19	1.6	44
Delaware	7.60	19	9.81	17	7.5	17
Florida	9.68	10	5.28	28	5.6	30
Georgia	10.30	7	41.27	2	5.6	30
Hawaii	5.86	35	-4.50	46	11.7	1
Idaho	11.15	2	13.62	12	8.5	12
Illinois	5.53	39	-1.79	40	2.9	39
Indiana	5.21	44	1.22	36	4.3	35
Iowa	4.59	47	5.85	26	9.5	7
Kansas	6.55	29	10.71	16	6.9	21
Kentucky	4.87	45	-3.30	43	5.8	28
Louisiana	5.55	38	3.89	30	5.8	28
Maine	7.61	18	-2.32	41	-0.9	49
Maryland	6.52	30	-24.39	50	4.2	36
Massachusetts	5.37	42	13.15	13	2.4	42
Michigan	4.85	46	15.86	11	6.2	26
Minnesota	5.46	41	28.18	5	7.2	19
Mississippi	6.72	24	18.50	9	6.3	24
Missouri	5.77	36	6.65	23	8.9	11
Montana	10.36	6	20.27	6	9.0	10
Nebraska	7.87	17	50.77	1	7.0	20
Nevada	8.93	13	18.26	10	10.1	5
New Hampshire	9.79	9	11.25	14	-9.4	50
New Jersey	7.05	20	6.83	22	0.8	46
New Mexico	9.15	12	18.98	8	5.5	32
New York	6.86	22	0.65	37	0.8	46
North Carolina	6.61	27	3.88	31	2.8	40
North Dakota	5.32	43	6.16	25	2.5	41
Ohio	3.83	50	0.24	38	1.7	43
Oklahoma	6.57	28	3.88	31	7.9	13
Oregon	10.72	4	28.50	4	9.2	9
Pennsylvania	4.36	49	-3.32	44	3.2	38
Rhode Island	7.89	16	-5.14	47	5.5	32
South Carolina	5.51	40	5.49	27	7.4	18
South Dakota	6.65	26	9.64	18	11.2	2
Tennessee	6.27	31	7.05	20	7.7	15
Texas	6.91	21	3.82	33	10.4	3
Utah	8.85	14	19.59	7	7.9	13
Vermont	8.00	15	-9.16	48	0.4	48
Virginia	6.69	25	4.96	29	1.0	45
Washington	13.02	1	6.57	24	10.4	3
West Virginia	6.14	34	0.07	39	6.4	23
Wisconsin	4.57	48	3.33	35	6.9	21
Wyoming	10.08	8	3.73	34	6.3	24

Entrepreneurial Energy Data Sources

Entrepreneurial energy – the ability of a state to produce new business – is a critical characteristic of a robust economic climate. The measures are:

- *New Companies*
- *Change in New Companies*
- *New Business Job Growth*

New Companies

New firms are defined as those that seek new account numbers from the state employment service.

Measure: Number of companies applying for new employment service account numbers, October 1993-September 1994, per 1,000 October 1994 workers (seasonally adjusted).

Source: U.S. Department of Labor, Employment and Training Administration, Unemployment Insurance Service, ETA581, "Contributing Operations Reports". Washington, DC: 1994.

Change in New Companies

This measure examines the trend in new company formations on a year-to-year basis.

Measure: Percentage of change in companies applying for new employment service account numbers, from the year October 1992-September 1993 to the year October 1993-September 1994.

Source: Same as New Companies.

New Business Job Growth

A good indicator of the impact of entrepreneurship in a state is the job growth associated with relatively young businesses. This measure gives a picture of the importance local entrepreneurs are making in a state economy through the creation of new jobs.

Measure: Percent growth in employment at firms four years old and younger, 1989-1993.

Source: David Birch, Anne Haggerty, William Parson. *Who's Creating Jobs?* Cognetics, Inc. Cambridge, MA: 1994.

The 1995 Development Report Card

159

Structural Diversity Data

State	Sectoral Diversity		Dynamic Diversity	
	Score	Rank	Score	Rank
Alabama	0.0423	4	1.97	26
Alaska	0.0982	40	45.70	48
Arizona	0.0609	23	25.55	45
Arkansas	0.0608	22	8.20	38
California	0.0467	8	8.63	39
Colorado	0.0429	6	-3.78	1
Connecticut	0.0738	37	10.13	41
Delaware	0.1823	48	0.19	22
Florida	0.0518	13	5.17	34
Georgia	0.0510	12	0.52	23
Hawaii	0.1121	42	60.01	49
Idaho	0.1138	43	13.15	43
Illinois	0.0482	11	0.04	20
Indiana	0.0598	20	-0.96	12
Iowa	0.0644	27	-1.41	9
Kansas	0.0719	34	-1.57	6
Kentucky	0.0472	9	-1.47	8
Louisiana	0.0649	28	5.14	33
Maine	0.0718	33	0.15	21
Maryland	0.0622	24	-0.80	15
Massachusetts	0.0538	14	11.41	42
Michigan	0.1391	47	-0.94	14
Minnesota	0.0591	19	1.91	25
Mississippi	0.0472	9	-1.06	10
Missouri	0.0427	5	-0.49	17
Montana	0.1205	46	1.41	24
Nebraska	0.1143	44	-0.98	11
Nevada	0.2911	50	99.48	50
New Hampshire	0.0708	32	2.54	28
New Jersey	0.0637	26	5.13	32
New Mexico	0.0605	21	8.70	40
New York	0.0690	31	3.13	30
North Carolina	0.0586	17	-0.66	16
North Dakota	0.1198	45	-2.06	5
Ohio	0.0578	16	6.82	36
Oklahoma	0.0665	30	-2.86	3
Oregon	0.0663	29	4.86	31
Pennsylvania	0.0411	2	-1.57	6
Rhode Island	0.0588	18	16.96	44
South Carolina	0.0722	35	-0.95	13
South Dakota	0.1926	49	7.05	37
Tennessee	0.0421	3	2.00	27
Texas	0.0546	15	-3.43	2
Utah	0.0375	1	29.73	47
Vermont	0.0727	36	-0.24	18
Virginia	0.0438	7	-2.64	4
Washington	0.0867	38	27.22	46
West Virginia	0.0918	39	6.64	35
Wisconsin	0.0630	25	2.80	29
Wyoming	0.1037	41	-0.16	19

Structural Diversity Data Sources

Two features of diversity are measured in this subindex: how diverse an economy looks in terms of earned income across many traded sector industries, and how diverse an economy acts, so that when employment in one industry is declining, employment in others is stable or growing. The two measures are:

- *Sectoral Diversity*
- *Dynamic Diversity*

Sectoral Diversity

One indication of diversity is the degree to which income generated by a state's traded sector is spread across a range of industries rather than concentrated in just a few.

Measure: Score based on the Herfindahl Index, indicating the degree of diversity among industries within the state's traded sector, 1993.

Source: U.S. Department of Commerce, Bureau of Economic Analysis. *State Personal Income Summary Tables, 1969-1993.* Washington, DC: August 1994. Calculations by Mt. Auburn Associates.

Note: A "0" score indicates perfect diversification; "1" indicates that the state is dependent on only one traded industry. See the Appendix: *Traded Sector & Structural Diversity* for more information on the Herfindahl Index and this measure.

Dynamic Diversity

This measure examines the extent of similarity in the percent of employment change year-to-year among each state's key traded industries. Thus, this measure reflects the diversity of employment change across traded industries. If all key industries in a state decline simultaneously, that reflects low dynamic diversity.

Measure: Index score indicating the degree to which the employment levels in a state's individual traded industries moved in concert with one another, 1984-1993.

Source: U.S. Department of Commerce, Bureau of Economic Analysis. "State Employment Tables." Washington, DC: August 1994. Calculations by Mt. Auburn Associates.

Note: The lower the score, the greater the degree of dynamic diversity. See the Appendix: *Traded Sector & Structural Diversity* for more information on this measure.

Development Capacity Index

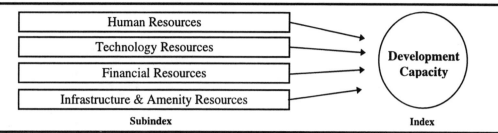

Human Resources	
Technology Resources	Development Capacity
Financial Resources	
Infrastructure & Amenity Resources	
Subindex	**Index**

To assess Development Capacity, twenty-four measures were gathered into four subindexes.

The Development Capacity Index examines a state's underlying resource base for a comprehensive picture of its competitive capacity.

Human Resources Subindex

The Human Resources subindex measures the education and skill levels of the state's workforce. The more skilled the people, the stronger and more lasting the structure of the economy they build. The three measures are:

- *High School Graduation*
- *High School Education Attainment*
- *College Education Attainment*

Technology Resources Subindex

This subindex identifies the extent to which new technologies and technically-proficient institutions and individuals are available in a state by measuring six indicators:

- *Ph.D. Scientists & Engineers in the Workforce*
- *Science & Engineering Graduate Students*
- *Patents Issued*
- *University Research & Development*
- *Federal Research & Development*
- *Small Business Innovation Research Grants*

Financial Resources Subindex

This subindex focuses on the availability and patterns of use of capital to meet the full range of business finance needs. The seven measures are:

- *Commercial Bank Deposits*
- *Loans to Deposits*
- *Loans to Equity*
- *Commercial & Industrial Loans*
- *Commercial & Industrial Loans to Total Loans*
- *Venture Capital Investments*
- *Small Business Investment Capital Financings*

Infrastructure & Amenity Resources Subindex

Roads, bridges, sewers, power, housing, and other basic economic building blocks are an essential part of the economic foundation of a state. To examine these areas, the following eight indicators are measured:

- *Highway Deficiency*
- *Bridge Deficiency*
- *Urban Mass Transit Availability*
- *Energy Cost*
- *Sewage Treatment Needs*
- *Urban Housing Costs*
- *Health Professional Shortage Areas*
- *Tourism Spending*

Data tables, measures, and sources for each subindex can be found on the pages that follow.

Human Resources Data

State	High School Graduation		High School Attainment		College Attainment	
	%	Rank	%	Rank	%	Rank
Alabama	66.1	44	76.6	41	16.0	47
Alaska	74.1	29	90.4	1	24.2	15
Arizona	72.7	33	83.7	15	23.3	19
Arkansas	78.3	19	75.2	43	14.8	48
California	68.6	40	82.4	23	26.3	10
Colorado	75.1	28	89.9	2	31.1	2
Connecticut	80.4	16	84.9	11	31.1	2
Delaware	69.6	38	81.8	24	24.1	17
Florida	65.0	45	81.3	28	21.0	26
Georgia	63.7	46	77.3	40	24.3	14
Hawaii	78.1	20	86.7	6	24.6	13
Idaho	81.1	12	82.8	21	20.2	28
Illinois	78.6	18	80.1	34	22.6	24
Indiana	76.0	27	77.4	39	14.8	48
Iowa	87.6	2	82.9	20	17.4	44
Kansas	80.5	15	85.9	9	23.0	20
Kentucky	69.8	37	71.3	48	17.8	41
Louisiana	52.9	50	71.9	46	17.3	45
Maine	81.1	12	83.5	17	19.9	30
Maryland	76.1	25	81.5	26	26.8	6
Massachusetts	79.1	17	85.0	10	31.3	1
Michigan	70.9	35	81.7	25	18.6	38
Minnesota	89.2	1	84.9	11	22.7	23
Mississippi	62.1	47	70.3	49	18.2	39
Missouri	73.2	32	80.7	33	20.7	27
Montana	85.5	5	84.4	13	21.5	25
Nebraska	87.2	4	86.4	8	18.8	37
Nevada	70.7	36	87.5	5	17.7	43
New Hampshire	78.1	20	83.6	16	26.4	7
New Jersey	84.1	7	82.5	22	28.9	4
New Mexico	67.8	42	81.1	30	25.4	12
New York	66.6	43	81.3	28	26.0	11
North Carolina	68.5	41	74.0	44	19.7	33
North Dakota	87.5	3	81.1	30	20.2	28
Ohio	72.4	34	81.4	27	19.9	30
Oklahoma	76.3	24	79.0	38	19.7	33
Oregon	73.5	31	83.9	14	22.9	21
Pennsylvania	81.5	11	79.3	37	19.8	32
Rhode Island	76.8	23	76.3	42	23.6	18
South Carolina	58.1	49	72.0	45	17.8	41
South Dakota	85.3	6	80.8	32	19.6	35
Tennessee	68.7	39	71.8	47	16.4	46
Texas	61.3	48	79.4	36	22.9	21
Utah	81.1	12	88.9	4	24.2	15
Vermont	82.4	9	83.5	17	26.4	7
Virginia	74.0	30	80.0	35	26.4	7
Washington	76.1	25	89.2	3	27.2	5
West Virginia	77.0	22	69.1	50	11.1	50
Wisconsin	82.2	10	83.2	19	19.2	36
Wyoming	83.8	8	86.5	7	18.1	40

Human Resources Data Sources

The skills of a state's workforce, and the extent to which those skills are adaptable to changing economic circumstances, are the most basic components of its human resource base. This subindex explores three educational measures:

- *High School Graduation*
- *High School Education Attainment*
- *College Education Attainment*

High School Graduation

In any economy where the minimum qualification for most jobs is high school completion, a state's economic competitiveness will be directly affected by its ability to produce new entrants to the workforce who meet the basic test of work-readiness. Despite differences from state to state in the level of competence associated with high school education today, this measure is still the best baseline we have available to gauge the basic skills level of tomorrow's workforce.

Measure: High school graduates as a percent of students entering 9th grade 4 years previously (Fall 1988), 1991-1992.

Source: National Center for Education Statistics, Department of Education. *Number of Public High School Graduates, by State.* Washington, DC: 1994.

High School Education Attainment

Another measure of the skills level of a state's existing workforce is how many of its citizens have already graduated from high school.

Measure: Percentage of heads of household with at least 12 years of education, 1991-1993.

Source: Jon Haveman, Purdue University. Calculations based on merged U.S. Current Population survey data tapes from March 1992, 1993, and 1994.

College Education Attainment

In today's economy, knowledge is itself a traded commodity. The higher the percent of college educated individuals in the population, the greater the capacity of the state's economy to compete.

Measure: Percentage of heads of household with at least four years of college, 1991-1993.

Source: Same as High School Education Attainment.

Technology Resources Data (part 1)

State	Ph.D. Scientists & Engineers in Workforce		Science & Engineering Graduate Students		Patents Issued	
	#	Rank	#	Rank	#	Rank
Alabama	3.08	38	1,428.26	28	80.09	47
Alaska	3.77	25	967.80	46	90.16	43
Arizona	3.38	33	2,034.20	9	258.09	17
Arkansas	1.92	50	537.50	50	64.90	49
California	4.94	10	1,414.77	30	330.67	8
Colorado	5.60	7	2,649.86	2	322.40	10
Connecticut	4.92	12	1,407.62	31	558.84	2
Delaware	10.94	2	2,263.77	4	635.21	1
Florida	2.20	48	1,151.52	41	164.44	27
Georgia	2.82	45	1,260.00	37	136.26	34
Hawaii	4.30	21	1,795.69	15	83.90	46
Idaho	4.51	16	1,465.42	26	323.89	9
Illinois	3.65	26	1,841.53	13	282.38	13
Indiana	2.92	42	1,746.47	18	202.61	24
Iowa	2.98	40	1,945.20	12	162.54	28
Kansas	2.90	44	2,127.78	8	128.24	36
Kentucky	2.49	47	934.04	47	88.51	45
Louisiana	3.14	36	1,337.76	34	102.31	41
Maine	3.61	28	688.71	49	112.90	39
Maryland	9.04	3	1,705.70	19	233.93	21
Massachusetts	7.71	4	3,606.67	1	438.58	3
Michigan	3.34	34	1,770.02	16	338.42	7
Minnesota	3.63	27	1,314.06	36	429.76	4
Mississippi	2.93	41	985.44	45	60.67	50
Missouri	3.44	32	1,324.28	35	143.75	32
Montana	4.49	17	1,481.71	25	113.95	38
Nebraska	3.13	37	1,454.66	27	114.20	37
Nevada	2.15	49	758.65	48	144.52	31
New Hampshire	3.91	22	1,013.51	44	395.61	6
New Jersey	5.71	5	1,407.19	32	411.01	5
New Mexico	11.01	1	2,147.47	7	157.58	29
New York	5.03	8	2,231.62	6	299.56	11
North Carolina	3.89	23	1,376.75	33	168.18	26
North Dakota	5.03	8	1,539.06	24	93.75	42
Ohio	3.48	31	1,977.22	10	278.56	14
Oklahoma	3.87	24	1,550.16	23	190.49	25
Oregon	4.38	20	1,415.44	29	252.43	19
Pennsylvania	4.43	19	1,628.31	22	255.85	18
Rhode Island	4.46	18	2,236.63	5	274.00	15
South Carolina	2.78	46	1,157.78	40	139.34	33
South Dakota	3.05	39	1,671.83	21	65.28	48
Tennessee	3.60	29	1,204.38	39	132.24	35
Texas	3.57	30	1,677.86	20	231.39	22
Utah	4.84	14	2,513.26	3	251.83	20
Vermont	5.64	6	1,256.14	38	294.83	12
Virginia	4.93	11	1,821.94	14	147.94	30
Washington	4.86	13	1,148.05	42	215.54	23
West Virginia	2.91	43	1,119.34	43	89.56	44
Wisconsin	3.19	35	1,753.29	17	273.82	16
Wyoming	4.54	15	1,946.81	11	108.33	40

Technology Resources Data Sources

The Technology Resources subindex examines the potential pool of innovators in a state and the pool of dollars devoted to research. The six measures which make up this subindex are:

- *Ph.D. Scientists & Engineers in the Workforce*
- *Science & Engineering Graduate Students*
- *Patents Issued*
- *University Research & Development*
- *Federal Research & Development*
- *Small Business Innovation Research Grants*

Ph.D. Scientists & Engineers in the Workforce

The larger the potential pool of innovators in a state, the greater the likelihood that the capacity for innovation will become reality.

Measure: Number of employed doctoral scientists and engineers per 1,000 workers, 1992.

Source: National Science Foundation, Division of Science Resource Studies. As expected to appear in *Characteristics of Doctoral Scientists and Engineers in the U.S.* Washington, DC: 1994.

Science & Engineering Graduate Students

This measure indicates how extensive science training is in a state, not how many degree recipients actually stay in the state after completing their education. Nevertheless, the history of industrial innovation indicates that new businesses are spawned, more often than not, in the same place entrepreneurs received their degrees.

Measure: Number of science and engineering graduate students in doctorate-granting institutions, per one million population, 1992.

Source: National Science Foundation. *Selected Data on Graduate Students and Postdoctorates in Science and Engineering: Fall 1992*, NSF 94-301, Washington, DC: 1994.

Patents Issued

This measure aims to capture the rate of innovation in a state. It is imperfect in that patents generally are issued at the location of the company headquarters, not necessarily at the location of the lab where the innovation is developed.

Measure: Number of patents issued per one million population, 1994.

Source: U.S. Department of Commerce, U.S. Patent & Trademark Office. "State-Country Counts from Calender Year 1994 Patent File." Technology Assessment and Forecast Database. Washington, DC: January 1995.

Technology Resources Data (part 2)

State	University R&D		Federal R&D		SBIR Grants	
	$	Rank	$	Rank	$	Rank
Alabama	67.16	28	520.24	4	5.04	17
Alaska	111.51	4	158.43	21	0.00	46
Arizona	78.94	20	166.54	19	6.93	10
Arkansas	30.53	47	28.68	49	0.27	43
California	76.26	22	518.32	5	10.93	9
Colorado	92.84	9	426.28	7	19.91	3
Connecticut	111.29	5	176.26	14	14.35	7
Delaware	75.18	23	62.55	40	5.54	15
Florida	35.72	45	209.99	13	2.99	25
Georgia	79.07	19	372.18	9	1.00	38
Hawaii	63.11	31	129.91	26	2.42	29
Idaho	44.38	43	280.69	11	0.71	42
Illinois	63.95	30	79.26	36	1.84	33
Indiana	53.00	40	64.82	39	0.85	40
Iowa	106.16	6	69.24	38	0.20	45
Kansas	60.89	33	36.15	47	1.30	35
Kentucky	32.31	46	19.09	50	0.82	41
Louisiana	59.41	34	39.56	45	1.22	37
Maine	20.08	50	49.07	42	6.09	14
Maryland	231.04	1	1,177.61	2	16.19	4
Massachusetts	178.95	2	538.16	3	42.38	1
Michigan	73.85	25	92.86	30	2.04	31
Minnesota	73.51	26	101.88	28	3.38	23
Mississippi	40.01	44	97.82	29	0.27	43
Missouri	65.83	29	141.25	23	0.90	39
Montana	57.31	35	86.77	34	3.55	22
Nebraska	84.47	17	44.27	44	2.57	27
Nevada	56.96	36	351.02	10	2.14	30
New Hampshire	88.42	10	140.50	24	15.27	5
New Jersey	47.48	42	211.43	12	6.54	12
New Mexico	115.56	3	1,398.67	1	24.28	2
New York	84.95	15	168.81	18	4.36	20
North Carolina	87.05	12	102.40	27	1.95	32
North Dakota	85.31	14	85.22	35	2.52	28
Ohio	53.27	39	169.15	17	3.76	21
Oklahoma	53.53	38	39.26	46	1.24	36
Oregon	74.46	24	76.08	37	4.78	18
Pennsylvania	84.56	16	149.42	22	4.65	19
Rhode Island	103.19	8	384.38	8	5.23	16
South Carolina	48.91	41	47.77	43	0.00	46
South Dakota	30.48	48	33.61	48	0.00	46
Tennessee	54.46	37	132.56	25	2.74	26
Texas	76.93	21	162.72	20	3.13	24
Utah	105.44	7	173.19	16	15.11	6
Vermont	86.53	13	90.00	32	6.55	11
Virginia	62.12	32	506.71	6	11.83	8
Washington	81.40	18	175.33	15	6.52	13
West Virginia	30.23	49	91.83	31	0.00	46
Wisconsin	88.17	11	61.45	41	1.55	34
Wyoming	69.27	27	88.84	33	0.00	46

University Research & Development

This measure gives us a sense of the scale of research and development spending at universities in each state and, indirectly, its capacity to generate technology-related business development.

Measure: Research and development expenditures at doctorate-granting institutions, dollars per capita, Fiscal Year 1993.

Source: National Science Foundation. *Selected Data on Academic Science and Engineering R & D Expenditures: Fiscal Year 1993.* Washington, DC: 1994.

Federal Research & Development

There is a correlation between federal R & D spending and new business spin-offs. However, their relationship varies significantly, depending upon what kind of research is underway. In states where much of the federal research is classified, the problem of getting the results "over the fence" and into the state economy can be considerable.

Measure: Federal obligations for research and development, dollars per capita, Fiscal Year 1992.

Source: National Science Foundation, Division of Science Resource Studies. *Federal Funds for Research and Development: Fiscal Years 1992, 1993, and 1994,* Volume 42, NSF 94-328. Detailed Statistical Tables. Washington, DC: National Science Foundation, 1994.

Small Business Innovation Research (SBIR) Grants

Study after study reveals that small businesses drive innovation and are more efficient innovators than large firms. The federal government recognizes the importance of small business in overall industrial research and development by requiring that all federal agencies with annual R & D budgets of over $100 million set aside 1.25 percent of these funds to assist small businesses. The level of SBIR grants in a state indicates how technologically sophisticated a state's business base is.

Measure: SBIR grants awarded (in dollars) per worker, Fiscal Year 1993.

Source: U.S. Small Business Administration, Office of Innovation, Research and Technology. As expected to appear in *Small Business Innovation Development Act: Eleventh Annual Report.* Washington, DC: SBA, 1994.

Financial Resources Data (part 1)

State	Commercial Bank Deposits $	Rank	Loans to Deposits Ratio	Rank	Loans to Equity Ratio	Rank	C&I Loans $	Rank	C&I to Total Loans %	Rank
Alabama	9,073.11	19	0.85	24	7.96	11	4,076.88	15	21.74	21
Alaska	6,654.87	45	0.68	41	3.98	50	3,245.79	23	30.28	5
Arizona	7,502.66	39	0.76	33	7.26	21	1,675.39	48	12.01	47
Arkansas	9,389.46	15	0.65	45	6.05	43	2,286.29	42	15.93	39
California	7,459.21	40	0.83	25	6.89	30	3,228.52	24	19.81	28
Colorado	8,023.45	33	0.65	45	6.76	34	1,858.95	46	16.97	36
Connecticut	7,364.64	41	0.79	29	7.46	18	2,929.56	29	23.44	18
Delaware	40,446.90	1	2.30	1	7.13	24	9,985.78	1	5.43	50
Florida	9,148.26	17	0.78	31	7.91	12	2,314.10	41	13.59	45
Georgia	8,898.16	22	1.00	8	7.10	26	4,965.97	11	26.01	11
Hawaii	9,808.51	12	1.12	4	6.97	29	5,764.37	8	23.63	16
Idaho	7,636.67	37	1.00	8	9.63	1	3,741.67	17	20.03	27
Illinois	11,914.07	5	0.80	28	6.12	42	6,541.56	5	31.64	3
Indiana	8,424.88	28	0.86	21	7.60	17	2,912.27	30	18.46	30
Iowa	11,009.29	7	0.74	35	6.37	38	2,842.71	32	16.26	37
Kansas	9,863.58	11	0.63	47	5.57	46	2,766.67	36	20.33	25
Kentucky	8,992.12	21	0.89	16	7.29	20	3,474.00	22	18.05	31
Louisiana	7,816.21	36	0.57	50	5.25	48	2,267.01	43	20.22	26
Maine	5,588.37	49	0.86	21	8.29	7	2,785.44	33	24.79	13
Maryland	8,320.53	30	0.79	29	6.53	36	2,781.81	34	17.87	33
Massachusetts	9,228.94	16	0.91	14	6.75	35	5,922.82	7	34.32	2
Michigan	8,138.83	32	0.88	18	8.50	5	5,197.38	10	31.51	4
Minnesota	9,629.56	14	0.88	18	7.63	15	4,315.49	13	25.71	12
Mississippi	7,934.27	34	0.67	42	6.15	41	2,391.67	38	17.49	35
Missouri	10,514.68	9	0.74	35	7.09	27	3,609.94	19	21.95	20
Montana	7,586.02	38	0.73	37	6.81	33	2,898.51	31	20.67	24
Nebraska	12,619.11	4	0.76	33	7.16	23	3,100.01	27	15.77	41
Nevada	6,855.61	43	1.32	3	5.41	47	1,194.70	49	6.52	49
New Hampshire	5,056.58	50	0.82	26	7.75	13	905.63	50	9.89	48
New Jersey	11,834.57	6	0.71	40	7.22	22	4,348.87	12	23.30	19
New Mexico	6,745.44	44	0.67	42	7.04	28	1,782.17	47	15.75	42
New York	13,292.49	3	0.96	11	4.06	49	8,467.21	2	28.44	7
North Carolina	8,625.79	25	1.10	5	9.09	3	5,586.52	9	27.88	9
North Dakota	10,580.49	8	0.72	39	6.49	37	3,198.47	25	19.32	29
Ohio	8,525.78	26	1.04	6	8.86	4	4,215.16	14	21.28	23
Oklahoma	8,254.50	31	0.61	49	5.64	45	3,044.69	28	23.55	17
Oregon	7,025.35	42	0.93	12	8.03	10	3,940.68	16	26.78	10
Pennsylvania	10,101.64	10	0.92	13	7.12	25	6,064.12	6	28.21	8
Rhode Island	8,711.76	24	1.01	7	7.69	14	7,120.58	3	35.17	1
South Carolina	6,002.42	48	0.88	18	8.06	8	1,929.72	45	15.96	38
South Dakota	15,248.45	2	1.55	2	6.88	31	6,737.53	4	13.23	46
Tennessee	9,071.62	20	0.77	32	7.38	19	3,198.28	26	21.33	22
Texas	7,838.76	35	0.66	44	6.36	39	3,515.82	21	28.85	6
Utah	6,149.16	47	0.90	15	6.83	32	1,932.39	44	15.93	39
Vermont	8,344.23	29	0.89	16	9.39	2	2,379.86	40	14.35	43
Virginia	8,818.30	23	0.81	27	8.04	9	2,770.00	35	17.98	32
Washington	6,498.43	46	0.97	10	8.40	6	3,607.56	20	24.73	14
West Virginia	9,129.84	18	0.73	37	6.23	40	2,442.36	37	13.75	44
Wisconsin	8,465.19	27	0.86	21	7.63	15	3,617.27	18	24.24	15
Wyoming	9,633.25	13	0.62	48	5.80	44	2,391.40	39	17.69	34

Financial Resources Data Sources

This subindex provides a general picture of the financial capacity of a state – focusing primarily on its commercial banks. Measures used are:

- *Commercial Bank Deposits*
- *Loans to Deposits*
- *Loans to Equity*
- *Commercial & Industrial Loans*
- *Commercial & Industrial Loans to Total Loans*
- *Venture Capital Investments*
- *SBIC Financings*

Commercial Bank Deposits

Since deposits form the base from which banks invest, this measure provides a basic indicator of capital availability within a state. The higher the level of deposits, adjusted for population size, the more dollars available to lend.

Measure: Deposits in insured commercial banks, dollars per capita, 3rd Quarter, 1994.

Source: Federal Deposit Insurance Corporation, Division of Research. Washington, DC: February 1995. Calculations by CFED.

Note: Figures refer only to domestic bank deposits.

Loans to Deposits

An indicator of a bank's aggressiveness is the ratio of a bank's loans to its deposits. Deposits represent the major resource base upon which banks are able to lend funds. The degree to which banks actually lend deposits, versus investing them in other vehicles like bonds, is a key factor in evaluating their overall aggressiveness.

Measure: Ratio of insured commercial banks' total domestic loans and leases to total domestic deposits, 3rd Quarter, 1994.

Source: Same as Commercial Bank Deposits.

Loans to Equity

Equity is the original investment of the bank's founders plus any accumulated undistributed earnings. The more aggressive the bank, the more this base is leveraged as loans. This measure is designed to indicate how aggressive commercial banks are at using their resources to further business investments and expansions in the state.

Measure: Ratio of insured commercial banks' total domestic loans and leases to total capital, 3rd Quarter, 1994.

Source: Same as Commercial Bank Deposits.

Commercial & Industrial (C & I) Loans

A good measure of how well financial institutions are serving businesses is to divide their total commercial and industrial loans by the number of nonagricultural employees in the state (to adjust for differences in the size of their commercial and industrial sectors). One weakness with this measure is that a bank can make loans to businesses located outside that state; such loans cannot be separated out of this measure.

Measure: Domestic commercial and industrial loans, dollars per worker on nonagricultural payrolls, 3rd Quarter, 1994.

Source: Same as Commercial Bank Deposits.

Commercial & Industrial (C & I) Loans to Total Loans

Another indication of how well commercial banks are serving businesses is the extent to which their total loans go to commercial and industrial concerns, versus housing and consumer purposes.

Measure: Domestic commercial and industrial loans as a percent of total domestic loans of commercial banks, 3rd Quarter, 1994.

Source: Same as Commercial Bank Deposits.

Financial Resources Data (part 2)

State	Venture Capital Investments		SBIC Financings	
	$	Rank	$	Rank
Alabama	12.63	20	2.46	33
Alaska	0.00	37	0.00	43
Arizona	19.91	18	4.72	24
Arkansas	0.00	37	1.03	39
California	150.78	2	8.17	11
Colorado	121.00	3	12.45	6
Connecticut	108.84	4	6.32	18
Delaware	0.00	37	2.45	34
Florida	22.24	15	3.23	32
Georgia	8.63	24	15.22	4
Hawaii	0.00	37	0.00	43
Idaho	0.00	37	3.45	30
Illinois	32.78	11	3.72	27
Indiana	2.34	32	6.84	14
Iowa	6.99	26	0.46	41
Kansas	0.00	37	3.64	28
Kentucky	6.99	26	4.30	25
Louisiana	1.46	33	6.53	15
Maine	18.84	19	0.00	43
Maryland	36.05	10	2.07	37
Massachusetts	202.68	1	8.05	12
Michigan	2.68	31	1.77	38
Minnesota	38.55	9	9.42	8
Mississippi	0.00	37	0.00	43
Missouri	22.99	14	14.94	5
Montana	0.00	37	3.54	29
Nebraska	6.35	28	7.08	13
Nevada	0.00	37	0.00	43
New Hampshire	43.87	7	5.59	21
New Jersey	54.16	6	6.23	19
New Mexico	0.75	35	2.29	35
New York	4.28	30	9.93	7
North Carolina	8.13	25	6.03	20
North Dakota	0.00	37	0.00	43
Ohio	9.68	23	4.96	22
Oklahoma	6.27	29	0.29	42
Oregon	29.23	12	17.92	2
Pennsylvania	21.31	17	6.44	17
Rhode Island	0.00	37	6.45	16
South Carolina	27.48	13	2.25	36
South Dakota	0.00	37	0.00	43
Tennessee	11.97	22	25.50	1
Texas	41.09	8	9.28	9
Utah	0.34	36	4.81	23
Vermont	1.15	34	3.30	31
Virginia	21.73	16	17.54	3
Washington	56.66	5	4.01	26
West Virginia	0.00	37	0.77	40
Wisconsin	12.10	21	8.78	10
Wyoming	0.00	37	0.00	43

Venture Capital Investments

Venture capital firms provide early-stage capital for businesses with high growth potential and, as a consequence, can be instrumental in the formation and expansion of growth industries. Active venture capital participation in a state is an indicator of a rapidly developing economy and multiple investment opportunities. It is useful to note here that the venture capital industry, despite the fact that it has grown sharply in recent years, is still quite small and focused in only a handful of states. This year we measure the amount of venture capital investments made in a state, adjusted by the state's employment.

Measure: Private equity raised through venture capital investments, dollars per worker, 1994.

Source: VentureOne. *VentureOne Research Partner Database.* San Francisco, CA: February 1995.

Small Business Investment Company (SBIC) Financings

SBICs are federally licensed investment companies that target financing to economically and socially disadvantaged entrepreneurs. SBICs offer hard-to-find, patient, growth-oriented capital in the form of long-term loans, equity, or convertible debt. In exchange for a pledge to invest exclusively in small businesses, SBICs qualify for federal Small Business Administration guarantees.

Measure: Total SBIC financings in a state, dollars per worker, 1993.

Sources: U.S. Small Business Administration, Investment Division. As expected to appear in *SBIC Program Statistical Package.* Washington, DC: 1995.

Infrastructure & Amenity Resources Data (part 1)

State	Highway Deficiency %	Rank	Bridge Deficiency %	Rank	Urban Mass Transit Miles Miles	Rank	Energy Cost ¢	Rank
Alabama	6.25	15	37.16	34	2.31	39	5.69	15
Alaska	16.25	41	23.31	7	3.82	28	9.67	42
Arizona	6.07	14	11.11	1	6.22	19	8.24	39
Arkansas	3.42	6	36.66	33	1.01	48	6.77	31
California	10.66	29	28.52	18	11.96	7	9.76	43
Colorado	7.00	20	24.81	12	8.82	11	6.09	20
Connecticut	5.47	13	36.51	32	5.93	22	10.30	46
Delaware	10.85	31	24.58	11	6.04	20	6.84	33
Florida	4.19	8	24.19	9	6.88	16	7.21	35
Georgia	0.16	1	29.42	21	7.34	15	6.80	32
Hawaii	10.95	32	52.53	48	15.76	4	10.66	48
Idaho	17.41	44	23.64	8	0.88	49	3.98	2
Illinois	6.76	19	27.19	14	16.71	3	6.60	28
Indiana	7.22	23	32.47	24	3.55	32	5.30	8
Iowa	1.55	2	31.14	23	2.66	35	5.95	18
Kansas	10.80	30	35.04	30	1.59	44	6.61	29
Kentucky	7.08	22	35.79	31	3.77	30	4.43	5
Louisiana	19.82	48	40.06	39	4.91	26	6.27	24
Maine	11.00	34	38.11	37	3.81	29	9.23	41
Maryland	10.22	28	34.90	29	7.77	12	6.96	34
Massachusetts	5.01	10	63.89	49	14.71	6	10.04	45
Michigan	13.33	39	34.64	28	5.36	24	7.21	35
Minnesota	17.00	42	21.75	5	5.96	21	5.66	14
Mississippi	29.58	50	42.17	40	0.84	50	6.21	22
Missouri	5.19	11	49.54	47	5.90	23	6.37	27
Montana	9.54	27	24.43	10	2.33	37	4.40	4
Nebraska	11.21	35	37.79	35	3.73	31	5.58	12
Nevada	4.47	9	20.93	3	5.00	25	5.89	16
New Hampshire	18.15	46	39.36	38	1.50	45	10.68	49
New Jersey	9.06	25	47.15	45	19.26	2	9.97	44
New Mexico	17.98	45	17.43	2	3.92	27	7.29	37
New York	7.00	20	66.00	50	31.90	1	10.73	50
North Carolina	19.45	47	37.88	36	2.32	38	6.68	30
North Dakota	6.34	16	33.43	26	2.17	40	5.89	16
Ohio	2.70	5	33.22	25	6.54	17	6.24	23
Oklahoma	10.99	33	42.65	42	2.16	41	6.03	19
Oregon	11.96	37	27.40	15	9.40	9	4.45	6
Pennsylvania	11.74	36	42.96	43	10.70	8	8.05	38
Rhode Island	21.31	49	47.12	44	6.42	18	10.39	47
South Carolina	2.24	4	21.06	4	2.09	42	5.63	13
South Dakota	6.40	17	31.10	22	1.46	46	6.20	21
Tennessee	8.26	24	33.73	27	3.35	33	5.30	8
Texas	4.08	7	25.94	13	7.65	13	6.35	25
Utah	2.06	3	27.57	16	9.01	10	5.31	10
Vermont	17.27	43	42.61	41	1.09	47	8.99	40
Virginia	9.26	26	28.23	17	2.92	34	6.36	26
Washington	5.42	12	29.08	19	14.96	5	3.72	1
West Virginia	6.56	18	48.58	46	2.41	36	5.22	7
Wisconsin	13.84	40	29.24	20	7.44	14	5.52	11
Wyoming	12.07	38	22.93	6	1.62	43	4.25	3

Infrastructure & Amenity Resources Data Sources

Physical infrastructure and amenities form the basic foundation upon which businesses build, and are crucial to attracting and keeping the employees that businesses need to be competitive. Eight measures are used to evaluate this subindex:

- *Highway Deficiency*
- *Bridge Deficiency*
- *Urban Mass Transit Availability*
- *Energy Cost*
- *Sewage Treatment Needs*
- *Urban Housing Costs*
- *Health Professional Shortage Areas*
- *Tourism Spending*

Highway Deficiency

In an economy where most goods are transported by truck, highway conditions are not just a measure of state infrastructure capacity; they are a fundamental measure of competitiveness as well. We measure the percent of rural and urban highway mileage with poor serviceability ratings.

Measure: Percentage of highway mileage rated in poor condition (2.5 or less for interstates, 2.0 or less for all other systems) – all functional systems, 1993.

Source: U.S. Department of Transportation, Federal Highway Administration. *Highway Statistics, 1993.* Washington, DC: GPO, 1994.

Bridge Deficiency

The percent of bridges structurally deficient and functionally obsolete is measured. These bridges are not all necessarily unsafe, but rather may have narrower widths or lower maximum loads than modern standards, inhibiting and impeding the flow of goods in certain areas.

Measure: Percentage of bridges on and off federal aid system rated as deficient, as of June 30, 1992.

Source: Eleventh Report of the Secretary of Transportation to the U.S. Congress, *Highway Bridge Replacement and Rehabilitation Program, 1993.* Washington, DC: GPO, April 1993.

Urban Mass Transit Availability

The extent of mass transit availability is an important asset for ensuring workforce mobility and overall transportation capacity.

Measure: Weighted measure of urban public mass transit systems' carrying capacity, in annual vehicle revenue capacity miles per capita, 1992.

Source: U.S. Department of Transportation. *Section 15 Annual Report, 1992* as in data diskettes from McTrans Center, University of Florida, Gainesville, 1994.

Energy Cost

Electrical energy continues to increase in importance as economies become more technology-intensive. Moreover, energy costs vary substantially from state to state and affect both business costs and living costs.

Measure: Average cost in cents of electricity per kilowatt hour (as measured by average revenue per kilowatt hour sold), 1993.

Source: Edison Electric Institute. *Statistical Yearbook of the Electric Utility Industry, 1993.* Washington, DC: October 1994.

Infrastructure & Amenity Resources Data (part 2)

State	Sewage Treatment Needs $	Rank	Urban Housing %	Rank	Health Professional Shortage Areas #	Rank	Tourism Spending $	Rank
Alabama	204.83	13	29.24	8	177.96	43	746.52	42
Alaska	342.37	33	34.93	35	152.04	40	2,247.89	3
Arizona	327.94	32	35.80	38	62.88	9	1,264.43	13
Arkansas	94.17	5	30.09	11	137.25	38	922.98	32
California	271.98	24	44.23	49	88.53	22	1,222.92	16
Colorado	158.21	11	31.84	22	65.99	11	1,712.14	6
Connecticut	668.90	45	35.53	37	59.25	7	638.65	49
Delaware	272.46	25	34.34	31	41.33	3	989.57	30
Florida	514.01	39	37.75	44	69.82	13	1,800.86	5
Georgia	288.00	28	32.86	26	138.60	39	1,442.16	8
Hawaii	233.62	16	55.77	50	24.78	1	4,424.14	2
Idaho	236.45	17	31.80	20	155.70	41	1,129.26	20
Illinois	270.77	23	33.88	30	81.14	18	1,052.51	24
Indiana	314.31	31	30.71	14	85.52	20	646.77	47
Iowa	28.83	1	29.23	7	86.45	21	863.38	37
Kansas	245.24	18	28.87	6	65.56	10	780.68	40
Kentucky	346.01	34	28.36	4	127.00	36	921.95	33
Louisiana	286.48	27	31.82	21	200.95	48	991.16	28
Maine	290.32	29	36.57	41	68.62	12	964.13	31
Maryland	306.92	30	35.49	36	29.92	2	848.52	38
Massachusetts	1,289.00	49	39.92	48	81.16	19	845.28	39
Michigan	391.31	36	32.34	24	106.67	30	687.16	45
Minnesota	216.96	15	31.74	19	49.55	4	1,143.55	18
Mississippi	252.11	19	33.28	28	270.85	50	699.69	44
Missouri	263.01	21	26.89	1	109.43	31	1,124.39	22
Montana	79.27	4	28.45	5	129.18	37	1,504.08	7
Nebraska	152.80	9	29.78	10	99.82	25	917.62	34
Nevada	124.06	6	37.52	43	123.91	35	8064.17	1
New Hampshire	771.17	46	36.09	39	57.56	6	867.09	36
New Jersey	610.91	43	38.43	45	53.62	5	1,141.80	19
New Mexico	77.85	3	36.26	40	199.28	47	1,256.59	14
New York	1276.82	48	37.13	42	117.03	32	990.56	29
North Carolina	591.37	42	31.89	23	118.42	33	1,120.74	23
North Dakota	59.38	2	31.31	16	190.35	44	1,226.46	15
Ohio	462.16	37	30.17	12	79.93	17	645.92	48
Oklahoma	144.24	8	30.32	13	103.49	27	1,033.57	25
Oregon	489.93	38	33.52	29	104.09	28	1,010.23	27
Pennsylvania	254.45	20	31.42	17	70.28	14	759.62	41
Rhode Island	928.71	47	38.99	47	105.24	29	470.52	50
South Carolina	188.33	12	32.80	25	197.56	46	1,148.51	17
South Dakota	153.52	10	31.56	18	218.13	49	1,015.08	26
Tennessee	367.93	35	29.52	9	101.80	26	1,432.02	9
Texas	263.48	22	34.54	34	99.33	24	1,127.29	21
Utah	127.07	7	34.42	33	76.24	16	1,355.59	11
Vermont	285.96	26	38.95	46	59.73	8	1,395.77	10
Virginia	534.01	40	34.36	32	72.63	15	1,300.41	12
Washington	588.52	41	33.18	27	98.44	23	898.25	35
West Virginia	666.30	44	28.30	3	172.30	42	653.47	46
Wisconsin	211.58	14	31.07	15	119.47	34	706.03	43
Wyoming	2,974.47	50	28.19	2	193.33	45	2,097.78	4

Sewage Treatment Needs

Without adequate sewage treatment facilities, existing businesses are constrained from growth and new businesses must seek other sites which can handle their sewage needs.

Measure: Total documented needs for publicly owned wastewater treatment facilities and other SRF eligibilities to meet estimated population for the next 20 years, millions of dollars per capita, 1992.

Source: U.S. Environmental Protection Agency. Office of Water. *1992 Needs Survey Report to Congress.* EPA 832-R-93-002. Washington, DC: September 1993.

Urban Housing Costs

Many areas of the nation face shortages of available housing that threaten to constrain development prospects, particularly in urban areas. However, no adequate state-by-state assessment of housing capacity is available at the present time. We assume a direct relationship between availability and cost, that is, the higher the demand for housing, the higher the cost.

Measure: Weighted annual average of fair market rent schedules for a standard two-bedroom unit of housing, metropolitan areas (1994), as a percent of per capita income (1992).

Source: U.S. Department of Housing and Urban Development. "Section 8 Housing Assistance Payments Program; Fair Market Rents Final Rule." *Federal Register*, September 28, 1994; and Department of Commerce, Regional Economic Analysis. Washington, DC: 1994. Calculations by CFED.

Health Professional Shortage Areas

We measure the availability of health services in a state by the proportion of a state's population that resides in health professional shortage areas, a federal designation that indicates an area is underserved by primary medical practitioners for either economic or geographic reasons. While this measure is not complete because it depends on the area or state applying for such designation, it offers a more direct way to measure the availability of health services to a state's residents than simply counting the number of doctors in a state.

Measure: State population without primary care within ready economic and geographic reach, per thousand population, December 1994.

Source: U.S. Department of Health and Human Services, Bureau of Primary Health Care, HRSA, Division of Shortage Designation, *Selected Statistics on Health Professional Shortage Areas.* Washington, DC: December 31, 1994.

Tourism Spending

Another way to understand whether "this is a good place to live" is to observe people's behavior, specifically observing the amount people spend to participate in recreation and tourism activities in a state. While this is an indirect measure ranging from amusement parks to campsites, it has the advantage of revealing how people value the amenities in a state.

Measure: U.S. domestic travel-generated business receipts, dollars per capita, 1991.

Source: U.S. Travel Data Center. *Impact of Travel on State Economies, 1991.* Table 5. Washington, DC: U.S. Travel Data Center, 1993.

Tax & Fiscal System Index

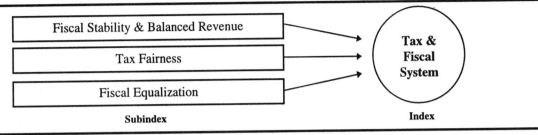

Fiscal Stability & Balanced Revenue

Tax Fairness

Fiscal Equalization

Subindex

Tax & Fiscal System

Index

Despite the tendency of state and local governments to use tax abatements and incentives to entice out-of-state businesses to relocate and encourage new business investments, recent research shows that, at best, these inducements have a marginal impact on business decisions. Thus, public sectors too often subsidize businesses for activities they would have undertaken anyway. Other factors, such as proximity to markets or access to skilled workers, are more important to employers and generally overwhelm any advantages created by tax differentials. This does not mean a state's tax and fiscal environment does not affect its economic climate. Rather, it is the soundness of a state's tax and fiscal system that impacts development:

- Government is an essential partner with businesses in making the strategic investments in people, institutions, and infrastructure that competitive firms require. Taxes are the "price" for such investments.

- Businesses seek predictable tax environments – revenues should not be falling or increasing erratically, nor should rates be changing annually. Fiscal stability is a large part of a state's economic climate, providing greater certainty for businesses and households. It also produces sufficient revenues, serving as a source of counter-cyclical funds in recessions.

- Over-reliance on any one tax source leads to unstable revenue streams. Inevitably, states with such systems will be forced to raise rates on remaining taxes.

- Even at the risk of some loss of stability and tax balance, a tax system must possess some "elasticity" – the tax base must be able to keep up with economic growth. If not, future development might be jeopardized by the inability of the fiscal system to invest enough in roads, clean air and water, an educated workforce, and crime-free communities.

- Taxes need to be broad-based in order to treat all taxpayers evenly, to keep tax rates low, to minimize the distortion of economic decisions, and to generate adequate revenues. (Thus, the worst thing tax officials can do is to create a tax base with lots of holes in the form of tax incentives for different types of companies.)

- Taxes must be fair. Tax systems should shield the poor's subsistence income from taxes, extract a reasonable contribution from those most able to pay, and treat businesses and households with the same incomes equitably.

- Not all communities within a state can afford an adequate level of public services. State governments are in an ideal position to "level the playing field" by assuming a proportion of local costs in key areas like education.

- Like the federal government, states are faced with structural deficit problems. Increased volatility in traditional economic sectors, federal mandates for public services (without accompanying increases in federal funding), and exploding (and hard to control) expenditures for criminal justice, education, and health care are bursting state budgets. These difficulties are even harder to address because state revenue systems are now out of touch with their economic base. The rise of the service sector at the expense of goods producers and the birth of multinational corporations mean the existing state tax systems are not yielding sufficient revenues. At the same time some sectors carry more than their fair share. Reforms are needed to create a tax system equipped to deal with today's global, information-based service economy.

- A tax system must be efficient in its administration and simple to understand. Structuring a system in this way decreases compliance costs and enhances public trust.

- State governments do face difficulties from interstate tax competition which raise politicians', businesses', and citizens' concerns about having a poor business climate. These are best dealt with by following the above tax guidelines and by making sure there is a fairly balanced, broad-based revenue base.

- A modern tax and fiscal system embodies a variety of appropriate (and often conflicting) goals – fiscal stability, balance, fairness, and revenue potential. No structure will perfectly realize all these objectives. Instead, policymakers must draw upon their understanding of their state's problems, opportunities, and political culture to "balance" these competing goals.

As a way of translating these guidelines into a simplified and workable assessment tool, CFED has created a Tax and Fiscal Index that measures three vital aspects of a state's tax system: Fiscal Stability and Balanced Revenue; Tax Fairness; and Fiscal Equalization. Because a state's tax system is not a driving factor in its economic climate, we do not grade this index. Instead, the 15 highest ranking states receive a plus (+), the lowest 15 receive a minus (–), and the remaining 20 receive a check (√).

Fiscal Stability & Balanced Revenue

The "best" state tax and fiscal environment has several identifiable and widely-recognized characteristics. First: major taxes are balanced – no individual tax is unduly burdensome, and all taxes, taken together, help insulate revenues from recession and economic shocks to the extent possible. Second: the tax system – combined with a fiscal system in which prudent controls guard against wide swings in tax levels and the quality of services – permits states to provide businesses the assurances needed to make long-term investments. South Carolina, North Carolina, and Minnesota lead in fiscal stability and balanced revenue.

Tax Fairness

It is occasionally argued that an equitably distributed tax system is antithetical to a good business climate – especially when a state lures branch plants and other footloose facilities via special tax breaks. But if state and local governments are to be credible, their current citizens and businesses must be convinced that their taxes are fair with no individual or company benefiting at the expense of others. California and Minnesota are the leaders in tax fairness.

Fiscal Equalization

State policies to promote fiscal capacity among local governments are essential to a sound business climate. Such policies assure that all communities have an equal ability to provide adequate public services to firms and individuals. New Mexico and Wyoming lead in equalizing fiscal capacity.

Scoring the Index

States can score up to 280 points in the Tax & Fiscal Index – a possible 100 points in Fiscal Stability & Balanced Revenue, 100 Points in Tax Fairness, and 80 points in Fiscal Equalization. The ranks in each sub-index and the Final Score are based on the total points in each category.

Tax & Fiscal System – Total Scores

State	Stability/ Balance		Tax Fairness		Fiscal Equalization		Final Score		
	Score	Rank	Score	Rank	Score	Rank	Score	Rank	Mark
Alabama	75.78	11	12.45	47	59.52	11	147.74	30	√
Alaska	40.34	46	42.10	21	65.75	3	148.19	29	√
Arizona	79.29	7	59.73	7	41.04	28	180.06	5	+
Arkansas	75.13	15	20.84	40	63.46	6	159.43	16	√
California	82.15	6	77.73	1	43.75	25	203.62	3	+
Colorado	83.24	5	54.44	9	22.84	48	160.53	15	+
Connecticut	72.40	21	50.59	13	30.55	44	153.54	23	√
Delaware	50.58	42	39.70	23	41.49	27	131.78	40	−
Florida	62.19	36	20.00	42	38.51	33	120.70	43	−
Georgia	74.05	18	22.05	39	50.70	17	146.81	31	√
Hawaii	69.68	28	28.70	36	59.62	10	158.00	19	√
Idaho	75.70	13	65.29	4	64.03	5	205.01	2	+
Illinois	56.50	40	47.42	17	31.91	41	135.82	37	−
Indiana	75.55	14	16.18	44	38.23	35	129.96	41	−
Iowa	70.11	24	48.63	15	38.25	34	161.80	14	+
Kansas	74.93	16	31.60	33	59.75	9	163.03	13	+
Kentucky	71.67	23	22.96	38	52.41	16	133.78	39	−
Louisiana	58.41	38	73.01	3	39.14	30	178.30	6	+
Maine	66.15	34	52.73	11	30.76	43	152.42	24	√
Maryland	68.93	29	42.73	19	33.22	40	144.47	35	√
Massachusetts	72.90	20	38.34	24	33.22	40	141.85	36	−
Michigan	69.99	25	35.47	27	36.39	37	208.41	1	+
Minnesota	85.73	3	76.82	2	45.86	23	208.41	1	+
Mississippi	69.96	26	30.98	34	64.84	4	165.77	12	+
Missouri	73.02	19	34.33	30	44.34	24	151.69	25	√
Montana	37.53	48	62.87	5	55.80	14	156.20	20	√
Nebraska	78.78	8	51.72	12	28.48	45	158.98	18	√
Nevada	41.66	45	17.40	43	49.52	20	108.58	45	−
New Hampshire	30.80	50	48.80	14	17.99	50	97.59	48	−
New Jersey	67.33	31	37.87	25	40.23	29	145.42	34	√
New Mexico	74.78	17	31.90	32	73.89	1	180.56	4	+
New York	66.51	32	42.81	18	39.01	31	148.33	28	√
North Carolina	85.94	2	29.73	35	57.75	13	173.42	8	+
North Dakota	66.25	33	56.25	8	49.77	19	172.27	11	+
Ohio	83.28	4	34.37	29	41.77	26	159.42	17	√
Oklahoma	69.95	27	20.36	41	59.84	8	150.14	27	√
Oregon	46.58	43	53.95	10	22.84	49	123.36	42	−
Pennsylvania	78.72	9	40.68	22	34.75	38	154.15	21	√
Rhode Island	72.15	22	36.70	26	37.72	36	146.58	32	√
South Carolina	86.11	1	42.11	20	45.96	22	174.19	7	+
South Dakota	53.18	41	6.10	50	25.42	47	84.71	50	−
Tennessee	60.86	37	11.20	48	33.92	39	105.98	46	−
Texas	44.60	44	12.80	46	38.58	32	95.98	49	−
Utah	75.75	12	42.72	19	54.81	15	173.28	9	+
Vermont	56.56	39	61.97	6	26.94	46	145.47	33	√
Virginia	67.85	30	35.00	28	30.94	42	133.79	38	−
Washington	31.91	49	10.40	49	59.90	7	102.20	47	−
West Virginia	65.42	35	25.99	37	59.21	12	150.62	26	√
Wisconsin	77.57	10	48.28	16	46.45	21	172.30	10	+
Wyoming	37.72	47	14.40	45	67.01	2	119.13	44	−

Fiscal Stability & Balanced Revenue Data (part 1)

State	Personal Income Tax %/Total Tax Revenue	Points	General Sales Tax %/Total Tax Revenue	Points	Property Tax %/Total Tax Revenue	Points	Corporate Income Tax %/Total Tax Revenue	Points
Alabama	21.74	15.00	30.20	14.85	12.13	9.10	4.08	15.00
Alaska	0.00	0.00	3.39	2.54	27.89	15.00	12.48	12.80
Arizona	16.01	12.01	32.85	12.86	33.32	12.51	4.64	15.00
Arkansas	23.40	15.00	33.73	12.20	17.23	12.92	5.23	15.00
California	23.63	15.00	25.98	15.00	28.60	15.00	9.70	15.00
Colorado	22.98	15.00	26.58	15.00	33.31	12.52	3.64	15.00
Connecticut	18.59	13.94	20.83	15.00	39.14	8.15	10.69	14.59
Delaware	32.41	15.00	0.00	0.00	14.11	10.58	8.49	15.00
Florida	0.00	0.00	32.80	12.90	38.38	8.71	4.61	15.00
Georgia	24.91	15.00	28.80	15.00	29.59	15.00	5.78	15.00
Hawaii	26.74	15.00	38.17	8.88	16.40	12.30	1.93	13.50
Idaho	28.22	15.00	23.14	15.00	25.08	15.00	5.36	15.00
Illinois	17.90	13.43	21.42	15.00	38.50	8.63	7.57	15.00
Indiana	25.26	15.00	27.50	15.00	31.80	13.65	9.49	15.00
Iowa	24.88	15.00	18.44	13.83	35.09	11.18	4.28	15.00
Kansas	16.88	12.66	23.89	15.00	37.06	9.71	6.69	15.00
Kentucky	31.15	15.00	20.75	15.00	16.92	12.69	4.83	15.00
Louisiana	12.27	9.20	38.58	8.56	16.73	12.55	5.62	15.00
Maine	22.24	15.00	21.56	15.00	38.21	8.84	4.25	15.00
Maryland	37.42	15.00	13.78	10.33	27.99	15.00	3.63	15.00
Massachusetts	34.86	15.00	12.92	9.69	34.32	11.76	9.24	15.00
Michigan	17.70	13.27	17.88	13.41	43.72	4.71	13.99	11.29
Minnesota	27.06	15.00	19.90	14.93	31.36	13.98	6.26	15.00
Mississippi	12.71	9.53	34.20	11.85	26.98	15.00	5.73	15.00
Missouri	23.85	15.00	30.14	14.90	24.12	15.00	3.52	15.00
Montana	22.10	15.00	0.00	0.00	39.96	7.53	7.53	15.00
Nebraska	20.17	15.00	23.82	15.00	36.07	10.45	5.19	15.00
Nevada	0.00	0.00	33.18	12.61	24.04	15.00	0.00	0.00
New Hampshire	1.49	1.12	0.00	0.00	64.09	0.00	12.70	12.58
New Jersey	17.93	13.44	17.70	13.27	43.33	5.01	7.27	15.00
New Mexico	15.74	11.81	42.19	5.86	12.15	9.12	3.26	14.83
New York	28.44	15.00	17.28	12.96	33.34	12.50	8.43	15.00
North Carolina	28.90	15.00	23.97	15.00	20.62	15.00	7.28	15.00
North Dakota	10.69	8.02	24.39	15.00	30.24	14.82	6.18	15.00
Ohio	30.02	15.00	20.46	15.00	29.31	15.00	5.30	15.00
Oklahoma	23.25	15.00	29.95	15.00	14.86	11.15	3.41	14.98
Oregon	35.66	15.00	0.00	0.00	41.23	6.58	5.60	15.00
Pennsylvania	24.87	15.00	17.28	12.96	27.79	15.00	8.85	15.00
Rhode Island	21.31	15.00	17.33	13.00	42.06	5.96	4.87	15.00
South Carolina	24.72	15.00	25.83	15.00	28.46	15.00	4.11	15.00
South Dakota	0.00	0.00	34.14	11.89	39.11	8.17	4.78	15.00
Tennessee	1.26	0.95	44.67	3.99	23.64	15.00	7.14	15.00
Texas	0.00	0.00	31.94	13.54	39.30	8.02	0.00	0.00
Utah	25.36	15.00	31.73	13.70	27.09	15.00	3.80	15.00
Vermont	20.82	15.00	12.05	9.04	41.80	6.15	4.11	15.00
Virginia	26.18	15.00	16.31	12.23	32.66	13.00	4.83	15.00
Washington	0.00	0.00	48.19	1.36	29.29	15.00	0.00	0.00
West Virginia	20.40	15.00	26.53	15.00	17.70	13.28	7.23	15.00
Wisconsin	27.07	15.00	19.03	14.28	35.34	10.99	6.18	15.00
Wyoming	0.00	0.00	21.59	15.00	42.46	5.65	0.00	0.00

Fiscal Stability & Balanced Revenue Data Sources

To measure balance within the tax system, we evaluate the share of total state and local tax revenues (exclusive of federal aid) provided for by four separate taxes: personal income taxes, general sales taxes, property taxes, and corporate income taxes. Points are then assigned based on how well each separate tax compares with an "ideal" range, one that would result in a well balanced and diversified revenue system. To measure the degree of revenue stability, we examine whether a state has a rainy day fund and the available revenues within that reserve, whether it has decoupled from the federal net operating loss carryback provision (and only allows a net operating loss carryforward), and whether it has a broad-based sales tax. The measures are:

Balance:
- *Personal Income Tax*
- *General Sales Tax*
- *Property Tax*
- *Corporate Income Tax*

Fiscal Stability:
- *Rainy Day Fund*
- *Net Operating Loss Carrybacks*
- *Breadth of Sales Tax Base*

Personal Income Tax

States receive 15 points if personal income taxes account for at least 20 percent of state and local tax revenues. Points are deducted at the rate of one point for every 1 1/3 percentage points below 20 percent, so that states with no income tax get zero points.

Measure: State and local individual income taxes as a percentage of revenues from all state and local taxes (Fiscal Year 1991-1992).

Source: U.S. Department of Commerce, Bureau of the Census, Government Finances Division. *Government Finances: 1991-1992 (Preliminary Report) GF/92.* Washington, DC: August 1994, and data disk.

General Sales Tax

States receive 15 points if general sales tax revenues account for 20 to 30 percent of state and local tax revenue. One point is deducted for every 1 1/3 percentage points outside this range. States with no sales tax get zero points.

Measure: State and local general sales taxes as a percentage of revenues from all state and local taxes.
Source: Same as Personal Income Tax.

Property Tax

States receive 15 points if general property tax revenues account for 20 to 30 percent of state and local tax revenue. Points are deducted at the rate of one point for every 1 1/3 percentage points outside this range.

Measure: State and local property taxes as a percentage of revenues from all state and local taxes.
Source: Same as Personal Income Tax.

Corporate Income Tax

States receive 15 points if corporate income taxes as a percent of state tax revenues are within a 50 percent range of the U.S. average of 6.85 percent (3.43 to 10.28). One point is deducted for every percentage point outside this range. States with no corporate income tax receive zero points.

Measure: State corporate income taxes as a percentage of total tax revenue, 1993.
Source: U.S. Department of Commerce, Bureau of the Census, Government Finances Division. Washington, DC: data disk.
Note: Due to reporting errors, Alaska's corporate income tax data is from 1992.

Fiscal Stability & Balanced Revenue Data (part 2)

State	Rainy Day Fund		Net Operating Carrybacks		Breadth of Sales Tax Base	
	%/Gen. Fund	Points	Allowed?	Points	Sales Tax Rev. as % Personal Inc. Per 1%	Points
Alabama	0.0	5.0	no	10	0.43	6.83
Alaska	6.6	10.0	yes	0	no state sales tax	0.00
Arizona	1.9	6.9	no	10	0.63	10.00
Arkansas	no	0.0	no	10	0.63	10.00
California	0.0	5.0	no	10	0.45	7.15
Colorado	3.9	8.9	no	10	0.43	6.83
Connecticut	0.0	5.0	no	10	0.36	5.72
Delaware	5.0	10.0	yes	0	no state sales tax	0.00
Florida	2.0	7.0	no	10	0.54	8.57
Georgia	0.0	5.0	yes	0	0.57	9.05
Hawaii	no	0.0	yes	0	1.26	20.00
Idaho	2.6	7.6	yes	0	0.51	8.10
Illinois	no	0.0	yes	0	0.28	4.45
Indiana	4.6	9.6	yes	0	0.46	7.30
Iowa	2.0	7.0	yes	0	0.51	8.10
Kansas	0.1	5.1	no	10	0.47	7.46
Kentucky	2.0	7.0	yes	0	0.44	6.99
Louisiana	0.0	5.0	yes	0	0.51	8.10
Maine	0.0	5.0	yes	0	0.46	7.30
Maryland	3.2	8.2	yes	0	0.34	5.40
Massachusetts	2.0	7.0	no	10	0.28	4.45
Michigan	8.0	10.0	no	10	0.46	7.30
Minnesota	5.8	10.0	no	10	0.43	6.83
Mississippi	7.7	10.0	yes	0	0.54	8.57
Missouri	0.5	5.5	yes	0	0.48	7.62
Montana	no	0.0	yes	0	no state sales tax	0.00
Nebraska	1.5	6.5	no	10	0.43	6.83
Nevada	0.0	5.0	no corp. tax	0	0.57	9.05
New Hampshire	2.1	7.1	no	10	no state sales tax	0.00
New Jersey	1.0	6.0	no	10	0.29	4.61
New Mexico	4.2	9.2	no	10	0.88	13.97
New York	0.5	5.5	yes	0	0.35	5.56
North Carolina	3.0	8.0	no	10	0.50	7.94
North Dakota	0.0	5.0	yes	0	0.53	8.41
Ohio	2.4	7.4	no	10	0.37	5.88
Oklahoma	1.2	6.2	yes	0	0.48	7.62
Oregon	no	0.0	no	10	no state sales tax	0.00
Pennsylvania	1.0	6.0	no	10	0.30	4.76
Rhode Island	2.8	7.8	no	10	0.34	5.40
South Carolina	2.7	7.7	no	10	0.53	8.41
South Dakota	3.6	8.6	no corp. tax	0	0.60	9.53
Tennessee	2.5	7.5	no	10	0.53	8.41
Texas	0.1	5.1	no	10	0.50	7.94
Utah	3.0	8.0	yes	0	0.57	9.05
Vermont	0.5	5.5	yes	0	0.37	5.88
Virginia	1.1	6.1	yes	0	0.41	6.51
Washington	1.5	6.5	no corp. tax	0	0.57	9.05
West Virginia	no	0.0	yes	0	0.45	7.15
Wisconsin	0.0	5.0	no	10	0.46	7.30
Wyoming	0.0	5.0	no corp. tax	0	0.76	12.07

Rainy Day Fund

States receive five points if they have a rainy day or budget stabilization fund: one more point is added for every percentage point up to five percent of general fund appropriations in their rainy day fund, allowing for a maximum total of ten points.

Measure: Budget stabilization funds, as a percent of state general fund appropriations, projected for the Fiscal Year 1995.

Source: National Conference of State Legislatures. State Budget Actions 1994. Denver, CO: National Conference of State Legislatures, November 1994.

Net Operating Loss Carrybacks

Profits are inherently a volatile tax base. The federal government allows corporations to carry operating losses forward to offset future profits, and it also allows them to carry losses backward to offset past profits – which means that they can obtain refunds of past tax liability. State allowance of such carrybacks can make corporate profit tax collections even more volatile and wreck havoc with forecasted revenues during recessions. Consequently, many states have "decoupled" from this federal provision and only allow carryforwards. States receive ten points if they have done so.

Measure: Does the state allow net operating loss carrybacks (1994)?

Source: William A. Raabe and Karen J. Boucher. *1995 Multistate Corporate Tax Guide,* Volume 1: Corporate Income Tax. New York: 1995.

Breadth of Sales Tax Base

The United States economy is becoming more service-based. Unfortunately, many states have not kept up with this change by making their sales tax much more comprehensive, thereby covering a wider variety of consumer and business services. This lessens the erosion of a state's tax base, caused by the decline of manufacturing and other goods producing sectors. There is a maximum of 20 points for the state with the most comprehensive sales tax base. States with no sales tax receive no points. For each .1% below the best, 1.59 points are deducted.

Measure: Sales tax revenue as a percent of personal income per 1% of tax rate, FY 1991.

Source: John F. Due and John L. Mikesell, *Sales Taxation, State and Local Structure and Administration,* Urban Institute Press, December 1994.

Tax Fairness Data (part 1)

State	Sales & Excise Tax Burden		Personal Income Tax Progressivity		Income Tax Threshold	
	%/Income	Points	Ratio	Points	$	Points
Alabama	8.2	7.2	1.10	2.37	4,600	2.88
Alaska	2.6	19.6	0.00	0.00	0	0.00
Arizona	7.9	9.6	3.60	7.76	15,800	9.88
Arkansas	9.3	4.0	3.26	7.03	11,700	7.31
California	9.4	3.6	11.60	25.00	22,600	14.13
Colorado	6.2	15.6	1.90	4.09	15,600	9.75
Connecticut	7.3	12.4	3.80	8.19	24,000	15.00
Delaware	3.4	19.2	2.38	5.13	8,600	5.38
Florida	7.8	10.0	0.00	0.00	0	0.00
Georgia	7.9	9.6	2.27	4.89	12,100	7.56
Hawaii	7.1	13.6	1.70	3.66	6,300	3.94
Idaho	7.2	13.2	4.39	9.46	16,200	10.13
Illinois	8.2	7.2	1.26	2.72	4,000	2.50
Indiana	7.4	11.2	1.15	2.48	4,000	2.50
Iowa	7.4	11.2	2.02	4.35	13,500	8.44
Kansas	8.0	8.0	3.48	7.50	13,000	8.13
Kentucky	6.6	15.2	1.52	3.28	5,000	3.13
Louisiana	11.3	0.8	2.45	5.28	11,000	6.88
Maine	7.6	10.4	6.20	13.36	14,800	9.25
Maryland	5.8	16.4	1.95	4.20	19,400	12.13
Massachusetts	4.9	18.0	1.32	2.84	12,000	7.50
Michigan	8.2	7.2	1.40	3.02	8,400	5.25
Minnesota	6.6	15.2	4.52	9.74	19,000	11.88
Mississippi	10.3	2.4	4.01	8.64	15,900	9.94
Missouri	8.1	7.6	1.47	3.17	9,700	6.06
Montana	3.5	18.8	2.12	4.57	7,200	4.50
Nebraska	9.0	4.4	3.34	7.20	16,200	10.13
Nevada	7.3	12.4	0.00	0.00	0	0.00
New Hampshire	3.5	18.8	0.00	0.00	0	0.00
New Jersey	5.2	17.2	3.50	7.54	5,000	3.13
New Mexico	11.0	1.6	7.01	15.11	16,300	10.19
New York	8.3	6.0	2.90	6.25	16,900	10.56
North Carolina	8.3	6.0	2.60	5.60	13,000	8.13
North Dakota	7.9	9.6	5.27	11.36	16,469	10.29
Ohio	7.3	12.4	2.51	5.41	10,500	6.56
Oklahoma	8.3	6.0	2.34	5.04	10,900	6.81
Oregon	2.5	20.0	2.15	4.63	10,900	6.81
Pennsylvania	5.7	16.8	0.99	2.13	10,800	6.75
Rhode Island	7.9	9.6	4.60	9.91	19,500	12.19
South Carolina	6.8	14.4	3.52	7.59	16,200	10.13
South Dakota	9.4	3.6	0.00	0.00	0	0.00
Tennessee	11.1	1.2	0.00	0.00	0	0.00
Texas	9.7	2.8	0.00	0.00	0	0.00
Utah	8.8	4.8	2.05	4.42	13,600	8.50
Vermont	4.9	18.0	9.70	20.91	20,900	13.06
Virginia	6.0	16.0	1.80	3.88	8,200	5.13
Washington	11.7	0.4	0.00	0.00	0	0.00
West Virginia	10.6	2.0	3.01	6.49	8,000	5.00
Wisconsin	7.2	13.2	2.24	4.83	16,400	10.25
Wyoming	6.8	14.4	0.00	0.00	0	0.00

Tax Fairness Data Sources

Tax fairness helps build political credibility for state and local governments, mitigating individual and business taxpayers' perceptions that the tax system may benefit others at their own expense. Measures are:

- *Sales & Excise Tax Burdens on Low-Income Families*
- *Personal Income Tax Progressivity*
- *Income Tax Threshold*
- *Property Tax Circuit Breaker*
- *Combined Corporate Reporting*
- *Tax Expenditure Budgets/Reports*

Sales & Excise Tax Burdens on Low-Income Families

This measure examines the level, or burden, of sales and excise taxes as a percentage of income for low-income families (poorest 20 percent of all families in the state). The maximum number of points a state can receive is 20, with .4 points (20 points divided by 50) subtracted for each position further from the best.

Measure: Percent of income spent on sales and excise taxes by the poorest 20 percent of a state's population, 1994.
Source: Citizens for Tax Justice. *State Sales and Excise Tax Burdens, 1994.* Washington, DC: February, 1995.

Personal Income Tax Progressivity

The personal income tax burden for the top one percent of all taxpayers is compared to the average tax burden for middle-income and low-income taxpayers (bottom 60%). The more progressive a state's personal income tax, the higher the share of taxes paid by the top-income taxpayers as compared to the average. There is a maximum of 25 points for states with the most progressive tax (this year California, with a ratio of 11.6), and states with no personal income tax receive no points. For each percent below the most

progressive rate, 2.155 points are subtracted (25 points divided by 11.6).

Measure: Ratio of income tax burden for top 1 percent of all taxpayers to average income tax burden for bottom 60 percent, 1994.
Source: Citizens for Tax Justice. *Personal Income Tax Progressivity Rankings for States with Broad-Based Personal Income Taxes, 1994.* Washington, DC: February 1995.

Income Tax Threshold

The income level at which state residents – specifically a family of four with two parents – begin paying taxes is measured. The maximum number of points is 15; the higher the income threshold, the more points a state receives. Points are deducted at the rate of one point for each $1,600 below the highest threshold, $24,000. States without a personal income tax receive no points.

Measure: State income tax thresholds for two-parent families of four, 1994.
Source: Center on Budget and Policy Priorities, Washington, DC: forthcoming release.

Tax Fairness Data (part 2)

State	Property Tax Circuit Breaker		Combined Reporting		Tax Expenditure Budgets	
	Type	Points	Required	Points	Budgets	Points
Alabama	none	0.0	no	0	no	0
Alaska	elderly/disabled renters	2.5	yes	20	no	0
Arizona	elderly/disabled owners	2.5	yes	20	yes	10
Arkansas	elderly/disabled owners	2.5	no	0	no	0
California	elderly, disabled	5.0	yes	20	yes	10
Colorado	elderly, disabled	5.0	yes	20	no	0
Connecticut	elderly, disabled	5.0	no	0	yes	10
Delaware	none	0.0	no	0	yes	10
Florida	none	0.0	no	0	yes	10
Georgia	none	0.0	no	0	no	0
Hawaii	all renters	7.5	no	0	no	0
Idaho	elderly/disabled owners	2.5	yes	20	yes	10
Illinois	elderly, disabled	5.0	yes	20	yes	10
Indiana	none	0.0	no	0	no	0
Iowa	all owners & renters	10.0	no	0	no	0
Kansas	elderly, disabled	5.0	yes	20	no	0
Kentucky	none	0.0	no	0	yes	10
Louisiana	none	0.0	no	0	yes	10
Maine	all owners & renters	10.0	yes	20	yes	10
Maryland	all owners & renters	10.0	no	0	yes	10
Massachusetts	none	0.0	no	0	yes	10
Michigan	all owners & renters	10.0	no	0	yes	10
Minnesota	all owners & renters	10.0	yes	20	yes	10
Mississippi	none	0.0	no	0	yes	10
Missouri	all renters	7.5	no	0	yes	10
Montana	elderly, disabled	5.0	yes	20	yes	10
Nebraska	none	0.0	yes	20	yes	10
Nevada	elderly, disabled	5.0	–	0	no	0
New Hampshire	none	0.0	yes	20	yes	10
New Jersey	all owners & renters	10.0	no	0	no	0
New Mexico	elderly, disabled	5.0	no	0	no	0
New York	all owners & renters	10.0	no	0	yes	10
North Carolina	none	0.0	no	0	yes	10
North Dakota	elderly, disabled	5.0	yes	20	no	0
Ohio	none	0.0	no	0	yes	10
Oklahoma	elderly/disabled owners	2.5	no	0	no	0
Oregon	elderly/disabled renters	2.5	yes	20	no	0
Pennsylvania	elderly, disabled	5.0	no	0	yes	10
Rhode Island	elderly, disabled	5.0	no	0	no	0
South Carolina	none	0.0	no	0	yes	10
South Dakota	elderly/disabled owners	2.5	–	0	no	0
Tennessee	none	0.0	no	0	yes	10
Texas	none	0.0	no	0	yes	10
Utah	elderly, disabled	5.0	yes	20	no	0
Vermont	all owners & renters	10.0	no	0	no	0
Virginia	none	0.0	no	0	yes	10
Washington	none	0.0	–	0	yes	10
West Virginia	elderly/disabled owners	2.5	no	0	yes	10
Wisconsin	all owners & renters	10.0	no	0	yes	10
Wyoming	none	0.0	–	0	no	0

Property Tax Circuit Breaker

A state receives 10 points if it has a state-financed property tax circuit breaker available to all taxpayers; 7.5 points if it's available either to all renters or all homeowners, 5 points if available only to the elderly and/or disabled, and 2.5 points if available *only* to either renters or homeowners who are either elderly or disabled.

Measure: Property tax circuit breaker programs for homeowners and renters, 1994.

Source: Scott Mackey and Karen Carter, *State Tax Policy and Senior Citizens*, 2nd edition. National Conference of State Legislatures, Denver, CO: 1994.

Combined Reporting

A growing share of business is being conducted by companies across state and national boundaries, and state tax systems have not adequately adapted to this shift. Sophisticated multistate businesses have been able to use this situation to avoid paying their fair share, thereby causing instate firms to be disproportionately taxed. States are now beginning to use the technique of apportionment to divide the total profits of a multistate enterprise among the states with jurisdictions to tax it. One leading approach is to apportion on a combined reporting basis. This method treats the profits of all the separate legal entities, such as a parent corporation and its subsidiaries, as a single "unitary" business. This prevents a multistate corporation from using various subsidiaries to shift income between states in order to minimize its total state tax bill. States receive 20 points if they used combined reporting in their corporate income tax. States without a corporate tax receive no points.

Measure: Does the state always require unitary business combination for tax reporting purposes (1994)?

Source: William A. Raabe and Karen J. Boucher. *1995 Multistate Corporate Tax Guide,* Volume 1: Corporate Income Tax. New York, NY: 1995.

Tax Expenditure Budgets/Reports

Many states erode their tax base and harm horizontal equity (treating taxpayers with the same income equally) by providing many tax incentives and breaks to both businesses and households. An effective way of increasing accountability and tracking the costs to the state in lost revenues from these incentives is to require that tax expenditure reports be compiled annually or biannually. States receive 10 points for having such a budgeting and reporting process.

Measure: States with tax expenditure budgets/reports, 1994.*

Source: Center on Budget and Policy Priorities. Washington, DC: forthcoming release.

* Notes on Tax Expenditure Budgets/Reports:

Virginia: Sales and use tax expenditures are examined only on a five-year cycle, i.e., each year the Department of Taxation releases a report that examines two categories of sales and use tax exemptions.

West Virginia: The Department of Tax and Revenue prepares reports on a three-year cycle; these reports analyze tax expenditures for most major state taxes.

Nebraska: The Department of Revenue prepares a tax expenditure report every even-numbered year.

Fiscal Equalization Data

State	Welfare %	Points	Local Education %	Points	Other State Aid %	Points
Alabama	97.59	19.52	70.91	40.00	8.44	0.00
Alaska	96.13	19.23	79.28	40.00	20.43	6.52
Arizona	84.05	16.81	49.26	19.26	18.89	4.98
Arkansas	99.76	19.95	68.61	38.61	18.81	4.90
California	50.99	10.20	61.11	31.11	16.35	2.44
Colorado	71.49	14.30	38.54	8.54	6.88	0.00
Connecticut	90.35	18.07	42.48	12.48	8.72	0.00
Delaware	99.50	19.90	51.59	21.59	12.06	0.00
Florida	95.60	19.12	49.39	19.39	11.43	0.00
Georgia	98.40	19.68	61.02	31.02	3.94	0.00
Hawaii	98.08	19.62	100.00	40.00	7.87	0.00
Idaho	92.34	18.47	71.70	40.00	19.47	5.56
Illinois	95.23	19.05	42.86	12.86	13.83	0.00
Indiana	85.82	17.16	45.10	15.10	19.88	5.97
Iowa	90.48	18.10	56.37	26.37	19.38	5.47
Kansas	96.25	19.25	49.00	19.00	10.89	0.00
Kentucky	98.75	19.75	82.10	40.00	11.07	0.00
Louisiana	98.50	19.70	62.71	32.71	8.25	0.00
Maine	97.37	19.47	49.67	19.67	10.03	0.00
Maryland	98.59	19.72	40.09	10.09	14.86	0.95
Massachusetts	98.56	19.71	35.71	5.71	21.71	7.80
Michigan	93.62	18.72	37.94	7.94	23.64	9.73
Minnesota	68.72	13.74	57.65	27.65	18.38	4.47
Mississippi	98.09	19.62	70.49	40.00	19.13	5.22
Missouri	97.27	19.45	54.88	24.88	10.19	0.00
Montana	91.93	18.39	58.93	28.93	22.39	8.48
Nebraska	93.90	18.78	39.70	9.70	13.69	0.00
Nevada	90.94	18.19	59.02	29.02	16.22	2.31
New Hampshire	89.97	17.99	15.16	0.00	9.90	0.00
New Jersey	81.73	16.35	46.78	16.78	21.01	7.10
New Mexico	96.05	19.21	86.89	40.00	28.59	14.68
New York	61.33	12.27	56.74	26.74	10.18	0.00
North Carolina	86.27	17.25	67.52	37.52	16.88	2.97
North Dakota	92.45	18.49	51.05	21.05	24.14	10.23
Ohio	79.64	15.93	49.91	19.91	19.85	5.94
Oklahoma	99.22	19.84	71.68	40.00	10.62	0.00
Oregon	97.91	19.58	31.03	1.03	16.14	2.23
Pennsylvania	88.87	17.77	45.17	15.17	15.71	1.80
Rhode Island	96.24	19.25	48.48	18.48	4.19	0.00
South Carolina	99.54	19.91	56.05	26.05	11.71	0.00
South Dakota	96.54	19.31	36.12	6.12	12.12	0.00
Tennessee	96.88	19.38	44.55	14.55	8.20	0.00
Texas	97.85	19.57	49.00	19.00	6.31	0.00
Utah	97.91	19.58	65.22	35.22	6.28	0.00
Vermont	99.85	19.97	36.96	6.96	13.92	0.01
Virginia	78.31	15.66	45.27	15.27	10.52	0.00
Washington	99.48	19.90	70.28	40.00	9.18	0.00
West Virginia	99.94	19.99	69.22	39.22	5.57	0.00
Wisconsin	75.15	15.03	43.94	13.94	31.40	17.49
Wyoming	96.75	19.35	57.66	27.66	34.96	20.00

Fiscal Equalization Data Sources

State policies that promote equal fiscal capacity among local governments are crucial for a sound business climate. These policies increase the ability of all communities to provide a sufficient level and quality of services to firms and individuals.

We measure fiscal equalization by the extent to which state governments finance key service costs and provide revenue sharing aid to communities by examining:

- Welfare
- Local Education
- Other State Aid

Welfare

States receive .2 points for every percentage point of total state and local welfare costs assumed by state government, up to a maximum of 20 points.

Measure: State government direct welfare expenditures as a percent of total state and local direct welfare costs, Fiscal Year 1991-1992.

Source: U.S. Census Bureau, Government Finances Division. *Government Finances: 1991-1992* (Preliminary Report), GF/92-5P. Washington, DC: August 1994 and data disk.

Local Education

States receive one point for every percentage point of total state and local K-12 education costs assumed by state government over 30 percent and up to 70 percent, with a maximum of 40 points.

Measure: State government intergovernmental primary and secondary education assistance to local governments as a share of total local government spending on primary and secondary education, Fiscal Year 1991-1992.

Source: Local data: same as Welfare. State data: U.S. Bureau of the Census, State Government Finances: 1992, series GF/92-3. Washington, DC: October 1993.

Other State Aid

States receive one point for every percentage point by which its other general revenue contributions to local governments exceed the U.S. average (13.91 percent), up to a maximum score of 20 points.

Measure: State intergovernmental assistance, not including primary and secondary education and public welfare assistance, as a share of local expenditures, less local spending on primary and secondary education and public welfare, Fiscal Year 1991-1992.

Source: Same as Local Education.

Note: For more background on business climate and taxes, see Karl Seidman. *The Role of Taxation in State Business Climate.* Washington, DC: The Corporation for Enterprise Development, 1987. For a discussion of the merits of a balanced revenue system, see Robert Kleine and John Shannon. *Characteristics of a Balanced and Moderate State-Local Revenue System,* and Steve Gold, *Reforming State Tax Systems.* Washington, DC: National Conference of State Legislatures, 1986.

Appendix

Rural/Urban Disparity

To augment the Equity subindex of the Economic Performance Index, CFED devised a rural/urban disparity measure to help gauge the difference between the performance of rural and urban counties within a state, based on a variety of indicators.

Why a Rural/Urban Measure?

One major finding that emerged from the *1988* and *1989 Development Report Cards* was that when the measures that constitute the main indexes were compared, many predominantly rural states scored lower than predominantly urban states.

The implication was fairly clear – the nation's rural areas had not enjoyed the prosperity born of the vaunted 1980's economic recovery. Yet, we knew that the mere fact of *being* rural did not preclude robust economic performance or hinder pursuing an aggressive development policy.

To further explore this finding, CFED developed the *1989 Rural Economic Climate Report* which included several new measures to assess the disparities between a state's rural and urban areas. Several measures from that report – including employment growth, unemployment, earnings growth, and average earnings – have been included in subsequent Report Cards to assess how much economic performance differs between rural and urban areas within a state. The larger the gaps between rural and urban areas in these key measures of economic performance, the lower the Rural/Urban Disparity score.

What is Rural?

The term "rural" can be defined using a variety of criteria from low population density, to agricultural base, to isolation from metropolitan areas. For *The Development Report Card,* we used the definition of "nonmetropolitan" from the Economic Research Service (ERS) at the U.S. Department of Agriculture. This definition is commonly used in government data collection and many private studies, though it is not the only one. The ERS defines a nonmetropolitan county as one which is outside the boundaries of any metropolitan statistical area (MSA). MSAs are comprised of socially and economically integrated counties with at least one city of 50,000 and a total area population of at least 100,000. Thus, these rural counties can differ significantly from one another – one with an urban area of 20,000 and another comprised solely of remote farms – yet they are all independent of any metro area.

For more information on rural economies see *Rethinking Rural Development*, and *The Regional Performance Benchmarks System*, both from The Corporation for Enterprise Development, Washington, DC, 1993; and *A State-Level Examination of Metro/ Nonmetro Per Capita Income Inequality 1979-87* (AGES 9108) and *An Update: The Diverse Social and Economic Structure of Nonmetropolitan America* (AGES 9063), both from The U.S. Department of Agriculture, Economic Research Service, Washington, DC, 1990.

Rural/Urban Disparity Index Measures

New Jersey has no counties classified as non-metropolitan, thus, it has no values for any Rural/Urban Disparity measure. A score and rank is assigned for New Jersey to keep it comparable with its rankings in the other three equity subindex measures. The data and data sources for the 1995 Rural/Urban Disparity measure follow.

Rural/Urban Disparity Data* (part 1)

State	Long-Term Employment %	Long-Term Employment Rank	Short-Term Employment %	Short-Term Employment Rank	Unemployment Difference %	Unemployment Difference Rank
Alabama	[1.62]	11	[0.27]	8	2.45	41
Alaska	12.16	44	[1.66]	38	3.17	44
Arizona	13.60	47	0.46	15	3.75	47
Arkansas	[0.06]	1	[0.55]	18	2.23	36
California	12.42	45	1.94	41	4.79	50
Colorado	6.01	33	0.95	29	1.20	16
Connecticut	10.87	42	1.00	31	0.37	6
Delaware	[1.25]	9	[0.64]	19	0.22	5
Florida	[1.06]	7	[0.27]	8	1.44	22
Georgia	[5.15]	27	[0.87]	20	1.15	15
Hawaii	6.04	34	0.52	17	3.92	48
Idaho	[5.21]	28	[0.13]	3	2.02	32
Illinois	6.59	36	1.59	37	1.59	23
Indiana	1.94	15	2.07	43	1.02	13
Iowa	[5.78]	32	[2.16]	44	0.45	7
Kansas	[3.95]	24	[1.26]	33	[0.05]	2
Kentucky	1.68	12	0.24	7	2.23	36
Louisiana	2.92	20	2.18	45	2.09	35
Maine	1.58	10	[0.93]	27	1.65	27
Maryland	0.63	3	0.74	20	2.04	33
Massachusetts	1.74	14	[0.17]	4	[0.55]	10
Michigan	11.05	43	2.68	48	2.00	31
Minnesota	[3.10]	22	1.31	34	1.94	30
Mississippi	[1.23]	8	[1.96]	42	2.33	39
Missouri	6.39	35	1.34	35	1.69	28
Montana	[2.13]	17	0.87	21	1.07	14
Nebraska	[1.00]	6	[0.19]	6	0.00	1
Nevada	[24.33]	50	[2.29]	47	1.60	24
New Hampshire	[2.91]	19	2.26	46	[0.75]	12
New Jersey	N/A	25	N/A	25	N/A	25
New Mexico	7.16	37	[1.76]	39	2.86	43
New York	10.37	40	0.40	13	[0.21]	4
North Carolina	[5.75]	31	[3.66]	50	1.79	29
North Dakota	[18.24]	49	[0.49]	16	2.04	33
Ohio	5.36	29	0.92	26	1.31	20
Oklahoma	[8.43]	38	[0.28]	11	1.37	21
Oregon	[9.05]	39	[0.88]	23	2.44	40
Pennsylvania	3.04	21	0.44	14	1.63	26
Rhode Island	[12.69]	46	[3.42]	49	0.49	8
South Carolina	[1.68]	12	[0.17]	4	3.41	46
South Dakota	[3.54]	23	[0.91]	24	0.50	9
Tennessee	4.62	26	[0.09]	2	2.57	42
Texas	[14.24]	48	[0.94]	28	0.58	11
Utah	0.44	2	0.95	29	1.23	17
Vermont	[10.44]	41	[0.27]	8	1.28	18
Virginia	[0.84]	5	0.05	1	2.32	38
Washington	[2.40]	18	1.89	40	3.29	45
West Virginia	[2.01]	16	[1.24]	32	4.22	49
Wisconsin	5.70	30	1.58	36	1.29	19
Wyoming	[0.68]	4	[0.29]	12	0.11	3

* *Ranking is based on absolute value. Bracketed data indicates states where the urban value for a measure was greater than the rural value. Unbracketed data indicates where the rural value exceeded the urban.*

Rural/Urban Disparity Data Sources

Long-Term Employment Growth Difference

Measure: Absolute value (in percentage points) difference between the state's nonmetropolitan and metropolitan counties' long-term employment growth rates, 1987-1993.

Source: U.S. Department of Commerce, Regional Economic Information System, as prepared by the U.S. Department of Agriculture, Economic Research Service, Agriculture and Rural Economy Division. Washington, DC: 1995. Calculations by CFED.

Short-Term Employment Growth Difference

Measure: Absolute value (in percentage points) difference between the state's nonmetropolitan and metropolitan counties' short-term employment growth rates, 1992-1993.

Source: Same as Long-Term Employment Growth Difference.

Unemployment Difference

Measure: Absolute value (in percentage points) difference between the state's nonmetropolitan and metropolitan counties' unemployment rates, 1993.

Source: Same as Long-Term Employment Growth Difference.

Rural/Urban Disparity Data* (part 2)

State	Average Earnings Ratio		Long-Term Earnings		Short-Term Earnings	
	Ratio	Rank	%	Rank	%	Rank
Alabama	79.87	30	0.06	1	[1.42]	37
Alaska	91.59	3	[1.52]	15	[0.37]	13
Arizona	86.79	14	0.86	6	0.16	5
Arkansas	83.38	19	3.01	31	[0.22]	6
California	72.83	43	[5.95]	41	[1.95]	42
Colorado	75.00	38	1.08	8	[0.57]	21
Connecticut	77.40	32	[9.46]	50	[0.55]	19
Delaware	69.19	45	[7.26]	47	[0.37]	13
Florida	83.15	20	[1.22]	12	[1.18]	35
Georgia	74.57	39	[1.18]	11	[0.81]	28
Hawaii	79.96	29	[2.86]	28	[2.61]	47
Idaho	88.55	9	[1.84]	17	[1.99]	43
Illinois	65.65	48	[4.45]	34	2.22	44
Indiana	82.35	23	[1.45]	14	1.83	40
Iowa	80.74	27	[2.97]	29	2.36	45
Kansas	74.43	40	2.26	20	0.45	17
Kentucky	80.00	28	0.53	4	0.33	12
Louisiana	83.41	18	2.52	24	0.29	9
Maine	90.84	6	[2.41]	23	0.38	15
Maryland	75.55	37	[1.07]	7	[0.55]	19
Massachusetts	73.17	42	[9.04]	49	0.30	10
Michigan	68.19	47	2.01	18	[0.28]	8
Minnesota	68.27	46	[7.10]	46	0.04	1
Mississippi	84.83	16	1.23	13	1.35	36
Missouri	63.59	49	1.70	16	1.64	39
Montana	88.14	10	1.14	10	[2.62]	48
Nebraska	84.80	17	5.07	39	[0.97]	31
Nevada	90.99	5	3.92	33	[2.43]	46
New Hampshire	84.94	15	[5.03]	38	[1.56]	38
New Jersey	N/A	25	N/A	25	N/A	25
New Mexico	88.57	8	[0.26]	3	[1.10]	32
New York	63.29	50	[6.39]	43	[3.93]	49
North Carolina	81.82	25	[2.08]	19	[1.10]	32
North Dakota	91.35	4	4.92	37	7.94	50
Ohio	82.65	21	[0.54]	5	0.60	22
Oklahoma	76.83	36	[0.13]	2	1.11	34
Oregon	82.39	22	[6.07]	42	[0.06]	2
Pennsylvania	77.00	34	[4.80]	36	[0.27]	7
Rhode Island	99.73	1	[6.78]	44	[0.72]	26
South Carolina	88.00	12	[3.12]	32	0.40	16
South Dakota	90.36	7	8.09	48	[0.30]	10
Tennessee	78.14	31	2.34	22	0.63	23
Texas	70.56	44	[2.62]	26	[0.54]	18
Utah	88.05	11	[5.48]	40	[0.69]	24
Vermont	82.33	24	[2.99]	30	1.91	41
Virginia	74.32	41	[4.70]	35	[0.92]	30
Washington	76.97	35	[6.98]	45	[0.76]	27
West Virginia	87.97	13	[2.70]	27	[0.90]	29
Wisconsin	77.36	33	[1.10]	9	0.13	4
Wyoming	96.56	2	2.31	21	0.09	3

* Ranking is based on absolute value. Bracketed data indicates states where the urban value for a measure was greater than the rural value. Unbracketed data indicates where the rural value exceeded the urban.

Average Earnings Ratio

Measure: Ratio of nonmetropolitan counties' to metropolitan counties' average annual labor and proprietor earnings, per full-time worker, 1992.

Source: U.S. Department of Commerce, Regional Economic Information System, as prepared by the U.S. Department of Agriculture, Economic Research Service, Agriculture and Rural Economy Division. Calculations by CFED.

Long-Term Earnings Growth Difference

Measure: Absolute value difference (in percentage points) between the state's nonmetropolitan and metropolitan counties' change in average annual labor and proprietor earnings, per full-time worker, 1987-1992.

Source: Same as Average Earnings Ratio.

Short-Term Earnings Growth Difference

Measure: Absolute value difference (in percentage points) between the state's nonmetropolitan and metropolitan counties' change in average annual labor and proprietor earnings, per full-time worker, 1991-1992.

Source: Same as Average Earnings Ratio.

Traded Sector & Structural Diversity

Despite the fundamental importance of competitiveness and industrial diversity to a state economy, there are no simple or straightforward measures that capture these dimensions in a state's business sectors. As part of *The Development Report Card's* Business Vitality Index, CFED, working with Mt. Auburn Associates, has devised four special indicators of industrial competitiveness and diversity.

Traded Sector Strength and Change in Traded Sector Strength reflect the value added by the key industries in a state, an important factor in assessing the state's competitiveness. Similarly, the levels of Dynamic Diversity and Sectoral Diversity indicate how vulnerable a state may be to downturns in one or several of its critical industries.

Because these measures are more complicated and less intuitive than, say, business failures or employment, we offer here a more extensive explanation of each.

Traded Sector Strength

The traded sector firms, comprised of those in-state businesses producing goods and services that compete with firms outside the state, bring new wealth into an economy by exporting goods and services, and/or they retain wealth in an economy by substituting for the goods and services that otherwise would have to be imported.

The ideal way to estimate traded sector income would be to use an up-to-date input-output table to calculate precisely the value of the goods and services that a state's businesses export.

Unfortunately, such up-to-date data does not exist; the most recent data are over a decade old.

As an alternative, we calculate the size of a state's traded sector by the amount of income it brings into the economy for each civilian worker. Using 1993 data, we estimate the amount of income that each state industry derives from its traded sector activities and then sum that income across all industries to arrive at traded sector income for the state.

Of course, the difficulty in designing such a measure is specifying which industries within an individual state's economy are, in fact, "traded". To determine the fully- and partially-traded industries for each state, we start with the U.S. Bureau of Economic Analysis (BEA) classification of industries (as designated by SIC codes) as fully-, partially-, and non-traded, and then augment the BEA classification with our own research.

Fully-traded industries include:

- *agricultural services*
- *coal mining*
- *farming*
- *fisheries*
- *forestry*
- *insurance carriers*
- *mail-order houses*
- *manufacturing (except for food processing and printing/publishing)*
- *metals mining*
- *petroleum mining*
- *pipeline transportation*
- *railroad transportation*
- *research and development*
- *water transportation*

The Corporation for Enterprise Development

Partially-traded industries differ from state to state according to the extent to which their activities are traded. For instance, although in most states banking is a local, non-traded activity, in states like New York and Delaware, much banking activity is traded. For any given state, partially-traded industries may include:

- *accounting*
- *advertising*
- *air transportation*
- *amusements and recreation*
- *banking*
- *communication*
- *eating and drinking places*
- *educational services*
- *engineering and architectural services*
- *federal government*
- *food processing*
- *health services*
- *hotels*
- *legal services*
- *management services*
- *motion pictures*
- *non-metals mining*
- *printing/publishing*
- *securities brokers*
- *transportation services*
- *trucking*
- *utilities*
- *wholesale trade*

We then use two steps to determine the extent to which the income from the partially-traded industries in each state should be counted as traded. First, we determine a "location quotient" for each industry in each state. A location quotient measures an industry's share of state employment relative to its share of national employment. A location quotient of 1.0 means that the industry has the same share of state employment as it does national employment. A quotient of 1.5 means that the industry's share of employment in the state is 50 percent more than its national share.

Next, starting with the BEA framework, we analyze the distribution of location quotients for each partially-traded industry to determine the appropriate formula for estimating the percent of industry income that is traded. In each industry, the higher the location quotient, the higher the percent of income that is attributed to the industry's trading activity. To calculate *Total Traded Sector Income*, incomes from the totally-traded and partially-traded sectors are added together. To arrive at the measure of *Traded Sector Strength*, we divide the sum of traded sector income by the number of civilian workers in a state, so as to be able to compare across states.

Structural Diversity Measures

In measuring *Structural Diversity* in a state's economic base, our analysis considers both how diverse a state's economic structure *looks* – for example, how its employment is distributed over a wide range of industries – and how diverse it *acts*.

The Sectoral Diversity measure examines the degree to which income generated by a state's traded sector is spread across a range of industries. We employ an index developed by an economist, Dr. Herfindahl, that adds the sum of the square of each traded sector industry's share of total traded sector income. A "0" score indicates perfect diversification; a score of "1" indicates that all the traded sector activity is in just one industry. So, for example, in comparing two states, each of which has only two traded industries, the state in which the split in total traded sector income is 50/50 is more diverse (a score of .5) than the state where the split is 75/25 (a score of .625).

We also examine how diverse a state's traded sector industries act, in a measure we call *Dynamic Diversity*. That is, in an economy that has dynamic diversity, when one industry is declining, others should be growing or stable. We are, therefore, interested in the diversity of employment change, which provides a measure of protection against downside risk – in other words, we do not want to see all of a state's major industries declining at the same time. Our attention is again focused on traded sector industries, since they are the industries that generate wealth in a state.

To estimate *Dynamic Diversity,* we measure the extent of similarity in employment change over time from industry to industry. Such a similarity in change is known in statistical terms as "covariance". When employment change is diverse, there is a significant amount of negative covariance between industries – so that when one industry is declining, another is growing, and vice-versa. Thus, the lower the score, the more diverse the economy.

For each state, the following two steps are used to calculate *Dynamic Diversity*:

Step 1. For every possible pair of the top twelve traded sector industries, a score is developed. The score is the covariance of employment change in those industries between 1985 and 1993, multiplied by the weight (based on employment size of sector) of one industry times the weight of the other.

Step 2. The score for each pair of industries is then summed to get the state's raw Dynamic Diversity score.

Obviously, it is important to adjust for the size of each industry, so our measure assigns an industry weight based on the percentage of traded sector employment it holds. The measure also takes into account the actual percentage change in employment in each industry – the higher the percentage, the greater the impact. So if two key industries both decline significantly, the measure is more unfavorably affected than if they both decline by a small amount.

The Corporation for Enterprise Development

Changes in Individual Measures in the 1995 Development Report Card

The Development Report Card provides a comprehensive range of indicators on the economic health and capacity for growth in each of the 50 states. In order to do so, diverse information must be gathered from a wide variety of sources. Because index grades are presented for the states for five years in order to evaluate performance over time, CFED must constantly balance the need for consistency in its data and sources against the increased value of using new data sources or measures which may be more timely or a better proxy for what is to be measured. While we have tried to be as consistent as possible, we believe that several changes were advisable for the 1995 Report Card. These changes are explained below.

Economic Performance Measures

Hazardous Waste: Last year's Report Card used the preliminary figures for 1991 Hazardous Waste production by state, a measure which is compiled biennially. This year's Report Card uses the final 1991 figures, which are essentially the same as the preliminary ones, except in the cases of Alaska, Massachusetts, New York, Virginia and Washington, all of which were very significantly adjusted by the Environmental Protection Agency and the states.

Business Vitality Measures

New Business Job Growth: This year's version covers a four year period instead of five (1989-1993 instead of 1987-1992) and is thus not strictly comparable to the data in the 1994 Report Card. Additionally, the measure's creators note that their methods of identifying new companies have improved.

Development Capacity Measures

Urban Mass Transit: Annual Vehicle Revenue Capacity Miles, introduced last year, was not available at press time for 1992. Therefore, a measure used in previous Report Cards, Actual Revenue Miles (as opposed to Revenue Capacity Miles which accounts for the average size of vehicles), was substituted. Although the raw figures differ significantly, the state's relative performances do not.

Acknowledgments

CFED Project Team

Project Director:
Daphne Clones

Writing and Analysis:
Carol Conway
Brian Grossman
Carl Rist

Research and Administrative Assistance:
Linda Keeney

Contributors

CFED Staff
Beverly Brandon-Simms
Brian Dabson
Bob Friedman
Lisa Kawahara
Andrea Levere
Debby Manley
Puchka Sahay
Bill Schweke
Anna C. Smith
Cicero Wilson
Shireen Zonoun

Capital Systems Group, Inc. (CSG) Staff
Joy Motheral
Korin Armstrong
Christopher Stathes

Special Assistance

Database Software & Analysis:
Capital Systems Group, Inc.
Christopher Stathes
Hemant Virkar

Research & Analysis:
Mt. Auburn Associates
Andrew Reamer
with: Anthony Ives
Howard Man

Tax & Fiscal System Index:
Michael Mazerov

Book Layout & Design:
Capital Systems Group, Inc.
Joy Motheral

Cover Design:
Marketing Options
Shelley Wetzel

Printing:
Linemark Printing

Report Card Funding

Funding for the research and production of *The 1995 Development Report Card* comes both from sales revenues and donations. Sponsoring organizations include labor unions and private foundations. *The Development Report Card* remains the work of CFED and does not necessarily reflect the specific views of any one sponsor. CFED thanks each of these generous contributors:

- *American Federation of Labor-Congress of Industrial Organizations*
- *American Federation of State, County & Municipal Employees*
- *American Federation of Teachers*
- *The Joyce Foundation*
- *The Levi Strauss Foundation*
- *Public Employee Department, AFL-CIO*
- *Service Employees International Union*

Working with

Adults with a Learning Disability

Alex Kelly

Speechmark Publishing Ltd
Telford Road, Bicester, Oxon OX26 4LQ, UK

Published by
Speechmark Publishing Ltd, Telford Road, Bicester, Oxon, OX26 4LQ,
United Kingdom

www.speechmark.net

002-3841/Printed in the United Kingdom/1010

British Library Cataloguing in Publication Data

Kelly, Alex
    Working with adults with a learning disability
    1. Learning disabled – Services for
    I. Title
    362.3

ISBN 0 86388 413 X
(Previously published by Winslow Press under ISBN 0 86388 231 5)

Contents

Preface

Working with adults with a learning disability (ALD) is still one of the least popular options for students coming out of college, and recruitment into ALD jobs remains difficult. Although I am sure that more could be done to improve the content of coursework and placements in ALD, I remain frustrated, mystified and determined to put the record straight. In my opinion, working with adults with a learning disability is the most varied, challenging, exciting, rewarding and fun job I could have, and after 14 years of working as a speech and language clinician, predominantly in ALD, I still love going to work. People with learning disabilities are still too rarely seen as having words and thoughts of value inside them, and so only too rarely are provided with a means of interpreting them or having them interpreted. It is hardly surprising, therefore, that these adults often give up the exhausting struggle to communicate, or that they express themselves in other, less appropriate ways. These thoughts and needs that are left unformed and unspoken become a storehouse of pain that can be incredibly damaging to the individual.

People who work with adults who have a learning disability have such an important role to play. We can help them to express those thoughts that have been locked away; we can help them to be listened to and understood; we can help them to have an effect on their surroundings and on their lives, and we can help them to be seen as more valued. What could be more rewarding?

This book is written predominantly for speech and language clinicians, although it is hoped that anyone working with adults with a learning disability will find it useful and interesting, as everyone has a role to play in improving communication. The book aims to provide an overview of all the aspects of working with adults with learning disabilities, and for ease of accessibility, each chapter covers a different aspect of work. However, it is not intended that each chapter should stand entirely on its own. Each person with a learning disability is an individual with their own individual strengths and needs, and an overview of learning disability is important in order to plan for their needs. It is therefore recommended that the reader does not simply focus on a specific chapter relevant to the diagnosis of the client they are currently working with, but rather views these discrete issues within the totality of the needs of this client group.

The introduction aims to give a theoretical background to working with adults with a learning disability. This includes how we define and understand learning disability, the causes of learning disability, and the needs of people with learning disabilities. In addition, an historical background to the services for people with learning disabilities is given, including an introduction to normalisation and how this has had an impact on current services.

The following chapters look at the areas of assessment, challenging behaviour, augmentative and alternative communication, the profound and the multiply-disabled client, social skills, dysphagia, group therapy, staff training, working in a community learning disability team, and enabling people to access the criminal justice system. In addition, there is a revised version of the Personal Communication Plan (PCP) (Hitchings and Spence, 1991) at the end of the book.

Acknowledgements

I would like to thank the following for all their support and encouragement in writing this book:

Kym Brown, Saxon Irving, Cheryl Noël, Alison Proudman, Brian Sains, Sue Smith, Kate South, Dani Williams and the West Specialist Health Care Team (Southampton).

I would like to thank Nicci Forshaw for writing the chapter on enabling people with learning disabilities to access the criminal justice system (Chapter 10). Nicci works as a specialist speech and language therapist for the North Warwickshire NHS Trust in the Forensic Services for people with learning disabilities.

I would also like to thank Robert Spence for permitting me to include a revised version of the Personal Communication Plan (PCP) for people with learning disabilities.

I would like to thank my mum and dad, and my sister Sue for all their extra help in looking after my children.

This book is dedicated to the four men in my life: my husband Brian Sains and my three children, Edward, Peter and George.

Foreword

This book is timely and helpful. It is written in a clear and direct style primarily for speech & language therapists but it will be of use to everyone working with adults with learning disabilities. It should act as a bridge between qualified and unqualified staff and facilitate informed discussion of the communication needs of individual clients and of the potential for communication in the social environment created by service organisations.

Meaningful communication is at the heart of good service provision. This book places communication in the context of normalisation and the five accomplishments showing how controlling language can cut off avenues for relating and making choices, how too many abstractions can create unhelpful 'noise' which drowns out important messages and how 'getting it wrong' can disempower people and leave them being spoken 'for' rather than 'with' or 'to'.

The book covers a broad agenda also taking in non-verbal communication (in the context of culture and individual impairment/need) and challenging behaviour. A further chapter sets out a guide to augmentative and alternative communication, which covers signing, symbols and aids. Profound and multiple disabilities are considered in detail and a form of assessment, which focuses on pre-verbal communication included. Social skills, self-awareness and body language are covered and guidelines for running groups are developed. Dysphagia (difficulty in swallowing) is also covered in detail. A final chapter is dedicated to helping people with learning disabilities access the criminal justice system.

The book demonstrates how comprehensive an agenda this is for service providers. Too often 'ordinariness' is assumed to be a matter of just being natural but this book helps to confront that simplistic notion and replace it with a model of careful and thorough assessment of the individual and their environment which enable services to provide an appropriate and empowering context for service users.

The book is well set out and referenced and has clear, user-friendly illustrations, bullet points, checklists and charts. Each chapter builds up to, and provides worked examples of, careful and useful assessment. It brings together ideas and strategies that are grounded in real issues and situations. As a text for speech & language therapists and an introduction to their colleagues in multi-disciplinary teams and service agencies it will be an invaluable reference book and guide.

Hilary Brown
Salomons: Canterbury Christ Church University College
October 2000

Copyrights

Blissymbols are reproduced by permission of Blissymbolics Communication UK.

Makaton signs and symbols are reproduced by permission of Makaton Vocabulary Development Project.

Picture Communication Symbols are reproduced by permission of Mayer-Johnson.

Rebus symbols are reproduced by permission of Widget Software.

Introduction

WHAT IS LEARNING DISABILITY?

What is learning disability? Immediately we find ourselves in a confusing area as there is so much disagreement in terms of definitions used for classification. Indeed there are a surprising number of terms which all describe the same group of people, such as:

◆ learning disability
◆ mental subnormality
◆ mental retardation
◆ special needs
◆ developmental disability
◆ mental handicap
◆ learning difficulty
◆ mental deficiency
◆ intellectual impairment

Following a long debate over the past 15 years about how best to describe the users of 'mental handicap' services, the Department of Health in England and Wales has agreed to use the term 'people with learning disabilities'. However, people remain confused, particularly when meeting with colleagues from other parts of the world. For example, in the United Kingdom the term 'learning disability' is most common, but 'mental handicap' and 'learning difficulties' are also sometimes employed, while in North America the terms 'mental retardation' or 'mental deficiency' are used, and in Australasia the term is 'intellectual impairment' (Sperlinger, 1997). An additional confusion is that in some countries 'learning disability' and 'learning difficulty' are sometimes used to describe children with difficulties such as dyslexia.

In this book, the term 'learning disability' will be used.

DEFINING AND UNDERSTANDING LEARNING DISABILITIES

How we define and understand 'learning disability' continues to be an interesting, if not sometimes confusing, question. As professionals, we speak with a great deal of confidence about what a learning disability is, but from a theoretical perspective and at an operational level it is not clear at all. We are not talking here about how we refer to our clients, but about how people with learning disabilities are defined. This is obviously important in order to calculate the size of this section of the population and analyse their needs and social and/or health resource requirements. Learning disability has been identified and defined using a number of different classifications, and these have included legislative definitions, intellectual ability, social ability, and the cause of the learning disability.

Gates (1997) defines learning disability as a term that is used to describe a group of people with 'significant developmental delay that results in arrested or incomplete achievement of the "normal" milestones of human development. These relate to intellectual, emotional, spiritual and social aspects of development. Significant delays in the achievement of one or more of these milestones may lead to a person being described, defined or categorised as having learning disabilities'.

The US Developmental Disabilities Act (1984, cited by Sinason, 1992) links mental and physical handicaps by defining mental or physical impairment (or a combination of the two) as something that is liable to continue indefinitely and results in substantial functional limitations in three or more of the following: self-care, receptive and expressive language, learning, mobility, self-direction, capacity for independent living and economic self-sufficiency. This definition is helpful because it reflects a person's need for interdisciplinary or generic care, treatment or services which are of lifelong or extended duration and are individually planned and coordinated.

The World Health Organisation (WHO) Classification of Mental and Behavioural Disorders (WHO 1993) states that mental retardation is 'a condition of arrested or incomplete development of the mind, which is especially characterised by impairment of skills manifested during the developmental period which contributes to the overall level of intelligence, ie, cognitive, language, motor and social abilities'.

Ian McDonald, Director of Brunel University's Mental Handicap Services Unit, has created his own definition of disability, which is: 'the irreconcilable difference between imagination and realisation' (1988, cited by Sinason, 1992), a definition which Sinason herself considers to be 'painfully emotionally accurate'.

Luckasson et al (1992) probably give us the clearest definition of learning disability and manage to capture most aspects of previous definitions. They state that learning disability can be defined as referring to:

◆ significantly sub-average intellectual functioning, ie, a score of an IQ of below 70 on standardised tests of intelligence;
◆ existing concurrently with related limitations in two or more of the following areas: communication, self-care, home living, social skills, use of community resources, functional academic skills, health and safety, leisure and work;
◆ manifested before the age of 18.

These can be considered to be the three core criteria for learning disability, and all three must be met for a person to be considered to have a learning disability. The British Psychological Society (1999) recommends that 'in accordance with the various definitions, classification of "learning disability" should only be made on the basis of assessments of both intellectual *and* adaptive/social functioning acquired before adulthood'.

People with *severe* learning disabilities will *in addition* (Emerson, 1995):

◆ Score below IQ 50 on standardised tests of intelligence.

- Show clear signs of significant disabilities in acquisition of adaptive behaviours from early in life, and will need considerably more support than their peers to take part in everyday activities.
- Show (most of them) some evidence of damage to their central nervous system.
- Have (many of them) additional sensory or physical handicaps.

To clarify the definition further, Sperlinger (1997) cites the following people who are *not* included in the definition of learning disability:

- People who develop an intellectual disability after the age of 18.
- People who suffer brain injury in accidents after the age of 18.
- People with complex medical conditions that affect their intellectual abilities and which develop after the age of 18 – for example, Huntington's Chorea, Alzheimer's Disease.
- People with some specific learning difficulties – for example, dyslexia, delayed speech and language development, and those with literacy problems.

LEGAL TERMINOLOGY

Throughout history many societies have described learning disabilities using legislative definitions. However, legal definitions that cover people with learning disabilities tend to be used for specific purposes and are not particularly helpful in enlightening us as to this group of people. There appear to be two broad types of context (Sperlinger, 1997):

1 *Definitions/assessment within criminal, civil, family and children's law* – for example, fitness to plead, fitness to stand trial, ability to instruct counsel, ability to be a witness, UK Police and Criminal Evidence Act 1984.
2 *Enabling legislation for various services and supports* – for example, in the UK, the Mental Health Act 1983, Registered Homes Act 1984, Local Government Finance Act 1988.

The terminology varies between pieces of legislation: for example, 'mental incapacity' and 'mental impairment' are used in the Mental Health Act 1983; 'mental deficiency' is used in the Sexual Offences Act 1956, and these have specific legal meanings (see Gates, 1997, for further explanation), but these terms are not commonly used elsewhere to describe people with learning disabilities.

Most definitions include some combination of the three main factors used in determining whether a person has a learning disability (Dawson, 1996):

- Organic impairment or abnormality (assessed by medical diagnosis).
- Level of intelligence (often assessed by IQ).
- Level of social functioning (often determined by social competence scales).

Other variables include:

◆ The necessity for the condition to have arisen during the 'developmental period'. This means while the brain is still forming (usually taken to be before the age of 18 years).
◆ The inclusion of criteria of behaviour (eg, abnormally aggressive).
◆ The inclusion of criteria concerning treatment.

THE INCIDENCE OF LEARNING DISABILITIES

In the UK, in 1999, it was estimated that over one million adults and children were mildly learning disabled, and that were are approximately 300,000 severely learning disabled people. The Department of Health in the UK (1995) estimated that mild learning disability may affect as many as 20 people in every 1,000 of the population, and that a further three to four in every 1,000 have a severe learning disability. The prevalence rates of severe and profound learning disabilities decrease with rising age due to the increased survival rates of children with severe and complex disabilities, and it is estimated that between 18.75 and 22 per cent of the total who have severe or profound learning disabilities are under the age of 16 (Audit Commission, 1987, cited by Sperlinger, 1997).

It is also estimated that:

◆ Approximately 20 per cent of people with learning disabilities live in hospitals or NHS units.
◆ Just over 25 per cent live in residential accommodation provided by Local Authority Social Service Departments or private or voluntary sectors.
◆ At least 50 per cent live with their parents or other carers.
◆ There are many thousands of people with a mild or moderate degree of learning disability who may require services at some stage in their life.
(Local Authority Circular, 1992, cited by Dawson, 1996).

However, it is difficult to estimate accurately the number of people who have a learning disability in an average district, for the following reasons (Kerr *et al*, 1996, cited by Sperlinger, 1997):

◆ Variation is associated with a variety of factors, such as the level of social deprivation within an area. For example, Ricks (1990, cited by Sinason, 1992) found that 80 per cent of the total number of learning disabled people in the UK are only mildly learning disabled; most of these are from social class V and have experienced a socially disadvantaged environment.
◆ Differential resettlement from hospitals to specific areas also accounts for considerable variation.
◆ Individuals with mild learning disabilities are difficult to identify.
◆ Identification is difficult as general service registers are not inclusive.

CAUSES OF LEARNING DISABILITY

Learning disabilities are diverse and can be the result of a number of different causative factors. Such conditions are manifested during the different stages of the developmental process – preconceptual, prenatal, perinatal and postnatal – and can be described as being genetic or environmental.

An understanding of the potential causes and manifestations of learning disabilities is essential for professionals working with this client group as it enables them to assess and plan appropriate intervention with relevant others in the person's life. It is also important if such professionals are involved in research, and when offering support and counselling to parents and carers. However, labelling individuals with a condition can have a very negative effect and should be avoided, as it can prevent professionals from seeing individuals for what they are and for the qualities they possess as opposed to the characteristics and traits associated with that condition. As in everything, a balance is needed.

The birth of a child with learning disabilities may be the result of genetic action, environmental influences or a mixture of the two. These will be looked at briefly under these two headings. Table 0.1 summarises the causes of learning disability:

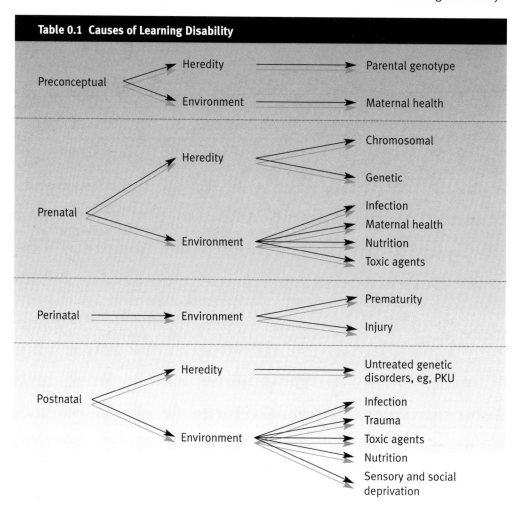

Table 0.1 Causes of Learning Disability

Preconceptual	Heredity	Parental genotype
	Environment	Maternal health
Prenatal	Heredity	Chromosomal / Genetic
	Environment	Infection / Maternal health / Nutrition / Toxic agents
Perinatal	Environment	Prematurity / Injury
Postnatal	Heredity	Untreated genetic disorders, eg, PKU
	Environment	Infection / Trauma / Toxic agents / Nutrition / Sensory and social deprivation

Genetic causes of learning disability

Hereditary material is passed from parents to child by genes which are attached to chromosomes. Abnormalities in the chromosomes or genes may result in a learning disability in the child (see Table 0.2 and Appendix I).

Table 0.2 Genetic Causes of Learning Disability

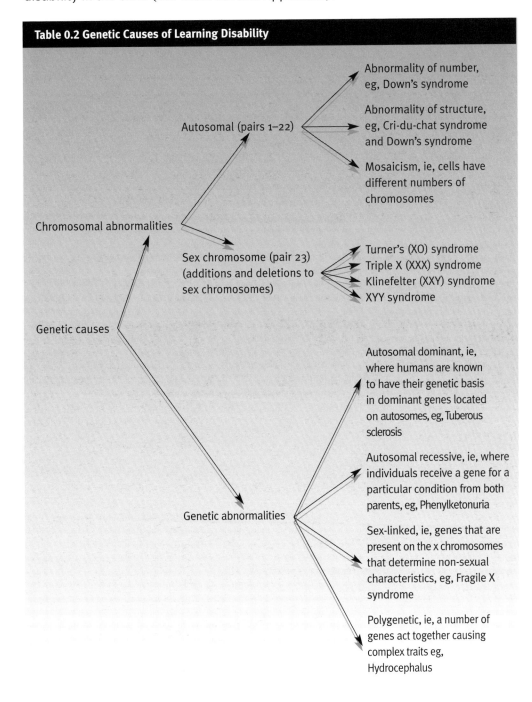

Environmental causes of learning disability

Characteristics such as health, body size and indeed intelligence are inextricably influenced by the environment. Someone deprived of food and vitamins is likely not to thrive, and similarly someone deprived of stimulation and education is at a disadvantage when developing intellectually, whatever their gene status. There are a number of significant points to consider when discussing environmental factors associated with causing learning disability, such as maternal health, nutrition and infection. These can be considered under the four following developmental stages: preconceptual, prenatal, perinatal and postnatal, as different factors are particularly relevant at different stages of the baby's development (see Table 0.3 and Appendix II).

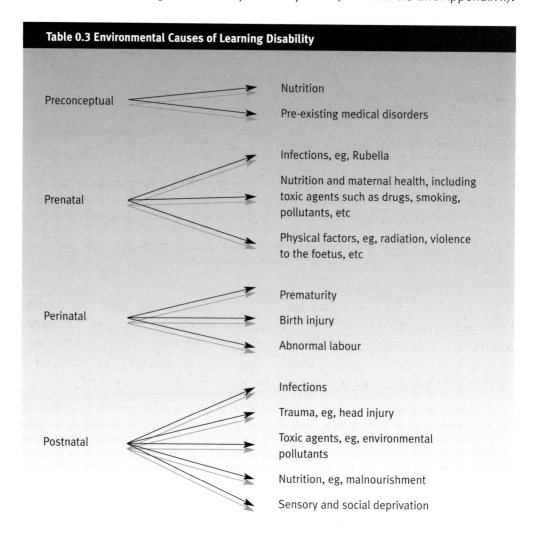

Table 0.3 Environmental Causes of Learning Disability

Preconceptual
- Nutrition
- Pre-existing medical disorders

Prenatal
- Infections, eg, Rubella
- Nutrition and maternal health, including toxic agents such as drugs, smoking, pollutants, etc
- Physical factors, eg, radiation, violence to the foetus, etc

Perinatal
- Prematurity
- Birth injury
- Abnormal labour

Postnatal
- Infections
- Trauma, eg, head injury
- Toxic agents, eg, environmental pollutants
- Nutrition, eg, malnourishment
- Sensory and social deprivation

HISTORICAL BACKGROUND TO SERVICES IN THE UK FOR PEOPLE WITH LEARNING DISABILITIES

History has revealed some differing responses to people with learning disabilities, and consequently services have been affected throughout the years. There was no clear differentiation made between learning disability and mental health in the UK until 1325 when an Act was passed that made provision for the ways in which the properties of people with learning disabilities and those with mental health problems were dealt with: 'fools were to have them protected, whereas lunatics were to have them protected until they recovered' (Gates, 1997). By 1689, Locke had attempted to make a qualitative distinction in the ways in which these two groups of people thought. He said 'In short herein seems to be the difference between idiots and madmen, that madmen put wrong ideas together, and so make wrong propositions, but argue and reason for them; but idiots make very few or no propositions and reason scarce at all' (Locke, cited by Gates, 1997).

Following the agricultural and industrial revolutions, various institutions were built to rid the new industrial cities of rogues, madmen, cripples, outcasts and any subgroup of humanity that did not quite belong to society. In 1869 Galton (cited by Gates, 1997) wrote his first important work on eugenics. He concluded that it would be possible to produce a gifted race of men by manipulating marriages and removing and segregating from society all people with learning disabilities. In 1904 a Royal Commission was set up to advise on the needs of the 'mentally defective' population. The four main recommendations from this commission were (Gates, 1997):

◆ People who were mentally defective needed protection from society, and indeed from themselves.
◆ All mentally defective people should be identified and brought into contact with caring agencies.
◆ Mentally defective people should not be condemned because of their condition.
◆ A central organising body should be established to work with the local caring agencies who would be responsible for the care of individual people.

This led to the enactment of the 1913 Mental Deficiency Act which introduced compulsory certification of 'defectives' admitted to institutions, clearly to segregate people with a learning disability from society. This resulted in large numbers of institutions being built, both for people with learning disabilities and for those with mental health problems, as the 1913 Act separated these two groups of people for the first time. The Act placed the management and responsibility for the care of people with a learning disability with local authorities, and it was not until the emergence of the NHS in 1946 that these asylums became hospitals, and the health service became the major provider of care for people with learning disabilities.

In 1959 the Mental Health Act introduced the terms 'mental subnormality', 'severe mental subnormality', 'mental disorder' and 'psychopathic disorder', and required local authorities to provide both day and residential services for people with a learning disability. It also made provision for voluntary attendance at a hospital rather than compulsory certification, which reflected a fundamental shift in the attitudes of legislators and society as well.

During the 1960s a series of scandals was reported concerning the care of people with learning disabilities in large hospitals. This resulted in the then Labour Government publishing an extremely significant document in 1971 known as 'Better services for the mentally handicapped' (DHSS, 1971). This promoted a model of community care with a decrease in hospital beds and increase in local authority provision. This shift in responsibility resulted in the Griffiths Report (1988), the Government's White Papers 'Caring for people'(1989a) and 'Working for patients'(1989b) and the 1990 National Health Service and Community Care Act.

These provided the final move from hospital-based care to community care, and also made local authorities responsible for acting as lead agents in the provision of care packages for people with learning disabilities.

Although the move to community care has been slow, it has been brought about by the belief that people with learning disabilities should live ordinary lives in ordinary houses, which means not only a tremendous shift by both planners and service providers, but also by society in accepting this to be right. Another significant development that contributed to the notion that people with learning disabilities should live ordinary lives was the impact of the developing concept of normalisation which has been influential in determining service provision today. It is therefore important to take time to fully understand the concept of normalisation and what it means to service providers, service users (clients) and society today.

However, before an explanation of normalisation is given, it is important to understand the concept of deviancy and how this has had a profound effect on how people with learning disabilities have been perceived, labelled and consequently treated.

NORMALISATION

An historical perspective on the use of labelling and the concept of deviancy

In order to fully understand the principle of normalisation and the consequent management of services today, it is important to understand the concept of deviancy. Wolfensberger (1972) states that a 'person can be said to be deviant if he is perceived as being significantly different from others in some aspect that is considered of relative importance, and if this difference is negatively valued'. Deviancy is therefore of our own making in that it is in the eyes of the beholder. An observed quality only becomes a deviancy when it is viewed negatively. A good example of this is obesity, which is valued in some Middle Eastern cultures, but in the Western culture is often viewed negatively. The results of this 'stigma' are obvious: low self esteem, higher unemployment and fewer successful relationships. Wolfensberger (1972) describes these as the negative effects that can occur when people become marginalised, and has identified eight social role perceptions of people with learning disabilities. Most of these socio-historical role perceptions reflect prejudices that have little relationship to reality; however, as with most prejudices, the lack of objective reasons is not a crucial element in the shaping of a social policy. Generally people play the roles they have been assigned; it is well known that people's behaviour is profoundly affected by the role expectations placed on them. Unfortunately, this 'role-appropriate' behaviour is viewed as the person's natural behaviour, rather than as behaviour that has been elicited through circumstance or an environment. This then permits those who define social roles to 'make self-fulfilling prophecies by predicting that someone cast into a certain role will emit behaviour consistent with that role' (Wolfensberger, 1972). The major roles that Wolfensberger describes are as follows:

1   Subhuman
2   Menace
3   Object of dread
4   Object of pity and burden of charity
5   Holy innocent
6   Sick
7   Object of ridicule
8   Eternal child

1 Subhuman

Throughout history, people with learning disabilities as well as other 'deviant' groups have been perceived as not fully human, and have therefore been denied full human status. It may be thought that this is of purely historical interest and that people with learning disabilities are now valued as equal citizens, but evidence of such belief can be found in relatively contemporary literature. An example of this was the case of the young woman with Down's syndrome who required a heart and lung transplant; an article in the London *Guardian* newspaper (Toolis, 1996) reported that no centre would accept anyone with Down's syndrome as a patient. The medical director of one such centre was reported as saying: 'As a doctor I see that my main aim is to make people live, and to become independent human beings that will live a fulfilled life... I have grave doubts as to whether, however good a Down's sufferer is, they will ever be able to lead a totally independent life. And in view of the shortage of organs, I feel that my priority, if asked to make a decision between a normal person and a Down's patient, is to go for the one who can become that independent person' (Toolis, 1996). More recently, in 1999, the *Sunday Times*, London, reported on the case of a nine-year-old girl who was refused a heart transplant because she had Down's syndrome. Her local health authority said that 'because she is a Down's syndrome child she is not eligible for any donor organ'.

The view of people with learning disabilities as being subhuman was central to the segregation of these people into large institutions. As Mittler (1979) commented: 'The late Victorians were so haunted by the spectre of a declining national intelligence that they pursued a ruthless segregationist policy which led to many thousands of people being identified as mentally handicapped and incarcerated in asylums and colonies. The fact that their names were later changed to hospitals does not alter the fact that they were sited and designed to meet the needs of the time to segregate the handicapped from the rest of society and to do everything possible to prevent them from multiplying.' (Mittler, 1979)

2 Menace

History is filled with incidents of people's persecution of other people, and therefore it is not surprising that one role perception in history is that of the deviant person as a menace. Even today, people with learning disabilities are seen as being a menace. It is common to experience problems when trying to relocate people from hospital into the community, as potential neighbours complain that they agree with the theory of living in the community but 'not in my backyard'. They typically complain about a drop in the value of their own property, or people 'wandering around' and generally 'being a menace'.

3 Object of dread

Related to the two previous role perceptions is the perception of the person with the learning disability as a dreadful entity or event. Because of this, when a child is either born with or diagnosed as having a learning disability, it is often regarded as a punishment from God. Prospective parents view the possibility of having such a child with dread. As Bannerman and Lindsay (1994) say, 'A family's investment in and expectation of their children is often very high and the arrival of a child with a disability may be the end of dearly held dreams about what that child would achieve in life'.

4 Object of pity and burden of charity

This role perception has arisen out of the view that the person with the learning disability is not enjoying the 'normality' of being human and is seen as 'suffering' from their condition. The pitied person is likely to be held blameless for their condition and possibly unaware of their deviance and unaccountable for their behaviour. Usually this form of the pity perception is accompanied by compassion and acceptance, but may be lacking in respect for the person. In some countries the church has had a historical involvement in the care of people with a learning disability, because they are seen as needing charity, as is evidenced by the institution of charitable homes to care for them. Such a perception may mean that the person with a learning disability is expected to be grateful and submissive in return for being 'kept'.

5 Holy innocent

A common perception of people with learning disabilities is that they are special children of God, and are in some way innocent of original sin. Because of this, and maybe to compensate in some way for their disability, they are seen to enjoy a special relationship with God. This religious role perception is certainly not recent. The first institution founded in the Western world (Valencia, Spain, in 1410) was called the 'Hospital of Innocents' and was intended to be for 'the innocent ones, that is, the insane'. In France, the 'retarded' person has been referred to as 'l'enfant du Bon Dieu' and in English the term 'Christling' or 'God's infant' has been used. The holy innocent perception is still particularly prevalent in Catholicism. There is a 'prayer for holy innocents' in the Roman ritual and a poem entitled 'Heaven's very special child'. The holy innocent perception is one of the most benign role perceptions; however, it does in one way imply a reverse form of dehumanisation, by elevating a human being almost above the human level and by suggesting a 'little angel' status.

6 Sick

Following the establishment of the National Health Service in the UK came the medicalisation of some services offered to people with learning disabilities. The asylums became 'hospitals' and a natural consequence was the development of a medical model of care. This implies the perception of the person with learning disabilities as being 'sick', and, after 'diagnosis', being given 'treatment' or 'therapy' for their 'disease' in a 'clinic' or 'hospital' by 'doctors' and 'therapists', all of which will hopefully lead to a 'cure'.

Although it is clear that people with learning disabilities do face particular challenges to their health that are not always met very well by generic services, this does not mean that services should be constructed for them that meet this distorted role perception of them being 'sick'. If perceived as sick, the person with learning disabilities may be seen as having the privileges that accompany being sick, for example, exemption from normal social responsibilities. In addition, the person must also want to 'get well' or at least better, and must seek suitable and appropriate remedy for their condition (Wolfensberger, 1972).

7 Object of ridicule

There is a great deal of evidence both from the past and present that people with learning disabilities are seen as 'thick' or 'incompetent', and thus it is often thought not inappropriate to ridicule them. In medieval society, people with learning disabilities were used as 'fools' and jesters in court entertainment, and in folk humour they are depicted as objects of ridicule.

8 Eternal child

This is probably the most common perception of people with a learning disability. It means that carers do not place strong or even reasonable developmental and adaptational demands on the person. They are not allowed to take risks or make their own choices, and their environment is adapted accordingly.

Society's management of 'deviancy'

It is apparent that people with learning disabilities are not perceived in the same way as other people in society. As we review society's efforts to handle this, we can classify these efforts into four categories (Wolfensberger, 1972): destruction of individuals, their segregation, reversal of their condition, or prevention of it. Destruction of the 'deviant' has often been advocated, even today, for reasons related to self-preservation or self-protection. The condoning of abortion of high-risk foetuses can be viewed as a variant of this theme. As a more humane option, the 'deviant' person can be segregated from the mainstream of society and placed at its periphery. The third and fourth alternatives are to reverse or prevent deviancy. Reversal is generally tried by means of education, training and treatment, which may also apply to prevention. Since 'deviancy' exists by social definition, 'it can also be prevented or reversed by social redefinition, eg by not attaching negative value to certain type of differentness' (Wolfensberger, 1972). Prevention and reversal of deviancy in essence underpin what normalisation is all about, and are the principles on which services today are based.

So, what is normalisation?

'Normalisation' is a confusing term to describe a powerful and useful way of looking at human services. It is confusing because it has little to do with 'normality' and 'abnormality'. It is *not* 'making people normal', or forcing people to do 'normal' things, ignoring people's needs and difficulties and thus exposing them to unnecessary danger and failure, and it is not just 'getting people out of institutions'. It has a lot to do with revaluing people with learning disabilities and enabling them to live ordinary lives in the community, with whatever support and assistance they require. 'Normalisation' is also known as 'principles of ordinary living'.

The father of the concept of 'normalisation' is widely acknowledged to be Neils Bank-Mikkleson, who sought to bring to people with a learning disability in Denmark the legal and human rights of all other citizens. In 1959 this was enshrined in legislation as an objective 'to create an existence for the mentally retarded as close to normal living conditions as possible' (cited by Dawson, 1996).

In 1969, Bengt Nirje in Sweden first used the term 'normalisation'. Nirje, like Bank-Mikkleson, believed that people with a learning disability should be afforded the same basic rights as others in the community, based upon a shared humanity. However, people with a learning disability were seen to carry three burdens:

1 The initial impairment.
2 An imposed or acquired disability resulting from the structures in society or from the behaviour of others towards the person with a disability.
3 The personal awareness of being a person with a disability (cited by Dawson, 1996).

Nirje believed that services could have an effect on the second burden and this would in turn have an effect upon the other two. He stated that service providers should seek to ensure that a person with a disability has the same opportunities as other people in society: the same chances to experience the 'normal' rhythms of life. This was the process of 'normalisation'. 'It did not mean changing the individual to gain a state of 'normality' but meant changing the environment and the experiences around the person with a learning disability. The emphasis for change was no longer on the person with a learning disability but on society.' (Dawson, 1996)

Central to his thinking was the concept of integration. All people should relate to one another as equals and have mutual respect. People with a learning disability should experience integration in all spheres of life. Nirje (1980) identifies six categories of integration (cited by Dawson, 1996):

◆ *Physical integration* means an individual should be able to experience the normal rhythm of life in 'ordinary' places.
◆ *Functional integration* means an individual should be able to function in and have access to 'ordinary' segments of society. This is an extension of physical integration.
◆ *Social integration* means that in the inter-personal relationships within the community, the person with a disability is afforded respect and esteem.
◆ *Personal integration* means the individual is enabled to maintain meaningful personal relationships with significant people.
◆ *Societal integration* means that the person with a learning disability should have the same rights as other citizens.
◆ *Organisational integration* means that the services provided to enable the above should be as similar as possible to those used by other people.

Wolf Wolfensberger published his text on normalisation in 1972 in the United States. He defined normalisation as: 'The utilization of culturally-valued means in order to establish and/or maintain personal behaviors, experiences and characteristics that are culturally normative or valued.' The normalisation principle is culture-specific because cultures vary in their norms. Services should therefore be typical to that culture and individuals should be enabled to act and look appropriate to that culture, while bearing in mind age and sex of the individual. The use of the term 'normative' is intended to have statistical rather than moral connotations, and could be equated with 'typical' or 'conventional'. We should therefore be enhancing the reputation of the individual and the cultural stereotype (social role) of a devalued group rather than 'normalising' their behaviour. Wolfensberger later used 'social role valorisation' as a preferred term for normalisation.

Wolfensberger argues that people who are handicapped, sick and old have traditionally been socially devalued and are marginalised as human beings. But why? He identified seven core themes in this whole devaluing process:

1 Unconsciousness
2 Role expectations (as described earlier in the chapter)
3 Deviancy magnification
4 Personal competence
5 Imitation
6 Dynamics of imagery
7 Social integration.

1 Unconsciousness

This relates to the powerful role of the unconscious in steering and maintaining destructive service dynamics. Brandon (1988) describes four different levels from awareness to levels of unawareness:

AWARE ⟶ BLIND SPOTS ⟶ HIDDEN AGENDAS ⟶ UNCONSCIOUSNESS

Blind spots are the areas which we can no longer easily see because we work in a service every day and do not notice that: the project name-plate is covered by a bush; the clocks do not tell the correct time; the building looks drab; the place smells... When these things are pointed out, maybe by a new member of staff, we may not feel much anger or pain, just a little cross with ourselves for having a 'blind spot'. We can see the need for change and how it can be achieved and we can see why it was not possible for us to notice it.

Hidden agendas reflect processes which are more painful, and we may therefore feel considerable anger when someone points out that the service we work in neglects clients' interests. For example: the service that fails to involve clients in making decisions may conceal an attitude that 'we know what is best for others', and the service that gives little privacy to clients may hide a crude desire to interfere in people's lives.

Unconsciousness occurs when we become disillusioned with work, and we share feelings of impotence and powerlessness with our client group: 'The managers take no notice of us anyway, so what is the point?'.

There is therefore a need for consciousness and clarity of ideology.

2 Role expectations

As described earlier, clients can become entrapped in a series of 'self-fulfilling' prophesies of the most negative and destructive kind. Service staff hold role expectations of clients that are mainly unconscious but are reflected in the structure of the environment, the language used and the activities on offer. It is then easy to become oblivious to ordinary standards of human behaviour in settings which are regarded as 'strange' anyway, and we become institutionalised. It also becomes difficult to see a person's potential through the dehumanising impact of institutional services as the services offer them only the narrowest and most negative of passive roles.

3 Deviancy magnification

'Congregating devalued people together in often quite large groups, magnifies perceived stigmata' (Brandon, 1988). Segregating and congregating people together creates huge barriers to communication and makes it difficult to see the individual as opposed to the disability. Either positively or negatively, people are judged by the company they keep. This is the point that the cat in Lewis Carroll's *Alice's Adventures in Wonderland* is making about madness:

'But I don't want to go among mad people,' Alice remarked.
'Oh, you can't help that,' said the cat. 'We're all mad here. I'm mad. You're mad.'
'How do you know I'm mad?' said Alice.
'You must be,' said the cat, 'or you wouldn't have come here.'

4 Personal competence

In order to enhance people's personal competence, we need to have the belief that they have potential and therefore can develop. So many services, however, have pessimism built into their fabric. We need to develop a realistic optimism and must assume that everyone needs opportunities to extend their levels of competence. The ingredients of competence are complex and multiple, consisting of feelings of self-worth and value, of being able to function and cope within an increasingly large number of human settings, and of becoming more experienced. The development of competence is an essential element in service provision because the way we appear and act either facilitates or hinders the possibilities for deepening relationships with others. Appearance and presentation are very important in beginning social relations, but people need to feel worthwhile as well as appear worthwhile.

5 Imitation

Imitation is a powerful process, but most human models available for devalued people are fairly negative in that they are often segregated from valued social patterns and put together with other socially devalued people. Good services offer people with learning disabilities valued social models to copy, such as roles about being a tenant, lover, citizen, committee member, or person of influence.

6 Dynamics of imagery

Symbols and imagery usually linked with people with learning disabilities are negative. Posters, radio and TV programmes, and newspaper articles try to elicit feelings of pity, sympathy, fear, superiority or ridicule. Tragic heroes and heroines are created as in the poster that says that 'Herb Ross will be eight years old for the rest of his life' (cited by Brandon, 1988), presenting Herb in the 'perpetual child' role, and as someone who is not capable of maturing and developing into an adult.

7 Social integration

Segregation reduces society's level of tolerance for diversity and means that we do not come to terms with 'rejected people'. A devalued person needs to be integrated into the valued social life of the community; to have the opportunity to be educated with non-devalued peers; to work alongside other people; to be involved in worship, recreation and shopping. The community therefore needs to be appropriately equipped and society able to respond positively.

The five principles of normalisation

Having identified Wolfensberger's main themes in the devaluing process, the implications for improving services to people with learning disabilities will be considered. To do this, it is important to understand the five principles or accomplishments of normalisation – that is the five basic elements which all people need and value in order to achieve a good quality of life. Brandon (1988) defines them as 'simple elements which are sources of our value, as experienced by us and seen by others'. They are:

1   Relationships or community participation
2   Choice
3   Respect
4   Personal development or competence
5   Community presence

All of us need to experience every one of these five principles in our life in order to achieve a 'good quality of life', and if any one of the principles is denied then there will be a general 'leakage' into the other aspects of life. For example, if you are prevented from going out into the community for a period of time, then this will have an effect on your relationships, your ability to make certain choices, your feelings of self-worth and your ability to develop in some areas, eg, the adult education class you had been attending.

So what do these principles actually mean in terms of improving services to people with learning disabilities? Each principle will be considered in turn.

1 Relationships or community participation

This is the experience of being part of a growing network of personal relationships which includes forming a wide range of close friendships, not only with other clients and service providers. O'Brien (1987) defines community participation as 'supporting and enabling people with a learning disability to make and maintain relationships with family and the wider community'. But what do we mean by a 'good relationship'? What ingredients go towards having a good relationship with others? Mostly we may say it just feels right and we feel appreciated by the other person. Elements like warmth, love, respect for sexuality, respect, sharing, friendship, giving time when needed, closeness, consideration and empathy are vital.

When considering the quality of relationships that people with learning disabilities have, it is important to look at the opportunities they have for developing relationships within the wider community, the diversity and quality of those relationships and what could be done to improve the situation (see O'Brien, 1981).

The implications for providing a service that respects the individual's right to having a variety of 'good' relationships are obvious, yet in practice it is not often that one goes into a service that has the policies and protocols to enable clients to enjoy different kinds of relationships.

The speech and language clinician has an important role to play in enabling people with learning disabilities to develop relationships. Communication is central to any relationship, whether that communication is verbal or non-verbal, and the moment communication breaks down, the relationship is in danger of breaking down. How many times have we said in our own lives that a friendship or sexual relationship failed because 'we stopped talking', or 'he didn't listen to me', or 'she didn't understand me'? People with good communication and social skills have a headstart in forming and keeping relationships; it is not any different for people with a learning disability. We therefore need to teach clients the skills necessary to achieve this and also to teach staff the skills to communicate effectively with the clients.

Consider this scenario: a speech and language clinician on a multidisciplinary team is asked to help assess the suitability of a community home for a client moving out of a hospital unit. The client's first language is Makaton and the home is a non-signing environment, where the other clients are all verbal and the staff group are untrained in the use of Makaton. Before this client can move, there is a great deal to be done to ensure that they will be able to communicate in their new home and form relationships with other clients and staff. However, when the home manager is approached about Makaton training for the staff and other clients living in this home he is not willing to allow either the staff or clients to be taught Makaton as he believes that signing 'makes the clients stand out as disabled'. If this client moved into this home, it would be easy to anticipate how their quality of life would be adversely affected and in particular their ability to have relationships with other people in their immediate environment.

2 Choice

This is the experience of growing autonomy in both small and large matters. Personal choice defines and expresses individual identity and people with learning disabilities should be consulted as individuals and should be part of any decision-making process. As O'Brien (1997) says, making choices means 'supporting people with a learning disability to make informed decisions about their lives'. We need to consider what opportunities the person with learning disabilities has to make real choices about food, drink, clothes, going out, holidays, activities, relationships and sexuality. How do they make their choices known and are decisions made for them, with or without consultation?

The issue of *real* choices needs to be stressed as too many services for people with learning disabilities offer the clients choices that are not real and therefore meaningless. A good example of this is where clients are encouraged to make choices about their environment: for example, the colour of their bedroom carpets. They may have limited understanding and expression and are shown samples of carpets in varying colours, and staff are asked to decide on the client's preference for colour by interpreting their eye gaze, pointing or verbal behaviour. If the clients do not understand what is being asked of them, then the choice is not real for them and is probably being done so that services can boast that 'individual preferences were taken into consideration and clients were able to choose the colour of their bedroom carpets, for example'. Imagine being one of those clients and smiling and gazing at the bright purple square of carpet (and of course, she does like the colour purple) and then having to sleep in a bedroom with a bright purple carpet... 'Who did this cruel thing to me?. . . and how can I tell them how much it upsets me?'

The speech and language clinician has an important role to play in enabling clients to make choices. We can teach clients to make a choice verbally or non-verbally through eye-pointing, gesture, objects, and we can help carers to respond to choices and change environments to enable more real choice in clients' lives.

3 Respect

This is the experience of having a valued place among a network of people, and valued roles in community life. This means that people with learning disabilities should not be relegated to a narrow range of low-status roles which restrict the opportunity to be valued as individuals, but should be enabled to have a voice about their own life. O'Brien (1987) defines respect as 'affording respect and dignity to individual service users and portraying a positive image to the general public'. The implications for this are that services need to share information with their clients so that they are informed about what is happening around them; clients need to be consulted and their opinions sought across all aspects of their life and then enabled to make decisions about their environment; advocates need to be provided to help represent clients who are unable to express their wishes for themselves; clients need to be given responsibility in managing some aspects of their life and environment.

The speech and language clinician has an important role in enabling the client to have a valued role in their life. For the client who is unable to communicate effectively, there is a barrier to being respected and less likelihood of having their opinion sought. We need to help our clients to be listened to and help others to do the listening.

4 Personal development or competence

This is the experience of having a growing ability to perform skilfully both functional and meaningful activities with whatever assistance is required. People with learning disabilities should be allowed the expectations, responsibilities, opportunities, learning experiences and assistance necessary for development and should be enabled to develop and maintain skills which will increase their independence and acceptance by others. This means that services need to cater for the individual needs of each person and for their likes and ambitions, enabling them to develop in the ways they wish to. As a person's ability to perform different tasks increases, so their self-esteem and confidence increases, enabling them to develop further. A barrier to this positive virtuous circle is often the expectations of carers and resources available to them.

The speech and language clinician is often involved in enabling clients to learn new skills and helping carers to facilitate the learning through their use of speech, signs and symbols.

5 Community presence

This is the experience of sharing the ordinary places, such as shops and libraries, that define community life. This means that we need to be narrowing the distance between people with learning disabilities and other people in the community and enabling them to experience community life in a positive way, ie, *not* going to the beach for a day's outing with a bus load of other people with learning disabilities. Genuine mixing involves planning and support for the person with the learning disability so that it becomes a positive experience both for the person with the learning disability and also for the people in the community. Too often a visit to the local pub, hairdresser, doctor, etc, can end up being a negative experience for all concerned because there was no planning and thought behind it.

A person's ability to communicate is central to facilitating good community presence. Therefore the speech and language clinician has a valid role in enabling clients to experience this in a positive way, for example, by teaching them the appropriate communication and social skills for ordering a pint, buying a newspaper, using the public swimming pool, and where necessary, teaching the local community to understand and respond appropriately to different methods of communication.

Normalisation – a summary

Normalisation is not something that is provided for people who have a learning disability, but is a system for designing and providing the life experiences necessary to fulfil each person's potential in achieving a good quality of life, both in their daily life and in planning for the future. It requires constant thought and self-appraisal from all involved. The effects of normalisation can be evaluated at three levels:

Client level: There should be an increase in the five principles (relationships, choice, respect, personal development and community participation), and thus an improvement in the quality of life.

Service level: There should be an increase in the effectiveness and quality of the service provided, more tailored to individuals' needs, and involving clients in all aspects of service delivery.

System level: There should be a reduction in misunderstanding and prejudice against people with learning disabilities, and an increase in acceptance and involvement of them by the community.

The message of the normalisation principle is therefore simple: people with a learning disability should not, by virtue of their disability, be deprived of ordinary possibilities for pleasurable life experiences, living circumstances and companions; people with learning disabilities have a right to a good quality of life.

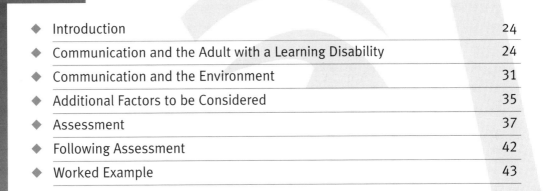

Chapter 1: Assessment

INTRODUCTION

This chapter will address the area of assessment of communication and the adult with a learning disability. The communication needs of this client group will be considered first, including an overview of the most common difficulties experienced and how these can have a profound effect on their ability to communicate successfully. Secondly, assessment of the adult with a learning disability will be considered, and in particular, assessment of expression, comprehension and the environment. This chapter will not describe areas of assessment that are covered in detail in other chapters, ie, assessment of the client who has challenging behaviour, a profound learning disability, social skills needs, or who needs an augmentative and/or alternative communication system. Finally, this chapter will consider how to use the assessment material to plan intervention and set appropriate goals.

The revised Personal Communication Plan (PCP) is included at the end of *Working with Adults with a Learning Disability* and it is intended that the reader will refer to the relevant sections of the assessment while reading this chapter.

COMMUNICATION AND THE ADULT WITH A LEARNING DISABILITY

Communication is an important part of our everyday life and central to many of the things we do. Crystal (1992, cited by Ferris-Taylor, 1997) summarises the main functions of communication as 'the exchange of ideas and information, emotional expression, social interaction, control of reality, recording facts, thinking and expressing identity'. In order to communicate these, a variety of verbal and non-verbal behaviours are used. Communication is also a two-way process, involving at least two people sending and receiving messages and information.

When working with people with learning disabilities, however, it is necessary to recognise a wide range of behaviours as potential communication, and to adopt a generous definition of communication. As Bell (1984) states, 'Behaviours not intended as communicative by the handicapped person can be regarded as such if they are interpreted in that way by the receiver'. This means that all behaviour has the potential to communicate a message, but it is often up to the carers to recognise and respond to it and in doing so, to give it a purpose.

The incidence of communication difficulties among people with learning disabilities is high. Depending on definitions and the population involved (eg, hospital or community), it has been estimated as 40–50 per cent (Mansell 1992, cited by Ferris-Taylor, 1997). This would suggest that there is an almost open-ended need for speech and language clinicians, and that communication is certainly a key consideration for all those who come into contact with people with learning disabilities.

So, what are the communication problems that face the adult with a learning disability? Adults who have a learning disability may have a huge range of communication difficulties and one person's needs will vary considerably from another's. However, it is possible to outline the most common difficulties experienced by this client group, and thus give the reader an overview of the range of communication needs that will be encountered in working with adults with learning disabilities.

Comprehension

Most people with learning disabilities have some difficulty in comprehending at some level, and it is therefore important to try to assess how much the person understands. Carers and other professionals often find it difficult to work out how much a person with a learning disability can understand, and are more likely to overestimate their ability than underestimate it. As Clarke-Kehoe and Harris (1992) state, 'our experience suggests that the ability of people with learning difficulties to understand verbal information is often overestimated by staff. How many times have we heard or used the expression; "she understands everything you say"?' This may happen for a variety of different reasons:

First, it is often assumed that a person's understanding and expression are on roughly equivalent levels, and yet this is not always the case. Some people with learning disabilities have developed effective social speech and learnt phrases which reap benefits in terms of social contact, but which are sometimes meaningless in terms of their content. They may also have good use of non-verbal skills which make them seem to be understanding even when they are not. It is not difficult to think of clients who eagerly approach people and say 'Hello . . . how are you today? . . . have you come to see me? . . . the weather's been good recently, hasn't it? . . .', etc. It must not be assumed that this person understands at the same level as they are expressing themselves as some, or all, of these phrases could be learnt social phrases. Conversely, a person may have relatively good understanding, but little or no speech, and this may lead to staff underestimating their understanding.

Second, for many people, non-verbal information such as gestures, routine, and peer behaviour often gives them enough information to respond to a verbal command correctly. It is not what was said that was understood, but the total situation. A complicated request such as 'Go and get your coat on now, the bus is here and it's time to go home' may be understood purely because of the routine and through peer behaviour. In addition there may be other cues, such as gesturing towards the coats, and sensory information, such as that it is getting dark outside. In this instance, people are receiving a variety of cues – time-related, visual and olfactory – and the verbal message is only one part of the situation. If someone is therefore reliant on additional cues to enable them to understand, and there is a lack of awareness of how much language is actually understood by that person, it can lead to unrealistic expectations and instructions later on. For example, the instruction 'Go and get your coat on, your mum is here and you're going to the dentist' may seem to be of similar complexity to the previous example, but is far more difficult for the person to understand because it is not home time and other clients are remaining seated.

There are some common factors which can be identified as often affecting someone's ability to understand and therefore making language difficult to follow for the adult with a learning disability:

Vocabulary

There are several reasons why people may have difficulties in this area:

◆ *Many different words are used to describe the same thing* – for example, the same drink may be referred to by different people as squash, pop, juice, a brand name or a name of a fruit. Everyday activities such as going out for a walk could be referred to as going for a stroll, a wander, a tramp, etc. Confusing at the best of times!

◆ *Some words have lots of different meanings, such as 'hand'* – for example, my hand, give me a hand, hand me that cup, etc.

◆ *Words are often used metaphorically and are liable to be either confusing or taken literally by someone with a learning disability* – for example, 'pull your socks up', 'blowing a fuse' or 'skating on thin ice'.

◆ *Understanding of words may be linked to particular contexts and experiences, and may not be correctly understood in other situations.* An example of this, cited by Ferris-Taylor (1997) is of the disabled child who was asked if she would like to go to the theatre. She declined the offer and looked quite fearful, as her main experience of the theatre was the operating theatre.

◆ *Vocabulary is also acquired according to relevance to the individual,* and the adult with learning disabilities may have acquired some complex vocabulary in relation to his or her needs – for example health needs – but may have gaps in their understanding of more basic vocabulary.

Complexity of ideas

Abstract concepts such as time can be very difficult for someone to understand. Words like tomorrow, later, yesterday, are often used when communicating with clients, and yet if they do not have a good understanding of time and duration, they are meaningless, and this can lead to frustration and repetition of questions, such as 'When am I going swimming?' In order to help people understand these concepts, they not only need help to understand time through the use of a calendar, diary, chart, etc, but they also need carers to be consistent in their use of words.

How many times have clients been told 'later' when the reality is 'not today, and maybe tomorrow if we're not short-staffed'.

Sentence construction

Some features of sentence construction can be particularly difficult. An example is negatives, as they can be embedded in sentences in a variety of ways: 'there's no bread', 'there isn't any bread', 'there's no more bread', 'it's not time for dinner', 'don't go to the toilet'. These can be easily missed and the person will therefore understand the sentence to have the opposite meaning. This obviously leads to confusion, and possibly to a belief that the person is being difficult.

Sentence length

Many people with learning disabilities respond to only one or two key words from any sentence, and even though they may understand the individual key components of a sentence, they may have difficulty in assimilating the whole. Sentence length is therefore important to maximise someone's ability to understand what is being said to them. The request: 'Go to the toilet and then go and get some dinner' would be easier to understand for some people if it was divided into two separate requests: 'Go to the toilet', and then 'Go and get some dinner now'. In addition, sentence length can be reduced if we cut out unnecessary information. The request: 'Please may I borrow your knife to cut my orange?' may be the most polite way to ask for the knife, but it would be easier to omit the reason why the knife is needed, and this may prevent the person misunderstanding the request and offering the orange.

Later in this chapter, the practicalities of assessing someone's understanding will be addressed. It is obviously important to know how much someone with a learning disability is able to understand, independent of other cues, in order to consider:

◆ How should people be communicating to the person, not only in general conversation but when giving important information and when teaching new skills?
◆ Would the person benefit from additional cues, such as signs, pictures or symbols, to help them understand others' communication? If this is the case, what needs to change in the person's environment? (For example, staff training in Makaton.)
◆ Why are inappropriate responses or challenging behaviour occurring, if any? Is it because of boredom, or because they are being uncooperative, or is it because they have not understood what is expected of them?

Expression

As with comprehension, most people with learning disabilities have some difficulty in expressing themselves at some level. Expressing oneself effectively is a complicated process and one that is affected by a number of different factors often associated with learning disability; for example, hearing impairment, dyspraxia and dysarthria. The ability to express one's needs effectively is so central to achieving a better quality of life for so many people with learning disabilities, that a large part of the speech and language clinician's work is in this area. Assessment of expressive skills is therefore an essential part of this work.

There are some areas of expression that can be identified as often affecting someone's ability to express themselves effectively and which therefore need to be considered within an assessment:

Method of expression

There are several ways to express the same message, both verbally and non-verbally. People can communicate through speech, gesture, sign language, body language, physical behaviour, etc, and most use several of these methods simultaneously without even thinking about it. People also have the choice, most of the time, to decide whether to say, for example, 'I'm very angry with you', or show that person they are angry through body language, or throwing something at them! Sometimes, all three are chosen. For many people with learning disabilities, they do not have the choice and their ability to express themselves has been reduced. People with learning disabilities are often described as 'not being able to express themselves or communicate in any way'. This is never true. Every behaviour, however small, has the potential to be communicative, and so for some clients this is the most important part of the assessment. Some of the difficulties may include:

◆ Large environments can mean that physical or challenging behaviour is more likely to be noticed than eye pointing, for example.
◆ It takes time and patience to enable some people to be able to express themselves non-verbally.
◆ The environment needs to be receptive and able to 'listen'.
◆ Skills that may have been taught to people in the past can be lost if the support is no longer there. For example, if people who need to express themselves through signing are in a non-signing environment, they will become de-skilled.

Vocabulary

The essential question to ask when assessing this aspect of someone's expressive skills is, 'Has this person got the important words/signs/symbols *for them* so that they can communicate *what they want to communicate*?' Some people have been taught to sign 'thank you' when they are given a drink, but have never been taught the sign 'drink'. The question that needs to be asked by the clinician, other relevant people, and the client if possible, is 'What are the most important things in this person's life that they need and want to communicate?' A small, appropriate and functional vocabulary is preferable to a larger, inappropriate one.

Complexity of utterances

Many people with learning disabilities express themselves in one or two key-word phrases, either verbally or non-verbally (signing or symbols), and this may be linked to their comprehension level or to the skills they have at their disposal. Once again, it is important to ascertain whether their level of expression, in terms of the complexity of their utterances, is appropriate to their needs and is effective in their environment.

Fluency

Difficulties with fluency of speech are not uncommon in adults with learning disabilities and can be linked with stammering behaviour, such as tension, altered breathing patterns and physical gestures. It is unusual to work on the fluency problem itself with this client group as it requires a great deal of self-awareness and self-monitoring and it can be difficult to maintain the speech modification techniques in everyday life. Ferris-Taylor (1997) states that there is considerable debate about whether 'stammering' in adults with learning disabilities is, in fact, stammering, or is part of a person's overall communication development. This means that 'stammering' could be seen to be normal dysfluency, which is found in children, and therefore should not be perceived as a difficulty. However, we do need to assess how much the dysfluency affects the ability of adults with learning disabilities to express themselves effectively, and to analyse when the difficulties arise and what emotions are linked to these situations.

Volume/Rate/Intonation/Pitch

These aspects of speech need to be assessed in terms of how appropriate they are, and whether the person can adapt them effectively (see Chapter 6).

Articulation

A large number of people with learning disabilities have some articulation difficulties. For example, the adult who has Down's syndrome is more likely to have unclear speech because of the physical manifestations of the disorder: large tongue, small mouth and high palate. It is very unusual for a speech and language clinician to work on improving articulation as it has been proved many times that clients find it incredibly difficult to transfer skills learnt in therapy into their everyday life, and success depends on a high level of awareness and commitment. As Ferris-Taylor (1997) said: 'Helping someone improve the clarity of their speech will probably be a very slow process, if it is appropriate at all within the context of their overall strengths and difficulties in communicating. There are likely to be severe limits to the changes which can be made by adulthood.' It is more likely that other ways will be considered to improve clarity, for example by teaching clients and their carers augmentative systems such as Makaton, or giving clients an additional means of expressing themselves, such as a symbolised communication book (see Chapter 3).

It is also important to consider the possibility that the client has a hearing impairment which may be affecting the production of certain sounds. If this is the case, then assistance in using a hearing aid may be beneficial, and some people may adjust their speech spontaneously when using their hearing aid because they can hear themselves more clearly.

Use of language

Many adults with learning disabilities appear to express themselves reasonably well, but closer assessment may show that their use of language masks underlying problems in their understanding. Two common features are echolalia and perseveration.

Echolalia or echoed speech is the repetition of words or sentences spoken by others. An example of this would be a person replying 'doing' when asked the question 'What are you doing?', or when offered a choice, always choosing the thing that was mentioned last. Echolalia can also be delayed, so that a phrase heard can be repeated over and over again, but without the person knowing what it means. Many autistic people use echoed speech, sometimes remembering long conversations, but it is important not to be misled into assuming their expressive language and comprehension is at a high level. Further specific assessment of the echolalia may be relevant (see Aarons and Gittens, 1992).

Perseveration means the continuation of speech (or activity) which was appropriate in one context but is now no longer appropriate. This can be seen in people who repeatedly ask for the same thing even when they have been responded to, or those who find it difficult if the topic of conversation changes. They may also always want to talk about the same topic and may only initiate conversations about the same subject. The cause of perseveration is often not known, but may be linked to a person's sole interest, or a distressing event, or memory problems. People who have such repetitive speech can be very difficult and irritating to be around, and they are sometimes labelled as having challenging behaviour, because of their speech. Assessment needs to show how much the person is able to understand, so that people can communicate at an appropriate level, and changes in the person's form or tone of voice need to be noted so that staff are cued into their emotional state.

Assessment of a person's expressive language is important so that the following can be considered:

◆ How is this person communicating their needs, and do they need to be further developed in order to improve their quality of life?
◆ Would the person benefit from an additional means to express themselves?
◆ What needs to change in the person's environment in order to facilitate better expression, either through the teaching of new skills or through increased awareness and understanding of existing skills?

Social skills

This is frequently an area of need for people with learning disabilities, and a common focus of work for speech and language clinicians working with adults with learning disabilities. As Spence and Hitchings (1992) state: 'It is often difficult for our clients to learn the skills of good social interaction incidentally, as the majority of us do. From an early age, they are expected to behave badly or differently because they are cognitively impaired.' The term 'social skills' includes non-verbal behaviour (body language and paralinguistic skills), verbal behaviour (listening and conversational skills) and assertiveness skills. Poor social skills are a real barrier to experiencing a good quality of life, and the client who has learned even a few good social skills is more likely to be interacted with and valued as a member of a community.

Chapter 5 should be referred to for a full description of social skills and the assessment of social skills difficulties.

COMMUNICATION AND THE ENVIRONMENT

If the communication difficulties that face the adult with the learning disability are to be really understood, it is necessary to look beyond their skills and their use of such skills. Everyone needs skills with which to communicate and the ability to use these skills effectively, but it is also essential to have a receptive and appropriate environment in which to communicate, and a motivation to communicate in the first place (See Figure 1.1).

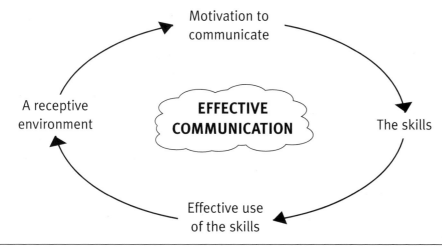

Figure 1.1.
A Model of Effective Communication

As Mittler (1988) says, 'Somehow we have to ensure that people *want* to communicate, that there is *someone* to communicate with, that they have *something* to communicate about and that we show them that communication is *enjoyable* and *brings results*.' For some people with learning disabilities, communication is not enjoyable because they are ignored, unstimulated or they have learnt that there is little point as it does not bring results. They may have some skills with which to communicate and they may be able to use these skills appropriately; what they do not have is a receptive or appropriate environment and the motivation to communicate. Assessment of someone's communication therefore needs to look not only at the person's skills but also at the environment they are in, to see where there is a breakdown in their ability to communicate effectively.

The environment

The five accomplishments of normalisation can be used to help assess the environment in terms of whether it is receptive and motivating, and to identify aspects that may need to be changed.

Relationships

This is the experience of being part of a growing network of personal relationships. Communication usually develops as part of a pleasurable, reciprocal and social process, and is dependent on people having varied and good relationships. For some people with learning disabilities, communication may not be enjoyable because they lack the opportunity to develop relationships with others. Most adults with learning disabilities are still segregated in special day centres, clubs, housing and other organisations, and this obviously means that their ability to develop relationships with non-disabled people (other than service providers) is limited. The person with communication problems is even more at a disadvantage.

Studies have shown that in settings for adults with learning disabilities, staff tend to use 'controlling speech' (ie, designed to begin, control or terminate activities) rather than conversational speech (ie, designed to explain, give or ask for information) (Van der Gaag and Dormandy 1993, cited by Ferris-Taylor, 1997). This means that in the reciprocal process of communication, carers may dominate and control the conversation, which may lead to the client not being able to fulfil their communicative potential. In addition, people with learning disabilities may inherently make fewer demands, either by sending fewer messages or else by sending messages that are not in a form carers can easily recognise, such as ambiguous gestures, or unintelligible sounds or words. If these attempts to communicate are met with little success, they are likely to decrease, having an adverse affect on the client's motivation, confidence and use of skills. This links to one of Wolfensberger's core themes of normalisation: role expectancy, that is, low expectations tend to be self-fulfilling (see Introduction).

Choice

This is the experience of growing autonomy in both small and large matters. Personal choice defines and expresses individual identity, and people with learning disabilities should be consulted as individuals and should be part of any decision-making process. The range and type of daily choices is likely to be restricted for people with learning disabilities compared to others of a similar age. Given that a primary motivation to communicate is to make choices and influence what happens next, it is important to assess this part of a person's environment. However, making choices that are real and meaningful is not a simple skill. Ferris-Taylor (1997) explains the complexity of the process by listing the following points to consider:

◆ People need to be aware that choices are possible and available.
◆ There needs to be the opportunity to make choices. Choices are often pre-empted, especially when someone has a communication difficulty, as it may be easier or quicker to choose for them or anticipate what they want. There are three levels of pre-empting described by Halle (1991, cited by Ferris-Taylor, 1997):
   1   *Environmental:* the desired item or activity is physically present or readily available, so there is no need to communicate in order to obtain it.
   2   *Non-verbal:* the person's need is anticipated by others who offer or provide it.
   3   *Verbal:* others notice the individual's likely need and verbally initiate or offer it before the person has a chance to express it themselves.
◆ People need to have an awareness or experience of what the choice means. For example, it is no good offering a person the choice of going horse-riding or roller-blading if they have not had the experience of one or both of these activities.
◆ People need to understand the consequences of choice – ie, that if you make a choice, you may not like what you have chosen, but you are often stuck with it! This element of learning by mistake is important, and one that people with learning disabilities are often protected from.

◆ People need to understand the financial constraints of choices and the impact of our choice on others. Given that people with learning disabilities are likely to be among the poorest people in society and are mostly living in group settings with others, their choices are going to be unduly constrained and compromises will have to be made.
◆ People need the assertiveness to carry through with their choices, even if others disagree with or dislike their choice. This is particularly difficult if choices are being suggested by a member of staff whom the person wants to please, and may link to fluctuations in choices.

- People need a means of expressing their choice, either spoken, signed or symbolised which is understood by others and acted upon.
- People need to be able to choose from a range of alternatives that is within their memory and understanding capabilities.

Respect and dignity

This states that all people have the right to have a valued place among a network of people and a valued role in the community. If someone with a communication difficulty is to be valued then they need to be listened to and this puts a responsibility on to the carer to be able to do this effectively. This may mean having a shared language with the client such as Makaton, or simply taking time to sit and understand what they are trying to communicate. Another way that people can be shown that they are valued is to be given responsibility within their everyday environment, and once again, people with communication difficulties may need to be enabled to do this.

Personal development

This is the experience of having a growing ability to perform skilfully both functional and meaningful activities, with whatever assistance is required. The person with communication difficulties may find it difficult to express their preferences for activities, or may be prevented from learning new skills because of their communication needs and the additional support they may need. People thrive on learning new things and this in turn motivates them to communicate (and maybe boast!) about them. The environment needs to be conducive to facilitating learning of all kinds and enabling people with communication problems to be part of this.

Community presence

This is the experience of sharing the ordinary places that define community life. Despite service aspirations towards community integration, most adults with learning disabilities are still segregated in some way. The person with the communication difficulty may have additional problems in using the community because the general public do not understand, for example, Makaton signs or symbols. This may mean that they are reliant on a member of staff to accompany them and 'speak for them'. This obviously has an adverse effect on the person's self-esteem and may reinforce a sense of helplessness and power imbalance. This, in turn, affects their motivation to communicate.

Assessment of the environment is an essential aspect of any comprehensive assessment of communication so that the following can be considered:

- Is the environment receptive and appropriate to the person's needs?
- Is the person motivated to communicate?
- Are there people with whom the person is able to communicate?
- Does the environment stimulate communication and interaction?
- Do those in the person's environment listen to and act upon communication?
- Does the environment offer opportunities for making choices and learning new skills?
- Is the environment respectful of the person's communication needs?

ADDITIONAL FACTORS TO BE CONSIDERED

Culture and race

Ferris-Taylor (1997) states: 'It is easy to overlook the cultural and racial background of someone with learning disabilities when it differs from that of the professionals involved.' She goes on to say that there are likely to be misunderstandings and inaccuracies in assessing someone's communication, especially if their first language is not English. Assessments may use materials that are unfamiliar or offensive to clients, and the involvement of an interpreter and careful planning for how to work together is crucial for effective assessment.

It is also important to remember that non-verbal communication is linked to language and culture, and there may be different rules, for example about eye contact, bodily proximity and touch. Gestures may also have different meanings in different cultures – for example, whereas in British culture a 'thumbs up' gesture is interpreted as having a positive meaning, for some Bengali-speaking people it may be interpreted as being quite rude (Ferris-Taylor, 1997).

Ferris-Taylor (1997, p.203) goes on to describe some general good practice guidelines:

- Use materials which are appropriate to the person's culture, in both assessment and any subsequent work.
- Ensure that the environment contains a range of images which include people of different races in a variety of roles; this can encourage relaxed and relevant conversation.
- Learn some key words in the person's first language and encourage other colleagues and peers to do so.
- Use an interpreter for an assessment or other important meetings or appointments.
- Ensure that you understand some of the cultural and non-verbal rules of the person's first language, to minimise misunderstandings.
- Avoid making assumptions about the person's preferences and customs based purely on culture. Find out from the person and their family, where possible.

Sensory information

Information from all of our senses is important in communication, but the most important ones for communicating effectively are hearing and vision. Many people with learning disabilities have additional difficulties in communicating because of sensory disabilities, and this needs to be considered when assessing their communication strengths and needs. Clarke-Kehoe (1992, cited by Ferris-Taylor, 1997) estimates that as many as 45 per cent of people with severe and profound learning disabilities may have some kind of visual or hearing impairment. In addition, sensory disabilities are more prevalent in elderly people: 34 per cent of people aged 60 and over have a significant hearing loss, which rises to 74 per cent in those aged over 70 (RNID 1990, cited by Ferris-Taylor, 1997).

Often, no allowances are made for sensory disability unless it has actually been diagnosed, and this can lead to unrealistic demands and expectations being placed on people. People may also be labelled and described as 'stubborn', 'inattentive', 'uncooperative', 'uncommunicative' or 'challenging', when they are struggling to cope with sensory loss that has not been diagnosed. These factors will have a direct effect on the communication assessment and it is therefore important to ascertain whether someone has a sensory impairment, and where possible to obtain a professional assessment. However, there are sometimes difficulties in having adults with learning disabilities seen for audiological or ophthalmological assessment. The professionals involved often feel insufficiently skilled in assessing our clients, or may feel that it is too time-consuming and not beneficial for someone with learning disabilities. However, the learning disability makes it even more important to obtain an accurate picture about a person's sensory abilities. As Ferris-Taylor (1997) says, 'Some people with learning disabilities may spontaneously attempt to compensate by using their other senses more fully . . . however, others may have great difficulty in adapting and learning new skills, and so extra help is vital.'

Ferris-Taylor (1997, p.207) goes on to describe some general good practice guidelines for communicating with someone with a hearing loss and someone with a visual impairment.

Communicating with someone who has a hearing loss

◆ Ensure you have the person's attention and that they are looking at you before you start talking. This helps them lip-read and watch your facial expression.
◆ Allow the person to see your face clearly by making sure there is enough light and that the light is shining on your face and not in their eyes.
◆ Slow your speech and use reasonable volume, but do not shout.
◆ Avoid exaggerating your lip patterns as this will distort the natural rhythms and visible patterns of speech.
◆ As far as possible, cut out any background noise.

◆ Get reasonably close to the person. If they use a hearing aid, the optimum distance apart is about one metre; beyond that, background noise will sound as loud as speech.
◆ Be aware that group situations will be more difficult for the person.
◆ Ensure that the person has had a recent ophthalmological assessment as good vision is obviously important.
◆ Use your facial expression, body language, gestures and Makaton signs to back up what you are saying.

Communicating with someone who has a visual impairment

◆ Use your speech to compensate for non-verbal cues which the person will be missing out on. For example, use the person's name especially when first beginning to talk, and say who you are; show the person you are listening by saying 'yes', 'mmmm', etc; and tell the person what is happening in their environment or what is about to happen, eg 'I am going to get your dinner'.
◆ Use language carefully where directional words are concerned. 'The box is next to the table' is more helpful than 'The box is over there'.
◆ Where appropriate, try to help the person understand the meaning of what you are saying by encouraging them to feel the object, or by demonstrating the appropriate action.
◆ If it is appropriate to use signs or symbols, these will need to be adapted, for example by using hand-over-hand signing and adapting the signs so that they are in contact with the person's body ('body signing').

ASSESSMENT

Introduction to core themes

In this section, assessment of comprehension, expression and the environment will be considered. In Chapters 2 to 6, assessment will be discussed in detail in relation to the client with specific difficulties, that is, challenging behaviour, alternative and augmentative communication needs, a profound learning disability, social skill difficulties and dysphagia.

Throughout this section, there are some core themes that run through all aspects of assessment, and these will be stated briefly here:

◆ Talk to, discuss with, involve and listen to the person's key worker, or most relevant person. They know the person best, they know what the environment is really like, and they will be the person who will probably be the key to success in terms of intervention. Little can be achieved without a good co-worker and ally.
◆ Observe the person in their everyday environment and see how they communicate with their peers and with staff. This will give any clinician, however experienced, most of what they need to know. A more formal assessment should add to, but never replace, an informal one.

◆ The person's communication should not be assessed in isolation from their environment as the two are inextricably linked, and any intervention agreed following assessment will inevitably have an effect on the person's environment. The action plan/programme has to work for the environment as well as for the person.

Background information

Responding to referral

Talk to the person making the referral and find out as much as possible about the reasons why this client was referred. It is surprising how often the initial reason for referral is misleading. Ask for advice with regard to who is the most appropriate person to meet with and collect the relevant background information.

Initial meeting with key worker/carer, and client, if appropriate

◆ Agree reason for referral.
◆ Collect bibliographical information: address, dob, etc.
◆ Find out about home and daytime environment.
◆ Find out about physical factors such as hearing, vision, medication and medical conditions, eg, epilepsy.
◆ Explore cultural factors.
◆ Discuss client's likes and dislikes.
◆ Find out about important people in their life.
◆ Clarify which people need to be involved in the assessment.

Plan of assessment

◆ Agree type of assessment; for example, observation of what and where.
◆ Agree date(s) and member of staff to liaise with/work with, preferably the person you have just met with.

See the Personal Communication Plan (PCP) at the end of the book, background information section.

Assessment of comprehension

Vocabulary

◆ Consider how adequate this is for the person's communication needs.
◆ What evidence is there that they misunderstand certain words?
◆ Is there a mismatch between the carer's expectation of the person's vocabulary and the person's actual understanding of words? Test this out with the help of the carer.
◆ Are there words that the person would benefit from understanding? If so, agree an achievable number and decide how best to enable the person to

understand them, for example, through speech, signing, pictures, etc. When choosing the words, consider the person's likes and dislikes, and what is important to them.

Sentence comprehension

- Observe staff interaction with the person and consider how much the client is understanding.
- How much are they able to understand in the context of their everyday environment, considering cues such as routine and peer behaviour?
- How much are they able to understand without any non-verbal cues? (This may need to be 'set up' by the clinician and carer.)
- Is their ability to understand affected by the environment they are in? Consider noise, visual distractions, etc.
- What is their understanding like in a quiet, calm room? Test out how many key words they can understand in a sentence, using objects and activities that are familiar to the person. Re-test them, as appropriate, using non-verbal cues in order to ascertain how much they are helped by these.
- How does the person cope in unfamiliar situations?
- Consider specific aspects of sentence comprehension, such as negatives, questions and tenses. Test these out as appropriate, in familiar settings.
- Discuss results of assessment with the carer/key worker and agree how to maximise the person's potential in terms of their ability to understand what is said to them. For example, using short one key word sentences; using gesture/signing/pictures, etc, in addition to speech.

Abstract concepts

- What is the person's understanding of time, not only in terms of the verbal labels, such as 'later', 'today' and 'tomorrow', but in terms of their ability to understand their daily routine and what is expected of them at certain times? How could this be improved? Consider visual prompts, written prompts and consistency in the use of words relating to time, eg, 'later'.
- What is the person's understanding of words relating to emotions and feelings? How could the person be enabled to understand these concepts more fully?

The PCP has a section on comprehension (see end of book), covering the above aspects, which is completed jointly by the clinician and relevant others following observation and assessment of the client. The CASP (Van der Gaag, 1988) has a section on assessing comprehension using pictures and objects, and which is completed by the clinician. Both assessments have an action-planning stage following assessment.

Assessment of expression

Method of expression

◆ Consider how the person expresses their needs.

◆ Observe verbal and non-verbal behaviour; for example, vocalisations, eye-pointing, body movements, physical behaviour.

◆ Observe the response that the person receives to each intent to communicate.

◆ Consider the environment the person is in and whether their method of expressing themselves is related to their surroundings; for example, eye-pointing to an object may not have been found to be effective in a noisy and busy environment, and so the person learns that screaming has a quicker response.

◆ If the person's method of expressing their needs is assessed to be inappropriate or ineffective, what could be done to improve this for them? Consider increasing skills in augmentative systems of communication, both the client's and staff's, or increasing awareness of the person's existing methods of expression and building upon them. For example, if a person is observed pacing up and down the corridor prior to being incontinent, then the staff could be encouraged to respond to their pacing by saying 'You need to go to the toilet' and signing (if appropriate) the word 'toilet'. This is then reinforced by signing again once the person is at the toilet. In this way, the person's individual method of expressing their need for the toilet is being responded to, whether it was intentional or not, and it can then be developed into a more easily recognised way to express 'toilet'.

◆ When considering the most effective method of expression for the person, consider also the environment. How much support would they need? How realistic is it, and are expectations being raised with the possibility of setting up the person to fail? An example of this may be giving a communication book to someone who lives with another client who eats or destroys anything made of paper.

Vocabulary

◆ Consider how adequate this is for the person's communication needs.

◆ Is this person able to express what they want to express?

◆ What are they doing in their life that is really important to them/motivates them, etc? Have they got the words/signs for these activities?

◆ Are there things that the person needs and wants to be able to express and at present cannot very effectively? If so, agree an achievable number with the key worker and decide how best to teach these to the client.

Expression at sentence level

◆ Is the person able to express themselves using sentences, and are these meaningful? Consider use of language and any evidence of echolalia and perseveration, for example.

- Is their ability to express themselves in sentences appropriate to their needs?
- If not, what would they benefit from improving on and how can this be achieved? It may be simply a case of modelling more complete sentences, for example when the client has said 'John drinking', the staff member could say, 'Yes, John's drinking a cup of tea'.

Fluency

- Is there evidence of dysfluency, and what form does this take; for example, repetition, blocking, tension?
- Observe when the difficulties arise and what emotions are linked to these situations?
- What is the general reaction to the person's dysfluency and could this be improved on? For example, by avoiding pressure on the person to speak, allowing the person time to finish speaking, maintaining eye-contact, or giving the person an alternative to speech in particularly stressful situations.

Volume/Rate/Intonation/Pitch

- Are these aspects of the person's speech appropriate, and can they adapt them effectively?
- If not, what can be done to increase the person's skills in this area? See Chapter 5 for suggestions on improving these non-verbal skills.

Articulation

- Is the person difficult to understand because of phonological difficulties?
- How much of a problem is this for the person, that is, do they get frustrated?
- What could be done to improve the person's ability to express themselves more clearly? This may include 'tuning in' to the person's speech by creating a glossary of approximations that the person uses, although this is only practical if their vocabulary is relatively small; building up a list of target words that are important to the person and which could be practised regularly; or encouraging the person to use additional non-verbal means to help clarify the verbal message – for example, gesture, facial expression, and signing.

The PCP (see end of book) has a section on assessing expression covering the above aspects, and which is completed jointly by the clinician and relevant others following observation and assessment of the client. The CASP has a section on assessing expression using pictures and observations of the client.

Assessment of the environment

As stated earlier in this chapter, assessment of the environment is an essential aspect of any comprehensive assessment of communication. It should be considered at the same time as one is considering the person's ability to understand and express themselves effectively, and therefore may not need a separate section.

Following the assessment of someone's communication, it will hopefully be possible for the clinician to answer most of the questions set out earlier in the chapter:

◆ Is the environment receptive and appropriate to the person's needs?
◆ Is the person motivated to communicate?
◆ Are there people with whom the person is able to communicate?
◆ Does the environment stimulate communication and interaction?
◆ Do those in the person's environment listen to and act upon communication?
◆ Does the environment offer opportunities for making choices and learning new skills?
◆ Is the environment respectful of the person's communication needs?

If some of these questions cannot be answered following assessment of comprehension and expression, then time needs to be given to answering them through observation and discussion with relevant members of staff. From this, areas of need may become apparent and actions need to be agreed with the staff.

Sometimes, however, the environment needs to be assessed in greater detail, particularly if it is a possible training need. The PCP has an environment section (see end of book) which assesses the five accomplishments of normalisation.

FOLLOWING ASSESSMENT

During assessment, strengths and needs will have been identified which will form the basis of any intervention or action plan for the client. As with any form of intervention, even if it consists of a few recommendations, it is essential that it is agreed jointly with relevant members of staff first. Often it is necessary to look at all the needs that have been identified during the assessment and agree priorities for action, because if too many actions are worked on at any one time, the chance of failure increases. It is therefore important to:

◆ Summarise all the information gained from the assessment.
◆ Identify the person's strengths in each area.
◆ Identify the person's needs in each area.
◆ Identify any environmental needs.
◆ Discuss with relevant members of staff and agree which needs should be prioritised for intervention.
◆ Discuss and agree the method of intervention.
◆ Write the programme or action plan.
◆ Talk through the action plan with all relevant members of staff to ensure there is no misunderstanding as to the purpose and content of the plan.
◆ Spend some time working alongside staff to support them in following the plan, and then give them the opportunity to discuss the plan with you.

The PCP has shared action planning forms to help the clinician complete this part of the assessment.

SUMMARY OF ASSESSMENT – WORKED EXAMPLE

NAME _____ David _____ DOB _____

ADDRESS _____ DATE _____

BACKGROUND INFORMATION

David is a 35-year-old man who lives in a small house with three other men of similar age. He has lived in this house for the past two years, prior to which he lived in a large hospital which had been his home for 24 years. There is a stable staff group at his home and his key worker is at present the deputy home manager, Steve, who has known David for two years. David has regular contact with his parents and brother, seeing them approximately twice a month on a Sunday. He does not attend any day services, but has a fairly active timetable, and he particularly enjoys walking, going to the local pub, shopping, watching music videos and having cups of tea. He spends some time with another resident, Ray, but it is reported that he has no close friendships with the other residents and prefers the company of staff. He is a physically able man with no visual or hearing impairments. He has been labelled in the past as having 'mild challenging behaviour', but staff report no recent incidents.

David was referred for a speech and language therapy assessment as staff felt that he was at times becoming frustrated in his ability to communicate his needs. They feel that he could potentially express himself more, but they wanted some advice on how to achieve this. He has been assessed over a period of a month on four separate occasions. This has included a meeting with his key worker and the head of home, a joint visit into the community and some observation time in his home.

LEVEL OF UNDERSTANDING

David often gives the impression of understanding everything that is being said to him as he smiles and nods and repeats a few of the last words heard. He does have a good understanding at a one-word level and his vocabulary is certainly adequate for his needs at present; however, assessment revealed some areas of need for David in his understanding:

1 David does not understand requests if they are more complex than a one key word utterance. He relies on non-verbal cues at these times, particularly gesture. He echoes back the last word if he still has not understood.

2 David does not have a good understanding of time, frequently asking when something is going to happen, and sometimes becoming upset if a desired activity does not happen immediately.

3 David understands the words 'no' and 'don't', but does not understand negatives within sentences, for example, 'We can't go to the shops now'.

SUMMARY OF ASSESSMENT – WORKED EXAMPLE

EXPRESSIVE SKILLS

David is able to use speech to communicate his needs. He mainly uses short phrases that can become quite repetitive, for example, 'cup of tea'. He also repeats sentences that have been said to him previously, copying intonation patterns, but with varying volume and facial expression depending on how he is feeling. For example, 'not today David' could be said calmly and quietly if he is feeling happy, or in a more agitated way and louder if he is unhappy about something. He paces up and down and rubs his face repeatedly if he is distressed. This behaviour has been observed at times when he seems unsure of what is happening next and has not understood the situation. He has a good basic vocabulary and is able to communicate immediate needs such as hunger, thirst and the need to go to the toilet. His speech is on the whole clear and easy to understand. Assessment has therefore revealed several needs for David:

1   David uses his speech and non-verbal behaviour sometimes to indicate that he has not understood what is expected of him, and if this is not recognised, he can become increasingly agitated.

2   David mostly speaks in short, incomplete sentences, for example, 'go walking', 'want a drink', but is able to repeat complete sentences if modelled by a member of staff.

SUMMARY AND RECOMMENDATIONS FOR INTERVENTION

David would benefit from having a better understanding of what is expected of him. This would be best achieved through increasing staff awareness into their use of speech and encouraging them to use short, simple sentences and simple gesture/Makaton when speaking to David. He would also benefit from a visual timetable to help him understand what is happening on that day.

David's speech often reflects the fact that he has not understood. Increasing staff awareness into his use of echolalia and encouraging them to respond by explaining what is happening in very clear and simple sentences would hopefully reduce David's anxiety. David often speaks using incomplete sentences, but this will not be worked on directly at present and will be considered as an area for action at his next review in three months' time.

SUMMARY OF ASSESSMENT – WORKED EXAMPLE

ACTION PLAN

1 STAFF TRAINING to cover the following areas: using one key word sentences; using simple negatives; recognising and responding to David's echolalia, and essential Makaton signs. Discuss action plan with all staff. Set dates for next staff meeting with a provisional review session one month later.

2 THREE JOINT SESSIONS set weekly for Alex to work alongside three different members of staff to help implement the programme and offer support as appropriate.

3 TIMETABLE to be put together jointly by Alex, Steve and David. To be done in one month.

Clinician _____A Clinician_____ Key worker _____Steve Martin_____

Chapter 2: Challenging Behaviour

INTRODUCTION

Aggression and violence remain a major topic of concern and have been for many years in services for people with learning disabilities. As McDonnell and Sturmey (1993) write: 'These behaviours are stigmatising and present a devalued image of the person to the general public and to carers. Maladaptive behaviours in general and extra-personal maladaptive behaviours in particular have been implicated in the breakdown of family placements, placement in more restrictive settings such as institutions, breakdown of community placements and subsequent readmission and reduced chance of discharge.' People who have learning disabilities and in addition have challenging behaviour continue to challenge the services and are saying – often wordlessly – something very important. The challenge that carers and services face is to find a way of 'listening' to their behaviour and providing an environment that enables people to communicate their needs and control their lives without having to use their challenging behaviour in order to effect change in their surroundings.

In this chapter, the role of the speech and language clinician in working with clients who present with challenging behaviour will be considered. First, 'challenging behaviour' as a term will be defined, and the different approaches of managing behaviour that is challenging will be described. The link between challenging behaviour and communication will then be considered, and finally the role of the speech and language clinician will be addressed in terms of assessment and intervention.

WHAT DO WE MEAN BY CHALLENGING BEHAVIOUR?

We all do things that other people find incredibly irritating or objectionable, but that would not be described as 'challenging'. Other people may ignore these behaviours; they may try to let us know that we are being irritating in the hope that we will change that behaviour; they may actively avoid us, or they may simply try to focus on our good points. Most people try to be reasonable and will negotiate where appropriate, and in turn, we usually try to behave in ways that are acceptable to other people, especially those close to us.

People with learning disabilities, like everyone else, vary in their behaviour and personalities, but some people with learning disabilities present extreme forms of behaviour which most people find objectionable, and which may result in those clients becoming isolated and having few friends. Examples of such behaviour might be the person who tries to become physically intimate with people they have known for only a short time, or who talks incessantly and uses offensive language irrespective of where they are. While it is recognised that they need help in learning social skills, it is not easy to know whether or not they will be described as having 'challenging behaviour'.

'Challenging behaviour' is generally used to describe behaviour which significantly impairs the person's quality of life and the ability of the service to meet that person's needs. Examples of severe challenging behaviour are:

- Physical aggression towards other people.
- Physical aggression towards themselves, or self-injury.
- Damage to materials or property.
- Sexually inappropriate behaviour.

Emerson *et al* (1987) define severely challenging behaviour as follows:

> By severely challenging behaviour we mean behaviour of such intensity, frequency or duration that the physical safety of the person or others is placed in serious jeopardy or behaviour which is likely to seriously limit or deny access to the use of ordinary community facilities. Ordinarily, we would expect the person to have shown the pattern of behaviour that presents such a challenge to services for a considerable period of time. Severely challenging behaviour is not a transient phenomenon.

Zarkowska and Clements (1988) describe challenging behaviour in a slightly different way:

> Behaviour may legitimately be regarded as a problem if it satisfies some or all of the following criteria:
> - The behaviour itself or its severity is inappropriate, given the person's age and level of development.
> - The behaviour is dangerous either to the person himself or to others.
> - The behaviour constitutes a significant additional handicap for the person by interfering with learning of new skills or by excluding the person from important learning opportunities.
> - The behaviour causes significant stress to the lives of those who live and work with the person, and impairs the quality of their lives to an unusual degree.
> - The behaviour is contrary to social norms.

As can be seen from these definitions, challenging behaviour is not about isolating specific behaviours as 'challenging', as most people have done things at times of extreme stress that could then be described as 'challenging'. It is more to do with the strength of the behaviour (frequency, duration and intensity), the context in which it occurs (where and at what time), the age or developmental status of the person concerned and the likely consequences of that behaviour.

The term 'challenging behaviour' is used (as opposed to other terms such as inappropriate, difficult or problem behaviour) for a number of reasons:

- It emphasises that behaviours are considered problematic because of their implications or consequences: they create a challenge for carers and members of staff.
- It is a term which reflects the social judgement implied in the identification of the problem behaviour.

◆ It reminds us that providers of services have a responsibility to respond to the challenge and to try to improve that person's quality of life.

◆ It reflects the relationship between behaviour and the conditions in which people live. In poor conditions, for example where few human needs are met, many people are likely to present challenges, but in settings where their needs are met they are less likely to present challenging behaviour. Therefore behaviour is not therefore a personal characteristic, but is something which changes according to circumstances (Harris and Hewett, 1996).

INCIDENCE OF CHALLENGING BEHAVIOUR IN PEOPLE WITH LEARNING DISABILITIES

It is difficult to find data on the actual incidence of challenging behaviour in adults with learning disabilities. Some services seem quick to label people as having challenging behaviour if they have at some time in the past 'got angry and hit out', whereas some services only describe people as having challenging behaviour after a large number of violent incidents. However, it is known that the incidence of significant challenging behaviour among people with learning disabilities is considerably higher than in the rest of the general population, and whereas many of the behaviours are similar to those which may be found in the rest of the general population (for example, tantrums, aggression, absconding), there are a number of behaviours less commonly found in the rest of the general population (repetitive and stimulatory behaviours; socially inappropriate behaviours such as masturbating, stripping and smearing; and self-injurious behaviours such as self-hitting, self-biting or eye-poking).

McDonnell, Dearden and Richens (1991) have speculated that the physical nature of violent incidents is dependent on the situation and the nature of the population studied. They maintain that it is relatively uncommon for people with learning disabilities to 'fight' in the same way as a 'hardened street fighter'. Therefore, the use of weapons is rare, as is punching and kicking when compared to hair pulling, biting and grabbing of clothes.

UNDERSTANDING THE CAUSES OF CHALLENGING BEHAVIOUR

When a violent incident occurs, one of the most common expressions used by carers is 'it happened out of the blue' or 'there was no reason for it'. Challenging behaviour does *not* tend to occur without a reason. Carers may not understand why it happened, but this does not mean that no cause existed. It is important to be always trying to understand human behaviour, no matter how confusing it may appear at first glance. Challenging behaviours are by their nature complicated and difficult to understand, and will always present a continuing challenge to those who work and live with people with learning disabilities.

Historically there has been a tendency to use rather simple models to understand challenging behaviour in people with learning disabilities, for example, as simply attention-seeking behaviour which has been learnt and which needs to be stopped. This reflects a lack of understanding of the special problems and needs of this group.

It is unusual to find a simple or single cause for challenging behaviour, and there are a number of factors which are likely to contribute and which may explain their high incidence in this group. Zarkowska and Clements (1988) describe these factors under four headings: biological, social, emotional and cognitive. **Biological factors** include organic brain dysfunction, epilepsy, hearing and visual difficulties, and certain temperamental characteristics such as a high intensity of emotional responding and poor adaptability to new situations. **Social factors** also have an important influence on behaviour. For example, people who receive poor quality care, or who are rejected by society, caregivers or peers are more likely to develop behavioural and emotional problems. Environments in which there is a high level of tension and interpersonal conflict are also more likely to result in people exhibiting challenging behaviour.

Emotional factors include aspects such as the experience of failure in many areas of life, and the fact that people with learning disabilities frequently remain highly dependent on others for their needs throughout their adult life, resulting in a poor self-concept and low self-esteem. These emotional factors can themselves be important determinants of challenging behaviour. Finally, **cognitive factors** include a number of important factors which have been associated with the occurrence of challenging behaviour and which are frequently encountered in people with learning disabilities. These include poor problem-solving skills, poor communication skills and poor social skills.

As Zarkowska and Clements say, any of the influences described above can affect a person's emotional adjustment and consequent behaviour, regardless of intellectual ability; however, people with learning disabilities are often exposed to a large number of these influences, and these are likely to interact with one another and cause a greater chance of challenging behaviour.

From a number of years' experience of working with people with challenging behaviour, McDonnell (1995) gives us a list of nine common causes of challenging behaviour which are instantly recognisable to those of us who work frequently with these clients:

1 Being unable to communicate a need

If a person cannot communicate their needs and wishes, this can lead to violent behaviour. It is possibly easy to imagine or think of actual examples when aggression or even physical violence has been caused by an inability to communicate something to someone who does not appear to be able to understand what is being said. It is not difficult to understand how frustrating this would be if this was a normal, everyday event.

2 Being confused

Challenging behaviour can often occur when people do not understand the demands being placed on them, and so they become confused. People frequently speak using grammatically complicated language and assume that they have been understood, and those who care for people with learning disabilities are more likely to over-estimate, rather than under-estimate, a client's ability to understand verbal information. Imagine being in a foreign country where no one speaks your language, and if they then shouted at you and seemed upset with you, it would be difficult for you to understand why and you would probably become confused and maybe frightened as well.

3 Being in pain

If a person has a communication problem, it is difficult for them to tell anyone that they are in pain. A person may behave in an uncharacteristic manner or even become aggressive if they have a headache, stomach ache or dental problem. Therefore illness should always be considered as a possible cause of challenging behaviour.

4 Medication change

Similar to the notion of being confused, changes in medication can have a number of behavioural side-effects. Most people, when prescribed medication, have an idea of what the medication they are taking is supposed to do, and research has shown that an individual can easily be confused and excited if medication is administered without explaining the side-effects. For example, if someone is given adrenaline but told that it is aspirin, dramatic behavioural effects will occur that the person will not understand. This can obviously be extremely frightening. A similar thing can happen to people with learning disabilities. Medication changes are often routine and well-intentioned, but a lack of explanation and a difficulty in a person's ability to comprehend verbal information may lead to a sequence of events that the person does not understand either. This will lead to confusion and can precipitate aggression and violence.

5 Inactivity

Challenging behaviour is often seen to decrease if the activity schedules of people with learning disabilities are increased. Providing a structured day with new experiences can have a dramatic effect on the incidence of challenging behaviour.

Boredom is therefore an important factor, because if a person is bored, violent and aggressive behaviours can provide that individual with a great deal of attention. If this is the case, we need to provide that attention in a more positive manner appropriate to the behaviour displayed.

6 Attention-seeking behaviour

While it is true that sometimes challenging behaviour is used to attract the attention of care staff, it is important to remember that seeking attention is a perfectly valid thing to do! It is more relevant to ask why it is that the person needs the attention of care staff, and how that attention can be available to them without their having to use difficult behaviour; and then to teach care staff to respond to altered signals.

7 Changes in routine

Changes in everyday routine can often lead to challenging behaviour, and this is particularly true for people with autism and people who have limited understanding. Routines help people to manage and understand their environment, and for those people who have difficulties in understanding, a familiar routine is something that they rely on in order to make sense of their world and what is expected of them. A change in routine can therefore be confusing and distressing, and can in turn lead to challenging behaviour.

8 Environmental effects

The environment can have a dramatic effect on people's behaviour, and many of these effects have been associated with violent and aggressive behaviour. Some of these include :

- The amount of personal space a person requires
- Heat
- Extreme noise
- Seating arrangements.

9 Delusional thoughts

Some people with learning disabilities may have mental health difficulties that can result in delusional thoughts and ideas which may or may not be apparent. They may hear voices which request that they do something violent, or similarly a person may become paranoid about particular individuals whom they think may be trying to kill or harm them. In all of these cases, a result of delusional thoughts can be challenging behaviour.

The above causes are summarised in **Handout 3** in Chapter 8.

It is important to remember that challenging behaviours do *not* occur without a reason, but are often a result of a number of different factors, which in turn result in behaviours being complicated and sometimes confusing, and often difficult to understand. It is important to always try to understand the behaviour that is seen to be challenging, and to understand how the person's communication difficulties may be influencing or directly affecting their challenging behaviour.

APPROACHES TO THE MANAGEMENT OF CHALLENGING BEHAVIOUR

Approaches to the management of challenging behaviour in people with learning disabilities, like the models for understanding the behaviour itself, have in the past been simplistic and often narrowly focused, according to the carer's professional background. The main approaches that the reader may come across will be discussed briefly, and current thinking in the management of challenging behaviour will then be described.

◆ *Biological approaches.* These have focused on pharmacological interventions, to reduce anxiety or suppress aggressive behaviour, for example, or to reduce obsessional and ritualistic behaviour.

◆ *Social approaches.* These emphasise the importance of 'normal' living environments, the need to treat people with learning disabilities with respect and dignity, and to give them greater autonomy in their own lives. The underlying assumption is that if people are treated well, they are more likely to behave well.

◆ *Educational approaches.* These emphasise the importance of increasing people's skills and experiences on the assumption that, in the absence of things to do and in the absence of more appropriate responses, people will use whatever skills they have available to meet their needs.

◆ *Psychological approaches.* These can be described under four different headings: behavioural, psychodynamic, cognitive and humanistic.

The behavioural perspective

Until very recently, the behavioural approach was most commonly used to help people who had challenging behaviour. This approach focuses specifically on observed behaviours rather than on people's thoughts or emotions. Behaviourists say that human behaviour, like animal behaviour, can be described as a stimulus-response chain. Learning is said to occur when observable behaviour changes as a result of associating certain actions with certain consequences: if the consequences gratify, the behaviour increases, if they displease, the behaviour decreases. Behaviourists describe actions which make the behaviour more likely to occur as reinforcers or rewards, and those that make it less likely to occur as punishers.

Within the traditional behavioural framework, challenging behaviours are analysed by looking at environmental factors (rewards, punishers, and triggers) and interventions aimed at building appropriate behaviours by teaching and reinforcing them through the manipulation of triggers, and consequences for both appropriate and inappropriate behaviours. Rewards (eg verbal praise, drinks, liked activity) may be given for the use of appropriate skills or behaviours, but punishment or withholding of reinforcers is no longer considered a suitable means of reducing inappropriate behaviour.

The psychodynamic perspective

This approach takes as its basic assumption the view that much of human behaviour is driven by unconscious processes. During development, basic drives and instincts, such as aggression and sex drive, may be punished and forbidden, and this serves to force them into the unconscious from where they may subsequently present as emotional problems. Helping people overcome these problems means that the unconscious basis of the difficulties needs to be understood, and the repressed emotions and drives need to be brought into awareness so that they can be dealt with in more rational ways.

The cognitive perspective

This relatively recent approach focuses on people's interpretations of events. According to the cognitive perspective, people's thoughts and interpretations influence their mood: thus negative thoughts lower mood and positive thoughts raise a person's mood and subsequent motivation. Thoughts can become distorted with adverse effects on both mood and motivation, and by accessing a person's unhelpful thoughts and interpretation of events they can be helped to develop more useful ways of thinking and better problem-solving strategies.

The humanistic perspective

This approach focuses on the inner life or subjective experience of the individual. People are viewed as motivated by a desire for personal growth and self-fulfilment. When difficulties arise, these desires are temporarily halted and people may need help to get them back on the road to self-fulfilment. This can be facilitated by relationships with people who show warmth, respect, and unconditional regard for the person.

A 'coming together' of approaches and perspectives

Nowadays, it is increasingly acknowledged that human behaviour is too complex to be viewed from any one perspective. Each perspective – the conscious mind, subjective experience, unconscious processes, environmental influence and the quality of relationships – has something to offer in relation to our understanding of people. Biological, social and educational perspectives are equally important in terms of the help that can be given.

The most influential model for understanding challenging behaviour in people with learning disabilities has traditionally been the behavioural model, and the most frequently used therapeutic interventions have been pharmacological and behavioural. Recent years, however, have seen increasing debate about the use of behavioural interventions, particularly the use of punishment as part of the intervention. Some behaviourists now promote positive, non-aversive ways of changing people's behaviour. The emphasis is still on behaviour, but the focus is much broader. These behaviourists address the person's total environment and look closely at the function of each behaviour that needs to be changed, and assess the meaning of the behaviour by using consequence analysis. The quality of someone's life is examined and if it is lacking something, recommendations are made for positive constructive improvement. However, even these behavioural interventions still assume that it is possible to control people by manipulating their environment and do not always take into consideration the person's intentions.

The STAR model is a multi-component approach that encompasses the many factors, as described earlier, that may be influencing a person's behaviour. It provides a framework for understanding and assessing challenging behaviour and planning therapeutic interventions. It is a broad problem-solving approach that separates the various factors that may be involved into four broad categories: (S) settings, (T) triggers, (A) actions, and (R) results. These will be described briefly, as it is important to have a basic understanding of approaches being used when working with people with challenging behaviour.

Settings

Settings are those factors that influence motivation and are the context in which actions occur. Among the most important environmental setting conditions are the physical climate (eg, noise, crowding), the social climate (eg, quality and style of interactions and relationships), and the occupational climate (eg, the quality, structure and appropriateness of activities). Among the most important personal setting conditions are the person's physical state, their psychological state and their cognitions, as what people think and how they interpret events influence a person's mood and subsequent behaviour.

Triggers

Triggers are the signals or stimuli that are present in a situation and which 'set off' specific actions. They occur immediately before the behaviour, and there are various reasons why triggers can set off behaviour. They may signal the availability of the thing that the person wants (eg, the smell of food), or the imminence of the thing that the person does not want. They may trigger habitual behaviour – a behaviour which always follows a stimulus because it has always done so – or they may directly elicit a behaviour – an automatic reaction to a stimulus. They may create emotional overload – as in a small occurrence being the 'last straw' – or they may cause a sharp and rapid increase in arousal or emotion.

Actions

Actions are the observable behaviours and the agreement upon the 'action' which is of concern is the starting point within the STAR model. Subsequently, actions that need to be encouraged or learned are also identified. Actions are influenced by many variables both directly and indirectly. They are in some ways determined by environmental settings and influenced by personal setting factors; they are set off by specific triggers and are likely to achieve a positive result for the individual on at least some occasions.

Results

Results are the events that follow an action, and they provide information about the appropriateness of that action in a given situation. They can also influence the likelihood of a person performing that action in similar situations on subsequent occasions. There are three classes of results which can follow an action: reinforcers, punishers and neutral results. *Reinforcers* strengthen or encourage behaviour. Positive reinforcement occurs when an action is followed by something that is desired, and negative reinforcement occurs when an action is followed by the cessation of something unwanted. *Punishers* weaken or discourage behaviour – for example, being ignored or deprived of privileges. *Neutral results* following an action are likely eventually to weaken the future use of an action. They are neither negative nor positive and the behaviour simply achieves little, if anything, for the individual.

CHALLENGING BEHAVIOUR: A WAY TO COMMUNICATE

In the past, challenging behaviour and communication were viewed as separate issues. It is only fairly recently that speech and language clinicians have been working alongside fellow professionals, such as clinical psychologists, to help assess and plan appropriate intervention techniques for people with challenging behaviour. From a pragmatic perspective, all behaviour can be considered to be communicative, as noted by Watzlawick *et al* (1967) and cited by Donnellan *et al* (1984): 'No matter how one may try, one cannot *not* communicate. Activity or inactivity, words or silence all have message value: they influence others and these others, in turn, cannot *not* respond to these communications and are thus themselves communicating.'

The task that is faced is to see the challenging behaviour as one way in which a person might be trying to say something – a form of communication rather than a result of pathology or malice. It is necessary to look underneath the behaviour to find possible reasons why the person is expressing themselves in this way, and to uncover what needs the person may have that are not being met. The behaviour is therefore not the focus of therapy, but part of a picture of someone's life that needs to be understood.

It is also important to be aware of this person's behaviour within the context of their present and past environments. People with challenging behaviour are often caught in a vicious circle whereby their behaviour has caused them to be removed from ordinary settings into segregated, barren environments which in turn reduce the likelihood that their needs will be attended to in an appropriate way. It is important to appreciate the conditions which prevailed in the large hospitals where many adults with a learning disability spent a large part of their lives, and to understand that the behaviours that are seen as challenging now, were possibly strategies that worked for them there, and were possibly even demanded by that setting. People learned appropriate skills in an abnormal living environment. The randomness of such behaviours may therefore be challenged, and the person presented as someone who has learned skills in the past which were valid and is therefore capable of learning further new skills. As Brown (1994, p.8) states: 'Sometimes people were actually taught to do things which now seem inappropriate; for example, women . . . were taught to lift their skirts up whenever they sat down to avoid wetting their clothes. Otherwise, individuals worked out for themselves, by trial and error, by testing out the responses which were available, how they could exert some control over what happened to them.'

Communication difficulties can be related to challenging behaviour in two ways. First, challenging behaviour can cause communication difficulties; for example, self injury can result in hearing loss or physical damage to the mouth. Second, challenging behaviour can itself be a form of communication, an effective way of sending a message: for example, 'I don't want to do this any more'. The behaviour either expresses a need or is a direct result of a comprehension difficulty. The behaviour can therefore be a symptom of an underlying need or difficulty rather than itself being the difficulty.

Impaired expressive skills may mean that the only way the person with learning disabilities is able to express pain, thirst or boredom is through challenging behaviour. Experience may also have shown them that their environment is more likely to respond if they are self-injuring than if they are standing by the tea trolley, looking at the cups. It is not difficult to imagine being in a foreign country where no one seems to understand *anything* you do or say, and needing to communicate something very important (or for that matter something that started off as trivial but grew in importance as time went on, eg, thirst, hunger, boredom). What lengths might someone go to in order to get their meaning across, and would any of them be similar to some of the behaviours that we see people with learning disabilities exhibiting?

Impaired receptive skills, or comprehension, can also have a devastating effect on someone's behaviour. Staff frequently assume that clients understand far more than they are actually able to, and often report that a particular client 'understands everything that you say to them . . . if they feel like it'. As was discussed in the Chapter 1, a client needs to understand only one key word in a phrase to have a good chance of following that instruction correctly, but equally sometimes incorrectly. For example, 'Come on George, it's time to pack up now. Go to the toilet and then you can go into lunch.' All George may need to understand is 'toilet' to be seen to be responding appropriately to that instruction, and indeed it can be easily argued that he does not need to even understand that if there was non-verbal information such as gesture, routine, or peer behaviour available. However, these cues are not always present and this may lead to problems and misunderstanding; for example, 'Come on George, it's time for lunch. Don't go to the toilet yet; Mary is in there.' If George has only understood the word 'toilet', then he will presumably respond to this request incorrectly. If staff are unaware that the person has difficulties in understanding verbal information, they may interpret inappropriate or bizarre responses as challenging behaviour.

The frustration arising from lack of understanding can further contribute to challenging behaviour. As Clarke-Kehoe and Harris (1992) explain, some of the main consequences that can arise from the person's impaired receptive skills and carer's lack of awareness are:

◆ The carer's expectations may be unrealistic.
◆ The person with the learning disability may receive only part of a message, or misinterpret the information and therefore respond in an inappropriate or bizarre way.

- When people do not respond appropriately they may be mistakenly described as unco-operative.
- Some people may be punished for not cooperating when they do not understand what they are meant to do.
- The person may come to perceive the world as a confusing place of mixed messages and disappointments.
- People can become frustrated at the inconsistencies they are constantly exposed to, and may exhibit their frustration as challenging behaviour.
- They may also feel it safer not to respond and appear to be withdrawn.

Therefore, if it can be assumed that challenging behaviour is a form of communication, then speech and language clinicians, with their specialist knowledge of communication, have an important role to play in interpreting the message behind the behaviour, both in giving the client a more effective way to express themselves and in facilitating the staff to respond to this communication effectively.

ASSESSMENT OF COMMUNICATION AND THE PERSON WITH CHALLENGING BEHAVIOUR

Introduction to assessment

As previously stated, it is obviously important not to view either the behaviour or the communication of a client in isolation, but to see them in the context of their everyday environment. It is as important to identify the client's skills and needs as it is to identify the staff's skills, needs and expectations, and in addition to be aware of the issues at service level that will have an effect on the staff and subsequently the client. If the work is to be effective, it is important to work and effect change at all levels, and not to expect a client to learn or adapt behaviour where there is not the environment to facilitate this (see Figure 2.1).

Assessment of expressive skills

It is important to begin by assessing the individual and how they signal or express that they are in need of something (see Figure 2.2).

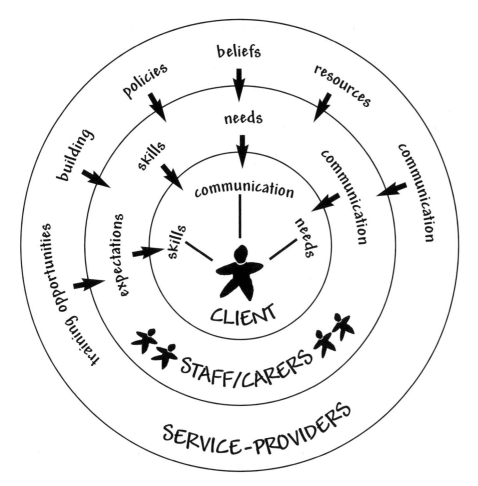

Figure 2.1 *The Client in the Context of their Everyday Environment*

THE CLIENT'S NEEDS **THE CLIENT'S EXPRESSIVE SKILLS**

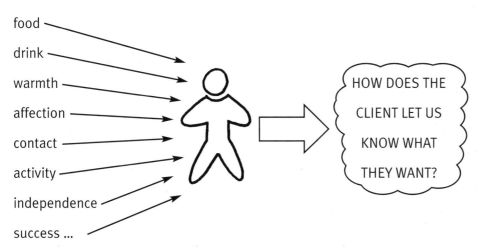

Figure 2.1 *Assessment of Expressive Skills*

Staff need to be enabled to think through the strategies that individuals use to make known their basic needs. By using the following format, which has been adapted from Clarke-Kehoe (1994), the clinician is helped to identify the needs that the client is able to convey, those they have no appropriate way of conveying and whether there is associated challenging behaviour. Following this, it is possible for staff and clinician to assess jointly the main areas of need in terms of improving the client's ability to express themselves, and to plan intervention as appropriate.

ASSESSMENT OF EXPRESSIVE SKILLS

NAME _____ DOB _____

ADDRESS _____

COMPLETED BY _____ DATE _____

HOW DOES THE PERSON TELL YOU WHEN THEY ARE ...	What does the person say? What noises do they make or signs do they use?	What does the person do with their hands, feet, body language and so on?
bored?		
tired?		
hungry?		
thirsty?		
feeling angry?		
feeling sad?		
feeling happy?		

ASSESSMENT OF EXPRESSIVE SKILLS

HOW DOES THE PERSON TELL YOU WHEN THEY ...	What does the person say? What noises do they make or signs do they use?	What does the person do with their hands, feet, body language and so on?
are in pain?		
want to go to the toilet?		
want to go out?		
want to be alone?		
need help?		
like someone?		
don't like someone?		

Other things you have noticed the person communicating; how do they do this?

_____

_____

_____

_____

Photocopiable

ASSESSMENT OF EXPRESSIVE SKILLS – SUMMARY SHEET

NAME _____ DOB _____

ADDRESS _____

COMPLETED BY _____ DATE _____

---

1 METHOD OF COMMUNICATION (verbal and nonverbal)

---

2 NEEDS THAT CAN BE EXPRESSED EFFECTIVELY

---

3 NEEDS THAT CANNOT BE EXPRESSED EFFECTIVELY

---

4 ACTION REQUIRED (including goals for client; training)

Photocopiable

©Alex Kelly, 2000

Assessment of comprehension

As was stated previously, the ability of people with learning disabilities to understand verbal information is often overestimated by staff and carers, and the consequences of this can be devastating for the client. When assessing comprehension in an adult who presents with challenging behaviour, the same principles apply as were discussed in Chapter 1. However, it is important to stress again that a formal assessment of a client's comprehension will have little functional relevance to improving their communication environment. It is much more relevant to spend time observing the client and staff interacting in their everyday environment and assessing by means of everyday activities. The comprehension assessment provides the clinician with a format for observing how much a person understands in their environment by assessing their responses to both verbal and non-verbal information. If possible, it is easier to video some staff/client interactions and then analyse the information from the recording.

The questions that we need to ask are:

◆ How many information-carrying words (key words) can the client understand in any one sentence?
◆ What non-verbal behaviour is necessary or beneficial to the client in order to help them understand?
◆ Where there appears to be inconsistency in a client's ability to understand, what other external factors in their environment may be affecting their comprehension skills?
◆ What communication methods help and hinder at times of challenging behaviour?
◆ What are the training implications in the above?

ASSESSMENT OF COMPREHENSION

NAME _____ DOB _____

ADDRESS _____

COMPLETED BY _____ DATE _____

SPEAKER

CLIENT

VERBAL REQUEST (actual words said)	NON-VERBAL BEHAVIOUR (gesture, signing, routine...)	RESPONSE (client's behaviour/action)

ASSESSMENT OF COMPREHENSION

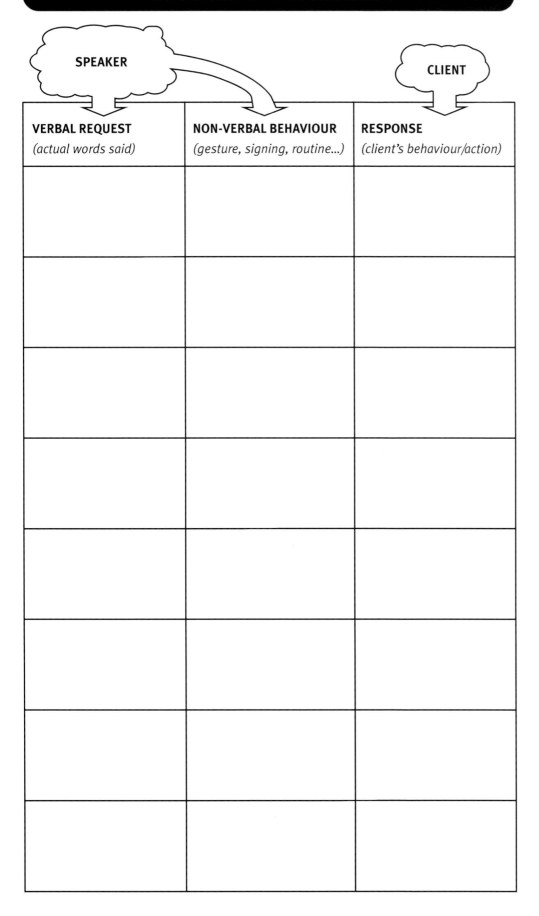

SPEAKER

CLIENT

VERBAL REQUEST (actual words said)	NON-VERBAL BEHAVIOUR (gesture, signing, routine...)	RESPONSE (client's behaviour/action)

Working with

Adults with a Learning Disability

④

ASSESSMENT OF COMPREHENSION – SUMMARY SHEET

NAME _____ DOB _____

ADDRESS _____

COMPLETED BY _____ DATE _____

---

1 METHOD OF COMMUNICATION (verbal and nonverbal)

---

2 ENVIRONMENTAL FACTORS/COMMUNICATION METHODS that aid comprehension

---

3 ENVIRONMENTAL FACTORS/COMMUNICATION METHODS that hinder comprehension

---

4 ACTION REQUIRED (including training implications, intervention...)

68

Assessment of the environment

Assessments are often carried out solely in terms of analysing specific skills and behaviours without really addressing the whole issue of a person's environment and the effect it is having on them. There is a very great need to assess the person's quality of life and the opportunities for achieving a better quality of life within their everyday environment. Speech and language clinicians can have a valid role in carrying out this assessment as communication is so central to an individual's ability to achieve a good quality of life.

The five principles of normalisation (see Introduction) can be used to assess how the person's behaviour and communication difficulties adversely affect them, and the extent to which the service is failing to make opportunities available to them because of their difficulties. As Brown (1994, p9) states:

> There is a commitment to work with people in such a way that they:
> - are not segregated or isolated because they are difficult to deal with (community presence)
> - are enabled to make choices and have their preferences respected (choice)
> - are encouraged to join in activities and relate to other people (relationships or participation)
> - are helped to present themselves positively and to be perceived by staff as worthwhile people despite their difficult behaviour (respect)
> - learn new skills and ways of meeting their needs (personal development or competence).

Assessment of a person's environment and quality of life will involve observation of that environment and detailed discussions with relevant members of staff. The environment section of the Personal Communication Plan (PCP), which is included at the end of this book, aims to identify a person's current opportunities for achieving a good quality of life within their everyday environment; the barriers that are currently present, and opportunities for improvement. There are five checklists to complete, each one addressing one of the accomplishments of normalisation, and it is obviously preferable to complete them jointly with relevant members of staff. Finally, there is a summary sheet provided in order to collate and summarise the material, and from which an action plan can be formulated.

INTERVENTION

Introduction to intervention

Following assessment, the actions that were identified during the assessment period will be used to form the basis of intervention or action plan for the person with challenging behaviour. As with any form of intervention, it is essential that any action plan is agreed jointly with all relevant members of staff and managers where appropriate, and that a realistic (ie, not too many) number of objectives are set. This means that the *actions* and *improvements* listed in the assessment sheets will need to be analysed and then prioritised for action. An example of this might be where a need has been identified for a client to learn some basic Makaton signs, and for the staff to have some initial training in Makaton. It is obviously important to address the staff training need prior to teaching the client the signs, otherwise the client may experience a new frustration. Also, the simpler the programme or action plan is and the easier it is to read and understand, the more likely it is to be implemented. It is always preferable to keep updating a programme than tearing up one that has not even been started! Another important part of ensuring a programme is implemented is to spend time with key members of staff demonstrating what is being recommended, and then observing and supporting staff in its implementation. It is unlikely that the speech and language clinician will be the most relevant person to teach the client new skills, but they are certainly the most relevant people to ensure that the communication programmes that have been put in place for clients are followed.

The three main areas of intervention are the same as in assessment and will be considered separately, even though in practice they are obviously very interlinked.

Improving expressive skills

As discussed previously in this chapter, the inability to express needs effectively can frequently lead to challenging behaviour, and therefore the focus for intervention is often to improve a client's expressive skills.

Using the information from the assessment it is important to decide:

(a) What clients need to be able to express that they are currently unable to do effectively.
(b) How they will most effectively communicate this, using as many of their existing skills as possible.
(c) The training implications for staff in implementing the above.

(a) What the client needs to be able to express

There will often be a number of things that the client cannot currently express; and these must be considered and then prioritised according to the client's needs,

rather than anyone else's. This means prioritising signs that motivate the client over ones that please other people, such as 'please' and 'thank you', which have no functional relevance for the client. It is therefore important at this stage to agree a limited number of things that the person would really benefit from learning to express, and also to choose things initially that happen regularly/daily as opposed to weekly. It is also critical at this stage to consult with a member of staff who knows the client well, and who will be able to advise on what motivates them and is important to them. Not all people with challenging behaviour and learning disabilities want to learn how to say or sign 'drink', 'toilet' and 'dinner'.

(b) How will the client do this?

It is important at this point to consider the person's current method of communicating and level of understanding and, where possible, current skills should be built on. Most frequently it is simply a choice between verbal or non-verbal communication, and for the latter a choice between signing, symbols or objects. Sometimes, for the more severely learning disabled person, it may be necessary to formalise their current vocalisations and body language so that carers respond consistently to one set of behaviours, and in turn the behaviours become more meaningful and communicative to both the staff and client involved. For example, it may be observed that sometimes John rocks in his chair and looks from side to side when he is thirsty; and so staff agree to respond consistently to this behaviour by offering him a drink. In time, John will learn that this behaviour is a successful way of expressing his need for a drink.

It is also important to consider the environment in which the person spends most time, and how their peers interact with one another. It may be important, for example, to teach one client some Makaton in addition to speech because the people with whom they live communicate solely through signing. Conversely, it is not desirable for staff to be signing to only one client because 'they need Makaton and the others don't'.

(c) The training implications

With any new programme, some element of staff training will probably be needed. This may be only a few joint sessions with an experienced member of staff and the client to ensure that the programme is workable, or it may mean a series of staff training sessions to teach them relevant skills (see Chapter 8). Whatever the level of training needed, it is obviously an essential part of ensuring that a programme is implemented successfully.

Improving comprehension

As discussed previously in this chapter, the capacity of people with learning disabilities to understand verbal information is often overestimated by staff and carers. Following assessment, a clearer idea of the individual's level of understanding will have been gained, and also the environmental factors and communication methods that help and/or hinder their ability to understand. Intervention at this level has to focus on changing that person's environment so that they are more able to understand what is expected of them and less likely to experience frustration and upset. Often, when assessing a person with challenging behaviour, it is also necessary to look separately at communication with the individual at times of challenging behaviour. It is sometimes appropriate for the communication environment to change at these times to enable the client to understand better what is being said or expected of them. For example, some clients' ability to understand verbal information decreases at times of challenging behaviour and so any speech needs to be simplified and repeated, possibly with additional signing to help the client focus on what is being said. Another example is the client who finds too much verbal information a trigger for further challenging behaviour, and so at such a time the communication environment needs to be one which offers minimal speech by only one member of staff.

If a person's environment is to be changed successfully, so that their ability to understand what is expected of them is increased, then this needs to be done with the full support of the staff and managers. How this is best achieved will vary from environment to environment and from clinician to clinician, and it is difficult to set down any meaningful guidelines. However, spending time working alongside the relevant members of staff, providing ideas and backing this up with some good (and fun) staff training (see Chapter 8) will achieve excellent results.

Improving the environment

Having carried out the assessment of the environment with other relevant carers and professionals, it is then simply a matter of prioritising the areas that were identified as needing improvement. As mentioned before, it is best to identify only a small number of objectives that are achievable for the client and the environment in which they are living or spending time.

Often it is not appropriate for clinicians to write separate programmes for improving the environment, but to be more involved in helping staff to write care plans for individual clients that then include the identified areas for improvement. For example, if a care plan is being written around managing a client's challenging behaviour at meal times in a busy day centre, clinicians could be involved in helping staff to consider how the environment could change. This could include enabling the client to enjoy mealtimes alongside their friends and not being segregated because of their behaviour *(relationships)*; enabling the client to make a meaningful choice about what they eat and drink *(choice)*; encouraging them to eat in a way that will decrease the likelihood of challenging behaviour *(personal development)*, and changing the way they are responded to at times of challenging behaviour so that they are not perceived negatively by other clients *(respect)*. These will, in turn, have an effect on their ability, one day, to use restaurants in the community *(community presence)*.

There are some definite advantages to including the principles of normalisation into individual clients' care plans as opposed to writing programmes specifically around 'improving choice', etc. Care plans that would have been written anyway but that are now possibly more detailed or with a slightly different focus, and that are also being supported by other professionals, are more likely to be followed than additional programmes set up specifically to improve choice or relationships within a setting. If there is a general need for change within an environment, this is probably best achieved through workshops with the staff (see Chapter 8).

Writing programmes

In general, programmes or action plans need to be clear, easy to read, well presented and, most importantly, relevant to the person's overall life and environment. Ideally they need to be written in conjunction with a key member of staff and then talked through with all members of staff, so that there is no misunderstanding as to the purpose and content of the plan. Time must be spent working alongside members of staff to support them in following the plan, and then having the opportunity for discussion afterwards. In addition, it is helpful sometimes to summarise all the information from the assessments and programmes on to a *communication profile* that can then be placed at the front of a client's file. The next few pages contain actual examples of different formats for programmes and profiles.

COMMUNICATION PROFILE

NAME _____ DOB _____

ADDRESS _____ DATE _____

METHOD OF COMMUNICATION

LEVEL OF UNDERSTANDING

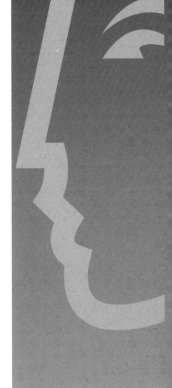

COMMUNICATION PROFILE

COMMUNICATION ENVIRONMENT

Speech and Language Clinician_____ Contact number_____

COMMUNICATION PROFILE – WORKED EXAMPLE

NAME _____John_____ **DOB** _____

ADDRESS _____ **DATE** _____

METHOD OF COMMUNICATION

John expresses himself predominantly through body language. He indicates that he wants something by either pointing or looking at it, or by actually leading someone by the hand. He indicates how he is feeling through his body posture and facial expression, and also by the way he walks, for example a slow pace with stooped posture and rigid face indicates that he does not want to do something. He has a few Makaton signs (drink, toilet, bus) and a few individual signs, for example both hands on his head indicates that he wants people to leave him alone, clapping his hands and high pitched vocalisations indicate that he is becoming agitated, and knocking on doors or windows indicates that he wants to go outside. John has no recognisable words, but uses vocalisations to indicate mood; generally the higher pitched sounds indicate distress or agitation, and lower pitched humming noises indicate that he is calm and happy.

John indicates 'yes' by smiling and 'no' by looking away.

LEVEL OF UNDERSTANDING

John understands at a one-word level if in a familiar situation. For example, if he is in the dining-room and he is asked if he would like a drink, he will understand and respond accordingly. Outside familiar settings he can easily become agitated and frightened if he does not understand what is expected of him. He can understand at a one-word level if sentences are kept very short, they are repeated several times and if Makaton is used for the key word in the sentence.

At times of challenging behaviour, John's ability to understand verbal information is reduced. He is more likely to respond to minimal speech, increased use of gesture and signing and physical contact.

COMMUNICATION PROFILE – WORKED EXAMPLE

COMMUNICATION ENVIRONMENT

John's body language needs to be observed and responded to accordingly and in a consistent way, as it is the main way in which he expresses himself. For example, if John is indicating that he is happy, staff will reflect this back, for example by saying, 'You feel happy today, John' (sign 'happy'). NB See also care plan on responding to John's challenging behaviour.

John needs to be spoken to in short, simple sentences with key words being signed. For example, 'Do you want to go to bed now?' (sign 'bed').

John often needs a quiet environment and quiet speech to calm him down. At times of agitation, only one member of staff should speak to John, and speech should be kept to a minimum.

Prior to taking John out of the building, explain where he is going using short, simple sentences, with signing, and repeat as necessary. Once out of the building, continue with clear explanations to reduce possibility of John becoming anxious (see relevant care plan).

Speech and Language Clinician __A Clinician__   Contact number___12345___

COMMUNICATION PROGRAMME

NAME _____ **DOB** _____

ADDRESS _____ **DATE** _____

AIM

ACTION PLAN

Speech and Language Clinician _____ Contact number _____

COMMUNICATION PROGRAMME – WORKED EXAMPLE

NAME_____Mark_____   DOB_____

ADDRESS_____   DATE_____

AIM

To improve Mark's ability to express his needs and feelings through using MAKATON. Initially to teach Mark the following signs: DRINK, FOOD, WALK, BATH, BED, PAIN and TABLET.

ACTION PLAN

1   Gain Mark's attention by using his name and touching his forearm if necessary before signing to him.

2   Every time Mark has a drink or some food, goes for a walk, has a bath or goes to bed, sign the relevant Makaton sign to him before, during and directly after the activity.

   For example,   'Mark,...do you want a drink?'
                    'Are you enjoying that coffee (sign 'drink')?'
                    'Mark,...you've finished your drink. Now we're going to...'

3   When Mark is agitated and obviously distressed, ask him if he has a pain (sign 'pain').

   For example,   'Mark,... have you got a pain?' (if he indicates yes or
                    continues being upset)
                    'I'll get you a tablet'.
                    'Mark,... here's a tablet for your pain.'

4   Record observations on attached sheet.

Speech and Language Clinician__A Clinician_____   Contact number_____12345____

COMMUNICATION PROGRAMME – RECORD OF OBSERVATIONS

NAME _____ DOB _____

AIM

DATE	OBSERVATIONS/COMMENTS	STAFF NAME

Speech and Language Clinician_____ Contact number_____

Chapter 3: Augmentative & Alternative Communication

INTRODUCTION

The inability to express oneself is possibly one of the most devastating and cruel things that can happen to a person. As Joseph (1986, cited by Beukelman *et al*, 1998) states: 'Speech is the most important thing we have. It makes us a person and not a thing. No one should ever have to be a "thing".'

Some people have their ability to communicate and express their needs taken away from them through illness or disease, but most adults with learning disabilities who have severe expressive problems have had these problems since they were born. It is impossible to imagine what it is like to spend long periods of time, sometimes years, unable to communicate our needs. Anne McDonald probably came closest to describing the experience, after spending 10 years working in an institution for people with learning disabilities: 'Crushing the personalities of speechless individuals is very easy: just make it impossible for them to communicate freely.' (Crossley & McDonald, 1984)

Similarly, it is difficult to imagine what it must be like to be *able* to communicate using augmentative and alternative strategies after months or years of silence. People with learning disabilities may not be able to communicate the feelings of freedom when suddenly they are given a means to express themselves, but Christy Brown gives us an insight into how it felt for him on the day he printed his first letter with a piece of chalk in his left foot:

> I drew it – the letter 'A'. There it was on the floor before me . . . I looked up. I saw my mother's face for a moment, tears on her cheeks . . . I had done it! It had started – the thing that was to give my mind its chance of expressing itself . . . That one letter, scrawled on the floor with a broken bit of yellow chalk gripped between my toes, was my road to a new world, my key to mental freedom. (1954, cited by Beukelman, 1998)

The area of augmentative and alternative communication (AAC) is perhaps one of the most important areas that speech and language clinicians need to have a good knowledge of when working with adults with learning disabilities. It is certainly an area that clinicians think about on a daily basis. Whether seeing the need for it, seeing it being used badly or well, or working directly with clients and staff to set up an effective AAC system, it is definitely a large part of their working week. It is therefore essential that clinicians know what is meant by AAC, and what systems are available. It is also important to be able to identify those people who would benefit from AAC and then to be able to assess them. Finally, clinicians need to be able to design an appropriate system for such people, and to ensure that it is implemented successfully. These issues will be addressed in this chapter, so that the reader will have a good understanding of AAC and will be able to work effectively with adults with learning disabilities who need an AAC system.

WHAT IS AUGMENTATIVE AND ALTERNATIVE COMMUNICATION?

Augmentative and alternative communication (or AAC for short) is described by Sally Millar (1994) as being 'any method of communicating that can supplement the ordinary methods of speech and handwriting, where these are impaired.' The American Speech and Hearing Association (ASHA) (1989) defines AAC as 'an area of clinical practice that attempts to compensate (either temporarily or permanently) for the impairment and disability patterns of individuals with severe expressive communication disorders (ie, the severely speech-language and writing impaired)'. Many people with physical or cognitive disabilities cannot rely on speech as their main means of communication, and so the main aim of augmentative communication is to provide support and to enhance the communication and the quality of life generally of such people.

The term 'AAC' does not refer to any one specific communication system or method, but to the general function, which may be put into practice in a wide variety of different ways. The overall idea of augmentative communication is to use to the full whatever abilities the person does have, in order to compensate for and/or bypass areas of weakness.

An **augmentative communication system** means the whole 'package' of techniques and technologies that makes up 'total communication' for a specific individual. Individuals might use their facial expression, body posture and gesture, eye-pointing, vocalisations and speech attempts to communicate; they might also use a more formalised system such as signing or symbols, and/or computer-based message storage with text-processing and synthesised voice output. All these may be described as their AAC system.

Alternatively, Janet Scott (1996) describes an AAC system as including four interlinking strands (adapted from RCSLT, 1989):

◆ *The communication medium* – how the meaning of the message is being transmitted. This can be 'unaided', for example by using facial expression, gesture or signing, or it can be 'aided', where the person communicates using some sort of device other than their body.
◆ *A means of access to the communication medium* – this may be, for example, via a keyboard or touch screen, or by using a switch.
◆ *A system of representing meaning* – when people speak, their meaning is represented by words that act as 'symbols'. Where a person is unable to speak, their meaning has to be represented by a different set of symbols.
◆ *Strategies for interacting with a communication partner* – for example being able to start up a conversation, or to sort out things when the other person does not understand.

Implementation of the whole system might be referred to as the *AAC programme*, and this is the really crucial part. Providing someone with an augmentative system is the easy bit; ensuring that it is implemented in an effective way, so that the person is able to use it in all parts of their life, is the challenging bit! This will be addressed later in this chapter.

DIFFERENT FORMS OF AAC

Initially, it is useful to divide AAC methods into *unaided* and *aided,* although it is important to remember that it is rarely an 'either-or' situation where a choice has to be made. Many AAC users employ a number of different forms of AAC – a mixture of unaided and aided communication systems.

Unaided communication

Millar (1994) describes this term as meaning 'an augmentative method of communication which does not require the use of any additional material or equipment'. Essentially this means gesture and/or signing. The advantages of unaided communication systems are that they are, precisely, unaided, and are therefore quick, immediate and practical and you can't forget to take them with you! They also can't be lost or broken.

Gesture is often used to include a number of different aspects of body language: facial expression, eye gaze, body movements and hand gestures. It is intuitive to everybody and often immediately intelligible to others, and can frequently be used with people with more profound learning and physical disabilities. However, it is limited to the here and now, which would be a definite disadvantage for some people if it was their only method of communication.

Signing is a more sophisticated form of unaided communication and is really a whole specialist subject in itself. There are a number of different forms of signing – some use restricted numbers of signs (a core vocabulary) as a support for speech, while others provide complex language to replace speech totally.

The Makaton vocabulary

Makaton is the most common form of sign language used with people with learning disabilities in the UK, and was originally designed to meet the needs of people who had a learning disability, a hearing loss and were living in a hospital. It was designed in the UK by Margaret Walker in the early 1970s and is now used widely with both children and adults with learning disabilities, whose communication difficulties may be related to a number of factors, not just hearing loss. It consists of a core vocabulary of 350 signs and symbols (the symbols will be discussed later), and an additional vocabulary of approximately 7,000. The signs are derived from British Sign Language (BSL) but have been standardised – that is, the dialectical variations in signs have been eliminated. The signs are, on the whole, iconic, which means that they are easy to learn and sometimes to recognise, even if you don't know any Makaton. This also means that Makaton can be used successfully by carers to aid understanding as well as to encourage more effective expression.

The core vocabulary is grouped into eight stages, designed as a guideline for teaching everyday essential vocabulary in a meaningful sequence, and progressing from simple to more abstract concepts. For example, in stage 1, everyday ideas such as 'drink', 'mum', 'I', 'you', 'where' and 'what' are included, while in stage 7, more abstract concepts occur such as 'late', 'early', 'how much' and 'how many'. However, an important feature of Makaton is personalisation of the vocabulary to suit individual needs, so at each stage, vocabulary should be selected which is relevant to the individual in terms of their interests, daily activities and environment. Makaton also recommend that the individual is initially taught a small selection of important everyday concepts, and that the vocabulary is expanded upon when necessary.

When using Makaton, carers should use normal grammatical speech and sign only the key words, although the number of words signed will obviously depend on the person being communicated with. For example, when talking to someone who has a small Makaton vocabulary, you might say (and sign) 'Shall we go and get on the bus (sign 'bus') now?'. When talking to someone with a slightly larger vocabulary, you might also sign the word 'go', and when talking to someone with an extensive vocabulary, you might sign 'we', 'go', 'bus' and 'now' (see Figure 3.2).

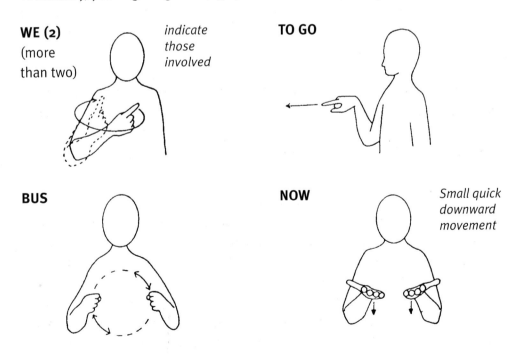

WE (2) (more than two)   *indicate those involved*

TO GO

BUS

NOW   *Small quick downward movement*

Figure 3.1
Examples of Makaton Signs

Aided communication

Millar (1994) describes aided communication as being 'systems which involve some physical object or equipment such as symbol charts or books, to microelectronic devices (... communication aids).' The aided communication system may be something very simple – for example an alphabet written on a piece of card – or it may be something highly sophisticated, such as a computer-based system specially programmed with a large vocabulary. Aided communication is mainly described in terms of systems that are 'low-tech', or *non-electronic,* and those that are 'high-tech', or *electronic.* This chapter will concentrate on 'low-tech' aids, as this is where the majority of the clinician's work lies, but it will also describe the essential aspects of 'high-tech' aids, including where clinicians might go for assessment and advice in this highly specialised area.

Advantages of aided communication

◆The biggest advantage of aided communication is the flexibility and the richness of communication that can be achieved by creating and/or customising vocabulary sets for individuals; by employing sophisticated methods of storage and retrieval; and by providing users with the special means of accessing them, if necessary.

◆ They can be used by non-readers and individuals with a profound and multiple disability, as many are based on simple pictures and symbols.

◆ Systems based on the alphabet, for those people who can use them, give access to a limitless range of communication.

◆ Low-tech systems can be quick and easy to use and are accessible to everyone.

◆ High-tech aids can be designed for operation by very minimal movements, for example a single switch press, and so can be accessible to people with severe physical disabilities.

◆ Electronic systems with voice output increase the independence of the individual, and provide the opportunity to take part in different types of communication – for example, phone calls.

Disadvantages of aided communication

◆ The biggest disadvantage of aided communication is the equipment itself. It can sometimes be forgotten, lost or broken.

◆ Sometimes the equipment is bulky and heavy and, certainly with high-tech aids, is often very expensive.

◆ There is often additional equipment that comes with the communication aid, such as wheelchair mountings, battery recharges or spare batteries.

◆ Technical problems do occur and so people who have a high-tech aid also need a low-tech aid as a back-up.

◆ Insurance is also needed.

◆ There is sometimes an unrealistic expectation of success and of the individual's communicative potential.

LOW-TECH AIDS

Introduction to low-tech aids

Millar (1994) defines low-tech systems as 'anything that doesn't involve electricity or electronics'. They can be as basic and 'low' as pen and paper, but this does not mean in any way that low-tech systems should be viewed as inferior to high-tech ones. Low-tech aids have many advantages:

◆ They can offer the user a quick, powerful and flexible way to communicate.
◆ They never have flat batteries or need to be charged up.
◆ They are not expensive and can easily be adapted and updated when necessary.
◆ They are less scary to people who are a bit technophobic.
◆ They don't mind falling down the stairs!

A low-tech system does not give the user the option of speech output or visual output to a screen or printer. The user relies on the listener to 'read' what they are indicating and then to translate or interpret. This can be described as 'listener-mediated' output. Low-tech communication systems therefore require both the user and the listener or communication partner to be actively involved in the interaction, and the responsibility for achieving effective communication is shared, with the listener taking a substantial part in working out the final message.

Accessing a low-tech communication system

The user of a low-tech aid needs to indicate to the listener, in some way, which symbol, letter or word is being selected. This may be achieved by direct selection, listener scanning and/or coded selection.

◆ *Direct selection.* This means that the user directly selects the desired item from the display of symbols, letters or words by pointing to or touching it. This can be achieved by finger or fist pointing, or by using another part of the body, such as in eye pointing.
◆ *Scanning.* Although people tend to think of scanning in terms of electronic aids, it is possible to use scanning to access a low-tech aid. This is called *listener-scanning.* The listener indicates, one by one or group by group, the items in the display and then the user indicates the desired one by performing a predetermined action. This method of accessing can be speeded up by using a row-column scanning method which can involve either a *manual scanning* system and/or a *verbal/auditory scanning* system. This means that the listener initiates the scanning either manually or verbally and waits until the user responds in the predetermined manner. Figure 3.2 shows an example of a low-tech communication system which uses both manual and verbal scanning by the listener in order to enable the user to access the desired symbol.

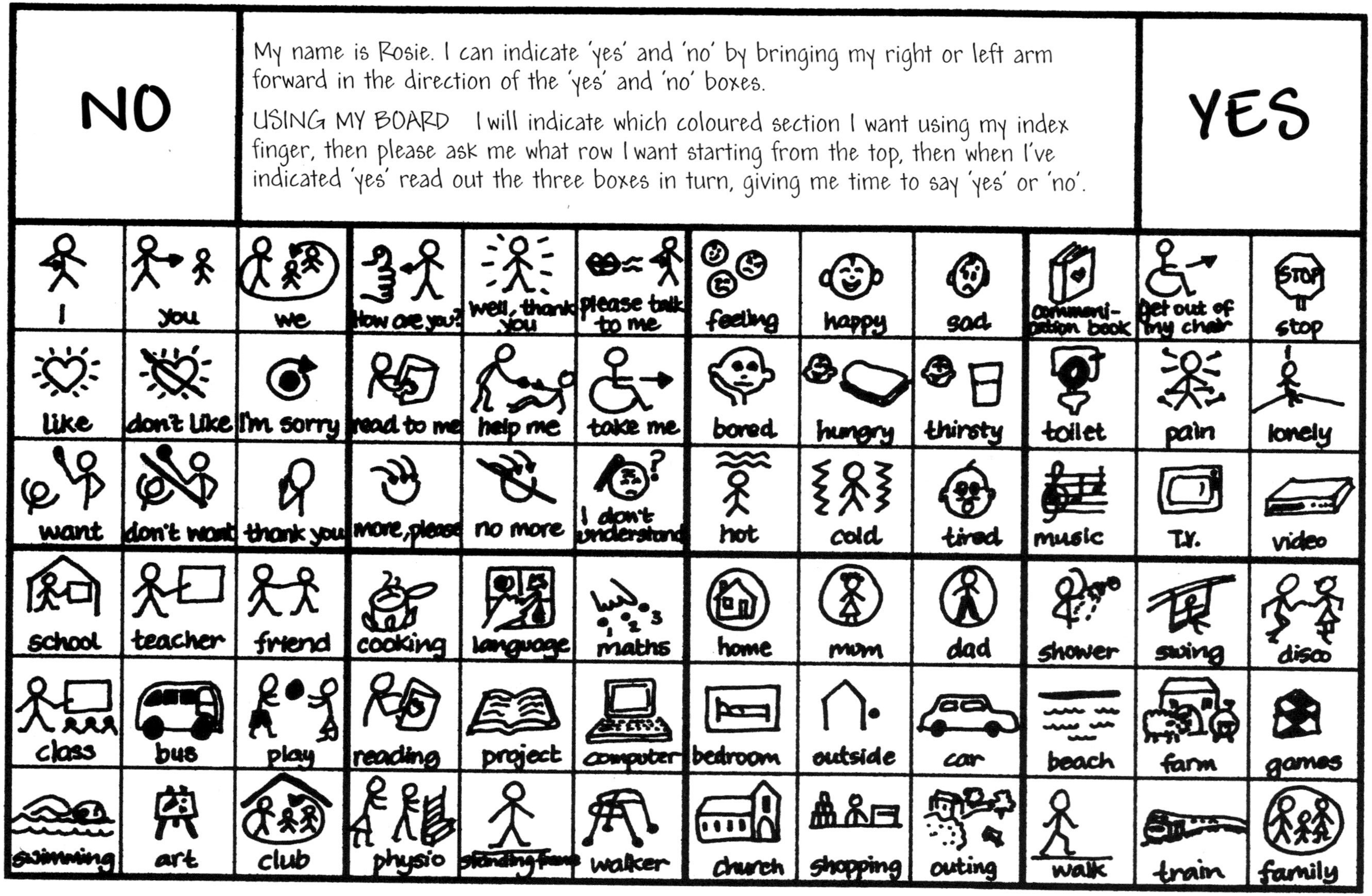

Figure 3.2 A Low-tech Communication System using Listener-Scanning and Direct Access

◆ *Coded.* This selection can be used with either direct selection or scanning. It involves the user accessing a symbol or word through the use of a code that may include colours, numbers, letters or pictures as its indicators. This can allow the user to access a larger vocabulary much more quickly than is possible by direct selection or scanning. Figure 3.3 shows an example of a communication book that uses a coded system to access a symbol. This is one page from a whole book with an index on the first page designed in the same manner so that the person can select the appropriate page using the same code.

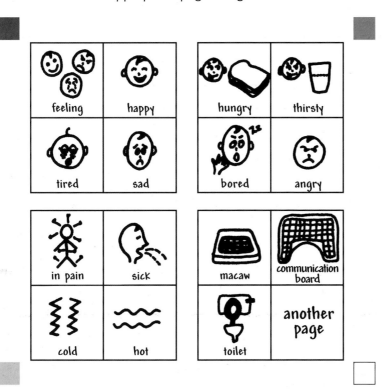

Figure 3.3
A Low-tech Communication System using Coded Access

Peter will indicate which coloured box he wants by fist pointing to the appropriate colour in the corner of the page. He will then indicate which symbol he wants in the same way.

The representational set

The development of a low-tech communication system will be based on a set of symbols which represent language. This may include graphic/pictorial symbols, textured symbols, photographic material, and three-dimensional tangible symbols. The choice of which symbol set to use is obviously dependent on the needs and abilities of the person and other people in their environment. The following will be considered:

◆ Graphic symbol systems
◆ Enhanced symbols
◆ Tangible symbols or objects of reference.

Graphic symbol systems

There are a large number of popular and versatile symbol communication systems which have been developed in the English-speaking world, mainly in North America (eg, PCS, Picsyms, Bliss), the United Kingdom (eg, Rebus, Makaton, Sigsymbols), and Australia (eg, Compic). In this chapter, PCS, Rebus, Makaton and Bliss will be described and compared.

Symbol sets and systems

Symbol communication systems vary from simple, finite sets of symbols to more sophisticated systems. The former will be more appropriate for someone who has a severe learning disability as they usually consist of clear, concrete pictures which are easy to recognise, and with which everyday needs can be expressed. The simplest level of picture sets are often home-made, either with photographs or clear, coloured pictures. There are also some commercially produced sets such as WordWise Stickers (Winslow Press). The more sophisticated systems, including Blissymbols, are more appropriate for someone who has a less severe learning disability as the symbols are more abstract.

Important features of symbol systems

It is important, when choosing a system for a person, not to be influenced by external factors such as the system that several other people are using or the one for which there already happen to be lots of photocopied symbols. As MacDonald (1994) states: 'Each potential communicator will have his own individual strengths and needs and these must always form the central part of the decision-making process.' She goes on to say that 'all systems have their particular advantages and disadvantages and these must be matched to the cognitive, linguistic, sensory and physical abilities of the candidates.' This means that for some people, a simple, concrete, picture-based set, which is not very flexible or expandable but is highly 'guessable' will be suitable. But for others it may be more important to offer a system that has the potential to grow with the individual and convey a wide range of abstract concepts and grammatical structures. It is therefore important to look at the construction, the level of symbolic representation and the flexibility of the symbol system.

1 *Construction.* This means their visual clarity and ease of reproduction. Many adults with learning disabilities have additional visual perception difficulties, and it is important to consider how visually busy or perceptually confusing the symbols are. It is also necessary to consider how easy the symbols are to draw, as it is sometimes important for the carers to be able to draw the symbols quickly and easily, for example to write up the user's news in a home book.

2 *Level of symbolic representation.* This means the degree to which the symbols effectively convey the concepts they represent and the level of iconicity in the representations. However, these two aspects of symbolic representation are

not always compatible as the more pictorial (iconic) symbols tend to depict only one particular example of a meaning. This is illustrated by MacDonald (1994) in the verb 'to save'. If it is depicted by a pictorial symbol of coins dropping into a money box, then this cannot effectively be used to mean 'to save from drowning'. A more abstract symbol representing the concept 'to keep for the future' would validly convey the whole meaning of the word, but the extent to which a user will be able to learn a less concrete symbol will depend on their developmental level.

3 *Flexibility.* This means the potential for vocabulary expansion and grammatical structure – that is, the ability to generate new meanings and to convey different meanings such as tense and negatives.

Summary of comparisons between systems

MacDonald (1994) gives a thorough comparison of the four most popular symbol systems, and the main points she makes in her chapter are summarised below:

1 Many Rebus and Makaton symbols do appear very similar. However, American Rebus symbols were designed by the Peabody Picture Rebus Scheme to encourage reading in people with a learning disability in the USA, and then British Rebus symbols were adapted from these to suit the British culture, and these are the ones that are used with the Widget Software. Makaton symbols were devised by the Makaton Vocabulary Development Project's Symbols Working Party.

2 Some pictorial symbols are overcrowded, for example the PCS symbol for 'garden'.

garden — PCS, Rebus, Makaton, Bliss

3 On the whole British Rebus and Makaton symbols are clearer and simpler than PCS, although the use of black silhouettes in PCS makes a few of the symbols very clear.

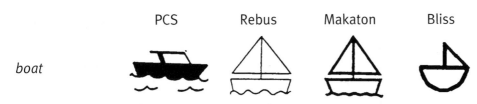

boat — PCS, Rebus, Makaton, Bliss

4 Blissymbols are very stylised and therefore less pictorial, but easy to reproduce.

5 Abstract vocabulary is always difficult to depict, and some systems have resorted to traditional orthography at times which seems to contradict the

main reason for using a symbol system in the first place. An example of this is 'for' in PCS.

6   Where the main attribute of a concept is easily illustrated, there is often a similarity across all four systems, for example, 'strong'.

strong

7   With pictorial symbols it is not always possible to encapsulate the full range of meaning, for example, 'to wash' in PCS, Rebus and Makaton. This means that the symbol is less conceptually complete and less versatile, but some systems provide different symbols for different situations, for example 'to wash hands' and 'to wash face'. For some clients these pictorial examples will be necessary, but they will obviously take up more space in their book or on their chart.

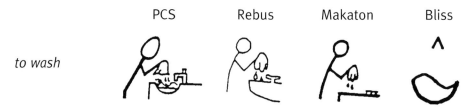

to wash

8   The only system which is able to offer really open access to vocabulary is Bliss. In order to interpret some of the symbols, however, the user needs to understand the underlying symbol elements, for example, 'suddenly' is made up of 'time' and 'lightening' ('sky' and 'electricity'). It is therefore more suitable for people who may require a wide and flexible vocabulary.

suddenly

9   Bliss has markers for word classes (verb, adjective, etc.) which allows for more versatility and makes the system more truly linguistic. This is unlikely to be relevant to some people with more severe learning disabilities.

10 Some symbol dictionaries offer two different sizes of symbols, others suggest they are enlarged or shrunk from the master set to suit individual users and their communication aids.

Enhanced symbols

It is sometimes necessary to 'enhance' or 'embellish' symbols in order to make them easier to learn, more eye-catching or visually interesting. It may be appropriate to make the outlines bolder, or to make them more tactile by making them out of material, or to use bright colours and glitter paint. Enhancements can also be made to highlight or draw attention to a particular part of the symbol. This can be particularly relevant when teaching someone Bliss, or when moving a child from a pictorial symbol system to a more abstract one such as Bliss. Careful assessment of the person's needs obviously has to precede any enhancing, and the clinician should never rush to the felt-tips because it would make the communication aid prettier!

Objects of reference or *tangible symbols* or *signifiers*

Objects of reference are defined as 'objects that have special meanings assigned to them . . . They stand for something, in much the same way as words do.' (Ockelford, 1994, cited by Park, 1997.) They are described by Park as having three main uses: as an aid to memory, to help understanding, and to communicate. Objects of reference are often used with people who are unable to make the representational leap from understanding an object or activity to understanding the meaning of a two-dimensional symbol relating to that activity. It is assumed that objects of reference are easier because they appear to have more common-sense appeal: they are permanent, concrete and manipulable and they can often closely resemble the thing they represent. However, it cannot be taken for granted that the person will understand the link between an object and an activity and as Park (1997) says: 'the meaning is not located in the object itself, but in the way in which it is used.'

Park (1997) describes three types of objects of reference (taken from the work of Peirce, 1932 and cited by Park):

◆ An **index** is an object or sign that relates to the thing it stands for because it comprises part of the activity. Examples of this may be a shopping bag to indicate 'shopping', a cup to indicate 'drink' and a coat to indicate 'going out'. All references to the use of 'functional cues' or 'object cues' will come in this category. Using objects of reference as indexes may be the most appropriate starting point for an individual who is severely learning disabled. Some writers, for example Rowland and Stremell-Campbell (1987), cited by Park (1997), describe the benefits of using 'object cues' which are everyday objects used consistently to provide specific information. They state that 'the object cues have the potential to reduce startle-behaviour and forms of inappropriate behaviour, as they let the learner know what is about to happen' (Park, 1997). Object cues are closely tied to personal need routines, and subsequently the learner can be encouraged to make a response to the cues.

◆ An **icon** is an object that is related to the thing it stands for by some visual and/or tactile resemblance, but unlike the index, it is not a functional component of the activity. The object of reference therefore has a degree of iconicity – visual (for example a miniature object), tactile (for example, a piece of towelling material for 'swimming') or auditory (for example, a chime bar for 'music'), or a combination of these. The significant difference from the previous category of index is that the object of reference is representational.

◆ A **symbol** is also an object that is separate from the thing it stands for, but in addition, bears no resemblance to it in the way that icons do; the connection between the object and the thing it stands for is arbitrary. An example of this might be a three-dimensional wooden shape that is attached to the door of the dining room, and the user then learns and is able to understand that the connection between the wooden shape and the dining room is an abstract one.

For many people with learning disabilities, the use of an object of reference as an index may be the most appropriate and necessary starting point. A spoon to represent 'eating' is a component of the whole activity of eating and will be seen as such before it is identified as a symbol for a meal. It is often very appropriate that real objects are used to begin with, as it is a good basis for developing the use of two-dimensional symbols – a gradual shift from the concrete to the abstract. Park (1997) cites an example of this process where a learner began to request a crisp by pointing to a full packet of crisps. Over time, the bag was emptied and then cut down until only the logo of the packet remained. The person was then able to request crisps by pointing to the two-dimensional symbol of the logo.

Park concluded his article by suggesting that the three types of objects of reference described initially by Peirce in 1932 can be used to formulate a developmental framework for the use of them.

1 *Indexes* – objects that relate to the thing they stand for because they participate in, or are actually part of, the event or object for which they stand. Also known as *functional cues* and *object cues*.
2 *Icons* – objects that are related to the things they stand for by virtue of some physical resemblance. These would include: *identical or real objects; associated objects* (eg purse for 'shopping'); *miniature objects; partial objects;* and *objects with shared features* (eg, rubber material for 'swing').
3 *Symbols* – objects that are related to the things they stand for by an arbitrary bond agreed upon by those who use the symbol. This includes *artificial or arbitrary objects* such as wooden shapes attached to doors, and a 3-D shape for 'finished'.

HIGH-TECH AIDS

What do we mean by 'high tech'?

High-tech communication aids can be defined as equipment which is electronic in nature and requires a power supply – either battery or mains powered. They can be divided into two main categories:

◆ Dedicated communication aids
◆ Computer-based communication equipment.

Dedicated communication aids

Dedicated communication aids were designed solely for the means of providing an alternative to oral speech, or to augment an individual's oral speech. There are many communication aids available on the market today and it is unrealistic to expect a speech and language clinician working with adults with learning disabilities to have a good knowledge of these. This is a highly specialised area and most regions have a specialist advice and assessment unit for communication aids where the clinicians will be able to assess and advise properly on appropriate aids for an individual. For this reason, high-tech aids will not be discussed in detail. However, this chapter will address briefly the factors that are considered when describing and choosing between different aids.

The four factors that need to be considered when describing and evaluating communication aids are:

1   Accessing the communication aid
2   Selection set
3   Output
4   Portability

1 Accessing the communication aid

There are two main ways that an individual can access a communication aid: *direct selection* or *indirect selection via scanning*.

Direct selection. Direct selection means that the person is able to select by physically touching the equipment. This could be a keyboard, touch-sensitive screen or membrane keypad. The term can be extended to include the use of a head pointer or a mouth stick.

Indirect selection. Indirect selection requires the user to activate a switch or number of switches connected to the communication aid. The aid must therefore be able to accept a switch and have some kind of scanning array available to the individual.

Jans and Clark (1994) list the commonly-used switches:

◆   Simple lever switches, operated by pressing on the hinged 'lid' of a lightweight box.
◆   Platform switches, requiring the user to press a large 'lid' or button resting on a few switches; light pressure on any part of the 'lid' activates one or other of the switches.
◆   Bead switches mounted on a necklace and activated by the chin or cheek.
◆   Head switches, mounted into a wheelchair/headrest.
◆   Push switches and joysticks – operated by pushing a handle or plate.
◆   Wobble switches and spring sticks – the user can hit the switch in any direction.

◆ Suck and puff switches.
◆ Tongue switches.
◆ Sound-operated switches.

2 Selection set

Communication aids can be used with different types of representational systems, and the system chosen is called the selection set. This is mainly a decision between using either symbols or text.

3 Output

Another important factor to consider when looking at communication aids is the output that is available.

Visual output. This refers both to a visual display unit such as a small screen and to a printed copy of the message through a printer. These can be either internally built into the communication aid or connected externally. Different communication aids vary in the size and clarity of their visual display and with the amount that is displayed at any one time.

Auditory output. There are two kinds of speech output: digitised and synthesised.
◆ *Digitised speech* is a real voice recorded into a communication aid, and obviously tends to sound more natural and acceptable to some listeners. It also means that different languages, accents, ages and gender of voices can be used to suit the individual.
◆ *Synthesised speech* is speech generated by a computer. The advantages of synthesised speech are that it uses less memory than digitised speech, and it is open-ended and allows the user to create new messages. However, these aids are more complicated and time consuming to program and the pronunciation often sounds 'strange'. They also depend on the user having fairly good reading and writing skills.

Feedback. Communication aids may also give feedback to the listener. This may be auditory, tactile, or visual feedback.

4 Portability

These days it is becoming much easier to find communication aids in a range of different shapes, sizes and weights. It is obviously important that the communication aid is portable and can be used in different situations. As Scott (1996) said: 'It may seem very obvious, but if the people using AAC do not have their communication aids available and accessible to them, they will not be used.'

Computer-based communication equipment

Computer-based communication aids consist mainly of software programs which can transform a computer into a communication aid, although most systems still maintain use of the equipment as a computer as well. One piece of equipment can therefore be used as a communication system and as a computer, minimising the amount of equipment someone has to deal with.

Computer-based communication systems are rarely used with adults with learning disabilities, and this is probably because they do not have the same experience of and access to computers as other adults, making it an expensive option for someone who simply needs a high-tech communication system. This will possibly change in future years as computers become more part of education in special needs schools, and adults become more computer literate.

ASSESSMENT OF THE INDIVIDUAL

This part of the chapter will address AAC assessment of an adult with a learning disability. Low-tech aids only will be considered, as assessment for high-tech aids should be carried out in communication aid centres by clinicians who are specialists in this field. As Light and Binger (1998) state: 'The assessment [of high-tech aids] should be conducted by a skilled team of professionals with expertise in AAC.'

AAC assessment involves 'the gathering and analysis of information so that . . . [the clinicians] can make informed decisions about the adequacy of current communication, the individual's communication needs, AAC systems and equipment, instruction, and outcome evaluation.' (Beukelman *et al*, 1998). The goal of assessment is therefore to gather enough information to make an informed decision that meets the person's current and future communication needs. Assessment cannot be viewed as a 'one-off' process, but as an ongoing one which reflects the client's changing needs. It is important to assess for today's needs and then for tomorrow's needs, and so on.

As with other areas of assessment, it is essential to assess both the individual and their environment, and these will be considered in turn.

Assessment of the individual needs to include:

1   Current expressive skills
2   Potential to use and/or increase speech
3   Potential to use AAC systems.

Assessing current expressive skills

The initial step in assessing communication is to determine the effectiveness and the nature of the individual's current communication system. Most people use a variety of communication techniques to express themselves, including natural speech, vocalisations, gestures, body language, signing, pointing, eye gaze, objects, etc. These need to be assessed in terms of their effectiveness, both in relation to their operational effectiveness – ie, how accurately the person is able to use a particular skill – and their social effectiveness – ie, whether the person is able to use the technique in an interactive and social situation. An example of this may be clients who are able to eye-point to an object if presented with a choice, and who are operationally effective at eye-pointing. However, they do not use it in their environment to request, because they have learnt that it is not an effective means of communication in the busy day centre, and so they are socially ineffective in their ability to use eye-pointing.

It is also important to assess the types of messages that the individual is communicating. Are they able to express everyday needs and wants effectively? Are they able to share information with others and join in everyday routines? Is their communication limited to the here and now and to objects in their environment? And are they able to communicate with strangers and access services in the community using current expressive skills?

The following two pages give the speech and language clinician a format for observing the client's expression and for discussing relevant issues with their main carer. They are also used to summarise information in the worked examples at the end of this chapter.

ASSESSMENT OF CURRENT EXPRESSIVE SKILLS 1

NAME _____ DATE _____

What skills/techniques is the person using to express themselves?

Techniques used	Examples	Other skills/ techniques	Accuracy	Socially effective

Summary

AUGMENTATIVE & ALTERNATIVE COMMUNICATION

ASSESSMENT OF CURRENT EXPRESSIVE SKILLS 2

NAME _____ DATE _____

What types of messages and communicative functions is the person able to use?

1 Ability to express needs and wants

2 Ability to communicate about something that is not in their immediate environment

3 Ability to socialise and share information with others

4 Ability to join in everyday routines

5 Ability to be part of their wider environment/community

Summary

Assessing the potential to use speech

Many people who are being assessed for AAC still have some ability to communicate using natural speech, and it is important to assess where an AAC system would fit into their existing skills. Elder and Goossens (1994) suggest that there are three 'levels of competency' and the AAC system would complement their speech accordingly:

1   The first group are those people who need to use the AAC system *as their primary communication mode*. These people may have no or little effective speech and any speech they do have will be used as a secondary mode of communication. An example of this would be people who have a mild to moderate learning disability and a severe physical disability which makes it extremely difficult for them to express themselves effectively verbally. They have a symbolised communication book attached to their wheelchair and this is their primary mode of communication. They also use their limited speech to gain attention, for example, and to indicate 'yes' and 'no', but this is their secondary mode of communication.

2   The second group are those people who need to use the AAC system *frequently to complement their speech*. These people need both their speech and the AAC system for effective communication. An example of this group would be people who have unclear speech and who use Makaton to be understood.

3   The third group are those people who use *speech as the primary communication mode*. These people may have faded the use of their AAC system as their speech improved, although this is more common in children than in adults with a learning disability, or they may have an AAC system that they use at particular times. An example of this would be people who have difficulty expressing themselves at times of stress, and who need an alternative means of expression at those particular times. In this case the vocabulary chosen may be very specific to a situation and a person, and may be the only experience of AAC that person has had and possibly will ever have.

As has already been discussed in Chapter 1, intelligibility of speech is not something that is easy to change in an adult with a learning disability. Therefore, even though a person may have a large vocabulary of spoken words, if they are not intelligible to a wide variety of people, they will usually benefit more from an AAC system to complement their speech than a course of articulation therapy.

Assessing the potential to use an AAC system

The three important areas to assess in order to devise an appropriate low-tech AAC system for someone are comprehension, vision and motor skills. The purpose of this is to identify strengths and abilities that will be used and built upon in the use of an AAC system. Without a good assessment of the client's capabilities, time and effort will possibly be wasted in devising a system that is not appropriate for that person's needs, and the person will experience increased frustration and a possible decrease in motivation to communicate. As Beukelman (1998) states: 'Technology alone does not make a competent communicator any more than a piano makes a musician or a basketball and a hoop make an athlete.'

Assessment of comprehension

We have already assessed the ways in which the client is currently expressing themselves and how effective this is. It is also important to know how much they are able to understand, and in particular their symbolic development. As people develop they are increasingly able to understand that representations of decreasing perceptual similarity to the original object may act as a symbolic reference. The following hierarchy was based on the work of Cooper, Moodley and Reynell (1978) and DeLoache (1987), and was confirmed by research by Mirenda and Locke (1989, cited by MacDonald, 1994).

Hierarchy of symbolic development

1   *Real objects:* The person is able to focus beyond themselves and recognise the significance of commonly used objects, and will use them or pretend to use them appropriately. At this stage of development, a person understands their world by the actual objects that are around them.
2   *Photographs:* The person is able to understand that clear, colour photographs are exact representations of the real item.
3   *Miniatures:* The person is able to understand that an object that differs significantly in size and in other visual features represents a real item. At this stage of development, a child plays appropriately with small dolls and an adult is able to understand the relevance of 'pretend food'.
4   *Coloured pictures:* The person is able to understand what two-dimensional but still fairly realistic pictures represent.
5   *Line drawings (realistic/sketches):* The person is able to understand pictures that are visually less realistic but still very picture-like.
6   *Line drawings (minimal/stylised):* The person is able to understand simplified outlines.
7   *Written words:* The person is able to understand completely abstract symbols, such as words, which relate to sounds rather than meaning.

A person's AAC system obviously needs to match their level of abilities, as there is little point in giving a symbolised communication chart to someone who only understands their world through objects. There is equally little point in giving an objects of reference communication system to someone who could have coped with realistic line drawings.

Once it has been established which level they are functioning at, it is important to assess their comprehension and vocabulary level. A more formal assessment, such as an adult version of the Derbyshire Language Scheme (Knowles & Masidlover, 1982), is sometimes useful to gain an idea of someone's level of comprehension. It is usually more appropriate, however, to assess their skills informally through observation, talking to relevant others and 'setting up' situations in their everyday environment (see Chapter 1 for a fuller discussion on assessing comprehension).

This information will be used to determine the extent of the vocabulary set that will be used and will influence factors such as page layout. For example, if someone is likely to want to put symbols together in order to form sentences, then symbols will need to be grouped accordingly. One of the most frustrating things that can happen to all concerned, especially the client, is devising an AAC system that is not right for that person. This is usually because they were not assessed adequately and the resulting symbolised communication book, for example, is either too simple, too complicated or does not have the relevant vocabulary for the individual concerned.

Assessment of vision

It is important to assess vision so that decisions can be made about the type, size, placement, spacing and colours of symbols. However, as Ferris-Taylor (1997) states: 'There are often difficulties in obtaining adequate assessment for adults. Staff in . . . ophthalmological services for adults may . . . be reluctant to see them at all, regarding the process as too time-consuming or not beneficial for someone with learning disabilities.' She goes on to give a checklist of behaviours or features which may indicate a visual impairment, but stresses the importance of professional assessment if a visual impairment is suspected:

◆ Poking or rubbing the eyes.
◆ Exploring items by touch.
◆ Not appearing to notice people or things unless they are very close; needing to examine things at close quarters.
◆ Reluctance to move around, especially when in new places.
◆ Reluctance to look for/search for things visually.
◆ Appearing startled when someone approaches.
◆ Dislike of predominantly visual tasks/reluctance to engage in such tasks.
◆ Visible signs of eye pathology, eg, inflammation, swelling.

If someone has been assessed as having a visual problem, then the AAC system will have to be adapted to suit their needs and strengths. For example, if the person is already using some signs to express needs, then new signs may need to be taught using hand-over-hand signing or 'body signing' – that is, where signs that are normally 'in space' are adapted so that there is always contact with the person. If the person is assessed to be suitable for symbols, then they will need to be adapted to be more tactile.

If the person is assessed as not having a visual problem, the clinician will still need to assess the following:

◆ How large does the person need the symbols to be?
◆ How many symbols can they visually (and manually) cope with on a page?

◆ Are they helped by the use of different colours either for use in an encoding system or for colouring in the symbols?

This assessment is probably best done informally in the person's environment, with help and advice from relevant carers.

Assessment of motor skills

Assessment of a person's motor capabilities is important when devising a low-tech communication aid, so that we can identify a motor technique that the person is able to use effectively and consistently, for example, signing, finger-pointing, etc. Assessment is usually best done initially through observation and interview and then through actual assessment of the person's range and accuracy of movement.

Observation and interviewing of the carers will give us information about what the person does now: for example, do they use gesture effectively?; do they point at objects?, etc. This information is obviously important so that we look at building on a person's existing skills rather than introducing new ones when they are not necessary.

Next, the assessment needs to test the individual's range and accuracy of movements. This is usually most relevant when deciding on layouts for symbol charts and on accessing of symbols. Factors that need to be included are:

◆ The degree of accuracy with which the person can use the technique to access targets of various sizes.
◆ The maximum range and number of targets that they can access.
◆ Whether adaptations such as textured surfaces, head or limb supports increase accuracy.

For some clients, it is essential that an assessment is done by a physiotherapist, especially if they are physically disabled, as it is important to assess the most effective seating position to maximise motor capabilities.

ASSESSMENT OF THE ENVIRONMENT

Assessment of the environment needs to include:

1 Policy and attitude barriers
2 Knowledge barriers
3 Skill barriers

1 Policy and attitude barriers

Policy barriers are the result of decisions that govern the situations in which users find themselves. For example, managers may have decided that normalisation principles mean that all the users need to appear as 'normal' as possible and therefore the use of something like Makaton would be actively discouraged as it 'makes the person look more disabled'. Alternatively, they may have a 'limited-use' policy that means that they may allow AAC systems as part of certain educational groups, but may not allow them to be taken outside into the community or back to their home.

Attitude barriers occur when the beliefs held by an individual, rather than an establishment, present a barrier to participation. This may mean that carers, families or other professionals will discourage the use of an AAC system. This may be done blatantly, for example by locking the book away in a cupboard or leaving it at home, or subtly and insidiously, for example by not encouraging the person to use their system or by not recognising communicative attempts made by the person using their AAC system. The result of most attitude barriers is that the people concerned have reduced expectations of the individual, which in turn limits their ability to participate and communicate. The most that can be done in these circumstances is for the clinician to keep challenging the people in authority and advocating on behalf of the client.

2 Knowledge barriers

A knowledge barrier refers to a lack of information on the part of someone other than the AAC user that results in limited opportunities for participation. Examples of this may be staff who have never been trained in Makaton; staff who do not know how to use a person's communication book or do not understand the encoding system; and staff who do not understand what the objects of reference are for. Assessment of the environment needs to identify these barriers in advance so that information and/or training can be given in order to eliminate or minimise them.

3 Skill barriers

Skill barriers occur when, despite even extensive knowledge, carers have difficulty with the actual implementation of an AAC technique or strategy. An example of this could be a member of staff who is sent on a Makaton course and becomes very proficient at the signs, but who doesn't change their practice once back in their place of work. It is important to assess the skill level of individuals who will be responsible for various aspects of the AAC user's communication intervention plan in order to identify skill impairments and to design interventions to reduce these barriers. Sometimes it is not possible to assess skill barriers until after an intervention strategy has been in place for a little while, and then the importance of ongoing assessment becomes paramount.

Following assessment of the individual and their environment, it is important to 'put it all together' and decide on the most appropriate AAC system for the individual. The following form gives the clinician a way of summarising all the information.

AAC ASSESSMENT SUMMARY SHEET

NAME _____ DOB _____

ADDRESS _____

COMPLETED BY _____ DATE _____

CURRENT EXPRESSIVE SKILLS

Techniques used

Communicative functions used

Use of speech

COMPREHENSION

Level of symbolic development and vocabulary size

VISUAL ABILITIES

Visual/perceptual abilities and difficulties

MOTOR SKILLS

Current use of motor skills and range and accuracy of movement

AAC ASSESSMENT SUMMARY SHEET

THE ENVIRONMENT

Current environment

Existing barriers

SUMMARY OF RECOMMENDATIONS

AAC system recommended and environmental recommendations

ACTION PLAN

Completed by _____ Date _____

INTERVENTION

Assessment will have given the clinician a clear idea of the following:

◆ The person's current communication strengths and needs and which techniques are most successful for the person.

◆ The person's level of symbolic development and comprehension, and therefore which representational set would be most appropriate.

◆ The person's visual and motor capabilities and therefore any adaptations that would need to be made and which mode of access the person would use.

◆ The person's environment and any barriers that exist to successful intervention.

◆ And finally, which AAC system would be most appropriate for the person and the steps that would need to be taken to maximise the chance of success.

Often intervention naturally follows assessment as the assessment has revealed what is needed. However, there are always factors that need to be addressed when starting to devise and implement AAC systems and these will be considered next. It is obviously difficult to talk generally about implementing AAC systems as every person's AAC system will need to be unique to their strengths and needs. However, it is possible to give a checklist of factors to consider when devising a system and these will be given under three categories:

◆ Devising and implementing a *symbol-based* system.

◆ Devising and implementing a *signing* system.

◆ Devising and implementing an *objects-of-reference* system.

1 Devising and implementing a symbol-based system

i) Determining symbol set

◆ Consider how extensive the vocabulary is likely to be; some symbol sets have larger numbers.

◆ Choose one symbol system as the predominant system and then add from other systems if necessary. You can mix and match to suit an individual's needs.

◆ Consider what symbol systems are being used around the person in their environment. Choosing a system that is already in use in their environment will maximise on existing staff skills and will increase the opportunity for peer interaction.

ii) Selecting vocabulary

◆ Involve significant others in vocabulary selection (see McCall *et al*, 1997). The speech and language clinician may know the *least* about what is going in the client's everyday life.

◆ Including irrelevant vocabulary is a major disincentive to the use of an AAC system (Murphy *et al*, 1996, cited by McCall, 1997).

- Vocabulary needs to be unique to the user and dependent on their age, gender, interests, culture and previous experience.
- Consider including vocabulary around social greetings, starting and ending conversations, chatting someone up, swearing, etc. This will motivate some users far more than being able to request a drink, for example.

iii) Symbol layout

- Consider word versus phrase-based messages. Having some phrases/sentences in one symbol will speed up the user's interaction but reduces flexibility. Consider, therefore, how likely the person is to want to create new sentences.
- Leave gaps so that symbols can be added at a later stage.
- Consider activity-based sections/charts.
- Consider frequently-occurring activities and motivating activities. It is obviously best to start with these and also to ensure they are placed in the system where access can be quickest and easiest. For example, if the user is reliant on listener-scanning, then the most used symbols need to be placed where there is minimum effort for all involved (see example below).

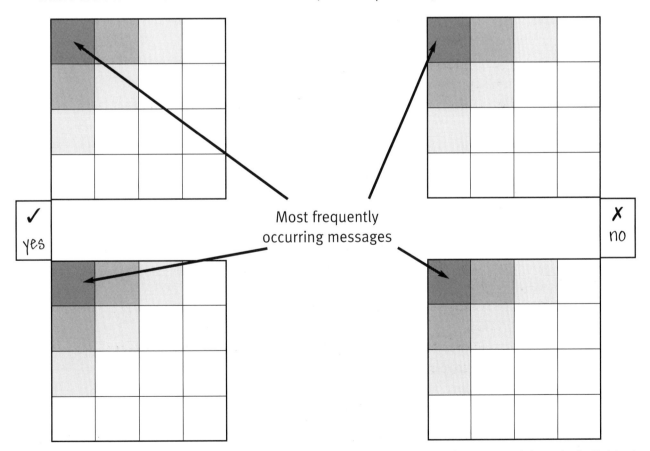

Example: The user eye-points to the box they want and the listener scans the rows and then the individual messages from left to right.

Figure 3.4. *An Example of Symbol Layout for Listener-scanning*

iv) Listener-friendly – clear instructions

◆ The easier the symbol system is to understand and the more attractive it looks, the more likely it is to be used by others to promote interaction, and the more likely it is to be used correctly.

◆ Consider menu pages, where appropriate, and clear instructions for the listener (see Figure 3.5 below).

Figure 3.5
*Instructions for
Listeners*

Example 1

> *My name is Mark. I will indicate one of the six main areas of my communication board with my fist. I will then look at one of the four colours at the corners of my board to show you which coloured square I need. Please ask me which row I want (horizontal) and then which symbol (left to right). I can say 'yes' and I indicate 'no' by turning my head away.*

Example 2

> My name is
>
> This is my communication book.
>
> I communicate with people by pointing to symbols or using sign language.
>
> When talking to me, please help me to understand you by using as much sign language or body language as possible.

Example of a menu page

Index

Grammatical Words Alphabet Numbers Colours		People
Actions/Hobbies Places Football Music		Feelings Body Parts
Everyday Objects		Time Months of the year Days of the week Weather
	Look in my diary	

v) Availability and accessibility

◆ The clinician needs to convince others of the need for the system to be available to the user in all the situations in which the user wants it. Motivation of everyone involved, but particularly the user, is often at its greatest when the AAC system is new, and efforts should be made to make the system available in all situations (see Murphy *et al*, 1996).

◆ In some environments it may be appropriate to design symbol communication charts in specific areas or for specific activities – for example, symbolised menu charts in the canteen, symbol charts for swimming (laminated!) – and then place them in an appropriate place – ie, where they can be seen and used. This will increase the accessibility of symbols for the user, increase the awareness and use of symbols by carers, and reduce the amount of symbols needed in the user's book or chart.

vi) Introducing the system

◆ Start with motivating and frequently-occurring activities.
◆ Choose symbols initially where the user will receive a motivating and immediate response.
◆ Do not present the user with a complete (and huge) book or chart – it will take them too long to learn to use it functionally. Start small and motivating, and build up gradually.

vii) Training staff

◆ Involving staff in the assessment and creation of an AAC system for a client will sometimes be the best training. They will have an understanding of the person's capabilities and what the AAC system is hopefully going to achieve. They will know the vocabulary that has been selected and the format of the system because they have been involved in making these decisions. They sometimes just need support in ensuring that the person is encouraged by others to use their system.

- Training does need to be an ongoing process in order to establish effective facilitative practices. This is often best done by modelling good use of the system during an activity. It is also important to discuss the different ways that carers could use the AAC system during various activities with as many relevant carers as possible – for example, discussing mealtimes with dinner staff, bus journeys with escorts and self-care with residential staff.
- Where barriers have been identified, training needs to be linked directly to improving the situation – for example, changing attitudes by running staff training that directly challenges those attitudes, perhaps through experiential exercises and group discussions.

viii) Displaying a symbol-based communication system

Various methods have been developed to store and display symbols for different users, and the method chosen will depend on its intended function. They may be designed to be task-specific, as an introduction to symbols, or as a total communication system. A user may also need a variety of formats to complement one another and to increase flexibility and use of symbols in their environment. The following is a list of some typical formats that may be chosen, but which is by no means intended to be exhaustive.

- *Communication boards:* symbols are based on a two-dimensional matrix. The size is determined by the physical ability of the user, their needs and the size of the wheelchair tray or desk the board is to be mounted on.
- *Communication books:* symbols are displayed on pages of, for example, clear plastic wallet books, photograph albums, ring binders, etc. The symbol layout depends on the user's capabilities and the book needs to be well organised if it is to be practical. Books are a good way of storing large amounts of vocabulary in a relatively small space.
- *Topic boards:* a restricted vocabulary of symbols is displayed on a two-dimensional matrix and is task- or topic-specific.
- *Communication wallets:* symbols are arranged on cards and inserted into 'credit card' sleeves. They are incredibly portable but able to contain only a very small vocabulary.
- *E-TRAN frames:* symbols are displayed on a frame usually made of perspex and accessed by eye-pointing.

2 Devising and implementing a signing system

i) Selecting vocabulary

- Involve significant others in vocabulary selection.
- Initial vocabulary needs to be around motivating and frequently-occurring activities.
- Choose signs that bring a reward, either physical, such as a drink, or social, such as an interaction with someone the user likes.

- Do not choose signs to please other people, such as 'thank you' and 'please'. These serve no purpose for the client.
- Consider signs that the user would really benefit from being able to use.
- Choose a small number to begin with and build up the repertoire gradually. This makes it easier for the user and the staff.

ii) Staff training

- Staff need to understand why the client is being introduced or encouraged to sign. Take time to talk it through and to win them over if necessary.
- Clients will never learn to sign if people don't sign to them. Giving staff the appropriate training to increase their knowledge of the signs is a good first step, but continued informal 'training' needs to occur in order to increase their skills in using signs appropriately.
- One-off training sessions in Makaton rarely, if ever, work, and each establishment needs to be encouraged to become more of a signing environment by whatever method possible. This could include having 'signs of the week' that are taught in staff meetings and displayed for everyone to see, or competitions between staff to be the best signer by maybe 'ratting' on those staff members seen not to be signing the signs of the week, etc. The more fun and light-hearted the training and follow-up is, the more likely the training is to be a success.
- Staff need to be trained informally through joint working in the way to use signs with the user and the way to encourage the user to sign. Staff need to be discouraged, for example, from saying 'show me the sign for "drink" and then you can have one', and should be encouraged to praise spontaneous signing and model the signs as appropriate.

iii) Clear instructions

- Draw up a clear intervention programme that states which signs are going to be used with the client, when they are going to be used and how they should be used. Include the line drawings of the signs, if practical, and put the programme somewhere noticeable so that all staff are aware of it.
- Do not just tell staff to 'start signing these five signs around John whenever possible'. Work alongside staff to help them learn the right way to sign right from the beginning; it is easier than trying to change bad working practices.
- Inform other relevant professionals so that they can sign when appropriate.

iv) Introducing the signs

- Start with a few signs around frequently occurring and motivating activities.
- Show the user the signs without making them sign back, for example 'shall we have a **drink** John?' . . . 'here's your **drink**' . . . 'are you enjoying your **drink**?' etc.
- Use photographs, if appropriate, for example, 'here's a picture of a **drink**'.
- Praise and reward the user for spontaneously signing, for example, by immediately giving them a drink if that is what they signed. Don't correct the

user if they sign inaccurately, just model the correct sign back, for example, 'that's right John, well done, it's **drink** time'.

3 Devising and implementing an objects-of-reference programme

i) Selecting vocabulary/objects

◆ Involve significant others in the selection of objects.
◆ Initially these need to be centred around motivating and frequently-occurring activities.
◆ Choose objects that bring a reward or immediate result.
◆ Choose objects that are consistent with the user's level of symbolic development. For example, if they understand their environment by actual objects, then choosing part of an object or an associated object will be confusing to the user.
◆ Select a small number to begin with and build up their system gradually.

ii) Staff involvement

◆ Meet with staff and explain why an objects-of-reference programme is being introduced.
◆ Decide on a sensible place to keep the objects so that the user and staff are able to access them easily.
◆ Choose someone whose responsibility it is to ensure that the objects are all there and that none are missing.

iii) Staff training

◆ This is best achieved through informal joint sessions where staff can watch the clinician model good use of the objects and they can then have the opportunity to practise skills in everyday situations.
◆ Ongoing support will be necessary to ensure continued good practice.

iv) Clear instructions

◆ Draw up a clear intervention programme which states the objects that are to be used with the user, when they are going to be used and how they should be used. Make sure everyone sees it who needs to.
◆ Work alongside staff to help them get it right.
◆ Inform other relevant professionals.

v) Introducing the programme

◆ Start with a few objects around frequently occurring and motivating activities.
◆ Ensure that the objects are used consistently, that is, they are used every time that activity occurs, and in the same way.
◆ Show the user the object and help them build up an association between the activity and the object by giving it to them immediately prior to an activity and during an activity. It may also be relevant for the user to help put the object

away in its designated place at the end of the activity. For example, 'It's nearly time for a drink, Mark' (shows the cup to Mark, and then hands it to him while they go to the kitchen); 'Let's have a drink now' (shows Mark the cup); 'Have you finished now? Let's put your cup back' (Mark puts his dirty cup in the kitchen and his other cup back on the shelf with his other objects of reference).

◆ Praise and reward the user for spontaneously accessing one of their objects by immediately responding to the request, even if it is felt that the 'person didn't mean anything by it'.

ASSESSMENT OF CURRENT EXPRESSIVE SKILLS 1 – WORKED EXAMPLE

NAME _____ Ian _____ DATE _____ March 2000 _____

What skills/techniques is the person using to express themselves?

Techniques used	Examples	Other skills/ techniques	Accuracy	Socially effective
SPEECH	'Mum' 'Home'	Sometimes uses gesture	Very difficult to understand	Yes, if understood. Mostly, no.
BODY LANGUAGE	Facial exp. & body posture to indicate feelings	Sometimes uses speech/ vocalisations	Yes	No – he's reliant on others to interpret
SIGNING	Has about 10 signs, eg. 'car'	Uses speech as well	No – very inaccurate	Yes, if understood. Mostly, no.
LEADING PEOPLE TO OBJECT	Shows you telephone	Uses speech to try to back up	Yes, if object is attainable	No – usually done as last resort & Ian is frustrated
POINTS AT OBJECTS/ PICTURES	Points at videos, photos	Sometimes uses speech as well	Yes	Yes, if meaning is understood
PHYSICAL BEHAVIOUR	Stamping feet; slams doors when frustrated	Shouts/ vocalises	Yes	No – leaves everyone feeling bad that Ian can't be understood

Summary

Current techniques Ian is using are not effective. Speech is used alongside all other techniques, but is not effective as a means of expression. Signing is inaccurate. Pointing is the most effective technique.

ASSESSMENT OF CURRENT EXPRESSIVE SKILLS 2 – WORKED EXAMPLE

NAME ___Ian_____ DATE __March 2000_____

What types of messages and communicative functions is the person able to use?

1 Ability to express needs and wants

Ian is limited to being able to express a few needs and wants that are either regularly expressed by him and so easily anticipated – eg, 'Mum' means he wants to phone his mother – or that are in his immediate environment.

2 Ability to communicate about something that is not in their immediate environment

Very limited. Ian is reliant on other people listing possible needs once he has got their attention. This is only successful if he is with someone who knows him well, but still can be long-winded and frustrating.

3 Ability to socialise and share information with others

Very limited. Ian is quite isolated in his residential placement. He hasn't made any friends even though he is a sociable and friendly young man with good comprehension. Has good relationship with key worker.

4 Ability to join in everyday routines

Has a busy timetable of activities, most of which are manual/practical and not reliant on speech. Ian joins in but remains a passive member of any group.

5 Ability to be part of their wider environment/community

Enjoys going out into the community, especially when at home as he is well known and liked, for example in the local pub. He is reliant on other people knowing him well enough to anticipate his needs.

Summary

Ian's ability to express different messages is limited to his immediate environment unless he is at home. His limited expressive skills mean that he is isolated from his peers and unable to fully participate in activities.

AAC ASSESSMENT SUMMARY – WORKED EXAMPLE SHEET

NAME _____ Ian _____ DOB _____

ADDRESS _____

COMPLETED BY _____ DATE _____

CURRENT EXPRESSIVE SKILLS

Techniques used

Ian uses a variety of techniques to express himself: speech, body language, signing, leading people to or pointing at objects & physical behaviour. None of these are accurate or socially effective & he is reliant on others knowing him well enough to interpret correctly. Pointing is probably the most effective technique.

Communicative functions used

Ian is limited to expressing his needs in his immediate environment when communicating with someone who doesn't know him well. He is socially isolated and unable to participate fully in activities.

Use of speech

Ian's use of speech is very limited and difficult to understand. It is used alongside other expressive techniques, but is not an effective means of expression.

COMPREHENSION

Level of symbolic development and vocabulary size

Ian does not read but is able to understand minimal line drawings (symbols). His comprehension is at a 2-3 word level. He understands emotions but is confused by time and negatives. He sometimes benefits from Makaton being used, for example in negatives.

VISUAL ABILITIES

Visual/perceptual abilities and difficulties

Ian has good vision. He is able to find a small symbol (2cm) from a page of 30 symbols.

MOTOR SKILLS

Current use of motor skills and range and accuracy of movement

Ian struggles to sign accurately, even when shown using hand over hand. He has very accurate and effective pointing skills.

AAC ASSESSMENT SUMMARY – WORKED EXAMPLE SHEET

THE ENVIRONMENT

Current environment

Ian has recently started living at a residential unit that offers a wide range of vocational day services. There are 11 other young men living there.

Existing barriers

3 staff, including Ian's keyworker, have been trained in Makaton. Ian's keyworker is the only member of staff who uses it effectively.

SUMMARY OF RECOMMENDATIONS

AAC system recommended and environmental recommendations

1   Ian would benefit from having a symbolised communication system that is portable and extensive enough to match his level of comprehension. A filofax has been agreed upon.

2   Ian benefits from people using Makaton at times, particularly when using negatives.

ACTION PLAN

1   Keyworkers and Ian to buy filofax.

2   Speech & language clinician and keyworker will meet with Ian to build up a vocabulary of symbols that he understands and can use. Eight sessions initially agreed.

3   Ian's parents have been contacted & agreed to provide vocabulary relevant to home. Meeting also arranged.

4   Filofax also to contain a symbolised timetable and a calendar to help Ian understand when he's going home.

5   Keyworker to work alongside other members of staff to increase their skills in using Makaton and the filofax (as appropriate).

6   Speech & language clinician to attend next staff meeting to discuss this action plan.

Completed by ___A. Clinician___   Date ___31 March 2000___

WORKING WITH ADULTS WITH A LEARNING DISABILITY

AAC ASSESSMENT SUMMARY – WORKED EXAMPLE SHEET

Example of 2 pages from Ian's communication book

FEELINGS

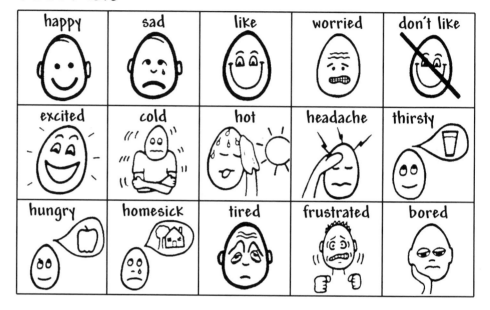

GOING OUT

ASSESSMENT OF CURRENT EXPRESSIVE SKILLS 1 – WORKED EXAMPLE

NAME James

DATE 5 April 2000

What skills/techniques is the person using to express themselves?

Techniques used	Examples	Other skills/ techniques	Accuracy	Socially effective
SPEECH	'Tea-tea' 'Bus-bus'	Sometimes uses Makaton sign or one of his own signs	Often very difficult to understand	Yes, if understood.
SIGNING	Has about 15 signs	Will vocalise/ speak at same time	Some signs are very accurate, some not	Yes, if understood.
LEADING PERSON TO OBJECT	Takes you to door if he wants to go out	Will vocalise & sign sometimes	Yes – you know what he wants	No – often gets a negative response
VOCALISA-TIONS	Different noises to indicate feelings	Will also use behaviour	Not very consistent	No. People tell him to be quiet or misinterpret
PHYSICAL BEHAVIOUR	Throwing objects when angry & bored	Will vocalise	No – can mean too many things	No – people get cross & don't find out what was wrong
POINTING AT PHOTOS/ PICTURES	Points to photo of him	Says 'Jay-Jay'	Yes	Yes – gets 1:1 interaction which he enjoys

Summary

James' most effective techniques to express himself are signing (when he signs accurately) and pointing at photographs.

AUGMENTATIVE & ALTERNATIVE COMMUNICATION

ASSESSMENT OF CURRENT EXPRESSIVE SKILLS 2 – WORKED EXAMPLE

NAME_____James_____   DATE __5 April 2000__

What types of messages and communicative functions is the person able to use?

1 Ability to express needs and wants

James' ability to express himself is limited to the 15 Makaton signs he knows, and objects that are in his immediate environment. He is often reliant on others interpreting his behaviour.

2 Ability to communicate about something that is not in their immediate environment

This is limited to a few activities that James has learnt a sign for, eg, 'bus', 'trampolining' and 'walk'.

3 Ability to socialise and share information with others

James loves 1:1 attention and is able to socialise with staff who use Makaton, or those who take time to listen to him & work out what he's communicating.

4 Ability to join in everyday routines

Joins in all activities but can get very angry & frustrated if he's not understood. This has meant he has been prevented from doing certain activities for a period of time, as a result.

5 Ability to be part of their wider environment/community

Enjoys going out, but does not interact with other people in the community.

Summary

James' ability to express different messages is greatly affected by the skills of the listener. His frustration can adversely affect his ability to participate.

AAC ASSESSMENT SUMMARY – WORKED EXAMPLE SHEET

NAME _____ James _____ DOB _____

ADDRESS _____

COMPLETED BY _____ DATE _____

CURRENT EXPRESSIVE SKILLS

Techniques used

James uses a variety of techniques to express himself, predominantly speech and signing. He is most effective when he signs accurately and when pointing to photographs.

Communicative functions used

James' ability to express different messages is adversely affected by his limited knowledge of Makaton and the skills of the listener.

Use of speech

James uses speech a great deal to back up other techniques. His speech is very unclear and is mostly difficult to understand.

COMPREHENSION

Level of symbolic development and vocabulary size

James understands at a 1-word level, although this can increase to a 2-word level if Makaton is used.

He does not understand line drawings (symbols), but understands photographs.

VISUAL ABILITIES

Visual/perceptual abilities and difficulties

James does not appear to have any visual or perceptual difficulties.

MOTOR SKILLS

Current use of motor skills and range and accuracy of movement

James has good motor skills – he is able to sign accurately (once he has learnt a sign) and can point to photos.

AAC ASSESSMENT – A SUMMARY – WORKED EXAMPLE

THE ENVIRONMENT

Current environment

James lives in a small residential unit.

Day activities are offered by support workers.

Existing barriers

James is in an environment that doesn't use Makaton consistently and effectively. Some staff are skilled, but some appear unsure of the benefits.

SUMMARY OF RECOMMENDATIONS

AAC system recommended and environmental recommendations

1   James would benefit from being able to express himself more through signs.
2   James needs to be in a signing environment.

ACTION PLAN

1   Initially 10 signs to be used consistently with James (see programme).
2   Joint sessions to be planned to work alongside key members of staff to ensure effective signing.
3   Communication book to be made using 20 photographs and corresponding Makaton sign. These to include the 10 signs in programme and 10 other key activities.
4   Speech and language clinician to attend next staff meeting to discuss this action plan.

Completed by ___A. Clinician___   Date ___5 April 2000___

COMMUNICATION PLAN FOR JAMES – WORKED EXAMPLE

AIM

To improve James' ability to use Makaton

ACTION PLAN

Staff to use the following signs immediately prior to and during the activity. These signs to be used regularly (ie, every day) and consistently (ie, every time that activity occurs).

Do not make James sign them, but praise any attempt made by James to sign.

MAKATON SIGNS – New to James

Bath

Food

Tap once

Bed

Mum

Tap twice

Outside

Ice-cream

Mime licking ice cream

Chocolate

'C' finger makes small anti-clockwise movement on chin

Cook

Cigarette

One movement only

Home

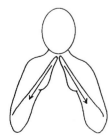

Makaton signs known to James –
Please; Toilet; Drink; Walk; Bus; Hot; Trampolining; Yes; No; Horse-riding; Biscuit; Hello; Cake; Bad; Sorry.

AUGMENTATIVE & ALTERNATIVE COMMUNICATION

INTRODUCTION

Working with adults who have profound and multiple disabilities will always present us with a challenge. These people are often described as having 'no communication skills' (Goldbart, 1994), and are therefore thought of as *non-communicators*. This issue, or perception of people with profound and multiple disabilities, is central to the challenge we face. If people are treated as non-communicators, they will never learn to communicate, but if we can get the message across to carers that *any behaviour is potentially communicative*, then we can begin to change their perceptions and help them to see people with profound and multiple disabilities as communicators. As Goldbart states, 'It is by being treated as communicators that we become communicators' (1994), and as Newson (1978) also says 'It is only because he (the child) is treated as a communicator that he learns the essential art of communication' (cited by Goldbart, 1994).

Caldwell (1998) feels that the challenge we face is to find a way to 'get in touch' with those people who have complex needs and may seem to be locked in a world of their own. She says that we need to try to understand how the person senses and perceives their world and we need then to find a way to establish contact. The challenge, therefore, is to 'find the key' to communicating with each person and so to 'open the door' so that they are enabled to experience more effective communication in their environment and a better quality of life. Caldwell (1998) quotes Han Fei Tzu (3rd century BC), who wrote: 'The greatest obstacle to conversation is not knowing the heart of the person one speaks to . . . only when people learn to speak to each other will they begin to be . . . equal.'

This chapter aims to give the reader an understanding of profound and multiple disabilities, the development of communication and, in particular, preverbal communication, assessment methods and strategies for intervention.

DEFINING AND UNDERSTANDING PROFOUND & MULTIPLE DISABILITY

This client group is defined by the complex range of disabilities with which they can present. Clients with a profound learning disability represent a small percentage (1-2 per cent) of all clients with a learning disability (DSM IV, 1994). As also described in the DSM IV, most of these clients have an identified neurological condition and display considerable impairments in their sensorimotor ability.

Profound learning disability has been defined in many different ways. The American Association on Mental Deficiency defines the degrees of learning disability in terms of intelligence quotients (IQs), and profound learning disability as an IQ of below 20 or 25 (Grossman, 1983). Other definitions have been based on a description of the person's functional skills or lack of them. Functional definitions have been given to us by Presland (1982), Sontag *et al* (1973) and Browning *et al* (1981), and all have been cited by Hogg (1986). They list similar characteristics of profound learning disability such as: clients are non-verbal, they are delayed in self-help, social and motor skill development, not toilet trained, and suffering from severe physical and sensory impairments. A further way of defining profound learning disability is in terms of the services people receive or need, therefore describing people with profound learning disability as mostly requiring some form of long-term residential care with higher staffing ratios.

Wake (1997) combines the latter two kinds of definitions by suggesting that 'Profound and multiple disability could be construed as referring to an individual who requires maximum assistance in all aspects of everyday life, in terms of 24-hour care and supervision. The person may have difficulty in communication, eating and drinking, continence and mobilisation, for example.'

In addition to their profound learning disability, clients will also present with a multiple disability and this means that the individual has additional needs, for example:

◆ *Sensory* – most commonly these will be visual or hearing impairments, but could also include impairment of any sensory channel, for example, hypersensitivity.
◆ *Physical* – for example, cerebral palsy, epilepsy, diabetes, and complex health needs.
◆ *Emotional/behavioural* – for example, autism, challenging behaviour, mental health problems.

The following additional needs will be briefly described in order to give the reader an understanding of the issues that may face the person with profound and multiple disabilities:

1   Physical disability
2   Visual impairment
3   Hearing impairment
4   Feeding difficulties
5   Cardiovascular problems
6   Poor oral hygiene
7   Respiratory problems
8   Incontinence
9   Epilepsy

1 Physical disability

Hogg and Sebba (1986) cite studies which state that between 35 and 50 per cent of people with profound and multiple disabilities are unable to walk. Many individuals are therefore completely dependent on their carers, and the need for input from the physiotherapist and occupational therapist is important. A physical disability also means that there needs to be consideration of the following:

◆ Promotion of the individual's potential so that they have the opportunity to develop everyday functional skills that will enhance the quality of their life.

◆ Strategies to minimise additional physical disabilities that can occur, such as muscle atrophy, contractures, loss of limb flexibility, increased difficulty in using seating, hoists and wheelchairs, and podiatry-related problems.
◆ Prevention of pressure sores.
◆ Strategies to enhance mobility, so that routine activities such as dressing and bathing can be done easily and quickly.

2 Visual impairment

The incidence of visual impairment in people with profound and multiple disabilities varies considerably between studies. For example Woods (1979, cited by Hogg, 1986) suggests that 42 per cent of children with severe to profound learning disabilities have a 'visual defect', while Browning *et al* (1981, cited by Hogg, 1986) found that 9 per cent of people with profound learning disabilities were blind and 12 per cent were partially sighted. Visual impairment can be caused by:

◆ *Retinopathy of prematurity* – where retinal blood vessels spasm and complete retinal detachment can occur.
◆ *Macular degeneration* – in which central vision deteriorates but peripheral vision is still present.
◆ *Glaucoma* – where there is a build-up of aqueous fluid in the ducts of the eyes, resulting in pressure on the optic nerve as well as on the retina.
◆ *Damage to the optic nerve and the areas of the brain associated with vision during pregnancy or postnatally* – owing to, for example, meningitis or trauma.
◆ *Cataracts* – which can seriously impair an individual's vision. It has been found that up to 50 per cent of people with Down's syndrome have cataracts (Lane & Stratford, 1985, cited by Wake, 1997).
◆ *Hemianopia* (absence of half of the normal field of vision), which is often associated with hemiparesis (paralysis of one side of the body).

3 Hearing impairment

It has been suggested that as many as one in 10 people with learning disabilities have some form of hearing impairment (Ball, 1991, cited by Wake, 1997), although definite statistics are difficult to obtain because the screening of such individuals is still inadequate. There are people who are more at risk of having a hearing impairment, and the risk factors include: premature birth, prenatal infection, maternal illness during pregnancy (eg, rubella and herpes zoster), neurological impairment such as severe cerebral palsy, meningitis and other central nervous system infection, and trauma (Wake, 1997). Care issues include maximising any residual hearing and developing effective means of communicating non-verbally.

4 Feeding difficulties

People with profound and multiple disabilities often have a number of specific problems concerned with eating and drinking, and these may be related to muscle tone around the mouth and face, or in the body generally. A person with severe cerebral palsy, for example, may have a problem with all of these and this will result in difficulties in seating position, as well as problems with their ability to suck, chew and swallow without aspirating. Important reflexes such as coughing and gagging may be limited, and the person may still have some of the reflexes that are present in infancy, such as the startle reflex (Wake, 1997). See also Chapter 6 on dysphagia.

5 Cardiovascular problems

A lack of physical mobility can predispose individuals to the risk of circulatory problems, such as peripheral vascular disease (Wake, 1997). Carers need to be aware of the importance of diet and passive and/or active physiotherapy routines which will help maintain the cardiovascular system's effective functioning.

6 Poor oral hygiene

Much criticism has been aimed at the level of priority given to such a basic need when caring for people with profound disabilities (Griffiths & Boyle, 1993, cited by Wake, 1997). However, maintaining good oral hygiene in people with profound and multiple disabilities may be difficult for carers because of:

◆ An exaggerated bite reflex
◆ Hypersensitivity around and in the mouth
◆ Malocclusion (where upper and lower teeth are abnormally related)
◆ Swallowing difficulties
◆ A build-up of food in the mouth because of chewing and swallowing difficulties
◆ Medication which predisposes the individual to gum problems.

7 Respiratory problems

People with multiple disabilities often have respiratory problems and there are many reasons for this, for example:

◆ Poor swallowing and/or gag reflex
◆ Poor cough reflex
◆ Immobility
◆ Inability to be in an upright position
◆ Common problems such as asthma and colds
◆ Conditions that are linked with various respiratory disorders, for example, Down's syndrome, Goldenhar syndrome, and Batten's disease.

8 Incontinence

Continence care can be a major issue for people with profound and multiple disabilities, and although it is important to ensure that there are no underlying factors that could add to the problem, such as urinary tract infections, the primary cause is likely to relate to the degree of learning and physical disability (Wake, 1997). Additional problems such as constipation are also associated with immobility, and it is therefore important for the individual to have a well-balanced diet and adequate fluid intake.

9 Epilepsy

Epilepsy is a condition that is often associated with profound and multiple disabilities (Kay *et al* 1995a, cited by Wake, 1997). Epilepsy is defined as 'recurrent, episodic, uncontrolled electrical discharge from the brain. Epilepsy is the term for recurrent, unprovoked seizures or convulsions' (McMenamin *et al* 1993, cited by Wake, 1997). The four common types of epilepsy are:

◆ *Generalised tonic-clonic seizures (or grand mal)* – the best known form of epilepsy, which involve two stages, tonic and clonic. The tonic stage involves loss of consciousness and the muscles go into extension giving the person a rigid appearance. The clonic period is where the muscles are alternately rapidly contracting and relaxing. After the convulsing has stopped, a period known as the postictal phase follows, in which the person is often very drowsy and may wish to sleep for a time.
◆ *Absence seizures (or petit mal)* – where the person has a brief loss of awareness, without any obvious jerking or falling down.
◆ *Simple partial seizures* – when the symptoms affect only one side of the body. The person remains conscious but often experiences 'unusual feelings' (Wake, 1997). They can often occur while the person is asleep.
◆ *Complex partial seizures* which more difficult to describe. The person may experience an aura beforehand – eg, an unusual smell, and automatisms – ie, repetitive behavioural responses such as 'finger flapping' – may be evident. The person is often said to be unaware of their surroundings, as consciousness is affected to a degree. The temporal lobe of the brain is associated with this type of seizure.

COMMUNICATION AND PEOPLE WITH PROFOUND & MULTIPLE DISABILITIES

In order to develop effective assessments and intervention strategies for people with profound and multiple disabilities, it is important to have an understanding of the different functions or purposes of communication, and also the way in which we learn to communicate. We need to be able to identify processes and strategies which might be of use in facilitating communication, and we need to have a good understanding of the early development of language so that we can recognise and value small changes in people moving from 'pre-intentional' to 'intentional' communication. Many clients with profound and multiple disabilities may appear to have extremely limited communication. The term 'preverbal' is frequently used to describe this group; however, this term on its own is far too broad to describe the wide range of ability within this client group. Clinicians need to have a clear understanding of the development of functional language and communication so that they are able to see how a client is communicating at present and how they can be moved up the hierarchy of functional communication in achievable steps.

Functions of communication

Several authors have categorised the different ways in which we can have an impact on others, the different functions or purposes of communication. Table 4.1 lists the functions of communication that were originally developed by Kiernan and Reid (1987). When considering communication in relation to people with profound and multiple disabilities, it is not necessary to think about a sophisticated system of language and grammar, but simply some ways of communicating the first four functions in the list.

Table 4.1 The Early Uses of Communication	
Seeking attention	The person 'asks' that their presence is acknowledged
Needs satisfaction	The person 'asks' that their needs are satisfied by the provision of things, people or personal services
Simple negation	The person acts so as to stop the activity of someone, to induce them to leave them alone
Positive interaction	The person uses positive behaviours to maintain an interaction, without reference to external objects or needs
Negative interaction	The person uses negative or provocative behaviour to control the other's attention
Shared attention	The person calls the other's attention to an interesting object or event, thus achieving shared attention
Giving information	The person tells others about or comments on objects, people or events
Seeking information	The person asks others or requests information on objects, people or events
Pretending	The person communicates about pretending or make believe
In general, the first three uses develop before the second three uses, which are acquired before the third three uses.	
Source: Goldbart et al (1994) – adapted from Halliday (1975) and Kiernan & Reid (1987).	

Development of early communication

The two main theoretical approaches to explaining the development of early communication are the *psycholinguistic* approach and the *sociolinguistic* approach. Although quite different in their approaches, they are not contradictory and each one has an influence on our practice. The psycholinguistic approach is a semantic-cognitive theory (see Coupe O'Kane & Goldbart, 1998). It suggests that children need experience of objects and events in their environment in order to learn language, and that this experience can be gained through interaction with people and objects and through play. This theory certainly explains a lot of what we see in the early utterances of young children, but it does not explain why language and communication develop. In the sociolinguistic approach, the emphasis is on the child being in a social setting, and suggests that 'language is acquired only if the child has reason to communicate' and 'as a more effective means of obtaining things' (Coupe O'Kane & Goldbart, 1998). In the same way, an adult with a learning disability will only learn to communicate if they have a reason, or purpose, for that communication, whether social or material. This approach also places importance on the person being an active participant in the process of learning communication, and having opportunity to communicate with mature language users.

These two theories are not mutually exclusive and can be used in a complementary way in order to help us to understand how language develops. The stages in development according to the psycholinguistic approach include aspects of cognitive, semantic and symbolic development. They are drawn from Piaget's findings on the sensori-motor period (Piaget, 1952, cited by Coupe O'Kane & Goldbart, 1998) (see Table 4.2).

The stages of development according to the sociolinguistic approach are more concerned with the way in which language learners come to acquire a functional use of language and communication (see Figure 4.1). From birth to about six

Table 4.2 Cognitive, Semantic and Symbolic Development in Piaget's Sensorimotor Period		
Stage	Age (months)	Description
1	0–1	Engaged mainly in exercises of reflexes. Selective looking.
2	1–4	Early undifferentiated schemes, eg, mouthing, looking, holding. The baby learns to repeat pleasurable actions with its own body.
3	4–8	First stage of intention. Baby learns to repeat actions (external to self), eg, making a mobile swing. Differentiated schemes, eg, shaking, banging, therefore cognitive roles being established.
4	8–12	Establishes goal prior to initiation of an activity, therefore intention is fully established. Appropriate use of familiar objects. Cognitive roles expand and semantic roles start to be expressed, eg, existence, repetition, disappearance.
5	12–18	New means of achieving ends through experimentation. Tools used. Exploration of containers. Showing and giving objects. Relational then self-pretend play. First words, categorised by semantic role.
6	18–24	New means of achieving ends through mental combinations, ie, showing insight in problem-solving. Predicts cause-effect relationships. Decentred then sequenced pretend play. Two-word utterances.
Source: Adapted from Coupe O'Kane & Goldbart (1998), and Goldbart, et al (1994).		

months, caregivers accept a wide range of the baby's actions and vocalisations as meaningful; for example, if the baby kicks his legs when put on the floor, the adult may say 'You like it down there, don't you?', or if the baby screws up his face and vocalises when being fed, the adult may say, 'Oh dear, you don't like this, do you?'

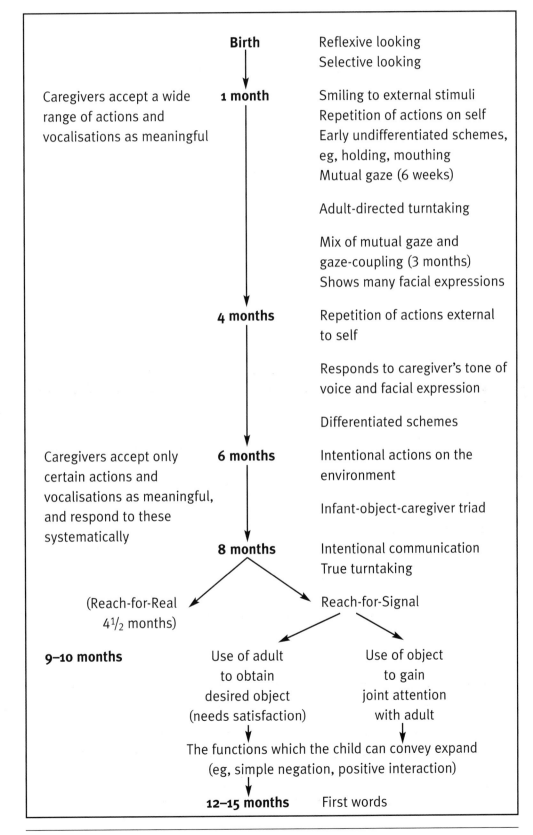

Figure 4.1
Development in the Functional Use of Language and Communication

The adult is 'imposing meaning, or richly interpreting, the infant's actions or vocalisations' (Coupe O'Kane & Goldbart, 1998), and is also directing and developing turn-taking by talking to the baby and then leaving spaces for the baby to fill with sounds or actions, thus creating a 'conversation'.

At around six months, the baby begins to demonstrate intention; caregivers become more selective, and will only interpret certain actions or gestures as meaningful. Thus, by accepting only more and more clearly defined behaviours as communicative, they shape intentional communication, and teach the child 'the concept that you can affect other people's behaviour by your own actions or vocalisations, that is, communication' (Coupe O'Kane & Goldbart, 1998). From this stage of intentional communication, children start to use the 'reach-for-signal', that is, they learn to gesture to something out of reach, look at the adult, and later to vocalise as well, to communicate that they want the thing they are reaching for. They also learn to direct the adult's attention to something they want to communicate about, therefore becoming more active, a directive partner in interactions. Children gradually show increasingly sophisticated ways of communicating, from looking to gesture to gesture-plus-vocalisation to words (or signs/symbols), and finally they are able to do increasingly varied things with their skills in communication.

Intention is an important aspect of early language development for people with profound and multiple disabilities. Much of the work of the speech and language clinician will be around assessing clients' preverbal skills, and enabling them to develop intention. In simple terms, a client who is an intentional communicator will be actively and deliberately using their communication skills to influence their environment and the people within it. A client who is pre-intentional will have a number of communicative behaviours which are interpreted and responded to (or not) by the people within their environment.

Pre-intentional communication can be further subdivided (Coupe O'Kane & Goldbart, 1998), as follows:

◆ *Reflexive stage* – clients have reflexive responses to their own body and their environment which familiar people interpret; for example, different cries to indicate hunger, cold, pain.
◆ *Reactive stage* – clients react to their own body and to their environment and people interpret this; for example, body stiffening is interpreted as dislike.
◆ *Proactive stage* – clients deliberately responds to objects and people, and people then assign communicative intent to them; for example, pursing lips and turning head is seen to mean 'don't want'.

Table 4.3 looks at the way in which this occurs: how clients and communication partners respond and the way that a client progresses from one stage to another.

Table 4.3 Development of Intentional Communication

Focal person	Interpretation	Action	Result
REFLEXIVE STAGE			
Crying due to hunger A purely reflexive response	Has a need	Carer goes to person, and their verbal response would indicate concern.	Person learns that crying can influence those in their environment. Also learns to link the carer's words and intonation to their action.
REACTIVE STAGE			
Reaching or looking for objects in immediate environment	Person either wants them, or wants you to do something with them.	Carer gives them to person or performs action with them. Also names object or describes action.	Person begins to learn that reach or look can be used in order to request. Also begins to link spoken words and real objects.
PROACTIVE STAGE			
Looking/ reaching to object and then reaching/ looking/ vocalising at carer	Person wants *you* to get them the object or carry out the action.	Carer carries out request and emphasises their interpretation, eg 'You want Mary to get a drink?'	Person is able to develop true intentional communicative control over their environment.

(Source: Descriptive stage terms taken from Coupe O'Kane & Goldbart (1998)

Several important points in relation to intervention and management can be made from our understanding of how language develops:

◆ Clients need to be given a diversity of experiences to enable them to develop a range of schemes for acting on the environment.

◆ The transition from actions relating to self to actions relating to objects and people is a particularly difficult area for people with profound and multiple disabilities. We need to be able to assess when a client has begun to develop intention and then to start shaping intentional communication.

◆ It is important to identify the best route for developing communication for each individual so that their existing skills are used to their maximum potential.

◆ It is necessary to assess the use of communication in everyday settings and provide strategies for promoting communication.

Symbolic development

In addition to understanding the development of early communication skills, it is also important for the clinician to have an understanding of a client's level of symbolic development. This is essential when facilitating formalised intentional communication – that is, where the client uses speech/signs/symbols to communicate a need in a consistent manner. The primary methods of communication used by this client group often are informal and non-verbal. However, this is sometimes difficult for carers to understand and they may wish the client to start using a more formalised method of expression, such as signing or symbols.

When deciding which methods of communication are going to be accessible to the client, it is important to assess the level of difficulty that this would present to them. Figure 4.2 looks at the abstract and concrete nature of different symbols which may be used for communication.

Figure 4.2
Symbolic
Development

REAL TREE   *MOST CONCRETE*
(Sensory support: colour of tree, size of tree, sound
and smell of tree, 3D; is situated in context)

MINIATURE OF TREE
(Sensory support: colour of tree, shape of tree, 3D)

PHOTO OF TREE (ACTUAL TREE)
(Sensory support: colour of tree, shape of tree)

PHOTO OF A TREE (ANY TREE)
(Sensory support: some aspects of colour and shape)

LINE DRAWING OF A TREE
(Sensory support: generalised shape)

SIGN FOR TREE (MAKATON)
(Sensory support: gross link to generalised shape of a tree)

WORD TREE
(Sensory support: none)

MOST ABSTRACT

As Figure 4.2 illustrates, the concrete or abstract nature of a symbol is determined to some extent by the degree of sensory support that it gives the person trying to understand it. In this case a real tree gives the person a wealth of sensory support to help them understand the concept of 'tree', whereas the spoken word gives none. As is also shown, commonly-used systems such as line drawings (eg, Rebus) and signs (eg, Makaton) give only very limited sensory support.

It is important to remember that for a client with a profound learning disability, abstract concepts are difficult to understand, and therefore the more concrete something is, and the more sensory support that can be given, the easier it is for that client to understand.

ASSESSMENT

Assessment of people with profound and multiple disabilities is generally most effective if it is done over a period of time in a structured and detailed way, and with people who know the person well. As we have seen in the first part of this chapter, many people have complex and multiple needs which must be understood and taken into account when devising an appropriate assessment procedure. Variables that may need to be considered during assessment include:

Internal factors
◆ Physical factors such as pain, fatigue, discomfort and hunger.
◆ Identified conditions such as epilepsy and diabetes.
◆ Sensory factors such as vision and hearing, and hyper- or hyposensitivity.
◆ Emotional issues that might be related to hormonal changes, mental health issues or difficulty with changes to routine.

External factors
◆ Noise
◆ Movement
◆ Familiarity of staff and activities
◆ Time of day
◆ Temperature
◆ Lighting.

Logically, if a client has very limited communication skills then a small change to these kinds of internal or external variables could have a major impact on the way in which they are able to demonstrate their skills. For example, a client with cataracts who is facing towards a light source such as a window can potentially be completely blinded, drastically affecting their apparent response to external stimuli.

Information-gathering

Gathering information is clearly going to be an important first part of the assessment process. Depending on the client's individual circumstances, the following sources may or may not be appropriate:

◆ *The carer* is usually the best person to talk to in the first place. It will be important to find out how the client communicates and how the carer understands and responds to them. It is also necessary to find out what motivates the person, what activities are disliked and how the carer knows this. The carer will also be able to give a description of any additional difficulties, such as sensory and physical, and will be able to tell you what medication the person is taking (if any). It will also be important to find out who the person likes and who would be the best person to work alongside for assessment purposes.

◆ *The client's notes.* These should give an overview of the client's needs and the services involved. Although it is important to make use of the often abundant notes available, it is also important to bear in mind that the situation may have changed and information should always be checked to make sure that it is relevant.

◆ *Relevant others.* This may include family, professionals, advocate, etc. If other professionals are currently working with the client, what are they working towards and, with all relevant others, how do they communicate with the client?

Checklists are the most effective way of gathering initial information about the client, and the *Personal Communication Profile* (see end of book) has a checklist that can be used for this purpose. Alternatively the clinician may wish to use the following checklist.

Assessment of early communication

Two assessment schedules will be described in detail in this section, both aimed at giving carers more information about individuals at very early stages of communication. The Affective Communication Assessment (Coupe *et al*, 1985) helps in the recognition of behaviours which are potentially communicative, and the Pre-Verbal Communication Schedule (Kiernan & Reid, 1987) helps to highlight the extent to which an individual is using each of the functions of communication described earlier. It also gives us a profile of the client's strengths and needs in a range of skills that contribute to communication. The way in which each of these assessments can be used for planning intervention will be considered.

The Affective Communication Assessment (ACA)

The ACA was developed to provide a systematic way of analysing the reactions of people with profound and multiple disabilities to a variety of experiences. More specifically, the ACA assesses whether the person has any consistent patterns of behaviour that a familiar adult could interpret as meaning that the person *likes, dislikes, wants, rejects, or is neutral to* the experience. All people with profound and multiple disabilities exhibit a range of behaviours through their bodies, facial expressions, etc, and it is likely that these will occur regularly in response to certain external stimuli. For the person who is functioning at the pre-intentional level, it is important that carers are sensitive to these responses, attach meaning to them and respond as if they were a communicative signal. In this way, a two-way process of communication can be facilitated which will incorporate some consistent responses to the person's feelings. Through observations of the person's behaviours, it is possible to identify 'consistent repertoires of behaviours which express feelings and responses. This information can then be utilised to draw up and implement relevant and specific programmes of intervention' (Coupe O'Kane & Goldbart, 1998).

COMMUNICATION CHECKLIST

NAME _____ **DOB** _____

ADDRESS _____

RELEVANT OTHERS

Name   Occupation/relationship to client   Contact number

DESCRIPTION OF COMMUNICATION

Primary mode of communication

Strategies for expressing needs/wants/yes/no, etc

Strategies to assist understanding and expression

LIKES	DISLIKES

PHYSICAL FACTORS

Physical disability

Sensory difficulties

Medical condition

Medication and side effects

Other

Completed by _____ Date _____

Using the ACA

The person being assessed should be seated in their optimum position and the adult should select stimuli and situations to which the person is already known to respond. These stimuli should take into account all sensory channels as well as the environment itself. Responses should be videotaped whenever possible as it is difficult to record the required range of behaviours just by watching. Using the Observation Recording Sheet (see Figure 4.3), these stimuli are presented in turn and any responses noted. At the same time, the adult interprets the meaning thought to be conveyed by the person to each stimulus, for example 'I want'/'I don't want' or 'I like'/'I don't like'. A period of time must be allowed between the presentation of successive stimuli and for the stimulus to be registered in order to observe a response.

Having collated and interpreted responses to a variety of stimuli, it is important to check for the consistency and quality of the behaviours by using the Identification Recording Sheet (see Figure 4.4). The clinician will need to select the strongest responses and list the behaviours exhibited by the client. The stimuli will then need to be re-presented, the behaviours recorded and the responses interpreted. A new set of experiences are then chosen and described in the columns at the top of the sheet and the behaviours and responses are recorded. At this stage, it is possible to assess whether the person has a consistent way of responding to things they like as opposed to things they dislike. These responses can then be shaped into intentional communication.

Using the ACA information to plan intervention

The ACA has identified patterns of responses – ie, potentially communicative behaviours – along with the stimuli and settings in which they are likely to occur. It is therefore possible to create optimum setting conditions in which the client can effectively communicate using a predicted repertoire of behaviours. The adult is then able to respond in a relevant and consistent way throughout the day. Thus, the frequency of the person's communicative behaviours is likely to increase. It is also important 'for opportunities to be presented where the child [or adult] is in a position to control or have an effect on the environment and the people within it. In this way, the child, however unintentionally, can initiate and respond to communication' (Coupe O'Kane & Goldbart, 1998). It is then possible to generalise and shape the affective communication towards intentional signalling.

Goldbart (1988) gives an example of this by describing Lisa. The ACA has shown that Lisa enjoys loud noises and vigorous physical activity and will respond to them by laughing and making a small breathy noise. A turn-taking sequence was set up where a member of staff would swing Lisa in her arms then pause, wait for a sound from Lisa, then swing her again. In this way Lisa's 'like' response is being shaped into a meaningful communication for 'more' or 'again'. In addition, the assessment has shown that she doesn't like water and shows this dislike by closing her mouth, putting her head back and frowning. At mealtimes, she is given a sip of water and

ACA OBSERVATION Recording Sheet		STIMULI											DATE					
CLIENT'S NAME:																		
HEAD	Turn – R/L, U/D																	
	Activity ↑ ↓																	
	Rotating																	
	Other																	
FACE	Frown																	
	Smile																	
	Anguish																	
MOUTH	Activity ↑ ↓																	
	Open/close																	
	Tongue activity																	
	Contact																	
EYES	Activity ↑ ↓																	
	Open/close																	
	Gaze																	
	Localise/search																	
HANDS	Activity ↑ ↓																	
	Finger activity ↑ ↓																	
	Contact																	
ARMS	Reaching																	
	Activity ↑ ↓																	
LEGS	Activity ↑ ↓																	
BODY	Activity ↑ ↓																	
VOCALISATION	Utterance																	
	Cry																	
	Laugh																	
	Other																	
	AFFECTIVE COMMUNICATION Interpretation of client's behaviour																	

Coupe J et al, 1985

Figure 4.3 ACA Observation Recording Sheet

ACA IDENTIFICATION Recording Sheet	STIMULI												DATE						
CLIENT'S NAME:																			
AFFECTIVE COMMUNICATION Interpretation of client's behaviour																			

Coupe J et al, 1985

Figure 4.4 *ACA Identification Recording Sheet*

when she indicates 'dislike', she is given a sip of orange juice. In this way, her responses are becoming more meaningful and communicative as she is being responded to in a consistent manner and *as a communicator*.

The Pre-Verbal Communication Schedule (PVCS)

The PVCS is made up of 28 sets of questions. Of these, 12 relate to pre-communicative behaviours like 'hearing and listening' and 'social interaction without communication'. Motor and vocal imitation are seen as bridging pre-communicative and communicative behaviour. A further 14 sets of questions assess communicative behaviour.

Using the PVCS

As with the ACA, this assessment needs to be completed by people who know the person well. Many of the questions can be answered from knowledge of the person, but some need to be assessed directly. Answers are recorded on the checklist and then these are scored in two ways. First, a profile of strengths and needs is drawn up using Score Sheet 1 (see Figure 4.5). This will give a picture of the overall performance of the person and some indication of their preferred means of communicating. Second, Score Sheet 2 in the PVCS looks at the person's communication in terms of the functional use of communicative responses, that is:

◆ Attention-seeking
◆ Need satisfaction
◆ Simple negation
◆ Positive interaction
◆ Negative interaction
◆ Shared attention
◆ Motor imitation
◆ Vocal imitation
◆ Understanding of non-vocal communication
◆ Understanding of vocalisation and speech.

Using the PVCS information to plan intervention

Using the PVCS profile and the category scores it should be possible to identify a client's preferred means of communicating and suggest ways of extending these towards the use of signs, symbols or speech. It is also possible to look at the purposes for which the person uses their communication and whether there are gaps that need developing. The PVCS manual (Kiernan & Reid, 1987) goes through each of the sections and indicates their significance in programme planning.

Other forms of assessment

Another approach to assessment is to look at the Individualised Sensory Environment (Bunning, 1997). This system aims to design a sensory environment

Score Sheet 1

Figure 4.5
*PVCS Score
Sheet 1*

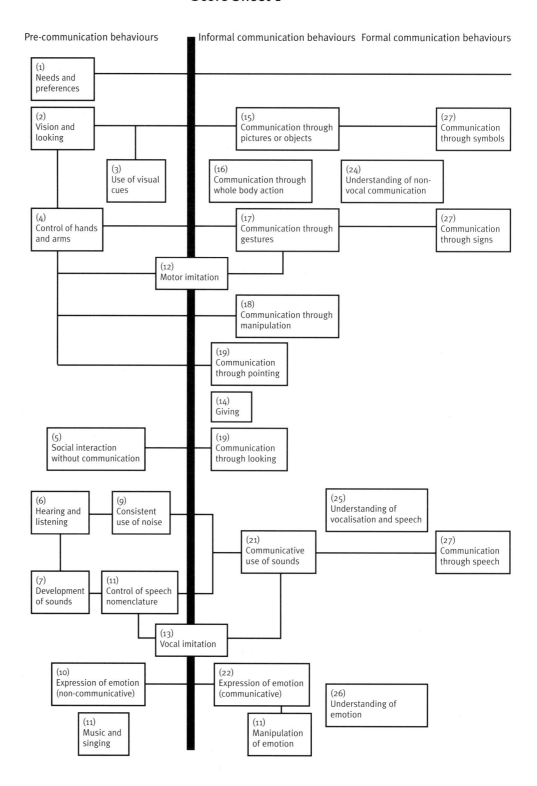

Pre-communication behaviours   Informal communication behaviours   Formal communication behaviours

(1) Needs and preferences

(2) Vision and looking

(15) Communication through pictures or objects

(27) Communication through symbols

(3) Use of visual cues

(16) Communication through whole body action

(24) Understanding of non-vocal communication

(4) Control of hands and arms

(17) Communication through gestures

(27) Communication through signs

(12) Motor imitation

(18) Communication through manipulation

(19) Communication through pointing

(14) Giving

(5) Social interaction without communication

(19) Communication through looking

(6) Hearing and listening

(9) Consistent use of noise

(25) Understanding of vocalisation and speech

(21) Communicative use of sounds

(27) Communication through speech

(7) Development of sounds

(11) Control of speech nomenclature

(13) Vocal imitation

(10) Expression of emotion (non-communicative)

(22) Expression of emotion (communicative)

(26) Understanding of emotion

(11) Music and singing

(11) Manipulation of emotion

for a person with profound and multiple disability which enables them to develop communicative control over their environment and identify at which pre-intentional stage they are operating. A detailed questionnaire is carried out with a keyworker which helps to establish the level at which the client is relating to objects, activities, and people. This can then be used as a baseline. Ongoing assessment involves identifying the prompt level required for a client to respond to a range of sensory stimuli, varying from the client being able to request the stimulus themselves to having to be given the stimulus as a prompt. One unique feature of this approach is that the prompts are given a numerical score which helps to measure at which prompt level the client is operating, and also to measure change across time.

A further approach is to analyse the communicative behaviour of clients and carers in specific situations. An example of this kind of approach is an unpublished assessment called 'Intent to Communicate' (East, 1981). This assesses reasons (functions) for communication – eg, gaining attention, requesting, protesting – and the methods of communication (channels) that the client is using – eg, eye-gaze to object, touch, vocalisation. In this assessment situations are set up to encourage the client to use their communicative skills, eg, to protest or request something. An example of such a situation may be drinking equipment placed just out of the client's reach, causing the client to gain attention and request a drink. The client should be given enough time to use their communicative skills before the carer responds. Situations are ideally recorded on video and analysed in order to assess the functions and channels of communication that the client and carer are using. This assessment helps to identify at which stage of pre-intentional development the client is; which functions and channels of communication they are able to use, and the way in which the carer is interacting with them. See Handouts 12 and 13 for checklists which can be used for this purpose and which have been adapted from 'Intent to Communicate' (East, 1981).

Other assessment approaches that could be used are those that are linked to staff training packages. Examples of this are ENABLE (*Encouraging a Natural and Better Life Experience*, Hurst-Brown & Keens, 1990) and INTECOM (Jones, 1990). These tend to involve checklist-style assessments which are intended to be carried out either with carers or for carers to do independently. The general principle is that following assessment clinicians and carers plan appropriate goals and monitor them together.

Following assessment, it is important not only to plan intervention, but to summarise a client's communication in a format that is accessible to everyone. The communication profile given later in this chapter is an example of how this could be done.

Working with

Adults with a Learning Disability

12

P

Photocopiable

©Alex Kelly, 2000

148

SITUATION PLAN

NAME	AIM	MATERIALS	DATE	INSTRUCTIONS	KEYWORKER	OUTCOME

SITUATION ASSESSMENT RECORD

NAME		DOB		KEYWORKER			
HOW?	SITUATION DATE		SITUATION DATE		SITUATION DATE		
Body language • Eyes • Face • Body • Hands							
Verbal/vocal							
Signing/gesture							
Physical contact • Moving away from object/person • Moving towards object/person							
Other							
Why?							

COMMUNICATION PROFILE

NAME _____ ATTENDS _____

PRIMARY MODE OF COMMUNICATION

STRATEGIES FOR COMMUNICATING

Include strategies for indicating 'yes' and 'no'

SIGNS/WORDS/PHRASES USED

PREFERRED ACTIVITIES FOR INTERACTION	DISLIKED ACTIVITIES

STRATEGIES TO ASSIST UNDERSTANDING AND EXPRESSION OF LANGUAGE

SENSORY DIFFICULTIES	PHYSICAL DIFFICULTIES AFFECTING COMMUNICATION
HEARING	
SIGHT	
OTHER	MEDICATION

Therapist _____ Date _____

PROMOTING COMMUNICATION

Kiernan and Reid (1983, cited by Goldbart, 1986, p164) state that people need four things in order to communicate:

◆ The 'idea of communication' – that is, the realisation that they can affect the behaviour of others by vocalisations or actions.
◆ 'Something to say' – in other words, the person must have wishes, needs or preferences that they want others to know about.
◆ 'Reasons for communication' – the person must believe that, by communication, they can get other people to satisfy their wishes, needs or preferences.
◆ 'A means of communication' – whether through words, natural gestures, signs, symbols, facial expressions, or any combination of these, the individual must have a way of expressing themselves.

Many people with profound and multiple disabilities will not yet have acquired the first of these four requirements; that is, their communication is 'pre-intentional' and assessment using the ACA or PVCS will have identified the appropriate intervention in order to shape their behaviour into intentional communication. Intervention will obviously be directed at teaching carers to respond consistently to identified behaviours, interpreting them as intentional and giving the required feedback. As Goldbart (1988) says, 'The aim here is to shape these behaviours from responses to experiences to communications about those experiences.'

Once some measure of intention has been established, intervention will focus more on carers providing further opportunities for the client to communicate. Initially this should include situations in which the client can indicate their needs and make choices according to their own preferences (need satisfaction), and contexts where their rejection or refusal of things, people or experiences can be accepted (simple negation). Once these are being reliably communicated, intervention could then be aimed at increasing opportunities for communication and extending the episodes. This could be achieved by developing skills of positive interaction, like turn-taking and attending to other people's communication.

In addition to individual intervention programmes, there are a number of general points that can be made, based on what we have learnt about the development of early communication, in relation to promoting communication in people with profound and multiple disabilities (Goldbart et al, 1994):

◆ It is necessary to provide a wide range of opportunities for engaging with objects, so as to promote the development of object-related schemes.
◆ It is necessary to provide responsive and supportive interactions with people, so as to promote early interaction skills.
◆ It is necessary to provide opportunities for the individual to affect their environment, so as to promote the development of intentionality.

◆ It is necessary to be sensitive to the point when intention has been acquired, so as to provide the consistent feedback required for the development of intentional communication.

◆ It is necessary to provide an environment which is conducive to the person's continued use of communication, so as to encourage the development of communicative functions/intentions, for example:
  – opportunities to request and choose things (need satisfaction)
  – opportunities to reject and refuse things (simple negation)
  – opportunities for turn-taking and for showing and giving things (positive interaction and shared attention).

◆ It is necessary to provide an environment with plenty of joint social activity involving other people, some focused on age-appropriate objects:
  – so as to encourage the acquisition of cognitive roles on which an understanding and later
  – the use of semantic roles (early meanings) is built
  – so that there is plenty for the person to communicate about.

MEASURING CHANGE

Measuring change and monitoring outcomes of intervention

Change with this client group is likely to be small, but, as stated in the introduction to this chapter, a small change to the communication skills of a person with multiple disabilities has the potential to change their whole lives. Because of the subtlety of change, it is vital to have clear ways of measuring this from the outset of therapy. In order to do this, goals need to be set in a way that allows a clinician and carer to see whether that goal has been wholly or partially achieved. The goals also need to be small enough and specific enough to show the change that has taken place. For example, it may be valid for a clinician to work on improving a client's attention skills, but a goal that states its aim as 'to improve attention skills' will be difficult to measure and monitor. It is also a goal that is likely to be repeated frequently through a client's life, and the result could be the appearance that the therapy never progresses. However, a goal that states its aim is 'to maintain attention for five minutes during a named activity' is easy to measure and therefore to monitor change. It is also more likely to be achieved because it is specific and hopefully achievable.

In the current climate of clinical governance, it is essential that we find ways of measuring outcomes with the clients we work with. It is particularly important if the work is going to be long-term. There are several published assessments that contain methods by which clinicians can monitor outcomes. The PCP encourages the clinician to set clear actions in relation to their assessment which can then be reviewed at the end of therapy; ENABLE (Hurst-Brown & Keens, 1990) uses a numerical system to assess both individuals and groups which could be conducive to outcome measurement; and the Individualised Sensory Environment (Bunning, 1997) intervention uses a numerical system to rate prompt levels required for the client to respond. This allows clinicians to present clearly to carers the way in which clients have progressed or maintained their skills.

A format is given in this chapter for clinicians to use in order to measure change and monitor outcomes (adapted from Smith, 1997). The clinician sets three specific, achievable and time-measured goals which are then scored at the end of a period of intervention. A score of 2 is given for totally achieved, 1 if partially achieved and 0 for no achievement of goal. This enables the clinician to score clearly a client's achievement level and to plan for future intervention.

THERAPY AGREEMENT

NAME _____

THERAPIST	KEYWORKER
DATE	REVIEW DATE

OBJECTIVES	COMMENTS	SCORE
1		
2		
3		
	TOTAL	

Total score of 0, 1, or 2 = discharge or re-evaluate therapy/environment,

3 or 4 = change goals which have been achieved,

5 or 6 = discharge or change all goals.

SIGNED

Clinician_____ Carer_____

COMMUNICATION PLAN – WORKED EXAMPLE

NAME ___John___   ATTENDS ___Local Day Service___

PRIMARY MODE OF COMMUNICATION

Eye-pointing & some limited finger-pointing

STRATEGIES FOR COMMUNICATING

Include strategies for indicating 'yes' and 'no'

Some vocalisations – particularly if distressed

SIGNS/WORDS/PHRASES USED

Points at objects (with eyes)
No recognisable signs

PREFERRED ACTIVITIES FOR INTERACTION	DISLIKED ACTIVITIES
Sensory room - bubble tube & switch Music - heavy rock.	Anything involving physical contact. Water.

STRATEGIES TO ASSIST UNDERSTANDING AND EXPRESSION OF LANGUAGE

Offer visual choices - eg, hold two objects in front of John.

SENSORY DIFFICULTIES HEARING	PHYSICAL DIFFICULTIES AFFECTING COMMUNICATION
May be poorer over winter time due to ear infections. SIGHT Needs to wear glasses, but not keen to.	Epilepsy - often less responsive if due to have a fit
OTHER Appears very sensitive to touch.	MEDICATION Anti-convulsant – may cause drowsiness

Therapist ___A Clinician___   Date ___25.5.00___

SITUATION ASSESSMENT RECORD – WORKED EXAMPLE

NAME John		DOB 01.01.70	KEYWORKER Gary

	SITUATION Choosing drinks in coffee bar	**SITUATION** Using bubble tube & switch	**SITUATION**
HOW?	**DATE** 7.6.00	**DATE** 9.6.00	**DATE**
Body language • Eyes • Face • Body • Hands	Eye gaze to object (coffee jar). Eye gaze to keyworker.	Eye gaze to object (tube). Some hitting of switch with hand. Smiling.	
Verbal/vocal	Loud vocalising – grunting while looking at keyworker.	Very quiet humming.	
Signing/gesture	None.	None.	
Physical contact • Moving away from object/person • Moving towards object/person	Paced back and forth between his chair and keyworker.	Face very close to bubble tube.	
Other	Very quickly becoming agitated.	Maintained attention for 20 minutes.	
Why?	Vocalising to gain attention. Eye gaze to request drink.	Potential for intentional use of switch to request tube.	

INTERVENTION PLAN – WORKED EXAMPLE

WHO?
John

WHERE?
Day service

WHEN?
Coffee time

WHICH STAFF?

All staff at coffee bar.

WHAT TO DO

Offer John visual choice of tea, coffee or juice while using Makaton signs.

STAFF RESPONSE

To give John the drink he eye- or finger-points to.
Verbally confirm what John has chosen, eg, 'You want coffee, John'.

EQUIPMENT

Tea, coffee and juice.

OUTCOME FOR CLIENT

For John to learn he can use his eye- and finger-pointing to make choices.

REVIEW DATE
September 00

SIGNED

Therapist _____ A Clinician _____ Date _____ 24.06.00 _____

PROFOUND & MULTIPLE DISABILITIES

SENSORY ASSESSMENT RECORD – WORKED EXAMPLE

NAME John		DOB 01.01.70	KEYWORKER Gary	
HOW?	**SITUATION/STIMULI** electric fan	**SITUATION/STIMULI** warm water in bowl	**SITUATION/STIMULI** rock music	
	DATE 27.6.00	**DATE** 27.6.00	**DATE** 27.6.00	
Body language • Eyes • Face • Body • Hands	Eye gaze to fan. Body very still. Smile.	Eye gaze to carer. Anxious expression. Hands pushed water away	Eye gaze to recorder. Eye gaze to carer. Ear up against recorder.	
Verbal/vocal	Very quiet.	Growling until water taken away.	Humming.	
Signing/gesture	None.	Pushing object away.	None.	
Physical contact • Moving away from object/person • Moving towards object/person	Moved close to fan, but did not touch.	Moved object away. Edged chair back from table.	Moved close to object.	
Other	Hands touching face.	–	–	
Why?	Liked it – was interested.	Disliked.	Liked.	

INTERVENTION PLAN – WORKED EXAMPLE

WHO?

John

WHERE?

Key group.

WHEN?

Morning key group time.

WHICH STAFF?

Support worker.

WHAT TO DO

Place fan or music linked to a switch just out of John's reach. Turn on for 30 seconds & then switch off.

STAFF RESPONSE

Wait for a signal from John (eye-point, finger-point or touch). Then bring switch to him.

EQUIPMENT

Fan, tape recorder, adaptor and switch.

OUTCOME FOR CLIENT

For John to use eye- or finger-pointing or touch to gain attention, and a switch to control/request an object.

REVIEW DATE

September 00

SIGNED

Therapist _____A Clinician_____ Date _____29.06.00_____

THERAPY AGREEMENT – WORKED EXAMPLE

NAME John

THERAPIST A. Clinician	KEYWORKER Gary
DATE 29.06.00	**REVIEW DATE** 29.09.00

OBJECTIVES	COMMENTS	SCORE
1 For John to be able to use finger- or eye-pointing to make a choice between tea, coffee and juice.		
2 For John to use eye- or finger-pointing or touch to gain attention.		
3 For John to use a switch to control/request an object.		
	TOTAL	

Total score of 0, 1, or 2 = discharge or re-evaluate therapy/environment,

3 or 4 = change goals which have been achieved,

5 or 6 = discharge or change all goals.

SIGNED

Clinician A Clinician   Carer G Carer

Chapter 5: Social Skills

INTRODUCTION

We are all social beings, regardless of culture, class, status or intellect. We all have social goals: to make friends, to persuade or influence someone, to extract or give information, to express feelings, etc. These goals are desired because they provide outlets for basic needs – affiliation, achievement and so on. Many adults lack the skills that are important for success in social interactions, and in particular people with learning disabilities often experience difficulties in this area, leading sometimes to isolation, frustration and prejudice. People with learning disabilities also often have communication difficulties that affect their ability to interact in groups, and this in turn has an effect on their quality of life. Speech and language clinicians have an important role to play in social skills training, as this is one way in which clients can be helped to learn the necessary skills in order to communicate more effectively in a variety of settings, thus having a profound effect on their quality of life.

In this chapter, social skills and social skills training will be considered. A definition and explanation of what is meant by the term 'social skills' will be given; a brief description of how social skills develop; what the possible causes are of social skills difficulties or social inadequacy; how to assess social skills; how to plan and carry out social skills training, including the importance of self awareness and some practicalities of running and evaluating social skills therapy.

WHAT ARE SOCIAL SKILLS?

Communication is complicated and as Rustin and Kuhr (1989) say, 'Many processes are involved and there is no unitary measure or single theory of communication skill/social skill that would encompass all aspects of social communicative behaviour.' But what is meant by social skills? It is probably best explained by considering what we mean by social inadequacy or social skill difficulties. As Trower *et al* (1978) say, 'A person can be regarded as socially inadequate if he is unable to affect the behaviour and feelings of others in the way that he intends and society accepts. Such a person will appear annoying, unforthcoming, uninteresting, cold, destructive, bad-tempered, isolated or inept, and will be generally unrewarding to others.' These impressions, and their opposites, are conveyed to others by the way in which people use the 'elements' of behaviour, or social communication skills, and these can be grouped into *NON-VERBAL* and *VERBAL BEHAVIOUR* and will be described in the next section of this chapter. The person who has social skills difficulties will be bad at using these skills and at understanding other people's use of them. Spence (1977) defines social skills as 'Those components of social behaviour which are necessary to ensure that individuals achieve their desired outcome from a social interaction . . . or as appropriate social behaviour within a particular social situation.'

Social skills can therefore be seen as the ability to communicate appropriately and effectively. Communication needs to be appropriate not only to the situation but also to age, sex, race, status, etc, and communication needs to be effective in that people communicate what they wanted to communicate.

Non-verbal behaviour

'Non-verbal communication is unavoidable in the presence of other people . . . a person may decide not to speak, or be unable to communicate verbally, but he still gives messages about himself to others through his face and body' (Wilkinson and Canter, 1982). Non-verbal behaviours have various functions. They can replace words, repeat what is spoken, emphasise a verbal message – especially the emotional type – regulate interaction, or contradict what is being said, revealing a true feeling. People are usually much less aware of their non-verbal communication than of the verbal content of their speech, and similarly non-verbal messages are also often received unconsciously. People form impressions of others based on their non-verbal behaviour, sometimes without knowing or identifying what it is about the person that gives rise to the belief that they are arrogant, friendly, shy, irritating, etc. Individuals are more likely to 'believe' non-verbal behaviour if it contradicts the verbal content. For example, if someone says they are happy but their body language 'says' they are unhappy, the non-verbal behaviour will be taken as the truth by the majority of people.

Non-verbal behaviour can be described in terms of the following skills, and these can be subdivided into body language and paralinguistic skills.

Body language is the way we use our bodies to communicate feelings, personality, social roles, likes and dislikes. During social interaction every part of our body is active; however, certain parts of our body convey more information than others, and do so in distinctive ways:

1   *Eye contact.* The main functions of eye contact are to indicate that we are attending to others, and to watch non-verbal signals from others. In addition, the amount and type of eye contact indicates interpersonal attitudes. Eye contact is closely coordinated with speech and serves to emphasise, provide feedback and attention, and manage speaking turns. For example, a period of eye contact usually starts a conversation during which the speaker may look away a good deal while the listener looks at the speaker. The speaker will then look at the listener, both to check that he is attending and to signify his turn to speak. Eye contact also expresses emotions and attitudes. A strong gaze can indicate dominance or aggression, and a person with little eye contact may indicate shyness or unhappiness. It is also a common means of expressing affiliation and intimacy.

2   *Facial expression.* The face is a specialised communication area which is used by animals to express their emotional state and their intentions towards other animals. In humans the face is more controlled, but it also communicates the

main emotions and provides a rapid and continuous commentary on speech, for example, by raising the eyebrows. Smiling and head nods also indicate agreement or willingness for the other person to continue speaking, and act as reinforcers. Information about personality and identity is also conveyed, for example, by typical and idiosyncratic expressions and by grooming. Facial expression is one of the most informative aspects of body language. The face can respond instantaneously and is the most effective way to provide feedback to another person, as feelings are often reflected in the face even when we want to disguise them.

3   *Gesture.* Hand gestures have been found to be second in importance to facial expression as a means of non-verbal communication (Argyle, 1969, cited by Wilkinson & Canter, 1982). The hands communicate by illustration of the object of discussion, by pointing and by sign language. Gestures can be used without words, eg, waving, and can be used to reinforce the verbal message, eg, by shaking a fist when angry or outlining the shape of something while describing it. The hands also indicate the level of arousal and anxiety, and give information about personality, feelings and attitude towards self through touching of others and self-touching. For example, scratching the face or picking at clothes may indicate anxiety or impatience, or may just be an idiosyncratic habit.

4   *Distance.* People communicate their like and dislike of others by how close they sit and stand to one another. Status is also signalled by distance and by using space symbolically, like sitting at the head of the table. Human beings also establish territory in the same way as animals, though by different methods. They also control the behaviour of others by changing the spatial arrangement and distance, for example by the position of a desk, or by moving closer or further away during conversations. There are also important individual differences, some people needing more personal space than others. Important factors appear to be culture, height – for example a tall person may need to stand further away from a short person to gain comfortable eye-contact – and social conventions – for example it is usually more acceptable to stand closer to work colleagues at a party than at the office.

5   *Touch.* This is the earliest form of communication used by infants and probably, for this reason, is a powerful signal later in life to indicate sexual, affiliative or aggressive attitudes. Touch can be used to communicate warmth, caring, love and affection, as well as to indicate emotional states such as fear, distress and exuberance. Touch is also used in a more ritualised way as a part of greetings and farewells, and may or may not have any emotional

significance in such situations, depending on the relationship of those people involved. Bodily contact is also controlled by elaborate social and

cultural rules: physical contact between adults, for example, is less common in Britain than in some other countries.

6 *Fidgeting.* People communicate their level of anxiety, arousal or boredom through the use of fidgeting. Most fidgeting is done with the hands but the feet can also convey information about the person's level of arousal.

7 *Posture.* Bodily posture varies mainly along the tense-relaxed continuum and usually indicates such. The positio the body and limbs reflects a person's attitude and feeling himself and his relationship to others. It can reveal warmt.., congruence with others, and status and power in relation to the other. A relaxed posture, for example, may be used by the higher status person during a social interaction to signal his status. Posture also changes depending on whether you like or dislike the other person. Leaning towards a person may indicate positive feelings, whereas turning away with a more closed posture (eg arms crossed) may indicate negative feelings. Posture also reflects a person's emotional state: for example, anger may be conveyed through a tense and rigid posture, and depression may be seen in a 'hunched' posture. Individuals also have their own characteristic styles of posture, which in turn reflect their own personalities and self-image.

8 *Personal appearance.* This is used primarily to send messages about ourselves, and not only affects our self-image but also our behaviour and the behaviour of those around us. Styles of dress and hair, cosmetics and badges all convey information about social status, occupation and personality, and constitute one of the main forms of self-presentation. Appearance also signals social attitudes, like sexual availability and rebelliousness, and is often a good indication of someone's emotional state. Personal appearance also usually provides a basis for first and sometimes long-lasting impressions.

Paralinguistic skills or vocal cues are concerned not with the content of speech, but with the way in which the words are spoken. They include:

1 Volume
2 Rate or speed
3 Clarity
4 Intonation
5 Fluency

They can significantly affect the meaning of what is said and therefore how it is received. The same sentence can have very different meanings by altering, for example, the intonation, speed and volume. The words 'I love you' can be said lovingly, teasingly, sarcastically or cruelly, meaning that the words themselves can be less important than the message conveyed. Paralinguistic skills are also indicators of emotional state, although this is very dependent on the individual as people express the same emotion in different ways. However, people who are anxious tend to speak more slowly, are more dysfluent and repetitious, while anger is usually expressed by a high-pitched, strong, loud voice. As with body language, people form judgements of others based on their paralinguistic skills. For example, people with varied intonation are likely to be seen as dynamic and extroverted, whereas those with a slow rate of speech and flat intonation are seen as sluggish, cold and withdrawn (Addington, 1968, cited by Wilkinson & Canter, 1982).

Non-verbal behaviour has to be seen as the basis or foundation on which all other social skills are built. These non-verbal elements are rarely used in isolation and the meaning conveyed is usually a result of a combination of non-verbal cues together with the verbal behaviour and the situation or context the person is in. The importance of good non-verbal behaviour also cannot be under-rated in terms of affecting someone's ability to not only express themselves successfully, but also be listened to and taken seriously. People are greatly affected by the non-verbal behaviour of others, quickly forming opinions based on, for example, their appearance, facial expression and tone of voice. And individuals have their own constructs which are used to form these 'opinions', meaning that the nose stud, the middle-class accent, the leather trousers, the fast speaker, will affect different people in different ways. Equally, everyone uses their non-verbal behaviour consciously, as well as unconsciously, to communicate individuality, or confidence, or feelings, etc. If natural body language and paralinguistic skills are altered for a particular situation, it is interesting to note the effects this has on someone's ability to communicate effectively and feel confident about themselves. For example, imagine going to work dressed in something very uncharacteristic and wearing no makeup (or lots of makeup). Our ability to get out of the car might be affected as well the ability to communicate to colleagues or clients!

The implications and importance of these skills to the adult with a learning disability is obvious, and the role we have in improving these skills cannot be underrated.

Aren't you coming into work today?

Verbal behaviour

'Speech is used for a variety of purposes, for example to communicate ideas, to describe feelings, to reason and argue' (Wilkinson & Canter, 1982). The words people use depend on a number of factors, including the situation they are in, their role in that situation, the topic of conversation and what they are trying to achieve.

Situations vary from intimate, informal ones to more formal ones, and vary in terms of the range and amount of speech acceptable in those situations and the role the person is in. In addition, each person brings their own style and personality into their verbal behaviour in terms of how much they speak, or the characteristic phrases they use. Similarly, the topic or content of speech varies from highly personal to impersonal, and from concrete, as in giving directions, to abstract, as in discussing political views. It can be about 'internal' matters, such as feelings, opinions and thoughts, or about 'external' matters, such as the layout of the office.

The main form of verbal behaviour is conversation, although the form the conversation takes varies significantly depending on the factors already mentioned. As Spence (1977) states: 'It is important for all individuals to be able to cope adequately at a very basic level of conversation,' and if they have difficulty in this area they are likely to find it hard to make friends or deal with a number of everyday situations. Verbal behaviour can be broken down into a number of processes which are described below. It is important to remember, however, that conversation does not consist of speech alone; but includes the use of non-verbal behaviour already described, and a person's non-verbal behaviour has an effect on their verbal behaviour and their ability to hold a conversation effectively.

1 *Listening.* Listening is an essential part of conversation and is important not only in understanding what is being said, but also in communicating interest and feelings about what is being said. It is the way in which feedback is given to the speaker who needs to know if they are being understood or accepted, and provides them with the necessary reinforcement for them to continue the conversation. Non-verbal skills are particularly important in listening: appropriate eye-contact, facial expression and posture all go together to indicate to the speaker that they are being listened to. Verbal aspects of listening include sounds or isolated words of agreement and encouragement, or a comment on what the person is expressing, eg, 'That sounds good', or 'I'm sorry, how awful'.

2 *Opening a conversation.* There are a number of different ways of starting a conversation and these vary according to the situation and the relationship of those people involved. Conversations often start with general statements of fact, followed by more specific details. Generally, conversations are started by:
    (a) Asking a question or requesting something, eg, 'Do you know what time it is?'
    (b) Comments about the environment, eg, 'You're very busy today.' 'It's hot today.'
    (c) Greetings, eg, 'Hello, how are you?'

(d) Exchanging information, eg, 'Hello, I'm Alex. I've just moved in next door.'

(e) Personal questions or remarks, eg, 'I like your dress.' 'You look happy today.'

3 *Maintaining a conversation.* How the conversation continues is obviously dependent to a large extent on how it was started; however, there are a number of skills that need to be learnt and used if a conversation is to be maintained successfully:

(a) Taking turns. The ability to take turns appropriately in a conversation is not a simple case of speaking alternately. It involves paying careful attention to the non-verbal behaviour of the other person as they will signal that they are ready to hand over the conversation by an increase in eye contact and inflection of voice as well as by the content, eg, by asking a question. The listener may also indicate that they wish to speak by altering their eye contact, facial expression and posture, and in this way the speaker and listener take turns. As Wilkinson and Canter (1982) state, 'In any satisfying conversation taking turns operates by mutual agreement but may not involve all parties making equal contributions. By careful timing, constant interruptions and prolonged silences are avoided.'

(b) Asking questions. This is used quite frequently at the beginning of a conversational sequence before the speaker and listener settle on a topic of mutual interest. Questions are also used to show that the speaker is being listened to, eg, 'Why did you feel upset?' and to explore a topic further, eg, 'That's really interesting. What happened after that?' They are also used to change the subject within a conversation, although this needs to be done after a suitable pause, eg, 'Talking of children reminds me I need a baby-sitter at the week-end. Would you be able to do it for me?'

(c) Answering questions. This involves listening to the other person and then answering the question appropriately.

(d) Relevance. 'In order to keep a conversation going and flowing smoothly, it is necessary to respond appropriately to the theme of the conversation by imparting some further information, disclosing feelings or asking a relevant question.' (Wilkinson & Canter, 1982)

Relevance therefore underpins most of the other skills in maintaining a conversation, as without it the conversation is almost definitely going to come to an end sooner rather than later!

(e) Repair. This is the ability to correct someone if they have misheard or misunderstood something, eg, 'No, I didn't say Mrs Smith died; I said my fish died.' Sometimes this is a straightforward correction of a sentence misheard, but sometimes it is a case of interrupting a person who has misunderstood and then correcting them. This is obviously much more difficult and probably something that everyone has struggled with at times.

3   *Ending a conversation.* The ability to end a conversation appropriately not only involves good verbal behaviour, eg, 'I must be going now', but also good non-verbal behaviour, eg, withdrawing eye contact and shifting your body posture.

As stated earlier, it is important to remember that a conversation cannot consist of verbal behaviour alone, but is dependent on good non-verbal behaviour as well. A person's non-verbal behaviour will therefore affect their verbal behaviour and their ability to hold a conversation successfully.

As well as considering the elements of social skills, ie, the non-verbal and verbal behaviour, the way people use these skills in order to be assertive needs to be considered. This is often an area of need for people with learning disabilities and, as with the skills already described in this chapter, is an area where the speech and language clinician can have an extremely important role to play.

Assertive behaviour

Assertive behaviour has been defined as 'behaviour which enables a person to act in his own interests, stand up for himself without due anxiety, and to express his rights without denying the rights of others' (Alberti & Emmons, 1974, cited by Wilkinson & Canter, 1982). Another definition of assertiveness is 'The ability to find a compromise where conflict exists' (Holland & Ward, 1990). Assertiveness can also be seen as self-expression, which is similar to the definition given by Wolpe (1969) who refers to assertion as 'the proper expression of any emotion other than anxiety towards another person' (cited by Wilkinson & Canter, 1982). It includes the ability to communicate feelings to others, to express friendship and affection, annoyance and anger, joy and pleasure, grief and sadness, and to both give and accept praise and criticism. If a person is unassertive, it means that he denies his needs and fails to express his feelings. He may have difficulty in saying 'no' to an unreasonable request, in asking someone to do something for him, in defending himself against accusation, in telling someone how he feels about them or something that is happening to him. A great number of people who have learning disabilities and who have lived in institutions have learnt to be unassertive because that is what the environment 'demanded' of them. As more people move into the community, assertiveness becomes more and more of a need in their new way of life.

There are many misconceptions about being assertive. Common responses to the question 'What does being assertive mean?' include: 'Getting my own way'; 'Winning all my arguments'; 'Speaking louder and faster than the other person'; 'Always having an answer'; 'Being able to stand up to anyone'. In fact, all these definitions describe aggressive behaviour rather than assertive behaviour, and being assertive does not mean being aggressive. Aggression may be some individuals' response in some situations where they find that they need to stand up for themselves or make their needs known, but the aggressive person, like the passive person, needs to learn how to be assertive.

There are many situations in which assertive behaviour would be appropriate. The following are examples of just a few of the situations in which many people report having difficulty, and which can be included in a social skills training programme. It is important to remember that assertive behaviour includes the use of non-verbal and verbal behaviour. A person's ability to be assertive, and to learn to be assertive, is dependent on their ability to use their body language, paralinguistic skills and conversational skills appropriately.

1 *Expressing feelings.* This can mean expressing negative feelings such as, 'I don't like that', or 'That hurts', as well as expressing positive feelings such as, 'I love you', and 'You make me feel happy'.

2 *Standing up for yourself.* This is relevant in a situation where someone has been cheated of something that is rightfully theirs, eg, 'I asked for six oranges and you only gave me five', or where someone's identity or beliefs are being belittled.

3 *Making suggestions.* It is important to be direct and positive, making the message as clear as possible. This could include asking someone out on a date or making a suggestion in a larger group of friends.

4 *Refusing.* How someone refuses something depends on the request made of them. For example, if it was a reasonable request, such as a date, the refusal needs to be accompanied by an excuse, eg, 'I'm sorry, I can't go out tonight as I've already arranged to go to the cinema with Sally.' If the request is unreasonable, an acknowledgement of the person's needs, accompanied by a definite 'no' without an excuse or a justifying account is necessary, eg, 'I realise you don't want me to go out tonight, but I'm going anyway'. If the person persists, it is important to point this out, eg, 'I've said no, don't go on about it.'

5 *Disagreeing.* It is important again to be clear and positive and where appropriate to give a reason, eg, 'I don't think we should smoke in here as we could get the sack if we're caught.'

6 *Complaining.* This is relevant in a situation where someone feels they have been cheated or wronged, eg, 'I bought this iron yesterday and it doesn't work' , or 'You didn't tell me that my sister phoned yesterday and needed me to phone her back urgently.' As with standing up for yourself, it is appropriate to do this in a firm and direct way without apologising.

7 *Apologising.* Being able to apologise is very necessary as everyone makes mistakes. If possible, it is best to make the approach first and to be clear and direct, and then to make good the situation, eg, 'I'm so sorry, I forgot all about you coming round last night and I went out. Would you like to come round tonight?'

8   *Requesting explanations.* This often includes the ability to interrupt appropriately and then ask someone to explain something again. This is often best done with an initial apology and then a clear and direct request, eg, 'I'm sorry, I don't understand exactly what you're saying. Are you telling me I can't see you again?'

Having described non-verbal, verbal and assertive behaviour, it is relevant to consider how these skills develop and to explore the possible causes of social skill difficulties, or 'social inadequacy'.

THE DEVELOPMENT OF SOCIAL SKILLS

In this section of the chapter, the acquisition of social skills will be considered, and why it is that some people fail to acquire them. When considering the adult with a learning disability, it is important to remember that a number of the factors described will have been and may still be relevant in their acquisition of social skills. It would obviously be necessary to be aware of these only if they were having an impact on the individual's everyday life, and more specifically on their ability to learn more appropriate social skills.

Trower *et al* (1978) state that 'Skills are acquired through various forms of learning, such as imitation, reinforcement and instruction, and through exposure to a wide range of environmental opportunities, and to skilled models such as parents, siblings, relatives, peers and others.' It would follow that failure to learn them would occur through a lack of either skilled models or social opportunities, although in practice it is not possible to separate these two influences.

Parents

The earliest environment and the first 'models' available to an infant are the parents, and studies have shown that there is a link between the social competence of parents and their children (Trower *et al*, 1978). As well as providing models for their children, parents instruct them in social behaviour, reinforcing appropriate and discouraging inappropriate behaviour. Instructions to the child may be quite explicit, showing that the parents have a good understanding of appropriate social behaviour. For example, commands such as, 'Look at me when I'm talking to you', 'Don't interrupt', 'Say hello' are all specific attempts to help the child learn appropriate-looking, turn-taking and greeting behaviours. As Trower *et al* (1978) say, 'It is probable that socially unskilled parents will be less accurate in their perceptions of what is appropriate, and therefore less likely to instigate and reinforce skilled responses in their children.'

Siblings

Most children are brought up in families with siblings, and brothers and sisters are an important part of a child's learning environment, in terms of particular modelling and environmental opportunities. However, these are affected by the child's position in the family, the age gap between siblings, and their sex.

Peers

In later childhood and adolescence, peers become more important as more time is spent with them. Studies have shown that children's groups have norms of their own to which children learn to conform, and that children use social techniques such as imitation to gain admission to groups (Trower *et al*, 1978). Peer groups provide models for imitation and opportunities for learning to influence others, etc, but little is known about whether behaviour established in earlier childhood is changed or reinforced by these experiences.

Other factors which contribute to the development of social skills include attitudes to the environment, deprivation, and cognitive abilities.

Attitudes to the environment

A number of writers have been interested in attitudes to the environment in relation to competence. Studies have shown that people who are socially unskilled are less likely to be able to control and manage the situations they are in (Trower *et al*, 1978). Feelings of powerlessness to control the environment, and experience of situations in which the individual has been unskilled, have been found to be significant factors in some socially unskilled people. The implications for adults with a learning disability are obvious. They are often treated as people with 'needs' as opposed to 'strengths', leading them to a belief that they are possibly 'incompetent'; they are often not given the opportunity to control their own environments, leading them to a possible state of 'learned helplessness'.

Effects of deprivation

There have been many studies into what happens to children who are brought up under conditions of deprivation, such as those in institutions, in broken homes or in families with disrupted relationships. Rutter (1972, cited by Trower *et al*, 1978) has concluded that 'Privation or poverty of stimulation, such as found in child-care institutions . . . can have negative consequences for cognitive development.' Deprivation involving family relationships, however, seems to have negative consequences for emotional and behavioural adjustment, and has a negligible effect on cognitive development. Other factors mentioned as being relevant and which are particularly pertinent to a person in an institution are the opportunities to develop attachments to other adults and the length of separations.

Cognitive abilities

'The social skills model requires cognitive abilities for processing information, for making inferences about the consequences of courses of action, for taking the role of the other person, and so on.' (Trower *et al*, 1978.) However, there is some disagreement as to at what age these abilities develop. Piaget (1956, cited by Trower *et al*, 1978) claimed that children were unable to make logical inferences until the age of seven, and yet Bryant (1974, cited by Trower *et al*, 1978) demonstrated these skills in children of three and four. Piaget also claimed that children were 'egocentric' under the age of seven and were unable to perceive the world from another person's point of view – a skill that is particularly relevant to social skills – until the age of nine. However, Borke (1975, cited by Trower *et al*, 1978) demonstrated that children as young as three could succeed on perceptual role-taking tasks, provided the task is made age-appropriate.

Conclusion

Adults with a learning disability may be at a disadvantage when considering the acquisition of social skills. They may have had an upbringing where they learned to be 'helpless' or 'incompetent', or where there were inadequate models. They may be cognitively at a level where it is difficult for them to acquire certain social skills. They may also be living in an environment that does not encourage or promote appropriate social skills, either due to inadequate models or deprivation. These factors all have a profound effect on their ability to learn appropriate social behaviour. Assessment, is therefore, an important first step in establishing whether it is appropriate to include someone in a social skills training programme.

ASSESSMENT OF SOCIAL SKILLS

Rustin and Kuhr (1989) state that 'The goal of assessment is to measure social skills competence in order to define changes required in the client's social interaction.' There are many ways of assessing social skills, but only some are relevant to this client group.

The interview is the traditional method of assessing social skills, and assumes that clients are potentially the richest source of information about themselves. When assessing an adult with a learning disability, the interview is more of an opportunity to observe the person interacting on a one-to-one basis and to give the person 'the opportunity to express the aspects of themselves which they perceive to be of most importance' (Rinaldi, 1992). It is also a valuable source of information about their self-awareness and awareness of others around them. *Talkabout* (Kelly, 1996) and the Social Use of Language Programme (SULP) (Rinaldi, 1992) both include a short client interview as part of the initial assessment procedure. In addition, *Talkabout* includes a self-assessment rating scale which enables clients to rate themselves on certain skills using 'smiley faces', and enables the therapist to assess how much awareness they have of their communication skills.

Rating scales are an extremely useful measure of change. Information can be obtained about the clients' behaviour by observing them in actual social interactions in their everyday environment, or in staged interactions or role play, and this information can be transferred on to a rating scale. Rating scales use either numbers or descriptions to rate each skill, and some use a combination of both.

The SULP includes several rating charts designed to be completed either from structured observation over a period of time and in different social contexts, or from the client's self-assessment. Rinaldi (1992) uses a four-point rating scale (0–3), where 0 = appropriate or 'no difficulty' and 3 = inappropriate or 'very difficult'. She also uses descriptions. For example, in the 'Communication Skills Rating Chart', the rating 1 for 'rate of speech' is described as 'fast but not difficult to follow' and 2 is 'too fast, difficult to follow'. In the other two rating charts, Rinaldi uses one description for each rating, for example 0 = 'no difficulty'.

The Personal Communication Plan (PCP) (see end of book) has a social skills section which assesses each skill on a five-point rating scale. Each number has a description, and results are transferred to a pictorial summary in order to identify quickly the areas of strength and need. This visual representation is also extremely useful for clients to help them understand their own communication skills.

Assessment of self-awareness

Good self-awareness is undoubtedly an asset to the client in social skills training, but how much should it be part of the assessment and therapy itself? Rustin and Kuhr (1989) emphasise the importance of self-awareness and self-monitoring by saying 'Clients need to have a better understanding of their behaviour ... If clients are trained in self-monitoring, self-reinforcement and other self-regulation procedures, they will be better able to accomplish the complex underlying rules of appropriate interaction.'

In SULP, self/other-awareness is seen as an important and integral part of therapy and is worked on alongside the interactive process of communication. The self/other-awareness exercises are graded according to degree of difficulty, starting with physical attributes, interests, strengths and weaknesses in Part One and moving on later to feelings, opinions and friendships in Part Two. In *Talkabout*, self- and other-awareness are seen to be starting points for therapy and prerequisites for success. The author found, through evaluating numerous social skills groups with young adults with learning disabilities, that the clients' success was directly related to their awareness of their communication strengths and needs. That is, clients with a poor awareness of their needs did not do as well in therapy as those clients who had good awareness. Success in improving clients' awareness of their communication strengths and needs was also found to be directly related to their self- and other-awareness. That is, clients with poor self- and other-awareness did not do as well at improving their awareness of their communication as did those clients who had a good basic awareness of themselves.

Conclusion

Assessment of social skills is therefore not necessarily a complicated issue. The most important part of the initial assessment is to ascertain whether the person with the learning disability is able to succeed in a social skills group. It is not enough to know that a person, or group of people, has difficulties with using appropriate eye contact and body posture, and to plan a group working on these skills. We need to know if they have a good awareness of themselves and other people, and then if they have a good understanding of their communication needs. The initial assessment in *Talkabout* provides clinicians with a quick method of assessing how much self- and other-awareness a client has, and gives them the ability to group clients according to their skills. The most effective way to improve a person's understanding of their communication skills is to work as a group on enabling the clients to assess their own communication. Level two of *Talkabout* is aimed specifically at this, and from there, clients can progress to improving their skills.

INTERVENTION – SOCIAL SKILLS TRAINING

Social skills training evolved to 'meet the needs of those who lacked adequate models and learning opportunities to function more appropriately within society' (Rustin and Kuhr, 1989). It therefore aims to 'increase the client's repertoire and awareness of social situations and offer him a wide variety of behavioural alternatives from which he is free to choose as, and when, he so wishes' (Wilkinson & Canter, 1982). Social skills training is based on the idea that skills are learned and therefore can be taught to those who lack them. However, as has been seen in this chapter, it is not as simple as that with a person who has a learning disability, and the training package offered must be appropriate to that person's strengths and needs.

It is essential to structure social skills therapy so that certain skills are taught first, with more complex ones taught last. Rustin and Kuhr (1989) describe 'foundation skills', which include among others non-verbal skills, as the 'basic skills and . . . fundamental to the development of more sophisticated social interactions . . . clients need to be well-versed in these skills before they can proceed to more complicated skills.' They go on to say that in some cases, for example in severe learning disability, social skills training may be entirely directed at this basic level. They describe 'interaction skills', which include verbal skills, as 'more complex than foundation skills as they require the combination of two or more skills being in operation at the same time'. Rustin and Kuhr progress to 'affective skills' and then 'cognitive skills'.

A hierarchical approach is obviously necessary if social skills training is to be effective and this structure, with the inclusion of self awareness and awareness of communication, is reflected in *Talkabout* (see Figure 5.1).

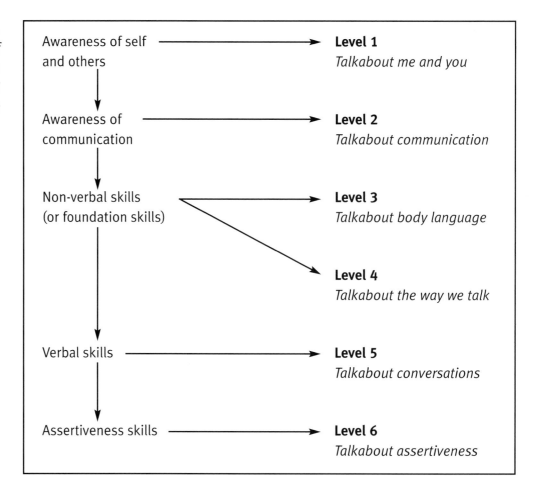

Figure 5.1
*The Hierarchy of
Social Skills
Training and
Talkabout*

Awareness of self
and others

Level 1
Talkabout me and you

Awareness of
communication

Level 2
Talkabout communication

Non-verbal skills
(or foundation skills)

Level 3
Talkabout body language

Level 4
Talkabout the way we talk

Verbal skills

Level 5
Talkabout conversations

Assertiveness skills

Level 6
Talkabout assertiveness

Each level in *Talkabout* has therapy aims, a suggested process for therapy, and worksheets to cover all topics. The main aims of *Talkabout* are that:

1 It is functional, relevant and fun.
2 Clients at all times assess and evaluate their own skills, thus ensuring ownership of the work by the individual.
3 It is easy to evaluate and show success.
4 It is flexible so that clients with different needs can start and end at different parts of the package.
5 It is possible to use the package without a speech and language clinician present, thus encouraging staff development generally.

The SULP also uses a hierarchical approach to training. It is divided into three parts and enables the clinician to progress through the stages as appropriate. In Part One clients become aware of and practise using the skills of the 'interactive process of communication' in game activities and simple conversation tasks, and work on basic self- and other-awareness. In Part Two clients apply the skills they learnt in part one to a range of social contexts which they practise in the classroom, and work on further self- and other-awareness. In Part Three the clients practise 'assignments' in real-life settings.

Improving awareness of self and others

As has been explained earlier in the chapter, the awareness of self and others is a prerequisite to effective social skills training, and therefore, if a person does not have good self- and other-awareness, this is the first stage of social skills training. This means that the clinician needs to help the person with a learning disability build up a good understanding and awareness of who they are, in the context of their everyday life. This includes what they look like, what they are like as a person, who is important to them in their life, their likes and dislikes, and their individual strengths and needs. As with all social skills training, this is best achieved within a group setting, and *Talkabout* gives the clinician a suggested process for therapy, and worksheets for group members to complete and keep to help them build up this picture of themselves.

The suggested process for improving self- and other-awareness is as follows:

Process

Physical appearance: What do we look like?
◆ Group discussions and games to look at how we describe people: eg, describing famous people, people in the group.
◆ Words we use to describe people.
◆ What do I look like?
◆ What does our group look like?
◆ What I have noticed about . . . observing others, including family members or a close friend.
◆ Changing one thing about the way I look.

Personality: What are we like?
◆ Group discussion on what we mean by 'personality'.
◆ What are people like?.. including famous people, people on TV.
◆ What words do we use to describe people? Do any of these words describe me? Do other people agree with me?
◆ How would we describe our best friend? And someone we don't like? Are there certain qualities we look for in a best friend?
◆ 'Labels' that have been given to me and words that have been used to describe me. How do they make you feel? What's the nicest thing someone has said about you?

People in our lives
◆ Group discussion on who are the important people in our lives. Why are they important?
◆ Who is the most important person in my life?

Likes and dislikes
◆ Group discussion on what we like and dislike doing.
◆ What do I like doing? Are there other people in the group who like doing the same things? Why do they like it?

- What do I not like doing?
- Group discussion on similarities within the group. Devise a group likes/dislikes list.

Strengths and needs: What are we good and not so good at?
- Group discussion on things that we are good at.
- I am good at . . . Collect ideas and devise a group 'circle' of all the skills the group possess.
- My feelings about this week. Group members are encouraged to complete a worksheet on things that they did well and things they did not do so well each day during one week.
- Group discussion on liking ourselves. Is it important? Is it important to not like some things about ourselves?
- Is there one thing I'd like to change about myself? Discussion of realistic versus unrealistic.

Problem-solving
- Brainstorm solutions to one of the group members' problems.
- Possible solutions are written on to a worksheet.
- The first five solutions are written out as a record of 'things to try'.
- The problem-solving process is repeated as many times as necessary in order to demonstrate that 'needs' are sometimes solvable!

Summing up
- Group discussion of what each person has learnt about themselves.
- Each person completes a worksheet on what they can now say about themselves and feeds this back to the group.

Improving awareness of communication

An important part of enabling someone to have a good awareness of their communication is allowing that person to assess themselves and to establish their own 'list' of strengths and needs. Obviously, before someone is able to do this, they need to understand what it is they are assessing. This part of the social skills training programme explores what is involved in communication and enables each group member to assess themselves on each skill. An action plan is then drawn up, based on what they need/want to work on. From this stage of therapy, a person can move on into a social skills group where the focus is on improving specific skills, for example eye contact. This should allow them a better chance of succeeding, because they will not only understand what eye contact is, but will also know that it is something they need to work on.

The suggested process for improving awareness of communication is as follows:

Process

How do we communicate?

◆ Group discussion/brainstorm on ways in which people communicate. Use video or role-plays to observe people talking to each other in different ways.

Body language

◆ Group discussion on what is meant by body language. Use video and/or role-plays to watch people's bodies. Which part of our bodies do we use to communicate with others?

◆ Body language . . . what am I like at it? Discussion of rating scale. What does very good/quite good and so on, mean?

◆ Video group members talking to one another. Each person rates self on scale with help from others in the group and from watching self on video.

The way we talk (paralinguistic skills)

◆ Group discussion on our voices. Do we all sound the same? Use video clips to facilitate five aspects of 'the way we talk'.

◆ How do we talk when we are . . .? Group members act out different emotions and look at what happens to the way they talk.

◆ The way we talk. Discussion of five aspects, and using cartoons/pictures to help, until group members are happy with their meaning.

◆ The way I talk . . . what am I like at it? Using video and role play, group members rate themselves on the worksheet.

Conversations

◆ Group discussion on the differences between a good and bad conversation. Use video clips and/or role play to demonstrate.

◆ A bad conversation =

◆ A good conversation =

◆ Conversation skills . . . what are they?

◆ What am I like at conversations?

Assertiveness

◆ Group discussion on aggression, using video clips/role plays.

◆ What does being aggressive mean?

◆ Group discussion on being passive, using video/role plays.

- What does being passive mean?
- Group discussion on being assertive.
- What does being assertive mean?
- Assertiveness . . . what am I like at it?

Summing up
- Group members transfer all their ratings for each section on to a summary worksheet and identify areas of strength and need.
- Group members complete an action plan of areas that they need/want to work on. This needs to be hierarchical, ie, body language should always precede other skills.

Improving non-verbal skills: body language

Suggested process

What do we mean by body language?
- Group discussion on what happens to people's bodies when they are communicating.
- What is body language?
- Recap on individual strengths and needs.

Eye contact
- Group discussion and exercises to experience poor eye contact. What happens and how does it make us appear?
- Good eye contact . . . what does it mean? How can I improve my eye contact?
- Group activities to help improve and monitor eye contact.

Facial expression
- What are our faces doing when we are talking and what do they tell us?
- Poor facial expression . . . what happens and how do we appear?
- Good facial expression . . . what does it mean? How can I improve it?
- Group activities to help improve and monitor facial expression.

Hand gestures
- Hands . . . why use them? Group discussion.
- Poor hand gesture . . . what happens, etc.
- Good hand gesture . . . what does it mean? How can I improve it?
- Group activities to help improve and monitor gesture.

Distance and touch
- How close can we get to people? Group discussion and exercises.
- Who can we get really close to? Who can we get quite close to? etc.
- When do we touch people and why do we touch people?
- When should we not touch people?

- Distance and touch . . . getting it right . . . and what to do if we get it wrong?
- Group assignments to monitor distance and touch.

Fidgeting
- What happens when we fidget? Why do we fidget?
- How can we improve our fidgeting? Group activities.

Posture
- Observing people's bodies . . . what do they tell us?
- Why is good posture important? How can we improve it? Group activities.

Personal appearance
- Group discussion on the different ways people look . . . what does it tell us about them?
- When do we change our appearance and why?
- What should we remember to do daily, regularly, etc.? Why?
- How can we improve our appearance?

Summary & evaluation
- Reassessment and evaluation.

Improving non-verbal skills: the way we talk

Suggested process

What do we mean by the way we talk?
- What happens to our voices when we feel different emotions?
- Introducing the five aspects and recapping on individual needs.

Volume
- Poor volume. When should we talk loudly/quietly?
- Good volume . . . what does it mean? How can we improve it?
- Group activities to help improve and monitor volume.

Rate
- Poor rate . . . when should we talk quickly/slowly?
- Good rate . . . what does it mean? How can we improve it? Group activities.

Clarity
- Poor clarity . . . when do we tend to mumble?
- What does speaking clearly mean? How can we improve it? Group activities.

Intonation
- Poor intonation . . . how do we feel and appear?
- Good intonation . . . how can we improve it? Group activities.

Fluency
- Poor fluency . . . how do we feel, etc? Stammering versus poor fluency.
- How can we become more fluent? Group activities.

Summary & evaluation
◆ Reassessment and evaluation.

Improving verbal skills

Suggested process

What do we mean by conversations?
◆ Experience and/or watch a bad conversation. What happens?
◆ Experience and/or watch a good conversation. What are the differences?
◆ Conversational skills . . . what are they? Recap on skills.
◆ Why is it important to be good at conversations?
◆ Recap on individual strengths and needs.

Listening
◆ Poor listening . . . what happens? How do we appear?
◆ How can we show we are listening? Watch people listening . . . what do they do?
◆ Good listening . . . what does it mean? How can we improve? Group activities.

Starting a conversation
◆ How not to start a conversation. What happens and how do we appear?
◆ How can we start a conversation? Discuss possible openers.
◆ Good conversation starters . . . what should happen? How can we improve?

Taking turns
◆ Introduce the idea of maintaining a conversation.
◆ How can we keep a conversation going?
◆ Poor turn-taking . . . what happens?
◆ Good turn-taking . . . what does it mean? How can we improve? Group activities.

Asking questions
◆ Asking questions . . . badly! What happens?
◆ Asking questions . . . well! What does it mean? How can we improve? Group activities.

Answering questions
◆ Answering questions . . . badly! What happens?
◆ Answering questions . . . well! What does it mean? How can we improve? Group activities.

Being relevant
◆ What does being relevant mean? Why should we be relevant?
◆ Group activities to help improve and monitor being relevant.

Repairing
◆ What does repairing a conversation mean? Discuss issues such as misunderstanding, correcting, slowing down, explaining. Why is it important?
◆ How can we improve? Group activities.

Ending a conversation
◆ How can we end a conversation?
◆ Good conversation endings. What should happen? What else should we remember? How can we improve? Group activities.

Summary & evaluation
◆ Reassessment and evaluation.

Improving assertive behaviour

As has been stated earlier in the chapter, assertive behaviour is reliant on effective non-verbal and verbal skills. For this reason, assertiveness should only be taught if the clients are sufficiently skilled in these areas to make it an achievable goal.

Suggested process

What do we mean by assertiveness?
◆ Group discussion on different kinds of behaviour. Consider different TV characters.
◆ Introduce idea of a scale from passivity to aggression. Where do we see ourselves most of the time?
◆ Discuss passivity and examples of when we have been passive. What could we have done differently?
◆ Discuss ways to appear less passive and more assertive.
◆ Discuss aggression and examples of when we have shown or seen aggressive behaviour. What could we have done differently?
◆ Discuss ways to appear less aggressive and more assertive.
◆ What can we do to appear more assertive?
◆ Coping with aggression, such as insults. How should we respond?
◆ Recap assertive behaviours that the group are going to look at and individual areas of strength and need.

Expressing feelings
◆ Group discussion on why we should tell people how we feel. How should we do it?
◆ Situations/group activities to practise expressing feeling effectively.

Standing up for yourself
◆ Why should we stand up for ourselves? When is it important and how should we do it?
◆ Situations/group activities to practise.

Making suggestions
◆ Why make suggestions? When is it important and how can we make them?
◆ Situations/group activities to practise.

Refusing
◆ Why should we be able to refuse? When is it important and how can we do it?
◆ Situations/group activities to practise.

Disagreeing

◆ Why should we be able to disagree? When is it important and how can we do it?

◆ Situations/group activities to practise.

Complaining

◆ Why should we be able to complain? When is it important and how can we do it?

◆ Situations/group activities to practise.

Apologising

◆ Why should we be able to apologise? When is it important and how can we do it?

◆ Situations/group activities to practise.

Requesting explanations

◆ Why is it important to ask for explanations? When is it important and how can we do it?

◆ Situations/group activities to practise.

Summary & evaluation

◆ Reassessment and evaluation.

PRACTICALITIES IN SETTING UP AND RUNNING GROUPS

It has been stated earlier in this chapter that the success of a social skills group has a lot to do with the ability of the clinician to assess the clients effectively and structure the therapy appropriately, so that the complexity of the skills is graded. This ensures that clients are not 'set up' to fail by trying to learn complex skills when the necessary foundation skills are not in place. However, there are also practicalities to consider when setting up and running a group, and some of these will be thought about in this section.

Size of the group

The size of the group should ideally be six to eight, not including the group leaders. It is important to remember that a great number of clients find it difficult to communicate and attend in larger groups, and so where this is unavoidable, it may be necessary to consider dividing the group for some of the session. It is also important to have enough people within a group to make role plays and group discussions feasible and interesting. Social skills groups run better with two leaders, especially as there is often a need to model behaviours, work video cameras and facilitate group discussions, sometimes all at the same time! It is also important for carryover, so the

co-leader should ideally be someone from their everyday environment, for example, college or centre. In fact, clinicians would be well advised to refuse to run a social skills group unless they have someone appropriate to run it with.

The group contract

A group contract is often important to set up and agree on prior to a group starting. This can include membership, time, place and duration of group, and rules. For examples, see Kelly (1996) or Hitchings (1992).

Format of the session

The format of the session will vary from time to time, but there are general guidelines which apply to most groups:

1   Group cohesion activity. This is an essential part of the group. It brings the group together and helps them to focus on the other group members and the purpose of the group. The activity should be simple and stress-free, and all members should participate and feel part of the group. An example of this activity might be throwing a ball to someone and asking what their favourite TV programme is.

2   Revision of previous session. In order to ensure cohesion between sessions, it is important to recap on relevant aspects of the previous sessions. It may also be appropriate to recap on the aims and rules of the group and change the session plan if something has occurred that needs attention. This is also the time when home assignments are discussed, if appropriate.

3   Introduction to the session theme. The theme for that session is introduced. This can be done through discussion, brainstorming, playing a game, watching a video, etc.

4   Main activity. This may include modelling of a new skill followed by role play by the clients and feedback, and then replay where necessary. The use of video has been found to be invaluable in enabling the clients to monitor their own skills accurately, and it is also a good record of progress.

5   Summing up. This may include setting home assignments which Rustin and Kuhr (1989) consider to be an important feature of generalisation: '*Homework assignments are carried out in the real world and indicate to the therapist how well clients are able to generalise their newly acquired skills.*'

6   Finishing activity. Each session should end with a group activity to bring the group back together again and to reduce anxiety if the clients have found any of the activities difficult. The activity should therefore be fun, simple and stress free.

The use of worksheets

The use of worksheets is an excellent way to help clients understand and remember the skills that are being taught. The worksheets should be simple and visually pleasing, for example through the use of cartoons. Clients should be encouraged to keep their own worksheets so that they have a visual reminder and cue for the group sessions. This also encourages more ownership of their work.

Evaluation

When evaluating groups throughout a social skills training programme, it is important to evaluate not only the clients' skills but also the sessions and the activities within the session. The following questions need to be considered:

1   The session: How did the session go?
                    What were the problems?
                    What went well?
                    Are there changes that need to be made in future sessions?
2   The activities: Were the activities at an appropriate level?
3   The clients: Did they enjoy the session?
                   Did they learn anything?
                   Are they improving?

Well-structured session notes are the best way to evaluate a session, but at the end of therapy, client improvement needs to be assessed. If rating scales have been used to assess the clients initially, then a re-test gives a clear indication of success. It is also valuable to gain some insight into whether the clients believe they have improved or not and if they have enjoyed the group. *Talkabout* (Kelly, 1996) has several evaluation forms for this purpose.

CONCLUSION

In conclusion, social skills training is an important area of the speech and language clinician's work with adults with a learning disability. However, the success of therapy is often dependent on the ability of the clinician to assess the clients effectively and structure the therapy and groups appropriately. It is important to assess the client's self- and other-awareness and to work on this, when appropriate, prior to moving on to actual social skills training. It is also important to involve the client as much as possible in the assessment and evaluation of their own skills, so that they have a good awareness and understanding of their own communication strengths and needs, and therefore what it is that they need to improve. Therapy also needs to be structured so that the complexity of the skills is graded. This means that non-verbal skills are always taught prior to verbal and assertiveness skills, and clients are never 'set up' to fail by trying to learn complex skills when they do not have the necessary foundation skills.

RESOURCE LIST OF BOOKS FOR GROUP ACTIVITIES

Brandes D & Phillips H, 1979, *Gamesters' Handbook: 140 games for teachers and group leaders,* Hutchinson, London.

Brandes D, 1984, *Gamesters' Handbook Two: another collection of games for teachers and group workers,* Hutchinson, London.

Dynes R, 1990, *Creative Games in Groupwork,* Winslow, Bicester.

Dynes R, 2000, *The Non-Competitive Activity Book,* Winslow, Bicester.

Kirby A (Ed), 1993, *Icebreakers,* Gower Publishing, Aldershot.

Rustin L & Kuhr A, 1989, *Social Skills and the Speech Impaired,* Taylor & Francis, London.

Chapter 6: Dysphagia

INTRODUCTION

Many excellent textbooks have already been written on this specialist subject, and it would obviously be foolish to try to condense all the wisdom and practical advice from these books into one chapter. Instead, we will give a brief explanation of swallowing, an overview of dysphagia and adults with learning disabilities, and some practical guidelines around assessment and intervention. This chapter aims to give clinicians more confidence to accept referrals for people who experience eating and drinking difficulties, and some practical advice on assessment and intervention. However, clinicians should be aware of the importance of ongoing training in this area, and of local policy statements on dysphagia which set out standards for working with clients with dysphagia.

A DEFINITION OF DYSPHAGIA

Dysphagia can be defined as a disorder of swallowing which 'can occur at any point during the passage of the bolus through the oral, pharyngeal, and oesophageal structures. Any difficulty with swallowing that interferes with its safe and comfortable resolution or, overall, with nourishment or control of oral secretions is a symptom of dysphagia' (Prontnicki, 1995).

THE NORMAL SWALLOW

The act of swallowing can be divided into three distinct stages (see Figure 6.1):

1 Oral
2 Pharyngeal
3 Oesophageal.

The oral (feeding) stage

This stage is 'the transfer of material from the mouth to the oropharynx' (Groher, 1997), and the activities of the oral stage are 'preparations for the activation of a swallow, when food and drink are involved' (Langley, 1988). The oral stage is voluntary in the sense that it can be initiated and stopped at will, unlike the other two stages, and this means that if it is impaired, there is greater possibility for therapeutic intervention. The stimulus needed for the oral stage to be completed is usually saliva, and the arousal of appetite produces an increase in the flow of saliva in the mouth and digestive juices in the stomach, which both have a role in preparing for the activation of swallowing. The presence or absence of hunger affects the strength of these responses, and can be aroused by a combination of the thought of food, and the smell and sight of food. At a later stage, the sensation of food on the tongue further stimulates the flow of saliva. The arousal of appetite is something that is sometimes overlooked, and yet is essential if we are to fully address swallowing problems.

The oral stage can be further divided into the *preparatory* and *executive phase.*

Preparatory phase

During this phase, a portion of food is placed somewhere in the oral cavity, where it is chewed and moved around until it has been dispersed, re-collected and reformed into a 'cohesive bolus drenched in saliva' (Langley, 1988). During this stage, the lips are closed and the jaw opened; the tongue and mandible move from side to side and in a rotary fashion, mixing the food with the saliva to form the bolus. The soft palate is lowered to prevent food spilling into the pharynx before the swallow reflex is triggered. Once the bolus is prepared, it is held by the anterior portion of the tongue in a cupped position against the hard palate, the entrance to the larynx is opened and the entrance to the oesophagus is closed.

Executive phase

During the executive phase, 'the lips and jaw are closed with the tongue progressively elevating anteriorly to posteriorly, propelling the bolus through the oral cavity' (Davies, 1999). A groove is created along the midline of the tongue, helping to guide the bolus. When the bolus reaches the base of the tongue and contacts the pillars of fauces, the swallow reflex is activated, the soft palate is raised, which prevents food from being regurgitated via the nasal passage, and respiration ceases. The backwards humping of the tongue, which is performed voluntarily, is the last act of the swallowing sequence to be so controlled, as subsequent activity is controlled by reflex and therefore its course cannot be interrupted voluntarily.

The pharyngeal (swallowing) stage

This stage of swallowing begins with the triggering of the swallow reflex. This reflex is triggered as the bolus comes into contact with the pillars of fauces towards the back of the oral cavity. This stage cannot be voluntarily interrupted and will not take place if the reflex has not been activated. Breathing is halted throughout the pharyngeal stage and resumed at the end of it. During the pharyngeal stage it is essential that there is efficient protection of the airway so that material is not ingested into the lungs, and that the whole sequence is completed rapidly so that breathing can be resumed.

The pharyngeal stage is amazingly complicated for something that lasts less than one second. In summary, however, the pharyngeal stage is as follows: the soft palate is raised and the base of the tongue retracts towards the pharyngeal wall, with the pharyngeal wall contracting towards the base of the tongue. This creates pressure in the pharynx, which helps to propel the bolus into the oesophagus. Elevation of the hyoid bone is initiated, with simultaneous elevation and anterior movement of the larynx. This tucks the larynx under the base of the tongue, helping to prevent material from entering the airway. The larynx then acts as a valve that closes at three levels. The first level of closure is at the true vocal cords, next the false vocal cords close, and then the base of the epiglottis is lowered until it makes contact with the aryepiglotic folds protecting the airway.

The oesophageal stage

During this stage the bolus is moved towards the stomach by peristalsis (a wavelike movement caused by alternate contraction and relaxation of the circular and longitudinal muscles). This stage is reflexive and none of the muscles and structures involved are subject to any form of voluntary control. Gravity assists the progress of the bolus down through the oesophageal tube, and reflex relaxation of the lower sphincter allows entry into the stomach.

Investigation and management of oesophageal stage dysphagia is usually carried out by a gastro-enterologist, and the majority of cases require surgical or medical management.

Figure 6.1
The Normal
Swallow

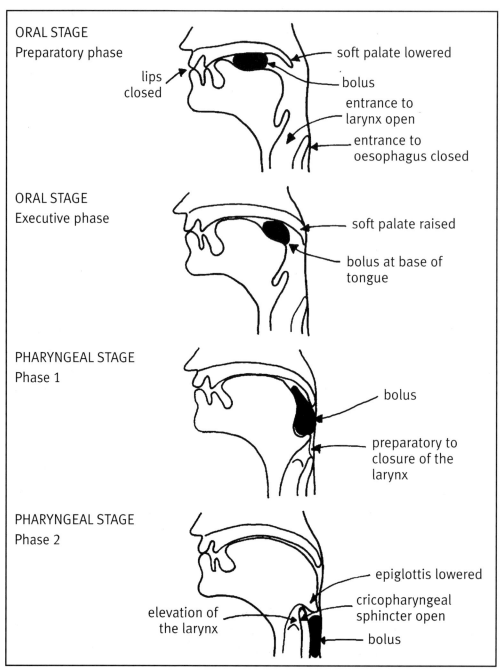

ORAL STAGE
Preparatory phase

lips closed — soft palate lowered — bolus — entrance to larynx open — entrance to oesophagus closed

ORAL STAGE
Executive phase

soft palate raised — bolus at base of tongue

PHARYNGEAL STAGE
Phase 1

bolus — preparatory to closure of the larynx

PHARYNGEAL STAGE
Phase 2

elevation of the larynx — epiglottis lowered — cricopharyngeal sphincter open — bolus

DYSPHAGIA IN ADULTS WITH A LEARNING DISABILITY

According to Hickman (1997) there appears to be some debate among speech and language clinicians around the notion of dysphagia in adults with a learning disability. Some Health Care Trusts make a clear clinical demarcation between the terms 'adults who acquire dysphagia' and 'adults with long-standing problems with eating and drinking'. Some clinicians would therefore feel that adults with a learning disability fall into the latter category and therefore do not present with 'dysphagia proper'.

However, this does not mean that these clients with 'long-standing problems with eating and drinking' can be disregarded just because the problems *are* long-standing ones and have not been acquired recently. Past and present research shows that the incidence of dysphagia in adults with learning disabilities is relatively high. Hickman (1997) cites several research studies, including Sloan (1977) who studied 40 children with cerebral palsy through barium swallows, and found a high proportion of incoordination at an oral and pharyngeal level. However, despite a high percentage having a delayed swallow reflex, they had sufficient laryngeal closure to prevent significant aspiration. Roger *et al* (1994, cited by Hickman, 1997) also found links between mealtime respiratory distress and ALD. Also, McCurley *et al* (1975, cited by Hickman, 1997) discovered a significant link between mortality rates and respiratory infections within this population, and concluded that aspiration is a significant health need for adults with a learning disability. Jenner and Hickman (1995, cited by Hickman, 1997) carried out a survey and comparison of dysphagia in adults with a learning disability in North Warwickshire and North Birmingham. They found an incidence of 36 per cent of clients having dysphagia within the long-stay residential setting and 5.3 per cent in the community. The most prevalent difficulty was in the oral phase (33 per cent and 4.6 per cent).

In addition, Dumble and Tuson (1998) carried out a survey of adults with learning disabilities for eating and drinking difficulties, following staff training and referral from staff. They were able to identify a further 10.2 per cent of clients with dysphagia, making a total of 23.9 per cent, including clients already known to them to have dysphagia.

Prontnicki (1995) states that dysphagia is more common in 'the developmentally disabled population' as there are many 'conditions' commonly associated with dysphagia: 'those causing problems primarily through neuromuscular control, cognitive impairment, interactive difficulties, or anatomic abnormalities'. She concludes by saying that people with learning disabilities 'frequently suffer from dysphagia . . . and nutrition and respiratory status may be compromised by the dysphagia.'

In summary, dysphagia is certainly relatively common in adults with learning disabilities, for whatever reason, whether recently acquired or of a long standing nature. Speech and language clinicians working with this client group therefore need the skills to assess and treat those people who are experiencing dysphagia, and to know when to refer to other professionals for more specialist assessment, such as videofluoroscopy (a radiographic investigation in which a radio-opaque substance – barium – is incorporated into small amounts of food or drink and is photographically recorded and viewed using a video-tape).

ASSESSMENT OF DYSPHAGIA

The most common reasons for referral are:

◆ Episodes of choking
◆ Possible aspiration
◆ Inappropriate rate of eating
◆ Excessive food loss.

However, people are often *not* referred for a swallowing assessment and this may be due to:

◆ Lack of staff awareness or knowledge
◆ Lack of time and staff support at meal times
◆ Lack of awareness that change is possible
◆ Habitual problems, ie, 'he has always coughed.'
◆ Lack of awareness of an individual's limitations.

If this is the case, then it is possibly appropriate to hold some staff training to increase staff awareness, and to encourage staff to refer clients for an assessment of dysphagia as necessary.

Method of assessment

Ideally, this should always be done as part of a team which should always include the client's main carer. It may also be relevant to assess jointly with other professionals, such as physiotherapists, occupational therapists, and dieticians.

The assessment should include some discussion with the carer, observation of the client in their everyday setting, oral examination (if necessary), reading medical notes and some structured observations by staff over a period of time.

Background information

The following information needs to be collected prior to observation of the client, and will give the clinician an idea of the likelihood of dysphagia and the urgency of assessment and intervention:

Is/are there any:

◆ Recent loss of weight?
◆ Evidence of dehydration?
◆ Frequent chest infections?

- Urinary tract infections?
- Coughing and choking at meal/drink times?
- 'Gurgly'-sounding voice after eating/drinking?
- Gasping for breath at mealtimes?
- Change of colour?
- Refusal to eat?
- Behaviour problems around mealtimes?

In addition, the following factors need to be considered and assessed prior to observation:

- *Physical difficulties* – including physical conditions that may be linked to oral skills, positioning, ability to self-feed, etc. Also include dental problems.
- *Sensory problems* – visual and perceptual problems, hearing difficulties, and sensitivity around the mouth.
- *Medication/medical status* – for example, if epileptic, type and frequency of seizures and whether they may have an effect on safety of swallow, or if medication may influence alertness levels. If the person is diabetic, this may affect alertness, anxiety and behaviour around mealtimes, and will also influence any recommendations made regarding consistency and dietary changes. Some medications related to muscle relaxation may have an effect on responsiveness, muscle response and general alertness.
- *Likes and dislikes* – food and drink that the person seems to like and dislike; and whether these have an effect on their swallowing.

Observation of client

The following factors need to be assessed during the observation of the client in their everyday setting:

- *Ability to self-feed,* and if assistance is needed, what kind and how much?
- *Meal/drink observed.* Description of food/drink and the consistency and appearance of it. Also need to know if this is typical, and whether the person would typically eat a wide range.
- *Environment.* What is the environment like? For example, is it noisy? relaxed? rushed? Consider distractions and level of staff support.
- *Positioning.* Consider client positioning, in particular: how upright are they, are they as close to 90 degrees as is realistic? Do they have a foot support? Are they well back in their seat? Are they comfortable and able to use their physical skills to their maximum? Are they able to support themselves? Does the seating inhibit any of the above? Consider also the seating of the keyworker, if appropriate. Are they at eye-level or as close as possible to the client? Are they able to offer support where needed?
- *Communication.* Consider general interaction with the client, for example, if it is at an appropriate level and pace, and if the environment inhibits interaction. Also consider the explanation by the keyworker to the client, for example, the temperature and nature of the food and when it is coming.

- ◆ *Eating.* Observation and description of the following:
  - Lips – what is lip closure like? Can they use their lips to remove food from the spoon? Any evidence of a bite reflex?
  - Tongue – is tongue movement normal? Is the tongue used to move food in the mouth in a normal way, or is there evidence of a suck/swallow pattern or tongue thrust?
  - Chew – is chewing adequate? Is there only up/down chewing, or also side-to-side? Is there a suck/swallow pattern? Is there any pouching of food?
  - Swallow – is there noticeable elevation, and does it occur once, or are there swallow rehearsals or several swallows to every mouthful? Is the swallow audible? Is it delayed? Is it consistent or does it vary, and if it varies, what seems to be affecting it?
  - Coughing/choking – does the client cough following a swallow? How often?
  - Other – include factors such as shortness of breath, change in complexion/ colour, refusal to eat, watery eyes, any tension or anxiety noted, etc.

- ◆ *Drinking.* Observation and description of the following:
  - Lips – for example lip seal on cup.
  - Swallow – as above.
  - Coughing – as above.
  - 'Gurgly' vocalisations.
  - Other – as above.

Effects of oral-stage disability

Langley (1988) p80, describes some manifestations of disability at the oral stage:

- ◆ *Drooling* – may be due to a combination of sensory and motor deficit affecting tongue, lips and face, or to salivary insufficiency or swallowing deficit (see pharyngeal stage).
- ◆ *Inability to clear the mouth of residues* – may be due to sensory deficiency in the oral cavity and/or motor impairment of the tongue.
- ◆ *Loss of taste and smell* – may be due to direct cranial nerve involvement or a side-effect of poor salivary distribution and reduced oral activity. This results in less enjoyment in food and less effective preparation.
- ◆ *(Reappearance of) primitive oral reflexes and tongue thrusting* – may be associated with diminished cortical control.
- ◆ *Impaired jaw-closing, lip-seal or naso-pharyngeal seal* – due to mechanical deficiency or motor impairment of the relevant structures and muscles. Consequences include ineffective biting, interference with swallowing and nasal regurgitation.
- ◆ *Chewing disability* – may be attributed to disordered sensory feedback and/or motor weakness or incoordination and results in limitations of diet.
- ◆ *Inability to manipulate a bolus* – as above (chewing disability).

DYSPHAGIA ASSESSMENT SHEET

NAME _____ DOB _____

ADDRESS _____

KEYWORKER _____ DATE _____

BACKGROUND INFORMATION

	Yes	No	Comments
1 Recent loss of weight?	___	___	_____
2 Evidence of dehydration?	___	___	_____
3 Frequent chest infections?	___	___	_____
4 Urinary tract infections?	___	___	_____
5 Coughing and choking at meal/drink times?	___	___	_____
6 'Gurgly' sounding voice after eating and drinking?	___	___	_____
7 Gasping for breath at mealtimes?	___	___	_____
8 Any change in colour?	___	___	_____
9 Refusal to eat?	___	___	_____
10 Behaviour problems around mealtimes?	___	___	_____

PHYSICAL DIFFICULTIES include difficulties relating to oral skills, positioning, ability to self-feed, dental problems.

SENSORY PROBLEMS visual/perceptual problems? auditory problems? sensitivity around mouth?

MEDICATION / MEDICAL STATUS include influence on alertness/behaviour.

Photocopiable

©Alex Kelly, 2000

DYSPHAGIA ASSESSMENT SHEET

LIKES/DISLIKES and the effect it has on eating and drinking skills.

OBSERVATION OF CLIENT

ABILITY TO SELF-FEED and description, and if assistance is needed, what kind and how much?

MEAL/DRINK OBSERVED description of food/drink, note consistency & appearance. Is it typical?

ENVIRONMENT consider noise, distractions, time, staff support.

POSITIONING

Client: include how upright they are, do they have any foot support? are they comfortable? are they able to use physical skills to maximum? does the seating inhibit any of the above?

Staff member: are they at eye-level? can they offer support when needed?

COMMUNICATION

General interaction: consider level of communication and environmental distractions.

Explanation: for example, nature, texture and temperature of food.

DYSPHAGIA ASSESSMENT SHEET

EATING

Lips: closure on spoon? ability to remove food from spoon? evidence of bite reflex?

Tongue: normal tongue movement? evidence of tongue thrust or suck/swallow pattern?

Chew: up/down only? side-to-side? suck/swallow pattern? pouching of food?

Swallow: noticeable elevation? swallow rehearsals? audible swallow? delayed?

Coughing/choking: incidence, immediately after swallow or after several mouthfuls?

Other: eg, shortness of breath, change in complexion/colour, watery eyes, anxiety or tension, refusal to eat.

DRINKING

Lips: lip seal on cup.

Swallow: as above.

Coughing: as above.

'Gurgly' vocalisations: watery sound to vocalisations after drinking?

Other: as above.

DYSPHAGIA ASSESSMENT SHEET

RECOMMENDATIONS

ACTION PLAN

Completed by _____ Date _____

- *Failure to project the bolus into the pharynx* – may be due to motor weakness or difficulty in initiating movement, and prevents or delays initiation of the pharyngeal stage.
- *Aspiration of liquid before the initiation of a swallow* – results from motor or other impairment of tongue function which allows liquids to be decanted into the pharynx before activation of the reflex.
- *Choking and coughing or discomfort at the pharyngeal stage* – caused by attempts to swallow a poorly collected or unsaturated and unchewed bolus. May result from poor tongue function, reduced sensation or loss of inhibitory controls over feeding.

Effects of pharyngeal stage disability

The effects of disability affecting the pharyngeal stage include *choking, coughing* and *aspiration*. These can occur when any of the following conditions are observed:

- *The swallow reflex fails to activate* – this means that the pharyngeal stage cannot take place and may result in an inability to swallow saliva which will cause drooling and/or pooling of secretions. This is usually associated with neurological causes involving the swallowing centre in the medulla or cranial nerve damage.
- *The swallow reflex is delayed* – this means that aspiration can occur.
- *Laryngeal protection is inadequate* – causes include surgical alteration of the relevant structures, recurrent laryngeal nerve palsy and the presence of tracheostomy tube restricting elevation of the larynx.
- *Aspiration is 'silent'; sensation in the larynx is reduced or absent* – causes of widespread loss of general sensation in the area are often neurological. The cough reflex fails to activate to clear the vocal cords of intrusive material and the cause of aspiration may be failure of the swallow reflex or of the laryngeal protective mechanism only.
- *Pharyngeal peristalsis is weak or non-existent* – this leads to aspiration after the swallow when uncleared residues can drop into the reopened airway.
- *The cricopharyngeal sphincter fails to relax, or relaxation is mistimed* – this can lead to aspiration because of pooling of material above the closed sphincter after reopening of the airway. Pooling often occurs in the pyriform sinuses, which form a recess on each side of the laryngeal opening.

INTERVENTION

It is sometimes difficult to distinguish between assessment and intervention when working with the person who has eating and drinking difficulties, as assessment has to continue throughout any period of intervention. However, the initial assessment will have given the clinician the basic awareness of where the difficulties arise and therefore, where intervention needs to start. There are many excellent textbooks available to the clinician on the management of dysphagia, but in this chapter those problems common to people with learning disabilities will be addressed, and the reader will be given some practical suggestions for intervention.

The following areas will be considered:

◆ The environment
◆ Positioning of the client
◆ Equipment
◆ Assisting someone at mealtimes
◆ Encouraging self-feeding
◆ Management of oral problems
◆ Management of swallowing problems
   – Continuing oral feeding
   – Alternatives to oral feeding
◆ Drawing up care plans and risk assessments.

The Environment

An appropriate environment can make mealtimes a much more pleasant experience for both clients and staff, and advice given on this area will depend on the individual's needs and their everyday setting. Factors that may need to be addressed are:

◆ The noise level
◆ Distractions
◆ Time
◆ Amount of staff support
◆ Lighting
◆ How crowded the dining space is.

Some suggestions for intervention may include:

◆ Allowing the person to eat their dinner in a quiet side room.
◆ Seating the person so that they are less distracted by their environment.
◆ Seating the person so that they can see what is going on, and are not always turning their head.
◆ Giving the person their meal first, so that they have plenty of time.
◆ Seating the person so that they can see clearly the member of staff who is supporting them.

Eating is usually a social activity and, as much as possible, this should be remembered and encouraged. However, some clients prefer to eat in privacy because of their dysphagia, and individual preferences should always be ascertained and catered for as far as circumstances allow.

Positioning of the client

The client's sitting position will affect the outcome of his attempts at feeding and swallowing. The recommended posture is seated with spine erect and central, both feet flat on the floor and head and neck slightly flexed. The arms should be free to manipulate equipment. If a client is unable to achieve this posture, the best possible approximation should be arranged, with guidance from a physiotherapist and occupational therapist.

For some clients with physical disabilities, it will be essential to work out a position that maximises their ability to concentrate on their oral skills while minimising their physical problems. Three examples are given below:

1 Extensor spasm

If a client has an extensor spasm (typically, arched back, arms up, legs down and mouth open), they are helped by bringing their head forward, moving their arms forward and to their midline and raising their knees, as this will inhibit the spasm.

2 Athetoid asymmetrical head reflex

If a client has an athetoid asymmetrical head reflex, which typically means their head goes to one side, they are helped by bringing their arms forward to midline, at which point their head may follow, but if it does not, then move their head to midline. This needs to be done from the front, as touching the back of their head will increase the spasm. Clients may also be helped if they hold on to a bar in front of them as this will help them to keep their head in midline.

3 Low tone

Clients with low tone may be helped by increasing the height of the table to support their arms, and this then fixes the muscles supporting the head. A standing frame could also be used to help fix the muscles.

Equipment

Appropriate equipment can help with problems such as bite reflex, poor lip closure, self-feeding skills and visual difficulties. Advice should be sought from an occupational therapist as to the most appropriate equipment for the individual client's needs.

Assisting someone at mealtimes

When advising about assisting clients at mealtimes, it is often important to model good practice as well as talk it through and write it down. The following factors may need to be considered:

Positioning

The person assisting in feeding needs to ensure that, wherever possible, they are seated at eye-level and to the front of the person they are feeding. Sometimes it is necessary for the member of staff to support the client physically, for example if the client has poor lip seal (see later), and then this will be more difficult, but the ideal position is opposite the client, at eye-level, so that food can approach in midline.

Spacing

The member of staff should keep a steady rhythm when assisting. It may be possible for the client to give the member of staff a signal to indicate when they are ready for the next mouthful, for example, by raising their eyes.

Sensory factors

Clients should be encouraged to smell the food before it enters their mouth. They need to be told what it is, and whether it is hot or cold. It is also important not to mix up the food, or if they need a pureed diet, that each food (meat and vegetables) is pureed separately, so that the client can distinguish between the components.

Communication

Communicating with someone at mealtimes is a natural and sociable thing to do, but staff sometimes feel inhibited about talking to the person they are feeding and are more likely to have a conversation with another client or member of staff. It is important that staff are encouraged to communicate with the client and they may be helped by a few suggestions, such as telling the client what is on the spoon, whether it is hot or cold, encouraging the client to look at the food, and telling the client what they are doing. The member of staff should also know how much the client is able to understand, so that they can communicate at an appropriate level.

Giving food

The member of staff may need to consider the following:

◆ Where is the food placed in the mouth? Is it worth experimenting between right and left to see which is preferred? Is it sometimes better to place the food between the teeth rather than on the tongue?
◆ Is it better for the client to come forward on to the spoon, if possible?
◆ Keep a consistent pace and check to see if previous mouthfuls are finished.
◆ Try different sizes and shapes of spoon.
◆ Keep different foods separate.
◆ Check for personal preference regarding seasoning and type of food.

Familiarity

It is preferable to have the same members of staff helping individual clients each time as they will get to know individual preferences, and this will ensure that the client is as relaxed as possible. If different helpers are used, it is important that records are kept as to the quantity of food eaten.

Encouraging self-feeding

While it is ideal for someone to be able to feed themselves, there are sometimes physical factors that will need to be considered first. Clients need to maintain balance for hand/eye coordination; they need to grasp a spoon effectively and be able to maintain the grasp in order to load the spoon; they need to know where their mouth is, and they need adequate lip control to take food from the spoon and keep the food in their mouth. Different equipment can help individual clients to achieve self-feeding, such as angled spoons, deep plates/dishes, and non-slip mats. The occupational therapist will be able to advise regarding these.

Self-feeding may not always be the best course of action for a client, particularly if it involves a great deal of effort and there is concern about nutrition and health. It may be more appropriate and pleasant for the client to be fed by someone else, or to self-feed for the first part of the meal only.

Management of oral problems

Disinhibited and/or disorganised eating

This is common in people who have lived in large institutions, and is manifested by rapid, over-eager eating, cramming the mouth full of food and taking insufficient time to clear the mouth. This can lead to choking and aspiration and needs an action plan that encourages the client to eat at a slower and more controlled pace. Increasing staff support and giving smaller portions (with second helpings) can be all that is needed, but in extreme cases, a soft diet may need to be considered to minimise the risk of airway obstruction.

Poor head position

(See earlier section on positioning of the client.) It may also be necessary to give the client some head support, and this needs to be done sensitively and minimally. Using the crook of your arm around the back of their neck and your hand on their chin while you feed with the other arm is often the most effective way of providing support. This will mean that the helper needs to sit alongside the client as opposed to facing them, but should not mean that they stand over the client. A client's head should never be pushed up by the forehead in order to feed them.

Coughing and choking

Coughing and choking is usually a sign that there is a problem at the pharyngeal stage (swallowing), but it may also occur because of problems at the oral stage of feeding. Examples of this may be disorganised feeding (see above), lack of tongue control which means that food and liquid are allowed to spill into the pharynx before the swallow reflex is triggered, and if nasal regurgitation also occurs, it may indicate poor or mistimed elevation of the palate. Advice about the kinds of liquid and food the client is given may enable this problem to be managed without risk to the client (see later in this chapter for different kinds of food/drink).

Poor lip seal

This can mean that there is messy collection of food from the spoon and drink from the cup, and there is spilling from the mouth during chewing or swallowing. Giving lip support with your fingers is usually the best option, but one that needs to be experimented with in order to find the best position for both the helper and the client. Three possibilities are given below:

Using support
around head as well

Absent or weak biting and chewing

Inadequate chewing and biting may mean that food is either pushed out or that it is swallowed without being broken down. Exercises can be given to improve chewing (see for example, Langley, 1988, and Morris & Klein, 1987), but alternative management strategies need to be considered to minimise the risk of choking – for example, a soft diet.

Poor tongue movement

This means that clients will have difficulty in manipulating the food and liquid in their mouths, and moving the bolus to the back of the mouth to initiate the swallow reflex. Food and drink may therefore be spilled over the sides of the tongue, or the client may use a suck/swallow pattern of eating. Food may also collect on the palate and in the sides of the mouth, and nasal regurgitation may also occur. Once again, exercises can be done to improve tongue movement (see Langley, 1988, and Morris & Klein, 1987, for examples), but other management strategies will also need to be considered, such as a soft or pureed diet and thickened liquids. Guidelines will also need to be given around good oral hygiene and checking procedures following meals.

Management of swallowing problems

Assessment will have revealed if a client has a swallowing problem and whether this is *acute* or *chronic*.

Signs of aspiration

ACUTE (immediately following oral feeding)

◆ Coughing or choking
◆ 'Gurgly' vocalisations
◆ Change of colour
◆ Gasping for breath
◆ Rapid heart rate.

CHRONIC (long-term)

◆ Loss of weight
◆ Malnutrition
◆ Dehydration
◆ Urinary tract infections
◆ Frequent chest infections
◆ Refusal to eat
◆ Coughing and choking
◆ Respiratory problems.

Protection from aspiration and the effects of aspiration are imperative as many clients are very vulnerable to aspirational pneumonia, which is life-threatening. The management decision will need to be either to continue oral feeding or to consider alternatives, in which case a full assessment of the person's swallowing will need to be carried out at a hospital, for example, through videofluoroscopy.

Continuing oral feeding

A list of factors which will affect the choice of food and drink suitable for the client with dysphagia is included here:

1 *Consistency and texture*
   Some people with swallowing problems are able to swallow one consistency successfully, but cannot manage another without choking or aspirating. This is the first factor to be assessed, and advice may need to be sought from the dietician. For example, if the person cannot swallow liquids safely because a delayed swallow reflex means that they are aspirating the liquid before the swallow takes place, they will need to have a more solid diet. Liquids can be thickened, for example by using a prescribed thickening agent, but, because some people find this unpalatable, this can lead to dehydration and constipation. Careful monitoring by the carers will obviously be essential.

2 *Temperature*

Hot foods are often not tolerated by people with swallowing problems, because they do not have the same oral control as someone with normal swallowing, and cannot therefore take the usual precautions. Warm food and drink is often most easily managed.

Cold foods and ice may be used to assist feeding with some people, but this should be tried with care and with extra reading, as it is certainly not a good idea if the person is hypersensitive or has dental cavities.

3 *Variety*

Some people with dysphagia will need to be given a pureed diet and it is important that time is spent in helping staff to be creative and not to limit the client to a diet of porridge, pureed cauliflower cheese and yoghurt! This is not only important for their sanity but also for their health, and once again it is important to gain the advice of a dietician. Staff should be encouraged to experiment and note down things that worked well and things that didn't, so that other staff can benefit from this.

Texture hierarchy

The choice of food and drink to be given to a person with dysphagia can be divided according to consistency and texture:

Spreading foods	*Type*
Fluids	milk, water
Thickened fluids	custard, yoghurt
Liquidised/pureed	food that a spoon can't stand up in
Semi-solids	ice cream, baby food
Soft solid	blancmange, soft-boiled egg
Mashed/minced	mashed potato

Solid foods	*Type*
Bite melt	chocolate
Bite crumble	digestive biscuits
Bite splinter	toast, crisps
Bite lump	apple, carrot
Bite mash	potato, banana
Bite tacky	bread, toffee, raisins
Bite chew	meat

The kind of diet chosen will obviously depend on the individual needs of the client. Two common examples are given below:

Pureed diet and thickened liquids

These would be appropriate for someone who has a delayed swallow reflex and is aspirating liquids prior to swallowing, and who is not coping with foods that are not of the same consistency, consequently aspirating the gravy, for example, prior to swallowing the mince. It may also be appropriate for someone with very poor oral control to minimise the risk of aspiration and choking.

Advice:

◆ Puree or liquidise all foods to a smooth consistency.
◆ Puree each food separately. (This could be done in bulk and frozen.)
◆ Thicken all drinks with two to three teaspoons of thickener, depending on how slow-pouring the liquids need to be.
◆ Keep written records on food and fluid intake, and monitor for dehydration and constipation.
◆ Display the written care plan where all staff will see it.

Pureed/soft diet and normal liquids

This would be appropriate for someone who has problems swallowing due to poor oral control – for example chewing – and who is therefore at risk of choking, but who copes well with liquids.

Advice:

◆ Puree or mash all foods to a smooth consistency.
◆ Display the written care plan somewhere for all staff to see.

Foods to avoid

Certain foods are known to be difficult for people with eating and drinking problems. These are listed below:

◆ Foods with mixed texture, such as minced meats
◆ Stringy foods, for example sausages with skins
◆ Tough meats
◆ Fish with bones
◆ Mixed vegetables
◆ Peas
◆ Chips
◆ Tablets.

Alternatives to oral feeding

For some clients it will be decided by a team of professionals that oral feeding is no longer safe. This is usually after a full assessment of their swallow in hospital by videofluoroscopy. Videofluoroscopy is a type of radiological examination of the swallow process and should reveal information about the three phases of the swallowing process: oral, pharyngeal and oesophageal. It is particularly useful in identifying those people who are aspirating, but the video should also identify the following:

- Aspiration
- Residue in the valleculae
- Residue in pyriform sinuses and valleculae leading to overspill
- Oral control of the bolus
- Tongue movement in swallow
- Base of tongue movement
- Hyoid/laryngeal movement
- Presentation of the bolus to the pharynx
- Pharyngeal peristalsis
- Cricopharyngeal opening
- Transit times
- Co-ordination of movements
- Clear swallow
- Oesophageal peristalsis.

There are two main alternatives to oral feeding: the nasogastric tube or gastrostomy.

1 *The Nasogastric tube*

This is an effective temporary means of providing nutrition, especially in the unconscious or debilitated patient. These tubes are inserted through the nose and passed down the pharynx and oesophagus into the stomach while the person is supine, and they are asked to 'swallow' the tube. If aspiration and vomiting are problems, a longer tube may be inserted into the small intestine and this is called a *nasojejunal tube*. Nasogastric and nasojejunal tubes are rarely used with adults with a learning disability as an alternative to oral feeding as they are unpleasant and is easily displaced.

2 *Gastrostomy*

These are often referred to as PEGs, which stands for Percutaneous Endoscopic Gastrostomy. They are the most common alternatives to oral feeding and are designed to provide a more permanent opening for the passage of food into the stomach. They can be inserted under either general or local anaesthetic – an opening is made in the abdomen and in the stomach and a tube is inserted. Food then passes directly into the stomach, and when this is not happening, the stoma is covered with a dressing. A *jejunostomy* is where the tube is inserted into the jejunum and this reduces the incidence of gastric reflux.

If a client is given a PEG as a long-term alternative to oral feeding, then our involvement in the management of their dysphagia will cease, and care will be taken over by the nurses and dieticians. The client may be given a PEG as a shorter-term solution to dysphagia, and then their ability to swallow may need to be reassessed periodically. It will also be important to maintain some 'tasting', so that they do not lose the ability to tolerate food.

DRAWING UP CARE PLANS AND RISK ASSESSMENTS

As with all intervention, it is important to draw up clear action plans or care plans so that everyone is aware of identified needs and agreed actions. When working with the client with dysphagia, it is essential that a risk assessment is also drawn up. As Prime (1992) says, 'Although we would all agree with the inevitability of risk, it does not follow that clients must be placed in dangerous situations liable to mischance, loss or injury.' She goes on to say that risks can be estimated through the assessment process, and a well-informed decision can then be made in terms of balancing risks and needs.

Assessment of the client with dysphagia will have identified the factors around eating and drinking that may cause a problem or have an adverse effect on their quality of life. This information will have been used to draw up an intervention plan, but in addition, areas of risk need to be discussed and actions agreed so that everyone is clear about responsibilities and procedures. A risk assessment will include:

◆ The identified risk
◆ The physical risk to the client
◆ The psychological risk to the client
◆ Actions that will minimise the risk
◆ A date for reviewing the action plan.

A format for risk assessment is given, although different organisations may have other risk assessment formats that they prefer to use.

Working with

Adults with a Learning Disability

17

RISK ASSESSMENT

NAME _____ DATE _____

RISK IDENTIFIED

PHYSICAL RISK TO CLIENT

PSYCHOLOGICAL RISK TO CLIENT

ACTIONS TO MINIMISE RISK

REVIEW DATE _____

Signatures _____ _____

Photocopiable

©Alex Kelly, 2000

210

DYSPHAGIA ASSESSMENT – WORKED EXAMPLE

NAME _____Bob_____ DOB _____1.1.1940____

ADDRESS _____

KEYWORKER _____ DATE _____

BACKGROUND INFORMATION

	Yes	No	Comments
1 Recent loss of weight?		✓	
2 Evidence of dehydration?		✓	
3 Frequent chest infections?	✓		2 in last 6 months
4 Urinary tract infections?	✓		3 in last year
5 Coughing and choking at meal/drink times?	✓		Has coughed as long as anyone remembers
6 'Gurgly' sounding voice after eating and drinking?	✓		After drinking
7 Gasping for breath at mealtimes?	✓		But only after severe coughing/choking
8 Any change in colour?	✓		As above
9 Refusal to eat?		✓	Enjoys food
10 Behaviour problems around mealtimes?		✓	

PHYSICAL DIFFICULTIES include difficulties relating to oral skills, positioning, ability to self-feed, dental problems.

Bob is in a wheelchair and his posture is affected by curvature of the spine. Has been assessed by physio & current posture is the best possible. Bob self feeds with spoon & has own teeth.

SENSORY PROBLEMS visual/perceptual problems? auditory problems? sensitivity around mouth?

Slight hearing loss.

MEDICATION / MEDICAL STATUS include influence on alertness/behaviour.

Medication for constipation.

DYSPHAGIA ASSESSMENT – WORKED EXAMPLE

LIKES/DISLIKES and the effect it has on eating and drinking skills

Bob has spent most of his life – until recently, in a large institution where mealtimes & drinks were very important to him. He will eat & drink anything & will do it quickly.

OBSERVATION OF CLIENT

ABILITY TO SELF-FEED and description, and if assistance is needed, what kind and how much.

Bob feeds himself with a spoon (RH). He needs his food cut up & benefits from a non-slip mat & high-rimmed dish.

MEAL/DRINK OBSERVED description of food/drink, note consistency & appearance. Is it typical?

Steak & kidney pie, mashed potato & peas.
Tinned fruit & custard. Water to drink. Will eat everything.

ENVIRONMENT consider noise, distractions, time, staff support.

Pleasant, relaxed atmosphere in small residential home.
Two staff to six clients.

POSITIONING

Client: include how upright they are, do they have any foot support? are they comfortable? are they able to use physical skills to maximum? does the seating inhibit any of the above?

Bob is not very upright in his chair but physio assessment shows that this is the most upright he can get. Seems comfortable & able to use his skills.
Staff member: are they at eye-level? can they offer support when needed?

N/A

COMMUNICATION

General interaction: consider level of communication and environmental distractions.

Good level of staff-client interaction. Radio on but didn't appear to be distracting.
Explanation: for example, nature, texture and temperature of food.

Adequate to Bob's needs. He was told that it was quite hot & what it was.

DYSPHAGIA ASSESSMENT – WORKED EXAMPLE

EATING

Lips: closure on spoon? ability to remove food from spoon? evidence of bite reflex?
Good – no apparent problems.

Tongue: normal tongue movement? evidence of tongue thrust or suck/swallow pattern?
Slight tongue thrust. Movement slightly limited.

Chew: up/down only? side-to-side? suck/swallow pattern? pouching of food?
Up/down chewing but not enough to really break down food.

Swallow: noticeable elevation? swallow rehearsals? audible swallow? delayed?
Noticeable elevation, but appeared delayed & uncoordinated.

Coughing/choking: incidence, immediately after swallow or after several mouthfuls?
Coughed badly twice while eating dinner. Staff report this is typical.

Other: eg, shortness of breath, change in complexion/colour, watery eyes, anxiety or tension, refusal to eat.
While coughing, he went very red/purple and his eyes watered. Breathing was fast afterwards.

DRINKING

Lips: lip seal on cup.
Good.

Swallow: as above.
Swallow delayed.

Coughing: as above.
Immediately following swallow.

'Gurgly' vocalisations: watery sound to vocalisations after drinking?
Vocalisations were very watery-sounding following drink.

Other: as above.
Drinks too fast & looks a bit panicy/anxious while drinking.

DYSPHAGIA ASSESSMENT – WORKED EXAMPLE

RECOMMENDATIONS

Bob has a delayed swallow reflex & poor oral skills which means he is at risk of aspiration & choking. Assessment showed that he already has significant health needs related to chronic aspiration & therefore needs to have a diet that minimises the risk of further problems. It is recommended that he is given a puréed diet & thickened liquids.

ACTION PLAN

1. Write care plan for intervention.

2. Staff training in puréed only diets & thickening liquids.

3. Staff to keep diary sheets of food & fluid intake & incidence of coughing/choking/distress, etc.

4. Meet with keyworker & manager to write risk assessment.

5. Review in 4 weeks.

Completed by _____A Clinician_____ Date _____

RISK ASSESSMENT – WORKED EXAMPLE

NAME _____Bob_____ DATE _____

RISK IDENTIFIED

Bob will choke on food that has not been puréed & will aspirate liquid that has not been thickened.

PHYSICAL RISK TO CLIENT

• Airway obstruction — painful and life-threatening.

• Aspiration — chest infection, aspirational pneumonia or life-threatening.

PSYCHOLOGICAL RISK TO CLIENT

• Distress

• Trauma

• Shock

ACTIONS TO MINIMISE RISK

1 All food to be puréed.

2 Access to non-puréed food should be restricted.

3 Opportunities to eat a wide variety of puréed food should be actively worked on by staff – a 'good ideas for Bob' book to be started.

4 All drinks/liquids to be thickened using three heaped teaspoons of thickener.

5 Access to unthickened drinks should be restricted.

6 Ensure Bob is regularly offered drinks & that he has 8-10 drinks per day.

7 Staff to complete daily diary sheets & speech & language therapist will be contacted if evidence of aspiration.

8 Staff training in first aid re. choking.

9 Reassess after four weeks.

REVIEW DATE _____4 weeks_____

Signatures ___A Clinician_____   _____A Manager_____

Chapter 7: Group Therapy

INTRODUCTION

Groups are important in everyone's life, and the skills that are needed for group functioning are vital to all of us. As Johnson and Johnson (1975) state: 'The quality of your life depends upon the effectiveness of the groups to which you belong, and this effectiveness is largely determined by your personal group skills and knowledge of group processes.' People are social animals who have a great need to communicate with each other, and groups can therefore be a very appropriate setting for people who share problems in talking.

But what is meant by a group? Baron and Byrne (1987) suggest the following definition: 'Groups consist of two or more persons engaged in social interaction who have some stable, structured relationship with one another, are interdependent, share common goals, and perceive that they are, in fact, a group.' This definition certainly seems to cover all aspects of what would be understood by a speech and language therapy group.

People with learning disabilities often have communication difficulties which affect their ability to interact in groups, and this inability to interact well within group settings has an effect on their quality of life. The clinician can therefore have an important role to play, not only in developing communication skills, but also in helping clients communicate more effectively in different group settings. In this chapter, the following areas will be addressed: why choose group therapy?; group structure and group dynamics; setting up a group; and running a group.

WHY CHOOSE GROUP THERAPY?

Working with people in a group setting has always seemed to be a popular option for both clinicians and clients, and as Smith (1992) says: 'The group forum, by its very nature, is an ideal one in which to learn about, change or practise any behaviour which is associated with social interaction and communication.' Also, for many clients in learning disability settings, group therapy appears to be logical and practical. Many people with learning disabilities live communally and share day-care services, and group therapy can be used to promote better interaction within their everyday environment. A group may have different functions:

The functions of a group

1   *Assessment*. The clinician may wish to assess the client(s) within a group setting using specific activities which are assessment-based. The clinician may also want to supplement the information already gained through assessment by observing the client(s) in a group, and it is easier to video people for assessment purposes in a controlled environment than in an unstructured environment.
2   *Skills teaching*. Assessment may have revealed a group of people with similar communication needs who would all benefit from being taught similar skills.

3   *Maintenance of skills.* A group may be part of a programme to help clients use
    skills they have been taught, and to encourage them to take these skills
    outside the group.

Assumptions about group therapy

Group therapy may be popular and may work for many clients, but it is important
to run groups for the right reasons, and before the advantages of group work are
discussed, a few commonly-held assumptions about group therapy need to be
examined:

'A group will encourage clients to interact with one another.'

This is an assumption that is often made when planning a communication group. It
is obviously correct to encourage interaction within the group, using Makaton for
example, and it is correct to assume that the clients' ability to interact with one
another within the group will improve. However, will it necessarily be correct to
assume that the skills learnt in the group will be taken into the clients' everyday
environment? Clients do not just start interacting with one another over tea
because they have recently finished a communication group. Additional factors will
need to be taken into consideration if this is to be a 'spin off' from the group, and
additional work will undoubtedly need to be done. The environment needs to be
assessed in terms of its ability to facilitate interaction; for example, if the group is
improving Makaton skills, but the environment is a non-signing one, then skills are
unlikely to be transferred from the group. Clients need to be helped to transfer
skills, through direct support from the clinician working alongside them in different
activities, and through staff training in order to change the environment.

'A group will provide some stimulation.'

Running a group will obviously provide some stimulation for the people in the group;
however, this should not be a reason why a communication group is planned and run
by a clinician. The group should be meeting the communication needs of the clients and
not the needs of their environment. It is very easy to be caught up in the creation of a
timetable in a large day centre, and to find a 'slot' has been allocated to speech and
language therapy on Thursday mornings, as not much else is going on. Sometimes, this
'slot' is very useful, but it is important that speech and language therapy is not being

seen simply as a part of the timetable and a provider of stimulation! Several factors need to be considered: if the speech and language therapy group is really going to be the highlight of a client's day, what is happening in their environment and their life to make it so unstimulating? What could be done to improve this? If the Thursday morning 'slot' is going to be used, then make sure that there are co-leaders from that environment who can run the group without the clinician if necessary.

'A group will increase our contacts.'

Groups are often used as a way of seeing more clients by under-resourced clinicians. This keeps the managers and health authorities happy, and keeps the clinicians in work and probably still under-resourced. Running groups obviously does increase contacts, but it should not be the reason why a group is planned. The clinician needs to be aware of this pressure and temptation, and if this is the case, to try to concentrate on demonstrating effectiveness of therapy for individual clients, whether this is through individual work or group work.

'Groups are a good way to train staff.'

Group work may provide an opportunity for the clinician to demonstrate and model ways of facilitating communication to staff and clients; however, Woods and Britton (1985, cited by Rose and Wotton, 1992), emphasise that training staff is not enough, and the skills learnt in a group are not necessarily applied outside the group setting. Georgiades and Phillmore (1980) stress the need for a supportive environment where trained skills can be practised. The clinician therefore needs to be aware that running groups jointly with staff does not necessarily mean that their communicative behaviour will change, and additional support may be required within their environment.

'Clients like being part of a communication group.'

This is yet another assumption which should not form the basis of a clinician's choice of group work over individual. There are people who prefer their own company, or who remain on the periphery when in the company of others, or who prefer one-to-one interaction. Personality differences need to be considered when choosing between group work and individual work, and when possible clients should be encouraged to state their preference.

The advantages of group therapy

If a group is being run for the *right* reasons, and taking the above into consideration, then group therapy can have many advantages in meeting the individual communication needs of people with learning disabilities. A term which is sometimes used in the literature is 'individualisation', and Payne *et al* (1981) define this as 'instruction appropriate to the individual even though it is not always accomplished on a one-to-one basis . . . Instruction should be organised in an efficient fashion to facilitate maximum learning by each student.' Thus while individualisation indicates that instruction/teaching/activities and services should be geared to the needs of the individual, it does not mean that this has to be provided on a one-to-one basis. In fact, Polloway *et al* (1986) state that 'Research . . . encourages the consideration of group training approaches as a primary instructional basis.' The advantages of group therapy may include:

◆ Greater peer interaction and generalisation of skills.
◆ Increased observational learning, as group members can offer additional models, reinforcement and feedback.
◆ Increased opportunity to generate ideas in problem-solving, and to set up role plays and simulation games.
◆ Opportunity for clients to try out new skills in a safe environment.
◆ Peer group pressure can motivate individuals.
◆ A more relaxed and comfortable environment in which to learn new skills.
◆ Opportunity to transfer skills to other staff, thus improving the chance of carryover into the clients' everyday environment.

GROUP STRUCTURE AND GROUP DYNAMICS

Clinicians working in groups will obviously be more effective if they have some understanding of group structure and dynamics, and as Fawcus (1992a), states: 'Whilst . . . the use of groups appears to be increasing, this increase is not always being matched by an awareness of the processes involved in successful group management.'

The life cycle of a group

Whitaker (1989) identified three phases in the development of a group: the formative phase, the established phase and the termination phase. In the formative phase, members are establishing themselves as a group and individuals are finding a place within the group. When this has occurred, the group is in the established phase. Whitaker has suggested that in a group with a structured programme of activities, the established phase is reached more quickly as members come together sharing the same common, identified need and with some roles already established – for example, leadership. The termination phase is the period during which members are prepared for the time when the group will finish. It is also the time when individual achievements can be reviewed and plans are made for the future.

Roles within the group

Within a small group setting, roles may either be assigned or they may develop informally over a period of time. In speech and language therapy groups, the role of leader is normally automatically assigned to the clinician running the group, as they are seen as the group member with the specific expertise for that role. Whether or not the clinician is an effective leader is another matter, and one that will be examined later in this chapter.

Sears *et al* (1988) have described two types of leadership: task leadership which is concerned with accomplishing goals, and social leadership which focuses on the social and emotional aspects of group interaction. Both of these are important for effective group functioning, whether they are fulfilled by one or two people. Certainly in the early stages of a group's life cycle we might expect the clinician to play both roles.

Different types of groups call for different styles of leadership, and Baron and Byrne (1987) state that the selection of a leader should involve a process of matching the individual's mix of skills and characteristics to the needs of that particular group of clients. In theory, the clinician may have the technical expertise but may lack are demanded of an effective leader. Lack of confidence alone does not mean that a clinician cannot become a good leader, as experience will generally resolve that problem. It is essential, however, that the clinician has a sound theoretical knowledge and has also planned the early group sessions with care and thought. Whatever the style of leadership, ultimately, as Sears *et al* (1988) comment, the most effective leader may be the person who can adapt their style to match the situation. In their transactional view of leadership, Baron and Byrne (1987) state that it is not simply a matter of some people having leadership qualities. Although the leader brings influences to bear on the group, group members also have an effect on the leader and may be responsible for changing the leadership style. They go on to comment that an effective leader needs to be receptive to the opinions and needs of the group, will actively seeking feedback from group members, and will then respond by taking it into account when planning group activities.

Brown (1986) has given us an extensive list of group roles which include the group initiator, the jester, the challenger, the harmoniser and the group recluse. Whitaker (1989) has suggested that a person entering a group will seek a role which is familiar and feels safe, and this could even be one of the leadership roles. The clinician needs to recognise these roles as they develop, and even encourage group members to take on roles in an attempt to acquire or restore their sense of identity. As Brown (1986) says, group members may not only collaborate in making the roles available, but may also 'lock' willing

And who wants to be the group recluse today?

uh?

er...

members into the roles they adopt. This may be a very important function of the group, but the clinician should ensure that group members have the opportunity to swap and try out new roles from time to time.

Performance in groups

Task performance can certainly be affected by being in a group situation. It may improve simply because other people are present, a process which Zajonc, cited by Fawcus (1992a), describes as social facilitation – being in the presence of others increases an individual's drive or motivation. However, such an effect will work only where the responses are innate or well-learned, and if they are not, then the presence of others may have a socially-inhibiting effect. The presence of others may also have an arousal effect, with associated feelings of tension and excitement, which in turn has the effect of increasing motivation and performance. However, the level of anxiety caused by 'performing' in front of others can lead to the total inhibition of the desired response. It is the clinician's responsibility to create an environment that develops an acceptable level of arousal and motivation, and that is balanced by an empathetic response to communication attempts.

It is important that the clinician makes sure that all members of the group participate equally, and that 'social loafing' does not take place (Baron & Byrne, 1987; Sears *et al*, 1988). Baron and Byrne (1987) found that social loafing was less likely to occur where there was 'high task-attractiveness', that is where the group was given some explanation of the value of the task and received some sort of incentive. Sears *et al* (1988) also suggest that social loafing can be counteracted by giving individuals a greater sense of responsibility and involvement. However, there is always the tendency for one or two people to do most of the talking in a group, and sessions can develop into a dialogue between the clinician and one other group member. The clinician must therefore ensure that all group members have an equal chance to communicate and contribute to the session.

Group cohesiveness

Cohesiveness tends to occur when there is a good match between individual needs and the group goals (Baron & Byrne, 1987), and it is obviously the clinician's responsibility to ensure that this match is made, as far as is possible. Sears *et al* (1988) added the following factors in achieving group cohesion: in the first place, it will be helped by interpersonal attraction; secondly, it will tend to depend on how successfully the group accomplishes its objectives; and finally, it will tend to depend on how harmoniously and effectively the group interacts. The clinician must therefore ensure that the goals set are realistic ones which can be achieved, and that every group member has the opportunity to contribute. The clinician should also be sensitive to the non-verbal behaviours which communicate information about each individual's emotional states and attitudes (Gahagan, 1975, cited by Fawcus, 1992a).

The need for an accepting and supportive environment is obviously important in developing group cohesion, but it would be unrealistic to believe that arguments and differences of opinion do not arise from time to time. As Combs (1989, cited by Fawcus, 1992a) observed, controversy and differences of opinion are vital dynamics of the group process, and within a cohesive group it is certainly safe for them to occur.

Feedback within the group

'The role of feedback is so important in facilitating change and personal development that it merits special attention' (Fawcus, 1992a). As Whitaker (1989, cited by Fawcus, 1992a) said: 'Receiving feedback from others within the group is one of the advantages of the group as a context for help. Group members can gain information about the impact of their behaviours on others which is not ordinarily available to them.' Clinicians obviously needs to ensure that all feedback is given in a constructive way so that group members are able to try out new communication skills and behaviours in a 'safe' environment, and in doing so, to know how successful they have been through constructive feedback from the group.

SETTING UP A GROUP

Setting up a group is no easy task, especially in new environments. There are many things that need to be considered and addressed before a group should start, and there are some factors that need to be assessed in order to ascertain whether it will be worthwhile to run a group in the first place. The following factors will be discussed in this part of the chapter:

◆ The client's environment
◆ Group membership and homogeneity
◆ Setting goals
◆ Accommodation
◆ The contract.

Consideration of the client's environment

Careful consideration of a client's environment is essential before anything else is done to set up a group, and clinicians and managers need to be realistic as to what can be achieved in each setting. Georgiades and Phillmore (1980) argued that training staff (for example, through group work) and sending them back as hero-innovators results in them being worn down by harsh institutional realities, and their attitudes may revert to pre-training levels. 'Hospitals, like dragons, eat hero-innovators for breakfast' (Georgiades & Phillmore, 1980). This suggests that changing individuals is not the answer; it is the whole environment that needs to be assessed and the individuals' interrelationships in the institutional system that need to be changed. Georgiades and Phillmore (1980) recommend that the institution is treated like a client, and that time is given to assessing and evaluating the strengths and needs of the environment, including areas such as:

◆ Philosophy of care
◆ Environmental factors
◆ Identification of supportive relevant others
◆ Routine
◆ Level and quality of current activity
◆ Quality of staff/resident interaction.

Philosophy of care

In many homes and units a philosophy of care may exist, and this will outline the aims of the unit for its residents and how these aims are going to be achieved. It is important for the clinician to be familiar with the philosophy and its objectives as, in some units, new staff may be selected on the basis of their willingness to work within the framework of the philosophy of care. Spending time in a unit or in a home will give the clinician the insight to know whether a philosophy of care exists and whether it is being worked towards.

Environmental factors

The physical environment can have a dramatic effect upon a person's level of well-being and ability. Aspects of the environment such as lighting, layout of room and seating, size of room and decor, and degree of privacy all have a direct effect on how much people interact. Encouraging the staff to take a fresh look at the environment and to make simple changes such as arranging seats into 'conversational clusters' may alter people's perceptions of residents and improve opportunities for interaction.

Identification of supportive others

Setting up and running groups requires the support and cooperation of others and the system. The clinician cannot work effectively alone and therefore should not start a group if this is likely to be the case. Georgiades and Phillmore (1980) suggest guidelines for those working within institutions, although the same principles apply to any residential or day unit:

1   Work with forces supportive of change. Find those who want to help rather than persuade those who do not.

2   To prevent isolation of the supportive individual, a critical mass of care workers should be developed. These will provide support and motivation for each other.
3   Work within organisationally healthy parts of the system.
4   Identify the natural leaders among care staff. These may not be designated senior staff, but without their support, all efforts may be rendered useless.
5   Have support and permission from top-level management.
6   Ensure you receive mutual support.

Routine

It is important for a clinician to know the routine of the environment before deciding to run a group. Staff may be available to co-run groups at particular times, and other professionals may have prior claim to certain 'slots' in the week.

Level and quality of current activity

It is important to assess what activities are currently being offered and whether they are already meeting the needs of the clients. The speech and language therapy group may have nothing different or better to offer and the clinician should be realistic about what is achievable. It may be better to support clients in existing groups rather than setting up a new one.

Quality of staff/resident interaction

Improving the communicative environment is an important role for the speech and language clinician, but the clinician cannot simply tell staff to talk to clients as this is unlikely to be effective. Rose and Wotton (1992) suggest that the following kinds of interaction need to be observed:

◆   Are interactions staff- or resident-initiated?
◆   Are some residents/staff better at interacting than others?
◆   Are there key times in the day when interaction is increased/decreased?
◆   What opportunities are there for increasing interaction?
◆   Are there any factors which increase or decrease interaction?

Following these observations, the clinician is then able to offer staff support in improving the communicative environment. It should always be recognised, however, that care staff mostly communicate with the clients far more than the clinician ever will, and they will have a better understanding of the effect of the client's disability on themselves and on others. They undoubtedly need support, not criticism, to facilitate any change.

Group membership & homogeneity of the group

Groups are very seldom entirely homogeneous. Even if all the group members have a similar level of communicative ability, there will be differences in personality, age, sex and background, which will all lead to diversity. It is, however, important to match group members for communicative strength and need, otherwise the clinician is in danger of not meeting anyone's needs and ending up feeling very frustrated and dispirited. A group is also far more likely to gel and work more cohesively if its members have similar needs and goals, as cohesiveness tends to occur when there is a good match between individual needs and the group goals (Baron and Byrne 1987).

The size of the group will depend on the goals of therapy and the type of group being run, but in general there should be no fewer than three and no more than eight clients in a group (Hitchings, 1992). It is obviously important to remember that a great number of clients find it difficult to communicate and attend in larger groups, and it is important that clients are offered groups where the number of group members will not adversely affect their opportunity to learn and communicate. Group membership should also ideally be closed, although it is sometimes necessary for clients to drop out of groups for either practical or therapeutic reasons.

Groups run better with at least two group leaders, and at least one of the co-workers should ideally be someone who can ensure that there is carryover from the group into their everyday environment. The group leaders need to agree on the aims of the group and on how the group should be organised and run, and they should both/all have a clear understanding of the individual group members' strengths and needs. A good working relationship between the group leaders is often the key to a successful group and time should always be allowed for planning and evaluating sessions. The group leaders also need to have certain skills in order to run the group successfully (see earlier in the chapter, in 'roles within the group'). Rustin and Kuhr (1989) suggested 'They need to be sensitive, both to the individual group member's needs as well as those of the group as a whole.' They also suggest that group leaders need 'Good observational skills, the ability to view the group objectively, honesty, and a sense of humour.' Flexibility is also important, as it is often appropriate to follow the needs of the group rather than to stick rigidly to the original session plan.

Setting realistic goals

The clinician has to ensure that the goals set for each client are realistic ones which can be achieved. If unrealistic goals are set, then the clients are being set up for failure, something which does little to improve motivation to communicate. As Emanuel (1992) said about working with young disabled children: 'There are distressing effects on parents when their children prove unable to fulfil the promise of the unrealistic and euphoric claims of some early intervention programmes. A desire to help must not obscure an appreciation of the level of disability.' Unrealistic goals can have distressing effects on carers, parents, and other professionals, and most of all on the clients themselves.

Accommodation

Groups are obviously nicer to run in nice rooms! However, there are some factors that need to be considered when seeking a suitable (and nice) room for a group:

◆ The room should be large enough for the size and purpose of the group. For example, a larger room will be needed if the group will be involved in role play and video.
◆ The room should have as much natural light as possible. This is particularly relevant for some clients with perceptual and visual problems, but it is also relevant when teaching skills such as signing and when a video is going to be used.
◆ The room needs to be physically comfortable – for example, warm and quiet – and needs to have appropriate seating for the clients.
◆ There should be a means of displaying materials or writing up information – for example, a flip chart, wipe board or blackboard.
◆ There should be electric sockets in suitable places if videos, televisions or tape recorders are going to be used.

Today our signing group has been moved to the cupboard.

The contract

Having decided on the function of the group, the group membership and group aims, and having found a suitable venue, a contract needs to be drawn up and agreed with the appropriate manager. The contract needs to include:

◆ How long the group will run.
◆ Who will be in the group.
◆ On what day the group will run and the time it will start and finish.
◆ Staff members who will support the group.
◆ What will happen in the event of staff shortages/sickness.
◆ The aims of the group.
◆ How the group will be evaluated.

RUNNING A GROUP

In running a successful group, there are several factors that need to be considered:

◆ Facilitating cohesiveness
◆ Agreeing group rules
◆ Structuring the session
◆ Evaluating the group.

Cohesiveness

As has been stated earlier, cohesiveness is more likely to occur when there is a good match between individual needs and the group goals. If the clinician has achieved this, then it is hoped there will be less work in ensuring ongoing group cohesion. However, the clinician does need to ensure that the group 'gels' initially and that they continue to gel and work well as a group. Factors that can help cohesiveness are:

1   Arrange the room prior to the group so that no-one feels left out by the positioning of their chair in the room. When possible, use a circle of chairs to make everyone feel equal.
2   Work hard to ensure that everyone feels valued in the group. If a group member is naturally quiet, then it may be possible to give them a non-verbal role in the group, such as putting up the posters or collecting a less able client for the group.
3   Work hard also to ensure that everyone feels part of the group and has an equal 'say'. This does not mean forcing the chatty client to be quiet for long periods or forcing the quiet client to talk when he clearly does not want to. What it does mean is involving all clients in discussions and activities, even if it means asking the quiet client, 'Do you agree, John?' and the chatty client, 'Tell us what you think, Sarah'.
4   Start each session with a relatively simple activity that is fun and stress-free, and which cues each member into the group. An example could be throwing a ball to someone in the group, saying their name and one thing about them. It is essential that all members participate so that they feel part of the group.
5   Finish each session with another activity that is fun and stress-free. This will help to decrease any anxiety that has been felt by group members, and will help them to leave the group feeling relaxed and happy.

Group rules

In the early stages of the group, whenever appropriate, it is important to discuss and agree on a set of group rules. Douglas (1990) suggests that people entering a group need to know these rules so that they can derive maximum benefit from it. These rules can be used or referred to when problems arise that affect the cohesion or running of the group – for example, continual late arrival of members or one person dominating discussion. Spending time establishing these rules can also help group cohesion and instils a shared sense of responsibility for how the group functions. Asking the group questions such as, 'What makes a group a good group or a bad group?' is a good basis for discussion around setting up group rules.

At the same time as discussing group rules, it is also important to help the group members understand the group contract – for example, how long the group will last and what the aims are for the group. Both the rules and group contract could be done in a written or pictorial format and referred to in later sessions.

Structure of the session

The structure of the group session will obviously be dependent on the function of the group, but a few rules can be applied to most groups:

1   *Group cohesion activity.* This is an important part of any group, especially with people who have a learning disability, as they may need more 'cueing' into a group. The purpose of the activity is to bring the group together so that they gel and work well as a group. The activity should be relatively simple and stress-free, and it is essential that all group members participate so that they feel part of the group. Examples of good group cohesion activities are: activities which involve giving or requesting information – for example 'my favourite food is . . .'; name games; and non-verbal games – for example, Chinese mimes (passing a mime from one person to the next).

2   *Revision of previous session.* Where relevant, it is important that the main aspects of the previous session are recalled to ensure cohesion between sessions. It is also important at this stage to recap on the aims of the group and the agreed rules. Sometimes it is necessary to alter the plan of the session if one or more group members are expressing confusion over last week's session, or have had a relevant experience that needs discussion.

3   *Introduction to the session theme.* The theme for the session is introduced and explained. This can be done through discussion, brainstorming an idea, drawing a picture or in whatever way is suitable for the group.

4   *Main activity.* When appropriate, this part of the session may be broken down into smaller components. An example of this would be when introducing a new skill in a social skills group. First, there is the demonstration of the skill through modelling, involving clients when appropriate. Second, there may be role play or a group activity for group members to practise the skill. Third, there is feedback and replay if necessary. It is during this part of the session that it is most important not to lose people's attention by allowing an activity to go on for too long, or one person to dominate the conversation.

5   *Summing up.* This involves summarising what has been done in the session and setting assignments where appropriate. This could take the form of asking group members to practise a skill before the next session, or to observe a skill in others.

6   *Finishing activity.* Each session should end with a group activity to bring the group back together again. This is especially important if the group has been stressful in any way, as a group activity will help decrease any anxiety felt by the group. As with the activity at the beginning of the session, it should be simple and stress-free, and should include everyone in the group.

Careful timetabling is therefore essential if a session is going to run smoothly. As Fawcus (1992b) states: 'The over-all aims of a group session can best be achieved where the pacing and timing of activities are skilfully managed.' She goes on to say that too slow a pace will lead to boredom and a low level of arousal, and too rapid a pace will mean that group members will not have enough time to process the information and respond. Timing is therefore crucial and this becomes particularly important when judging the length of any specific activity. Fawcus (1992b) feels that 'Quit when you're winning' should be a golden rule in group management as it is better to change an activity at a point where everyone is still 'obtaining optimum satisfaction', than to persevere to a point where performance is beginning to deteriorate and interest is lost. Judgements around timing develop obviously with experience, but the clinician should always closely observe group members for signs that it is time to change the activity.

Evaluation

Time should always be given to evaluate the session with the other group leaders. This means preparing in advance a method for evaluation, for example, a form to complete after each session. Otherwise, there is the danger of slipping into . . . 'Did you think it went OK?' . . . 'Yes, great.' . . . 'See you next week then.' A form with a few questions on it or a box to fill in may increase the quality of post-group discussions. Questions that need to be answered are:

◆   Were the aims of the session met, and if not, why?
◆   How did the activities go? Would you change anything next time?
◆   Did everyone take part, and if not, what could be done next time to improve this?
◆   Are clients improving/learning new skills, and if not, what needs to change?
◆   What needs to be addressed in the next session that has not been planned for?

At the end of a group, it is also important to evaluate clients' skills, and this is normally done through reassessment. It is becoming increasingly important to evaluate the clinician's work and show that clients are improving. This has to be done by the clinician initially through assessing each client, agreeing a realistic goal or goals, and then reassessing that client on that specific skill at the end of the group. It could be simply a case of assessing a skill in terms of:

0 = skill not present
1 = skill emerging
2 = skill present but not consistent
3 = skill present and consistent.

This would enable the clinician to quantify improvements as well as evaluate the group qualitatively.

When possible, it is also useful to find out if the group members enjoyed the group and if they thought that they had learned something. This is not only helpful in discovering how enjoyable or boring groups are, but also in deciding if the clients learned as much as the clinician thought they did. This is best done with the use of pictures or symbols to help the client understand what it is that is being asked of them.

SOCIAL COMMUNICATION SKILLS GROUP – WORKED EXAMPLE

GROUP MEMBERS   Eight clients, aged 19–21, attending a Further Education College.

GROUP LEADERS   Speech and language clinician and Year Tutor.

AIM OF GROUP   To improve conversational skills.

TIMING & FREQUENCY One-hour sessions once a week for 12 weeks. Planning time with co-leader for half an hour after session.

EQUIPMENT USED   Worksheets from *Talkabout* (social skills package). Magazines to use as conversation material. Video camera and television.

ACTIVITIES USED   Group cohesion activities. Problem solving. Brainstorming. Modelling. Role play with video feedback. Homework assignments.

EVALUATION   Re-assessment of group members using the rating scale of conversational skills in *Talkabout*.

Group members to evaluate group using evaluation worksheets in *Talkabout*.

SOCIAL COMMUNICATION SKILLS GROUP – WORKED EXAMPLE

A SESSION PLAN for session 5

10.00 – 10.10   *Group cohesion activity – 'Change three things'*
Each group member takes it in turn to leave the room and change three things about their appearance; for example, removing a necklace, undoing a shoe lace. The rest of the group try to see what is different about them.

10.10 – 10.20   *Recap previous session*
Each member tries to remember one thing about what a good conversation means. Then the group recap on how we know if someone is listening.

10.20   *Introduction to session*
'Starting a conversation'.

10.20 – 10.45   *Main activity*
'How not to start a conversation.' Brainstorm ideas on to a sheet of paper.

Leaders role-play different scenarios to add to brainstorm. How do we appear to others if we start conversations badly? Discuss and write down ideas.

'How can I start a conversation?' Discuss possible openers and write down.

Group members take turns to try to start a conversation with the co-leader.

Group leader videos role plays to show next week.

10.45 – 10.50   *Homework*
Each group member thinks of someone in their life that they are going to try to start a conversation with this week. Group leaders make a note of these.

10.50 – 11.00   *Finishing activity – Chinese mimes*
Group members divide into two teams. A mime is passed down the line and the other group sees how much it stays the same.

Chapter 8: Staff Training

INTRODUCTION

Training staff who work with adults with learning disabilities is an important aspect of the work of a speech and language clinician. As Cullen (1988, cited by Chatterton, 1999) states: 'In order to change the communication skills of the clients, it may be essential to first change the behaviour of the staff.' Chatterton (1999) went on to say that the staff who spend the most time with the clients are the people who are the most able to effect communication change, and she quoted van der Gaag and Dormandy (1993) as saying that staff training is an 'essential and ongoing commitment' for speech and language clinicians working within this speciality.

People who have had communication difficulties for many years are often referred to clinicians, and some of their carers may have become complacent of their inability to express themselves, or may even disbelieve in their potential to improve. The challenge here is not to work with the person with the learning disability, but to effect change in the staff through whatever medium is most effective and appropriate. This will involve different kinds of staff training and the more effective the clinician is as a 'trainer', the more effective the outcome for the client will be. This is true with all the people with whom speech and language clinicians work with, as a client would rarely be seen for speech and language therapy without involving the staff group and advising on the relevant communication issues. This is all staff training.

There are additional problems specific to working with adults with learning disabilities: the clinician is often working alongside staff with little or no training, especially in residential units. As Tully (1986) states: 'Until a few years ago, with the exception of a few senior workers with nursing or clinical qualifications, helpers in residential facilities were untrained; what knowledge and skills they acquired resulted from working alongside more experienced but equally untrained colleagues. There was virtually no understanding that this way of operating imposed major limitations on the quality of help given to clients, and also no awareness that many staff were, despite their efforts, far from competent.' (p209.) The situation has improved in that there is a growing awareness of the need for training, and as a result there has been a rapid growth in tertiary-level courses, such as NVQs, for residential workers; however, the basic fact remains the same: residential staff are predominantly untrained.

An additional problem is that staff turnover is high. As Brown (1992) states: 'The difficulties associated with attracting and retaining staff have been a constant concern over the years.' He goes on to say that we need to be 'updating the knowledge-base and skills of trained staff and providing in-service training for unqualified staff.'

Staff training is not always specific to speech and language therapy and the communication needs of clients; work is often within a multidisciplinary context, and training should therefore reflect this. It is often not helpful to separate the different needs of a client, such as their communication needs, mental health needs, skill development needs, etc, or to provide separate training around these different areas. Where practicable, the clinician needs to help staff to see the person holistically by offering joint training sessions with other members of the multidisciplinary team. This is also a good way to increase the clinician's own skills and knowledge base.

In this chapter, the whole issue of staff training will be discussed. Initially staff training generally will be addressed, in terms of *why* train, *what* to train, *how* to train, *when* to train and *who* should train; some examples of staff training will then be considered and the reader will be given some ideas about aims and content of training, practical exercises, transferring skills and further reading/resources. It is obviously not possible to cover all aspects of training, as so much of it is centred around individual clients, but this chapter aims to give some principles and ideas that can be used with any training package being put together.

WHAT IS TRAINING?

Clements and Zarkowska (1994) state that training is 'Any systematic attempt to influence the knowledge, skills and values of staff.' This may be done in a variety of ways, for example:

◆ Off-site courses
◆ On-site courses
◆ Short training sessions in the working day
◆ On-the-job modelling and coaching
◆ Personal study.

Training should therefore not be seen as predominantly formal training. The majority of training happens informally: when clinicians meet with a keyworker and discusses action plans for clients; when they join a staff meeting and talk about a client's communication needs; when they spend time working alongside members of staff, maybe trying out different communication strategies or modelling them; and when they go out to the pub after work with colleagues and end up signing songs in Makaton!

WHY TRAIN?

Training can help to enhance motivations such as curiosity, the wish to know, the desire to learn, and the wish to develop as an individual. However, motivation is not enough. Staff need to understand exactly what is required of them and then be capable of carrying out the necessary actions. As Clements and Zarkowska (1994) state: 'Training is a way to help people carry out their work effectively.' They go on to say, however, that training is not necessarily the only way or the best way. There is sometimes little carryover from training to job functioning and this needs to be addressed if quality work is to be implemented and sustained. They stated that 'Training has an important but limited influence on staff performance.'

Tully (1986) lists four benefits of training staff who work in residential situations:

- *Benefits for clients* – staff who are trained have an increased awareness of client need and are more capable of giving appropriate help and support to enhance personal and social development.
- *Benefits for colleagues* – effectively-trained staff understand the relevance of teamwork and are more likely to work effectively alongside others.
- *Benefits for organisations* – staff who have been trained are likely to be more objective about what is happening within their organisation, and can contribute to its effectiveness.
- *Benefits for the individual worker* – the confidence that comes with training helps staff to be more effective. They are more likely to be motivated, more confident, will have the necessary skills to succeed, and will therefore experience increased job satisfaction.

WHAT TO TRAIN?

Training staff is not just about teaching them skills, as possessing skills is not enough to change human behaviour. Consider the act of driving: most people learn the *skills* involved in actually driving a car, but they also need to have a good understanding or *knowledge* of the rules of driving. In addition, if they are to become good drivers, they need to hold *values* around courtesy, turn-taking, value of human life, etc. All three areas interact, and a deficiency in any of the three will adversely affect a person's ability to drive safely and effectively. The same is true when training staff in communication. Their skills, their knowledge and the values they hold all need to be considered; and all of these can be influenced by training.

Knowledge

Knowledge covers aspects such as general information about clients and their needs, and the rationale/theory behind why certain skills are important. This is the foundation on which staff can build skills and working practices (values). For example, staff who have a good knowledge of a client's communication strengths and needs and a good understanding of what that client needs to promote more effective communication are more likely to learn and use the relevant skills effectively.

Skills

Training staff in specific skills can successfully influence how they behave at work. They need to learn skills which will enable them to become more competent at work, including communicating with people at an appropriate level, observing and responding to clients' communicative behaviour, and using skills in order to facilitate and encourage appropriate interaction. Staff not only need to be trained in specific skills such as Makaton, but also need to be trained to use these skills appropriately and effectively within their environment.

Knowledge and skills are not directly related – a member of staff can be very skilful without being knowledgeable, or very knowledgeable without being skilful. However, if a member of staff can have knowledge and skills, they are more likely to be more flexible in their approach, initiate and respond to situations more effectively, and be more innovative in their work practice. In addition to training staff in knowledge and skills, training needs to address the values held by individuals and the environments in which they work, as this will underpin all aspects of staff functioning.

Values

Values are based on the attitudes and policies that surround a service. They provide the rationale for why and how a service is delivered and are often linked to ideologies of care, such as the five service accomplishments of normalisation. Clements and Zarkowska (1994) state that training is often seen as an important vehicle for: 'conveying to staff the values that underpin a service; influencing staff values; and giving the moral answer to the question "why?".'

In reality, values can be hard to change if they have been held by an individual or an establishment for a long period of time, and it may be a case of gradually challenging them in a constructive manner. An example of this is a home manager who believes that normalisation means that clients should be encouraged and enabled to become as 'normal' as possible and should be discouraged from using or doing anything that will make them stand out in society as 'abnormal'. This home manager has strong values that mean that his clients would never, for example, be encouraged to use Makaton, even if it was their only means of expressing themselves, as in the manager's eyes, using Makaton is 'not normal'. However many Makaton training courses the manager went on and however knowledgeable they became in what their clients' communication needs were, they will probably never use their skills and knowledge to improve their working practice because their underpinning values do not complement them.

Values such as these often affect other less experienced staff and they may end up adopting them through ignorance. These staff are often easier to challenge and influence through training and by asking the question, 'Why do we do what we do?'

IDENTIFYING TRAINING NEEDS

The first step in devising any training programme is to identify the different types of training needs which can be divided into:

◆ Individual staff training needs
◆ Workplace training needs
◆ Organisational training needs.

This means assessing the knowledge, skills and values held by the staff and the environment in which they work. Whatever the training needs, it is necessary to determine which of these needs can be met with the training resources available. As Druce (1992) says: 'In an ideal world a comprehensive training programme would be formulated which would address all the needs which have been identified. In a world of limited resources this is not always possible and any particular programme may be designed to tackle only one particular prioritised training need at a given point in time.'

It therefore has to be the decision of the manager and the clinician to determine this and agree on the appropriate content. However, it is also important to involve the staff in this process of determining the content, and to give them some influence on the content of training. As Clements and Zarkowska (1994) state:

- the more actively that the learner is involved in the training process the more likely it is that learning will occur;
- staff will have more intimate knowledge of the job in practice and their own learning needs so that training can be directed more efficiently;
- consultation demonstrates respect for staff, an important support to motivation in general.

Therefore, what goes into training will be the knowledge, skills and values that are relevant to the staff's needs, but the precise content should be determined by their job requirements, their current competencies and their preference.

Having identified the training needs and the needs that are going to be addressed, it is important to set clear aims and objectives for the training programme, including the support that will be given to staff after any formal training to ensure effective transference of skills. Again, this is important to carry out jointly with the relevant managers/members of staff. Lastly, it is important to agree on the method and format of the training. It may be appropriate to draw up a contract at this stage which summarises the content and format of the training being offered and what is expected from the staff being trained, or the organisation in which they work – for example, to release an agreed number of staff for training at an agreed time.

HOW TO TRAIN?

Several factors should be considered when planning training in order to maximise the effectiveness of it. These include learner involvement, the training medium, the training environment, the packaging of information, and the social aspects of training.

Learner involvement

◆ Learning is enhanced by active involvement. This includes the learner having some say over the content of the course and participation in the training process itself. As Clements and Zarkowska (1994) state: 'Passively receiving information is not a good recipe for change.'

◆ When information has to be presented, this needs to be supplemented by learner activity, for example, asking and answering questions; discussing topics; problem-solving; making action plans; relating skills and knowledge to individual clients; carrying out assignments.

The training medium

◆ For *skills* training, it is essential that the training process involves actual practice of the skills, including demonstration, role-play and practice in the actual workplace. This is enhanced by feedback on the group member's performance.

◆ *Knowledge* tends to be verbally encoded and so training in this area will contain a stronger verbal element.

◆ *Values* training needs to have a strong verbal element, but values are often linked to emotions such as joy, guilt, anger (see Clements & Zarkowska, 1994). Values training therefore needs to contain an emotional element and this could be effected by powerful visual images, telling anecdotes, witness accounts and practical exercises that involve going through the same experience as the people with learning disabilities.

The training environment

◆ Distractions will reduce the effectiveness of training. This includes factors such as heating, lighting, seating, intrusions or interruptions, and behaviour of the presenter – for example, distracting habits.

◆ Extremes of arousal will also reduce the effectiveness of training. This will include evoking extreme anxiety or anger in participants; physical climate variables; and monotonous presentation techniques.

◆ The time of day may also be taken into consideration, as people vary in how alert they are at different times of the day. In general, it is assumed that learning is better in the first half of the day (Clements & Zarkowska, 1994).

The packaging of information

◆ People's concentration span when passively engaged in watching or listening should not be assumed to be much more than 20 minutes, and so it is important to use only short stretches of passive involvement.

◆ There is a limit to the number of new items of information or key points that can be taken on board at any one time; Clements and Zarkowska (1994) suggest three to five as a crude guide. It is important, therefore, to present only a limited number of points at one time.
◆ Repetition enhances learning and so it is important to go over the key points more than once.

The social aspects of training

◆ There are advantages to learning with others and these include: the chance to learn from each other as well as from the trainer; the chance to take part in role-plays and other practical exercises; and the motivational elements of group work, such as peer support and competition.
◆ Occasionally, a trainer may experience a member of the group who is destructive to the learning process because of their negative attitude or behaviour. They need to be challenged and dealt with assertively if they are going to be prevented from adversely affecting the whole training session.
◆ Group size should be considered, as if the group becomes too large, it is difficult for the trainer to keep close contact with all the staff.

In summary . . . effective training will:

◆ Be participative.
◆ Be individualised.
◆ Contain demonstration, practice and feedback when teaching skills.
◆ Contain emotional elements when training staff around values.
◆ Be delivered in short, manageable chunks, in a distraction-free environment, at optimum levels of arousal.
◆ Be organised on an individual or small-group basis.

THE USE OF GAMES

People often have reservations about playing games, especially on issues which are real or painful, as they see it as making light of things, and there is a danger that real learning may be trivialised by the mechanics of learning. However, there are advantages to playing games and they can be valuable, as long as they are carefully planned and thought through. Games work by 'encouraging people to suspend judgement at least for a little while. They develop a momentum of their own which works by getting people locked into rituals . . . which keep their attention . . . and they demand that people take turns [which] ensures that each member of the group has a say and underlines the intention to clarify rather than defend or attack one's own or others' attitudes' (Brown, 1992).

As with any training activity, games are useful only if they generate change, and there is nothing more annoying than being asked to play a game that seems to have little relevance to the content of the training course.

Checklist for using games in training

As a trainer, it is important, therefore, to check through a series of questions when planning a game (adapted from Brown, 1992):

◆ What is the aim of the game or exercise?
◆ Is the content directly related to the staff's experience? If not, how can it be adapted?
◆ Is the process appropriate to the hoped for outcomes?
◆ What will staff actually learn from the game?
◆ Does it work? If you're not sure, play it through yourself.
◆ Do you understand the rules, and can you explain them clearly?
◆ Can you explain the purpose of the game clearly?
◆ Does the exercise relate to the staff's own work/role? If not, adapt it so it does.
◆ Are people going to be left feeling uncomfortable at the end? If so, allow time to let people talk this through.
◆ Will people need de-roling? If so, are you clear about how to do this well?
◆ Have you allowed time for feedback after the exercise?

WHEN TO TRAIN?

For training to have the greatest impact, the content of the course should have immediate relevance to the staff being trained. Therefore training has to be closely tied to the current competencies required by the staff, and preferably should focus on skills that they need for their job. Ideally, effective training will be delivered 'just in time', before staff have begun to feel under pressure at work for not feeling competent, or have started avoidance behaviours or 'bad habits'. If staff are trained in skills for which there is no immediate requirement or relevance, then these skills are much more likely to be lost or not become consolidated.

DELIVERING TRAINING

Clements and Zarkowska (1994) suggest that: 'The traditional training format of assembling large groups together and running courses is not ideal.' With high staff turnover, there is an ongoing need for training activity which may be met by repeating training courses on a regular basis and making them readily accessible to relevant staff, or by a more open approach to training, such as practical assignments with tutor supervision.

A recent study by Money (1997, cited by Chatterton, 1999) compares the efficacy of different speech and language therapy approaches in improving the communication skills of people with learning disabilities and the staff who work with them. The approaches were:

1 Direct one-to-one work with the client and the key member of staff.
2 Indirect work via a training course to develop the communication skills of the key member of staff.
3 A combination of the two approaches.

Money (1997, cited by Chatterton, 1999) measured changes in the communicative behaviour of both the staff and clients, and results showed that all three approaches resulted in positive changes, but that the combination of direct work and training demonstrated the greatest number of statistically significant changes. As Chatterton (1999) says, 'This implies that for maximum effectiveness for both staff and service users communication skill training needs to be combined with a direct approach.'

WHO TRAINS? . . . THE SKILLS OF THE TRAINER

The most essential qualities of the trainer have to be:

◆ To know the subject inside out.
◆ To be able to train effectively.

Factors such as time, money and expertise will obviously affect whether in-house or external trainers are used. There is also the concept of the 'outsider effect' – that a message delivered by someone not involved in an agency has more impact than someone you are familiar with. However, using charismatic outsiders may also undermine the credibility of in-house resources and also does not make follow-up and transference of skills as easy.

Wood (1992a) said that trainers should at least be:

- alive to the issues
- able to formulate training programmes in a variety of presentations
- be a good model as a practitioner, leader and manager working with individuals and groups in motivating people
- support the production of good material
- encourage contributions and learning that reflects collaboration with others (p95).

Mansell *et al* (1987, cited by Wood, 1992a) identifies five categories of skills required by good trainers:

1 *Training for service development.* This includes identifying priorities for change in a service and in individuals, and gathering appropriate information about them.

2 *Planning and managing change.* This means setting objectives and making contracts, negotiating the input of other people, delegating tasks and responding to conflict within groups and organisations.

3 *Intervention skills.* These include presentation skills, group facilitation, designing learning material and experiential exercises, making group processes and values explicit, confronting appropriately and effectively and offering models of good training practice.

4 *Evaluation.* This involves giving and receiving clear feedback, using criticism effectively, defining appropriate criteria against which to measure success, and setting up positive monitoring relationships.

5 *Redesign.* Skills that are required for this are incorporating feedback into the design of new training, setting out a comprehensive training strategy, negotiating a mandate on the basis of this strategy, and learning from failures and successes.

EVALUATION

The purpose of evaluation

'Training which has minimal impact on what people do or achieve when they work in the lives of other people has no justification.' (Wood, 1992b.) It is important to evaluate the effect of training on the knowledge, skills and values of the people who undertook the training and then to assess whether the knowledge gained is applied in their workplace. Evaluation therefore has to be an integral part of the training process, not merely the last stage of that process, and it needs to answer the following questions:

◆ Has the training done anything for the staff; in what way and to what extent?
◆ Has the training affected the way staff behave in their place of work?

What needs to be evaluated?

The main areas on which evaluations can focus are shown in Figure 8.1 below (see Wood, 1992b):

Figure 8.1 *MAIN AREAS OF FOCUS FOR EVALUATION*

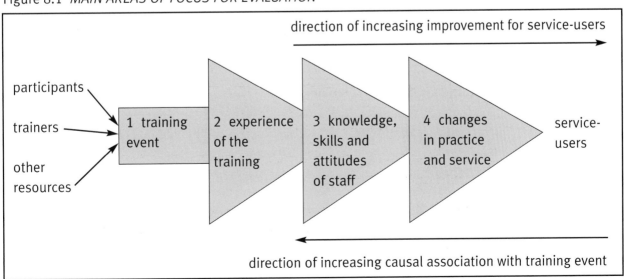

Shifts in staff values, knowledge and skills are easier to examine than changes from the perspective of the client. While it might be assumed that improvements in the values, etc, of staff will mean that clients will be influenced, this cannot be guaranteed. Evaluation needs to take account of these difficulties, and to attempt to be not just an examination of staff.

Evaluation methods

The choice of method used to evaluate training often depends on timescale and resources, but most trainers would probably ideally like to use a combination of methods if they had the resources to do so. There are three basic techniques:

1 *Pencil and paper assessment.* This is generally used to evaluate knowledge and values, and usually involves scales, ratings, formalised schedules or tests.
2 *Interviews and staff reports.* This is used to establish basic patterns of improvement, changes in values and knowledge, and to assess generalisation of any specific changes.
3 *Observational analyses.* This assesses qualitative improvements in the application of skills, and is used to infer generalisation of the staff's use of the training.

Stages of evaluation

Wood (1992b) suggests there are four stages of evaluation:

1 *The preparation phase,* which entails setting the terms of reference, deciding on the method(s) of evaluation and designing research tools.
2 *The execution phase,* which means the collecting of information.
3 *The analysis phase,* where data are examined and interpreted.
4 *The communication phase,* which is where the results are shared with relevant people and implications are drawn.

In summary

Chatterton (1999) states that, 'With the current emphasis on measuring outcomes, efficiency and cost-effectiveness within the NHS, it is important that the efficacy of training to develop communication between staff and service users is evaluated.' Evaluation is therefore an essential and integral part of any training package. It is important to establish whether the training has had an impact on what people do or achieve in their place of work, and whether it has had an impact on the lives of the clients in that service. The challenge is first to try to evaluate not only the skills, knowledge and values of staff who have received training, but also the effect it has had on the service to the clients; and second to make the conclusions meaningful to service planners and staff, and to relate them to people's needs. While doing all of this, it is necessary to remain as objective as possible, something which is relatively hard if the news is not good.

In the next sections of this chapter, different models of staff training relevant to the speech and language clinician working with adults with learning disabilities will be looked at. These will be divided into whole-establishment training and training small groups of staff.

WHOLE-ESTABLISHMENT TRAINING

The whole-establishment training model offers a basic framework that can be applied to either short or extended training activities. As Scragg (1992) states, 'It is a form of training where all staff of a unit are trained together, usually in their work setting, with the content of training focusing directly on service-related issues.' Whole-establishment training covers a wide field of activity. It can be a short discussion group only loosely related to practice, or a programme of workshops spread over many months as an integral part of service development.

Stages

The model of whole-establishment training described here has four stages:

Stage 1 A contract is agreed between a service and a trainer to meet a specified training need.
Stage 2 A training programme is designed that meets the needs identified in stage 1.
Stage 3 The programme is conducted using active learning methods relevant to the needs of the participants.
Stage 4 The programme is evaluated to check that objectives have been met and to help redesign future programmes.

Advantages of whole-establishment training

Training is essential in order to develop staff skills and competencies, and to enable them to support clients in the most effective way. However, Scragg (1992) states that staff often report that new skills are hard to transfer into their work place 'In the face of resistance at both organisational and individual levels'. In addition, Scragg cited Mittler (1984) who reviewed the effectiveness of training and concluded that 'Even the best designed training courses suffer from the fundamental misunderstanding that training by itself can have a significant impact on staff.' He emphasised that designing effective training meant giving particular attention to *the environment* where the training is to be applied, *the constraints of the system* and *existing staff practices*. This contradicted the traditional view that if enough training was thrown at a problem, it would eventually lead to an improvement in a service. Training should therefore take account of organisational constraints when the contract is being negotiated, and the training activities should be designed to integrate theory with practice relevant to participants' needs.

The model of whole-establishment training is therefore designed to help overcome the resistance faced by staff returning from training sessions into practice, and should ideally involve *all* staff from a particular unit (including the managers), and should be held within their own organisational context.

Stage 1: The training contract

The contract stage is essential if the training is going to meet the needs of the service and its staff. Time needs to be given to visiting the service in order to meet staff and to discuss with them what issues concern them and what skills they wish to develop. Staff will be more motivated by the training programme if time has been given to listening to their needs and then to designing the training around them. It is also important to meet the clients so that their needs can be kept in mind when designing the programme.

The following checklist has been adapted from Scragg (1992) and can be used prior to agreeing the contract.

Checklist

- ◆ What is the training problem or issue?
- ◆ Can desired outcomes be described?
- ◆ How many participants will be involved?
- ◆ How will participants be selected?
- ◆ Have their training needs been assessed?
- ◆ What previous training have they completed?
- ◆ What is the budget for the programme?
- ◆ Is there a venue?
- ◆ What dates are proposed?
- ◆ Who will take the responsibility for communicating with the participants?
- ◆ How will the programme be evaluated?
- ◆ Are there any service policies that are relevant to this training?
- ◆ What level of management support will there be?

Stage 2: Designing the training programme

This stage involves drawing up a clear statement of what staff will be able to do following training, developing a programme that includes teaching procedures that meet the learning objectives, and activities that enable the staff to practise the skills. It also includes planning the training environment and preparing handouts/videos, etc. The following checklist can be used when designing the programme:

Checklist

- ◆ *Write the learning objectives.* These should be observable and precise and can refer to things, people or behaviour.
- ◆ *Identify the different kinds of learning needs* – knowledge, skills and values.
- ◆ *Select teaching procedures to provide experiences that meet the learning objectives* – for example presentations, demonstrations, group activities, role-plays.
- ◆ *Plan the sequence of the programme* – for example, start and finish times, break times, and order of activities.

◆ *Prepare materials* – for example, handouts and videos.
◆ *Organise the environment* – for example, agreeing on reducing distractions, comfortable seating, provision of tea/coffee, and necessary equipment (TV, OHP, flipchart).

Stage 3: Conducting the training programme

The effective training programme is dependent on several factors: the presentation of learning activities, the management of the learning environment and the behaviour of the trainer. All three factors will interact and all three need to be appropriate to the context if the training is to be effective. The following checklist for ensuring an effective learning environment has been adapted from Loughary and Hopson (1979, cited by Scragg, 1992):

Checklist

◆ Send participants a programme at least two weeks prior to the event.
◆ Welcome participants, provide name badges if appropriate and encourage them to chat to other people on arrival.
◆ Check all facilities, including teaching rooms, equipment and domestic arrangements.
◆ Start and finish on time.
◆ Allocate time for a warm-up activity to build relationships in the group and make people feel more at ease.
◆ Learn participants' names and use them.
◆ Establish credibility by describing briefly own relevant experience.
◆ Show confidence in the subject and enthusiasm for the material/exercises, etc.
◆ Speak positively and assume the participants are interested. Use examples from practice to bring the subject to life.
◆ Provide encouragement and feedback on completion of tasks.
◆ Use participant-centred learning models rather than presenter-dominated models.
◆ Use learning approaches based on a cycle of short, focused presentations followed by longer periods of active involvement rather than passive listening.
◆ Use small-group work which is conducive to open discussion, risk-taking and learning from others.
◆ Use high quality audio-visual materials to maintain attention.
◆ Have previously-prepared handouts in sufficient numbers.
◆ Take tea, coffee and lunch with the participants – this is when a lot of people will ask questions and give feedback on how it is going.

Stage 4: Evaluating the training programme

The final stage in the process is evaluation which has two purposes:

1 To enable participants to check on the progress they have made towards achieving their learning objectives.

2 To provide feedback to the trainer on the content of the training so that future training courses can be improved.

The first stage of evaluation is an evaluation of the training session and this is usually achieved by participants completing a simple questionnaire, either using a rating scale (see Figure 8.2) or more open questions (see Figure 8.3), or a mixture of both.

Figure 8.2 *Evaluation Questionnaire: Rating Scale*

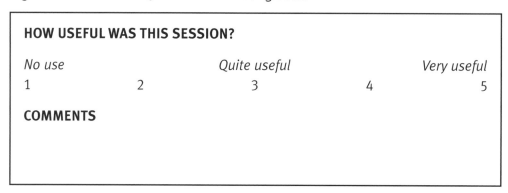

HOW USEFUL WAS THIS SESSION?

No use		*Quite useful*		*Very useful*
1	2	3	4	5

COMMENTS

Figure 8.3 *Evaluation Questionnaire: Open Questions*

WHAT DID YOU FIND MOST USEFUL ABOUT THIS SESSION?

WHAT DID YOU FIND LEAST USEFUL ABOUT THIS SESSION?

The second stage of evaluation is to observe how far skills developed during the session and whether these skills have been transferred into their work environment. Scragg (1992) gives a checklist for helping people transfer skills to practice:

Checklist

◆ Review the skills developed during the workshop and list those you want to introduce into practice.
◆ Write down the barriers that will limit the potential to implement new practice.
◆ List opportunities that will help you improve chances of implementing new practice.
◆ Develop strategies for overcoming barriers using opportunities identified.
◆ Write an action plan based on your selected strategy.

STAGE 1 THE TRAINING CONTRACT – WORKED EXAMPLE

INITIAL TRAINING REQUEST

A Makaton training programme was requested by the manager of a small unit for people with challenging behaviour, two of whom were known to have used Makaton in the past and one of whom was currently trying to communicate using Makaton.

INITIAL MEETING WITH MANAGER

It was agreed that time should be spent on the unit prior to drawing up a contract for the training, and that the next staff meeting would be an ideal opportunity to meet all the staff on the unit and to discuss the training programme.

VISIT TO THE UNIT

A visit to the unit revealed the following:

- Clients were expressing themselves predominantly non-verbally, for example through body-language, eye-gaze, behaviour and vocalisations. Only one Makaton sign was observed. Informal assessment showed that the clients had significant problems in understanding what was expected of them and often relied on situational cues.

- Staff were very skilled in managing challenging behaviour, but often used inappropriately complex speech and did not always identify the different modes of expression used by the clients. Staff had also had some training in normalisation and were trying to implement the philosophy of an ordinary life into the unit; however, they were unable to adapt their communication to suit the individual clients, for example when offering choices, and this sometimes resulted in incidents of challenging behaviour.

- The environment was physically attractive, but noisy as the TV remained on all the time in one room and the radio was on in the other communal room.

- Informal discussions with staff showed that some were keen to learn Makaton and some thought it would be a waste of time because the clients did not use it. Some felt that that they needed more information on the clients' communication needs and strategies for encouraging more effective communication.

STAGE 1 THE TRAINING CONTRACT – WORKED EXAMPLE

STAFF MEETING

The following points were discussed and agreed at the next staff meeting:

- The training need is greater than a need for Makaton training. A need for a greater awareness of the communication needs of the clients who live in the unit, and the link between challenging behaviour and communication was identified. Increased strategies for communicating effectively with individual clients were also identified.

MEETING WITH MANAGER

A further meeting with the manager of the unit confirmed the following:

- A date and venue for the one-day training workshop.

- All staff, including the manager, to attend and the unit to be covered by agency staff.

- Other relevant professionals were identified to invite; for example, the occupational therapist who works regularly at the unit.

- An outline of the course would be sent two weeks prior to the course and would be circulated to all staff by the manager.

- Evaluation of the course would include a written evaluation of the day, and follow-up visits to the unit to assess staff skills through joint working and evaluation of the aims and objectives set for each client on the course.

STAGE 2 DESIGNING THE TRAINING PROGRAMME – WORKED EXAMPLE

LEARNING OBJECTIVES AND LEARNING NEEDS

IMPROVING KNOWLEDGE

- For staff to be able to describe the communication needs of all the clients.

- For staff to be able to understand the link between challenging behaviour and communication.

- For staff to be able to describe the relevant strategies for improving effective communication with individual clients.

- For staff to be able to plan communication programmes for each client.

- For staff to be able to describe why Makaton is important.

IMPROVING SKILLS

- For staff to be able to use their communication skills appropriately with individual clients.

- For staff to be able to sign stages 1 and 2 of Makaton confidently.

TEACHING PROCEDURES

- **Presentations** – explanation of the model for effective communication; presentation of the causes of challenging behaviour; description of impaired expressive and receptive skills.

- **Demonstrations** – video of unknown client; video of clients in the unit; Makaton signs.

- **Group activities** – brainstorm how and why we communicate; group discussion on receptive environments; breakdown of communication; discussion on individual clients; formulating action plans for each client; Makaton signing; role-playing different communication strategies.

- **Group games** – warm-up activity; exercise on trying to communicate without using words.

PROGRAMME/HANDOUTS – see next section of worked example.

STAGE 3 CONDUCTING THE TRAINING PROGRAMME – WORKED EXAMPLE

PROGRAMME SENT TO PARTICIPANTS

Workshop on communication and challenging behaviour

Date and venue

9.30–9.40	Arrive and coffee
9.40–9.55	Introduction to day
9.55–10.40	What is effective communication?
10.40–10.50	What is a receptive environment?
10.50–11.15	Communication breakdown
11.15–11.30	Coffee
11.30–11.50	Causes of challenging behaviour and the link to communication
11.50–12.30	Expressive skills and level of understanding and the link to behaviour
12.30–1.30	Lunch
1.30–2.00	Video – where is communication breaking down and what is needed to make communication more effective?
2.00–2.45	Video and small-group discussion on clients in unit
2.45–3.00	Tea
3.00–3.30	Action-planning for the clients
3.30–4.00	Makaton stages 1 & 2
4.00–4.30	Summary and evaluation

WORKSHOP ON COMMUNICATION AND CHALLENGING BEHAVIOUR

<u>Timetable</u>		<u>Activities</u>
9.30–9.40	Arrival	1 Welcome participants
		2 Participants encouraged to talk and have coffee
9.40–9.50	Introduction	1 Introduce self
		2 Warm-up exercise
9.50–9.55	Workshop details	1 Go through aims and plan of day and check if OK
		2 Describe domestic arrangements
9.55–10.10	Group exercise	1 Introduce 'effective communication'
		2 Brainstorm 'How do we communicate?'
10.10–10.20	Presentation & demonstration	1 Describe how verbal and non-verbal behaviours are used in combination
		2 Demonstrate different scenarios to elicit comments on first impressions, the importance of non-verbal behaviour
10.20–10.30	Group exercise	1 Brainstorm 'Why do we communicate?'

STAGE 3 CONDUCTING THE TRAINING PROGRAMME – WORKED EXAMPLE

10.30–10.40	Presentation	1 Describe model of effective communication (flipchart) using answers given in brainstorm activities as examples 2 Give handout on model (Handout 1)
10.40–10.50	Group exercise	1 Discussion on what do we mean by a 'receptive environment'? List ideas on model on flipchart 2 Give handout on effective communication (Handout 2)
10.50–11.00	Presentation & demonstration	1 Introduce 'breakdown of communication' – can occur at any place in the model/cycle 2 Describe/act out scenario where communication has broken down, eg, argument at home (a funny example that is real is best) – why did it break down and where in the cycle did it occur?
11.00–11.10	Group exercise	1 Participants pair up and think of examples of communication breakdown – where did it occur in the cycle?
11.10–11.15	Feedback	1 Feedback from exercise and any questions
11.15–11.30	Coffee break	
11.30–11.50	Presentation & group exercise	1 Introduce 'the link between communication and challenging behaviour' 2 Brainstorm the causes of challenging behaviour 3 Present nine causes of challenging behaviour & give handout (Handout 3) 4 Group discussion on how many of these are linked to communication difficulties
11.50–12.00	Presentation	1 Impaired expressive skills – how does the person with challenging behaviour express their needs?
12.00–12.15	Group exercise	1 In pairs, try to communicate the sentence given to you to your partner without using words or sign language (see practical exercise, Handout 5) 2 Everyone feeds back – how did it feel?
12.15–12.25	Presentation & demonstration	1 Impaired receptive skills – explanation of 'key word phrases' 2 Give examples of different commands – how many words do they need to understand? Discuss cues.

STAGE 3 CONDUCTING THE TRAINING PROGRAMME – WORKED EXAMPLE

12.25–12.30	Group exercise	1 Group list reasons why it is important to know how much someone understands.
		2 Give handout (Handout 4)
		3 Session feedback
12.30–1.30	Lunch	
1.30–1.40	Presentation	1 Introduction to the afternoon – linking what was learnt in the morning to people with challenging behaviour
		2 Introduction to unknown client on video
1.40–2.00	Video & group exercise	1 Video
		2 Group discussion on what are her expressive and receptive skills like? Where is communication breaking down and what does she need to make it more effective?
2.00–2.45	Group exercise & video	1 Divide into small groups – exercise explained
		2 Short video clips of every client in the unit
		3 Each group discusses one client and completes a model of effective communication for them on a flipchart
		4 Feedback to large group
2.45–3.00	Tea break	
3.00–3.30	Group exercise	1 Action planning for individual clients in small groups – what needs to change? Agree on an action plan
		2 Feedback to large group
3.30–4.00	Demonstration & group exercise	1 Teach Makaton stages 1 & 2
		2 Participants sign some useful phrases
4.00–4.30	Summary & evaluation	1 Summary of main points and action agreed for clients
		2 Evaluation of session and finish

STAGE 4 EVALUATING THE TRAINING – WORKED EXAMPLE

EVALUATION OF WORKSHOP ON COMMUNICATION AND CHALLENGING BEHAVIOUR

SESSION EVALUATION

- Questionnaire completed by all participants at the end of the session.

EVALUATION OF TRANSFERRING OF SKILLS

- Action plans devised during the workshop were reviewed one month later jointly by speech and language clinician and keyworker.

- Joint working sessions were organised to evaluate progress of action plans and staff skills.

- Reports written jointly with key workers on all clients to summarise needs and action plans agreed. Reports copied to relevant others.

- Trainer attended staff meeting three months after the workshop to discuss ongoing issues.

TRAINING SMALL GROUPS OF STAFF

It is not always practical or appropriate to train a whole establishment, and in some places it is more effective to start training a limited number of staff. This is an 'incrementalist approach' and relies on staff who have been trained affecting the skills of others by example.

Mansell (1988) defines the priorities for this kind of training model as:

◆ A clear focus on exemplary service models – providing ideas and opportunities which people can aim for – and helping to establish innovative projects which demonstrate these ideas in practice.
◆ Developing local competence and creating effective local change agents by helping people acquire skills and a mandate to effect change.
◆ Matching the focus on organisational change with training interventions which develop individuals who can make use of the opportunities that a supportive environment provides.
◆ Directing training towards maintaining innovation and sustaining good practice beyond the initial period of enthusiasm and attention.

The small-group training model should be planned and implemented using the same stages and checklists as the whole-establishment training model, although there will obviously be some adaptations. For example, in stage 1, the training contract, the main difference will be the decision as to *who* will be included in the training programme.

SMALL GROUP TRAINING MODEL – WORKED EXAMPLE

Training was requested by a residential and day unit for 20 young people with learning disabilities, in order to help the unit become a receptive communication environment for several clients who used signs and symbols to communicate.

The contract

A meeting with the manager and staff was arranged and the following was agreed:

- Four key members of staff, including the manager, were identified to train initially. Criteria for selection included being the key worker for a client who used signing and/or symbols to communicate and the ability to attend all four training sessions.

- Four training sessions were organised to be held within the establishment, and to run weekly over a period of a month.

- Commitment was given to providing a room free of distractions.

- If the training was evaluated as being successful, a second training programme would be organised for a further four members of staff. This would continue until all key members of staff had received training. This would mean three training programmes being completed over a six-month period, as there would be a month between each course to allow time for individual work with those members of staff who had recently received training.

The learning objectives

- For staff to be able to understand the importance of augmentative systems of communication.

- For staff to be able to identify improvements needed in the environment in order to make it more appropriate to clients' communicative needs.

- For staff to be able to describe relevant strategies for improving effective communication with individual clients.

- For staff to understand how communication can be facilitated and how it can break down.

- For staff to be able to plan communication programmes for individual clients.

- For staff to be able to sign stages 1–4 of Makaton confidently and identify and learn other signs relevant to the needs of the home.

- For staff to be able to use their communication skills appropriately with clients.

Teaching procedures

- *Presentations* – explanation of the model of effective communication; description of impaired expressive and receptive skills; description of various augmentative systems.

- *Demonstrations* – Makaton signs; use of symbol boards/communication books.

- *Group activities* – brainstorming; group discussion on the clients and environment; formulating action plans for the clients and for changing the environment; Makaton signing; role-playing different communication strategies; homework assignments.

SMALL GROUP TRAINING MODEL – WORKED EXAMPLE

- *Group games* – warm-up activities; experiential learning games on communicating without speech, etc.

Content of session (each one three hours long)

Session 1:
- What is effective communication?
- What is a receptive environment?
- Communication breakdown.
- Explanation of impaired expressive and receptive skills.
- Homework assignments: assessment of a client in terms of their communication and where it is breaking down.

Session 2:
- Explanation of different methods of augmentative communication.
- Feedback from homework.
- Videos of clients.
- Group exercise on formulating action plans for individual clients.
- Homework assignments: assessment of the communication environment of the home and how it could become more 'receptive'.

Session 3:
- Feedback from homework.
- Group exercise on formulating one or two action plans based on ideas brought back from homework.
- Demonstration of and practice in stages 1 and 2 of Makaton.
- Homework assignment: identify other important signs to learn from the vocabulary.

Session 4:
- Homework feedback.
- Makaton demonstration and practice.
- Explanation and discussion on the use of symbols.
- Role-play on using appropriate communication strategies with different clients.
- Discussion of agreed action plans for clients and the environment and review meetings set up over next four weeks.

Evaluation methods
- Pre- and post-workshop questionnaires on client's communication strategies and needs to determine if knowledge has been gained.
- Questionnaire at end of workshop to evaluate content of course.
- Joint working sessions and review meetings to evaluate effectiveness of action plans and transference of skills.

A MODEL OF EFFECTIVE COMMUNICATION – HANDOUT 1

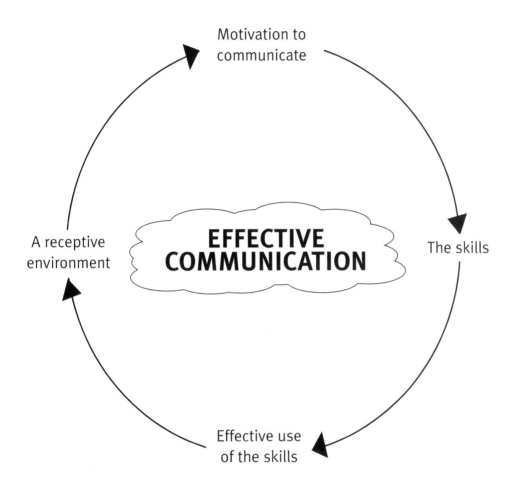

Motivation to communicate

A receptive environment

EFFECTIVE COMMUNICATION

The skills

Effective use of the skills

'Somehow we have to ensure that people **WANT** to communicate, that there is **SOMEONE** to communicate with, that they have **SOMETHING** to communicate about and that we show them that communicating is **ENJOYABLE** and **BRINGS RESULTS**.' (Mittler, 1988)

EFFECTIVE COMMUNICATION – HANDOUT 2

HOW DO WE COMMUNICATE?

VERBALLY	*NON-VERBALLY*
Speech	Body language
Content of speech	Facial expression
Noises	Eye contact
Listening	Posture & gait
Tone of voice	Gesture
Volume	Sign language
Rate of speech	Distance
Clarity of speech	Touch
Fluency	Personal appearance
	Body movements
	Behaviour
	Pictures/symbols

- Most of us use verbal and non-verbal skills in combination all the time, to reveal feelings, attitudes, etc.
- Most of our true communication is non-verbal.

Every behaviour, regardless of form or intention can communicate, that is any behaviour has the potential to send a message.

WHY DO WE COMMUNICATE?

To:

- Tell someone what we want
- Express feelings
- Obtain information
- Give information
- Get attention
- Make friends or for pleasure/social reasons
- Put our views across

WHAT IS A RECEPTIVE ENVIRONMENT?

An environment that provides:

- Someone to talk to
- Someone to listen and act on what you are saying
- Someone who understands you – a SHARED LANGUAGE
- Time to talk/express yourself
- Respect
- Stimulation without distraction
- An appropriate environment for the activity

Photocopiable

©Alex Kelly, 2000

COMMON CAUSES OF CHALLENGING BEHAVIOUR – HANDOUT 3

ref. McDonnell (1995): *Staff Training in the Management of Challenging Behaviour.*

1 Being unable to communicate a need

If a person cannot communicate their needs and wishes, this can lead to challenging behaviour. It is possibly easy to imagine, or think of actual examples, when we have become aggressive or even physically violent ourselves when we have been trying to communicate something to someone and they appear not to be able to understand what we are saying. It is not difficult to understand how frustrating it would be if this occurred on a daily basis.

2 Being confused

Challenging behaviour can often occur when people do not understand the demands that are being placed on them and so they become confused. We frequently speak to people using grammatically complicated language and assume that we have been understood, and we are more likely to overestimate, rather than underestimate, a client's ability to understand verbal information. It may be like being in a foreign country where no-one speaks your language, and if they then shouted at you and seemed upset with you, it would be difficult for you to understand why and you would probably become confused and maybe frightened as well.

3 Being in pain

If a person has a communication problem, it is difficult for them to tell you they are in pain. A person may behave in an uncharacteristic manner or even become aggressive if they have a headache, stomach ache or dental problem. Illness should always therefore be considered when investigating the cause of challenging behaviour.

4 Medication change

Similar to the notion of being confused, changes in medication can have a number of behavioural side-effects. Most people, when prescribed medication, have some idea of what the medication they are taking is supposed to do. Research has shown that an individual can easily be confused and excited if medication is administered without explaining the side-effects. Medication changes are often routine and well-intentioned, but a lack of explanation and a difficulty in a person's ability to comprehend verbal information may lead to a sequence of events that the person does not understand either. This will lead to confusion and can precipitate aggression and violence.

5 Inactivity

McDonnell states that research shows that challenging behaviour decreases if we increase the activity schedules of people with learning disabilities. Boredom is therefore an important factor, because if a person is bored, violent and aggressive behaviours can provide that individual with a great deal of attention. If this is the case, we need to provide that attention in a more positive manner appropriate to the behaviour displayed.

COMMON CAUSES OF CHALLENGING BEHAVIOUR – HANDOUT 3

6 Attention-seeking behaviour

While it is true that sometimes challenging behaviour is used to attract attention, it is important to remember that seeking attention is a perfectly valid thing to do. We need to ask why it is that the person needs attention and how can we ensure that attention is available to them without having to use difficult behaviour.

7 Changes in routine

Changes in everyday routine can often lead to challenging behaviour, and this is particularly true for people with autism and people who have limited understanding. Routines help us to manage and understand our environment, and for those people who have difficulties in understanding, a familiar routine is something that they rely on in order to make sense of their world and what is expected of them. A change in routine can therefore be confusing and distressing and can in turn lead to challenging behaviour.

8 Environmental effects

The environment we live in can have a dramatic effect on our behaviour and many of these effects have been associated with violent and aggressive behaviour. Some of these include:

- the amount of personal space a person requires
- heat
- extreme noise
- seating arrangements.

9 Delusional thoughts

Some people with learning disabilities may have mental health difficulties, and this can result in delusional thoughts and ideas which may or may not be apparent. A result of delusional thoughts can be challenging behaviour.

Challenging behaviours do *not* occur without a reason but are often a result of a number of different factors. We need to try to understand how the person's communication difficulties may be influencing or directly affecting their challenging behaviour.

COMMUNICATION AND CHALLENGING BEHAVIOUR – HANDOUT 4

Communication and challenging behaviour are linked. Challenging behaviour can itself be a form of communication, an effective way of sending a message, for example, 'I don't want to do this any more'. The behaviour either *expresses* a need or is a direct result of a *comprehension difficulty*. The behaviour can therefore be a symptom of an underlying need or difficulty rather than itself being the difficulty.

Expressive skills

The impact of impaired expressive skills on behaviour cannot be overestimated. We all have needs and we all need to express those needs. We need to look at how the person with challenging behaviour signals or expresses that they are in need of something.

THE CLIENT'S NEEDS   **THE CLIENT'S EXPRESSIVE SKILLS**

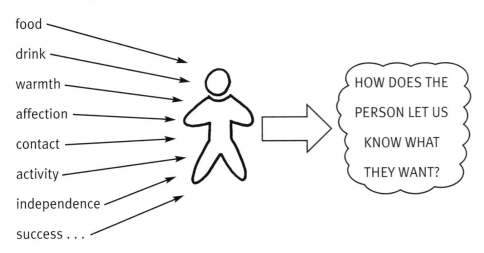

food
drink
warmth
affection
contact
activity
independence
success . . .

HOW DOES THE PERSON LET US KNOW WHAT THEY WANT?

- What lengths would you go to in order to express something if you were unable to communicate verbally?

Comprehension

Impaired receptive skills or comprehension can also have a devastating effect on someone's behaviour. People frequently assume that clients understand far more than they are actually able to, and clients are sometimes described as being able to 'understand everything that you say to them . . . if they feel like it'. A client needs to understand only one key word in a phrase to have a good chance of then following that instruction correctly, but equally sometimes incorrectly. If staff are unaware that a client has difficulties in understanding verbal information, they may interpret inappropriate or bizarre responses as challenging behaviour.

COMMUNICATION AND CHALLENGING BEHAVIOUR – HANDOUT 4

We need to know if someone has a comprehension difficulty, because otherwise there may be negative consequences:

- **our expectations may be unrealistic;**

- **the person with a learning disability may receive only part of a message, or misinterpret the information and therefore respond in an inappropriate or bizarre way;**

- **when people do not respond appropriately they may be mistakenly described as uncooperative, when in fact they do not understand what they are meant to do;**

- **the person may come to perceive the world as a confusing place;**

- **people can become frustrated at the inconsistencies they are constantly exposed to and may exhibit their frustration as challenging behaviour; and**

- **they may also feel it safer not to respond and appear to be withdrawn.**

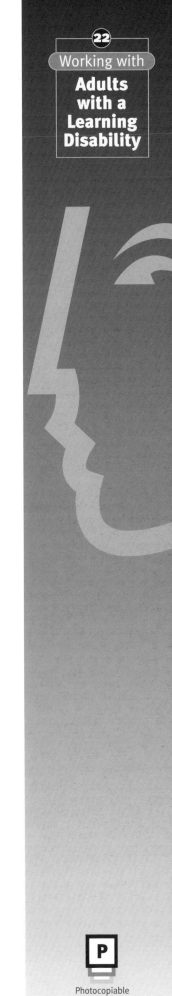

PRACTICAL EXERCISE – COMMUNICATION WITHOUT SPEECH – HANDOUT 5

Sentences

'WHERE IS ANDY' . . . THE MEMBER OF STAFF
WHO NORMALLY WORKS TODAY. 'I MISS HIM AND FEEL
WORRIED THAT HE IS NOT HERE.'

'I HAVE A PAIN IN MY HAND . . . MIKE HURT ME
YESTERDAY BY PULLING AT MY HAND.'

'I FEEL SAD . . . IT IS A YEAR AGO TODAY THAT MY DAD DIED.'

'I AM FRIGHTENED . . . THERE IS A HUGE
SPIDER UNDER YOUR CHAIR.'

'I AM FRIGHTENED OF YOU . . .
YOU TALK TOO LOUDLY.'

'I WANT YOU TO LEAVE ME ALONE.'

'I AM FED UP AND WANT TO GO HOME.'

'I FEEL EXCITED . . . I AM LOOKING FORWARD
TO GOING SWIMMING.'

Chapter 9: Working in a Community Learning-Disability Team

INTRODUCTION

Working as part of an effective multidisciplinary team has to be one of the most rewarding and exciting ways to work as a clinician. A team unites rather than isolates the specialist skills of each professional group, and the client is the catalyst who initiates interaction between the interdisciplinary team members. If a team *is* effective, then clinicians can achieve much more than they could as individuals.

However, not all teams are effective and simply bringing together staff from diverse professional backgrounds and with different experiences and skills is not sufficient to produce good joint working. In this chapter the issue of what makes an effective team will be addressed initially, and how effectiveness can be measured. The advantages of team work will be discussed briefly, as will the qualities needed to make a good team member. The role of the speech and language clinician in a multidisciplinary team will then be considered under four headings: individual work with clients; joint work with other team members; advice and support to other team members; and training team members. An example of joint working is described using the area of counselling, and in particular we consider the role of the speech and language clinician in supporting professionals involved in counselling people with learning disabilities.

Teams in the UK have a variety of names, including 'Specialist Health Care Team', 'Community Team for People with Learning Disabilities', and 'Community Learning-Disability Team'. In this chapter, the last will be used and will be abbreviated to CLDT, but the principles will remain the same in whatever country/environment teams are functioning.

WHAT MAKES AN EFFECTIVE TEAM?

The idea of CLDTs was first promoted in the UK in the 1970s by the Development Team for the Mentally Handicapped, and by the end of the 1980s most localities had some form of team or grouping of professionals. The *raison d'être* of CLDTs has been to 'confront head-on those concerns . . . that care-provision for people with a mental handicap was fragmented, that services were inaccessible, and that organisational and professional boundaries prevented continuity of care.' (Brown & Wistow, 1990) But CLDTs vary in their size, membership, function and effectiveness. So, what makes a team effective?

Pauline Barrett in Stewart (1987) said: 'The successful team may look as if it happened by magic but you can be sure that it did not . . .'. Barr (1993) suggests that an effective team has 'Clearly-defined goals, agreed values, and a commitment from members', and Ovretveit (1990, cited by Stewart, 1987), says that the quickest way to establish effective teamwork is to have 'a clearly defined leader'. Other important factors include having clear roles and responsibilities, good communication, good use of team resources, good links with other agencies, and systems to review and measure team performance and effectiveness.

The team leader

Gilbert and Scragg (1992) states that the leader's responsibility is to 'Enable the team to develop a shared commitment to a common purpose, and the recognition that a team needs the efforts of every one of its members to achieve this.' When this has happened, the team will see itself as a team, it will have a team direction and will be able to establish ways of working together. If this is achieved then membership of a team that works well can bring benefits that cannot be overestimated. Malin (1995) also suggests that the team leader will usually take on a coordinating role, including allocation and monitoring of caseloads, conflict resolution, review of team policy and practice, and representing team matters in general management. However, the team leader is reliant on committed support from team members, and without this such tasks are virtually impossible.

A clear purpose

A team needs to have a purpose or a 'mission' which is a long-term statement of intent and which describes how the team will meet the main goal of the service. They need to establish at the outset what the nature of the team is, what the client group is and what the core problems of that client group are. With this information it should be possible to determine who are the key team members and to reach agreement with the team and their managers on roles and an operational policy.

Clear roles and responsibilities

Team members need to have a clear idea of their role within a team and the limits of their responsibilities in order to achieve coordinated patterns of working. They also need to have a good understanding of the roles of other team members. Different professions have different methods of working and may have different value systems and priorities, and if they do not have a clear understanding of one another's work this can damage relationships between team members and reduce the effectiveness of the team. As Thompson and Mathias (1992) state: 'Before a group of people can cooperate and work together to achieve the best results, the role and function of each member of the group must be fully understood. Everyone must be aware of the part played by each team member in the overall programme.'

Communication

Communication is seen as a key element for the development of effective and enjoyable team working. It is important for three reasons (Gilbert & Scragg, 1992): to achieve the common task, to maintain the unity of the team, and to meet individual needs. Factors that will promote more

effective communication are: regular team meetings that make effective use of time and ensure contribution from team members; clear procedures for all written information – for example, case notes, minutes of meetings, client reviews; and office layouts that facilitate interaction between team members – for example, shared offices, access to meeting rooms, shared administration support.

Good use of team resources

The contribution of members is invaluable and unique, and the team leader needs to review the team continually, asking (Gilbert and Scragg, 1992):

◆ How well is the talent of the team being used?
◆ Are all members contributing and active?
◆ Are there any passengers?
◆ Are team meetings too long?
◆ Would any members be better re-deployed?

Links with other agencies

In the UK, services for people with learning disabilities are complex and often depend on the cooperation of multiple agencies and their staff, as well as users of services, their relatives and carers. CLDTs need to create 'open communication and harmonious activity with the main teams around it' (Cormack, 1987, cited by Gilbert, 1992), and need to be aware of the risks of focusing inwards and ignoring external relationships and communications that are crucial for the overall success of the service. In addition, the CLDT plays a key role in service-planning for people with learning disabilities in the community, and as Grant and Jenkins state (in Brown and Wistow, 1990): 'Theirs (CLDTs) is a juxtaposition between all the key groups who could claim a stake in community care.'

MEASURING TEAM PERFORMANCE AND EFFECTIVENESS

In the UK, The Department of Health paper *A First Class Service* (1998) states that services will be measured for quality and effectiveness by national service frameworks – for example NICE (National Institute of Clinical Excellence) – and clinical governance. However, as Taylor (1991, cited in Aylott & Toocaram, 1996) suggest, services for people with learning disabilities are not easily measurable, and it is therefore a challenge to produce evidence of an effective and efficient service to purchasers and service-users. Poulton and West (1993) use team innovation as indicators of team effectiveness, and Pearson and Spencer (1997) state that the top indicators through their research were: agreed aims, goals and objectives, effective communication, clearly-defined roles, and patients receiving the best possible care. They add that where people have clear set targets, performances are improved. It is therefore possible to conclude that if a team has a good team leader, a clear purpose and clear roles and responsibilities, good communication and use of team resources, and good links with other services, then they will be able to measure team performance and effectiveness.

ADVANTAGES OF TEAM WORK

As can be seen from the previous points, effective teams do not happen overnight and continue to need hard work and dedicated workers. However, being part of a CLDT has many advantages for the individual clinician. Pougher (1997) gives four reasons why working as part of a team is an advantage over working individually:

◆ Teamworking is an effective means of promoting organisational change. Staff are more likely to support change if they have been involved in it.
◆ Working in teams supports cooperation within an organisation rather than competition. It should improve communications between departments and help build trust and develop interdependence.
◆ People can bring into a team a wide range of skills and experience that can be shared. Thus a greater number of problems can be solved than could be tackled by one individual.
◆ The standard of decision-making in teams tends to be high, and recommendations from teams are therefore more likely to be implemented.

WHAT MAKES A GOOD TEAM MEMBER?

However, what do clinicians need to have in order to be good 'team players'? While Thompson and Mathias (1992) give 17 requirements for a good member of a CLDT team, the following are the most essential:

1 To be flexible and tolerant of many different views.
2 To have a holistic attitude to the client.
3 To be willing to share knowledge and skills and acquire new skills.
4 To be able to give and take in relationships with colleagues.
5 To have a positive and realistic approach to working with people with learning disabilities.
6 To be skilled in communication.
7 To be a good listener.
8 To be tolerant and patient.
9 To be able to motivate self and others.
10 To have a sense of humour.

These 10 requirements are obviously applicable to all people working as part of a team, but the chapter will now address the role of the speech and language clinician working in a CLDT.

THE ROLE OF THE SPEECH & LANGUAGE CLINICIAN

The role of the clinician can be divided into four main areas, although obviously these should not be viewed as independent from one another:

1 Individual work with clients

The clinician will accept referrals for clients who have difficulty with their communication (understanding or expression) or who have swallowing or feeding problems. They will liaise with other team members already involved with the client, and if the client is not known to the team, they may need to complete an initial screening assessment which would be brought back to the team prior to any intervention (emergency intervention excluded). Individual work is fed back to the team at client review meetings, and clinicians are required to keep working notes in the team's central files so that other team members can access them. Clinicians are expected to have a holistic attitude towards the client and should not be purely focusing on communication. They need to liaise with other professionals as appropriate and make inter-team referrals if this is agreed as a good course of action. They may also need to consider their individual work alongside other individual work that is occurring, and priorities for intervention may need to be agreed to prevent the client being overwhelmed by so much therapy.

Clinicians are also expected to manage their case loads effectively, operating waiting lists when appropriate and developing criteria for intervention when necessary. They also need to measure effectiveness through setting objectives to monitor the success of therapy and through peer review.

2 Joint work with other team members

In many cases, it is appropriate and most effective to work jointly with another member of the CLDT. As Thompson and Mathias (1992) state, working with team members 'is essential if the clients are going to reach their full potential'. Some examples of joint work are:

◆ The client who is referred for eating and drinking difficulties and initial assessment from the speech and language clinician reveals issues around posture and manual skills as well as swallowing problems. A three-way assessment between the physiotherapist, occupational therapist and speech and language clinician is agreed to be the most effective way of addressing all of the clients needs.

◆ The client who is initially referred to psychology for challenging behaviour, but initial assessment revealed that there are communication issues and also issues around daily living skills. The speech and language clinician and occupational therapist both become involved in assessing this client and the three professionals liaise regularly in terms of what the action plan for this client may be. If staff training is identified as a need, then they will organise and run it together.

◆ The client who is referred because his speech has deteriorated recently. Initial assessment of the client and discussions with his carers reveal that the client is showing some signs of depression and there is a question as to whether his lack of clarity is linked to this. The psychiatrist becomes involved and together with the speech and language clinician decides upon an appropriate course of intervention for this client.

◆ The client who is referred to occupational therapy for support in accessing a new community facility. The client has a symbolised communication book with which they communicate, but has no symbols that communicate this new activity. The speech and language therapist works jointly with the occupational therapist to create some new symbols for this client.

3 Advice and support to other team members

The speech and language clinician has a valuable role to play within a CLDT in offering advice and support to other professionals working with certain clients. They should act as a resource to others with regard to their knowledge of:

◆ A client's level of understanding
◆ A client's level and method of expression
◆ A client's eating and drinking difficulties.

It is often essential that work being done by another member of the CLDT is supported through advice from the speech and language clinician so that they can:

◆ Communicate at an appropriate level with that client.
◆ Understand what the client is communicating and be able to facilitate this through additional appropriate communication methods – for example, signing.
◆ Be aware of specific difficulties a client has and act accordingly – for example, ensuring drinks are thickened to an appropriate consistency if this is required.

4 Training team members

Communication is central to everyone's ability to achieve a good quality of life. As a specialist team of professionals working with adults with a learning disability, the CLDT has to be aware not only of the importance of enabling a person to communicate their needs, but also of their own ability to do so. All team members need to be trained to communicate effectively and appropriately with their clients ,and it is the role of the speech and language clinician on the team to do this. This can obviously be done through formal workshops, informal training sessions – for example at the end of team meetings – and joint working. Ideally, it should be done by a combination of all three.

COUNSELLING: AN EXAMPLE OF JOINT WORKING

There is evidence to suggest that people with learning disabilities often have life experiences which create the need for therapeutic interventions (Beaill & Warden, 1995; Sinason, 1986; Emerson, 1977). Despite this evidence, the availability of therapeutic intervention such as counselling as a method of treatment is limited.

Communication is probably the biggest single factor in restricting opportunities for counselling for people who have learning disabilities (Bungener & McCormack,

1994; Dalton, 1994). There is a wide assumption that if a person has no speech they have no need for, or cannot benefit from, certain types of help. Resources that have traditionally been dependent on a person speaking have therefore been denied them, and those people with a learning disability who also have a communication difficulty have been subjected to the devaluing pressures of inequality. But as Moulster (1997) says: 'The biggest problems exist, not for the person who has difficulty in communicating with us, but for those of us who are trying to understand. It is very easy to assume that if a person has a difficulty in communicating then it's their problem. The reality is that this is our problem. We need to find ways of understanding people's needs and enable people to communicate more effectively.'

In Moulster's dissertation on facilitating counselling opportunities for people who have learning disabilities (1997), she interviewed a number of counsellors who identified some of the 'problems' they experienced in counselling people with learning disabilities. Many of these addressed communication issues, and included:

◆ 'One of the main issues is around communication and how you actually put information across in a way that people can understand. Not relying on words helps break down barriers.
◆ Clients' verbal skills are often very limited. One advantage of joint working could be clarification and to aid communication.
◆ The skills I would like to have include a greater ability to help learning disabled people who do not communicate very readily or easily, who do not have verbal ability or the ability to reflect on their feelings and thought processes . . .
◆ There is so very little that has been done about encouraging other people [who have communication difficulties] to talk, helping people to open up – this is a skill we all need to develop. There is an enormous need for research in communication and counselling. In the past we have said it is very difficult to communicate with Jimmy and put Jimmy aside and blamed Jimmy – **he** cannot communicate.

The role of the speech and language clinician is therefore to give the counsellors the necessary skills to understand people's needs, to communicate with them effectively, and to enable people with learning disabilities to express themselves in an environment that is receptive to their needs. They may be able to do this through training staff in the use of alternative and augmentative systems of communication and in increasing awareness and understanding of the needs of clients with specific comprehension difficulties. However, there are also communication issues that are pertinent to counselling that need to be addressed by the counsellor and speech and language clinician. These are:

1   The person's ability to understand the concept of counselling
2   The person's ability to understand confidentiality
3   The person's ability to understand and talk about their feelings.

1   *Understanding counselling.* Moulster (1997) found that the issue of a client's ability to understand the concept of counselling was an important one. All the

counsellors interviewed expressed concern about the fact that they felt people who have learning disabilities do not understand the concept of counselling. Once again, it was considered to be an area where the counsellors needed support and skill-development in enabling the client to understand why they were having counselling and what this meant. The speech and language clinician can advise on this and can help the counsellor create pictorial or symbolic representations of counselling that are meaningful to the person.

2   *Understanding confidentiality.* This can be difficult in two ways: first, carers are not used to confidentiality and often expect to be told what is being discussed in the sessions, and second, it is difficult for counsellors to help the client to understand and to believe that the counselling sessions are confidential. People with learning disabilities are certainly not used to this and are more used to their lives/health needs/sexuality, etc, being common knowledge and openly discussed. The counsellor therefore needs to find an effective way of communicating the idea of confidentiality to the client and may ask the speech and language clinician for advice on this. Once again, pictures or symbols may be used to represent confidentiality and this could be incorporated into a contract with agreed rules between the counsellor and client.

3   *Understanding and expressing feelings.* Talking about feelings and thoughts is a central part of counselling sessions and many people with learning disabilities have difficulty with understanding and expressing abstract concepts such as emotions. If a person does have a difficulty in this area which is not addressed in the counselling, then potentially they will be confused and will not benefit from any discussion about their thoughts and feelings. It is therefore important for the person's understanding and expression of feelings to be assessed prior to, or right at the beginning of, counselling. Counsellors then need to be confident in working on this area through the use of pictures/symbols, etc, in order to meet the person's needs. The speech and language clinician can be involved in the assessment of the client and in providing advice on the best communication methods to use in the counselling sessions in order to meet the client's needs.

MULTIDISCIPLINARY WORKING – WORKED EXAMPLE

INITIAL REFERRAL
JS referred to the CLDT because of aggressive outbursts at the day centre. Clinical psychologist accepts referral.

INITIAL SCREENING
Summary: JS is a 38-year-old man who attends a large day centre five days a week and lives at home with his elderly mother. His father died one year ago, but he has never been told this and did not attend the funeral. Mother does not want to upset him. JS is a fairly independent man with good daily living skills and self-care skills. He appears to have good comprehension, but does not speak much. His behaviour started deteriorating about eight months ago and is now so bad that he is being threatened with exclusion from the centre. He throws furniture and attacks members of staff 'for no apparent reason'.

Needs identified: support staff in managing challenging behaviour, and refer JS for bereavement counselling.

CLINICAL PSYCHOLOGY
Ongoing intervention agreed with staff re-analysing and managing JS's behaviour.

COMMUNITY NURSING
Referral accepted by community nurse who has specialist training in counselling. Referral to speech and language therapy for assessment of communication needs prior to counselling starting.

SPEECH & LANGUAGE THERAPY
Assessment of JS revealed good functional level of understanding (two- to three-word level), but specific difficulties in verbal understanding of abstract concepts such as time and emotions. Showed a good understanding of pictures and symbols, even though he has never used symbols to help him communicate. JS's expressive skills are limited. He uses vocalisations, body language and, more recently, behaviour to express himself. He can also be echolalic. Recommendations: to work with JS and his key worker to put together a symbol communication book, and to liaise with community nurse re communication methods in counselling.

Liaison with speech & language clinician
Period of bereavement counselling

REGULAR MULTIDISCIPLINARY REVIEWS

DISCHARGE

INTRODUCTION

Given that the speech and language clinician's aim is to support people's progress towards fulfilling the 'principles of normalisation' (see Introduction), it is not surprising that clinicians are increasingly working with the specific aim of enabling clients to access other services (see, for example, Chapter 9, where the speech and language clinician's role in supporting clients to access a counselling service is explored).

A rapidly developing and challenging area of involvement for clinicians is the criminal justice system. More and more clinicians are becoming involved in supporting clients within different aspects of legal processes; for example, supporting clients in police interviews, having some input in the rehabilitation of offenders, providing an opinion on someone's ability to understand the implications of answering questions/pleading in court, etc. Speech and language clinicians may also become involved with the wider legal system in a number of capacities (eg, in cases of litigation, as an expert witness or witness of fact) but the remit of this chapter is **enabling people with learning disabilities to access the criminal justice system whether they are a witness, victim or suspect**.

This is a new and potentially huge area of work for clinicians, and it is hoped that this chapter will provide a basis for discussion and development within the profession. In order to explore some of the issues and the role that speech and language clinicians can play, this chapter aims to:

- Provide an overview of the components of criminal justice systems.
- Explore why the needs of people with cognitive and communication. impairments must be addressed, with particular consideration of the needs of clients with borderline to mild learning disabilities.
- Identify the potential barriers for people with cognitive and communication impairments.
- Explore the role that speech and language clinicians can play to increase client access to a criminal justice system.
- Discuss the implications for the speech and language therapy profession.

THE CRIMINAL JUSTICE SYSTEM

In order to consider a clinician's input to a criminal justice system, it is first necessary to have some understanding of: (i) its function, (ii) the agencies involved, and (iii) the principles and systems that have been established to enable agencies to work together in order to achieve the overall aims. Criminal justice systems are huge and highly complex and vary from one country to another – eg, the systems in England and Wales, and Scotland have evolved independently and therefore differ in certain aspects and in the terminology used. Whatever country a speech and language clinician is working in, it is important that they commit to learning about the system that is being applied to their clients. For the purposes of this chapter it will be helpful to highlight some of the basic characteristics of criminal justice systems. It is hoped that this will help clinicians to seek out the most relevant information about the criminal justice system in their area.

What are the aims of a criminal justice system?

- ◆ Protecting the public by preventing and deterring crime, by rehabilitating offenders and incapacitating others who constitute a persistent threat to the community
- ◆ Upholding and promoting the rule of law and respect for the law, by ensuring the due process and proper treatment of suspects, arrestees, defendants and those held in custody, successfully prosecuting criminals and acquiting innocent people accused of crime
- ◆ Maintaining law and order
- ◆ Punishing criminals with regard to the principles of just deserts
- ◆ Registering social disapproval of censured behaviour by punishing criminals
- ◆ Aiding and advising victims of crime. (Davies 1995)

Although this list of aims has been written with the criminal justice system in England and Wales in mind, it is applicable in general terms to other criminal justice systems. Identifying and highlighting the aims of a criminal justice system in this way helps to clarify the mind: criminal justice systems have been set up primarily to deal with criminals, and with a secondary role of supporting victims. Many speech and language clinicians working with people with learning disabilities may not have considered the possibility of coming into contact with the criminal justice system, crimes, victims or criminals as part of their work (and may not have come into contact with it out of work!). However, the more that clinicians embrace the principles of normalisation and that clients have the right and potential to increasingly access 'mainstream' services, the less of a surprise a communication specialist's involvement becomes.

What agencies are involved in the criminal justice system?

Any clinician beginning to work within a criminal justice system needs to be aware of the agencies that are involved at different stages. Table 10.1 (below) summarises the agencies involved in just one criminal justice system and their roles. Although this table is based on the system that applies to England and Wales, it is useful to help us consider the implications for speech and language clinicians.

Even though this table presents a highly simplified overview (eg, in England and Wales there are in fact six different types of criminal court, and the role of lawyers has been omitted) of only one system, it serves to give us a feel for the complexity of criminal justice systems in general: Davies *et al*, 1995, writing about the criminal justice system in England and Wales, suggest that

> Problems may arise where agencies are expected to cooperate with each other. There may, for example, be competition between agencies over the allocation of responsibilities or funding. Different working

Table 10.1 Agencies and their Roles	
Agency	**Main role**
Police	Investigate and prevent crime
Crown Prosecution Service	Identify and filter out weak cases Prepare prosecution cases
Courts	Process cases, decide on guilt, pass sentence, hear appeals against conviction
Prisons	Hold prisoners, rehabilitate offenders and prepare them for release
Probation	Prepare pre-sentence reports, undertake pre-release and aftercare work with offenders who have been given a probation and/or community service order

cultures which derive different perceptions of the goals of the system may lead to mistrust between agencies.

They went on to explain that

Differing models may be followed: the police, who have traditionally been seen as following a crime-control model, may have difficulties in communicating with lawyers whose role derives from the due process model, or with social workers, who may be more committed to a rehabilitative model.

This raises some pertinent issues for clinicians; they need to be well-informed and to have insight into the differing agencies and their aims and cultures. These are likely to vary hugely between different systems, and clinicians need to be active in seeking out information and developing contacts within different agencies on an ongoing basis. Clinicians also need to be very clear about their own role and 'culture', and to be aware of how their own 'therapeutic' background may affect their perception of various aspects of the system. Traditionally, a speech and language clinician's role has been perceived as a 'helping' one, but this needs to be defined within the context of **enabling** people with communication disabilities to access the criminal justice system: clinicians must be clear that their role is **not** to 'get clients off' or to 'get a confession' (in the case of a suspect), or to make a victim report a crime or 'disclose abuse'. Clinicians must be prepared to state and explain this explicitly to personnel from all the other agencies involved as they may come with certain misconceptions about what clinicians are trying to achieve for clients. In order to achieve a clinician's aim for clients, they need to remain neutral to all other parties. It may be that some clinicians will find it too difficult to become involved in a process that may result in a client being convicted of a crime, for example, where a clinician has strong beliefs about people with learning disabilities being systematically victimised throughout their lives because of their communication and cognitive disability; if this causes the clinician to see the 'crime' as being 'understandable', and the sole responsibility not of the client but of society at large, this may make it difficult for them to facilitate communication in a situation that potentially leads to the client being punished. This is not to say that such beliefs do not have any validity, but they may compromise a clinician's ability to act neutrally within a situation that demands it. It is essential that clinicians seek opportunities to examine their own belief systems, and that they are positively supported by managers to recognise when it is not appropriate for them to get involved in a case when personal beliefs may jeopardise the clinician's ability to fulfil the required role within a particular context.

What are the principles driving the system, and what are the processes involved?

Adversarial systems

The principles and systems that drive criminal justice systems vary from country to country, and clinicians need to find out those that apply in their area. The criminal justice systems in Britain and the United States are **adversarial**: within them there is an acceptance that the individual has rights, and the legal process starts with the premise that a person is innocent until proven guilty or has admitted guilt. A trial does not establish innocence, but whether there is sufficient evidence, 'beyond reasonable doubt', to establish guilt. It is the duty of the prosecution to prove the guilt of the accused 'beyond reasonable doubt', whereas it is the duty of the defence lawyer to plant the 'reasonable doubt' in the minds of magistrates, jury, etc. Davies *et al* (1995) highlight how this adversarial nature of criminal trials has important consequences for other parts of the system, and how it affects the way the police, prosecutors and the probation service perceive and discharge their respective roles. Speech and language clinicians need to be aware of the adversarial nature of criminal justice systems when getting involved, because the culture (and the associated inter-agency issues) can otherwise be a shock and difficult to deal with.

Diversion protocols

Of particular relevance when working with people with learning disabilities is the existence of legislation and/or protocols that enable an offender with learning disabilities to be diverted out of the criminal justice system. McGee and Menolascino (1992), writing about the criminal justice system in America, pointed out: 'A number of diversion models have evolved . . . Prisons are the most undesirable settings for these individuals because other inmates take advantage of them, subjecting them to physical brutality, rape, and extortion. Correctional pesonnel often lack the knowledge and skills to deal with them, and rehabilitation programs are rare.' In England and Wales, the legislation of the Mental Health Act, 1983 includes provision for diverting mentally-disordered offenders from custody to care. The act defines mental disorder as 'Mental illness, arrested or incomplete development of the mind, psychopathic disorder and any other disorder or disability of mind'. (Mental Health Act, 1983) There is an emphasis on inter-agency working between criminal justice agencies, health and social services in order to achieve this. The Mental Health (Northern Ireland) Order 1986 and the Mental Health (Scotland) Act 1984 serve similar functions. Speech and language clinicians need to familiarise themselves with any diversion systems that exist locally as they vary in terms of legislation and in implementation.

An overview of the process

In order to enable people with learning disabilities to access the criminal justice system, it is necessary for speech and language clinicians to have some awareness of the overall process that our clients may experience. Figures 10.1 and 10.2 provide a highly simplified overview of the processes that suspects and victims may progress through.

Figure 10.1
Summary of the Process for a Suspect

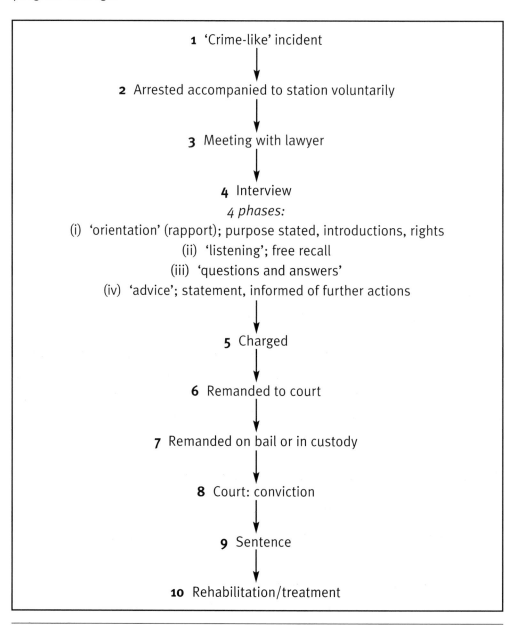

1 'Crime-like' incident

↓

2 Arrested accompanied to station voluntarily

↓

3 Meeting with lawyer

↓

4 Interview
4 phases:
(i) 'orientation' (rapport); purpose stated, introductions, rights
(ii) 'listening'; free recall
(iii) 'questions and answers'
(iv) 'advice'; statement, informed of further actions

↓

5 Charged

↓

6 Remanded to court

↓

7 Remanded on bail or in custody

↓

8 Court: conviction

↓

9 Sentence

↓

10 Rehabilitation/treatment

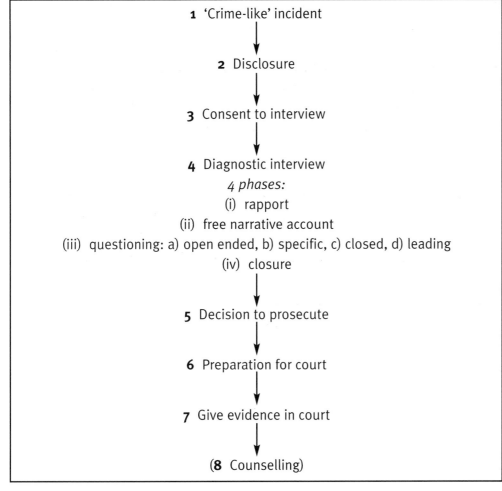

Figure 10.2
Summary of the Process for a Victim or Witness

1 'Crime-like' incident

2 Disclosure

3 Consent to interview

4 Diagnostic interview
4 phases:
(i) rapport
(ii) free narrative account
(iii) questioning: a) open ended, b) specific, c) closed, d) leading
(iv) closure

5 Decision to prosecute

6 Preparation for court

7 Give evidence in court

(**8** Counselling)

It is often the case that speech and language clinicians are initially asked to get involved with a specific situation – for example, supporting a client in an interview – but there are clearly a host of other situations within which the client's communication needs must be identified, acknowledged and addressed, such as in discussions with lawyers, in court, in counselling/treatment. This is a 'mind blowing' concept for all involved, not least for clinicians! However, speech and language clinicians specialising in working with people with learning disabilities have specific qualifications, skills and experience that make them ideally placed to: (i) raise awareness of the communication needs of people with learning disabilities, and (ii) find ways of working with others to ensure that clients' communication needs are met. Many clinicians already see these functions as central to their clinical role in supporting their clients within other settings.

WHY MUST CLIENTS' COMMUNICATION NEEDS BE MET?

The demands of the criminal justice system

Any criminal justice system places high demands on the communication skills of everyone coming into contact with it:

◆ The circumstances associated with coming into contact with the criminal justice system, whether as a suspect, victim or witness, are usually emotionally charged, and this has an impact on most people's communication skills.

◆ Criminal justice systems are highly complex, so understanding what is happening and what the consequences of taking various courses of action would be is extremely demanding, even for someone without a learning disability. This is exagerated by the fact that those parties trying to prove guilt beyond reasonable doubt, or to demonstrate that doubt exists, will use their verbal skills to the limit and the whole process has its own extensive terminology.

◆ Each interaction within the system stretches everyone's communication skills to the limit. If we consider briefly the communication demands on someone in just one aspect of the process, we quickly begin to realise why communication impairments must be recognised and addressed if the implementation of the criminal justice system is to be meaningful.

Table 10.2 lists some of the demands that are made on someone's ability to communicate while being interviewed as a suspect.

Table 10.2 Communication Demands on Someone being Interviewed as a Suspect
The interviewee needs to be able to: **hear, listen, concentrate** **identify salient points in spoken language**
Understand: what is happening, why it is happening, the significance of the situation, what the police want, what the police are asking, the likely consequences of taking different courses of action, the role of the solicitor, the solicitor's advice, their rights, the role of others (eg, the 'appropriate adult' if one is present), what the outcome is, what will happen next, etc.
Verbally express themselves in the following ways: ask for rights/information, seek clarification, ask questions, provide clarification, repair, monitor listener's understanding, provide a verbal account of past events, explain, justify, etc.
To do this someone needs to be able to: have the necessary vocabulary, retrieve the required words, sequence ideas, sentences and words logically, use sentence structure and grammar, use speech, voice, fluency, speed, intonation, volume, etc.
This verbal understanding and expression takes place within a social context, so someone also needs: (i) skills in understanding and using the appropriate non-verbal communication (eg, eye-contact, proximity, gesture, body language, facial expression), and (ii) knowledge of how to interact in a range of social situations (eg, turn-taking, developing a topic, being aware of the listener's needs/perspective)

The communication needs of people with learning disabilities

People with learning disabilities present a diverse and complex range of cognitive and communication disabilities that potentially affect their ability to participate fully within the criminal justice system. (See Chapter 1 for discussion of this client group's communication needs.)

It will be useful here to consider briefly the range of cognitive and communication impairments that people with borderline–mild learning disabilities may present, particularly as this client group's needs may often go unrecognised for much of a person's life, and because this client group is one that is traditionally neglected by speech and language therapy services. People with borderline–mild learning disabilities may present any of the following areas of impairment:

◆ *Cognitive impairments:* impairments of memory/retrieval, attention, sequencing, generalisation, problem-solving, coping strategies, impulse control, abstract reasoning, etc.
◆ *Mental illness:* McGee and Menolascino (1992) highlight that 'The presence of mental illness multiplies the impact of mental retardation on a person's behaviors, social perception and moral reasoning . . . Thus it is critical to consider the possibility of a host of allied psychiatric disorders, such as schizophrenia, bipolar affective disorders, and personality disorders . . .'
◆ *Communication impairments:* impairments of listening/attention, interpreting and responding to social situations, perspective-taking, understanding complex language/abstract concepts, understanding non-verbal communication, using verbal and non-verbal communication, suggestibility, acquiescence, confabulation, reading, writing, self-esteem, assertiveness, over-compliance, etc.

It will be useful here to consider the concepts of **suggestibility** and **acquiescence** as they apply to people with learning disabilities; although the precise definitions may not be familiar to some speech and language clinicians, they are factors that they have awareness and experience of. Speech and language clinicians have relevant knowledge and expertise that potentially enable them to contribute to the:

(a) identification of the presence of these factors within communication contexts
(b) minimisation of their effects through the awareness raising and training of others.

Interrogative suggestibility

Gudjonsson and Clarke (1986) define this as 'The extent to which, within a closed social interaction, people come to accept messages communicated during formal questioning, as a result of which their subsequent behavioural response is affected.' They proposed that five interrelated components form the interrogative process: a social interaction, a questioning procedure, a suggestive stimulus, acceptance of the stimulus and a behavioural response. The 'suggestive stimulus' may be a 'leading question'; Gudjonsson (1992) pointed out that 'Questions can be leading because they contain certain premises and expectations, which may or may not be informed and well founded . . . also . . . questions can be leading because of the context in which they appear.'

Acquiescence

This is the tendency to say 'yes' to 'yes/no' questions, and Clare and Gudjonsson (1993) found that 'acquiescent responding is related to poor intellectual skills.'

It is the author's experience that carers and professionals working with people with learning disabilities often routinely adopt a questioning style that is heavily dependent on leading and closed (including a high proportion of 'yes/no') questions when interacting with clients. They are usually unaware of what they are doing and oblivious to the potential consequences. This means that many day-to-day client responses are potentially 'unreliable' and do not reflect a real understanding or expression of opinion, feeling or experience; this pattern of daily interaction is reinforced so that a client who may already be susceptible to being suggestible and/or acquiescent becomes less and less able to overcome the expectation to respond in a certain way. The author has also experienced police officers saying 'We don't use leading questions', and then proceeding to use them from the outset in an interview!

A person may present any combination of the above-listed cognitive impairments, mental health problems and communication impairments, and therefore have difficulty accessing the criminal justice system, but added to this is the perception of people working within the criminal justice system that decisions are often made about a client's ability to participate meaningfully, based on a patchy knowledge of learning disabilities and without specialist assessment of someone's cognitive and communication needs. Figure 10.3 illustrates how the criminal justice system's perceptions of who can access the system may differ from a speech and language clinician's perceptions.

Figure 10.3 *Perceptions of Who Can Access the System*

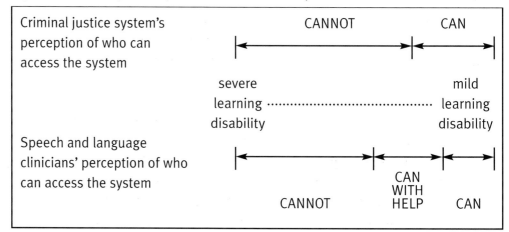

Figure 10.3 shows how speech and language clinicians are likely to believe that people at both ends of the learning disability spectrum are not effectively accessing the criminal justice system; ie, some people who have borderline to mild learning disabilities may be believed to be accessing the system when in fact they are not; their communication skills are being overestimated. At the moderate to severe end of the spectrum, people's communication skills are not underestimated so they do not receive the opportunity or support to enable them to access the system.

The consequences of communication breakdown

Within the context of the criminal justice system, the consequences of communication breakdown are potentially devastating. If a person's communication needs are not identified and met then there is an increased likelihood of their:

◆ Not understanding what is happening.
◆ Not understanding information.
◆ Not understanding their rights.
◆ Not understanding the implications of taking a particular course of action.
◆ Not understanding questions put to them.
◆ Not being able to give an account of an event.
◆ Not being able to provide a description.
◆ Not being able to make an informed decision about what to do at any stage.
◆ Not being able to understand conditions of bail, etc.
◆ Not being able to benefit from treatment/counselling, etc.

This has implications for all interactions throughout the process for an individual client, whether they be with police officers, psychiatrists, police surgeons (forensic medical examiner), social workers, probation officers, prison officers, solicitors/lawyers, barristers, judges, etc, and it is clear that the whole purpose of the criminal justice system is potentially undermined if communication issues are not addressed.

A particular area of concern is that of false confession, and a significant body of literature explores suggestibility, confabulation and acquiescence in relation to people with learning disabilities. Clare and Gudjonsson (1993) concluded that people with mild learning disabilities 'Were more suggestible than their average ability counterparts (Full scale IQ: 83–111) because they were much more susceptible to "leading questions". They also confabulated more and were more acquiescent. Overall, the data emphasised their potential vulnerability to giving erroneous testimony during interrogations.'

Bonnie (1992) highlighted the issues in relation to the American criminal justice system: 'Substantial reliability concerns are raised whenever a defendant with mental retardation pleads guilty . . . Limited conceptual skills, biased responding, and submissiveness to authority may mask significant doubts about criminal liability, especially in relation to culpability elements. The risk of unreliable pleas is further magnified by all the structural arrangements in criminal justice administration that encourage negotiated pleas. Public defenders or appointed lawyers often spend little time probing the more subtle aspects of criminal liability that may be most pertinent in the defence of persons with mental retardation.'

Disability Rights

This is an important area of development in many parts of the world, as highlighted in the Introduction where the principles of normalisation are discussed. An example of how legislation is being developed to ensure that such principles are upheld in practice is the UK Disability Discrimination Act, 1995. Service providers now have a duty not to discriminate against people with disabilities, for example, by 'failing to make alterations to a service or facility which makes it impossible, or unreasonably difficult, for a disabled person to use', and Government literature states that once the provisions within the Act are implemented, 'A service provider may have to make alterations to the way its service is provided: service providers will be expected to make reasonable changes to policies, practices or procedures that make it unreasonably difficult for disabled people to use the service.' (Booklet, 1996, The Disability Discrimination Act; access to goods, facilities and services; on behalf of the Minister of Disabled People)

Similarly, in the United States, The Developmental Disabilities Assistance and Bill of Rights Act of 1978 requires that each state and territory establish a 'Protection and Advocacy System' to protect and advocate for the legal and human rights of people with developmental disabilities. Wherever clinicians are working, it is important that they have up-to-date knowledge of the relevant legislation and agencies that operate in their area. This information can be vital in providing the necessary 'leverage' to enable clinicians to get their client's communication needs taken seriously and met. Nowadays, few people are completely ignorant of equal rights issues, and would prefer to avoid being accused of having discriminatory practices.

WHAT ARE THE POTENTIAL COMMUNICATION BARRIERS WITHIN THE CRIMINAL JUSTICE SYSTEM?

Society's attitudes

Society's attitudes towards people with learning disabilities have changed significantly over recent years; this is reflected in the way that service provision has developed, with the aim of enabling clients to attain O'Brien's 'ordinary life principles' (see Introduction). There is, however, some way to go before discriminatory attitudes are eliminated.

Diesfield (1996) illustrated this when she stressed that 'It is essential to challenge the stereotype that people with learning disabilities are not credible witnesses. Often when abuse is reported in services, managers fail to respond because they have swallowed the myth that, by definition, people with learning disabilities cannot make credible or reliable witnesses.' (Fairbairn et al, 1995)

'Historically, people with learning disabilities have been discriminated against in sexual matters. They tend to be seen either as "over-sexed" and somehow out of control, or as completely innocent and asexual, in which case they were given no information or support to express themselves sexually or to keep themselves safe.' (Brown *et al*, 1996) It is easy to see how attitudes like these, if left unchallenged, will have an impact on policy and legislation development in the future, to the detriment of people with learning disabilities.

Another example of how society's attitudes can bar the way to services is highlighted by Hill and Hordell (1998); through their work on the adaptation of the prison service Sex Offender Treatment Programme they came to believe that they have 'to some extent managed to scotch the commonly held belief that people with learning disabilities cannot work within a cognitive behavioural framework.' As long as people hold such beliefs and fail to appreciate what can be achieved by addressing communication needs (ie, by changing how they, as professionals, present information and treatment) then people with learning disabilities will continue to be deprived of opportunities to develop. Thornburgh (1992) also illustrated how ignorance of the abilities and needs of people with learning disabilities can lead to inappropriate decision-making within the criminal justice system, by citing the case of a 'Woman who is not even considered for programmes offering alternatives to incarceration, such as pre-trial diversion or probation, because those making the decision do not think she can benefit from them.'

Inadequate education about the criminal justice system

It is widely acknowledged that people with learning disabilities may have experienced an impoverished education, have significant difficulties communicating and learning, and may have limited social experiences. This potentially leaves them vulnerable to not having the opportunity to learn about the criminal justice system, for example, in relation to (i) what the laws of the land are, (ii) what happens to you if you break the law, (iii) what can be done if a crime is committed against you, and (iv) your rights within the system, etc.

The use of complex spoken language

Criminal justice systems and their associated language are extremely complex and difficult to understand for the lay person. Criminal justice systems have a huge specialised terminology to describe all the personnel, processes, places, offences, etc. Gudjonsson *et al* (1992) investigated people's understanding of the 'Notice to Detained Persons' (England and Wales). This is a leaflet that is given to detailed people, and this study explored people's understanding of the language within it. The study found that 'A mean of only 11 per cent of the sentences in the "Notice" were understood by the "intellectual disabilities" group compared with 68 per cent by their "general population" counterparts . . . only 8 per cent of the participants with intellectual disabilities (compared with 80 per cent of their average ability counterparts) understood the caution fully' (Clare & Gudjonsson, 1995).

Conley (1995), writing in the United States, cites Ellis, 1989 (a professor of law):

> The courts have held that there is independent value in the right to counsel and the right to be free from coerced, self-incriminatory statements that are independent of guilt or innocence. People with disabilities are the ones least likely to be able to exercise these rights . . . know of one case where a person thought 'rights' were the opposite of 'lefts' and that 'waiving' was a gesture . . . He also thought that guilt meant that you felt badly because something *had happened*.

(The writer is referring to the 'Miranda' warnings which are read to suspects by investigators in the United States.)

Another example of the use of complex language presenting a barrier to people with learning disability is within treatment programmes to address offending behaviour. Several years ago, the prison service in the UK identified the need to adapt existing cognitive-behavioural treatment for sex offenders so that people with learning disabilities can access it. Prior to 1996, sex offenders with an IQ of less than 80 were excluded from the national sex offenders treatment programme.

Compounding the effect of complex language being embedded into protocols and processes for people with communication impairments is the fact that most personnel working within criminal justice systems have little or no training or experience of working with, and communicating with, people with cognitive and communication impairments.

The use of written language

◆ Leaflets are routinely used to explain rights, responsibilities and procedures.
◆ A great deal of written documentation takes place as a case proceeds; for example, a written record of an interview may require signing, a written statement may be required.
◆ Forms may need to be completed; for example, applying for legal aid.
◆ Letters are sent to summon people to appear in court.
◆ Written confirmation of the process; for example, charge sheet, bail sheet, probation order, etc.
◆ Written handouts/activity sheets may be given as part of a treatment programme.
◆ Written notices and signs are posted around buildings.

Protocols and procedures

The legislation within the criminal justice systems requires that certain procedures are carried out in prescribed settings – for example, police stations, courts. To those who do not work within these settings they can be unfamiliar, strange and potentially frightening places. People finding themselves in such surroundings are likely to experience strong emotions that potentially affect their ability to communicate effectively. For example, police stations, or their equivalent, are likely to be busy places with a certain amount of background noise and with personnel from different agencies present; noise levels and surrounding activity can affect someone's ability to hear, listen and concentrate; officers of the law across the world wear uniforms that make them identifiable, but this also conveys authority which may contribute to a person's desire to please and to not request clarification, etc.

Davies *et al* (1995) graphically highlighted some of the atmosphere of a UK criminal court: 'A Crown Court trial has some of the appearance of a theatrical performance with costumes, ceremony, dramatic setting and seating for an audience.' (Davies *et al*, 1995); this is clearly not an environment that is conducive to enabling people to communicate to the best of their ability, and although there are examples of settings being modified, this is not systematic or based on thorough assessment of an individual's needs.

Another example of how procedures can be a barrier to effective communication is the generally-applied protocol of the same investigating officer(s) following a case through; it has been the author's experience that interviews have sometimes had to wait for up to a week until the relevant officer(s) are back on duty. This has the potential to affect someone's ability to talk about past events; for example, someone who has difficulty in identifying past time-scales, beyond 'yesterday', could give a reliable account of what happened 'yesterday' but not 'last Saturday' because they would be unsure of which day was being referred to.

Cognitive and communication needs not being identified or met

Suspects

When someone is arrested and taken to a police station it is initially up to the police to identify anyone who has a learning disability or to refer to specialist personnel for assessment. Given that most police officers have little or no experience of either of these client groups, and no specific training or skills in identifying them, it is not surprising that studies in many countries have shown that a significant number of people remain unidentified as having special needs. This is significant because in various jurisdictions some provision is made for people with learning disabilities. For example, in England and Wales, the Police and Criminal Evidence Act 1984 contains provisions for people with learning disabilities, and legislation in the United States deals differently with defendants with learning disabilities.

However, in order to benefit from any legislation that is in place, the learning disability must first be identified. Ellis and Luckasson (1985) pointed out: 'Efforts that many mentally retarded people typically expend in trying to prevent any discovery of their handicap may render the existence or magnitude of their disability invisible to criminal justice system personnel.'

Nemitz (1996) described a study where a significant number of 'vulnerable' people were not identified while in police custody, and Gudjonsson (1992) concluded that 'Those who are only mildly mentally handicapped are least likely to be identified, especially if their social functioning seems relatively satisfactory.' He spoke from a wealth of experience when he wrote:

> Possibly the most common reason for the failure of police officers to identify mental handicap prior to or during custodial interrogation is that many mildly mentally handicapped adults function quite well socially . . . This can disguise their more subtle disabilities. Another problem is that many police officers appear unaware of how to identify suspects with a mild mental handicap, and why they may be vulnerable to giving unreliable information during interrogation . . .

He went on to say that he came across numerous cases where prison medical officers and psychiatrists grossly overestimated the intellectual functioning of defendants, and he pointed out that such mistakes could lead to miscarriages of justice.

Bonnie (1992) concluded that:

> The low rate of referral for pre-trial forensic evaluation suggests that some defendants with mental retardation who "should" be found incompetent are now being convicted. But the more significant problem is that lawyers are probably providing inadequate representation for the much larger number of marginally competent defendants whose disabilities can be counteracted by skilful interviewing and counselling. This problem can be ameliorated by providing thorough forensic assessment and consultative assistance by appropriately trained clinicians . . . and by appointing trained representatives to assist persons with mental retardation.

Here Bonnie argued for some form of assistance to be put in place for people with learning disabilities within the American system. In the Police and Criminal Evidence Act 1984 (England and Wales) there is provision for the presence of an 'appropriate adult' during police interviews with suspects who have learning disabilities. It states:

> It is important to bear in mind that although the mentally disordered or mentally handicapped are people often capable of providing reliable evidence, they may, without knowing or wishing to do so, be particularly prone in certain circumstances to provide information which is unreliable, misleading or self-incriminating. Special care should therefore always be exercised in questioning such a person, and the appropriate person/adult involved if there is any doubt about a person's mental state or capacity.

The codes go on to say that the presence of an appropriate adult is intended to minimise these risks.

Victims and witnesses

The needs of victims and witnesses are also increasingly being recognised; this is reflected in the fact that in England and Wales recommendations are beginning to be made at government level: The 'Speaking up for Justice Report' (1998) made recommendations that aimed to enable 'vulnerable' people to give evidence. There are a number of recommendations that are of particular relevance to speech and language clinicians; they serve to provide clinicians with some insight into the way that legislation might proceed, and they potentially provide clinicians with extra confidence when advocating for their clients' communication needs; ie, they are not a lone clinician saying that these things are required; they have been identified in a government-level report. As criminal justice systems vary from one area to another, it is essential that clinicians seek out the latest legislation, reports and papers that apply to their geographical area of work. The relevant recommendations made in the 'Speaking up for Justice Report' referred to the need for:

◆ The police to identify a 'vulnerable' witness as early as possible in the investigation process. A person is defined as 'vulnerable': 'If the witness by reason of significant impairment of intelligence and social functioning/mental disability or other mental or physical disorder, or physical disability, if the witness requires the assistance of one or more special measures to enable them to give best evidence'.
◆ Making provision for the special needs of witnesses.
◆ Consulting the witness, and others who know them, about their communication.
◆ Planning the way in which a statement should be taken and what measures might be needed to assist the witness before and during the trial.
◆ The presence of a 'supporter', 'whose role would need to be clearly-defined'.
◆ The need for courts to develop further material to assist vulnerable witnesses to prepare for court attendance.
◆ 'The use of means to assist the witness in communicating, whether through an interpreter, a communication-aid or technique, or communicator or intermediary, where this would assist the witness to give best evidence . . . provided that the communication can be independently verified.' The report states that such communicators/intermediaries should be accredited.
◆ Agencies to undertake joint training to raise awareness of vulnerable witness issues.

Speech and language clinicians clearly have a role to play in enabling personnel within criminal justice systems to identify 'mild' communication impairments associated with borderline disabilities. It is essential that clinicians are proactive in raising public awareness of this client group's needs, particularly because society's attitudes and responses have caused, and continue to cause, people with mild learning disabilities to go to great lengths to cover up their difficulties and to keep everyone else happy. Those people with learning disabilities who do have the self-esteem and confidence to say they have difficulties may be prevented from doing so by their communication impairment, which is likely to be confounded by aspects of the system, as discussed previously; for example, someone who is able to communicate functionally in day-to-day situations may be communicatively disabled by the personnel and procedures within the criminal justice system.

THE ROLE OF THE SPEECH & LANGUAGE CLINICIAN IN ENABLING A PERSON WITH LEARNING DISABILITIES TO ACCESS THE CRIMINAL JUSTICE SYSTEM

Informing personnel within the criminal justice system of the person's needs

When speech and language clinicians become aware that one of their clients is, or is about to be, involved in a criminal justice system, they need to be proactive in informing everyone involved of the client's cognitive and communication needs. This will be more comprehensive and likely to carry more weight if the information provided is part of a fuller evaluation of the client that is presented by a multidisciplinary clinical team. In many circumstances it is the opinion of the specialist psychiatrist that is sought and heard by legal personnel; speech and language clinicians therefore need to invest time in working with psychiatrists and in raising the profile of the role that speech and language clinicians can play in identifying and supporting clients' communication needs.

'Competence', 'capacity', 'fitness'

A speech and language clinician has much to contribute to assessments of 'competence', 'capacity' or 'fitness', whether it be in relation to interviewing, assisting in own defence, consenting to a relationship or sexual act, etc. Evaluations in this area include assessing a person's understanding of a situation and/or information and assessing their understanding/beliefs about what the consequences of different courses of action may be. It is not appropriate for a speech and language clinician to take sole responsibility for assessing capacity or competence; there are other factors that need consideration, such as the client's ability to remember information, generate alternatives, reason through the short- and long-term consequences of taking different courses of action, appreciate the impact of these consequences in real terms on their life, manipulate the information in their mind in order to weigh up the different options, implement the action necessary to follow up a decision, etc. A client's needs will best be met if such an assessment is undertaken within a multidisciplinary context. Speech and language clinicians also have an invaluable role to play in terms of taking the necessary steps to maximise a person's ability to understand information and therefore increase the possibility of them being found 'competent', 'fit', etc.

Speech and language clinicians need to be prepared to explain and demonstrate the value of the contribution that they can make to this process, and there is the potential for them to be called to testify as an 'expert witness'.

Establishing the context

Clinicians need to find out as much as possible about the circumstances that surround the client's involvement, or potential involvement, with the criminal justice system. Legislation and procedures vary depending on whether someone is being interviewed as a witness, victim or suspect (and in the case of a suspect, whether they have been arrested or are being questioned 'informally'), and from one geographical area to another. Having some knowledge of those rules that apply in a particular situation will enable clinicians to advocate more effectively for a client's communication needs: (i) they will be able to utilise procedural requirements to enable them to put the client's communication needs on the agenda; (ii) they will earn credibility with personnel within the criminal justice system and will therefore be more likely to be taken seriously; and (iii) they will be able to provide the most relevant information about someone's communication needs as applied to that specific situation.

Which areas of communication?

Depending on the specific situation and the demands that are going to be placed on someone's communication skills, the information needed will vary; for example, the communication demands of a court are different from those within a treatment group. It is likely that information about the following areas of the client's communication ability will be of particular relevance in a range of situations:

◆ Understanding of abstract information.
◆ Receptive and expressive vocabulary as relevant to the specific situation.
◆ Ability to remember and reason with abstract information.
◆ Understanding of time-scales, sequential information.
◆ Understanding of the full range of question forms.
◆ Ability to understand idiom.
◆ Expressive skills.
◆ Suggestibility.
◆ Acquiescence.
◆ Ability to perceive different ages and understanding of language related to ages.
◆ Understanding of truth/lies.
◆ Understanding of right/wrong.
◆ Ability to perceive and interpret emotions in others.
◆ What the client believes is happening, why and what the likely consequences are.
◆ Ability to communicate past events reliably.
◆ Compliance.
◆ Ability to use spoken or other forms of communication within a social context, pragmatic skills.
◆ Ability to perspective-take.

Brown *et al* (1996), also recommend the assessment of the interviewer's ability to communicate,

◆ The interviewer's ability to communicate (ability to assess understanding and to modify their communication accordingly).
◆ The interviewer's ability to understand (the interviewee's communication).

They also recommend the involvement of a speech and language clinician in such an assessment.

Advising on how a client's communication needs can or cannot be met

The speech and language clinician needs to specify the manner, level and pace of communication that (i) the person requires in order to understand, and (ii) the person uses in order to express themselves – ie, what communication strategies all parties interacting with that client need to use in order to ensure effective communication. In such situations it is not uncommon to hear police, solicitors, carers and other professionals indicating that they know that they need to 'keep things simple', particularly if they have experience of people with learning disabilities. It is the author's experience, however, that this often reflects a huge oversimplification of the issues. Speech and language clinicians need to develop their skills in breaking down the concept of 'simplifying' things, so that others can appreciate what is involved and the skills needed in order to do this appropriately for an individual client within a particular situation with a particular communication partner. It is also common for other parties to have little or no awareness of the potential for the use of forms of communication other than spoken and written language; for example, drawing, mime, gesture and manual signs such as Makaton, symbols, high-tech communication aids, etc.

The speech and language clinician needs to recommend strongly that joint planning takes place in order to ensure that a client's communication, cognitive and emotional needs are catered for. In some circumstances it may also be helpful to emphasise the possible consequences of not identifying clients' communication and cognitive needs, for example:

1   That the information obtained may be unreliable.
2   That for an investigative interview, the methods used to interview the client may be examined later in court, and that if there is evidence that a person had identified communication needs that were not addressed, then there is a risk that the evidence obtained in any interview would not be considered admissible.
3   That failure to address someone's communication needs is likely to reduce the effectiveness of treatment.
4   That failure to address a person's communication needs comprises a form of disability discrimination.

Training others

Speech and language clinicians can raise others' awareness of communication issues and promote good practice through formal and informal training. This has been explored in Chapter 8. Clinicians can promote the long-term development of communication skills in criminal justice system personnel by establishing an ongoing approach to training. Each situation and client will present different challenges, and personnel will be most empowered to meet clients' communication needs if a reflective and problem-solving approach is fostered. Joint working and video reviewing are valuable tools in achieving this, but clinicians also need education in training and 'supervising' others.

Although some general principles can be addressed with all people working within the criminal justice system, training needs to be targetted at personnel needs, depending on their specific area of work.

Facilitating communication between the client and personnel within the criminal justice setting

As discussed earlier, there is an increasing recognition of the need for someone to bridge the gap between the communication skills of personnel within the criminal justice system and a person with a communication impairment. If a mismatch between the two has been identified, then there is the potential for a facilitator to be involved, whatever the situation. Speech and language clinicians need to assess the need for a facilitator in all aspects of the process that the client is involved in.

What are the aims of facilitation?

Brown *et al* (1996) argued for the involvement of a facilitator or, as they referred to it, an 'unofficial interpreter whose job it would be to:

◆ help the person with learning disabilities to understand by rephrasing the questions of the interviewer in a way that makes sense to them
◆ help the person with learning disabilities to answer by offering careful alternative suggestions in the event that they rely exclusively on yes/no responses
◆ support or make sense of the interviewee's communication.

Similarly, Elliott and Forshaw (2000) propose that someone is required to: facilitate communication . . . in specific situations when the communicative partner is unable to fully meet the client's communication needs. This may involve:

◆ Enabling the communicative partner to identify breakdowns in communication
◆ Enabling them to be aware of the needs of the client
◆ Enabling them to adapt their communication, eg utilising total communication. This may involve developing specific resources.
◆ Modelling effective communication strategies.

Who should facilitate?

There is currently very little guidance available about who should act as a facilitator and what skills and knowledge a facilitator needs. Under the *Notes for Guidance in the Codes of Practice of the Police and Criminal Evidence Act*, 1984, it was suggested that for people with learning disabilities: 'It may, in certain circumstances, be more satisfactory for all concerned if the appropriate adult is someone who has experience or training in their care rather than a relative lacking such qualifications.'

Part of the role of an appropriate adult is to 'facilitate communication'. Gudjonsson (1992) points out that the role is usually fulfilled by social workers and only occasionally by psychologists and psychiatrists; he makes no mention of speech and language clinicians, and highlights that the effectiveness of the 'appropriate adult' as a social support system is not known.

If a person's communication needs are to be identified and met fully, facilitators need:

◆ Specialist knowledge of communication and people with learning disabilities.
◆ Knowledge of the legal processes and the roles of personnel relevant to the situation.
◆ Communication assessment skills.
◆ Skills in responding flexibly to the communication needs of a situation.
◆ Skills in identifying and repairing communication breakdown.
◆ Skills in using the full range of communication strategies.
◆ Team-working skills.
◆ Adequate confidence and assertiveness to enable them to represent a client's needs in difficult and stressful situations.
◆ Skills in assessing the communication process, as it is happening, without bias.
◆ An ability to work under pressure.

In the author's experience of working within specialist residential and community services for people with learning disabilities, and of talking to clinicians working in other geographical areas, speech and language clinicians are increasingly being asked to take up the role of communication facilitiator. Perhaps this is a reflection of:

1 The steady increase in understanding of communication issues of people within criminal justice systems.
2 The increase in the number of speech and language clinicians who are seeing facilitation as part of their clinical role.

Considerations for speech and language clinicians acting as facilitators

◆ In suspect interviews or during court proceedings it is likely to be important that the communication facilitator is impartial; this is most likely to be the case if they are not clinically involved with the client. It may therefore be appropriate to refer to another speech and language clinician/facilitator.
◆ It is not appropriate to act as communication facilitator with a suspect if the clinician has any information relevant to the investigation.
◆ In the case of a victim or witness, it is likely to be preferable if the facilitator is known to the client.
◆ The facilitator needs to seek out information about the person's communication skills; the speech and language clinician may already have detailed knowledge; or this may be achieved by liaising with the client's speech and language clinician, other involved professionals and carers, or brief assessment before the actual interview. This will provide invaluable information about the general communicative ability and needs of a person, but the clinician must remain open-minded within the interview situation; the client's needs must be assessed in the light of that specific interaction. The facilitator needs to be careful not to

make assumptions about what a person does or does not understand based on information obtained in a very different setting(s).

◆ The facilitator should arrange to meet the client before the interview in order to explain their role and to gain the client's informed consent to them acting as a facilitator. Where it is felt that a client is unable to give informed consent, it would be good practice to involve the wider multidisciplinary team in deciding whether it is in the client's 'best interests' for the clinician to act as communication facilitator.

◆ The facilitator should be prepared to explain to all parties that they are impartial, not 'on anyone's side', and do not have any preconceived ideas about what has or has not happened.

◆ It follows that if a client needs someone to facilitate communication in a suspect interview with the police then there are likely to be similar needs when the client is interacting with a lawyer. If the lawyer requests such input then it is not appropriate for the same person to facilitate communication in both situations because being party to the discussion between the client and their lawyer may compromise the facilitator's impartiality during the police interview. It may be acceptable to all parties if the person acting as appropriate adult facilitates communication with the client just to ensure that the client understands the lawyer's role, but if facilitation is needed beyond that, then the lawyer needs to make arrangements for someone else to facilitate in that situation.

◆ The facilitator should negotiate with all parties about how they are going to fulfil their role in the situation; it will be useful to explain how they think they will need to facilitate communication, or it may otherwise be a surprise and perceived as disruptive when they try to stop proceedings to check understanding or introduce another form of communication such as drawing!

◆ Throughout the interview, it is helpful if the facilitator states their perceptions and actions; for example, an interviewing officer tells the person their rights and asks them if they understand them. The interviewee nods their head and says 'yes'. The facilitator states 'There isn't any evidence that _____ understands their rights.' The interviewing officer then asks the person to explain it back in their own words and some misconceptions are revealed; the officer looks to the facilitator for help. The facilitator says '_____ doesn't see, to understand _____, I will explain it and will use drawing to show what I mean,' etc.

◆ It is important to keep a record of the process and the client's actions and ensure that, where applicable, any representations that they make to the police are logged in the custody record or its equivalent.

◆ It is invaluable for clinicians acting as facilitators to have an opportunity for debriefing in order to reflect on issues/feelings that the situation raised and to ensure that learning points are identified. It is unlikely that any competent clinician is going to feel that they have done a good job! There is so much to consider and so many barriers to meeting clients' communication needs, not least the fact that the role of a 'communication facilitator' has yet to be defined!

Adapting written information

Speech and language clinicians have skills in breaking down language, simplifying vocabulary, organising information, presenting information visually – for example, using pictures, etc – and are therefore increasingly being asked to advise on producing 'written' materials for people with literacy difficulties. The audience for a leaflet can effectively be widened by considering the typeface, the size of print, the contrast between the print and the background, the layout, the use of pictures, the order of information, the prominence of contact details, the use of an audio tape and so on.

Advising policy makers

A highly effective way of ensuring that clients' communication needs are met is to influence policy-makers at all levels. Policies and procedures need to be developed from the outset with the communication needs of people with learning disabilities in mind, and with the involvement of people who have specialist knowledge of the communication needs of this client group. This would increase accessibility of the system, and enable speech and language clinicians to fulfil their role in supporting their clients within the system.

IMPLICATIONS FOR THE SPEECH & LANGUAGE THERAPY PROFESSION

This chapter has discussed the communication needs of people with learning disabilities within the context of criminal justice systems. It has shown that if speech and language clinicians familiarise themselves with the relevent legislation and guidance, then there are some routes available to them to try to ensure their clients' communication needs are recognised and addressed. In order for speech and language clinicians to meet the challenge of enabling clients with learning difficulties to access the criminal justice system meaningfully, then the profession needs to address the following areas:

Awareness-raising and training of others

As specialists in the area of communication, speech and language clinicians have a duty of care to highlight:

1 Their clients' needs.
2 Their role in meeting clients' needs.

They need to do this at every level with all relevant personnel, and so they need to take a proactive approach and foster good working relationships with relevant agencies. They need to be prepared to:

- Respond to Government consultation documents.
- Try to influence service management and policy makers at a local level.
- Raise awareness among the multidisciplinary team.
- Offer specialised training to criminal justice system personnel.

To be successful, they need to give very clear messages about their specialist skills and role in terms of supporting clients' communication needs.

Knowledge, skills and resource development

Clinicians need to:

◆ Develop their knowledge of agencies, protocols and procedures.
◆ Explore the specific areas of communication that have particular relevance within this context so that they can assess and advise effectively.
◆ Develop specific skills, for example in facilitating communication and acting as an expert witness.
◆ Debate within the profession and the development of good-practice guidelines for therapists.
◆ Develop resources for assessment and facilitation.

Support

Working within a criminal justice system potentially presents huge challenges to clinicians at both a personal and professional level, due to a combination of the following factors:

◆ The complexity of an unfamiliar system that is adversarial in nature.
◆ Society and therefore legal systems as yet do not fully acknowledge the cognitive and communication needs of people with learning disabilities.
◆ The small amount of relevant guidance is open to interpretation, and everyone involved struggles to interpret it meaningfully in individual situations.
◆ The nature of the work brings clinicians into contact with crime and therefore with victims and perpetrators.
◆ A clinician's involvement carries with it a big responsibility.
◆ This is a new and developing area of work for clinicians, so many are likely to feel poorly equipped to tackle situations that raise so many issues.

Clinicians are more likely to (i) feel able to try to ensure their clients' needs are met within the criminal justice system, and (ii) be successful, if they have access to supportive management that acknowledges the above factors and works with them to tailor effective support systems to meet the individual clinician's needs. Communicating Quality 2 (1996) emphasises the importance of clinical supervision for all therapists, and this area of work is no exception. It has also been the author's experience that debriefing following high-intensity work is essential, and access to personal counselling can be extremely helpful when work-related stresses jeopardise work performance. As in other areas of work the mutual clinical and personal support of an effective multidisciplinary team is invaluable; it is particularly advisable that clinicians do not work in isolation when trying to meet clients' needs within the criminal justice system, and a proper account of personal safety should always be taken.

Working within the criminal justice system can seem a daunting area for involvement for speech and language clinicians, particularly while it is in its infancy. However, there is real evidence of a developing awareness of the communication needs of people with learning disabilities in society and in aspects of the criminal justice system; this represents an exciting opportunity for clinicians to ensure that people's communication needs are increasingly identified, appreciated and met.

Appendices

Appendix I

GENETIC CAUSES OF LEARNING DISABILITY: CHROMOSOMAL ABNORMALITIES

Autosomal (pairs 1–22)

Examples	Description
Down's syndrome	Incidence of 1:650–700. Caused by an extra chromosome on autosome 21 (trisomy 21). Characteristics associated with Down's syndrome are: floppiness (hypotonia) in the neonatal period; small & round head; flat face; small ears with underdeveloped lobes; upward- & outward-slanting eyes; poorly developed bridge of the nose & mouth breathing; small mouth with a high narrow palate & large tongue; distinctive hands (and feet) with a wide gap between thumb and first finger. People with Down's syndrome are often small & broad in stature; have an increased risk of respiratory tract infections due to mouth breathing; have a tendency to hypotonia & the joints have an abnormal range of movement; and reduced fertility.
Edwards syndrome	Incidence of 1:3,000. Caused by an extra chromosome on pair 18 (trisomy 18). Prognosis is poor & most babies die in first few weeks. Degree of learning disability is severe, with associated physical disabilities including congenital abnormalities of the heart, nervous system, abdominal organs, kidneys & ears.
Cri-du-chat	Estimated incidence of 1:50,000. Caused by a deletion of the short arm of chromosome 5. Condition is characterised by a high-pitched crying believed to be caused by a laryngeal defect. Birthweight is low & general failure to thrive & poor suckling reflex. Degree of learning disability is normally severe & development of speech limited.

Sex Chromosome (pair 23)

Examples	Description
Turner (XO) syndrome	Incidence of 1:5,000–10,000 female births. Characterised by diminished secondary sexual characteristics, such as a lack of ovarian tissue. Typically short, have webbing of the neck, a low hairline at the back of the neck & widely-spaced nipples.

Triple X (XXX) syndrome	Around 0.1 per cent of all females have a XXX karyotype, have no physical abnormalities but varying degrees of learning disabilities. Skeletal & neurological problems and pychotic disorders have been associated with XXX syndrome.
Klinefelter (XXY) syndrome	Incidence of 1:1,000 male births. Caused by an additional X chromosome. Development appears normal until puberty, when secondary sexual characteristics fail to develop. Many people are of normal intelligence and those with a learning disability mainly have a mild learning disability.
XYY syndrome	Incidence of 1:1,000 male births. Most do not have a learning disability. They have a normal appearance with an above average stature.

GENETIC CAUSES OF LEARNING DISABILITY: GENE ABNORMALITIES

Autosomal dominant

◆ Where a human trait is known to have its genetic basis in dominant genes located on autosomes.
◆ Genetic disorders caused by dominant genes are fairly uncommon as they usually result in the death of the developing foetus.

Examples	Description
Tuberous sclerosis	Incidence of 1:30,000 (60 per cent have learning disabilities). Rare condition caused by a gene of poor penetrance. Distinctive features are skin lesions, learning disability and epilepsy.
Neurofibromatosis	Incidence of 1:3,000. Presence of six or more pigmented spots over 1.5cm & characteristic *café-au-lait* appearance is an indication that the gene is present. About one-third of sufferers have one or more serious problems, including optic glioma, cerebral & spinal tumours, & mild or moderate learning disabilities.
Prader-Willi syndrome	Incidence of 5–10:100,000. Caused by the absence of a defined area of chromosome 15. Associated with a variety of temperamental & behavioural characteristics, including extreme food-seeking behaviour, self-injury through skin picking, temper tantrums, liability of mood & sleep abnormalities, & stubbornness. Degree of learning disability is usually mild.

Autosomal recessive

- To be affected, individuals must receive the gene for a particular condition from both parents.
- People can be carriers of a disease & show no evidence of it, but can pass it on to their offspring.
- Many autosomal recessive disorders are associated with learning disabilities.

Examples	Description
Phenylketonuria	Incidence of 1:14,000. A disorder of protein metabolism that can be detected by a blood test. If left untreated, can result in learning disabilities and a number of associated conditions.
Galactosaemia	A condition where there is an abnormality of galactose metabolism. If the child survives, learning disability is evident.
Tay-Sachs disease	An autosomal recessive disorder of the lipid metabolism. Usually develops early in life & no treatment available. With delayed onset, occurring in the sixth or seventh year of life, death is likely to occur in the mid-teens. This is called *Batten's disease.* Deterioration is accompanied by spastic paralysis, blindness & convulsions.
Hurler syndrome	Condition in which there is abnormal storage of mucopoly-saccharides in the connective tissue. Often referred to as gargoylism because of physical appearance of those affected. Death usually occurs in adolescence as a result of physical & mental deterioration.

Sex-linked

- There are a number of genetically determined conditions associated with learning disabilities that are inherited in an X-linked manner.
- Females may be carriers of the condition with males being affected.

Examples	Description
X-linked hydrocephalus	Rare form of hydrocephalus – the aqueduct of Sylvius fails to develop fully.
Hunter syndrome	Similar to Hurler syndrome except that it affects only males. Slower rate of physical & mental deterioration – individuals usually survive into adulthood.

Fragile X syndrome	Incidence of 1:2,000 males (most commonly inherited cause of learning disability & accounts for 4–8 per cent of all males with a learning disability).
	Causes a non-specific form of learning disability without major dysmorphic features or severe neurological abnormalities.

Polygenetic

◆ Occurs when a number of genes act together causing complex traits.
◆ Risk of inheritance is smaller than single gene inheritance.
◆ There are a number of conditions that can be linked to leaning disability & can be considered to be of polygenetic origin, some of which are very rare.

Examples	Description
Sturge-Weber syndrome	Rare condition of unknown cause characterised by a facial naevus.
	Epilepsy & spasticity are common features & hemiplegia occurs on opposite side of the body to the facial naevus. Degree of learning disability can be severe.
Cornelia de Lange syndrome	Incidence of 1:40,000.
	Has also become known as Amsterdam dwarfism. All affected individuals have some degree of learning disability, which is often severe.
Hydrocephalus	Incidence of 2:1,000.
	Associated with an excessive amount of fluid in the brain. Severe damage to the brain occurs when the condition is untreated.
Hypothyroidism	A name given to a group of conditions caused by a deficiency of thyroxine. Learning disability is often severe & speech is delayed until seven or eight years of age.

Appendix II

ENVIRONMENTAL CAUSES OF LEARNING DISABILITY

Preconceptual

Cause	Example	Description
Nutrition	Healthy, balanced diet	Reduces incidence of neural tube defects & cleft lip & palate.
Pre-existing medical	Phenylketonuria	If mother has ceased to take her special diet, then there is a risk of foetal deformity & LD.

Prenatal

Cause	Example	Description
Infection	Rubella virus	Degree of LD is linked to time of contracting the virus.
	Cytomegalovirus	Common infection that affects four out of 1,000 pregnant women. Half pass on the virus to the foetus & 10 per cent of these will have a handicap: deafness, blindness, cerebral palsy and LD.
	Varicella zoster/ chicken pox	Can cause LD as well as other malformations if contracted in first five months of pregnancy.
	Toxoplasmosis	Infection can result from contact with animal excrement, undercooked meat & unwashed vegetables. LD & hearing impairments occur.
Maternal health and nutrition	Smoking	Linked to low birth-weight, spontaneous abortion, perinatal death & prenatal complications leading to LD.
	Alcohol	Linked with spontaneous abortion, low birth-weight & foetal alcohol syndrome.
	Drugs	May have a direct effect on the foetus or may interact with a nutrient, as in the case of the drug thalidomide which may have interacted with riboflavin.
	Environmental pollutants	Lead pollution in the atmosphere is known to cause stillbirth & congenital damage to the brain & CNS.

| Physical factors | Excessive use of X-rays Rhesus factor incompatibility Direct violence to the foetus Anoxia | All known to cause damage to the developing foetus. |

Perinatal

Cause	Example	Description
Problems during birth	Prematurity	Increased likelihood of subsequent developmental problems.
	Asphyxia	Main cause of CNS damage before & after birth, usually because of a prolonged second stage of labour or the umbilical cord around the baby's neck.
	Birth trauma	Usually caused by instrument delivery & may result in LD.
Immediately following birth	Hypocalcaemia Hypernatraemia Hypoglycaemia	If left untreated, can cause brain damage.

Postnatal

Cause	Example	Description
Infections	Encephalitis Meningitis Gastroenteritis	All carry the risk of brain damage & LD, if untreated.
Trauma	Head injury	Can result in brain damage.
Toxic agents	Neurotoxins, eg, lead	Can be detrimental in the developmental period.
Nutrition	Malnutrition	May experience both mental & physical developmental delay if malnourished.
Deprivation	Maternal, sensory & environmental	Deprivation may have an effect on physical and intellectual development.

NOTES ON THE AUTHORS

The PCP was written by Alex Hitchings (now Kelly) and Robert Spence and has been revised by Alex Kelly for inclusion within *Working with Adults with a Learning Disability*.

Robert Spence MSc DipCST MCSLT qualified from the School for the Study of Disorders in Human Communication in 1980. He has worked in a variety of clinical specialities and from 1985 to 1989 he was a member of the Islington Community Team for people with learning disabilities. At present, Rob is working as Chief Speech and Language Therapist for Community Services in Camden and Islington.

Alex Kelly (née Hitchings): see cover.

ACKNOWLEDGEMENTS

I would like to thank Rob Spence for allowing me to rewrite the PCP and include it in *Working with Adults with a Learning Disability*.

The Personal Communication Plan

Explanatory Notes

WHAT IS THE PCP?

The Personal Communication Plan (PCP) is a functional assessment and planning tool involving as many relevant others as possible in looking at the communication of the person with the learning disability in the context of their everyday life and environment.

The PCP is divided into five sections. The first four comprise the assessment, while the fifth section is the action plan.

1   **Background information.** This section summarises information on the person's home and daytime environment, social and physical factors and the plan for assessment. See Chapter 1.
2   **Speech and language profile.** This section assesses the person's expressive skills and comprehension. See Chapter 1.
3   **Social skills.** This section assesses the person's non-verbal, verbal and assertiveness skills using a five-point rating scale. Descriptions for each rating will also be given later in the explanatory notes.
4   **Environment.** This section describes and assesses the person's environment using the five accomplishments of normalisation as a framework. See Chapter 1.
5   **Action plan.** Identified needs from previous sections are summarised as action points and steps are agreed on to meet these actions. See Chapter 1.

USERS AND USES OF THE PCP

Users of the PCP

The PCP was designed to be used jointly by speech and language clinicians and relevant others in the person's life – for example, carer, key worker, or family. The person being assessed should also be involved in the completion of the PCP whenever possible. The PCP can be coordinated and completed by anyone involved in the process, but a speech and language clinician should coordinate the completion of the speech and language profile.

Uses of the PCP

The PCP is a flexible assessment and can either be used in total (ie, all five sections), or the four assessment sections can be selected to reflect a specific need as appropriate to the individual client. Below are examples of when different sections could be used.

◆   *All sections.* All sections should be used if a comprehensive assessment of communication is needed, or if all sections are considered to be relevant after completing the background information section. From this, an action plan is developed which will incorporate all aspects of communication.

- *Sections 1 and 2*. These sections (background information and speech and language profile) can be used together to provide information about the person's level of understanding and expressive skills. They can be used as a screening assessment, for example to identify potential caseloads in new environments, or to identify those clients who may need a more comprehensive assessment.
- *Sections 1 and 3*. These sections (background information and social skills) can be used to assess social skills. The graphic section at the end of Section 3 enables the clinician to plan intervention and evaluate progress, and also to identify common needs when assessing for groups.
- *Sections 1 and 4*. These sections (background information and environment) can be used to provide information about the person's communication environment, and in particular to identify opportunities to improve their quality of life. These sections can be particularly useful when assessing people with challenging behaviour or who are non-verbal, and as a basis for staff training.

COMPLETING THE SOCIAL SKILLS SECTION

This section uses a five-point rating scale in order to assess the person's non-verbal, verbal and assertiveness skills:

1 = Always inappropriate
2 = Mostly inappropriate
3 = Sometimes appropriate
4 = Mostly appropriate
5 = Always appropriate

The following descriptions will help the clinician to use the rating scale effectively and consistently.

Non-verbal skills

A Eye-contact

1   Avoids eye-contact at all times during conversations or continually stares.
2   Frequently avoids eye-contact, or frequent inappropriate staring.
3   Some inappropriate use of eye-contact.
4   Minimal avoidance of eye-contact or inappropriate staring, eg, when under stress.
5   Effective and appropriate use of eye-contact in all situations.

B Facial expression

1   Inappropriate to situation. May include scowling, grinning, blank expression.
2   Frequent inappropriate use of facial expression.
3   Some appropriate use of facial expression.
4   Frequently appropriate use of facial expression.
5   Effective use of a range of facial expressions changing according to the situation, eg, expresses own moods and feelings through facial expressions.

C Hand gestures

1   Uses inappropriate hand gestures excessively, or no use of hand gestures.
2   Frequent inappropriate use or non-use of hand gestures.
3   Occasional inappropriate use of hand gestures.
4   Can use gestures effectively, but occasional inappropriate use.
5   Uses hand gestures effectively, ie, for emphasis or substitution of speech.

D Proximity

1   Excessive proximity or distance when communicating, causing discomfort to others.
2   Frequent inappropriate proximity or distance.
3   Occasionally inappropriate.
4   Usually appropriate to situation, but may break down in stressful or unfamiliar situations.
5   Adapts proximity or distance appropriately and effectively, ie, according to relationships and social situations.

E Touch

1   Excessive use or avoidance of touch which causes embarrassment or anger in others.
2   Frequent use or avoidance of touch which is inappropriate to the situation.
3   Occasional inappropriate use of touch.
4   Mostly appropriate, but will very occasionally use touch inappropriately.
5   Effective and appropriate use of touch, ie, a degree of touch which is acceptable to others and/or the situation.

F Fidgeting

1   Excessive, continuous fidgeting, eg, whole-body movements.
2   Frequent excessive fidgeting.
3   Occasional excessive fidgeting, particularly in stressful situations.
4   Occasional minor fidgeting, eg, foot tapping, head scratching.
5   Rarely fidgets.

G Posture and gait

1   Usually inappropriate to situation, eg, obvious rigid or flaccid muscle tone.
2   Frequently inappropriate.
3   Some inappropriate posture or gait.
4   Mostly appropriate, but may break down when tense or under pressure.
5   Normal posture and gait – appropriate to all situations.

H Personal appearance

1   Habitually unkempt appearance and/or inappropriate clothing to season or situation.
2   Frequently unkempt and/or inappropriate appearance.
3   Occasionally unkempt and/or inappropriate appearance.
4   Usually appropriate, but may deteriorate, eg, if under pressure.
5   Maintains and adapts appearance to different situations, seasons and age. Uses appearance to create different impressions.

I Volume

1   Mostly uses inappropriate volume, eg, voice too loud or too quiet for the situation.
2   Frequently uses inappropriate volume.
3   Occasionally uses inappropriate volume.
4   Uses appropriate volume in most situations, but some difficulty in adapting.
5   Uses and adapts volume appropriately in all situations.

J Intonation

1   Consistently inappropriate, eg, monotonous or exaggerated.
2   Frequent inappropriate use of intonation.
3   Occasionally uses inappropriate intonation, particularly evident in stressful situations.
4   Uses appropriate intonation in most situations, but is affected by mood changes.
5   Intonation is used effectively and appropriately, ie, adapted to situation and content of speech.

K Rate

1   Continuous inappropriate rate, eg, too fast/slow/fluctuating between two extremes.
2   Frequently inappropriate rate of speech.
3   Occasionally inappropriate rate of speech, especially evident in stressful situations.
4   Appropriate rate of speech in most situations.
5   Rate of speech is appropriate and adapted effectively, eg, increasing rate when there is a sense of urgency, or slowing rate when others show confusion or misunderstanding.

L Clarity

1   Habitual use of indistinct speech, eg, mumbling.
2   Frequently mumbles to self and others.
3   Occasionally mumbles, particularly in stressful situations.
4   Generally speaks clearly, but will occasionally mumble.
5   Speech is consistently clear and easily understood.

M Fluency and hesitations

1 Continual dysfluency of speech, eg, severe blocking, struggle, prolongation, repetition, hesitation.
2 Frequently dysfluent. May also include excessive use of 'um' and 'er'.
3 Occasionally dysfluent with less evidence of struggle behaviour.
4 Some mild dysfluencies, eg 'um' and 'er', particularly in stressful situations.
5 Speech is fluent.

Verbal skills

A Listening: focusing

1 Finds difficulty in focusing attention in one-to-one situations, with no external distractions.
2 Can attend in one-to-one situation, but is easily distracted.
3 Can attend well in one-to-one situation, but is easily distracted in small group situation.
4 Can attend well in small groups, but finds noisy, crowded environments distracting.
5 Can attend well in a noisy, crowded environment.

B Listening: reinforcing

1 Total absence of verbal and non-verbal reinforcement, eg, nodding while listening, conveying to speaker that the focal person is not listening.
2 Infrequent use of reinforcers.
3 Occasional use of reinforcers, but still inadequate.
4 Frequent use of reinforcers, but with some inadequacy or inappropriateness.
5 Effective and appropriate use of reinforcers such as 'mm', 'I see', 'ah ha', nodding, etc.

C Listening: responding

1 Total absence of verbal responses while in the listening role.
2 Infrequent verbal responses and inappropriate responding, eg, interrupting.
3 Occasional use of verbal responses, eg, asking appropriate questions.
4 Frequent use of verbal responses, eg, reflecting back, sympathising. However, not always appropriate.
5 Good verbal responding skills, including asking for clarification, self-disclosure, empathy, achieving a good balance between listening and responding.

D Opening a conversation

1 Rarely initiates a conversation with others.
2 May initiate conversation, but usually inappropriate to context or situation, eg, habitual subject manner, interrupting, initiating conversations with strangers, personal remarks.

3   Initiates conversations, but mostly uses inappropriate or stereotyped phrases.
4   Often initiates conversations effectively, but occasionally uses inappropriate openers, especially when stressed.
5   Is able to initiate conversations successfully.

E Maintaining a conversation: turn-taking

1   Continually talks and monopolises the conversation, or does not contribute.
2   Minimal listening with frequent interruptions or few contributions.
3   Appears to listen using some appropriate responses, but occasionally interrupts inappropriately.
4   Generally takes turns in conversations effectively, with occasional difficulty.
5   Uses good turn-taking skills (eg, can interrupt when appropriate) and effectively responds to cues (eg, to natural breaks, eye-contact, questioning, adding information).

F Maintaining a conversation: asking questions

1   Does not ask questions during conversations, or seek further information when needed.
2   Rarely asks questions and questions asked are inappropriate.
3   Occasionally asks questions effectively.
4   Often asks questions, but occasionally these are ineffective or inadequate.
5   Asks questions with appropriate frequency, especially when gaining information to maintain a conversation.

G Maintaining a conversation: responding to questions

1   Does not respond to questions during conversations, due to misunderstanding or poor listening.
2   Rarely responds to questions with minimal utterances, eg, 'yes' or 'no'.
3   Occasionally responds to questions, but may be inappropriate, eg, echolalia.
4   Usually responds appropriately. Occasional use of inappropriate and/or stereotypical responses.
5   Responds to questions effectively and appropriately to maintain a conversation.

H Maintaining a conversation: relevance

1   Extreme difficulty in following the topic of the conversation, eg, introduces irrelevancies or continuous unrelated ideas.
2   Considerable difficulty in keeping to the topic. However, able to respond appropriately for one or two sentences or questions.
3   Some difficulty in keeping to topic, especially after about four or five connected responses.
4   Usually follows and maintains topic of conversation, but may occasionally introduce unrelated ideas.
5   Can maintain and develop a topic effectively and appropriately.

I Maintaining a conversation: repair

1 Does not seek clarification or further information when misunderstanding occurs.
2 Rarely seeks clarification or further information.
3 Sometimes seeks clarification or further information.
4 Usually seeks clarification or further information.
5 Consistently seeks clarification or further information when misunderstanding occurs.

J Ending a conversation

1 Demonstrates great difficulty in ending conversation. May appear embarrassed or walk off without adequate closure.
2 Demonstrates frequent difficulty in ending conversations.
3 Has some difficulty ending conversations.
4 Rarely has difficulty in ending conversations, but may occasionally do so with unfamiliar people or circumstances.
5 Consistently ends conversations proficiently and effectively, with appropriate non-verbal behaviour and verbal behaviour, eg, preparing for closure, using closing phrases, getting up.

Assertiveness skills

A Compliment-giving

1 Does not show appreciation or pay compliments, or only uses them inappropriately, eg, subject matter, non-verbal behaviour.
2 Rarely gives compliments appropriately.
3 Occasionally gives compliments appropriately.
4 Frequently gives compliments appropriately. May be some inappropriate non-verbal behaviour.
5 Gives compliments effectively, ie, uses appropriate non-verbal behaviour and content (not too personal or effusive).

B Compliment receiving

1 Does not receive compliments or appreciation, eg, lack of, or inappropriate, response.
2 Rarely receives compliments appropriately.
3 Occasionally gives appropriate responses to compliments.
4 Frequently responds appropriately, but may show some embarrassment or awkwardness.
5 Responds appropriately both verbally and non-verbally when given compliments, eg, 'thank you', smiling, nodding.

C Expressing feelings and needs

1 Does not express feelings or needs verbally. May appear passive or isolated. May appear aggressive or disruptive.
2 Rarely expresses feelings or needs effectively or appropriately.
3 Occasionally expresses feelings or needs.
4 Frequently expresses feelings or needs, but may sometimes experience some difficulty in communicating these effectively.
5 Effective expression of feelings or needs, ie, reports feelings with appropriate facial expression, body language and vocabulary.

D Standing up for self

1 Does not stand up for self or rights. May appear passive or inappropriately aggressive.
2 Rarely stands up for self or rights.
3 Occasionally shows an ability to stand up for self.
4 Frequently stands up for self and rights, with occasional hesitation or aggression.
5 Stands up for self and rights effectively, ie, can represent own views and feelings in an assertive, non-aggressive way.

E Making suggestions and giving opinions

1 Does not make suggestions or give opinions. May appear passive, easily led or disruptive.
2 Rarely makes suggestions or gives opinions, or has considerable difficulty in communicating these.
3 Occasionally makes suggestions or gives opinions, but may have difficulty in communicating these.
4 Frequently makes suggestions or gives opinions, but may be affected by situations.
5 Makes suggestions and gives opinions effectively and in the correct context.

F Refusal

1 Will always comply with requests, even when against their will. May appear passive or easily influenced.
2 Will frequently comply with requests, even when against their will.
3 Will occasionally comply with requests, even when against their will. Attempts to refuse but often ineffectively.
4 Rarely complies with requests against their will and often demonstrates effective refusal.
5 Has well-developed skills in refusal which are used effectively and appropriately, ie, ability to oppose something they do not agree with and to use appropriate non-verbal skills to reinforce refusal.

G Disagreeing

1 Does not disagree with opinions or statements when appropriate. May appear passive, easily influenced or aggressive.
2 Rarely disagrees with others, or communicates disagreement inappropriately, eg, aggression or disruption.
3 Will occasionally disagree with others when appropriate.
4 Frequently able to disagree appropriately.
5 Disagrees with opinions and statements effectively and appropriately. Puts forward own opinion and argues this with appropriate verbal and non-verbal behaviours.

H Complaining

1 Does not complain when appropriate to the situation, or may communicate dissatisfaction inappropriately, eg, aggression.
2 Rarely complains when appropriate. Easily influenced and dissuaded.
3 Will occasionally complain when appropriate.
4 Complains when appropriate, but occasionally communicates inappropriately.
5 Complains effectively and appropriately according to the situation by stating reasons for dissatisfaction lucidly and assertively.

I Making apologies

1 Does not apologise when appropriate to the situation, and when socially expected.
2 Rarely apologises when appropriate. May be defensive, aggressive or evasive.
3 Occasionally apologises when appropriate. Often makes attempts to apologise, but these are ineffectual or inappropriate.
4 Will usually apologise when appropriate, but with occasional difficulty.
5 Apologises effectively and appropriately, ie, recognises when an apology is necessary and can express this appropriately verbally and non-verbally.

J Requesting explanations

1 Follows requests, directions or decisions without question, even when unhappy, or may respond inappropriately to them.
2 Rarely questions requests, directions or decisions which require further clarification.
3 Occasionally questions these issues and requests further explanation.
4 Will usually request further explanation when appropriate, but with occasional difficulty.
5 Shows effective skills in requesting further explanations when necessary, eg, 'I don't understand why I have to...'.

PERSONAL COMMUNICATION PLAN – BACKGROUND INFORMATION

NAME _____ **DOB** _____

ADDRESS _____

HOME ENVIRONMENT (include important people in person's life)

Contact person _____ Telephone no. _____

DAYTIME OCCUPATION (include important people in person's life)

Contact person _____ Telephone no. _____

REASON FOR REFERRAL

DESCRIPTION OF COMMUNICATION

PHYSICAL FACTORS

Hearing difficulties

Visual or perceptual difficulties

Medical condition and medication including side-effects

CULTURAL FACTORS

LIKES AND DISLIKES

ACTIONS AGREED

Sections of PCP to be completed: Circle Y (yes) or N (no):

Speech & Language Profile Y N   Social skills Y N   Environment Y N   Other _____

Completed by _____ Date _____

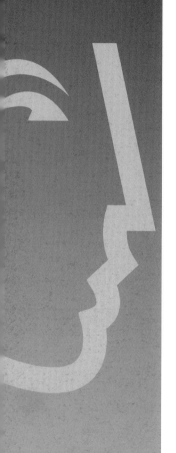

PERSONAL COMMUNICATION PLAN – SPEECH & LANGUAGE PROFILE

NAME _____ DOB _____

PERSON(S) COMPLETING SECTION _____ DATE _____

EXPRESSIVE SKILLS   ACTION

METHOD OF EXPRESSION How does the person express their needs?

Speech Y N   Eg _____
                              _____   ☐

Non-verbally Y N   Vocalisations? _____

                              Gesture? _____

                              Body language? _____

                              Physical behaviour? _____

                              Other? _____
                              _____   ☐

Augmentative system Y N   _____
                              _____   ☐

HOW EFFECTIVE IS THE PERSON'S METHOD OF EXPRESSION?

What could be done to improve this?
                                                                     ☐

What are the environmental considerations?
                                                                     ☐

VOCABULARY

Is the person's vocabulary (words/signs) adequate for their needs?   Y N   ☐

Can the person express a wide range of messages?   Y N

• Basic needs and wants? _____
  _____

• Something outside their immediate environment? _____
  _____

• Ability to socialise? _____
  _____

PERSONAL COMMUNICATION PLAN – SPEECH & LANGUAGE PROFILE

EXPRESSIVE SKILLS   **ACTION**

• Ability to join in everyday activities? _____

  _____

• Ability to be part of their wider community? _____

  _____

• What else would the person benefit from being able to express?_____

  _____

EXPRESSION AT SENTENCE LEVEL (words/signs)

Is the person able to use sentences effectively?   Y N

  Eg _____

  _____

  _____

Is the person's use of language appropriate?   Y N

  Eg _____

  _____

Any evidence of echolalia or perseveration?   Y N

  Eg _____

  _____

What could be done to improve the person's ability to join words/signs, etc? ☐

NON-VERBAL ASPECTS OF SPEECH

Evidence of dysfluency?   Y N

  Eg _____

Appropriate use of volume?   Y N

  Eg _____

Appropriate rate?   Y N

  Eg _____

Appropriate intonation?   Y N

  Eg _____

Appropriate pitch?   Y N

  Eg _____

What could be done to improve the person's skills in this area? ☐

P

Photocopiable

©Alex Kelly, 2000

PERSONAL COMMUNICATION PLAN – SPEECH & LANGUAGE PROFILE

EXPRESSIVE SKILLS   **ACTION**

ARTICULATION

Is the person difficult to understand because of phonological difficulties?   Y N

Eg _____

_____

What could be done to improve the person's ability to express themselves more clearly?

☐

ADDITIONAL COMMENTS

☐

SUMMARY OF ACTIONS TO IMPROVE EXPRESSIVE SKILLS

PERSONAL COMMUNICATION PLAN – SPEECH & LANGUAGE PROFILE

COMPREHENSION   **ACTION**

VOCABULARY

Is this adequate for the person's needs?   Y N

Is there evidence that the person sometimes misunderstands certain words?   Y N

What could be done to improve the person's understanding of words?
Consider likes and dislikes, and use of augmentative systems such as
signs, symbols.

☐

SENTENCE COMPREHENSION / LEVEL OF UNDERSTANDING

How much is the person able to understand within familiar environment?

- 1-key-word phrases? Y N   Eg _____
  _____

- 2-key-word phrases? Y N   Eg _____
  _____

- 3-key-word phrases? Y N   Eg _____
  _____

- Other, eg, negatives,   Eg _____
  questions . . .   _____
  _____
  _____
  _____

How much is the person able to understand without any non-verbal cues,
such as routine, peer behaviour?

- 1-key-word phrases? Y N   Eg _____
  _____

- 2-key-word phrases? Y N   Eg _____
  _____

- 3-key-word phrases? Y N   Eg _____
  _____

- Other, eg, negatives,   Eg _____
  questions . . .   _____
  _____
  _____
  _____
  _____

PERSONAL COMMUNICATION PLAN – SPEECH & LANGUAGE PROFILE

COMPREHENSION   **ACTION**

SENTENCE COMPREHENSION / LEVEL OF UNDERSTANDING (continued)

What does the person need to enable them to understand to their full potential?
Consider changes to environment, carers' speech, use of augmentative systems.

☐

ABSTRACT CONCEPTS

Can the person understand the concept of time?   Y N
    Eg _____
    _____

Can the person understand the vocabulary of moods or emotions?   Y N
    Eg _____
    _____

What could be done to improve the person's ability to understand
abstract concepts?

☐

ADDITIONAL COMMENTS

☐

SUMMARY OF ACTIONS TO IMPROVE COMPREHENSION

Completed by _____ Date _____

PERSONAL COMMUNICATION PLAN – SOCIAL SKILLS

NAME _____ **DOB** _____

PERSON(S) COMPLETING SECTION _____ **DATE** _____

RATING SCALE: 1 – Always inappropriate
2 – Mostly inappropriate
3 – Sometimes appropriate
4 – Mostly appropriate
5 – Always appropriate

NON-VERBAL SKILLS	**ACTION**

A   EYE-CONTACT

Rating   1 2 3 4 5   Description   ☐

B   FACIAL EXPRESSION

Rating   1 2 3 4 5   Description   ☐

C   HAND GESTURES

Rating   1 2 3 4 5   Description   ☐

D   PROXIMITY

Rating   1 2 3 4 5   Description   ☐

E   TOUCH

Rating   1 2 3 4 5   Description   ☐

F   FIDGETING

Rating   1 2 3 4 5   Description   ☐

G   POSTURE AND GAIT

Rating   1 2 3 4 5   Description   ☐

H   PERSONAL APPEARANCE

Rating   1 2 3 4 5   Description   ☐

I   VOLUME

Rating   1 2 3 4 5   Description   ☐

PERSONAL COMMUNICATION PLAN – SOCIAL SKILLS

RATING SCALE: 1 – Always inappropriate
2 – Mostly inappropriate
3 – Sometimes appropriate
4 – Mostly appropriate
5 – Always appropriate

NON-VERBAL SKILLS	ACTION

J   INTONATION

Rating   1 2 3 4 5   Description

☐

K   RATE

Rating   1 2 3 4 5   Description

☐

L   CLARITY

Rating   1 2 3 4 5   Description

☐

M   FLUENCY AND HESITATIONS

Rating   1 2 3 4 5   Description

☐

SUMMARY OF NON-VERBAL SKILLS

SUMMARY OF ACTIONS

VERBAL SKILLS	ACTION

A   LISTENING: FOCUSING (ability to attend)

Rating   1 2 3 4 5   Description

☐

B   LISTENING: REINFORCEMENTS (use of reinforcers such as 'mm')

Rating   1 2 3 4 5   Description

☐

C   LISTENING: RESPONDING (use of verbal responses while listening)

Rating   1 2 3 4 5   Description

☐

PERSONAL COMMUNICATION PLAN – SOCIAL SKILLS

RATING SCALE: 1 – Always inappropriate
2 – Mostly inappropriate
3 – Sometimes appropriate
4 – Mostly appropriate
5 – Always appropriate

VERBAL SKILLS	ACTION

D   OPENING A CONVERSATION

Rating   1 2 3 4 5   Description

☐

E   MAINTAINING A CONVERSATION: TURN-TAKING

Rating   1 2 3 4 5   Description

☐

F   MAINTAINING A CONVERSATION: ASKING QUESTIONS

Rating   1 2 3 4 5   Description

☐

G   MAINTAINING A CONVERSATION: RESPONDING TO QUESTIONS

Rating   1 2 3 4 5   Description

☐

H   MAINTAINING A CONVERSATION: RELEVANCE

Rating   1 2 3 4 5   Description

☐

I   MAINTAINING A CONVERSATION: REPAIR

Rating   1 2 3 4 5   Description

☐

J   ENDING A CONVERSATION

Rating   1 2 3 4 5   Description

☐

SUMMARY OF VERBAL SKILLS

SUMMARY OF ACTIONS

Photocopiable

Working with

Adults with a Learning Disability

PERSONAL COMMUNICATION PLAN – SOCIAL SKILLS

RATING SCALE: 1 – Always inappropriate
2 – Mostly inappropriate
3 – Sometimes appropriate
4 – Mostly appropriate
5 – Always appropriate

ASSERTIVENESS SKILLS	**ACTION**

A COMPLIMENT-GIVING

Rating   1 2 3 4 5   Description   ☐

B COMPLIMENT-RECEIVING

Rating   1 2 3 4 5   Description   ☐

C EXPRESSING FEELINGS AND NEEDS

Rating   1 2 3 4 5   Description   ☐

D STANDING UP FOR SELF

Rating   1 2 3 4 5   Description   ☐

E MAKING SUGGESTIONS AND GIVING OPINIONS

Rating   1 2 3 4 5   Description   ☐

F REFUSAL

Rating   1 2 3 4 5   Description   ☐

G DISAGREEING

Rating   1 2 3 4 5   Description   ☐

H COMPLAINING

Rating   1 2 3 4 5   Description   ☐

I MAKING APOLOGIES

Rating   1 2 3 4 5   Description   ☐

332

PERSONAL COMMUNICATION PLAN – SOCIAL SKILLS

RATING SCALE: 1 – Always inappropriate
2 – Mostly inappropriate
3 – Sometimes appropriate
4 – Mostly appropriate
5 – Always appropriate

ASSERTIVENESS SKILLS   **ACTION**

J   REQUESTING EXPLANATIONS

Rating   1   2   3   4   5   Description

☐

SUMMARY OF ASSERTIVENESS SKILLS

SUMMARY OF ACTIONS

Completed by _____ Date _____

PERSONAL COMMUNICATION PLAN – SUMMARY OF SOCIAL SKILLS

Ratings for each skill are transferred on to the chart by shading the appropriate number of sections.

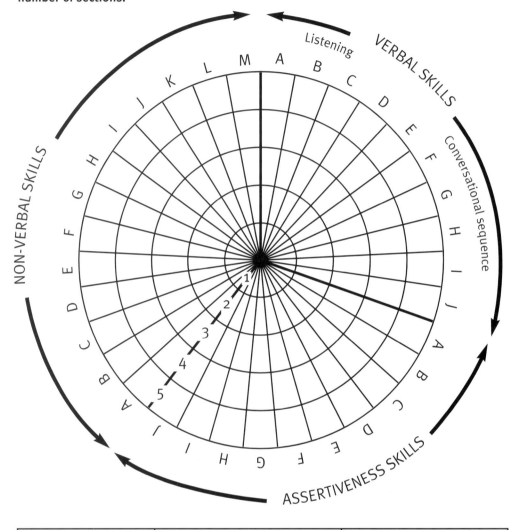

Non-verbal skills	Verbal skills	Assertiveness skills
A Eye-contact	A Listening – focusing	A Compliment-giving
B Facial expression	B Listening – reinforcing	B Compliment-receiving
C Hand gestures	C Listening – responding	C Expressing feelings
D Proximity	D Opening a conversation	D Standing up for self
E Touch	E Maintaining a conversation – turn-taking	E Making suggestions
F Fidgeting	F Maintaining a conversation – asking questions	F Refusal
G Posture and Gait	G Maintaining a conversation – responding to questions	G Disagreeing
H Personal appearance	H Maintaining a conversation – relevancy	H Complaining
I Volume	I Maintaining a conversation – repair	I Making apologies
J Intonation	J Ending a question	J Requesting explanations
K Rate		
L Clarity		
M Fluency/ hesitations		

PERSONAL COMMUNICATION PLAN – ENVIRONMENT

NAME _____ DOB _____

PERSON(S) COMPLETING SECTION _____ DATE _____

RELATIONSHIPS/COMMUNITY PARTICIPATION   **ACTION**

---

1   CONTACT & QUALITY OF RELATIONSHIPS
*   Consider with whom the person spends most time, and the diversity and quality of these relationships.

*   Consider current opportunities for developing relationships.

---

2   CURRENT BARRIERS TO IMPROVING RELATIONSHIPS
*   What are the barriers to improving relationships in the person's life? Consider personal barriers such as communication skills, and external barriers such as lack of opportunity.

---

3   IMPROVING OPPORTUNITIES
*   What could be done to improve opportunities for developing relationships? Consider the support and action necessary to achieve this.

☐

---

4   ADDITIONAL COMMENTS

Photocopiable

PERSONAL COMMUNICATION PLAN – ENVIRONMENT

CHOICE   **ACTION**

1   OPPORTUNITIES FOR CHOICE & CHOICE-MAKING SKILLS
- Consider the number of choices the person makes on a daily, weekly or occasional basis.

- How does the person make their choices known?

- Are choices made for the person, with or without consultation? Consider aspects of the environment, such as rigid routines, set menus, etc.

2   CURRENT BARRIERS TO IMPROVING CHOICE
- What are the barriers to improving choice in the person's life? Consider personal barriers, such as communication skills, and external barriers, such as lack of opportunity.

3   IMPROVING CHOICE
- What could be done to improve opportunities for increasing decisions? Consider aspects such as personal skills in decision-making and environmental changes which would facilitate choice.

4   ADDITIONAL COMMENTS

PERSONAL COMMUNICATION PLAN – ENVIRONMENT

RESPECT   **ACTION**

1   CURRENT OPPORTUNITIES TO BE VALUED
- Does the person have a valued role in their life? Consider aspects such as whether their opinions are sought and responsibilities are given.

- Is the person able to express individuality? Consider whether they can use their skills and interests in these roles.

- Consider current opportunities that exist for the person to become involved in the planning and management of their everyday life and environment.

2   CURRENT BARRIERS TO IMPROVING RESPECT
- What are the barriers to the person assuming a valued role and being perceived more positively? Consider personal barriers, such as communication skills, and external barriers, such as lack of opportunity.

3   IMPROVING RESPECT
- What could be done to improve the person's opportunity to have a valued role in their life? Consider the support and action necessary to achieve this.

☐

4   ADDITIONAL COMMENTS

PERSONAL COMMUNICATION PLAN – ENVIRONMENT

PERSONAL DEVELOPMENT/COMPETENCE	ACTION

1 CURRENT OPPORTUNITIES FOR PERSONAL DEVELOPMENT

- Identify the skills the person has developed over the past two years.

- Consider the support that has been necessary in order to facilitate this.

2 CURRENT BARRIERS TO IMPROVING PERSONAL DEVELOPMENT

- What are the barriers to the person developing or improving skills? Consider personal barriers, such as communication skills, and external barriers, such as resources, support and stereotyped perceptions of disability.

3 IMPROVING OPPORTUNITIES

- What could be done to improve the person's ability to learn new skills? Consider the support and action necessary to achieve this.

☐

4 ADDITIONAL COMMENTS

PERSONAL COMMUNICATION PLAN – ENVIRONMENT

COMMUNITY PRESENCE   **ACTION**

1   CURRENT OPPORTUNITIES FOR ACCESSING COMMUNITY FACILITIES
- Identify facilities to which the person has regular access and how frequently they use them.

- Does the person use these facilities independently? If not, how much support do they need?

2   CURRENT BARRIERS TO IMPROVING COMMUNITY PRESENCE
- What are the barriers to improving the person's ability to access facilities in the community? Consider personal barriers, such as communication skills, and external barriers, such as lack of opportunity and resources.

3   IMPROVING OPPORTUNITIES
- What could be done to improve the number and variety of community facilities the person could use? Consider the person's interests, and facilities that they would benefit from and enjoy using. Consider the support and action necessary to achieve this.

4   ADDITIONAL COMMENTS

PERSONAL COMMUNICATION PLAN – SUMMARY OF ENVIRONMENT

NAME _____ DOB _____

PERSON(S) COMPLETING SECTION _____ DATE _____

ACTIONS AGREED	ACTION

- **Relationships**

- **Choice**

- **Respect**

- **Personal development**

- **Community presence**

Completed by _____ Date _____

NAME

DATE

PERSONAL COMMUNICATION PLAN – ACTION PLANNING 1

Actions	Steps	By whom?	By when?	Notes on attainment

THE PERSONAL COMMUNICATION PLAN

341

PERSONAL COMMUNICATION PLAN – ACTION PLANNING 2

NAME _____ DOB _____

ADDRESS _____ DATE _____

AIMS

ACTION PLAN	BY WHOM?	BY WHEN?

REVIEW DATE	NOTES ON ATTAINMENT

Signed _____ Date _____

Bibliography

Aarons M & Gittens T, 1992, *The Autistic Continuum: an Assessment and Intervention Schedule,* NFER-Nelson, Windsor.

American Speech and Hearing Association (ASHA), 1989, *Competencies for Speech-Language Pathologists Providing Services in Augmentative Communication,* ASHA, 31, pp107–110.

Aylott J & Toocaram J, 1996, 'Community Learning Disability Teams', *British Journal of Nursing*, Vol 5.

Bannerman M & Lindsay M, 1994, 'Evolution of services', Shanley E & Starrs T (eds), *Learning Disabilities. A Handbook of Care*, Churchill Livingstone, Edinburgh.

Baron RA & Byrne D, 1987, *Social Psychology: Understanding Human Interaction* (5th edn), Allyn & Bacon, Massachusetts.

Barr O, 1993, 'Reap the benefits of a co-operative approach – understanding inter-disciplinary teamwork', *Professional Nurse*, Vol 4.

Beaill N & Warden S, 1995, 'Sexual abuse of adults with learning disabilities', *Journal of Intellectual Disability Research*, 39 (5).

Bell I, 1984, 'Communication and language in mental handicap: meaningful terms', *British Institute of Mental Handicap,* 12 March 1984.

Beukelman D & Mirenda P, 1998, *Augmentative and Alternative Communication,* Paul H Brookes Publishing, Baltimore.

Bonnie RJ, 1992, 'The competency of defendants with mental retardation to assist in their own defence', Conley RW, Luckasson R & Bouthilet GN, 1992, *The Criminal Justice System and Mental Retardation: Defendants and Victims,* Paul H Brookes Publishing, Baltimore.

Bradley H, 1991, *Assessing Communication Together (ACT),* MHNA Publications.

Brandon D, 1988, *A Handbook on the Practical Application of Ordinary Living Principles,* Good Impressions Publishing.

British Medical Association, 1994, *Health Care of Detainees in Police Station,* British Medical Association, Medical Ethics Committee, London.

British Psychological Society, 1999, *Learning Disability: Operational Definitions (draft D),* The British Psychological Society, Leicester, England.

Brown A, 1986, *Group Work.* Gower, Aldershot.

Brown H, 1992b, 'Using training materials in multidisciplinary settings', *Learning Together: Shaping New Services for People with Learning Disabilities*, Edited and published for CCETSW by Learning Materials Design, Central Council for Education and Training in Social Work (CCETSW), London.

Brown H, 1994, *Understanding and Responding to Difficult Behaviour,* Pavilion Publishing, Brighton.

Brown H, Egan-Sage E, Barry G & Mckay C, 1996, *Towards Better Interviewing. A Handbook for Police Officers and Social Workers on the Sexual Abuse of Adults with Learning Disabilities,* NAPSAC, Nottingham.

Brown J, 1992a, 'Professional boundaries in mental handicap: a policy analysis of joint training', Thompson T & Mathias P, *Standards and Mental Handicap: Keys to Competence*, Bailliere Tindall, London.

Brown S & Wistow G (eds), 1990, *The Roles and Tasks of Community Mental Handicap Teams,* Gower, Aldershot.

Bungener J & McCormack B, 1994, 'Psychotherapy and learning disability', Clarkson, P & Pokorny M (eds), *The Handbook of Psychotherapy*, Routledge, London.

Bunning K, 1997, 'The role of sensory reinforcement in developing interactions', Fawcus M (ed), *Children with Learning Difficulties – a Collaborative Approach in their Education and Management,* Whurr Publishers, London.

Caldwell P, 1998, *Person to Person – Establishing Contact and Communication with People with Profound Learning Disabilities and Extra Special Needs,* Pavillion Publishing, Brighton.

Clare ICH & Gudjonsson GH, 1993, 'Interrogative suggestibility, confabulation, and acquiescence in people with mild learning disabilities (mental handicap): implications for reliability during police interrogations', *British Journal of Clinical Psychology*, 32, pp295–301.

Clare ICH & Gudjonsson GH, 1995, 'The vulnerability of suspects with intellectual disabilities during police interviews: a review and experimental study of decision-making', *Mental Handicap Research*, 8, 2.

Clarke-Kehoe A, 1994, *Understanding and Responding to Difficult Behaviour,* Pavilion Publishing, Brighton.

Clarke-Kehoe A & Harris P, 1992, '. . . It's the way that you say it', *Community Care*, 9 July 1992.

Clements J & Zarkowska E, 1994, *Care Staff Management: A Practitioner's Guide,* John Wiley & Sons, Chichester.

COMMUNITY QUALITY 2, 1996, Royal College of Speech and Language Therapists, London.

Conley RW, 1992, 'Observations from the field', Conley RW, Luckasson R & Bouthilet GN, *The Criminal Justice System and Mental Retardation: Defendants and Victims,* Paul H Brookes Publishing, Baltimore.

Coupe O'Kane J, Barton L, Barber M, Collins L, Levy D & Murphy D, 1985, *The Affective Communication Assessment (ACA),* Manchester Education Committee, Manchester.

Coupe O'Kane J & Goldbart J, 1998, *Communication before Speech: Development and Assessment,* 2nd edn, David Fulton Publisher, London.

Crossley R & McDonald A, 1984 , *Annie's Coming Out,* Viking Penguin, New York.

Dalton P, 1994, *Counselling People with Communication Problems,* Sage Publications, London.

Davies M, 1995, *Criminal Justice: An Introduction to the Criminal Justice System in England and Wales,* Longman, Harlow.

Davies S, 1999, 'Dysphagia in acute strokes', *Nursing Standard*, 13, 30, pp49–54.

Dawson C, 1996, *Understanding Learning Disabilities,* Folens Ltd. Available from Winslow Press, Bicester.

DHSS, 1971, *Better Services for the Mentally Handicapped,* Cmnd 4683, HMSO, London.

Diesfield K, 1996, 'Witness credibility in cases of sexual abuse against adults with learning disabilities', *Tizard Learning Disability Review*, 1, 4.

Disability Discrimination Act, The, 1996, *Access to Goods, Facilities and Services*, DL 80, April 1996, Issued on behalf of the Minister of Disabled People.

DOH, 1988, *Community Care: Agenda for Action (Griffiths Report),* HMSO, London.

DOH, 1989a, *Caring for People: Community Care in the Next Decade and Beyond,* Cm849, HMSO, London.

DOH, 1989b, *Working for Patients,* Cm555, HMSO, London.

DOH, 1995, *The Health of the Nation: A Strategy for People with Learning Disabilities,* HMSO, London.

DOH, 1998, *A First Class Service: Quality in the New NHS,* HMSO, London.

Donnellan A, Mirenda P, Mesaros R & Fassbender L, 1984, 'Analyzing the Communicative Functions of Aberrant Behavior', *JASH* , 9, 3.

Douglas T, 1990, *Basic Groupwork,* Tavistock/Routledge, London.

Druce P, 1992, 'Steps in Formulating Training Programmes', In *Learning Together: Shaping New Services for People with Learning Disabilities,* Edited and published for CCETSW by Learning Materials Design, Central Council for Education and Training in Social Work (CCETSW), London.

DSM IV, 1994, *Diagnostic and Statistical Manual of Mental Disorders* (4th edn), American Psychiatric Association.

Dumble M & Tuson W, 1998, 'Identifying Eating and Drinking Difficulties', *Speech and Language Therapy in Practice*, Winter 1998.

East K, 1981, 'Intent To Communicate (ITC)', unpublished assessment, Southampton.

Elder P & Goossens C, 1994, *Engineering Training Environments for Interactive Augmentative Communication: Strategies for Adolescents and Adults who are Moderately/Severely Developmentally Delayed,* Southeast Augmentative Communication Conference Publications Clinician Series, USA.

Elliot K & Forshaw N, 2000, 'People with Borderline–Mild Learning Disability', France J & Kramer S (eds), *Communication and Mental Illness*, Jessica Kingsley Publishers, London.

Ellis JW & Luckasson R, 1985 'Mentally Retarded Criminal Defendants', *George Washington Law Review,* 53(3–4), pp414–93.

Emanuel R, 1992, 'Use of Groups to Facilitate Communication Development in Young Learning Disabled Children', Fawcus M (ed), *Group Encounters in Speech and Language Therapy*, Far Communications.

Emerson E, 1995, *Challenging Behaviour: Analysis and Intervention in People with Learning Disabilities,* Cambridge University Press, Cambridge.

Emerson E, Barrett S, Bell C, Cummings R, McCool C, Toogood A & Mansell J, 1987, *Developing Services for People with Severe Learning Disabilities and Challenging Behaviours,* Institute of Social and Applied Psychology, University of Kent.

Emerson E, McGill P & Mansell J, 1994, *Severe Learning Disabilities and Challenging Behaviour,* Chapman Hall, London.

Emerson P, 1977, 'Covert Grief Reactions in Mentally Retarded Clients', *Mental Retardation*, 15 (6).

English J & Card R, 1994, *Butterworth's Police Law,* Butterworth, London.

Fairbairn G, Rowley D, & Bowen M, 1995, *Sexuality, Learning Difficulties, and Doing What's Right,* David Fulton Publishers, London.

Fawcus M, 1992a, 'Group Structure and Group Dynamics', Fawcus M (ed), *Group Encounters in Speech and Language Therapy*, Far Communications.

Fawcus M, 1992b, 'Group work with the aphasic adult', Fawcus M (ed), *Group Encounters in Speech and Language Therapy*, Far Communications.

Ferris-Taylor R, 1997, 'Communication', Gates B (ed), *Learning Disabilities*, Churchill Livingstone, Edinburgh.

Gates B, 1997, *Learning Disabilities*, Churchill Livingstone, Edinburgh.

Georgiades N & Phillmore L, 1980, 'The myth of the hero-innovator and alternative strategies for organisational change', Kiernan C & Woodford F (eds), *Behavioural Modification with the Severely Retarded*, Associated Scientific Publisher, New York.

Gilbert P & Scragg T, 1992, *Managing to Care,* Community Care/Reed Business Publishing Group.

Goldbart J, 1986, 'The Development of Language and Communication', Coupe J & Porter J (eds), *The Education of Children with Severe Learning Difficulties*, Croom Helm, London.

Goldbart J, 1988, 'Communication', Sebba J (ed), *The Education of People with Profound and Multiple Handicaps*, Manchester University Press in association with BIMH, Manchester.

Goldbart J, 1994, 'Opening the Communication Curriculum to Students with PMLDs', Ware J (ed), *Educating Children with Profound and Multiple Disability*, David Fulton Publishers, London.

Goldbart J, Warner J & Mount H, 1994, *The Development of Early Communication and Feeding for People who have Profound and Multiple Disabilities. A Workshop Training Package for Parents and Carers,* Mencap PMLD Section, Manchester.

Groher M, 1997, *Dysphagia: Diagnosis and Management,* Butterworth-Heinemann, London.

Grossman HJ (ed), 1983, *Classification in Mental Retardation,* American Association on Mental Deficiency, Washington, DC.

Gudjonsson G, 1992, *The Psychology of Interrogations, Confessions and Testimony,* John Wiley & Sons, Chichester.

Gudjonsson G, 1995, 'Fitness for interview during police detention: a conceptual framework for forensic assessment', *The Journal of Forensic Psychiatry*, 6, 1, pp185–97.

Gudjonsson GH, Clare ICH & Cross P, 1992, 'The revised PACE "Notice to detained persons": how easy is it to understand?' *Journal of the Forensic Science Society,* 32, pp289–99.

Gudjonsson GH & Clarke N, 1986, 'Suggestibility in police interrogation: a social psychological model', *Social Behaviour*, 1, pp83–104.

Halliday M, 1975, *Learning How to Mean: Explorations in the Development of Language,* Edward Arnold, London.

Harris J & Hewett D, 1996, *Positive Approaches to Challenging Behaviours,* BILD, Kidderminster.

Hayes S, 1997, 'Recent research on offenders with learning disabilities', *Tizard Learning Disability Review*, 1, 3.

Hickman J, 1997, 'ALD and dysphagia: issues and practice', *Speech and Language Therapy in Practice*, Autumn 1997.

Hill J & Hordell A, 1998, 'Creative work', *Nursing Standard*, 2 December, 3, 11.

Hitchings A, 1992, 'Working with adults with a learning disability in a group setting', Fawcus M (ed), *Group Encounters in Speech and Language Therapy*, Far Communications.

Hitchings A & Spence R, 1991, *The Personal Communication Plan (PCP) for People With Learning Disabilities,* NFER-Nelson (OOP). Revised Edition: Kelly A, 2000, 'The Personal Communication Plan (PCP) for People with Learning Disabilities', in *Working With Adults with a Learning Disability,* Winslow Press, Bicester.

Hogg J & Sebba J, 1986, *Profound Retardation and Multiple Impairment. Volume 1. Development and Learning,* Croom Helm.

Holland S & Ward C, 1990, *Assertiveness: A Practical Approach,* Winslow Press, Bicester.

Hurst-Brown L & Keens A, 1990, *Encouraging a Natural and Better Life Experience: A Systematic Approach to the Facilitation of the Functional Communication Skills of People with a Learning Difficulty,* Forum Consultancy.

Jans D & Clark S, 1994, 'High technology aids to communication: an overview of devices and access methods', Millar S & Wilson A (eds), *Augmentative Communication in Practice: An Introduction,* CALL Centre, University of Edinburgh, Edinburgh.

Johnson D & Johnson F, 1975, *Joining Together: Group Theory and Group Skills,* Prentice Hall, Englewood Cliffs, NJ.

Jones S, 1990, *Intecom,* NFER-Nelson, Windsor.

Keirnan C & Reid B, 1987, *Pre-Verbal Communication Schedule (PVCS),* NFER-Nelson, Windsor.

Kelly A, 1996, *Talkabout: A Social Communication Skills Package,* Winslow Press, Bicester.

Knowles W & Masidlover M, 1982, *Derbyshire Language Scheme,* Ripley, Derbyshire (private publication).

Langley J, 1988, *Working with Swallowing Disorders,* Winslow Press, Bicester.

Light J & Binger C, 1998, *Building Communicative Competence with Individuals who use Augmentative and Alternative Communication,* Paul H Brookes Publishing, Baltimore.

Luckasson R, Coulter DL, Polloway EA, Reiss S, Schalock RI, Snell ME, Spitalink DM, & Stark J, 1992, *Mental Retardation: Definition, Classification and Systems of Support,* American Association of Mental Retardation, Washington DC.

MacDonald A, 1994, 'Symbol systems', Millar S & Wilson A (eds), *Augmentative Communication in Practice: An Introduction,* CALL Centre, University of Edinburgh, Edinburgh.

Malin N, 1995, *Services for People with Learning Disabilities,* Routledge, London.

Mansell J, 1988, 'Training for service development', Towell D (ed), *An Ordinary Life in Practice: Lessons from the Experience of Developing Comprehensive Community-Based Services for People with Learning Disabilities*, King's Fund Centre, London.

McCall F, Markova I, Murphy J, Moodie E & Collins S, 1997, 'Perspectives on AAC systems by the users and their communication partners', *EJDC*, 32, pp235–56.

McDonnell A, 1995, *Staff Training in the Management of Challenging Behaviours*, Studio III Training Systems.

McDonnell A & Sturmey P, 1993, 'Managing violent and aggressive behaviour: towards better practice', Jones RSP & Eayrs C (eds), *Challenging Behaviours and People with Learning Difficulties: a Psychological Perspective*, BILD, Kidderminster.

McDonnell A, Dearden B, & Richens A, 1991, 'Staff training in the management of violence and aggression', *Mental Handicap*, 19, BIMH Publications.

McGee JJ & Menolascino FJ, 1992, 'The evaluation of defendants with mental retardation in the criminal justice system', Conley RW, Luckasson R, & Bouthilet GN, 1992, *The Criminal Justice System and Mental Retardation: Defendants and Victims*, Paul Brookes Publishing, Baltimore.

Memorandum of Good Practice, 1992, The Stationary Office, London.

Mental Health Act 1983, *Code of Practice*, The Stationary Office, London.

Millar S, 1994, 'What is augmentative and alternative communication? An introduction', Millar S & Wilson A (eds), *Augmentative Communication in Practice: An Introduction*, CALL Centre, University of Edinburgh, Edinburgh.

Mittler P, 1979, *People not Patients: Problems and Policies in Mental Handicap*, Methuen, London.

Mittler P, 1988, foreword in Coupe J & Goldbart J (eds), *Communication Before Speech*, David Fulton Publishers, London.

Morris S & Klein M, 1987, *Pre-Feeding Skills*, Therapy Skill Builders.

Moulster G, 1997, 'A descriptive study which explores some initiatives introduced by different professionals to facilitate counselling opportunities for people who have learning disabilities', unpublished paper in University of Reading, Dept of Community Studies, Reading.

Murphy J, Markova I, Collins S, & Moodie E, 1996, 'AAC Systems: Obstacles to effective use', *EJDC*, 31, pp31–44.

National Development Team for Mentally Handicapped People, 1985, *Fourth Report 1981–1984*, HMSO, London.

Nemitz T, 1996, *The appropriate adult and support for vulnerable suspects in the police station*, NAPSAC Bulletin, June 1996.

O'Brien J, 1981, *The Principle of Normalisation: A Foundation for Effective Services*, Georgia Advocacy Office, Atlanta, Georgia.

O'Brien J, 1987, 'A guide to lifestyle planning', Wilcox B and Bellamy J (eds) *The Activities Catalogue: An Alternative Curriculum for Youth and Adults with Severe Disabilities*, Paul H Brookes Publishing, Baltimore.

Park K, 1997, 'How do objects become objects of reference? A review of the literature on objects of reference and a proposed model for the use of objects in communication', *British Journal of Special Education*, 24, 3.

Payne J, Polloway E, Smith J, & Payne R, 1981, *Strategies for Teaching the Mentally Retarded,* Charles E Merrill, Columbus, Ohio.

Pearson P & Spencer J, 1997, *Promoting Teamwork in Primary Care: A Research Based Approach,* Arnold, London.

Police and Criminal Evidence Act, 1984, *Codes of Practice*, The Stationery Office Books, London.

Polloway E, Cronin M & Patton J, 1986, 'The efficacy of group versus one-to-one instruction: a review', *Remedial & Special Education*, 7.

Pougher J, 1997, 'Providing quality care', Gates B (ed), *Learning Disabilities,* Churchill Livingstone, Edinburgh.

Poulton B & West M, 1993, 'Effective multidisciplinary teamwork in primary health care', *Journal of Advanced Nursing*, 18.

Prime R, 1992, 'Balancing risks and needs', Thompson T & Mathias P (eds), *Standards and Mental Handicap: Keys to Competence*, Bailliere Tindall, London.

Prontnicki J, 1995, 'Presentation: symptomatology and etiology of dysphagia', Rosenthal S, Sheppard J & Lotze M (eds), *Dysphagia and the Child with Developmental Disabilities*, Singular Publishing Group, San Diego.

RCSLT, 1989, *Augmentative and Alternative Communication (AAC) – Position Paper,* Royal College of Speech and Language Therapists.

Report on the Advisory Group on Video Evidence, 1989, Home Office, London. *Rights and Entitlements for Persons in Custody:* West Midlands Police, Witness in Court, Home Office.

Rinaldi W, 1992, *The Social Use of Language Programme (SULP),* NFER-Nelson, Windsor.

Rose G & Wotton G, 1992, 'Group work with the elderly', Fawcus M (ed), *Group Encounters in Speech and Language Therapy*, Far Communications.

Rustin L & Kuhr A, 1989, *Social Skills and the Speech Impaired,* Taylor & Francis, Basingstoke.

Scott J, 1994, 'Low tech methods of augmentative communication: an overview', Millar S & Wilson A (eds), *Augmentative Communication in Practice: An Introduction,* CALL Centre, University of Edinburgh, Edinburgh.

Scott J, 1996, 'Unlocking the potential of AAC', Millar S & Wilson A (eds), *Augmentative Communication in Practice: An Introduction,* CALL Centre, University of Edinburgh, Edinburgh.

Scragg T, 1992, 'Whole establishment training', In *Learning Together: Shaping New Services for People with Learning Disabilities.* Edited and published for CCETSW by Learning Materials Design, Central Council for Education and Training in Social Work (CCETSW), London.

Sears DO, Peplau A, Freedman JL & Taylor SE, 1988, *Social Psychology* (6th edn), Englewood Cliffs, Prentice Hall.

Sinason V, 1986, 'Secondary mental handicap and its relationship to trauma', *Psychoanalytic Psychotherapy*, 2, 2.

Sinason V, 1992, *Mental Handicap and the Human Condition: New Approaches from the Tavistock,* Free Association Books, London.

Smith H, 1992, 'Group therapy for dysphonia', Fawcus M (ed), *Group Encounters in Speech and Language Therapy*, Far Communications.

Smith S, 1997, 'Outcome measures with people with learning disabilities', *Bulletin*, CSLT Feb 97.

Speaking Up For Justice, 1998, Report of the Interdepartmental Working Group on the Treatment of Vulnerable or Intimidated Witnesses in the Criminal Justice System, Home Office, London.

Spence S, 1977, *Social Skills Training with Children and Adolescents*, NFER-Nelson, Windsor.

Spence R & Hitchings A, 1992, 'Assessing pragmatic skills of people with learning disabilities', *Human Communication*, May 1992.

Sperlinger A, 1997, *Introduction to Adults with Learning Disabilities: A Practical Approach for Health Professionals*, O'Hara T & Sperlinger A (eds), John Wiley & Sons, Chichester.

Stewart D, 1987, *Handbook of Management Skills*, Gower, Aldershot.

Thompson T & Mathias P, 1992, *Standards and Mental Handicap: Keys to Competence*, Bailliere Tindall, London.

Thornburgh D, 1992, Foreword in Conley RW, Luckasson R & Bouthilet GN, 1992, *The Criminal Justice System and Mental Retardation: Defendants and Victims*, Paul H Brookes Publishing, Baltimore.

Toolis K, 1996, 'A heart for Jo', *Weekend Guardian*, 10 August 1996.

Trower P, Bryant B & Argyle M, 1978, *Social Skills and Mental Health*, Methuen.

Tully K, 1986, *Improving Residential Life for Disabled People*, Churchill Livingstone, Edinburgh.

Van der Gaag A, 1988, *CASP*, Winslow Press, Bicester.

Wake E, 1997, 'Profound and Multiple Disability', Gates B (ed) *Learning Disabilities* (3rd edn), Churchill Livingstone, Edinburgh.

Whitaker DS, 1989, *Using Groups to Help People*, Routledge, London.

Wilkinson J & Canter S, 1982, *Social Skills Training Manual*, John Wiley & Sons, Chichester.

Wolfensberger W, 1972, *The Principle of Normalisation in Human Management Services*, National Institute of Mental Retardation, Toronto.

Wood J, 1992a, 'The changing job of the trainer', In *Learning Together: Shaping New Services for People with Learning Disabilities*. Edited and published for CCETSW by Learning Materials Design, Central Council for Education and Training in Social Work (CCETSW), London.

Wood J, 1992b, 'Evaluation', in *Learning Together: Shaping New Services for People with Learning Disabilities*. Edited and published for CCETSW by Learning Materials Design, Central Council for Education and Training in Social Work (CCETSW), London.

World Health Organisation, 1993, *Describing Developmental Disability: Guidelines for a Multiaxial Scheme for Mental Retardation (Learning Disability)*, *10th revision*, WHO, Geneva.

Zarkowska E & Clements J, 1988, *Problem Behaviour and People with Severe Learning Disabilities, The STAR Approach*, Chapman & Hall, London.